THE GRE TRAINER

THE GRE TRAINER is written by Mike Kim.

Trainer Test Prep, New York 10028
© 2025 Trainer Test Prep, LLC
All rights reserved. Published 2025.

25   1 2 3 4 5

ISBN: 978-0-9890815-7-3

THE GRE TRAINER

A remarkable self-study guide for
the self-driven student

CONTENTS

Introduction to the GRE

Hello, and welcome to *The GRE Trainer*. My name is Mike Kim, and I'll be your instructor. I understand how important success on the GRE is to your future, and I've done everything I can to make this study guide the most effective resource it can be. Thank you for putting your trust in me; I'm excited to get started with you.

In this introductory chapter, I'll review the basics of the GRE, such as how to register and the different sections of the exam. I'll also explain how this study guide is organized. Additionally, I'll offer advice to ensure that your study time is effective and that you will put yourself in a position to achieve your best possible score.

About the GRE

The GRE consists of five main sections: an essay section, two scored verbal sections, and two scored quantitative sections. In September 2023, Educational Testing Service (ETS), the makers of the GRE, significantly updated the exam and shortened it from nearly four hours to just under two hours. All the information in this guide relates to the most recent format of the GRE.

The Essay Section

The essay section consists of one "Analyze an Issue" essay. You will have 30 minutes to complete the essay, which is scored on a scale of 0–6 in half-point increments. For more information on the essay section, please refer to Chapter 22.

The Verbal Sections

The two scored verbal sections each consist of 27 questions: 12 questions in the first section and 15 in the second section. You will receive a total of 41 minutes (18 minutes for the first section and 23 minutes for the second section) to complete the verbal sections. There are three types of verbal questions:

- Text completion: requires you to fill in blank spaces in a sentence with the best of provided choices
- Sentence equivalence: requires you to fill in a blank space in a sentence with two synonymous words from a list
- Reading comprehension: tests your ability to understand and interpret text

The questions within each section are static; that is, they are preset and do not change based on your performance. You can jump around and return to any of the previous questions. However, the test is adaptive from section to section—how you perform on the first verbal section will determine the difficulty level of your second verbal section. You actually want to get to as difficult a second verbal section as possible in order to maximize your score, as the grading scale gets more forgiving as the difficulty increases.

The Quantitative Sections

Similar to the verbal sections, the two scored quantitative sections each consist of 27 questions: 12 questions in the first section and 15 in the second section. Unlike the verbal sections, you will have 47 minutes in total to complete the two sections (21 minutes for the first section and 26 minutes for the second section). The questions in this section do not test advanced math concepts; rather, they are based on math that you likely learned in high school or earlier: arithmetic, number properties, algebra, geometry, and data analysis.

The question types are multiple choice with one correct answer, multiple choice with one or more correct answers, numeric entry questions for which you have to fill in the answers, and quantitative comparison questions for which you are asked to compare two quantities. For more information on each of these different question types, please refer to Chapter 2.

Similar to the verbal sections, each quantitative section is static, and you can jump around, skipping and returning to questions as you wish; however, the test as a whole is adaptive, and how you perform on the first quantitative section will determine the difficulty level of the second quantitative section.

How the Verbal and Quantitative Sections Are Scored

The verbal and quantitative sections are scored on separate 130–170 scales. Each scaled score corresponds to a percentile rank reflecting a comparison with other test takers. Below is a sample of scaled scores and corresponding percentiles for a particular administration of the exam.

Scaled Score	Verbal Reasoning	Quantitative Reasoning
170	99	94
166	96	80
162	89	68
158	77	55
154	60	42
150	41	30

Data based on performance of individuals who tested between July 1, 2019, and June 30, 2022.

Each question within a section has the same weight, and there is no guessing penalty. **Therefore, never leave questions unanswered.** I also recommend you do not overinvest time on some questions at the expense of missing others, and you should practice allocating your time in a way that allows you to maximize your potential gains. You'll practice and develop these strategies with this guide.

Importance to Admissions

The importance of the GRE to admissions varies based on the type of graduate program to which you are applying and your particular circumstances. Additionally, different types of graduate programs emphasize different parts of your score (e.g., some science, technology, engineering, and math (STEM) programs may expect a relatively high quantitative reasoning score). Finally, there may be other considerations, such as grants or financial aid, in which GRE scores are used as selection criteria and thus serve as an added incentive to achieve your best score.

As you probably know, because each situation varies, I encourage you to research how much weight the GRE will have in your specific circumstances to determine if you should prioritize studying for a particular section of the test.

Registering for the Exam

You can register for the exam at: ets.org/gre/test-takers/general-test/register.html

As of the writing of this guide, the cost of taking the GRE is $220 in the United States and varies slightly in other locations. You can take the exam at a testing center or at home (the at-home option generally offers greater flexibility and availability in terms of both date and time). Although the exam content is identical for either option, there are some minor differences in the overall testing experience, such as the involvement of online proctoring methods, that you may want to research ahead of time. Another notable difference is that you are expected to work with a whiteboard (or sheet of paper inside a transparent sheet protector) and dry-erase markers for the at-home option instead of the scratch paper and pencil you would use at a test center.

You can take the GRE once every 21 days and up to five times within any continuous 12-month period. This limitation applies even if you've canceled one or more of your scores within that period.

Reporting Your Scores

As of this writing, ETS offers a few different options for reporting your GRE scores on test day and afterward.

On test day, if you choose not to cancel after viewing your scores at the test center, you can designate up to four schools to receive your scores at no additional cost. You can choose to send either only the score you **just received** or **all scores** for all the GREs you have taken over the past five years.

After test day, you can send your scores to additional schools for a fee. In this case, you can choose to send either your **most recent** score or **any selection** of scores from any GREs you have taken over the past five years.

How to Study for the GRE

The GRE is a very learnable exam. It is not a test of advanced reasoning ability, it does not include any questions that encourage ingenuity or "outside the box" thinking, and it is not designed to give an advantage to those with unique training in any particular field.

As long as you have the time and the motivation, you should expect that your studies will lead to significant score improvement. I have written this book to help make sure that you achieve this goal.

Throughout the study process, some students may not see significant score improvement. Why not? And, more important, how can we make sure this doesn't happen to you?

I recommend thinking of your studies as a three-legged stool that consists of learning, practice, and self-assessment. Whether you study for one month or six months, the key to your success depends on coordinating these three components. If you miss one of these key components, it can disrupt your entire study process. Let's discuss each individually in more detail and then bring them together again.

Learning

Learning for the GRE consists of learning about the GRE and learning about the concepts *tested* on the GRE.

Learning about the GRE involves understanding the different question types and how they work, including their tendencies and nuances. I will give you the most important details in this book, and you will pick up more details on your own throughout your exam preparation.

The study process also involves learning optimal strategies for all the different challenges the GRE presents. If you are new to the GRE, you will quickly discover that it is not chess—it does not require complex strategies, and in fact, overthinking your strategies can often be detrimental to your performance. However, you should develop smart strategies for approaching the challenges you expect to encounter on the GRE and master them through practice before test day. I will expand on this point later in this section.

Most importantly, preparation for the GRE involves learning the underlying content tested in the verbal and quantitative sections. For the verbal sections, a key factor is simply vocabulary, so I encourage you to enhance your vocabulary while studying for the GRE. For the quantitative sections, you will need to understand the underlying math rules, which I will cover in great detail in this guide.

Practice

The second key component of your GRE preparation is practice. The most realistic GRE practice is obtained using the official GRE materials. Of course, you will also obtain much practice with this study guide.

Performing well on the GRE requires an understanding of the underlying material. However, your practice is the "muscle-building" component of your training—it is how you develop the skills and habits that will help you perform better on the exam.

Ideally, you want targeted and mixed practice: a set of geometry questions is an example of targeted practice, and a practice test is an example of mixed practice. Make sure that you know which questions to use for any situation. Again, this study guide has been designed to give you plenty of experience with both.

I recommend you avoid burning through official questions and tests created and released by ETS, the makers of the exam. Although I provide materials that mimic the official exam, materials created by the actual test writers will best approximate what you'll see on test day. ETS offers a limited sample of practice questions and tests. These official questions offer the most important clues to your eventual success, and you will want to maximize their benefit. You can use official questions to find out what to expect on test day and to deepen your understanding of the question types, the underlying issues, how these issues are tested, and your strengths and weaknesses.

Combining the *Trainer* with Official Practice Materials

As discussed, the most accurate GRE preparation materials are those created by ETS, the actual makers of the GRE. Unfortunately, they offer students a limited amount of study materials. So, it's important to make sure you understand the options available to you and to maximize the utility you get from all the materials at your disposal.

As of this writing, on the ETS website, students are offered five practice exams and a new program titled GRE Mentor. Two of the five practice exams are free, and three require an additional fee of $44.95 per exam. GRE Mentor, for $149, offers access to the largest bank of GRE questions available—as of this writing, 640 official questions, an additional official exam (that you could purchase separately otherwise), and additional instructional materials.

In addition, ETS offers official printed guides: one large guide that covers the test as a whole and two smaller guides that focus on the quantitative and verbal sections, respectively.

When you combine your learning in the *Trainer* with your practice with official materials, my advice is twofold:

(1) Focus more on learning earlier in your studies and more on practice later in your studies.

(2) Whenever possible or helpful, cycle between the two so that your learning impacts your practice, and your practice drives what you choose to study.

Suggestion: Create a GRE Notebook

An effective GRE notebook can be an invaluable tool during your study process. It can help you cement your learning and work as a database of essential material, and it can serve as a road map to a higher score.

Here are a couple of key suggestions for optimizing the use of a study notebook:

1. Write down every challenge you face in both *The GRE Trainer* and official preparation material (e.g., the way a challenging question was written, a difficult concept or vocabulary term, a math concept you have not applied in years). Try not to stress too much when you encounter a challenge. Just do your best to describe, as honestly as possible, why it is problematic for you.

As you study, work to eliminate these challenges. Keep returning to your notebook, and use it as your guide. Each time you overcome a challenge, you will get better at the exam. Trust that many of these issues will resolve themselves, and you will learn and develop smarter ways to address the remaining issues. Work to "fix" each problem that you write down, and by the time you have resolved each of these issues, you will be ready for the test.

2. Think of your notes as constantly evolving. Be comfortable with messy notes and multiple drafts. I recommend that you take notes in a format that makes them easy to work with and move, such as loose-leaf paper in three-ring binders. If you follow these steps, by the end of this process, your notes, while not perfect, will tell the story of your study journey. You may be proud of how messy your notes became! Correctly answering questions may make you feel good, but working on challenges will lead to improvement in the long run, and the messiness can often be a testament to that hard work.

Self-Assessment

The final component of your GRE preparation is self-assessment. By evaluating your aptitude for the exam, your strengths and weaknesses, and your skills and habits, you can adjust your learning and practice to address your particular needs and to best serve your interests.

You can divide your self-assessment into two components: (1) what needs to be assessed and (2) your own assessment of your readiness. For example, one category to consider would be (1) different types of math concepts and (2) your comfort level with each of these concepts. You can also think more broadly in terms of issues such as vocabulary or verbal question types.

Note the difference between self-assessment and personal bias. You might believe you are strong or weak at math or have traditionally performed better in English classes than in quantitative classes, but results on standardized tests such as the GRE often do not align with expectations. Be as clinical as possible, recognize that this exam is learnable, and know that the study preparation will require you to invest time, effort, and energy. Use self-assessment to know where to concentrate that energy.

Bringing it All Together

Test takers underperform relative to their capacities when they cannot or do not prepare. They also underperform when they do not prepare as efficiently or as effectively as they might have. I want to help you avoid these barriers to success and maximize the returns you get for the work you put in.

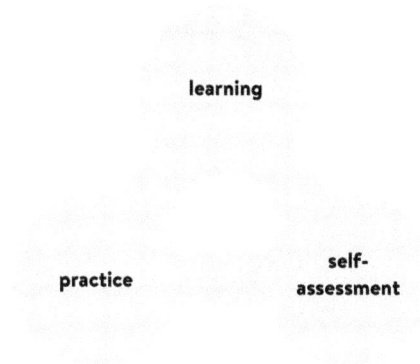

learning

practice

self-
assessment

Students who underperform relative to their efforts often do so because they failed to address one or more of these three critical components (learning, practice, and self-assessment) or failed to combine them, leading to the classic image of a rocky stool. Examples are a student who devotes all her exam preparation to attending courses and reading guides but does not practice or review or a student who takes numerous practice tests without mastering the underlying mathematical concepts.

Exam preparation is effective when learning, practice, and self-assessment come to-gether—when the material that is learned informs how you solve problems, when your experiences with questions deepen your understanding of the material, and when you understand and build on your strengths and weaknesses. **Every time you form a bond between these components, you get better at the GRE.**

Looking Ahead

In the next lesson, I'll begin by reviewing the basics of the quantitative sections and then move to six quantitative chapters that cover arithmetic and algebra.

Then, I will move on to a block of seven verbal lessons, reviewing all that you need to know about text completion, sentence equivalence, and reading comprehension.

Next, I will return for the second half of the math instruction, which will include data analysis and geometry.

I will then conclude with a lesson on the essay and some additional verbal practice.

A few months of concentrated studying for the GRE may be the key to opening doors that might be significantly harder to open otherwise. I am excited to join you on this journey. Let's get started.

2 Intro to Quantitative Reasoning

QUANTITATIVE REASONING

Why Is There Math on the GRE?

To succeed in graduate school, you will need a certain baseline of mathematical skills. Academic research, even in the humanities, almost always involves quantitative information or statistical analysis of some kind.

But that is only part of it.

What's more important is that math provides a level playing field for testing something else: your ability to understand context, correctly identify a task, and infer the information required to complete that task.

No matter your field of study, you will not excel unless you can consistently understand and organize context, correctly determine your tasks or priorities, and figure out how to accomplish your tasks or get the information that you need. That's exactly what's being tested here (albeit with prime numbers and hot dog stands).

Let's take a look at some sample questions.

Sample Questions

On the following pages, you'll take a look at each of the four types of questions that you'll face in the quantitative reasoning sections of the GRE: Multiple Choice (one answer), Multiple Choice (all that apply), Free Response (i.e., Numeric Entry), and Quantitative Comparison.

Please note that on the actual exam, Multiple Choice (one answer) and Quantitative Comparisons are the most common question types. Multiple Choice (all that apply) and Free Response appear significantly less often—usually just a few times per section.

Also, note that I've assigned a rough gauge of difficulty to each question for your reference, but please don't feel discouraged if you miss an easier problem or two. You might be a little rusty with some of these quantitative concepts and operations, and, well, that's what I am here for.

Multiple Choice (One Answer)

These are multiple-choice questions that ask you to select exactly one answer choice. There will always be five answers to select from, and if you ever arrive at an answer that is not among the answer choices, you will know that you've solved the question incorrectly; that is, one of the answer choices will always be correct.

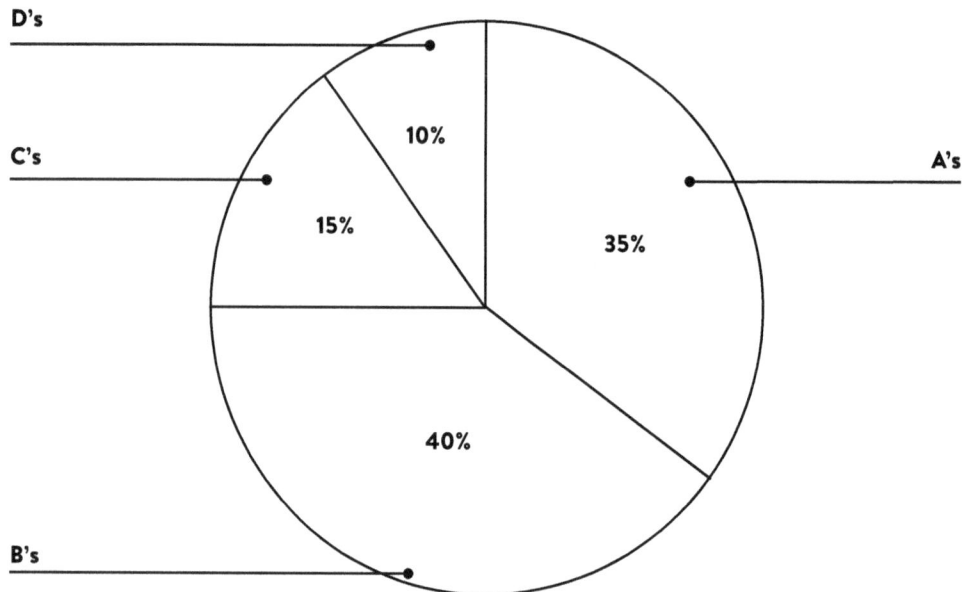

A teacher has exactly 200 students in a class and distributes grades according to the above percentages. How many more students received B's than D's?

(A) 30
(B) 40
(C) 50
(D) 60
(E) 70

If two students are selected at random, the probability that neither of them received an A is approximately

(A) 22%
(B) 42%
(C) 46%
(D) 52%
(E) 65%

Multiple Choice (All that Apply)

These are multiple-choice questions that ask you to select **one or more** answers from a list of choices. Note that the question may or may not specify the exact number of choices to select, and the number of available answer choices to select from will vary from question to question. **The answers to these questions are marked with square boxes rather than ovals.**

If $x \neq 0$, which of the following is equivalent to $\frac{1}{x^2}$?

Indicate <u>all</u> such choices.

- [A] x^{-2}
- [B] $x^4 - x^2$
- [C] $(x^2)^{-1}$
- [D] $x^{-1} + x^{-1}$
- [E] $(x^{-1})(x^{-1})$

If $(x - 3)(x - 5)$ is even, which of the following must be odd?

Indicate <u>all</u> such choices.

- [A] $(x - 1)(x + 1)$
- [B] $x(x + 3)$
- [C] x^{x+1}
- [D] $3x - 4(x + 1)$

On-Screen Calculator

The test makers provide an on-screen calculator that can be accessed anytime during the quantitative section by clicking the "calc" button and icon at the top of your screen.

Here are a few important notes about the operations and functions of the calculator:

- The +/− symbol converts a positive number into its negative opposite or vice versa.

- The parentheses cannot be nested; you cannot input an equation with a pair of parentheses inside another pair.

- Use "C" to clear your current equation and start fresh, or "CE" to clear only your latest input.

- You can use the memory buttons "MR," "MC," and "M+" to store, recall, or add different values while solving an equation. You don't need to use them, and in general, we recommend only doing so if you are already familiar with them.

- For Numeric Entry questions, clicking the "Transfer Display" button will transfer your result into the blank space.

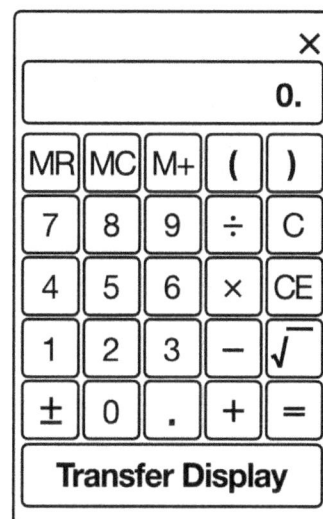

Quantitative Comparison

Quantitative Comparison questions provide you with information and then ask you to compare two quantities—Quantity A and Quantity B. The answer choices for Quantitative Comparison questions are reproduced in the box to the right.

Select answer choice (A) if you can determine that Quantity A is greater than Quantity B. Select answer choice (B) if you can determine that Quantity B is greater than Quantity A. Select answer choice (C) if you can determine that the two quantities are equal. Select answer choice (D) if you cannot determine the relationship between Quantity A and Quantity B from the information that's been given to you.

(A) Quantity A is greater.

(B) Quantity B is greater.

(C) The two quantities are equal.

(D) The relationship cannot be determined from the information given.

A certain coworking space charges members a set monthly fee of $35 and an additional $17 charge for each day of use.

Quantity A	Quantity B
The total monthly charge for a member who uses the coworking space for 8 days in a particular month	$170

A. Quantity A is greater.
B. Quantity B is greater.
C. The two quantities are equal.
D. The relationship cannot be determined from the information given.

A certain tea company offers its products in two different types of packages: a cylinder with a base radius of 2 centimeters and height of 5 centimeters and a cube with side lengths of 4 centimeters. For both types of packages, the company places a label that covers all sides but not the top and not the bottom.

Quantity A	Quantity B
The area of the label on the cylindrical package	The area of the label on the cubic package

A. Quantity A is greater.
B. Quantity B is greater.
C. The two quantities are equal.
D. The relationship cannot be determined from the information given.

Free Response

Free Response, or Numeric Entry, questions ask you to simply enter your answer directly rather than selecting among given answer choices. You will have the option of inputting your answer as an integer or decimal in a single box or as a fraction in two separate boxes. Note that you are <u>not</u> required to simplify fractional responses.

By weight, liquid X makes up $\frac{1}{4}$ of solution A and $\frac{1}{10}$ of solution B. If a new solution, solution C, is created by mixing equal weights of solutions A and B, what percentage of solution C will be made up of liquid X?

[ ] %

A certain list consists of the following 6 terms: 17, 28, 16, 25, x, $x - 6$. The mean of the list is x.

What is the value of x?

$x = $ [ ]

Multiple Choice (One Answer) Solutions

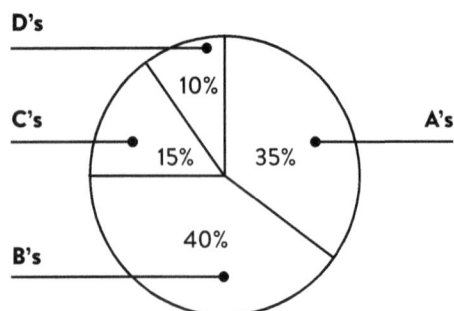

A teacher has exactly 200 students in a class and distributes grades according to the above percentages. How many more students received B's than D's?

Ⓐ 30
Ⓑ 40
Ⓒ 50
Ⓓ 60
Ⓔ 70

Solution (Difficulty: Easy)

Notice that the chart gives you information about the percentage of students who receive each grade, but the question concerns a number of students.

According to the pie chart, 40% of students received B's, and 10% received D's. The difference between 40% and 10% is 30%, meaning that the difference between the two groups represents 30% of the total number of students.

30% of 200 = (0.3)(200) = 60

Alternatively, you could have calculated the number of students who received B's and the number of students who received D's and solved for the difference:

(0.4)(200) = 80
(0.1)(200) = 20
80 – 20 = 60

In either case, (D) is the correct answer.

If two students are selected at random, the probability that neither of them received an A is approximately

Ⓐ 22%
Ⓑ 42%
Ⓒ 46%
Ⓓ 52%
Ⓔ 65%

Solution (Difficulty: Hard)

To satisfy the given condition, you need to select two students, neither of whom received an A.

Since 35% of students received an A, for the first selection, the odds of selecting a student who did not receive an A are 65%, or 0.65, or $\frac{130}{200}$.

Once the first student is selected, assuming that the student did not receive an A, there are now $\frac{129}{199}$ students remaining who also did not receive an A.

Thus, the odds of selecting two students in a row who did not receive A's, which requires first selecting a student who did not receive an A and then, from the remaining pool, selecting another student who also did not receive an A, are:

$\left(\frac{130}{200}\right)\left(\frac{129}{199}\right)$, which is ≈ 0.42136

(B) is the correct answer.

Multiple Choice (All that Apply) Solutions

If $x \neq 0$, which of the following is equivalent to $\frac{1}{x^2}$?

Indicate <u>all</u> such choices.

A x^{-2}
B $x^4 - x^2$
C $(x^2)^{-1}$
D $x^{-1} + x^{-1}$
E $(x^{-1})(x^{-1})$

Solution (Difficulty: Medium)

Note that this question requires you to be fresh and familiar with exponent rules. If it's been a while, no worries. Check out the Number Properties lesson, or keep in mind that I'll cover everything you need to know when you get there.

Let's evaluate each answer choice separately.

[A] A term with a negative exponent is the reciprocal (the flipped version) of the same term with a positive exponent, so x^{-2} is equivalent to $\frac{1}{x^2}$.

[B] When you add or subtract terms with exponents, you don't add or subtract the exponents themselves. The only way to algebraically simplify this statement is to factor out x^2: $x^2(x^2 - 1)$. This is not equivalent to $\frac{1}{x^2}$.

[C] When you raise a power to a power, you multiply the exponents together. So, $(x^2)^{-1} = x^{-2}$, or $\frac{1}{x^2}$, which is the same as the original statement.

[D] $x^{-1} + x^{-1} = \frac{1}{x} + \frac{1}{x} = \frac{2}{x}$. This is not equivalent to $\frac{1}{x^2}$.

[E] When you multiply exponential terms, you add their exponents. So, in this case, $(x^{-1})(x^{-1}) = x^{-2}$, or $\frac{1}{x^2}$, and this is equivalent to the original statement.

Therefore, answer choices [A], [C], and [E] are all correct.

If $(x - 3)(x - 5)$ is even, which of the following must be odd?

Indicate <u>all</u> such choices.

A $(x - 1)(x + 1)$
B $x(x + 3)$
C x^{x+1}
D $3x - 4(x + 1)$

Solution (Difficulty: Hard)

If $(x - 3)(x - 5)$ is even, that means that $x - 3$ and $x - 5$ must be even, meaning x itself must be odd.

If x were even, $x - 3$ and $x - 5$ would both be odd, in which case the resulting product would also be odd. Here are some examples to illustrate.

If x were 7: $(7 - 3)(7 - 5) = (4)(2) = 8$, which is even.
If x were 6: $(6 - 3)(6 - 5) = (3)(1) = 3$, which is odd.

Thus, x must be odd, and this is the key inference that unlocks this question. Knowing that x is odd, let's evaluate the answer choices.

[A] When x is odd, $(x - 1)$ is even, and $(x + 1)$ is even. Even times even is even, so [A] does not have to be odd.

[B] Odd + 3 = even, and odd times even is even, so [B] does not have to be odd.

[C] An odd number taken to any positive integer exponent will be odd (imagine, for example, 3, 9, 27, 81, 243...), so [C] must be odd.

[D] If x is odd, $3x$ must be odd. $4(x + 1)$ must be even. Odd minus even is odd, so [D] must be odd.

[C] and [D] must be odd.

Quantitative Comparison Solutions

A certain coworking space charges members a set monthly fee of $35 and an additional $17 charge for each day of use.

Quantity A	Quantity B
The total monthly charge for a member who uses the coworking space for 8 days in a particular month	$170

Ⓐ **Quantity A is greater.**
Ⓑ Quantity B is greater.
Ⓒ The two quantities are equal.
Ⓓ The relationship cannot be determined from the information given.

Solution (Difficulty: Easy)

For Quantity A, since the person is using the coworking space for 8 days, the total charge for the month would equal:

$$35 + 17(8) = 35 + 136 = 171$$

Thus, Quantity A is greater than Quantity B.

A certain tea company offers its products in two different types of packages: a cylinder with a base radius of 2 centimeters and height of 5 centimeters and a cube with side lengths of 4 centimeters. For both types of packages, the company places a label that covers all sides but not the top and not the bottom.

Quantity A	Quantity B
The area of the label on the cylindrical package	The area of the label on the cubic package

Ⓐ Quantity A is greater.
Ⓑ **Quantity B is greater.**
Ⓒ The two quantities are equal.
Ⓓ The relationship cannot be determined from the information given.

Solution (Difficulty: Medium)

If the cylinder has a radius of 2 centimeters, its circumference ($2\pi r$) is 4π centimeters, and the area of its label would thus be 20π centimeters, or approximately 62.8 square centimeters.

For the cube, the height of the label would be 4 centimeters, and the length would be 16 centimeters, for an area of 64 square centimeters.

The label on the cubic package would be larger, so Quantity B is greater than Quantity A.

Free Response Solutions

By weight, liquid X makes up $\frac{1}{4}$ of solution A and $\frac{1}{10}$ of solution B. If a new solution, solution C, is created by mixing equal weights of solutions A and B, what percentage of solution C will be made up of liquid X?

| 17.5 | % |

Solution (Difficulty: Medium)

Since you are adding equal weights of each solution, the resulting mixture will be 50% solution A and 50% solution B. So, the amount of liquid X will be $\frac{1}{4}$ of 50% plus $\frac{1}{10}$ of 50%:

$\frac{1}{4}$ of 50% = 12.5%

$\frac{1}{10}$ of 50% = 5%

12.5% + 5% = 17.5%

17.5% is the correct answer.

A certain list consists of the following 6 terms: 17, 28, 16, 25, x, $x - 6$. The mean of the list is x.

What is the value of x?

$x =$ | 20 |

Solution (Difficulty: Medium)

If the average of all the terms is x, you can set up the following equation and solve for x:

$$\frac{17 + 28 + 16 + 25 + x + x - 6}{6} = x$$

$17 + 28 + 16 + 25 + x + x - 6 = 6x$

$86 + 2x - 6 = 6x$

$80 = 4x$

$20 = x$

The correct answer is 20.

The Design of GRE Questions

You can think of all GRE quantitative questions, regardless of type, as being designed in the same way:

1. The question provides you with **context**.
2. It then presents you with a **task**.
3. In order to accomplish this task, you have to make some sort of **inference**.

Context	**Task**	**Inference(s)**
If $2x = 8$...	What is x?	$x = 4$

Of course, certain questions are easier, and others are more challenging. Certain questions make your task obvious, and others cloak it a bit more. However, thinking about all GRE quantitative questions in this way can help clarify your habits and categorize your challenges.

How to Study GRE Quantitative Reasoning

To answer any one particular question correctly, you need to:

1. Accurately assess the context.
2. Gain a clear sense of the task being presented.
3. Be comfortable with the math principles involved.
4. Find the missing pieces of information required to complete the task.

Why might you miss questions?

1. You misunderstand the context.
2. You identify the wrong task or lose sight of the task during your process.
3. You are uncomfortable or unfamiliar with the math principles involved.
4. You can't find the missing pieces of information required to complete the task.

How to Study Effectively

Developing effective study habits leads to consistently strong performance. As I've discussed, this process involves a combination of three components:

- **Learning** about the nuances of GRE questions and, most important, about quantitative topics.
- **Practice** topic-specific drills or question sets and integrated practice sections or full exams.
- **Self-Assessment**, which involves earnest review, careful consideration of strengths and weaknesses, and decision-making about the work that needs to be done to achieve mastery.

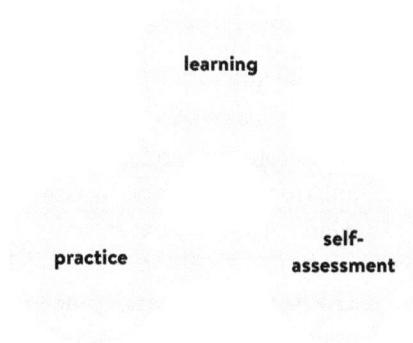

learning

practice

self-assessment

As discussed, the key to efficient and effective studying is coordinating these components—learning, practice, and assessment—so that they influence each other positively. On the flip side, be careful of disconnects between your learning, practice, and assessment. Do all you can to integrate the three.

Suggestion: Keep an Error Log

I strongly suggest keeping a running list of the questions you missed during your studies (perhaps in your GRE notebook) and reviewing this list periodically. You can take notes on each question: Did you have difficulty understanding the context, getting a sense of your task, or completing your task? What was it about the question that made it a challenge? And then, of course, once you have the proper understanding and experience, you can practice solving the question in a correct and ideal manner. Keep coming back to your error log, and keep reviewing each question that caused you trouble until you find that the questions no longer cause you any trouble.

Keeping such a log serves multiple benefits. Obviously, it can help you recognize and address isolated and unique concerns. Beyond that, it can help you notice patterns that you may not notice otherwise, and as test day approaches, it can give you a much stronger sense that you've covered all your bases and addressed all your weaknesses.

Context, Task, Inference

Let's quickly discuss how two of the previous questions fit into our framework for how GRE quantitative questions are designed.

A certain coworking space charges members a set monthly fee of $35 and an additional $17 charge for each day of use.

Quantity A	Quantity B
The total monthly charge for a member who uses the coworking space for 8 days in a particular month	$170

Ⓐ Quantity A is greater.
Ⓑ Quantity B is greater.
Ⓒ The two quantities are equal.
Ⓓ The relationship cannot be determined from the information given.

Context: You are told that the certain coworking space charges a set monthly fee of $35 and an additional $17 charge for each day of use, that Quantity A is equal to the total monthly membership charge for someone who uses the coworking space for 8 days in a particular month, and that Quantity B is equal to $170.

Task: You need to figure out whether you have enough information to know which value is greater, and, if so, which value is greater.

The Key Inference(s): Since you know Quantity B, you need to see if you can determine Quantity A, and per the information given in the question stem, you can.

$35 + 17(8) = 35 + 136 = 171$

Therefore, you can determine that Quantity A is greater and (A) is the correct answer.

If $(x - 3)(x - 5)$ is even, which of the following must be odd?

Indicate all such choices.

A $(x - 1)(x + 1)$
B $x(x + 3)$
C x^{x+1}
D $3x - 4(x + 1)$

Context: You are told that $(x - 3)(x - 5)$ is even.

Task: You need to identify which of the answer choices is odd.

The Key Inference(s): The key inference is that x is odd.

Knowing that x is odd, you can evaluate each answer choice individually, and once you do so, **you find that answer choices [C] and [D] must all be true.** *(Please see the problem solution for further discussion.)*

3 Arithmetic and Algebra

QUANTITATIVE REASONING

Welcome! This jam-packed lesson is full of essential fundamentals and covers the basics of arithmetic and the building blocks of algebra. Arithmetic and algebra are often separated in instructional books, but they are closely related. Arithmetic is simply the math that you do when combining or separating numbers. Algebra is math that uses placeholders called variables to represent unknown values. Any arithmetic problem that includes a variable to represent an unknown is also an algebra problem, so the fundamentals of arithmetic and algebra are often tested together.

Keep in mind that when it comes to the GRE, **fundamental does not mean easy**. Plenty of challenging GRE quantitative questions are built upon simple math concepts. Being familiar with these math topics does not mean you should skip this lesson. You'll want to know how these concepts are tested on the GRE, and I want to make sure you get plenty of practice. Let's go ahead and get started.

Order of Operations

There are certain essential rules of arithmetic, one of which is the order of operations.

Instead of going from left to right exclusively, in math, you follow a set order of arithmetic operations. You may have learned an acronym for this order when you were younger, PEMDAS: (P)arentheses, (E)xponents, (M)ultiplication and (D)ivision, (A)ddition and (S)ubtraction.

$3 + 2 \times 4 \neq 5 \times 4$

$3 + 2 \times 4 = 3 + 8$

$7 - (2 + 3) \neq 5 + 3$

$7 - (2 + 3) = 7 - 5$

P E MD AS

Parentheses serve several important functions in mathematical expressions. One such function is to indicate terms that need to be grouped together. For example, $2x + 3$ is very different from $2(x + 3)$, which is equivalent to $2x + 6$ (the 2 is distributed through the parentheses, or multiplied by each term inside the parentheses). Any time you replace a variable in an expression or equation with a number, you should use parentheses. For example:

- The value of $-x^2$ when $x = 2$ is $-(2)^2$, or -4. Start with the E (exponent) and calculate $2^2 = 4$, then multiply by -1.
- However, the value of $(-x)^2$ when $x = 2$ is $(-2)^2$, or 4. In this case, start with the P (parentheses), multiply the 2 by -1, then square the result.

Just a quick note on a potential misread of PEMDAS: you do not need to multiply before dividing or add before subtracting; think of the "M" and "D" going together and the "A" and "S" going together. In a series of operations that are just multiplication and division, or just addition and subtraction, simply go left to right.

$$20 \div 4 \times 3 = 5 \times 3 = 15$$

PEMDAS Drill

Solve the following equations:

1. $7 + 3(5 - 1)^2 =$

2. $\left(\frac{1}{4}\right)\left(\frac{2}{3}\right)\left(\frac{1}{5}\right) =$

3. $\sqrt{(4 - 2)^2 + 5} =$

4. $0.6(7 + \sqrt{7}) =$

5. $\dfrac{5}{\frac{1}{4}} - (3)(2)^2 =$

6. $(7)(6)(5)(4)(3)(2)(1)(0) =$

7. $(1 + 0.02)^3 =$

8. $10^3 - 0.1^3 =$

Exponents and Roots

It's important to spend a little bit of extra time on exponents and roots because they operate by a unique set of rules. You might not use them in everyday life, but they are particularly common on the exam.

An exponent represents the number of times that a base (a number or variable) is multiplied by itself. The term a^3 represents a base of a that is multiplied by itself 3 times in total.

$$a^3 = (a)(a)(a)$$
$$x^7 = (x)(x)(x)(x)(x)(x)(x)$$
$$x^1 = x$$

Thus, it is also true that any variable or number can be written as a base and exponent quantity by using an exponent of 1. For example:

a can be rewritten as a^1
4 can be rewritten as 4^1

Before I delve too deeply into exponent rules, please remember that PEMDAS always applies in any quantitative context.

In the expression $2a^3$, the exponent (3) is attached only to the base of a. The number 2 is attached to the quantity a^3 via multiplication. Therefore, you can understand that expression as $(2)(a^3)$, and if you knew that $a = 4$, you would calculate the expression's value as follows:

$(2)(4^3)$

You have no parentheses (P), so the next step in order of operations is exponents (E). The value of $4^3 = 64$. Then multiply (M) the quantity 64 by 2 to get 128.

However, in the expression $(2a)^3$, you do have parentheses that let you know that $(2a)$ is a quantity that must be grouped together (performing the multiplication action inside the parentheses first) before moving on to the exponent (E).

So $(2a)^3 = (2a)(2a)(2a)$, or $8a^3$.

If you know that the value of $a = 4$, then you can proceed in either of two ways:

$(2 \times 4)^3 = 8^3 = 512$
$(8)(4^3) = (8)(64) = 512$

PEMDAS Drill Solutions

1. $7 + 3(5 - 1)^2 =$

    $7 + 3(4)^2$

    $7 + 3(16)$

    $7 + 48$

    55

2. $\left(\frac{1}{4}\right)\left(\frac{2}{3}\right)\left(\frac{1}{5}\right) =$

    $\left(\frac{(1)(2)(1)}{(4)(3)(5)}\right)$

    $\frac{2}{60}$

    $\frac{1}{30}$

3. $\sqrt{(4 - 2)^2 + 5} =$

    $\sqrt{(2)^2 + 5}$

    $\sqrt{4 + 5}$

    $\sqrt{9}$

    3

4. $0.6(7 + \sqrt{7}) =$

    $\mathbf{4.2 + 0.6\sqrt{7}}$

5. $\dfrac{5}{\frac{1}{4}} - (3)(2)^2 =$

    $\dfrac{5}{\frac{1}{4}} - (3)(4)$

    $(5)\left(\frac{4}{1}\right) - (3)(4)$

    $20 - 12$

    8

6. $(7)(6)(5)(4)(3)(2)(1)(0) =$

    0

7. $(1 + 0.02)^3 =$

    1.02^3

    1.061208

8. $10^3 - 0.1^3 =$

    $1{,}000 - 0.001$

    999.999

Common Bases

The first set of exponent rules addresses typical situations in which all of the terms have the same base (a "common base"), whether that's a number such as 5 or a variable such as a. It is important to note that in these situations, that common base is preserved in the resulting term—what changes is the exponent attached to that common base.

1. $a^3 \times a^2$

If you write out the multiplication instead of using exponents, you get this:

$[(a)(a)(a)][(a)(a)]$, which is the same as a^5.

So, $(a^3)(a^2) = a^5$.

<u>Rule</u>: When multiplying exponential terms with the same base, add the exponents. Note that the resulting term preserves the common base of a.

2. $\dfrac{a^5}{a^2}$

Here, divide five a's by two a's, or

$$\frac{(a)(a)(a)(a)(a)}{(a)(a)} = \frac{(a)(a)(a)\cancel{(a)}\cancel{(a)}}{\cancel{(a)}\cancel{(a)}} = (a)(a)(a)$$

So, $\dfrac{a^5}{a^2} = a^3$

<u>Rule</u>: When dividing exponential terms with the same base, subtract the exponents. Note that the resulting term preserves the common base of a.

Be careful in situations where the exponents are expressions rather than integers. You should always use parentheses when subtracting one expression from another because that will remind you to distribute the negative sign. For example:

$\dfrac{5^{x+y}}{5^{x-y}}$

$5^{(x+y)-(x-y)}$

$5^{x+y-x+y}$

5^{2y}

3. $(a^4)^2$

Another way to write this would be $(a^4)(a^4)$.

You are multiplying four a's by four a's.

$[(a)(a)(a)(a)][(a)(a)(a)(a)] = a^8$

So, $(a^4)^2 = a^8$

Rule: When raising a base and exponent quantity to another exponent, multiply the exponents. Note that the resulting term preserves the common base of a.

4. $\dfrac{a^3}{a^3}$

Here, you have three a's being divided by three a's:

$$\frac{(a)(a)(a)}{(a)(a)(a)}$$

If you apply the rule for dividing base and exponent quantities with a common base, you get a^{3-3}, which results in a^0. The expression 0^0 is undefined, so a question such as this one would have to include the context that $a \neq 0$.

So if $a \neq 0$, what is the value for a^0? Well, as long as you know that the denominator of a fraction is not equal to 0 (a violation of the permanently implied context that the GRE tests only real numbers), then a fraction in which the numerator and denominator are equal has a value of 1. Therefore, a^0 must equal 1.

Rule: If $a \neq 0$, $a^0 = 1$. This rule applies to any base, whether a variable or a number. If you ever see an equation such as $9^{2x+3} = 1$, it's important to recognize that $9^0 = 1$, so you can set $2x - 3 = 0$. Solve for $x = \dfrac{3}{2}$ or 1.5.

Other Exponent Issues

Common Exponents

Next, we will consider situations in which we have terms with *different bases* but *common exponents*. An exponent can be distributed across two terms that are multiplied or divided.

$$(xy)^2 = x^2y^2$$

$$\left(\frac{x}{y}\right)^2 = \frac{x^2}{y^2}$$

This process works in both directions—two terms with different bases and the same exponent can be multiplied or divided, with the exponent staying the same:

$$x^2y^2 = (xy)^2$$

$$\frac{x^2}{y^2} = \left(\frac{x}{y}\right)^2$$

Note: This process works only for multiplication and division, not for addition or subtraction.

$$(x + y)^2 \neq x^2 + y^2$$

$$(x - y)^2 \neq x^2 - y^2$$

These two common exponent rules are the keys to solving difficult base and exponent questions. Let's discuss some important applications of these rules.

Getting to Common Bases: Change of Base

Sometimes, terms that do not initially share common bases can be rewritten so they do share a common base. A useful tip is to watch for terms with bases that are powers of 2, 3, or 5 (the first three prime numbers):

Powers of 2: 2, 4, 8, 16, 32…
Powers of 3: 3, 9, 27, 81…
Powers of 5: 5, 25, 125…

It is easy to rewrite quantities with bases like these. For example, because $8 = 2^3$, you can rewrite 8^4 by replacing the base of 8 with its equivalent expression 2^3, giving you $(2^3)^4$. Then, use the rule for raising a base and exponent quantity to another exponent to generate 2^{12}. Thus, 8^4 can be rewritten as 2^{12}, which can be helpful as shown below.

Here are some examples that use this strategy to generate common bases so that terms can be properly combined:

$$2^5 8^2 = 2^5 (2^3)^2 = (2^5)(2^6) = 2^{11}$$

$$\frac{5^{11}}{125^3} = \frac{5^{11}}{(5^3)^3} = \frac{5^{11}}{5^9} = 5^2$$

$$3^4 9 = 3^4 (3^2) = 3^6$$

$$\frac{(10^{-2})(10^5)}{100^2} = \frac{10^3}{(10^2)^2} = \frac{10^3}{10^4} = \frac{1}{10}$$

The change of base strategy also works with terms whose exponents contain variables. Here is a simple example to illustrate:

If $3^8 = 9^n$, what is the value of n?

You know that 9 is 3^2, so you can substitute 3^2 for 9 and rewrite the equation.
$$3^8 = (3^2)^n$$
$$3^8 = 3^{2n}$$

From this, you can see that $8 = 2n$, and $n = 4$.

There's a good reason to rewrite base and exponent quantities so that they have prime bases such as 2, 3, and 5. Remember our discussion of the power of prime factorization? Prime factors don't interact with other prime factors—for example, without knowing the numerical value of the prime factorization $(2^3)(5^7)(7^4)(11)$, you know with certainty that it isn't divisible by 3. Why? Because its prime factorization contains no 3s. No matter how many 2s, 5s, 7s, and 11s you multiply together, you'll never generate a number that is divisible by 3.

Let's apply that insight to base and exponent equations. Consider the following equation:

$$(2^x)(3^y) = (2^5)(3^2)$$

None of the 2s on the left are useful for generating the 3^2 on the right, nor are any of the 3s on the left useful for generating the 2^5 on the right. Therefore, you can create two separate equivalences, both of which must be true for the equation to be true:

$2^x = 2^5$, so $x = 5$
$3^y = 3^2$, so $y = 3$

One warning: you cannot make these separate equivalences if you have terms with non-prime bases anywhere in the equation. There is a separate process for rewriting terms with bases that aren't powers of prime numbers, but I'll discuss a bit later in the chapter.

Combining Quantities with Different Bases

If $(x^2)(y^2) = (xy)^2$, that means that different bases can be combined if they share the same exponent. For example, $(3^3)(5^3)$ can be rewritten as $(3 \times 5)^3$, which can be rewritten as 15^3. It's somewhat rare to want to combine different bases in this way, but let's look at a question in which this strategy is useful.

Example: How many zeros will appear before the first nonzero digit in the terminating decimal $\dfrac{1}{(2^5)(5^6)}$?

This is a difficult question, but it hinges on the key fact that when you multiply a decimal number by 10, you move the decimal one place to the right, and when you divide a decimal number by 10, you move the decimal one place to the left. In this type of question, it's useful to create as many 10s as you can, in this case, in the denominator of the fraction.

In the current denominator of your fraction, you have quantities with different bases that do not share a common exponent. But you can rewrite the denominator as follows:

$(2^5)(5^5)(5^1)$

You've simply replaced 5^6 with the equivalent expression of $(5^5)(5^1)$.

Now, you can combine $(2^5)(5^5)$ into 10^5, which gives you the following fraction:

$\dfrac{1}{(10^5)(5^1)}$

Leave the 10^5 quantity alone for now, and focus on the fraction $\dfrac{1}{5^1}$. Use the calculator to generate the decimal equivalent of 0.2. You can rewrite your expression as:

$\dfrac{0.2}{(10^5)}$

Every time you divide 0.2 by 10, move the decimal in 0.2 one place to the left. Therefore, you start with 0.2 and move the decimal 6 places to the left, and each place will be occupied by a 0. In other words, 0.000002, or 5 zeros before the first nonzero digit of 2. The answer to the question is 5.

Getting to Common Bases: Rewriting Terms with Non-Prime Bases

There's also an important application of the rule that $(xy)^2 = (x^2)(y^2)$, and here we return to the concept of common bases to discuss how to rewrite a base and exponent quantity with a base that is not a power of a prime number.

Consider a quantity such as 6^4, which has a non-prime base. You can rewrite 6 as $(2)(3)$, meaning that you can rewrite 6^4 as $(2 \times 3)^4$, and therefore as $(2^4)(3^4)$. Now you've turned 6^4 into quantities with prime bases, and now you can create the separate equivalences demonstrated in our initial discussion of common bases.

Example: If $(25^7)(8^6) = (2^4)(10^k)$, what is the value of k?

Here you have a number of terms with non-prime bases. Let's rewrite each of them:

25^7 can be rewritten as $(5^2)^7$, or 5^{14}
8^6 can be rewritten as $(2^3)^6$, or 2^{18}
2^4 has a prime base, so it does not need to be rewritten
10^k can be rewritten as $(2 \times 5)^k$, which can be rewritten as $(2^k)(5^k)$.

Now, you can rewrite the original equation as follows:

$$(5^{14})(2^{18}) = (2^4)(2^k)(5^k)$$

Let's combine terms with a common base on the right side:

$$(5^{14})(2^{18}) = (2^{4+k})(5^k)$$

You can now make separate equivalences:

$5^{14} = 5^k$, so $14 = k$

You have already solved for k, but let's confirm that the other equivalence works:

$2^{18} = 2^{4+k}$, so $18 = 4 + k$, so $14 = k$

Let's look at another situation in which changing a quantity with a non-prime base into one with prime bases can be very useful.

Consider the quantity 300^{200}. That's a very, very large number, one that the GRE calculator simply cannot handle. However, you can rewrite this quantity in a way that can help you evaluate it. Let's start by prime factoring the base of 300:

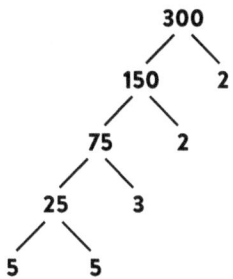

```
            300
           /   \
         150     2
        /   \
      75      2
     /   \
   25      3
  /  \
 5    5
```

factor tree for 300

Thus, you see that your base of 300 can be rewritten as $(2^2)(3^1)(5^2)$. Therefore, you can rewrite your quantity as $[(2^2)(3^1)(5^2)]^{200}$, which becomes $(2^{400})(3^{200})(5^{400})$. How is that useful?

Question: What is the greatest integer value of n such that 300^{200} is divisible by 2^n? Remember that divisibility questions should always be set up as fractions, with divisibility demonstrated when terms in the numerator can cancel out all of the terms in the denominator. So you should write the following fraction:

$$\frac{(2^{400})(3^{200})(5^{400})}{2^n}$$

The numerator will be divisible by the denominator as long as terms in the numerator can cancel out all of the terms in the denominator. Remember that primes don't interact with one another, so the 2^{400} in the numerator has to cancel out the 2^n in the denominator. Therefore, n can be as large as 400, but no greater. The answer is 400.

Note that if you had 2^{401} in the denominator, after you canceled out the common 2s, you'd have the following fraction:

$$\frac{(3^{200})(5^{400})}{2^1}$$

No matter how many 3s and 5s are in the numerator, they cannot cancel even a single 2 in the denominator, so this fraction will generate a non-integer number, and thus, the numerator of 300^{200} would not be divisible by 2^{401}.

Fractional Bases with Negative Exponents

The second rule, that $\left(\frac{x}{y}\right)^2 = \frac{x^2}{y^2}$, helps to explain how to efficiently rewrite base and exponent quantities with fractional bases and negative exponents. Let's first discuss negative exponents in general, then I'll discuss the particular case of a fractional base.

Consider the expression $\frac{a^2}{a^5}$.

$$\frac{(a)(a)}{(a)(a)(a)(a)(a)} = \frac{1}{(a)(a)(a)} = \frac{1}{a^3}$$

According to the second rule, this gives you a^{2-5}, or a^{-3}.

Thus, we have shown that $a^{-3} = \frac{1}{a^3}$.

One way to summarize the demonstration above is to say that any base with a negative exponent needs to be moved to the other side of a fraction line, which turns the exponent from negative to positive. If you think of a^{-3} as the fraction $\frac{a^{-3}}{1}$, then you can rewrite it as $\frac{1}{a^3}$.

If you have an expression such as $\frac{1}{y^{-2}}$, you can rewrite that as $\frac{y^2}{1}$, or simply y^2.

If a fraction line is given to you, then rewriting is even easier:

$$\frac{(x^{-2})(y^3)}{(x^4)(y^{-1})}$$

Simply rewrite as:

$$\frac{(y^1)(y^3)}{(x^2)(x^4)}$$

Then, combine terms with equal bases to get $\frac{y^4}{x^6}$.

Now, we can discuss the particular case of rewriting terms with fractional bases and negative exponents.

Consider the expression $\left(\frac{1}{5}\right)^{-2}$. It can be rewritten as $\frac{1^{-2}}{5^{-2}}$, and using the fraction line strategy, you can rewrite that as $\frac{5^2}{1^2}$, or simply 5^2. It's useful to memorize the following: If a fraction is taken to a negative exponent, you can take the reciprocal of the fraction and thereby make the exponent positive. So $\left(\frac{1}{5}\right)^{-2}$ can be rewritten in one step as $\left(\frac{5}{1}\right)^2$, or simply 5^2.

Common Exponential Equivalents

Please fill in the missing components and turn the page for full solutions.

This is the same as...	...this.
$2^4 5^4$	10^4
$3^5 2^5$	
$\dfrac{12^7}{4^7}$	3^7
$\dfrac{36^4}{3^4}$	
	21^2
$\dfrac{4^3 5^3}{2^3}$	

Advanced Common Base Questions

Sometimes, the test writers can make it far more challenging for you to see how the bases can align with one another. Below are two such examples. Please take a minute to see how you can find common bases and match exponents to solve for the variables in the following examples.

If $2^x + 2^x = 2^6$, what is the value of x?

It is important to avoid the common mistake of simplifying the left side of this equation as 2^{2x}. The rule is to add the exponents when *multiplying* terms with the same base. The rule doesn't apply when you are asked to *add* terms with the same base!

You can solve this problem with two good methods. The first method is to remember that adding two identical terms together is the same as multiplying that term by 2. In other words: $3 + 3$ can be rewritten as $3(2)$, as both expressions equal 6. So:

$(2^x)(2) = (2^6)$

Recall from the beginning of this chapter that 2 can be written as 2^1, giving you $(2^x)(2^1) = (2^6)$.

You can use the multiplication rule to write the left side of the equation as 2^{x+1}, so $2^{x+1} = 2^6$.

If quantities with the same base are set equal to one another, then the exponents of those quantities must be equal, so set $x + 1 = 6$ and $x = 5$.

Common Exponential Equivalents Solutions

This is the same as...	...this.
$2^4 5^4$	10^4
$3^5 2^5$	6^5
$\dfrac{12^7}{4^7}$	3^7
$\dfrac{36^4}{3^4}$	12^4
$7^2 3^2*$	21^2
$\dfrac{4^3 5^3}{2^3}$	10^3

Multiple answers possible

For our second method, remember that you can *factor out shared terms* from certain expressions!

Consider the original equation: $(2^x) + (2^x) = (2^6)$

On the left side, you are adding two terms that share a common factor: 2^x. You can rewrite the equation as $(2^x)(1 + 1) = 2^6$.

That simplifies to $(2^x)(2) = 2^6$. From there, follow the same solution path you followed in the first method.

Let's consider an example that demonstrates the flexibility of the second method.

If $3^6 - 3^3 = (26)(3^a)$, what is the value of *a*?

Again, there is no rule for *subtracting* base and exponent quantities, even ones with common bases, but you can factor out the common factor on the left side:

$(3^3)(3^3 - 1) = (26)(3^a)$

Using the calculator, you can calculate that the value of $(3^3 - 1) = 26$. So you have $(3^3)(26) = (26)(3^a)$.

Divide both sides by 26 to get $3^3 = 3^a$, and solve for $a = 3$.

One more example: Consider the expression $\dfrac{3^{15} - 3^{14}}{2}$

In the numerator, factor out the shared term 3^{14}: $3^{14}(3^1 - 1)$, which can be rewritten as $3^{14}(2)$.

Now the expression $\dfrac{3^{14}(2)}{2} = 3^{14}$, so you have determined that your original expression can be simplified to 3^{14}.

Fractional Exponents

Fractional exponents are also uncommon on the GRE, but let's briefly discuss them in case you happen to run into them on your exam. Fractional exponents work the same way as any other exponents, and they follow the same rules. Here are a few examples to illustrate:

$$x^{\frac{1}{3}}x^{\frac{1}{3}} = x^{\frac{2}{3}}$$

$$(x^{\frac{1}{3}})^{\frac{1}{2}} = x^{\frac{1}{6}}$$

$$x^{\frac{1}{2}}y^{\frac{1}{2}} = (xy)^{\frac{1}{2}}$$

Finally, it's important to note and remember the relationship between roots and fractional exponents. Taking the root of a number is the equivalent of taking the number to an inverse exponent, as per the following examples:

$$\sqrt{x} = x^{\frac{1}{2}}$$

$$\sqrt[3]{x} = x^{\frac{1}{3}}$$

$$\sqrt[6]{x^5} = x^{\frac{5}{6}}$$

You can generalize the rule for converting between roots and fractional exponents as:

$$x^{\frac{a}{b}} = \sqrt[b]{x^a}$$

Again, in much the same way that dividing by 2 and multiplying by $\frac{1}{2}$ are equivalent, taking a square root and taking a number to an exponent of $\frac{1}{2}$ are also equivalent.

Roots

Roots are a way of representing the inverse of exponents. $5^2 = 25$, so $\sqrt{25} = 5$; $4^3 = 64$, so $\sqrt[3]{64} = 4$. There is one key way in which roots, or radical expressions, differ from exponent expressions.

You know that if $x^2 = 25$, then $x = 5$ or -5 because either number squared would equal 25.

However, $\sqrt{x}$ is defined as the non-negative square root of x. Therefore, if you are given the expression $\sqrt{25}$, the answer is only the non-negative root of 25, or positive 5.

Aside from the exception noted above, roots follow the same rules of exponents that we've been discussing. Here are some examples to illustrate:

$$\sqrt{8}\sqrt{2} = \sqrt{16} = 4$$

$$\frac{\sqrt{8}}{\sqrt{2}} = \sqrt{4} = 2$$

As with base and exponent quantities, sometimes it makes sense to rewrite the numbers inside a given radical.

Example: $\sqrt{32} - \sqrt{8}$

$\sqrt{32}$ can be rewritten as $\sqrt{16}\sqrt{2}$, so $\sqrt{32}$ can be simplified to $4\sqrt{2}$.

$\sqrt{8}$ can be rewritten as $\sqrt{4}\sqrt{2}$, so $\sqrt{8}$ can be simplified to $2\sqrt{2}$.

Now you have $4\sqrt{2} - 2\sqrt{2}$, which resolves to $2\sqrt{2}$.

Example: $\sqrt{(2.5)(10^7)}$

It makes sense that you would want to see perfect squares inside radicals because perfect squares have integer square roots. 2.5 is not a perfect square, but 25 is. Why not borrow a 10 from the 10^7 quantity (leaving 10^6) and use it to turn 2.5 into 25?

$\sqrt{(25)(10^6)}$ is the same as $\sqrt{25}\sqrt{10^6}$.

You know that $\sqrt{25} = 5$, so let's consider $\sqrt{10^6}$. You learned earlier in the chapter that $\sqrt{x}$ is equivalent to $x^{\frac{1}{2}}$, so if you write $\sqrt{10^6}$ as $(10^6)^{\frac{1}{2}}$, you get 10^3. You know that $10^3 = 1{,}000$, so $(5)(1{,}000)$ gives you an answer of 5,000.

You can use the equivalence of $\sqrt{x}$ to $x^{\frac{1}{2}}$ to figure out how to simplify even large numbers via the magic of prime factorization.

Example: $\sqrt{7{,}200}$

The prime factorization of $7{,}200 = (2^5)(3^2)(5^2)$, so $\sqrt{7{,}200} = \sqrt{(2^5)(3^2)(5^2)}$.

You know that you can rewrite $\sqrt{(2^5)(3^2)(5^2)}$ as $[(2^5)(3^2)(5^2)]^{\frac{1}{2}}$.

The $\frac{1}{2}$ power interacts well with even exponents but not as well with the 2^5. So rewrite 2^5 as $(2^4)(2^1)$.

Now you have $[(2^4)(2^1)(3^2)(5^2)]^{\frac{1}{2}}$.

$(2^4)^{\frac{1}{2}} = 2^2 = 4$, so you can bring that outside the radical.

$(3^2)^{\frac{1}{2}} = 3^1 = 3$, so you can bring that outside the radical.

$(5^2)^{\frac{1}{2}} = 5^1 = 5$, so you can bring that outside the radical.

You now have $(4)(3)(5)\sqrt{2}$, which simplifies to $60\sqrt{2}$.

Roots are less common on the GRE, but I will offer some practice so that you'll be ready if you happen to run into them.

The Unusual Exponential Behavior of Different Types of Numbers

It is important to note that different types of numbers behave differently when taken to exponents. More specifically, numbers behave differently according to whether they fit into one of four different categories: less than –1, between –1 and 0, between 0 and 1, and greater than 1.

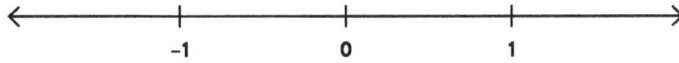

To illustrate, let's take the simple example of squaring x, and let's take a look at four different samples, one each from the different groups: -2, $-\frac{1}{2}$, $\frac{1}{2}$, and 2. Here are the results that you get:

x	x^2	Result
-2	4	$x < x^2$
$-\frac{1}{2}$	$\frac{1}{4}$	$x < x^2$
$\frac{1}{2}$	$\frac{1}{4}$	$x > x^2$
2	4	$x < x^2$

When x is a positive number greater than 1, it gets greater when squared. When x is a negative number, it gets greater when squared, but when x is between 0 and 1, it gets less when squared.

Knowing such results can tell you something about a number, and when you don't know whether a term is positive or negative, or what its value might be, you want to consider the various possible behaviors.

Exponential Behavior Drill

Determine whether each statement must be true, could be true, or must be false per each potential value of x.

Statement	$x < -1$	$-1 < x < 0$	$0 < x < 1$	$1 < x$
$x^2 > x$	must be true	must be true	must be false	must be true
$x^3 > x$				
$x^3 > x^2$				
$x^4 > x^3$				

<u>Solutions</u>

You can think about each of these relationships by testing hypothetical terms. For example, you can use –0.5 for x to see that:

If $x = -0.5$
$x^2 = 0.25$
$x^3 = -0.125$
$x^4 = 0.0625$

You can use these values to evaluate the various relationships you are asked about, and see that when x is between –1 and 0, x^2 must be greater than x, and so on.

Alternatively, inequalities, such as those presented in the columns to the left, can be considered and simplified algebraically. For example, you can evaluate $x^4 > x^3$ as follows:

Is $x^4 > x^3$?
$x^4 - x^3 > 0$
Is $x^3(x - 1) > 0$?

Then, you can evaluate the different potential values of x using positive/negative rules from here.

Exponential Behavior Drill Solutions

Statement	$x < -1$	$-1 < x < 0$	$0 < x < 1$	$1 < x$
$x^2 > x$	must be true	must be true	must be false	must be true
$x^3 > x$	must be false	must be true	must be false	must be true
$x^3 > x^2$	must be false	must be false	must be false	must be true
$x^4 > x^3$	must be true	must be true	must be false	must be true

Sample Questions

1. $x > 1$

<u>Quantity A</u>   <u>Quantity B</u>

$\dfrac{x^3 x^5}{x^2}$ $\dfrac{(x^2)^3}{x}$

Ⓐ Quantity A is greater.
Ⓑ Quantity B is greater.
Ⓒ The two quantities are equal.
Ⓓ The relationship cannot be determined from the information given.

Solution

$$\frac{x^3 x^5}{x^2} = \frac{x^8}{x^2} = x^6$$

$$\frac{(x^2)^3}{x} = \frac{x^6}{x} = x^5$$

If $x > 1$, then x^6 must be greater than x^5; thus, **Quantity A must be greater than Quantity B**.

2. If $-1 < x < 0$, which of the following must be true?

Indicate <u>all</u> such choices.

A $x^2 < x$
B $x^3 < x$
C $x^4 < x^2$
D $x^3 < x^5$
E $x^{-2} < x^{-1}$

Solution

You can choose a sample value, such as -0.5, to test and consider each answer. You can also choose a fraction such as $-\frac{1}{2}$ if you find that computation more comfortable.

For [A], the square of a negative number will always be positive and thus greater than the original number, so [A] must be false.

[B] does seem to hold true for all such numbers in absolute terms: numbers such as 0.5 get lesser and lesser as they get taken to greater exponents, but this gets turned around when the decimals are negative. For example, $-0.5^3 = -0.125$, which is greater than -0.5. So [B] must be false as well.

If you test out [C] with -0.5, you get $(-0.5)^2$, which is 0.25, and $(-0.5)^4$, which is 0.0625. You can extrapolate from this that x^2 will always be greater than x^4 for all values between -1 and 0, and [C] must be true.

If you test out [D] with -0.5, you get $(-0.5)^3$, which is -0.125, and $(0.5)^5$, which is -0.03125. You can extrapolate from this that x^5 will always be greater than x^3 for all values between -1 and 0 and [D] must be also true.

Finally, if you test out [E] with -0.5, you get $(-0.5)^{-2} = \frac{1}{(-0.5)^2} = \frac{1}{0.25} = 4$, and $(-0.5)^{-1} = \frac{1}{-0.5} = -2$. As -2 is not greater than 4, [E] does not have to be true.

Therefore, [C] and [D] are the correct answers.

The Exponent Rules You Need to Know

$a^5 a^3 = a^8$	If $a^x = a^y$, $x = y$
$\dfrac{a^5}{a^3} = a^2$	$a^0 = 1$
$a^{-2} = \dfrac{1}{a^2}$	$\dfrac{1}{a^{-2}} = a^2$
$(a^2)^3 = a^6$	$\sqrt{a} = a^{\frac{1}{2}}$
$a^3 b^3 = (ab)^3$	$\sqrt[x]{a^y} = a^{\frac{y}{x}}$
$5a^3 + 2a^3 = 7a^3$	

Exponents and Roots Practice Drill

Simplify the following expressions.

1. $\dfrac{4^{12} 6^{12}}{24^{11}}$	2. $4\sqrt{3} + 3(3)^{\frac{1}{2}} + 3(2)^{\frac{1}{2}}$
3. $\dfrac{3^2 5^3}{3^3 5^2}$	4. $(4\sqrt{3})(3\sqrt{3})(2\sqrt{2})$
5. $[(x^4)(x^3)](x^6)$	6. $\dfrac{x^{-5}}{x^{-8}}$
7. $\dfrac{5^x 6^x}{3^x}$	8. $(4\sqrt{18})(2\sqrt{2})$

Exponents and Roots Practice Drill Solutions

1. $\dfrac{4^{12}6^{12}}{24^{11}}$ $\dfrac{24^{12}}{24^{11}}$ **24**	2. $4\sqrt{3} + 3(3)^{\frac{1}{2}} + 3(2)^{\frac{1}{2}}$ $4\sqrt{3} + 3\sqrt{3} + 3\sqrt{2}$ $\mathbf{7\sqrt{3} + 3\sqrt{2}}$
3. $\dfrac{3^2 5^3}{3^3 5^2}$ $\dfrac{5}{3}$	4. $(4\sqrt{3})(3\sqrt{3})(2\sqrt{2})$ $(12)(3)(2\sqrt{2})$ $(36)(2\sqrt{2})$ $\mathbf{72\sqrt{2}}$
5. $[(x^4)(x^3)](x^6)$ $(x^7)(x^6)$ $\mathbf{x^{13}}$	6. $\dfrac{x^{-5}}{x^{-8}}$ $\dfrac{x^8}{x^5}$ $\mathbf{x^3}$
7. $\dfrac{5^x 6^x}{3^x}$ $\dfrac{30^x}{3^x}$ $\mathbf{10^x}$	8. $(4\sqrt{18})(2\sqrt{2})$ $\sqrt{18} = \sqrt{(9)(2)} = 3\sqrt{2}$ so $\therefore\ 4\sqrt{18} = (4)(3\sqrt{2}) = 12\sqrt{2}$ and $\therefore\ (4\sqrt{18})(2\sqrt{2}) =$ $(12\sqrt{2})(2\sqrt{2})$ $(24)(2)$ **48**

Introduction to Algebraic Translation

If one or more values in an arithmetic equation are unknown, you replace those elements with placeholders called **variables**. The letter x is often used as a variable to represent an unknown value, but any letter can be used as a variable.

Two additional terms you should know are **coefficient** and **constant**. A coefficient is a number attached to a variable through multiplication—for example, in the term $3x$, 3 is a coefficient of x and indicates that you should multiply x by 3. A constant is a letter that replaces a fixed number rather than a variable. For example, if a is a constant, then the value of a is a number such as 3, and that value cannot change over the course of the problem. We'll work more with constants in a later chapter.

For example, you could have the simple equation $5 + 3 = 8$. Or, you could have $5 + x = 8$.

Typically, in this kind of situation, your task is to isolate the unknown:

$5 + x = 8$
$x = 8 - 5$
$x = 3$

To solve for a variable, you want to bring together all terms that involve that variable and work to isolate that variable from exponents, coefficients, and so on. Once you have the variable by itself, you will know its value.

Here are a few more examples where you solve for a variable:

$5x - 9 = 56$ $3x + 13 + 4x - 3 = 24$ $\dfrac{6}{x-1} = \dfrac{9}{x}$
$5x = 65$ $7x + 10 = 24$ $6x = 9x - 9$
$x = 13$ $7x = 14$ $9 = 3x$
                          $x = 2$ $3 = x$

Inequalities

Equations and inequalities generally work in the same fashion, and again, in both cases, your task is typically to isolate the variable to solve for it.

Here's an equation you just worked on:

$5x - 9 = 56$
$5x = 65$
$x = 13$

And here's how it might look as an inequality:

$5x - 9 < 56$
$5x < 65$
$x < 13$

Remember that for inequality relationships, the relationship changes, or, casually speaking, the sign "flips," if you multiply or divide by a negative term (please note that the sign doesn't change if you add or subtract from both sides). Here are some examples of multiplying and dividing by negative terms:

If $-5x > 20$, then $x < -4$

If $\frac{x}{-2} \leq -6$, then $x \geq 12$

This property of inequalities is easy to forget—and therefore, important to keep in mind—if you ever consider multiplying or dividing an inequality by an unknown variable that could be positive or negative.

For example, consider a question that presents the inequality $ac > bc$. You need to look for any context given in the question—does it specify any number properties for a, b, and c?

If, for example, a, b, and c are all positive numbers, then you can simplify the inequality by dividing both sides by c without having to flip the inequality sign! The given inequality $ac > bc$ would be equivalent to the inequality $a > b$.

Isolate x Drill

1. $5x - 13 > 3x + 9$

2. $5^{x-1} > 125$

3. $\dfrac{6\sqrt{6-x} - 11}{3^2 - 2^3} = 1$

4. $\dfrac{75}{7x - 3} = 3$

5. $\dfrac{1}{3}x + \dfrac{1}{4}x < 14$

6. $\dfrac{4x - 8}{8 - x} = 4$

7. $4x^3 - 2x^2 + 18x + 17 = 2x^3 - 2x^2 + 18x + 71$

8. $5\sqrt{x} = 15 + 2\sqrt{x}$

9. $x + x + 1 + x + 2 + x + 3 = 48 - 2x$

Isolate x Drill Solutions

1. $5x - 13 > 3x + 9$

   $2x > 22$

   $\boldsymbol{x > 11}$

2. $5^{x-1} > 125$

   $5^{x-1} > 5^3$

   $x - 1 > 3$

   $\boldsymbol{x > 4}$

3. $\dfrac{6\sqrt{6-x} - 11}{3^2 - 2^3} = 1$

   $\dfrac{6\sqrt{6-x} - 11}{9 - 8} = 1$

   $6\sqrt{6-x} - 11 = 1$

   $6\sqrt{6-x} = 12$

   $\sqrt{6-x} = 2$

   $6 - x = 4$

   $\boldsymbol{x = 2}$

4. $\dfrac{75}{7x - 3} = 3$

   $75 = 3(7x - 3)$

   $75 = 21x - 9$

   $84 = 21x$

   $\boldsymbol{4 = x}$

5. $\dfrac{1}{3}x + \dfrac{1}{4}x < 14$

   multiply everything by 12 to

   remove denominators

   $4x + 3x < 168$

   $7x < 168$

   $\boldsymbol{x < 24}$

6. $\dfrac{4x - 8}{8 - x} = 4$

   $4x - 8 = 4(8 - x)$

   $4x - 8 = 32 - 4x$

   $8x = 40$

   $\boldsymbol{x = 5}$

7. $4x^3 - 2x^2 + 18x + 17 = 2x^3 - 2x^2 + 18x + 71$

   $2x^3 = 54$

   $x^3 = 27$

   $\boldsymbol{x = 3}$

8. $5\sqrt{x} = 15 + 2\sqrt{x}$

   $3\sqrt{x} = 15$

   $\sqrt{x} = 5$

   $\boldsymbol{x = 25}$

9. $x + x + 1 + x + 2 + x + 3 = 48 - 2x$

   $4x + 6 = 48 - 2x$

   $6x = 42$

   $\boldsymbol{x = 7}$

If c is identified as a negative number, you can simplify the inequality by dividing both sides by c and flipping the inequality sign! The given inequality $ac > bc$ would be equivalent, in this context, to the inequality $a < b$.

However, if no context is given for your variables, you don't know whether dividing by c would require you to flip the inequality sign! You, therefore, would not be able to conclude whether $a > b$ or $a < b$.

There is also value in approaching certain problems by combining two inequalities into one. For example:

Cindy purchases a car that costs $\$p$ and also pays a sales tax of 4.5% of the purchase price. If the total amount of her purchase payment is between $25,000 and $30,000, which of the following could be $\$p$, the price of the car before the application of sales tax?

Cindy's total payment can be written as $(1.045)(p)$. You, therefore, know that $1.045p > \$25{,}000$, and that $1.045p < \$30{,}000$.

If you choose, you can write this as the single inequality expression:

$\$25{,}000 < 1.045p < \$30{,}000$

This inequality has three segments, and the rule is that whatever you do to the middle segment has to be done to the left and right segments, as you are really simplifying two separate inequalities at the same time. So if you divide all three segments by 1.045, you get:

$\$23{,}923.44 < p < \$28{,}708.13$

You now know that the purchase price (if represented in integer form) would have to be greater than $23,924 but less than $28,709.

Introduction to Word Translation

Many GRE quantitative questions will require you to interpret situations in words and convert them into mathematical expressions. You want to be proficient with this, and you want to note any particular instances that cause you difficulty.

The Importance of "Is"

Almost all word problems involve the word "is" or its equivalents (e.g., "equals" or "represents"), and these words are vitally important for setting up mathematical equations. "Is" tells you which elements are equal to one another, or, in the case of "is greater than," etc., the "is" tells you of other relationships.

Start there, and then think of how components link to this relationship. If, for example, you are told that Sean *is* 5 years older than David, in mathematical terms, you can say $S = D + 5$ because Sean's age is David's age plus 5.

If Tom *is more than* twice as old as Barry, in mathematical terms, you can say $T > 2B$ because Tom's age is more than 2 times Barry's age.

Additional Basic Relationships

Here are other types of relationships common among mathematical terms and examples of how they might be presented in a word problem.

x + 7
7 more than x
Sum of x and 7
x increased by 7

x − 4
4 less than x
x decreased by 4
x minus 4

6x
6 times x
The product of 6 and x
x multiplied by 6

$\dfrac{x}{3}$
The quotient of x and 3
x divided by 3
The ratio of x to 3

$\dfrac{1}{x}$
The reciprocal of x

$\sqrt{x}$
The square root of x

x^2
The square of x

Advanced Algebraic Translations

It is helpful to be able to construct an average equation by dividing the sum of a set of values by the number of values in the set.

For example, "the average of x, y, and 7" can be translated as $\frac{x + y + 7}{3}$.

If you have a number represented as a decimal (and an integer such as 3 can, if you choose, be represented as the decimal 3.0), then moving the decimal one place to the right means multiplying the original number by 10, and moving the decimal one place to the left means dividing the original number by 10.

For example, if the decimal point of a certain positive decimal number x is moved 3 places to the right, you can translate that as $(x)(10^3)$. If the decimal point of a certain positive decimal number x is moved 3 places to the left, you can translate that as $\frac{x}{10^3}$.

Word Translation Drill

Here are a few phrases for you to practice translating. Please write out the mathematical equivalents.

6 more than 3 times the value of x is equal to 18.
The sum of x, y, and $2z$ is 32.
$3x$ decreased by $2y$ is 19.
x is 4 more than one-third of y.
The value of x is less than or equal to y minus $2z$.
The product of x and y is greater than the ratio of x to y.

Word Translation Drill Solutions

6 more than 3 times the value of x is equal to 18. **$3x + 6 = 18$**
The sum of x, y, and $2z$ is 32. **$x + y + 2z = 32$**
$3x$ decreased by $2y$ is 19. **$3x - 2y = 19$**
x is 4 more than one-third of y. **$x = \frac{1}{3}y + 4$**
The value of x is less than or equal to y minus $2z$. **$x \leq y - 2z$**
The product of x and y is greater than the ratio of x to y. **$xy > \frac{x}{y}$**

Solving with Two (or More) Unknowns

GRE quantitative questions often begin with several unknowns; you are then commonly asked to solve for one of them and are given information about the others. This is perhaps one of the most fundamental ways inferences work in math.

Here's a simple example to illustrate: Imagine that $x = y + 2$, and I tell you that $y = 4$. In this case, you can plug 4 in for y and solve for x:

$x = y + 2$
$x = 4 + 2$
$x = 6$

Notice that this can work with any number of unknowns. You can imagine that $x = y + z$, and you may be told that $y = 4$ and $z = 6$. In this case, you can solve for x this way:

$x = y + z$
$x = 4 + 6$
$x = 10$

Substitution and Elimination

Next, I will go over a couple of other ways in which you can convert situations that start with multiple unknowns into those with just one (or no) unknowns through processes known as substitution or elimination.

In substitution, you substitute one equation into the other to get rid of a variable. Here's a simple example to illustrate:

$x + y = 6; y = 2x$

You can substitute $2x$ for y in the first equation and solve for x:

$x + 2x = 6$
$3x = 6$
$x = 2$

Now that you know that $x = 2$, you can find y by plugging 2 into either original equation in place of x. For example, you go to the original equation $y = 2x$ and write it as $y = (2)(2)$, so $y = 4$.

In elimination, you combine entire equations through addition or subtraction to eliminate one or more variables, allowing you to use the resulting combined equation to solve for a remaining variable. Here are two simple examples to illustrate:

Addition

$3x + y = 26; x - y = 2$

Notice here that if you add the two equations together, you can eliminate the y variable and be left with just x:

$$
\begin{array}{rl}
3x + y &= 26 \\
x - y &= 2 \\
\hline
4x\quad\ &= 28 \\
x\quad\ &= 7
\end{array}
$$

Now that you know the value of x, you can insert it into either equation to solve for y:

$7 - y = 2; y = 5$

Subtraction

$3x + y = 26; x + y = 2$

Note here that combining these two equations using addition will not eliminate a variable. However, subtracting the second equation from the first will eliminate the y variable. Just be sure to remind yourself at each step that you are subtracting the second equation's term from the first equation's term.

$$
\begin{array}{rl}
3x + y &= 26 \\
x + y &= 2 \\
\hline
2x\quad\ &= 24 \\
x\quad\ &= 12
\end{array}
$$

Plugging 12 into the second original equation in place of x gives you:

$12 + y = 2$
$y = -10$

Note that subtracting the second equation from the first is equivalent to multiplying both sides of the second equation by (–1) and then combining them through addition. Some students feel more comfortable with that approach:

Given equations: $3x + y = 26; x + y = 2$

Rewrite second equation as: $-x - y = -2$

Combine equations via addition:

$$3x + y = 26$$
$$\underline{-x - y = 2}$$
$$2x\phantom{{}+y} = 24$$
$$x\phantom{{}+2y} = 12$$

There is another useful application for combining equations via addition or subtraction. Sometimes a question will ask you to find the value of an expression including both x and y variables rather than simply solving for the value of one or the other. In such cases, sometimes combining the equations can directly produce the correct answer without having to solve for the values of each variable individually. For example:

If $3x + 5y = 27$, and $2x - 3y = 13$, what is the value of $5x + 2y$?

Asking for the value of an expression such as $5x + 2y$ is often an indication that you can generate that exact expression through addition or subtraction of equations.

Align the equations and combine via addition:

$$3x + 5y = 27$$
$$\underline{2x - 3y = 13}$$
$$5x + 2y = 40$$

Our solution is 40, and you generated it directly by adding the equations. That is much more efficient than solving for x, then plugging x into an original equation to find y and then calculating the value of $5x + 2y$.

Solve for *x* with *y* Warm-up Drill

Here are sample situations for you to practice. For each set of equations, practice solving for x and y.

1. $3x - 2y = 7$; $y = 4$	2. $2x + y = 13$; $y = x - 2$
3. $6x + 4y = 10$; $3x + 4y = 1$	4. $x = 3y$; $y^3 = 27$
5. $0.5x - 0.3y = 2.6$; $x = 2y + 1$	6. $3x + 2y = 29$; $3x - 2y = 13$
7. $y = \frac{1}{2}x$; $x + y = 6$	8. $\frac{1}{3}x + \frac{1}{4}y = 4$; $y = x + 2$

Solve for *x* with *y* Warm-up Drill Solutions

1. $3x - 2y = 7$; $y = 4$ $3x - 2(4) = 7$ $3x - 8 = 7$ $3x = 15$ **$x = 5$**	2. $2x + y = 13$; $y = x - 2$ $2x + x - 2 = 13$ $3x = 15$ **$x = 5$; $y = 3$**
3. $6x + 4y = 10$; $3x + 4y = 1$ $6x + 4y = 10$ $-(3x + 4y = 1)$ $3x = 9$ **$x = 3$; $y = -2$**	4. $x = 3y$; $y^3 = 27$ **$y = \sqrt[3]{27} = 3$** **$x = 3(3) = 9$**
5. $0.5x - 0.3y = 2.6$; $x = 2y + 1$ $0.5(2y + 1) - 0.3y = 2.6$ $y + 0.5 - 0.3y = 2.6$ $0.7y + 0.5 = 2.6$ $0.7y = 2.1$ **$y = 3$; $x = 7$**	6. $3x + 2y = 29$; $3x - 2y = 13$ $3x + 2y = 29$ $+(3x - 2y = 13)$ $6x = 42$ **$x = 7$; $y = 4$**
7. $y = \frac{1}{2}x$; $x + y = 6$ $2y = x$ $2y + y = 6$ $3y = 6$ **$y = 2$; $x = 4$**	8. $\frac{1}{3}x + \frac{1}{4}y = 4$; $y = x + 2$ $4x + 3y = 48$ $4x + 3(x + 2) = 48$ $7x + 6 = 48$ $7x = 42$ **$x = 6$; $y = 8$**

Sample Question

If 20 percent of m is equal to 30 percent of l, and 50 percent of l is equal to 25 percent of k, what is the value of m when $k = 200$?

   (A) 100
   (B) 125
   (C) 150
   (D) 180
   (E) 280

Solution

If 50% of l is equal to 25% of k, and if $k = 200$, you can set up the following equation to solve for l:

$0.5l = 0.25(200)$
$0.5l = 50$
$l = 100$

If 20% of m is equal to 30% of l, and if $l = 100$, you can set up the following equation to solve for m:

$0.2m = 0.3(100)$
$0.2m = 30$
$m = 150$

The correct answer is (C).

Multi-Variable Comparatives

On the GRE, when you are given multiple situations involving multiple variables, you often won't be able to find exact values, and frequently that won't be your main task. Instead, you'll be required to think about how the variables compare to one another, and you'll have to consider whether or not you have enough information to know this relationship.

Sample Question 1

$x > 2y$

Quantity A   Quantity B
$5x$ $10y$

ⓐ Quantity A is greater.
ⓑ Quantity B is greater.
ⓒ The two quantities are equal.
ⓓ The relationship cannot be determined from the information given.

Solution

In this case, you never need to know the exact values of x and y, but you know enough about them to know that **Quantity A must be greater than Quantity B**, for if x is greater than $2y$, then $5x$ must be greater than $10y$. (If $x > 2y$ then $5x > (5)(2y)$, i.e., $5x > 10y$.)

Here's another example:

Sample Question 2

$x = 0.3z$ and $y = 0.4z$.

Quantity A   Quantity B
$0.2x$ $0.2y$

ⓐ Quantity A is greater.
ⓑ Quantity B is greater.
ⓒ The two quantities are equal.
ⓓ The relationship cannot be determined from the information given.

Solution

The answer depends on knowing whether x or y is greater. It's easy to assume that y would be greater, in which case Quantity B would be greater, but that depends on whether z is positive or negative. If z is negative, x would actually be greater; in that case, Quantity A would be greater.

Thus, in this situation, it cannot be determined, so **the correct answer is (D)**.

y = mx + b

One of the most fundamental and useful relationships in math involves having an *input*, commonly noted with *x* (but can be any variable), and a resulting *output*, commonly noted with *y*.

Imagine that at a certain amusement park, customers have to pay $5 for admission and $2 per ride. You could set up the following equation to figure out how much a certain person spends on admissions and rides:

y = 2x + 5

- **5** is a **constant** amount that must be paid regardless,
- *x* is the unknown **input** (i.e., the number of rides taken)
- **2** is a **multiplier** because it's the cost per ride, and
- *y* is the resulting **output** (i.e., final price).

Now, you can use the equation to figure out the cost based on how many rides the person takes.

Number of Rides	Formula	Cost
0	y = 2x + 5	5
1	y = 2x + 5	7
2	y = 2x + 5	9
3	y = 2x + 5	11

y = mx + b Drill

Convert each given statement into an equation. Solve for y when given x and for x when given y.

1. A certain plant starts the year at 15 inches tall and grows at a constant rate of 3 inches per month.

A. Write an equation to represent the situation.

B. How tall will the plant be after 6 months?

C. How long will it take for the plant to reach 4 feet in height?

2. A certain person starts with $400 in their savings account and puts $150 into it each month.

A. Write an equation to represent the situation.

B. Assuming they earn no interest, how much will they have in their savings account after 3 months?

C. Assuming they earn no interest, how long will it take them to accumulate $1,000 in their savings account?

3. A certain bathtub is filled with 42 gallons of water. The water drains at a rate of 6 gallons per minute.

A. Write an equation to represent the amount of water in the tub after x minutes.

B. How many gallons of water will be in the tub 3 minutes after draining has started?

C. How long will it take to drain the tub completely?

$y = mx + b$ Drill Solutions

1. A certain plant starts the year at 15 inches tall and grows at a constant rate of 3 inches per month.

A. Write an equation to represent the situation.

$y = 3x + 15$

B. How tall will the plant be after 6 months?

$y = 3(6) + 15$
$y = 18 + 15$
$y = 33$ inches

C. How long will it take for the plant to reach 4 feet in height?

$48 = 3x + 15$
$33 = 3x$
$11 = x$
$x = 11$ months

2. A certain person starts with $400 in their savings account and puts $150 into it each month.

A. Write an equation to represent the situation.

$y = 150x + 400$

B. Assuming they earn no interest, how much will they have in her savings account after 3 months?

$y = 150(3) + 400$
$y = 450 + 400$
$y = \$850$

C. Assuming they earn no interest, how long will it take them to accumulate $1,000 in their savings account?

$1,000 = 150x + 400$
$1,000 = 150x + 400$
$600 = 150x$
$4 = x$
$x = 4$ months

3. A certain bathtub is filled with 42 gallons of water. The water drains at a rate of 6 gallons per minute.

A. Write an equation to represent the amount of water in the tub after x minutes.

$y = -6x + 42$ (or $y = 42 - 6x$)

B. How many gallons of water will be in the tub 3 minutes after draining has started?

$y = -6(3) + 42$
$y = -18 + 42$
$y = 24$ gallons

C. How long will it take to drain the tub completely?

$0 = -6x + 42$
$0 = -6(7) + 42$
$x = 7$ minutes

Practice Questions

1. A coworking space charges a set monthly fee that includes free member access to the space for 5 days during the month. Members can pay for additional days at the space at a rate of $24 per day. If a certain member spent 20 days during a particular month at the coworking space and was charged a total of $500, what is the set monthly fee?

(A) $20
(B) $80
(C) $120
(D) $140
(E) $180

2. If $6x - 5 < 3 - 2x$ and $4x + 5 > 2x - 3$, which of the following could be the value of x? Indicate all such values.

A 3
B 1
C −1
D −3
E −5
F −6

3. If $5x - 2y = 9$ and $y = 3x$, what is the value of x?

$x =$ [ ]

4. Both x and y are positive, and $x = 2y$.

Quantity A

$\frac{1}{5}x$

Quantity B

$\frac{1}{10}y$

(A) Quantity A is greater.
(B) Quantity B is greater.
(C) The two quantities are equal.
(D) The relationship cannot be determined from the information given.

5. Deb earns a base wage of $45 per hour worked as well as a yearly bonus. During a certain year, she worked 50 weeks at an average of 40 hours per week. Deb's total pay for the year consisted of her base wages plus her bonus. If her bonus was equal to 25% of her total pay for that year, what was her total pay for the year?

$ [ ]

6. Which of the following is equivalent to 10,000?

(A) $(2^4)(5^5)$

(B) $(2^4)(5^4)$

(C) 10^5

(D) $\dfrac{10^6}{10^3}$

(E) $10^3 + 10^1$

7. $x = \dfrac{a+b}{c} + 1$

$y = \dfrac{a}{c} + b + c; c \neq 0$

Quantity A	Quantity B
x	y

(A) Quantity A is greater.
(B) Quantity B is greater.
(C) The two quantities are equal.
(D) The relationship cannot be determined from the information given.

8. If $\dfrac{(x-2)^2 - 1}{3} + 2 = 7$, what could be the value of x?

$x = \boxed{}$

9. For a certain board game, players receive 4 points for each red card they collect and 5 points for each purple card that they collect. They also lose 3 points for each gray card that they collect. Sarah collected 3 red cards, 3 purple cards, and 3 gray cards. Jonathan collected 4 red cards, 3 purple cards, and 4 gray cards.

Quantity A	Quantity B
Net points for Sarah	Net points for Jonathan

(A) Quantity A is greater.
(B) Quantity B is greater.
(C) The two quantities are equal.
(D) The relationship cannot be determined from the information given.

10. $0 < x < y < 1$

Quantity A	Quantity B
x^{-5}	y^{-4}

(A) Quantity A is greater.
(B) Quantity B is greater.
(C) The two quantities are equal.
(D) The relationship cannot be determined from the information given.

Practice Question Solutions

1. A coworking space charges a set monthly fee that includes free member access to the space for 5 days during the month. Members can pay for additional days at the space at a rate of $24 per day. If a certain member spent 20 days during a particular month at the coworking space and was charged a total of $500, what is the set monthly fee?

(A) $20
(B) $80
(C) $120
(D) **$140**
(E) $180

Solution

If this member spent 20 days during a particular month at the space, 5 of which were free, they paid for 15 days at a rate of $24 per day. Thus, we can set up the following equation to solve for s, the set monthly fee:

$500 = s + 15(24)$
$500 = s + 360$
$140 = s$

The correct answer is (D).

2. If $6x - 5 < 3 - 2x$ and $4x + 5 > 2x - 3$, which of the following could be the value of x? Indicate all such values.

A 3
B 1
C –1
D –3
E –5
F –6

Solution

Let's simplify each inequality by working to isolate the x term, which we can do by moving everything with x to the left of the inequality and simple numbers to the right of the inequality:

$6x - 5 < 3 - 2x$
$8x < 8$
$x < 1$

$4x + 5 > 2x - 3$
$2x > -8$
$x > -4$

Thus, we know that $-4 < x < 1$.

[C] and [D] satisfy the conditions.

3. If $5x - 2y = 9$ and $y = 3x$, what is the value of x?

$x = $ | **−9** |

Solution

We can substitute $3x$ for y in the initial equation and solve for x:

$5x - 2y = 9$
$5x - 2(3x) = 9$
$5x - 6x = 9$
$-x = 9$
$x = -9$

4. Both x and y are positive, and $x = 2y$.

Quantity A	Quantity B
$\frac{1}{5}x$	$\frac{1}{10}y$

Ⓐ **Quantity A is greater.**
Ⓑ Quantity B is greater.
Ⓒ The two quantities are equal.
Ⓓ The relationship cannot be determined from the information given.

Solution

One way to evaluate how the answers compare to one another is to substitute $2y$ for x in Quantity A.

$$\frac{1}{5}x = \left(\frac{1}{5}\right)(2y) = \frac{2}{5}y$$

If y is positive, $\frac{2}{5}y$ will always be greater than $\frac{1}{10}y$, so **Quantity A must be greater than Quantity B**.

Solutions Continued

5. Deb earns a base wage of $45 per hour worked as well as a yearly bonus. During a certain year, she worked 50 weeks at an average of 40 hours per week. Deb's total pay for the year consisted of her base wages plus her bonus. If her bonus was equal to 25% of her total pay for that year, what was her total pay for the year?

$ | **120,000** |

Solution

50 weeks at 40 hours per week is 2,000 hours worked. At $45 per hour, she earned $90,000 in hourly wages.

There are several ways to solve this from here, but if her bonus is equal to 25% of her total pay, that means her wages are equal to 75% of her total pay.

If 90,000 = 0.75 times her total pay, **her total pay =** $\frac{\textbf{90,000}}{\textbf{0.75}}$**, or \$120,000.**

6. Which of the following is equivalent to 10,000?

Ⓐ $(2^4)(5^5)$

Ⓑ $(2^4)(5^4)$

Ⓒ 10^5

Ⓓ $\frac{10^6}{10^3}$

Ⓔ $10^3 + 10^1$

Solution

$(2^4)(5^4)$ can be rewritten as $[(2)(5)]^4 = (10)^4 = 10,000$.

The correct answer is (B).

In terms of the other answers,

For (A), $(2^4)(5^5) = (16)(3,125) = 50,000$.
(C) $10^5 = 100,000$
(D) $\frac{10^6}{10^3} = 10^3 = 1,000$
(E) $10^3 + 10^1 = 1,000 + 10 = 1,010$

We can see that none of them is equal to 10,000.

7. $x = \dfrac{a+b}{c} + 1$

$y = \dfrac{a}{c} + b + c; c \neq 0$

Quantity A	Quantity B
x	y

Ⓐ Quantity A is greater.
Ⓑ Quantity B is greater.
Ⓒ The two quantities are equal.
Ⓓ **The relationship cannot be determined from the information given.**

Solution

$x = \dfrac{a+b}{c} + 1 = \dfrac{a}{c} + \dfrac{b}{c} + 1$

$y = \dfrac{a}{c} + b + c$

In comparing the two values, we can see that they share the component $\dfrac{a}{c}$, and whether x or y is greater is dependent on whether $\dfrac{b}{c} + 1 > b + c$, or vice-versa.

We don't have enough information to answer that question. For example, if b and c were both –1, then $\dfrac{b}{c} + 1 > b + c$, and $x > y$. But if b and c were 2 and 3, respectively, then $\dfrac{b}{c} + 1$ would not be $> b + c$, and x would not be $> y$.

Therefore, the correct answer is (D).

8. If $\dfrac{(x-2)^2 - 1}{3} + 2 = 7$, what could be the value of x?

$x =$ | **6 or –2** |

Solution

If $\dfrac{(x-2)^2 - 1}{3} + 2 = 7$, we can peel away the other elements to eventually isolate x.

First, we can subtract 2 from both sides and then multiply both sides by 3:

$\dfrac{(x-2)^2 - 1}{3} + 2 = 7$

$\dfrac{(x-2)^2 - 1}{3} = 5$

$(x-2)^2 - 1 = 15$

Now we can add 1 to both sides, and we get:

$(x-2)^2 = 16$

At this point, we can infer that $x - 2$ must be 4 or –4. If $x - 2 = 4$, $x = 6$. If $x - 2 = -4$, $x = -2$.

Thus, x can be equal to 6 or –2.

Solutions Continued

9. For a certain board game, players receive 4 points for each red card they collect and 5 points for each purple card that they collect. They also lose 3 points for each gray card that they collect. Sarah collected 3 red cards, 3 purple cards, and 3 gray cards. Jonathan collected 4 red cards, 3 purple cards, and 4 gray cards.

Quantity A	Quantity B
Net points for Sarah	Net points for Jonathan

 (A) Quantity A is greater.
(B) Quantity B is greater.
 (C) The two quantities are equal.
 (D) The relationship cannot be determined from the information given.

Solution

Option 1: If we notice the difference between the two, we can see that Jonathan has 1 more red card and 1 more gray card than Sarah does. The 1 more red card gives him 4 more points and the extra gray card 3 less points, giving him 1 more point total.

Option 2: We can calculate the net points for each:

Sarah: 3 red cards: $(3)(4) = 12$; 3 purple cards: $(3)(5) = 15$; 3 gray cards: $(3)(-3) = -9$.

Total points: $12 + 15 - 9 = 18$

Jonathan: 4 red cards: $(4)(4) = 16$; 3 purple cards: $(3)(5) = 15$; 4 gray cards: $(4)(-3) = -12$.

Total points: $16 + 15 - 12 = 19$

Quantity B is greater than Quantity A.

10. $0 < x < y < 1$

Quantity A	Quantity B
x^{-5}	y^{-4}

(A) Quantity A is greater.
 (B) Quantity B is greater.
 (C) The two quantities are equal.
 (D) The relationship cannot be determined from the information given.

Solution

Since x and y are numbers between 0 and 1, they become lesser and lesser when taken to exponents.

If $x < y$, then x^5 will be less than y^4.

That means x^{-5}, or $\frac{1}{x^5}$, must be greater than y^{-4}, or $\frac{1}{y^4}$, and thus Quantity A must be greater than Quantity B. If you weren't sure how to solve this conceptually, you could do so by testing numbers, which would yield the same results.

4

QUANTITATIVE REASONING

Number Properties

In this lesson, I'll focus on **number properties**, or the characteristics of numbers. Many topics I'll cover will likely fall into the category of things that you haven't needed to think about in a while, such as odd and even numbers, factors, digits, and remainders. I'll cover one topic at a time and discuss only what you need to know for the GRE.

GRE quantitative questions often provide context for individual questions, but some implied context applies to all quantitative questions: all numbers used in the test are real numbers. That means you need to be familiar with certain expressions that are "undefined" on the GRE:

- For every number x, the expression $\frac{x}{0}$ is not defined. Note that if you try to divide any number by 0 in the onscreen GRE calculator, you will receive the ERROR message.
- Any even root (e.g., a square root) of a negative number is undefined. Again, attempting to find the square root (or any even root) of a negative number on the GRE calculator will generate the ERROR message.
- The expression 0^0 is also undefined.

The Number Line

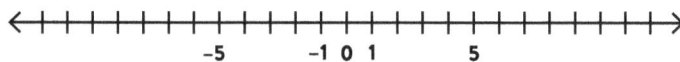

All real numbers can be placed on a number line where distance can be measured between points. Positive numbers go to the right from 0, and negative numbers go to the left from 0. Numerical values **increase** as you move along the number line to the **right** and **decrease** as you move to the **left**.

For example, –100 is less than $-\frac{1}{2}$, and 2 is greater than –500.

Sample Question

Point x is 4 units away from 0 on a number line where each unit is 1 away from another, and point y is within 2 units of x on the number line. Which of the following could be the value of y?

Indicate <u>all</u> such values.

A 6.2
B 5.4
C 2.1
D −1.8
E −5.9
F −6.2

<u>Solution</u>

If x is 4 units away from 0 on the number line, x can be either 4 or −4. If y is within 2 units of x on the number line, it can be either between 2 and 6 or between −2 and −6.

The answer choices that fit those ranges are [B], [C], and [E].

Positive and Negative Numbers

Numbers that are less than 0 are negative, and numbers that are greater than 0 are positive. 0 is neither positive nor negative. Non-negative and non-positive numbers include 0.

- If you multiply or divide two positive numbers, you get a positive result.
- If you multiply or divide two negative numbers, you get a positive result.
- If you multiply or divide a positive by a negative number or vice versa, you get a negative result.
- If you add two positive numbers, you get a positive result.
- If you add two negative numbers, you get a negative result.
- If you add a positive and negative number, you may get a positive or negative result; it depends on the values of the numbers.

Sample Question

If m is a positive number and n is a negative number, which of the following must be positive?

Indicate <u>all</u> such choices.

A $2m + n$
B $m - 2n$
C mn^2
D $(mn)^2$
E $(mn)^3$

<u>Solution</u>

To evaluate each answer, it can be helpful to think about when they might **not** be positive.

[A] If m is a very small positive, such as 2, and n is a very large negative number, such as −100, then [A] does not have to be positive.

[B] Since m is positive, and subtracting a negative number is equivalent to adding a positive one, the result must be positive.

[C] As long as n isn't 0, and it isn't, n^2 will be positive, so mn^2 will be positive as well.

[D] mn is negative, but a negative number squared becomes positive, so $(mn)^2$ will be positive.

[E] mn is negative, and a negative number cubed will remain negative.

[B], [C], and [D] are answers that must be positive.

Integers, Decimals, and Fractions

The next key characteristic of a number is whether it's an integer or not. **Integers** are whole numbers and their negative equivalents, terms such as −3, −2, −1, 0, 1, 2, 3. Numbers such as −3.2 or $\frac{1}{4}$, which must be written as decimals or fractions, are not integers. I'll focus more on decimals and fractions in the next lesson.

The remaining characteristics that I'm going to cover in this lesson will relate to integers.

Odd and Even Numbers

Integers can be odd or even. Even numbers can be divided by 2 with no remainder, while odd numbers cannot be. –6, 8, and 204 are examples of even numbers. –15, 7, and 613 are examples of odd numbers. Numbers that are not integers cannot be even or odd.

Odd (and Even) Behavior

Note that both positive and negative numbers can be odd or even, but a number must be an integer (i.e., not a decimal or fraction) to be considered odd or even.

Just as with positives and negatives, odds and evens follow certain patterns when multiplied, divided, added, and subtracted, and the test writers make use of these patterns to gauge your ability to make inferences.

Here are the fundamental patterns to know about how odd and even numbers behave when combined with one another:

- odd +/– odd = even; $3 + 3 = 6$
- odd +/– even = odd; $3 + 4 = 7$
- even +/– even = even; $4 + 4 = 8$
- odd × odd = odd; $(3)(3) = 9$
- odd × even = even; $(3)(4) = 12$
- even × even = even; $(4)(4) = 16$

It's interesting to note that if you multiply many integers together, all it takes to have the result be even is to have just one of the terms be even. Meanwhile, the only way to generate an odd product from multiplying many integers together is for all of them to be odd.

Sample Question

If x and y are both integers and $x - y$ is even, which of the following must also be even?

Indicate <u>all</u> such choices.

- [A] $x + y$
- [B] $2x + y$
- [C] xy
- [D] $\dfrac{x}{y}$
- [E] $x^2 - y^2$

<u>Solution</u>

For $x - y$ to be even, either both x and y must be even, or both x and y must be odd.

Knowing this, let's evaluate each of the answer choices.

[A] If both are even, $x + y$ will be even, and if both are odd, $x + y$ will be even. In both situations, $x + y$ must be even.

[B] If both x and y are even, $2x + y$ will be even, but if both are odd, $2x + y$ will be odd. [B] does not have to be even.

[C] If both x and y are odd, xy will be odd, so [C] does not have to be even.

[D] You haven't been told that y divides without a remainder into x, and there are also many situations where $\frac{x}{y}$ can produce an odd result (such as if $x = 6$ and $y = 2$), so [D] does not have to be even.

[E] Finally, if both x and y are even, x^2 and y^2 will both be even, and $x^2 - y^2$ will be even. If both x and y are odd, x^2 and y^2 will both be odd, and $x^2 - y^2$ will be even. So, [E] must be even in both situations.

[A] and [E] are correct.

Prime Numbers

Prime numbers are positive integers with exactly two positive factors (1 and themselves). 1 itself is NOT a prime number because 1 has just one positive factor.

There is no formula you can use to derive prime numbers. You have to memorize them or test terms; the way to test whether a number is prime is by seeing whether or not you can multiply other integers together to get that number. A number that you can multiply other integers together to get is a **composite number**.

List of prime numbers up to 100:

2, 3, 5, 7, 11, 13, 17, 19, 23, 29, 31, 37, 41, 43, 47, 53, 59, 61, 67, 71, 73, 79, 83, 89, 97

Note that 2 is the least prime number and the only even prime. If a question asks you to use prime numbers, make sure to consider 2, as it can behave differently from all other prime numbers.

Sample Question

If the sum of two distinct prime numbers is 12, what is the product of those two terms?

[   ]

Solution

Note that "distinct" means "different from each other." The only combination of distinct prime numbers that adds up to 12 is 5 and 7.

$(5)(7) = $ **35**

While on the topic of prime numbers, I want to introduce the concept of prime factorization, a key strategy for the quantitative portion of the GRE. Prime factorization refers to breaking down composite numbers into their multiplicative building blocks, otherwise known as their prime factors. A prime factorization of a composite number is like a fingerprint—no two numbers have the same prime factorization.

In order to prime factor a composite number, create a factor tree like the examples below:

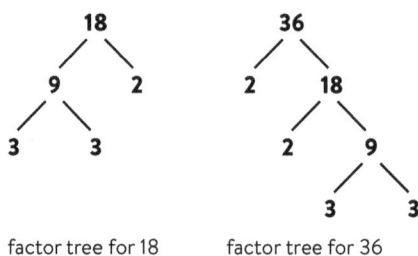

factor tree for 18   factor tree for 36

Note that 18 can be written as $(2)(3^2)$ and 36 can be written as $(2^2)(3^2)$—these are their prime factorizations. A number's prime factorization is useful in many ways, some of which I will discuss now and some of which will appear in later chapters.

You can tell from a number's prime factorization whether that number is the square of an integer (sometimes called a "perfect square"). Numbers that are squares of integers are composed solely of pairs of each prime factor. For example, the prime factorization of 36 contains a pair of 2s and a pair of 3s and no additional unpaired prime factors. 18 is not the square of an integer because while its prime factorization does contain a pair of 3s, it also contains an unpaired 2.

Note that if you are asked to find the least positive integer x such that $18x$ is the square of an integer, the answer would be 2, because $(18)(2)$ would have a prime factorization of $(2^2)(3^2)$. Cubes of integers can be identified by individual prime factors in sets of three—for example, $216 = (2^3)(3^3)$, so 216 is the cube of an integer.

Prime factorization can also help you quickly evaluate a number's divisibility. For example, a number with a prime factorization of $(2^2)(3)(7^3)$ is NOT divisible by 5—if it were, it would have a 5 in its prime factorization. However, that number is divisible by 14 because it contains a 2 and a 7 in its prime factorization, and $(2)(7) = 14$.

Factors and Multiples

x is a **factor** of y if x is able to divide into y cleanly without leaving a remainder. For example, 10 is a factor of 40 because $\frac{40}{10} = 4$. 9 is NOT a factor of 40 because $\frac{40}{9} = 4.444444444...$, which is NOT an integer.

x is a **multiple** of y if y multiplied by an integer equals x. For example, 40 is a multiple of 10 because $(10)(4) = 40$. 40 is NOT a multiple of 9 because there is no integer you can multiply 9 by to get 40.

Each of the following is a way the test might ask whether x is cleanly divisible by y:

- Is the fraction $\frac{x}{y}$ an integer?
- Is x a multiple of y?
- Is y a factor of x?

Note that any integer is both a factor and a multiple of itself. For example, 3 is a factor of 3 because $\frac{3}{3} = 1$, and 3 is a multiple of 3 because $(3)(1) = 3$.

The **greatest common factor** is the greatest number that can divide cleanly without a remainder into two or more terms. For example, the greatest common factor of 16 and 24 is 8. No number greater than 8 is a factor of both 16 and 24.

The **least common multiple** is the least number that can be divided cleanly without a remainder by each of two or more terms. For example, the least common multiple of 8 and 12 is 24. No number less than 24 is a multiple of both 8 and 12.

If you ever have trouble calculating a greatest common factor or least common multiple, you can once again use prime factorization to your benefit. For example, if you are asked to find the greatest common factor and least common multiple of 12 and 18, you can begin by prime factoring each number.

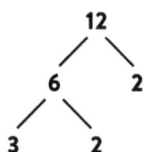

factor tree for 12   factor tree for 18

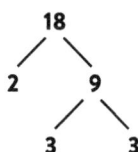

Next, you can create a Venn diagram that displays visually which prime factors these numbers have in common and which prime factors appear in only one of the numbers.

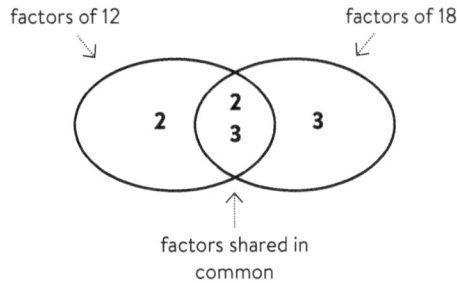

factors of 12   factors of 18

2   (2 / 3)   3

↑
factors shared in
common

The greatest common factor of two numbers is derived by multiplying the factors they share. If, for example, you were asked to consider the greatest common factor of 12 and 18, you can see they share the prime factors 2 and 3; therefore, their greatest common factor is (2)(3) = 6.

The least common multiple of two numbers is derived by multiplying the least number of prime factors required to create either of those two numbers. Your Venn diagram can provide you with this information. In this case, you'd need two 2s and two 3s: (2)(2)(3)(3) = 36, so your least common multiple is 36.

GCF LCM Drill

Find the greatest common factor and the least common multiple of the two given terms.

First Term	Second Term	Greatest Common Factor	Least Common Multiple
50	100		
21	35		
30	24		
36	48		

Solutions

50 is the greatest term that goes into both 50 and 100, and 100 is the least number that both 50 and 100 can go into.

For the remaining examples, always start with the greatest common factor, which is the greatest number that divides all terms, or the product of all common factors. Between 21 and 35, that would be 7; between 30 and 24, that would be 6; and between 36 and 48, that would be 12. To find the least common multiple, you need a term that is a product of all the other factors required to make each number.

factors of 50   factors of 100   factors of 50   factors of 100

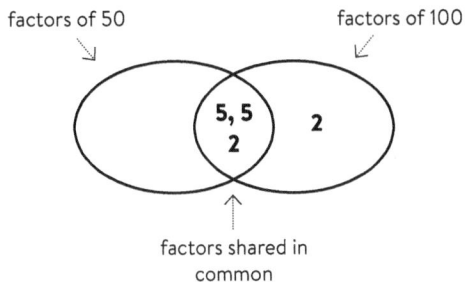

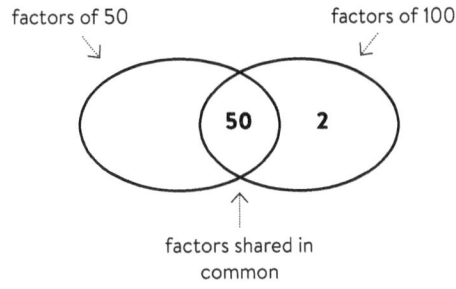

or

factors of 21   factors of 35

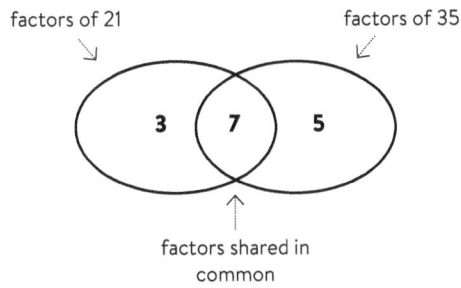

factors of 30   factors of 24   factors of 30   factors of 24

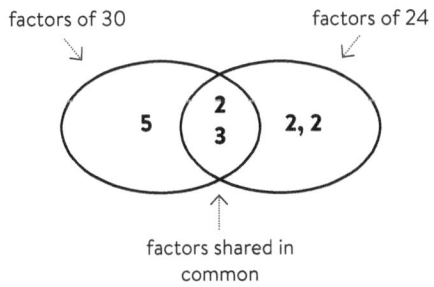

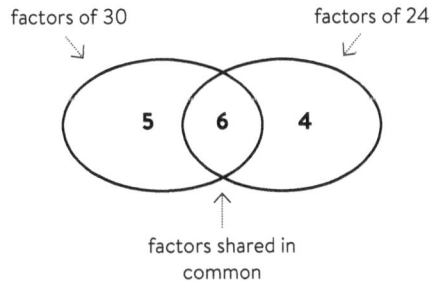

or

factors of 36   factors of 48   factors of 36   factors of 48

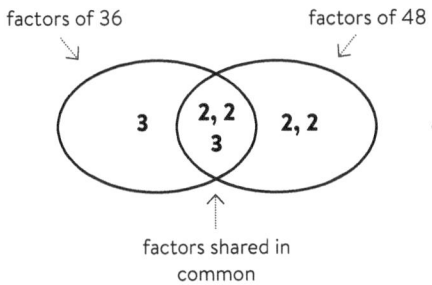

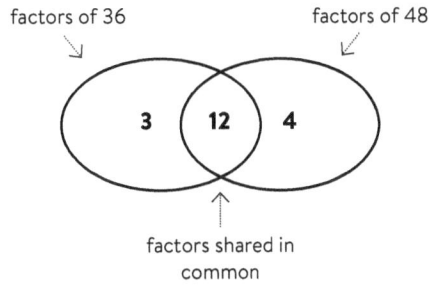

or

GCF LCM Drill Solutions

First Term	Second Term	Greatest Common Factor	Least Common Multiple
50	100	**50**	**100**
21	35	**7**	**105**
30	24	**6**	**120**
36	48	**12**	**144**

Sample Question

Class *A* can be divided evenly into groups of 6, 8, or 9. Class *B* can be divided evenly into groups of 3, 5, or 7.

Quantity A
The least number of people who could be in class *A*

Quantity B
The least number of people who could be in class *B*

Ⓐ Quantity A is greater.
Ⓑ Quantity B is greater.
Ⓒ The two quantities are equal.
Ⓓ The relationship cannot be determined from the information given.

Solution

The number of students in class *A* must be a multiple of 6, 8, and 9. Their least common multiple must have the factors (2)(3)(2)(2)(3) = 72.

The number of students in class *B* must be a multiple of 3, 5, and 7. Their least common multiple must have the factors (3)(5)(7) = 105.

So the least number of people who can be in class *B* is greater. **The answer is (B)**.

Remainders

When one number doesn't divide cleanly into another, the quotient will include digits to the right of the decimal (e.g., $\frac{7}{2}$ = 3.5) or will be expressed as a mixed number (e.g., $\frac{7}{2}$ = $3\frac{1}{2}$). You can also describe this situation by stating the whole number remainder left over after division (e.g., when 7 is divided by 2, there is a remainder of 1).

There is a way to express remainder situations algebraically. Take the example of $\frac{7}{2}$ = 3 remainder 1. That suggests the generalized expression of $\frac{a}{b}$ as $a = b(c) + d$, where *c* is the number of times *b* goes fully into *a*, and *d* is the whole number remainder.

Here are a few things to keep in mind when working with remainders:

- A lesser number divided by a greater number (e.g., $\frac{3}{7}$) will always generate a remainder equal to the lesser number. In other words, 7 goes into 3 zero times with a remainder of 3. You can demonstrate this using the algebraic expression noted above: $3 = 7(0) + 3$.
- If any integer is divided by another integer n, then there are always n possible remainders ranging from 0 through $(n - 1)$. For example, if x is an integer, then $\frac{x}{7}$ can leave a remainder of 0 (if x is a multiple of 7) or the numbers 1, 2, 3, 4, 5, or 6. It is not possible for a remainder to be greater than or equal to the divisor: $\frac{x}{7}$ will never have a remainder of 8 because 7 would divide into x one additional time and leave a remainder of 1.

Generally, questions that ask about remainders are actually testing your understanding of divisibility rules. That is, you'll be able to determine the remainder because you know how a particular divisibility rule works.

Divisibility Rules

Here are some commonly known tools for testing whether a certain term is divisible by another.

x is divisible by 2 if it ends in an even number.
x is divisible by 3 if its digits add up to a multiple of 3.
x is divisible by 4 if its last two digits form a number divisible by 4.
x is divisible by 5 if its last digit is 0 or 5.
x is divisible by 6 if it is divisible by both 2 and 3.
x is divisible by 8 if you can divide it in half 3 times.
x is divisible by 9 if its digits add up to a multiple of 9.
x is divisible by 10 if its last digit is 0.

Sample Question

x is an integer such that x divided by 10 has the same remainder as x divided by 5.

Quantity A	Quantity B
The units digit of x	6

- Ⓐ Quantity A is greater.
- Ⓑ Quantity B is greater.
- Ⓒ The two quantities are equal.
- Ⓓ The relationship cannot be determined from the information given.

<u>Solution</u>

When an integer is divided by 10 or 5, its last digit—the units digit—determines the remainder.

When an integer is divided by 10, its units digit is the remainder (for example, 1,637 divided by 10 would have a remainder of 7).

When an integer is divided by 5, if its units digit is less than 5, that digit itself will be the remainder (for example, 1,632 divided by 5 would have a remainder of 2). If the units digit is greater than 5, the remainder will be that units digit minus 5 (for example, 1,637 divided by 5 would have a remainder of 7 – 5 = 2).

If x is a number such that the remainder is the same when divided by 10 or 5, it must be an integer with a units digit less than 5.

Therefore, **Quantity B must be greater**.

Digits

As you just saw in that example, one final way that you'll be asked to think about numbers is in terms of their digits. Here are the official titles given to the different digits of a number, in order:

9	8	7	6	5	4	3	2	1	.	1	2	3	4	5	6	7	8	9
hundred millions	ten millions	millions	hundred thousands	ten thousands	thousands	hundreds	tens	ones		tenths	hundredths	thousandths	ten thousandths	hundred thousandths	millionths	ten millionths	hundred millionths	billionths

The test writers will often use digit questions to test your ability to round numbers or evaluate unknown possibilities.

Sample Question

How many positive 2-digit integers are there such that one digit is twice the other?

Ⓐ 4
Ⓑ 5
Ⓒ 6
Ⓓ 7
Ⓔ 8

Solution

You can solve this by systematically listing the different possibilities:

12, 24, 36, 48, 21, 42, 63, 84

The correct answer is 8, (E).

Sample Question

The number 4,3_2, which is a multiple of both 3 and 4, is missing its tens digit.

Quantity A	Quantity B
The missing tens digit	2

Ⓐ Quantity A is greater.
Ⓑ Quantity B is greater.
Ⓒ The two quantities are equal.
Ⓓ The relationship cannot be determined from the information given.

Solution

If 4,3_2 is a multiple of 4, the last two digits must be a multiple of 4. That gives you 4,312, 4,332, 4,352, 4,372, and 4,392 as your possibilities.

If 4,3_2 is a multiple of 3, the digits must all add up to a multiple of 3. Of your limited options, the only two that fit the criteria are 4,332 and 4,392.

In either case, the missing tens digit, which is 3 or 9, is greater than 2, so **Quantity A is greater**.

Practice Questions

1. How many 3-digit numbers are there such that the 3 digits add up to 3?

(A) 4
(B) 5
(C) 6
(D) 7
(E) 8

2. x is less than -1.

Quantity A	Quantity B
$\dfrac{x}{x+1}$	$\dfrac{-x}{-x+1}$

(A) Quantity A is greater.
(B) Quantity B is greater.
(C) The two quantities are equal.
(D) The relationship cannot be determined from the information given.

3. If x is a prime number greater than 10, which of the following could also be prime?

Indicate all such expressions.

A | $x + 4$
B | $x + 7$
C | $3x - 1$
D | $4x + 2$

4. $m = 4.62673$

Quantity A	Quantity B
m rounded to the nearest thousandth	m rounded to the nearest ten thousandth

(A) Quantity A is greater.
(B) Quantity B is greater.
(C) The two quantities are equal.
(D) The relationship cannot be determined from the information given.

5. If m and n are both prime numbers and $n = 3m + 1$, which of the following is a multiple of mn?

(A) 24
(B) 45
(C) 56
(D) 90
(E) 110

6. If m is a 2-digit number that has a remainder of 3 when divided by 23 and a remainder of 2 when divided by 7, what is the value of m?

$m = \boxed{}$

7. If a and b are consecutive integers, which of the following must be odd?

Indicate all such choices.

A | $a(a + b)$
B | $a - b$
C | $(a - b)(a + b)$
D | $2a - b$
E | $a - 3b$

8.

Quantity A	Quantity B
The sum of the prime factors of 70	The sum of the prime factors of 90

(A) Quantity A is greater.
(B) Quantity B is greater.
(C) The two quantities are equal.
(D) The relationship cannot be determined from the information given.

Practice Question Solutions

1. How many 3-digit numbers are there such that the 3 digits add up to 3?

Ⓐ 4
Ⓑ 5
Ⓒ 6
Ⓓ 7
Ⓔ 8

Solution

You can answer this question by systematically coming up with a list of all the possibilities:

102
111
120
201
210
300

The correct answer is 6, (C).

2. x is less than –1.

Quantity A	Quantity B
$\dfrac{x}{x+1}$	$\dfrac{-x}{-x+1}$

Ⓐ **Quantity A is greater.**
Ⓑ Quantity B is greater.
Ⓒ The two quantities are equal.
Ⓓ The relationship cannot be determined from the information given.

Solution

If you multiply the numerator and the denominator of Quantity B by –1, you get $\dfrac{x}{x-1}$.

At this point, you can see that what you are being asked to compare is x over 1 more than x versus x over 1 less than x, when x is a negative term less than 1.

It's tough to conceptualize this answer because of all the negatives, so you can test out a few terms.

$x = -2, -3, -4$
$x + 1 = -1, -2, -3$
$x - 1 = -3, -4, -5$

$$\frac{x}{x+1} = \frac{2}{1}, \frac{3}{2}, \frac{4}{3}$$

$$\frac{x}{x-1} = \frac{2}{3}, \frac{3}{4}, \frac{4}{5}$$

You can see a pattern where the numerators will always be the same, but the denominators for $\dfrac{x}{x+1}$ will always be 2 less than those for $\dfrac{x}{x-1}$, meaning that $\dfrac{x}{x+1}$ will always be the greater term.

(A) is correct.

Solutions Continued

3. If x is a prime number greater than 10, which of the following could also be prime?

Indicate <u>all</u> such expressions.

A. $x + 4$
B. $x + 7$
C. $3x - 1$
D. $4x + 2$

Solution

If x is a prime number greater than 10, it must be odd. [B], [C], and [D] all represent situations that must result in even numbers that, if greater than 2, cannot be prime.

[A] is the only viable choice, and one example of a pair of primes that makes [A] work would be 13 and 17.

4. $m = 4.62673$

Quantity A	Quantity B
m rounded to the nearest thousandth	m rounded to the nearest ten thousandth

(A) **Quantity A is greater.**
(B) Quantity B is greater.
(C) The two quantities are equal.
(D) The relationship cannot be determined from the information given.

Solution

m rounded to the nearest thousandth is 4.627.

m rounded to the nearest ten thousandth is 4.6267.

Quantity A is greater.

5. If m and n are both prime numbers and $n = 3m + 1$, which of the following is a multiple of mn?

(A) 24
(B) 45
(C) **56**
(D) 90
(E) 110

Solution

If $n = 3m + 1$, one must be even and the other odd, and if both are primes, and you know, per the given equation, that n must be greater than m, you can infer that $m = 2$ (the only even prime) and $n = 3(2) + 1 = 7$.

mn = 14, and (C), 56, is the one answer that is a multiple of 14.

6. If m is a 2-digit number that has a remainder of 3 when divided by 23 and a remainder of 2 when divided by 7, what is the value of m?

$m =$ | **72** |

Solution

You can derive the full list of 2-digit numbers that have a remainder of 3 when dividing by 23 by adding 3 to each of the multiples of 23:

$23 + 3 = 26$
$46 + 3 = 49$
$69 + 3 = 72$
$92 + 3 = 95$

Of these, 72 is the only term that gives you a remainder of 2 when divided by 7, so $m = 72$.

Solutions Continued

7. If a and b are consecutive integers, which of the following must be odd?

Indicate all such choices.

[A] $a(a + b)$
[B] $a - b$
[C] $(a - b)(a + b)$
[D] $2a - b$
[E] $a - 3b$

Solution

If a and b are consecutive integers, one must be even and one odd. Knowing this, let's evaluate each answer choice to see which must be odd.

[A] If a is odd, then $a(a + b)$ will be odd, and if a is even, then $a(a + b)$ will be even. So [A] does not have to be odd.

[B] Even minus odd and odd minus even always produce odd results, so [B] must be odd.

[C] $a - b$ must be odd, and $a + b$ must be odd, so $(a - b)(a + b)$ must be odd.

[D] If a is odd and b is even, [D] will be even, so this answer does not have to be odd.

[E] If a is odd and b is even, then $a - 3b$ must be odd. If a is even and b is odd, then $a - 3b$ must be odd as well. So [E] must be odd.

The correct answers are [B], [C], and [E].

8.

Quantity A	Quantity B
The sum of the prime factors of 70	The sum of the prime factors of 90

(A) **Quantity A is greater**.
(B) Quantity B is greater.
(C) The two quantities are equal.
(D) The relationship cannot be determined from the information given.

Solution

The prime factors of 70 are 2, 5, and 7, which add up to $2 + 5 + 7 = 14$.

The prime factors of 90 are 3, 3, 5, and 2, which add up to $3 + 3 + 5 + 2 = 13$.

Quantity A is greater.

5

QUANTITATIVE REASONING

Fractions, Decimals, and Percents

In this lesson, I will focus on key issues related to fractions, decimals, and percents. I will, of course, devote the most space and time to the issues that appear most often on the GRE.

Fractions

You can think of a fraction as part of a whole, and you can represent the same fraction in many different ways. If you imagine cutting a pie into 2, 4, 8, or 16 slices, you can see that $\frac{1}{2} = \frac{2}{4} = \frac{4}{8} = \frac{8}{16}$.

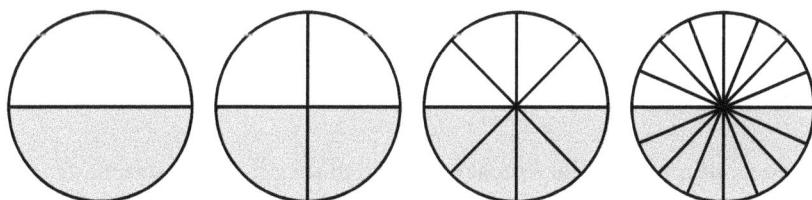

Simplifying Fractions

If you want to simplify a fraction, you can do so by dividing both the numerator and denominator using the same term. Here are some examples:

$$\frac{4}{6} = \frac{4 \div 2}{6 \div 2} = \frac{2}{3}$$

$$\frac{3x}{4x} = \frac{3x \div x}{4x \div x} = \frac{3}{4}$$

$$\frac{14x}{35y} = \frac{14x \div 7}{35y \div 7} = \frac{2x}{5y}$$

Occasionally, you might run into a radical in the denominator. In such situations, it is common practice to get rid of the radical in the denominator, and questions are written in such a way (e.g., with answer choices that don't have radicals in denominators) that expect you to be able to do so. In these cases, you can eliminate a radical in the denominator by multiplying both the numerator and the denominator by the same radical:

$$\frac{2}{\sqrt{3}} = \frac{2\sqrt{3}}{\sqrt{3}\sqrt{3}} = \frac{2\sqrt{3}}{3}$$

Mixed Numbers

A mixed number, such as $2\frac{1}{3}$, is one that has a whole number component and a fractional component. In general, you want to convert mixed numbers into improper fractions to perform any computation with them. You can convert mixed numbers into improper fractions by multiplying the whole number by the denominator of the fraction and adding the result to the numerator. Below are some examples.

$$4\frac{1}{3} = \frac{12}{3} + \frac{1}{3} = \frac{13}{3}$$

$$5\frac{3}{4} = \frac{20}{4} + \frac{3}{4} = \frac{23}{4}$$

$$-2\frac{1}{6} = -\frac{12}{6} + -\frac{1}{6} = -\frac{13}{6}$$

Adding and Subtracting Fractions

You can add or subtract fractions most easily when they have a common denominator. To change the denominator of a fraction without changing its overall value, you must multiply the numerator and denominator of a fraction by the same number.

$$\frac{1}{3} + \frac{2}{5} = \frac{(1)(5)}{(3)(5)} + \frac{(2)(3)}{(5)(3)} = \frac{5}{15} + \frac{6}{15} = \frac{11}{15}$$

$$\frac{1}{2} - \frac{2}{3} = \frac{(1)(3)}{(2)(3)} - \frac{(2)(2)}{(3)(2)} = \frac{3}{6} - \frac{4}{6} = -\frac{1}{6}$$

Multiplying and Dividing Fractions

You don't need common denominators to multiply or divide fractions. Simply multiply fractions straight across. Divide fractions by flipping and multiplying, as shown below.

$$\left(\frac{x}{5}\right)\left(\frac{7}{4}\right) = \frac{7x}{20}$$

$$\frac{\sqrt{5}}{4} \div \frac{3}{5} = \left(\frac{\sqrt{5}}{4}\right)\left(\frac{5}{3}\right) = \frac{5\sqrt{5}}{12}$$

Comparing Fractions

The exam will ask you to compare fractions to one another. You will know the answers to some questions instinctively. When you need to investigate further, you can convert fractions to decimals using your calculator or create common denominators.

$$\frac{3}{5} > \frac{2}{5}$$

If two fractions share the same denominator, the one with the greater numerator is greater.

$$\frac{3}{4} > \frac{3}{5}$$

If two fractions share the same numerator, the one with the lesser denominator is greater.

For example, if you were required to compare $\frac{3}{7}$ and $\frac{2}{5}$, you can use your calculator to see that $\frac{3}{7} \approx 0.429$, and $\frac{2}{5} = 0.4$, so $\frac{3}{7} > \frac{2}{5}$; alternatively, you can put them both over a common denominator, such as 35, and see that $\frac{3}{7} = \frac{(3)(5)}{(7)(5)} = \frac{15}{35}$, and $\frac{2}{5} = \frac{(2)(7)}{(5)(7)} = \frac{14}{35}$, which again shows that $\frac{3}{7} > \frac{2}{5}$.

Fractions Drill

For each pair of fractions, compare values to see which one is greater.

1. $\left(\frac{3}{4}\right)\left(\frac{1}{2}\right) + \frac{1}{2} - \frac{1}{4}$ *vs.* $\left(\frac{2}{3}\right)\left(\frac{1}{3}\right) + \frac{1}{3}$ 2. $\frac{2}{5} - \frac{2}{3}\left(1 - \frac{2}{3}\right)$ *vs.* $\frac{2}{3} - \frac{1}{5}\left(1 - \frac{5}{3}\right)$

3. $x > 0$; $\frac{2x}{3} + \frac{x}{2}$ *vs.* $\frac{\frac{x}{2}}{\frac{3}{5}}$ 4. $\frac{\frac{1}{3} + 2}{\frac{1}{2} + 3}$ *vs.* $\frac{3 - \frac{1}{4}}{4 - \frac{1}{3}}$

5. $\frac{1}{2} - \frac{\left(\frac{1}{2} - \frac{1}{4}\right)^2}{\frac{1}{8}}$ *vs.* $\frac{1}{2} - \frac{1}{3} + \frac{1}{4} - \frac{1}{5}$ 6. $2 - \frac{1}{\sqrt{5}}$ *vs.* $\frac{5}{4} + \frac{5 - 2\sqrt{5}}{12}$

Fractions Drill Solutions

1. $\left(\frac{3}{4}\right)\left(\frac{1}{2}\right)+\frac{1}{2}-\frac{1}{4}>\left(\frac{2}{3}\right)\left(\frac{1}{3}\right)+\frac{1}{3}$

$\quad \frac{3}{8}+\frac{4}{8}-\frac{2}{8} \qquad\qquad \frac{2}{9}+\frac{3}{9}$

$\quad \frac{5}{8} \qquad\qquad\qquad \frac{5}{9}$

2. $\frac{2}{5}-\frac{2}{3}\left(1-\frac{2}{3}\right)<\frac{2}{3}-\frac{1}{5}\left(1-\frac{5}{3}\right)$

$\quad \frac{2}{5}-\frac{2}{3}\left(\frac{1}{3}\right) \qquad\qquad \frac{2}{3}-\frac{1}{5}\left(-\frac{2}{3}\right)$

$\quad \frac{2}{5}-\frac{2}{9} \qquad\qquad\qquad \frac{2}{3}+\frac{2}{15}$

$\quad \frac{18}{45}-\frac{10}{45} \qquad\qquad \frac{10}{15}+\frac{2}{15}$

$\quad \frac{8}{45} \qquad\qquad\qquad \frac{12}{15}$

3. $x>0;\ \dfrac{2x}{3}+\dfrac{x}{2}>\dfrac{\frac{x}{2}}{\frac{3}{5}}$

$\quad \frac{4x}{6}+\frac{3x}{6} \qquad\qquad \left(\frac{x}{2}\right)\left(\frac{5}{3}\right)$

$\quad \frac{7x}{6} \qquad\qquad\qquad \frac{5x}{6}$

4. $\dfrac{\frac{1}{3}+2}{\frac{1}{2}+3}<\dfrac{3-\frac{1}{4}}{4-\frac{1}{3}}$

$\quad \dfrac{\frac{1}{3}+\frac{6}{3}}{\frac{1}{2}+\frac{6}{2}} \qquad\qquad \dfrac{\frac{12}{4}-\frac{1}{4}}{\frac{12}{3}-\frac{1}{3}}$

$\quad \dfrac{\frac{7}{3}}{\frac{7}{2}} \qquad\qquad\qquad \dfrac{\frac{11}{4}}{\frac{11}{3}}$

$\quad \left(\frac{7}{3}\right)\left(\frac{2}{7}\right) \qquad \left(\frac{11}{4}\right)\left(\frac{3}{11}\right)$

$\quad \frac{2}{3} \qquad\qquad\qquad \frac{3}{4}$

5. $\dfrac{1}{2}-\dfrac{\left(\frac{1}{2}-\frac{1}{4}\right)^2}{\frac{1}{8}}<\dfrac{1}{2}-\dfrac{1}{3}+\dfrac{1}{4}-\dfrac{1}{5}$

$\quad \dfrac{1}{2}-\dfrac{\left(\frac{2}{4}-\frac{1}{4}\right)^2}{\frac{1}{8}} \qquad \frac{30}{60}-\frac{20}{60}+\frac{15}{60}-\frac{12}{60}$

$\quad \dfrac{1}{2}-\dfrac{\left(\frac{1}{4}\right)^2}{\frac{1}{8}} \qquad\qquad \frac{13}{60}$

$\quad \dfrac{1}{2}-\left(\frac{1}{16}\right)\left(\frac{8}{1}\right)$

$\quad \dfrac{1}{2}-\dfrac{8}{16}$

$\quad 0$

6. $2-\dfrac{1}{\sqrt{5}}>\dfrac{5}{4}+\dfrac{5-2\sqrt{5}}{12}$

$\quad 2-\dfrac{(1)(\sqrt{5})}{(\sqrt{5})(\sqrt{5})} \qquad \frac{15}{12}+\frac{5-2\sqrt{5}}{12}$

$\quad 2-\dfrac{\sqrt{5}}{5} \qquad\qquad \frac{20-2\sqrt{5}}{12}$

$\quad \dfrac{10-\sqrt{5}}{5} \qquad\qquad \dfrac{10-\sqrt{5}}{6}$

Sample Question

If $a = \frac{1}{3}$ and $b = \frac{1}{4}$, what is the value of $\frac{ab}{a+b}$?

Ⓐ $\frac{1}{12}$

Ⓑ $\frac{1}{7}$

Ⓒ $\frac{7}{12}$

Ⓓ $\frac{12}{7}$

Ⓔ 7

Solution

If $a = \frac{1}{3}$ and $b = \frac{1}{4}$:

$$ab = \left(\frac{1}{3}\right)\left(\frac{1}{4}\right) = \frac{1}{12}$$

$$a + b = \frac{1}{3} + \frac{1}{4} = \frac{4}{12} + \frac{3}{12} = \frac{7}{12}$$

$$\frac{ab}{a+b} = \frac{\frac{1}{12}}{\frac{7}{12}} = \left(\frac{1}{12}\right)\left(\frac{12}{7}\right) = \frac{1}{7}$$

The correct answer is (B).

Decimals

Decimals are another way to express values that are not integers. Make sure you are comfortable converting between fractions and decimals (and vice versa), working with repeating decimals, and rounding.

Converting Fractions and Decimals

To convert a fraction to a decimal, simply divide the numerator by the denominator:

$$\frac{1}{4} = 0.25 \qquad\qquad \frac{6}{5} = 1.2 \qquad\qquad \frac{3}{200} = 0.015$$

To convert a decimal into a fraction, you see what position the decimal is taken to, and use that to determine the denominator of the fraction:

$$0.4 = \frac{4}{10} \qquad\qquad 0.08 = \frac{8}{100} \qquad\qquad 0.525 = \frac{525}{1,000}$$

You can then simplify the fractions as you would normally:

$$\frac{4}{10} = \frac{2}{5} \qquad\qquad \frac{8}{100} = \frac{2}{25} \qquad\qquad \frac{525}{1,000} = \frac{21}{40}$$

Repeating Decimals

Certain decimals never terminate but rather repeat indefinitely. One example is the decimal equivalent of $\frac{1}{3}$, which is 0.3333...

Represent a repeating decimal with this symbol:

$0.\overline{3}$

The component with the bar over is the part that will repeat.

Examples:

$0.\overline{4} = 0.44444...$
$0.\overline{53} = 0.53535353...$
$0.6\overline{2} = 0.622222...$

Terminating Decimals

Some decimals terminate, meaning that they have a finite number of digits to the right of the decimal point. The numbers 1.2, 3.75, and 6.125 are terminating decimals. There is an interesting quantitative question type that draws upon knowledge of terminating decimals. Consider the following fraction-to-decimal conversions:

$\frac{1}{2} = 0.5$

$\frac{1}{3} = 0.\overline{33333}$

$\frac{1}{4} = 0.25$

$\frac{1}{5} = 0.2$

$\frac{1}{6} = 0.1\overline{66666}$

$\frac{1}{7} = 0.\overline{142857}$

$\frac{1}{8} = 0.125$

$\frac{1}{9} = 0.\overline{11111}$

You can use these examples to generalize that whenever n is an integer, $\frac{n}{2}, \frac{n}{4}, \frac{n}{5}$, and $\frac{n}{8}$ will form terminating decimals, whereas $\frac{n}{3}, \frac{n}{6}, \frac{n}{7}$, and $\frac{n}{9}$ will form repeating decimals (more about those in a moment). But you can go even further—after all, 2, 4, and 8 are powers of 2, and 5 is a power of 5. Therefore, if the denominator of a fraction is composed entirely of powers of the prime factors 2 and 5, in any combination, then as long as the numerator is an integer, the resulting decimal will be a terminating decimal.

Example: the fraction $\frac{7}{(2^3)(5^5)}$ will form a terminating decimal.

On the other hand, if the denominator of a fraction contains powers of any prime factor other than 2 or 5, then no integer in the numerator will result in a terminating decimal.

Example: the fraction $\frac{2}{(2^2)(3)(5^2)}$ will NOT form a terminating decimal.

Rounding

Rounding is the act of replacing a number with a simpler, shorter approximation of it. You round to a particular place in the number—for example, the nearest thousand, integer, or hundredth. You round up if the digit after the one you are rounding to is equal to or greater than 5, and you round down if the digit after the one you are rounding to is less than 5.

Example: Round to the nearest tenth:

5.46 = 5.5
0.55 = 0.6
0.349 = 0.3

Sample Question

Which of the following is equal to $\frac{262}{999}$?

Indicate all such choices.

A 0.262262262
B $0.\overline{26}$
C $2.\overline{62}(10^{-1})$
D $0.262\overline{262}$
E $2.\overline{622}(10^{-1})$

<u>Solution</u>

$\frac{262}{999}$ is equal to 0.262262262262262262262..., or $0.\overline{262}$. Let's evaluate each answer choice and see which is equivalent.

[A] 0.262262262 starts out similar, but because it terminates and the number goes on indefinitely, this answer is not equivalent.

[B] $0.\overline{26}$ is equal to 0.262626262626..., which is not the same as the initial term. This answer is not equivalent.

[C] For $2.\overline{62}\,(10^{-1})$, you can see that $2.\overline{62} = 2.6262626262626...$, which, regardless of the impact of 10^{-1}, doesn't align with the original decimal. This answer choice is not equivalent.

[D] $0.26\overline{2262}$ equals 0.262262226222622262..., which is not equivalent to the original term.

[E] Finally, $2.\overline{622}$ equals 2.622622622622..., which, when multiplied by 10^{-1} (i.e., $\frac{1}{10}$), becomes 0.2622622622622.... This is equivalent to the original term.

[E] is the only correct answer.

Percents

A percentage is an alternative way to represent a decimal. The term "per cent" is an old way of saying "per one hundred," so, for example, the decimal 0.25, which is 25 one hundredths or $\frac{25}{100}$, becomes 25 percent, or 25%.

Any value expressed as a percentage can be written as a fraction with that value in the numerator and the number 100 in the denominator. That can help with problems that mention values such as x%; it's often helpful to turn x% into the fraction $\frac{x}{100}$.

Any decimal value can be represented as a percentage by multiplying it by 100. We've already seen that 0.25 is equivalent to 25% because (0.25)(100) = 25.

It is very easy to overlook small errors when it comes to decimals and percentages. The test writers know this, so be careful when dealing with them.

One common trap is the difference between quantities such as 0.01 and 0.01%.

In the case of the decimal number 0.01, multiply it by 100 to convert it to the quantity 1%, and you can write 1% as $\frac{1}{100}$. So 0.01 is equivalent to $\frac{1}{100}$, or 1%—the form you choose depends on the type of problem you are considering.

In the case of 0.01%, you can begin by translating it into the fraction $\frac{0.01}{100}$. You can then multiply the top and the bottom of the fraction by 100 to generate the fraction $\frac{1}{10,000}$, or one ten-thousandth.

Sample Questions

1. A certain item was discounted by 20%, and then the sales price was discounted again by 25%. The new price represents what percentage of the original price of the item?

Ⓐ 50%
Ⓑ 52%
Ⓒ 55%
Ⓓ 60%
Ⓔ 77.5%

Solution

If the price of the item was x, it would be $0.8x$ after the initial discount and $(0.75)(0.8x)$ after the second discount, which gives you:

$(0.75)(0.8)x = 0.6x$

Alternatively, you could have plugged in $100 as the price of the original item, in which case you could see that it would be $80 after the initial discount; then, after being discounted another 25% from $80, it becomes $60.

In either case, you can see that **the correct answer is (D)**.

2. x and y are both > 0, and x is 40% greater than y.

Quantity A	Quantity B
50% of x	75% of y

Ⓐ Quantity A is greater.
Ⓑ Quantity B is greater.
Ⓒ The two quantities are equal.
Ⓓ The relationship cannot be determined from the information given.

Solution

If x is 40% greater than y, you can think of it as $1.4y$. 50% of that would be $0.7y$.

As long as y is positive, 75% of y will always be greater than 70% of y; thus, **Quantity B is greater than Quantity A**.

Percentage Translation

A common type of percentage question uses the terms "is" and "of"—for example, 12 *is* what percent *of* 60? There are two good methods to approach this question.

The first method takes you back to algebraic translation—remember that the word "is" can be translated as an equal sign, and the word "of" often denotes multiplication. As shown above, you can translate "what percent" by using x as your unknown and translating that into a percentage by writing the fraction $\frac{x}{100}$. The result:

$12 = \left(\frac{x}{100}\right)(60)$
$12 = \frac{60x}{100}$
$1{,}200 = 60x$
$20 = x$, so 12 is 20% of 60

The second method is to write a fraction in the form is/of, use the calculator to generate a decimal result, and multiply that result by 100 to get the correct percentage. In the example, 12 is the "is" and 60 is the "of," so $\frac{12}{60} = 0.2$. Because $(0.2)(100) = 20$, you know that 12 is 20% of 60.

These methods work even for percentages that are not in the typical range of 1 through 100. Consider the following examples:

30 is what percent of 10?

Method 1

$30 = \left(\frac{x}{100}\right)(10)$

$30 = \frac{10x}{100}$

$3,000 = 10x$

$300 = x$, so 30 is 300% of 10

Method 2

$\frac{30}{10} = 3.0$

$(3.0)(100) = 300$, so 30 is 300% of 10

2 is what percent of 2,000?

Method 1

$2 = \left(\frac{x}{100}\right)(2,000)$

$2 = \frac{2,000x}{100}$

$200 = 2,000x$

$0.1 = x$, so 2 is 0.1% of 2,000

Method 2

$\frac{2}{2,000} = 0.001$

$(0.001)(100) = 0.1$, so 2 is 0.1% of 2,000

If you are given a number and a percentage, it's generally easiest to write an equation that translates the percentage into a decimal. Consider the following examples:

What is 34% of 68? (Round to the nearest tenth.)

$x = (0.34)(68)$, so $x = 24.12$, but rounded to nearest tenth is 24.1

51 is 30% of what number?

$51 = (0.3)(x)$

$\frac{51}{0.3} = x$

$170 = x$

Percentage Translation Drill

Let's practice solving percentage translation problems. Two of the three columns are filled in. Your job is to find the missing piece using either of the two methods we've discussed.

Part =	Percentage of	Whole
6	40%	15
84	200%	
16	8%	
	25%	300
12	40%	
$\sqrt{7}$		$5\sqrt{7}$

Percentage Increase/Decrease

Because any number is worth 100% of its own value, if it increases by a certain percentage, it will be worth that percentage plus 100%, and if it decreases by a certain percentage, it will be worth 100% minus that percentage. For example, if a number goes up 30%, it will be worth 30 + 100 = 130% of its original value, and if it goes down 30%, it will be worth 100 – 30 = 70% of its original value.

It is important to be able to correctly translate percentage increases and decreases so that you can efficiently solve for the value resulting from the increase or decrease. For example:

A number increased by 30% equals 26. What is that number?

As demonstrated above, if a number x is increased by 30%, the result will be 130% of its original value. Therefore, you want to translate this question into the following equation:

$(1.3)(x) = 26$
$x = \frac{26}{1.3}$, so $x = 20$

Ashley bought a sweater that was discounted 45% from its original price. If she paid $110 for the sweater, what was its original price before the discount?

If the original price of the sweater (let's call it p) was discounted by 45%, then the price Ashley paid was 55% of the original (100% – 45% = 55%).

$(0.55)(p) = 110$
$p = \frac{110}{0.55}$
$p = 200$

Percentage Translation Drill Solutions

Part =	Percentage of	Whole
6	40%	15
84	200%	**42**
16	8%	**200**
75	25%	300
12	40%	**30**
$\sqrt{7}$	**20%**	$5\sqrt{7}$

Percentage Increase/Decrease Drill

Let's practice percentage increase and decrease with a few terms below.

The five columns below represent:

1. an original term
2. a percentage increase or decrease
3. the percentage by which you should multiply the original term
4. that percentage represented as a decimal
5. the new resulting term

Original	Increase/Decrease	Multiply by %	As Decimal	New
10	Increase by 10%	110%	1.1	11
16	Decrease by 25%			
25		120%		
36				54
42	Increase by 200%			
80				64

Percentage Increase/Decrease Drill Solutions

Original	Increase/Decrease	Multiply by %	As Decimal	New
10	Increase by 10%	110%	1.1	11
16	Decrease by 25%	**75%**	**0.75**	**12**
25	**Increase by 20%**	120%	**1.2**	**30**
36	**Increase by 50%**	150%	1.5	54
42	Increase by 200%	**300%**	3	**126**
80	**Decrease by 20%**	80%	**0.8**	64

If you are asked to calculate the percentage by which a quantity has increased or decreased, use the equation $\left(\frac{\text{New} - \text{Old}}{\text{Old}} \right)(100)$. By "Old," I mean the original number; by "New," I mean the number resulting from the increase or decrease, regardless of whether the new number is less or greater than the original. If the (New – Old) quantity is negative, that simply means that the resulting answer represents a percentage decrease.

Consider the following questions:

The price of a sweater was increased from $40 to $70. By what percent was the price increased?

Old price: $40
New price: $70
Percent increase: $\left(\frac{70 - 40}{40} \right)(100)$
Percent increase: 75%

The price of a sweater was discounted from $70 to $40. What was the percentage by which the price was discounted? Please round your answer to the nearest 0.1%

Old price: $70
New price: $40
Percent discounted: $\left(\frac{40 - 70}{70} \right)(100)$
Percent discounted: 42.9% (rounded to nearest 0.1%)

Note in the examples above that though the price was changed in both cases by $30, the resulting percentages of increase/decrease differ! That's because in each case you compare the $30 change to the Old or Original amount to generate a percentage change.

The explanation above explains the difficulty inherent in another common percentages question type.

If a number x is increased by 50% and then the result is decreased by 50%, the final number is what percent of x?

You cannot simply work with the two 50% quantities because they are percentages of different numbers! Instead, you can solve this problem using one of two methods:

Method 1: x increased by 50% can be written as $1.5x$. Then you take the $1.5x$ quantity and reduce it by 50%, writing that as $(1.5x)(0.5)$. That results in a final quantity of $0.75x$, which can be read as 75% of the original x, or an overall decrease of 25% (100% of x minus 25% of x = 75% of x).

Method 2: plug in the number 100 for x. Increase 100 by 50% to get 150. Then decrease 150 by 50% to get 75. 75 is what percent of 100? $\frac{75}{100}$, or 0.75 as a decimal, which translates to 75%.

100 works well as a plug-in number for percentage questions because any number x compared to an original 100 is x% of 100. So if the original number is x and the resulting number is 39, the resulting number is 39% of x, and the resulting number is also a 61% decrease from x.

Percentage Questions Using the Terms "Greater Than" and "Less Than"

In the questions above, you differentiated between the Old/Original and the New/Resulting value because it is critical to compare the arithmetic difference between numbers to the Old/Original value (or starting point). Sometimes these questions are phrased as follows:

"70 is what percent greater than 40?"

The number that follows the word "than" is the number to which the arithmetic difference between the two numbers should be compared. The two numbers differ by 30, but the question asks what percent greater than 40.

So you place $\frac{30}{40}$ to get 0.75, or 75%. It is correct to say that 70 is 75% greater than 40 because you would have to increase 40 by 75% to get to 75.

"40 is what percent less than 70? Please round your answer to the nearest 0.1%"

The arithmetic difference is still 30, but now compare that number to 70. $\frac{30}{70}$ generates the decimal 0.428571, which you can represent as 42.9% rounded to the nearest 0.1%. It is correct to say that 40 is roughly 42.9% less than 70.

Watch out for these greater than/less than percentage questions in word problem form. For example:

In one minute, Bob types 25% more words than Sam does. If Bob types 100 words in one minute, how many words per minute does Sam type?

It is very tempting to see the number 100 and the quantity 25% and think that the answer is 75. However, that approach erroneously applies the quantity 25% to Bob's rate rather than Sam's—note that what follows the word "than" is Sam's rate, not Bob's!

The correct approach is to translate that question as follows:

Let Sam's rate = s. Bob's rate is therefore $1.25s$. So $100 = 1.25s$. Divide both sides by 1.25 to get $80 = s$. Sam can type 80 words per minute.

Working backward, see that if you start with Sam's rate of 80 and increase that by 25% of 80, you get $80(1.25) = 100$, which is correct for Sam's rate.

Compound Interest and Compound Growth and Decay

Compounding percentage growth and decay questions are rare on the GRE, but it is helpful to recognize the equations that result from proper translation.

Sally's checking account offers 10% interest compounded annually. If she makes an initial deposit of $500, how much money will she have at the end of 6 years?

Consider how you might approach this problem one year at a time—that will help you generalize the proper equation. After the first year, the amount of money Sally will have (let's call it s) would be:

$s = 500(1.1)$

In other words, you would increase her original deposit by 10% by multiplying 500 by 1.1 to generate 110% of the original $500 deposit. After one year, she would have $550, but we're going to use, for now, the expression $[(500)(1.1)]$ as the amount she has after one year.

Annually compounding interest means that the interest applies each year to the total resulting from the previous year's calculator. So after the second year, Sally would have $[(500)(1.1)](1.1)$, which you could write as $(500)(1.1)^2$

Note that at the end of each year, you multiply the previous year's result by 1.1, which means that after 6 years, Sally's total would be $(500)(1.1)^6$.

You can therefore generalize the equation as:

Final amount = (Initial amount)$\left(1 + \frac{r}{100}\right)^n$, where r is the percentage interest rate for the term of compounding (often annually, as in Sally's case), and n is the number of compounding terms (6 in Sally's case, because her interest compounded once yearly for a total of 6 years).

If the initial quantity is decreasing (or decaying) by 10% compounded annually, then your equation would be:

Final amount = (Initial amount)$\left(1 - \frac{r}{100}\right)^n$.

For example: If an initial supply of 3,000 candles decreases at a rate of 10% compounded annually, how many candles will be left after 4 years?

Final = $(3,000)(0.9)^4 = 1,968.3$, or 1,968 whole candles

Now, let's consider a quite difficult question that can be solved using this type of equation.

If an investment of T dollars doubles every 3 years, what will be the value of the investment, in dollars, 15 years from today?

First, some considerations:

When a quantity "doubles," it reflects a 100% increase from the original value. For example, if 2 doubles to 4, that is an *increase* of 2, which is a *100% increase.*

If the term of compounding is every 3 years, then 15 years is a total of 5 compounding terms $\left(\frac{15}{3} = 5\right)$.

Using the equation Final = Initial $\left(1 + \frac{r}{100}\right)^n$, where r is the percentage interest rate for the term of compounding and n is the number of compounding terms:

Final = $(T)\left(1 + \frac{100}{100}\right)^5$, which simplifies to:

Final = $T(2)^5$

$T(2)^5$ can be written as $32T$, and the answer could well be presented in that form.

A second possible method for the question above is to plug in numbers. Let's start with $100 and generate a table like the following:

Years after initial deposit	Value using *T* = $100
0 (initial deposit)	$100
3 (end of first compounding term)	$200
6 (end of second compounding term)	$400
9 (end of third compounding term)	$800
12 (end of fourth compounding term)	$1,600
15 (end of fifth compounding term)	$3,200

Note that the initial value for *T* was $100, and the final value is $3,200, so an answer of $32T$ correctly reflects the final value you generated by plugging in numbers.

Ratios

Imagine that you purchased from Jen's Candy Company a bag containing 50 solid-colored candies, each of which is red, blue, green, or yellow. Imagine that you have the following numbers of each color of candy:

Color	Number
Red	9
Blue	17
Green	8
Yellow	16
Total	50

While it would be correct to say that the ratio of green to total is $\frac{8}{50}$, which can be reduced and expressed in lowest terms as $\frac{4}{25}$, ratios on the GRE are *typically* $\frac{\text{part}}{\text{part}}$ comparisons, e.g., the ratio of red to blue is $\frac{9}{17}$.

The ratio of red to blue can be expressed in any of the following three ways:

$\frac{9}{17}$

9:17

9 to 17

Note that the order matters in each ratio expression, so a $\frac{9}{17}$ ratio of red to blue implies a blue to red ratio of $\frac{17}{9}$ (or 17:9, or 17 to 9).

If asked to double the ratio of red to blue, write the ratio as a fraction and then multiply the fraction by 2, which doubles the numerator but NOT the denominator:

$$\left(\frac{9}{17}\right)\left(\frac{2}{1}\right) = \frac{18}{17}$$

If asked to double the ratio of blue to red, re-write the ratio as $\frac{17}{9}$ and then follow the same process:

$$\left(\frac{17}{9}\right)\left(\frac{2}{1}\right) = \frac{34}{9}$$

The typical use of ratios to express $\frac{part}{part}$ relationships can lead to errors that you should guard against.

For example, imagine a collection of 10 marbles, of which 4 are green and 6 are yellow. The ratio of green to yellow is $\frac{4}{6}$, which reduces to $\frac{2}{3}$. If asked a question such as "What fraction of the marbles are green?," students often look at the ratio fraction and answer $\frac{2}{3}$. However, the question asked what fraction "of the marbles" are green, so you need to place green over the total. To do so, add the parts of the ratio together to get the whole, then compare part to whole. In this situation (with no other colors to worry about), a $\frac{2}{3}$ ratio of green to yellow would produce the following information:

Green marbles are $\frac{4}{10}$, or $\frac{2}{5}$ of the marbles.
Green marbles are 40% of the marbles.
The probability of selecting a green marble in a random selection from the collection is $\frac{4}{10}$, which reduces to $\frac{2}{5}$ (or 0.4 expressed as a decimal).

Because ratio fractions are typically expressed in lowest terms, the numbers in a ratio do not necessarily match the numbers of items in any given set or situation. For example, a $\frac{2}{3}$ ratio of green marbles to yellow marbles could mean that you have 5 total marbles (2 green and 3 yellow), but it could also represent a situation in which you have 500 total marbles (200 green and 300 yellow).

For that reason, it is often very useful to turn ratio values into coefficients attached to a single unknown. For example, a $\frac{2}{3}$ ratio can be expressed as $\frac{2x}{3x}$, where x is an unknown multiplier that has to be the same for each ratio term. That allows you to handle situations in which you aren't given the complete data.

Consider this question:

In a group of 217 people, the ratio of people who own cars to people who don't own cars is 2:5. How many people in the group own cars?

If you express the ratio of owners to non-owners as $2x:5x$ or $\frac{2x}{5x}$, then you can create an equation: $2x + 5x = 217$. You then solve for x, which equals 31; but note that you haven't yet answered the question you were asked! If your multiplier x is 31, then the number of car owners is $2x$, or $2(31)$, which equals 62.

You can use this technique to solve questions with more than two quantities in a ratio. For example:

In an office building containing a total of 72 offices distributed across 4 floors, the ratio of offices on the first, second, third, and fourth floors is 1:4:2:2. What is the difference between the number of offices on the second and third floors?

$1x + 4x + 2x + 2x = 72$, so $9x = 72$, so $x = 8$. The second floor contains $4(8) = 32$ offices, and the third floor contains $2(8) = 16$ offices, so the difference is $32 - 16 = 16$.

Many ratio questions involve items such as people, marbles, or (as in the example above) offices that must exist in integer quantities. In such cases, the total number of items must be a multiple of the sum of the parts of the ratio. For example, in the four-floor office building example, the sum of the parts of the ratio was $9x$, so the number of offices MUST be a multiple of 9.

However, in other situations such as mixtures of ingredients, you might need to work with fractions or decimals. The good news is that the process remains the same! For example:

A bean salad recipe calls for a 5:2:1 ratio of black beans:pinto beans:corn. If you follow the recipe and make 4.2 pounds of this salad, how many pounds of pinto beans will the resulting bean salad contain?

$5x + 2x + 1x = 4.2$, so $8x = 4.2$, so $x = 0.525$. Pinto beans are $2(0.525)$, so the salad would contain 1.05 pounds of pinto beans.

Proportions

A proportion is an equation that sets two ratios equal to each other, and it can be useful to solve for unknowns.

Remember Jen's Candy Company and their 50-piece bags of candy? Here's that table again.

Color	Number
Red	9
Blue	17
Green	8
Yellow	16
Total	50

Imagine that Jen's also offers jumbo bags with 250 pieces of candy instead of 50. These jumbo bags have the same proportions of each color, and you want to know how many pieces of candy in this jumbo bag are going to be blue.

You know that $\frac{17}{50}$ pieces in the smaller bag were blue, so if you use "x" for the number of blue pieces in the jumbo bag, you can set up the following equation and solve for x:

$$\frac{17}{50} = \frac{x}{250}$$

$$x = \frac{17}{50}(250)$$

$$x = 17(5)$$

$$x = 85$$

So you know that $\frac{85}{250}$ pieces in the jumbo bag are blue.

Direct and Inverse Proportions

Sometimes, a question will tell you that two numbers or quantities are proportional in a specific way. You can use helpful equations to solve these questions, as shown below.

For example, if a question states any of the following:

y is directly proportional to x
y varies directly as/with x
y and x vary in such a way that the value of the quotient $\frac{y}{x}$ is constant

Then you should write down the equation $y = kx$, where k is a constant. Note that this equation is equivalent to the equation $\frac{y}{x} = k$, expressing that the quotient of y and x will always remain constant. In a direct proportion, if one quantity increases, the other must also increase proportionally; similarly, if one quantity decreases, the other must also decrease proportionally.

For example: In a certain factory, the number of widgets made is directly proportional to the number of hours the factory operates. If the factory produces 3,000 widgets in 4 hours of operation, how many widgets will it produce in 7 hours?

Note that you can solve this question using the method discussed at the beginning of the Proportions section:

$\frac{3,000}{4} = \frac{x}{7}$, so $4x = 21,000$ and $x = 5,250$

But you can also use the equation $w = kh$. In the first situation, $3,000 = k(4)$, so $750 = k$. Remember that k is a constant, so you now know what value you can use for k in expressing the second situation.

$w = (750)(7)$, so $w = 5,250$

Why use the equation $y = kx$ when you can simply use a proportions approach that sets two ratios equal to each other? Well, for one reason, a question could state something like:

"y is directly proportional to the square of x," and it's probably simplest to approach this question with the equation $y = k(x^2)$.

However, the main reason to know how to write this type of equation is when addressing an **inverse** proportion question, where a typical proportion method of setting two equal ratios will NOT produce a correct answer.

If a question states any of the following:

y is inversely proportional to x
y varies inversely as/with x
y and x vary in such a way that the value of the product xy is constant

Then you should write down the equation $y = \frac{k}{x}$, where k is a constant. Note that this equation is equivalent to the equation $xy = k$, expressing that the product of x and y will always remain constant. In an inverse proportion, if one quantity increases, the other must decrease proportionally.

For example: If y is inversely proportional to x, and y equals 8 when x equals 5, what is the value of y when x is 7?

Please note that setting up the proportion $\frac{8}{5} = \frac{y}{7}$ will result in an INCORRECT answer, as that approach assumes a direct proportion!

Instead, write down $y = \frac{k}{x}$ and follow the process. The first relation gives you $8 = k(5)$, so $k = \frac{8}{5}$. Now that you know the value of the constant k, express the second relation as $y = \left(\frac{8}{5}\right)(7)$, and infer that $y = \frac{56}{5}$, or 11.2.

But it can get even trickier! Sometimes, you will be called upon to recognize an inversely proportional relationship that is not described using that terminology. Consider the following:

If 8 workers working at the same rate can finish a certain job in 9 hours, how many hours will it take 5 workers to finish the same job?

It's tempting to set up a direct proportion, but note that if you reduce the number of workers, expect the job to take longer to complete! As the number of workers decreases, the number of hours needed to complete the job will proportionally increase—a classic inverse proportion.

Set up the equation $w = \frac{k}{h}$. You know that $8 = \frac{k}{9}$, so $72 = k$. Then you know that $5 = \frac{72}{h}$, so $5h = 72$, and $h = 14.4$ hours.

Sample Questions

1. A certain 12-ounce can of soda contains 39 grams of sugar.

Quantity A   Quantity B
The number of 12-ounce cans required   6
to exceed 240 grams of sugar

- Ⓐ Quantity A is greater.
- Ⓑ Quantity B is greater.
- Ⓒ The two quantities are equal.
- Ⓓ The relationship cannot be determined from the information given.

Solution

If each 12-ounce can contains 39 grams of sugar, 6 total cans would contain $(39)(6) = 234$ grams of sugar. It would take more than 6 cans to exceed 240 grams of sugar; thus, **Quantity A is greater than Quantity B.**

2. Between $\frac{2}{7}$ and $\frac{3}{7}$ of all voters in a certain region cast a vote during the most recent election. If 7,325 people in the region cast a vote, how many total voters could be in the region?

Indicate <u>all</u> such numbers of voters.

- [A] 16,923
- [B] 19,324
- [C] 26,020
- [D] 27,921
- [E] 32,632

Solution

If 7,325 is $\frac{2}{7}$ of all voters, the region would have roughly 25,637.5 voters (which you could calculate using this equation: $7{,}325 = \frac{2}{7}x$).

If 7,325 is $\frac{3}{7}$ of all voters, the region would have roughly 17,091.7 voters (which you could calculate using this equation: $7{,}325 = \frac{3}{7}x$).

If 7,325 represents between $\frac{2}{7}$ and $\frac{3}{7}$ of the total number of voters, that must mean that the total number of voters is between roughly 25,637 and 17,092.

Only answer choice [B] fits the criterion, and it is the only correct answer.

3. A certain bag of candy has red, green, and blue pieces in a ratio of 3 to 4 to 2. If there are no other colors of candy in the bag, and there are 180 pieces of candy total, how many pieces of candy are blue?

- (A) 24
- (B) 40
- (C) 48
- (D) 60
- (E) 64

Solution

If the ratio of red to green to blue pieces is 3:4:2, that must mean that $\frac{2}{9}$ of all the pieces of candy must be blue (that is, 2 pieces out of 3 + 4 + 2 = 9).

If there are 180 pieces of candy total, then $\left(\frac{2}{9}\right)(180) = 40$ of them must be blue, and **(B) is the correct answer.**

Practice Questions

Contents of Investment Accounts A, B, and C

Account	Stocks	Bonds
A	$5,624	$2,254
B	$24,223	$8,901
C	$16,435	$12,417

Questions 1–3 are based on the above table.

1. The amount invested in bonds in account B represents approximately what percentage of the total amount invested in both stocks and bonds in all 3 accounts?

(A) 0.08
(B) 0.13
(C) 0.16
(D) 0.19
(E) 0.32

2. Which of the following is closest to the ratio of the amount of money invested in stocks in account A to the amount of money invested in bonds in account B?

(A) $\frac{4}{15}$

(B) $\frac{14}{25}$

(C) $\frac{3}{5}$

(D) $\frac{16}{25}$

(E) $\frac{4}{5}$

3. Which of the following ratios is greater than the ratio of the amount invested in stocks in account A to the amount invested in bonds in account A?

Indicate all such ratios.

[A] Amount invested in stocks in account B to amount invested in bonds in account B
[B] Amount invested in stocks in account C to amount invested in bonds in account C
[C] Amount invested in stocks in all accounts to amount invested in bonds in all accounts
[D] Total amount in all accounts to total invested in stocks in all accounts
[E] Total amount in all accounts to total invested in bonds in all accounts

4. m and n are both negative integers. $m > n$.

Quantity A	Quantity B
$\frac{m}{m+n}$	$\frac{n}{m+n}$

(A) Quantity A is greater.
(B) Quantity B is greater.
(C) The two quantities are equal.
(D) The relationship cannot be determined from the information given.

Practice Questions Continued

5. Which of the following is equivalent to multiplying a term by 1,000?

Indicate all such operations.

A Dividing the term by $\left(\frac{1}{10}\right)^3$

B Dividing the term by 0.001

C Multiplying the term by 10^3

D Multiplying the term by $\left(\frac{1}{10}\right)^{-3}$

6. Students and administrators rode on two buses to a field trip. On the first bus, the ratio of students to administrators was 8:1. Overall, the ratio of students to administrators was 6:1. If there were 54 students overall, 24 of whom rode on the first bus, how many administrators rode on the second bus?

┌──────────────┐
│   │
└──────────────┘

7. If $5 \leq m \leq 6$ and $n = m + 1$, which of the following could be the value of $\frac{m}{n}$?

Indicate all such values.

A 0.81
B 0.82
C 0.83
D 0.84
E 0.85

8. $a = \frac{4}{7}$, $b = 0.76$, and $c = a + b$.

Quantity A	Quantity B
a rounded to the nearest tenth + b rounded to the nearest tenth	c rounded to the nearest tenth

Ⓐ Quantity A is greater.
Ⓑ Quantity B is greater.
Ⓒ The two quantities are equal.
Ⓓ The relationship cannot be determined from the information given.

9. Erwin earns $37.50 per hour and works 20 hours per week. Bruce makes $12.50 more than Erwin per hour and works 10 more hours per week than Erwin. Bruce earns what percentage of what Erwin earns per week?

Ⓐ 40%
Ⓑ 50%
Ⓒ 80%
Ⓓ 100%
Ⓔ 200%

10. Erwin earns $37.50 per hour and works 20 hours per week. He changes positions at his work so that he works 10 more hours per week and earns $12.50 more per hour. By what percentage does Erwin's weekly pay increase?

- (A) 40%
- (B) 50%
- (C) 80%
- (D) 100%
- (E) 200%

11. A certain recipe includes only ingredients m and n. The ratio of m to n is k to $k + 2$, where k is a constant.

Quantity A	Quantity B
$\dfrac{m + n}{m}$	$\dfrac{7}{2}$

- (A) Quantity A is greater.
- (B) Quantity B is greater.
- (C) The two quantities are equal.
- (D) The relationship cannot be determined from the information given.

12. Frank bought a shirt at a 20% discount from its original price and a jacket at a 40% discount from its original price. He paid a total of $162, excluding taxes. If the original price of the jacket was twice the original price of the shirt, what was the original price of the shirt?

$ [   ]

13. A certain investor bought 50 shares of Company X. She sold 25 shares at a 50% profit and the remaining shares at a 75% profit. She was then required to pay $\frac{1}{3}$ of the profit earned in taxes. If the initial 50 shares initially cost $300 each, how much money did she earn from the investment after taxes?

$ [   ]

14. Triangle t has a base of m and a height of n. Rectangle r has a width 20% longer than the base of triangle t and a length 20% shorter than its height.

Quantity A	Quantity B
The area of a triangle t	One half of the area of rectangle r

- (A) Quantity A is greater.
- (B) Quantity B is greater.
- (C) The two quantities are equal.
- (D) The relationship cannot be determined from the information given.

Practice Question Solutions

Contents of Investment Accounts A, B, and C

Account	Stocks	Bonds
A	$5,624	$2,254
B	$24,223	$8,901
C	$16,435	$12,417

Questions 1–3 are based on the above table.

1. The amount invested in bonds in account B represents approximately what percentage of the total amount invested in both stocks and bonds in all 3 accounts?

(A) 0.08
(B) 0.13
(C) 0.16
(D) 0.19
(E) 0.32

Solution

If you add up all amounts in all accounts, you get $5,624 + $24,223 + $16,435 + $2,254 + $8,901 + $12,417 = $69,854.

$\frac{8,901}{69,854}$ = 0.127, so (B) is the correct answer.

2. Which of the following is closest to the ratio of the amount of money invested in stocks in account A to the amount of money invested in bonds in account B?

(A) $\frac{4}{15}$

(B) $\frac{14}{25}$

(C) $\frac{3}{5}$

(D) $\frac{16}{25}$

(E) $\frac{4}{5}$

Solution

The ratio of the amount of money invested in stocks in account A to invested in bonds in account B is $5,624 to $8,901, which is roughly equivalent to 0.632.

Of the answer choices, (D) is the closest to this; therefore, it is the correct answer.

For reference, here are decimal approximations for each of the answer choices:

(A) $\frac{4}{15} \approx 0.267$

(B) $\frac{14}{25} = 0.56$

(C) $\frac{3}{5} = 0.6$

(D) $\frac{16}{25} = 0.64$

(E) $\frac{4}{5} = 0.8$

3. Which of the following ratios is greater than the ratio of the amount invested in stocks in account A to the amount invested in bonds in account A?

Indicate all such ratios.

A **Amount invested in stocks in account B to amount invested in bonds in account B**

B Amount invested in stocks in account C to amount invested in bonds in account C

C Amount invested in stocks in all accounts to amount invested in bonds in all accounts

D Total amount in all accounts to total invested in stocks in all accounts

E **Total amount in all accounts to total invested in bonds in all accounts**

Solution

The ratio of the amount invested in stocks in account A to the amount invested in bonds in account A $= \dfrac{5,624}{2,254}$ ≈ 2.49.

Let's take a look at each of the answer choices to compare.

[A] Amount invested in stocks in account B to amount invested in bonds in account B ≈ 2.72
[B] Amount invested in stocks in account C to amount invested in bonds in account C ≈ 1.32
[C] Amount invested in stocks in all accounts to amount invested in bonds in all accounts ≈ 1.96
[D] Total amount in all accounts to total invested in stocks in all accounts ≈ 1.51
[E] Total in all accounts to total invested in bonds in all accounts ≈ 2.96

Answer choices [A] and [E] are greater than the ratio of stocks in account A to bonds in account A, and, therefore, correct.

4. m and n are both negative integers. $m > n$.

Quantity A	Quantity B
$\dfrac{m}{m+n}$	$\dfrac{n}{m+n}$

A Quantity A is greater.
B **Quantity B is greater.**
C The two quantities are equal.
D The relationship cannot be determined from the information given.

Solution

The fact that this question involves negative numbers makes it a bit tougher to conceptualize. So it can help to pick some numbers.

Let's imagine that $m = -2$, and $n = -3$.

$$\frac{m}{m+n} = \frac{-2}{-2+(-3)} = \frac{-2}{-5} = \frac{2}{5}$$

$$\frac{n}{m+n} = \frac{-3}{-2+(-3)} = \frac{-3}{-5} = \frac{3}{5}$$

Having gone through the example, you can see that the denominators for both are the same, and the numerators are just positive versions of the initial terms. No matter what values you choose for m and n, if n is more negative than m, **Quantity B will always be greater than Quantity A**.

Solutions Continued

5. Which of the following is equivalent to multiplying a term by 1,000?

Indicate all such operations.

A Dividing the term by $\left(\frac{1}{10}\right)^3$

B Dividing the term by 0.001

C Multiplying the term by 10^3

D Multiplying the term by $\left(\frac{1}{10}\right)^{-3}$

Solution

Let's look at each of the answer choices separately:

[A] Dividing the term by $\left(\frac{1}{10}\right)^3$ is equivalent to dividing a term by $\frac{1}{1,000}$. Dividing by $\frac{1}{1,000}$ is the same as multiplying by 1,000, so this is equivalent to the original operation.

[B] Dividing the term by 0.001 is equivalent to dividing by $\frac{1}{1,000}$, which, as discussed above, is equivalent to multiplying by 1,000, so this is equivalent to the original operation.

[C] Multiplying the term by 10^3 is equivalent to multiplying by 1,000, so this is equivalent to the original operation.

[D] Multiplying the term by $\left(\frac{1}{10}\right)^{-3}$ is equivalent to multiplying by $\left(\frac{10}{1}\right)^3 = 1,000$, which is equivalent to the original operation.

[A], [B], [C], and [D] are all equivalent to the original operation.

6. Students and administrators rode on two buses to a field trip. On the first bus, the ratio of students to administrators was 8:1. Overall, the ratio of students to administrators was 6:1. If there were 54 students overall, 24 of whom rode on the first bus, how many administrators rode on the second bus?

$$\boxed{6}$$

Solution

If there were 24 students on the first bus, and the ratio of students to administrators was 8 to 1, there must have been 3 administrators on the first bus because $\frac{24}{3} = \frac{8}{1}$.

If there were 54 students overall and the ratio of students to administrators was 6 to 1, there must have been 9 administrators because $\frac{54}{9} = \frac{6}{1}$.

If there were 9 administrators overall and 3 rode on the first bus, 9 − 3 = **6 must have ridden on the second bus, and the answer is 6**.

7. If $5 \leq m \leq 6$ and $n = m + 1$, which of the following could be the value of $\frac{m}{n}$?

Indicate all such values.

A 0.81
B 0.82
C 0.83
D 0.84
E 0.85

Solution

You can think about the range of results for $\frac{m}{n}$ by trying to plug in 5 and 6 for m.

When $m = 5$, $n = 6$, and $\frac{m}{n} = \frac{5}{6}$, which is $= 0.8\overline{3}$.

When $m = 6$, $n = 7$, and $\frac{m}{n} = \frac{6}{7}$, which is ≈ 0.857

Correct answers will fit within that range, so the correct answers here are [D] and [E].

8. $a = \frac{4}{7}$, $b = 0.76$, and $c = a + b$.

Quantity A | Quantity B
a rounded to the nearest tenth + b rounded to the nearest tenth | c rounded to the nearest tenth

Ⓐ **Quantity A is greater.**
Ⓑ Quantity B is greater.
Ⓒ The two quantities are equal.
Ⓓ The relationship cannot be determined from the information given.

Solution

For Quantity A, $\frac{4}{7}$ is ≈ 0.57, which, when rounded to the nearest tenth, is 0.6, and 0.76 rounded to the nearest tenth is 0.8, so a rounded to the nearest tenth + b rounded to the nearest tenth $= 0.6 + 0.8 = 1.4$.

For Quantity B, $\frac{4}{7}$ (approximately 0.57) + 0.76 ≈ 1.33, which rounds to 1.3.

Quantity A is greater.

Solutions Continued

9. Erwin earns $37.50 per hour and works 20 hours per week. Bruce makes $12.50 more than Erwin per hour and works 10 more hours per week than Erwin. Bruce earns what percentage of what Erwin earns per week?

(A) 40%
(B) 50%
(C) 80%
(D) 100%
(E) **200%**

Solution

If Erwin earns $37.50 per hour for 20 hours, he earns $750 per week.

If Bruce earns $37.50 + $12.50 = $50 per hour for 20 + 10 = 30 hours, he earns $1,500 per week.

Bruce earns twice as much as Erwin does per week, so he earns 200% as much. **The correct answer is (E)**.

10. Erwin earns $37.50 per hour and works 20 hours per week. He changes positions at his work so that he works 10 more hours per week and earns $12.50 more per hour. By what percentage does Erwin's weekly pay increase?

(A) 40%
(B) 50%
(C) 80%
(D) **100%**
(E) 200%

Solution

If Erwin earns $37.50 per hour for 20 hours, he earns $750 per week.

If he earns $37.50 + $12.50 = $50 per hour for 20 + 10 = 30 hours, he earns $1,500 per week.

Since his pay doubled, it increased by 100%. **The correct answer is (D)**.

11. A certain recipe includes only ingredients m and n. The ratio of m to n is k to $k + 2$, where k is a constant.

Quantity A	Quantity B
$\dfrac{m + n}{m}$	$\dfrac{7}{2}$

(A) Quantity A is greater.
(B) Quantity B is greater.
(C) The two quantities are equal.
(D) **The relationship cannot be determined from the information given.**

Solution

If the ratio of m to n is equal to $\dfrac{k}{k + 2}$, then, in terms of proportions, you know that $m + n = k + k + 2$, or $2k + 2$.

Therefore, $\dfrac{m + n}{m} = \dfrac{2k + 2}{k}$.

Must this always be greater or less than $\dfrac{7}{2}$ for some reason? At this point, there are a couple of ways you could go with what you have (or you could leave it alone and start testing some numbers).

One thing you could do is to divide $2k + 2$ by k:

$$\frac{2k + 2}{k} = 2 + \frac{2}{k}$$

This doesn't make things crystal clear, but it does simplify the matter a little bit. At this point, you can test a couple of different values for k and see what Quantity A gives us.

If $k = 1$, $2 + \dfrac{2}{k} = 2 + \dfrac{2}{1} = 4$

If $k = 2$, $2 + \dfrac{2}{k} = 2 + \dfrac{2}{2} = 3$

So depending on the value of the unknown constant k, either Quantity A or B could be greater, and **the correct answer is (D)**.

12. Frank bought a shirt at a 20% discount from its original price and a jacket at a 40% discount from its original price. He paid a total of $162, excluding taxes. If the original price of the jacket was twice the original price of the shirt, what was the original price of the shirt?

$\boxed{\quad 81 \quad}$

Solution

If you label the original price of the shirt x, then the original price of the jacket is $2x$.

Frank paid $0.8x$ and $0.6(2x)$ for a total of $162. You can set up and solve the following equation for x:

$0.8x + 0.6(2x) = 162$

$0.8x + 1.2x = 162$

$2x = 162$

$x = 81$

$81 is the correct answer.

Solutions Continued

13. A certain investor bought 50 shares of Company X. She sold 25 shares at a 50% profit and the remaining shares at a 75% profit. She was then required to pay $\frac{1}{3}$ of the profit earned in taxes. If the initial 50 shares initially cost $300 each, how much money did she earn from the investment after taxes?

$ [6,250]

Solution

If each share initially cost $300, for the 25 shares she sold at 50% profit, she earned (0.5)(300) = $150 each, or (25)($150) = $3,750 total.

If each share initially cost $300, for the 25 shares she sold at 75% profit, she earned (0.75)(300) = $225 each, or (25)($225) = $5,625 total.

Thus, she made a total profit of $3,750 + $5,625 = $9,375.

If she had to pay $\frac{1}{3}$ of that in taxes, that means she got to keep $\frac{2}{3}$ after taxes, which is $(\$9,375)\left(\frac{2}{3}\right) = \$6,250$.

14. Triangle t has a base of m and a height of n. Rectangle r has a width 20% longer than the base of triangle t and a length 20% shorter than its height.

Quantity A
The area of a triangle t

Quantity B
One half of the area of rectangle r

Ⓐ **Quantity A is greater.**
Ⓑ Quantity B is greater.
Ⓒ The two quantities are equal.
Ⓓ The relationship cannot be determined from the information given.

Solution

The formula for the area of a triangle is one half its base times its height.

The area of a triangle with a base of m and a height of n is $\left(\frac{1}{2}\right)mn$, or 0.5mn.

If the rectangle has a width of 1.2m and a height of 0.8n, its area is equal to (1.2m)(0.8n) = 0.96mn.

Half of this area is 0.48mn.

Thus, Quantity A is greater than Quantity B.

6

QUANTITATIVE REASONING

Absolute Value, Functions, and Quadratics

Over the next two lessons, I'll isolate and master specific mathematical situations that utilize many of the rules that we've been discussing and practicing. In this lesson, I'll focus on three in particular: absolute value, functions, and quadratic equations. Let's get started.

Absolute Value

A number's **absolute value** is its distance from 0. For example, the absolute value of 7 is 7, because it's 7 away from 0, and the absolute value of –5 is 5, because –5 is 5 away from 0.

In a practical sense, the absolute value symbol gives us the non-negative version of whatever is inside it.

For example:

$|7| = 7$
$|-5| = 5$
$|0| = 0$

If you are asked to solve for an unknown inside the absolute value, you have to consider whether it could be positive or negative.

For example, if you are told:

$|x| = 9$, you know that x must be 9 or –9.
$|2x + 3| = 7$, you know that $2x + 3$ must $= 7$ or –7. (If $2x + 3 = 7$, $x = 2$; if $2x + 3 = -7$, $x = -5$.)

Sample Questions

1. If $y = |x - 7|$, what is the value of y when $x = 4$?

2. If $|x - 7| = 3$, what are the two possible values of x?

Solutions

1. If $y = |x - 7|$, when $x = 4$,

$y = |4 - 7| = |-3| = $ **3**

2. If $|x - 7| = 3$, you know that $x - 7$ must be equal to 3 or -3. You can therefore set up the following two equations to solve for x:

$x - 7 = 3$
$x = 10$

$x - 7 = -3$
$x = 4$

Absolute Value Inequalities

Now, let's consider absolute value inequalities.

If you imagine that $|x| > 5$, you know that x must either be greater than 5 (for example, 6, 7, 8, or 1,000 all have absolute values greater than 5) or be less than -5 (for example, -6, -7, -8, or $-1,000$, also all have absolute values greater than 5).

Another example:

If $|x| < 7$,
$x < 7$ or $x > -7$

Let's state in words a useful strategy for working with absolute value inequalities in which you have isolated the absolute value expression on one side of the inequality:

Turn absolute value inequalities into two separate inequalities:

1. The first simply removes the absolute value signs but otherwise preserves the original inequality.
2. The second removes the absolute value signs, flips the inequality sign, and negates the "other side" of the original inequality (the side without the absolute value signs).

For example:

If $|x - 4| \geq 9$,
$x - 4 \geq 9$ or $x - 4 \leq -9$,
$x \geq 13$ or $x \leq -5$

If $|2x + 1| < 11$,
$2x + 1 < 11$ or $2x + 1 > -11$,
$2x < 10$ or $2x > -12$
$x < 5$ or $x > -6$

Sample Question 1

If $y \geq |12 - x|$, which of the following accurately represents all possible values of y when $x = 28$?

Ⓐ $y \leq -40$
Ⓑ $y \geq -40$
Ⓒ $y \leq -16$
Ⓓ $y \geq -16$
Ⓔ $y \geq 16$

Solution

When $x = 28$:

$y \geq |12 - x|$
$y \geq |12 - 28|$
$y \geq |-16|$
$y \geq 16$

(E) is the correct answer.

Sample Question 2

If $y = |2x - 3|$, which of the following accurately represents all possible values of x when y is less than or equal to 9?

Ⓐ $x \leq -3$ or $x \geq 6$
Ⓑ $-3 \leq x \leq 6$
Ⓒ $x \leq -15$ or $x \geq 15$
Ⓓ $-15 \leq x \leq 15$
Ⓔ $-6 \leq x \leq 3$

<u>Solution</u>

If y is less than or equal to 9, you know that $|2x - 3|$ must, therefore, be less than or equal to 9, and you can set up the following inequality to learn more about x:

$9 \geq |2x - 3|$

This means that $2x - 3$ must be less than or equal to 9 or greater than or equal to –9 (for example, –8, –7, etc.).

$2x - 3 \leq 9$
$2x \leq 12$
$x \leq 6$

or

$2x - 3 \geq -9$
$2x \geq -6$
$x \geq -3$

You know that x must be less than or equal to 6 or greater than or equal to –3, so $-3 \leq x \leq 6$.

(B) is the correct answer.

Functions

Functions are a mathematical way to describe the relationship between inputs and results, and they are very similar to the traditional x and y relationships with which you are more familiar.

For example, if you know that $y = x + 3$ and $x = 4$, you can input 4 for x and solve for y, which is 7.

Similarly, the test writers could tell us that $f(x) = x + 3$ and $x = 4$. You can input 4 for x and solve for $f(x)$, which is 7.

If you are told that $y = |x - 4|$ and $x = 1$, you could input 1 for x, solve for y, and see that $y = 3$.

Similarly, you could be told that $f(x) = |x - 4|$ and $x = 1$, so $f(x) = 3$.

In short, in the world of functions, $y = f(x)$. In a traditional x and y relationship, a solution might take the form of an ordered pair (x, y). In a function, a solution might take the form of an ordered pair $(x, f(x))$.

Here are a few translations that can help you work with functions:

"What is $f(3)$?" can be translated as "What is the output $f(x)$ of the function when the input $x = 3$?"

"If $f(x) = 27$, what is x?" can be translated as "What input value of x would produce an output $f(x)$ value of 27?"

Functions can also be graphed on the xy-plane, but I'll discuss that in a later chapter.

Symbols

Note that other types of symbols can be used to notate a function relationship. These symbols don't follow particular conventions, and you don't need to know them ahead of time. Rather, they are created for the specific question, and they gauge your ability to translate and work in a flexible manner. In this situation, the test writers will tell you what these symbols mean, and you'll have to implement the rules properly.

Sample Question

Let $*x* = 2x + 3$. What is the value of $*8*$?

Solution

If $*x* = 2x + 3$, then $*8* = 2(8) + 3$.

$*8* = 2(8) + 3 = 16 + 3 =$ **19**

Multi-Step Function Questions

Function questions can be more complicated when they require you to think about multiple outputs for multiple inputs. You can be asked to add or subtract functions from one another, or, commonly, you'll be asked to input a number into a function, get a result, input that result, and see what comes out, which is symbolized as $f(f(x))$.

Let's take a look at a couple of examples that illustrate these challenges:

Sample Question 1

If $f(x) = x - 3$, what is $f(5) + f(4)$?

Solution

To answer this question, you must first solve for $f(5)$ and $f(4)$.

$f(5) = 5 - 3 = 2$
$f(4) = 4 - 3 = 1$

Therefore, $f(5) + f(4) = 2 + 1 =$ **3**

Sample Question 2

If $f(x) = 2x + 2$, what is $f(f(3))$?

<u>Solution</u>

To solve for $f(f(3))$, you first must solve for $f(3)$.

$f(x) = 2(x) + 2$
$f(3) = 2(3) + 2$
$f(3) = 6 + 2$
$f(3) = 8$

Thus, you know that $f(f(3))$ is equal to $f(8)$, and you can now solve for $f(8)$ to get your final answer:

$f(x) = 2(x) + 2$
$f(8) = 2(8) + 2$
$f(8) = 16 + 2 = \mathbf{18}$

Quadratics

Quadratic equations contain one term in which the unknown or variable is taken to the second power (i.e., squared), and no term is raised to a higher power.

Solving Quadratic Equations

You solve quadratic equations through a process known as **factoring**.

To illustrate, start by imagining you must multiply the following terms together:

$(x - 3)(x + 5)$

Multiply these terms through a process known as **FOIL**—multiply the first terms together, the outside terms together, the inside terms together, and the last terms together:

First: $(x)(x) = x^2$
Outside: $(x)(5) = 5x$
Inside: $(-3)(x) = -3x$
Last: $(-3)(5) = -15$

If you bring it all together, you get the following:

$x^2 + 5x - 3x - 15$
$= x^2 + 2x - 15$

Now, imagine that you are given this equation:

$x^2 + 2x - 15 = 0$

Our task is to solve for x.

You can start by factoring, and you can do so by thinking about what numbers multiply to -15 and add up to 2. Those numbers would be 5 and -3. You can then factor:

$(x + 5)(x - 3) = 0$

In this case, since the product is 0, you know that either $(x + 5) = 0$ or $(x - 3) = 0$.

Thus, x must equal either -5 or 3.

The most common quadratic equation situations involve setting one side equal to 0, and then factoring to find solutions.

Let's take a look at another example:

$3x^2 - 12x - 18 = 18$

This equation looks a bit more complicated, but you can quickly simplify it by first moving everything over to one side, and then factoring out a 3 from each term:

$3x^2 - 12x - 18 = 18$
$3x^2 - 12x - 36 = 0$
$3(x^2 - 4x - 12) = 0$

You're left with $x^2 - 4x - 12$ to factor, and you can do so by figuring out which two numbers multiply to -12 and add to -4: -6 and 2. Now, you can rewrite the equation and solve x:

$3(x - 6)(x + 2) = 0$
$x = 6$ or -2

Here are a few more examples of quadratic equations that can be solved by factoring:

$x^2 + 2x - 35 = (x + 7)(x - 5) = 0; x = -7, 5$
$x^2 - 7x + 12 = (x - 4)(x - 3) = 0; x = 4, 3$
$4x^2 + 28x + 40 = 4(x + 2)(x + 5) = 0; x = -2, -5$

When quadratic equations are graphed on the xy-plane, they form parabolas. I'll discuss parabolas in a later chapter.

Special Factoring

Some of the most common quadratic factoring situations involve the squaring of sums or what's known as a difference of squares. Let's discuss each quickly.

<u>Square of a Sum</u>

Here are a few examples of sums that are squared:

$(x + 5)(x + 5) = x^2 + 10x + 25$
$(x - 4)(x - 4) = x^2 - 8x + 16$
$(5 - y)(5 - y) = 25 - 10y + y^2$
$(\sqrt{x} + 7)(\sqrt{x} + 7) = x + 14\sqrt{x} + 49$

It will help us to recognize when trinomials can be factored into perfect squares:

$x^2 - 12x + 36 = 0$
$(x - 6)^2 = 0$
$x = 6$

$x^2 + 4x + 4 = 0$
$(x + 2)^2 = 0$
$x = -2$

<u>Difference of Squares</u>

Even more common on the GRE is a factoring situation known as a difference of squares. Here are a few examples:

$(x + y)(x - y) = x^2 - y^2$
$(x + 5)(x - 5) = x^2 - 25$
$(x - 9)(x + 9) = x^2 - 81$
$(4 - \sqrt{x})(4 + \sqrt{x}) = 16 - x$

Be on the lookout for situations where you can factor a difference of squares.

If you know:

$x^2 - 9 = 0$

You can solve for x: $(x - 3)(x + 3) = 0$; $x = 3, -3$

If you are told $x^2 - 4y^2 = 0$ and asked about the relationship between x and y, here's how you could find it:

$(x - 2y)(x + 2y) = 0$; $x = 2y$ or $-2y$

Sample Question 1

$(2x + 3)(x - 1) + (x - 3)(x + 5)$ is equal to which of the following?

Ⓐ $3x^2 + 2x - 18$
Ⓑ $3x^2 + 3x - 16$
Ⓒ $(x + 3)(x - 2)$
Ⓓ $2(x + 3)(x - 2)$
Ⓔ $3(x + 3)(x - 2)$

<u>Solution</u>

If you foil and then combine like terms, you get the following:

$(2x + 3)(x - 1) + (x - 3)(x + 5) =$
$2x^2 - 2x + 3x - 3 + x^2 + 5x - 3x - 15$
$2x^2 + x - 3 + x^2 + 2x - 15$
$3x^2 + 3x - 18$

So far, you don't have a match for any of the answer choices.

Notice you can factor a 3 out from all of the terms: $3x^2 + 3x - 18 = 3(x^2 + x - 6)$

Then you can factor what remains:

$3(x^2 + x - 6) = 3(x + 3)(x - 2)$

(E) is correct.

Sample Question 2

If $(\sqrt{x} - \sqrt{2})(\sqrt{x} + \sqrt{2}) = 7$, what is the value of $(x - 3)(x + 3)$?

- Ⓐ 9
- Ⓑ 18
- Ⓒ 27
- Ⓓ 49
- Ⓔ 72

Solution

If you recognize the left side of the equation as a difference of squares, you can rewrite the equation as $x - 2 = 7$, in which case $x = 9$.

If $x = 9$, $(x - 3)(x + 3) = (6)(12) = 72$, and **(E) is the correct answer**.

Practice Questions

1. If $|x| > |y|$, which of the following must be true?

(A) $|x + 2| > |y|$
(B) $|x| > |y - 2|$
(C) $xy > 0$
(D) $x + y > 0$
(E) $x^2 - y^2 > 0$

2. The function f is defined for all numbers x by $f(x) = (x - 1)^2$.

Quantity A   Quantity B

$f(5)$ $f(-5)$

(A) Quantity A is greater.
(B) Quantity B is greater.
(C) The two quantities are equal.
(D) The relationship cannot be determined from the information given.

3. If a and b are two solutions to the equation $(x + 4)(x - 4) = 9$, what is the value of ab?

$ab = \boxed{}$

4. If $x^2 - 49 = 0$, which of the following must be false?

(A) $x^2 + 4x - 21 = 0$
(B) $x^2 + 9x + 14 = 0$
(C) $x^2 - 7x - 18 = 0$
(D) $x^2 + 5x - 14 = 0$
(E) $x^2 - 5x - 14 = 0$

5. The operation $m \Diamond n$ is defined by $m \Diamond n = 4m - 3n$. If $m = 2n$ and $m \Diamond n = 35$, what is the value of m?

(A) 7
(B) 9
(C) 11
(D) 12
(E) 14

6. The function f is defined for all numbers x by $f(x) = 4x - 8$.

Quantity A   Quantity B

$f(x + 5) - f(x)$ 20

(A) Quantity A is greater.
(B) Quantity B is greater.
(C) The two quantities are equal.
(D) The relationship cannot be determined from the information given.

Practice Questions Continued

7. If x is an even integer, which of the following must be odd?

Ⓐ $\left(\frac{x}{2}\right)^2 - 1$

Ⓑ $(x + 2)(x + 5)$

Ⓒ $(x - 4)(x - 2)$

Ⓓ $(x + 1)(x + 7)$

Ⓔ $(x + 4)(x - 3)$

8. $x^3 < x$, and $|4x - 8| = 16$.

Quantity A	Quantity B
x	6

Ⓐ Quantity A is greater.

Ⓑ Quantity B is greater.

Ⓒ The two quantities are equal.

Ⓓ The relationship cannot be determined from the information given.

9. The function f is defined for all numbers x by $f(x) = -2x(-1)^x$. If $f(f(x)) = 16$, what is the value of x?

$x =$ ☐

10. If $y = |x - 12|$ and if $y > x$, what is the value of x when $y = 42$?

$x =$ ☐

11. $|x + 4| \leq 9$, and $|y - 2| \leq 9$.

Quantity A	Quantity B
The greatest possible value of $|xy|$.	91

Ⓐ Quantity A is greater.

Ⓑ Quantity B is greater.

Ⓒ The two quantities are equal.

Ⓓ The relationship cannot be determined from the information given.

12. If $x - 10\sqrt{x} + 25 = 4$, what is one possible value of x?

$x =$ ☐

Practice Question Solutions

1. If $|x| > |y|$, which of the following must be true?

(A) $|x + 2| > |y|$
(B) $|x| > |y - 2|$
(C) $xy > 0$
(D) $x + y > 0$
(E) $x^2 - y^2 > 0$

Solution

If the absolute value of x is greater than that of y, then regardless of whether x is positive or negative, or a positive or negative decimal, x^2 will always be greater than y^2, therefore, **(E) must be true and is correct**.

One way to verify this is to come up with sample sets of terms that prove that none of the other answer choices have to be true.

For example:

(A) $|x + 2| > |y|$ does not have to be true if $x = -4$ and $y = 3$.
(B) $|x| > |y - 2|$ does not have to be true if $x = 5$ and $y = -4$.
(C) $xy > 0$ does not have to be true if either x or y is negative.
(D) $x + y > 0$ does not have to be true if both x and y are negative, or if x is negative and y positive.

2. The function f is defined for all numbers x by $f(x) = (x - 1)^2$.

Quantity A	Quantity B
$f(5)$	$f(-5)$

(A) Quantity A is greater.
(B) **Quantity B is greater.**
(C) The two quantities are equal.
(D) The relationship cannot be determined from the information given.

Solution

If $f(x) = (x - 1)^2$:

$f(5) = (5 - 1)^2$
$= 4^2$
$= 16$

$f(-5) = (-5 - 1)^2$
$= (-6)^2$
$= 36$

Quantity B is greater than Quantity A.

Solutions Continued

3. If a and b are two solutions to the equation $(x + 4)(x - 4) = 9$, what is the value of ab?

$$ab = \boxed{-25}$$

Solution

If $(x + 4)(x - 4) = 9$, you can solve for possible values of x:

$(x + 4)(x - 4) = 9$
$x^2 - 16 = 9$
$x^2 - 25 = 0$
$(x - 5)(x + 5) = 0$

Therefore, the two solutions are 5 and −5, and the product of them is (5)(−5) = −25.

4. If $x^2 - 49 = 0$, which of the following must be false?

Ⓐ $x^2 + 4x - 21 = 0$
Ⓑ $x^2 + 9x + 14 = 0$
Ⓒ $x^2 - 7x - 18 = 0$
Ⓓ $x^2 + 5x - 14 = 0$
Ⓔ $x^2 - 5x - 14 = 0$

Solution

If $x^2 - 49 = 0$, x must be either 7 or −7.

Knowing this, let's think about which of the five answers must be false.

You can factor (A) as $(x + 7)(x - 3) = 0$, and this could be true when $x = -7$.
You can factor (B) as $(x + 7)(x + 2) = 0$, and this could be true when $x = -7$.
You can factor (C) as $(x - 9)(x + 2) = 0$, and this cannot be true when x is either 7 or −7.
You can factor (D) as $(x + 7)(x - 2) = 0$, and this could be true when $x = -7$.
Finally, you can factor (E) as $(x - 7)(x + 2) = 0$, and this could be true when $x = 7$.

(C) is the only answer that must be false and is, therefore, the correct answer.

5. The operation $m \Diamond n$ is defined by $m \Diamond n = 4m - 3n$. If $m = 2n$ and $m \Diamond n = 35$, what is the value of m?

(A) 7
(B) 9
(C) 11
(D) 12
(E) **14**

Solution

If $m = 2n$, you can substitute this information into the given equation. Everywhere you see an "m," replace it with "$2n$":

$m \Diamond n = 4m - 3n$
$= 4(2n) - 3n$
$= 8n - 3n$
$= 5n$

If $m \Diamond n = 35$, then it must be true that:
$5n = 35$, so
$n = 7$

If $n = 7$ and $m = 2n$, then $m = 14$.

The correct answer is (E).

You can confirm your work by plugging terms back in:

$m \Diamond n = 4m - 3n$
$35 = 4(14) - 3(7)$
$35 = 56 - 21$
$35 = 35$

6. The function f is defined for all numbers x by $f(x) = 4x - 8$.

Quantity A	Quantity B
$f(x + 5) - f(x)$	20

(A) Quantity A is greater.
(B) Quantity B is greater.
(C) **The two quantities are equal.**
(D) The relationship cannot be determined from the information given.

Solution

If $f(x) = 4x - 8$, then $f(x + 5) = 4(x + 5) - 8$.

$f(x + 5) - f(x) = 4(x + 5) - 8 - (4x - 8)$

$= 4x + 20 - 8 - 4x + 8$

$= 20$

Quantity A and Quantity B are equal; the correct answer is (C).

Solutions Continued

7. If x is an even integer, which of the following must be odd?

(A) $\left(\frac{x}{2}\right)^2 - 1$
(B) $(x + 2)(x + 5)$
(C) $(x - 4)(x - 2)$
(D) **$(x + 1)(x + 7)$**
(E) $(x + 4)(x - 3)$

Solution

Let's reason through each answer choice to see whether you can tell if it's going to be even or odd when x is even.

With (A), when x is even, $\left(\frac{x}{2}\right)^2$ could be even or odd, so the final result could be even or odd. For example, if $x = 4$, $\left(\frac{x}{2}\right)^2 = 4$, and $4 - 1 = 3$, and if $x = 6$, $\left(\frac{x}{2}\right)^2 = 9$, and $9 - 1 = 8$.

With (B), when x is even, $(x + 2)$ must be even, and $(x + 5)$ must be odd, meaning $(x + 2)(x + 5)$ must be even.

With (C), when x is even, $(x - 4)$ must be even and $(x - 2)$ must also be even, meaning $(x - 4)(x - 2)$ must be even.

With (D), when x is even, $(x + 1)$ must be odd, and $(x + 7)$ must be odd, meaning $(x + 1)(x + 7)$ must be odd.

Finally, with (E), when x is even, $(x + 4)$ must be even, and $(x - 3)$ must be odd, meaning $(x + 4)(x - 3)$ must be even.

(D) is the correct answer.

8. $x^3 < x$, and $|4x - 8| = 16$.

Quantity A	Quantity B
x	6

(A) Quantity A is greater.
(B) **Quantity B is greater.**
(C) The two quantities are equal.
(D) The relationship cannot be determined from the information given.

Solution

If $|4x - 8| = 16$, you know that $4x - 8$ must be equal to either 16 or −16. You can use the two equations to solve for possible values of x:

$$4x - 8 = 16$$
$$4x = 24$$
$$x = 6$$

$$4x - 8 = -16$$
$$4x = -8$$
$$x = -2$$

Since you are told that $x^3 < x$, x can't be equal to 6 and must be equal to −2.

So, in this case, Quantity B is greater.

9. The function f is defined for all numbers x by $f(x) = -2x(-1)^x$. If $f(f(x)) = 16$, what is the value of x?

$x = $ [4]

10. If $y = |x - 12|$ and if $y > x$, what is the value of x when $y = 42$?

$x = $ [−30]

Solution

For the sake of simplicity, let's substitute z for the $f(x)$ inside the parentheses.

So instead of $f(f(x)) = 16$, write $f(z) = 16$.

If $f(z) = 16$, you know that:

$16 = -2(z)(-1)^z$

Note that the final component of the equation, $(-1)^z$, doesn't impact the absolute value of the term but rather whether the term is positive or negative. $(-1)^z$ is positive if z is even and negative if z is odd.

To get to 16 from the $-2(z)$, you need z to be -8.

If $z = -8$, then $(-2)(z) = (-2)(-8) = 16$, and (-1) taken to $(-8)^2 = (-1)^{64} = 1$.

So when $z = -8$, you can confirm that $f(z) = (-2)(-8)(1) = 16$.

Remember, you initially substituted z for $f(x)$, so this tells us that $f(x) = -8$.

Now, let's go back into the function to solve for x:

$f(x) = (-2x)(-1)^x$
$-8 = (-2x)(-1)^x$
$4 = (x)(-1)^x$

4 = x

Solution

If $y = |x - 12|$ and $y = 42$, you know that $x - 12$ could be equal to 42 or -42. You can use the two equations to solve for possible values of x:

$x - 12 = 42$
$x = 54$

$x - 12 = -42$
$x = -30$

Since you're told that $y > x$, you know that in this case, $x = -30$.

Solutions Continued

11. $|x + 4| \leq 9$, and $|y - 2| \leq 9$.

Quantity A	Quantity B
The greatest possible value of $|xy|$.	91

Ⓐ **Quantity A is greater.**
Ⓑ Quantity B is greater.
Ⓒ The two quantities are equal.
Ⓓ The relationship cannot be determined from the information given.

Solution

If $|x + 4| \leq 9$, you know that $|x + 4|$ is either less than or equal to 9 or greater than or equal to –9. You can set up the following inequalities:

$x + 4 \leq 9$
$x \leq 5$

$x + 4 \geq -9$
$x \geq -13$

Therefore, $-13 \leq x \leq 5$.

Similarly, if $|y - 2| \leq 9$, you know that $|y - 2|$ is either less than or equal to 9 or greater than or equal to –9. You can set up the following inequalities:

$y - 2 \leq 9$
$y \leq 11$

$y - 2 \geq -9$
$y \geq -7$

Therefore, $-7 \leq y \leq 11$.

In this case, the greatest possible value for $|xy| = |(-13)(11)| = |-143| = 143$.

Quantity A is greater.

12. If $x - 10\sqrt{x} + 25 = 4$, what is one possible value of x?

$x = \boxed{\textbf{9 or 49}}$

Solution

Option 1: If you recognize the left side of the equation as a perfect square, you can rewrite it $(\sqrt{x} - 5)^2 = 4$.

From here, you can see that for this to be true:

$\sqrt{x} - 5 = 2$
$\sqrt{x} = 7$
$x = 49$

or

$\sqrt{x} - 5 = -2$
$\sqrt{x} = 3$
$x = 9$

Option 2: Alternatively, you could move everything over, set it equal to 0, and then factor to solve:

$x - 10\sqrt{x} + 25 = 4$
$x - 10\sqrt{x} + 21 = 0$
$(\sqrt{x} - 7)(\sqrt{x} - 3) = 0$
$\sqrt{x} = 7$ or 3
$x = 49$ or 9

7

QUANTITATIVE REASONING

Sequences, Rates, and Mixtures

Let's finish this block of lessons by discussing a few other specific mathematical situations: sequences, rates, and mixtures.

Sequences

In general, a sequence is a series of terms that follows a rule of progression or a pattern of repetition. GRE quantitative questions tend not to use the precise terms or formal notation I'll use below, but if a question includes the word "sequence" or a notation such as $\{a_1, a_2, a_3, ..., a_n\}$, then your approach should be guided by the information in this section.

Sequences are composed of terms with numerical values that are identified by the numbered position they occupy in the sequence (first term, second term, nth term. The position of the term in the sequence is often presented as a subscript. A notation such as a_1, for example, denotes the *value* of the term in the *first* place in a given sequence.

Common sequence questions include:

What is a_3?
Translation: "What is the value of the third term in the sequence?"

If $a_n = 25$, what is the value of n?
Translation: "What position in the sequence does the term with a numerical value of 25 occupy?"

It's almost always helpful to write out the first few terms of any sequence, as shown below, with the term's position written below each dash and the value of that term written on each dash.

Value of Term	_____	_____	_____	_____	_____
Term #	1	2	3	4	5

Arithmetic Sequence

A commonly tested sequence on the GRE is the arithmetic sequence, where each term after the first is equal to the previous term plus a numerical constant. For our purposes, we'll call this constant d, though the test writers can (of course) use any letter.

For example, {2, 5, 8, 11, ..., n} is an arithmetic sequence with a d of 3. Note that the value of d can be positive or negative: {4, 2, 0, –2, –4, ..., n} is also an arithmetic sequence, one with a d of –2.

Any increasing set of consecutive integers can be considered an arithmetic sequence with a d of 1; similarly, any increasing set of consecutive even or consecutive odd integers can be considered an arithmetic sequence with a d of 2.

Most sequences on the GRE will be **finite** sequences: they will have first and final terms rather than proceeding to infinity. For example, "the set of positive multiples of 5 through 200" is a finite arithmetic sequence with a d of 5: {5, 10, 15, ..., 200}.

You might remember a formula to find a term in an arithmetic sequence:

$a_n = a_1 + (n - 1)(d)$.

Translation, from left to right: "In an arithmetic sequence, the value of the nth term [a_n] equals the value of the first term [a_1] plus the number of terms minus 1 [$n - 1$] times the difference between terms [d]." This formula certainly works, though I'll present something a little easier to remember and use in a moment.

In the arithmetic sequence {2, 5, 8, 11, ..., n}, if a_1 = 2, what is the value of the 65th term?

a_{65} = 2 + (65 – 1)(3)
a_{65} = 2 + (64)(3)
a_{65} = 194

The value of the 65th term in the sequence is 194.

But let's consider a simpler form of notation. If the value of the first term is a_1, then the value of the second term is $a_1 + d$, the value of the third term is $a_1 + 2d$, etc.

Instead of {a_1, a_2, a_3, ...}, you can write {a_1, ($a_1 + d$), ($a_1 + 2d$), ...}:

Value of Term	a_1	$a_1 + d$	$a_1 + 2d$	$a_1 + 3d$	$a_1 + 4d$
Term #	1	2	3	4	5

Note that the coefficient attached to the d is always one less than the term's numbered place in the sequence. Therefore, the 65th term in this arithmetic sequence can be written as ($a_1 + 64d$), which in the case above means that a_{65} = 2 + (64)(3), or 194.

There's one cool feature of arithmetic sequences that you should memorize: in any arithmetic sequence (no matter the first term or the difference between terms), the mean and the median are equal! Furthermore, both the mean and the median are the average of the first and last numbers in the finite sequence! Consider some simple examples:

$\{1, 7, 13, 19, 25, 31\}$

Mean = $\frac{96}{6}$, so mean = 16

Median is the average of 13 and 19, so median = 16

$\frac{1 + 31}{2} = 16$

$\{3, 7, 11, 15, 19\}$

Mean = $\frac{55}{5}$, so mean = 11

Median is the middle number, which is 11

$\frac{3 + 19}{2} = 11$

Finding the Number of Terms in a Finite Arithmetic Sequence

There's a useful way to find the number of terms in any finite arithmetic sequence if you know the values of the first and final terms and the constant d.

For example: How many positive multiples of 5 are there through the number 200?

$\{5, 10, 15, \ldots 200\}$, arithmetic sequence with d of 5. We'll refer to the constant d as the "step size" below:

Formula: $\frac{\text{last term} - \text{first term}}{\text{step size}} + 1$

$\frac{200 - 5}{5} = 1$

$\frac{195}{5} + 1$

$39 + 1 = 40$

There are 40 terms from the first term of 5 through the final term of 200.

Note that in a finite set of consecutive integers with a step size of 1, calculating the number of terms simplifies to (last − first) + 1.

How many consecutive integers are there from 205 through 431?

$431 + 205 + 1 = 227$ integers

Sum of a Finite Arithmetic Sequence

There's one more important feature of finite arithmetic sequences: you can break them down into pairs of numbers that add to the same constant total.

Returning to a previous example: {1, 7, 13, 19, 25, 31}
Consider the first and last numbers: 1 + 31 = 32
Now consider the second and second to last numbers: 7 + 25 = 32
How about the third and third to last numbers?: 13 + 19 = 32

What if you have an odd number of terms?: {3, 7, 11, 15, 19}
Consider the first and last numbers: 3 + 19 = 22
Now consider the second and second to last numbers: 7 + 15 = 22
There's an unpaired number in the middle of the sequence, but its sum is 11—half of a pair.

You can now find the sum of a finite arithmetic sequence: it is the sum of each pair times the number of pairs in the sequence. How do you find the number of pairs in the sequence? Use the method above for finding the number of terms in the sequence, and divide by 2. If you have an odd number of terms, then the number of pairs will end in 0.5, which will correctly add the value of half a pair for the unpaired term in the middle of the sequence.

Let's practice:

What is the sum of the positive multiples of 2 through 204?

Arithmetic sequence is {2, 4, 6, …204}
Value of each pair is (first + last), so (2 + 204) = 206
Number of terms is: $\frac{204 - 2}{2}$ + 1, so 102 terms
$\frac{102}{2}$ = 51 pairs
Sum of sequence is (51)(206) = 10,506

Let A(n) denote the sum of the positive integers from 1 to n. For example, A(30) = 1 + 2 + 3 + … + 30 = 465. What is the value of A(175)?

Arithmetic sequence is {1, 2, 3, … 175}
Value of each pair is (first + last), so (1 + 175) = 176
Number of terms is (175 – 1) + 1, so 175 terms
Number of pairs is $\frac{172}{2}$ = 87.5
Sum of sequence is (87.5)(176) = 15,400

Let's consider one more situation together: imagine that you are told that the sum of 30 consecutive integers is 645, and you need to find the least of these integers.

You can define the least as x, and you can imagine the list of integers as:

$x, x + 1, x + 2, ..., x + 27, x + 28, x + 29$

In this case, you know that each of the pairs is equal to $x + (x + 29) = 2x + 29$, and you have 15 pairs of terms.

$(2x + 29)(15) = 645$
$30x + 435 = 645$
$30x = 210$
$x = 7$

In this case, you know that the least of the integers in the sequence must be 7.

Geometric Sequences

In a geometric sequence, each term after the first is the result of multiplying the previous term by the constant r, called the "common ratio." For example, the following is a geometric sequence with a first term of 3 and a common ratio of 4: $\{3, 12, 48, 192, ... n\}$. The common ratio r can be found by dividing any term in a geometric sequence by the previous term, for example: $\frac{192}{48} = 4$, $\frac{48}{12} = 4$, etc.

Consider the following way of generalizing a geometric sequence with first term a_1 and common ratio r:

Value of Term	a_1	$(a_1)(r)$	$(a_1)(r^2)$	$(a_1)(r^3)$	$(a_1)(r^4)$
Term #	1	2	3	4	5

Note that the exponent attached to the base term r is always one less than the term's numbered place in the sequence. Therefore, the 8th term in this arithmetic sequence can be written as $(a_1)(r^7)$.

Note that in a geometric sequence, the increase between terms is not constant in arithmetic terms, but rather constant in percentage terms. In the example sequence $\{3, 12, 48, 192, ... n\}$, both of the following statements are true:

Each term is 400% of the previous term.
Each term represents a 300% increase from the previous term.

Other Types of Explicit Sequences

Sequences can also be presented with explicit rules for forming each term based on its position in the sequence. For example:

In sequence S, the value of the nth term is $\frac{2}{n}$. What is the value of the 5th term in the sequence? Writing out the first 5 terms shows that the value of the 5th term is $\frac{2}{5}$.

Value of Term	2	1	$\frac{2}{3}$	$\frac{1}{2}$	$\frac{2}{5}$
Term #	**1**	**2**	**3**	**4**	**5**

Finding a Particular Value

Finding a particular value in a sequence is very much like working with functions or traditional input-output relationships; in this case, the input is determined by where in the sequence the term lies (e.g., the 5th term or the 100th term), and the output is the value of that term.

Let's take a look at a couple of simple situations to illustrate.

For the sequence S, the nth term in the sequence is $2n - 1$.

1. What is the third term of the sequence?

2. 19 is which term of the sequence?

Here are the answers:

1. What is the third term of the sequence?

To find the third term, you can simply substitute 3 for n in the given expression:

$2n - 1$
$2(3) - 1$
$6 - 1$
5

The value of the third term in the sequence is 5.

2. 19 is which term in the sequence?

To determine which term 19 is, you can set up an equation and solve for n:

$2n - 1 = 19$
$2n = 20$
$n = 10$

So you know that 19 is the 10th term in the sequence.

Here are some examples of sequences first presented in notation form, then with the first few elements listed, and with a few missing elements for you to fill out.

In sequence S, the nth term is $n^2 - n$

Value of Term	0	2	6		
Term #	1	2	3	4	5

In sequence S, the nth term is $n(-1)^{n-1}$

Value of Term	1	-2	3		
Term #	1	2	3	4	5

Recursive Sequences

There is yet another type of sequence known as a recursive sequence. Whereas explicit sequences give you a formula that allows you to calculate the value of a particular term, recursive sequences give you a set of rules that allow you to find the value of a specific term based on other terms in the sequence (usually the previous term).

For example, imagine that you are told the following: $a_1 = 4$ and $a_n = (a_{n-1})(2) - 3$.

One way to generate the first few terms is to write out a series of equations:

To find a_2, where $n = 2$: $a_2 = (a_1)(2) - 3$
$a_2 = (4)(2) - 3$
$a_2 = 5$

To find a_3, where $n = 3$: $a_3 = (a_2)(2) - 3$
$a_3 = (5)(2) - 3$
$a_3 = 7$

You can quickly generate the following first 5 terms:

Value of Term	4	5	7	11	19
Term #	1	2	3	4	5

There's a more efficient method, however. In recursive sequences, it's helpful to translate a_n as "the value of any term" and a_{n-1} as "the value of the previous term." In other words, you can translate the recursive formula as:

"The value of any term is equal to 3 less than twice the value of the previous term."

So each term is created by doubling the previous term, then subtracting 3. Double 4, minus 3 = 5. Double 5, minus 3 is 7. Double 7, minus 3 is 11, etc.

Note that the recursive formula $a_n = (a_{n-1})(2) - 3$ is exactly the same as the recursive formula $a_{n+1} = (a_n)(2) - 3$. Why? Because a_{n+1} is the next term to the right of a_n.

Solution

$n^2 - n$:

Value of Term	0	2	6	12	20
Term #	1	2	3	4	5

$n(-1)^{n-1}$:

Value of Term	1	-2	3	-4	5
Term #	1	2	3	4	5

On the GRE, recursive sequences will often be presented in words. For example:

In a certain sequence of numbers, each term after the first term is found by multiplying the previous term by 4 and then adding 2 to the product. If the 5th term in the sequence is 426, what is the value of the 2nd term? :

Let's start with the following visual representation, labeling the unknown value of the 4th term as x:

Value of Term				x	426
Term #	1	2	3	4	5

Then set up the equation $4x + 2 = 426$, so $x = 106$ (value of the fourth term).

Then use x to represent the 3rd term: $4x + 2 = 106$. $x = 26$ (value of third term).

Then use x to represent the 2nd term: $4x + 2 = 26$. $x = 6$ (value of the second term).

Note that if this were a multi-answer question presenting you with a list of numbers and asking you which numbers are in the sequence, you'd need to look in both directions from 426. In other words, 6, 26, 106, and 426 are in the sequence, but so too are 1,706 (the 6th term), 6,826 (the 7th term), etc.

Patterned Sequences

A final kind of sequence is one in which a certain number of terms repeat. For example, consider the following repeating sequence:

$\{2, 4, 6, 8, 2, 4, 6, 8, ...\}$

The first 8 terms are written out to demonstrate the pattern, but the key is that the minimum unit of repetition is 4 terms: $\{2, 4, 6, 8\}$

If $a_1 = 2$, and you are asked to find the 55th term in the sequence, you are essentially faced with a remainder question. Every 4th term in the sequence will be an 8: $a_4 = 8$, $a_8 = 8$, $a_{12} = 8$, etc. So how many times will a 4-term pattern repeat completely within 55 terms?

One way to determine that is to enter $\frac{55}{4}$ into the calculator. That gives you 13.75—but decimal quantities can be tricky. A safe way to proceed is to note that the pattern repeats fully 13 times, and (4)(13) = 52, so the 52nd term will be the number 8. Then count forward 3 more terms, as shown below, to find that the 55th term will be a 6.

Value of Term	8	2	4	6
Term #	52	53	54	55

Note that this is the same as saying that $\frac{55}{4}$ = 13 remainder 3, so the 55th term will be the same as the 3rd term, i.e., 6.

If the numbers are manageable, some people prefer to count forward in multiples of 4 until they reach the final whole multiple of 4 less than the target number (in this case, until they reach 52), then count forward from the beginning of the pattern until they reach the target number. "If the 52nd term is 8, the 53rd is 2, the 54th is 4, and the 55th is 6."

Given the same repeating pattern {2, 4, 6, 8, 2, 4, 6, 8, …}, you might be asked to find the sum of the first 55 terms in the sequence.

Again, the key is to work with the minimum unit of repetition and find that the sum of the first 4 terms is 20. Each repeating set of 4 terms will sum to 20, so you'll have 13 sets of 20 followed by the numbers 2, 4, 6.

(20)(13) + 2 + 4 + 6 = 272

Specific Patterned Sequences to Watch For

It's important to be aware of number properties that result in (well-disguised) patterned sequences. One such example is the repeating pattern of unit digits in base and exponent progressions.

Example: What is the units digit of 7^{18}?

Let's see what happens with lesser integer powers of 7.

7^1 = 7 (units digit of 7)
7^2 = 49 (units digit of 9)
7^3 = 343 (units digit of 3)
7^4 = 2,401 (units digit of 1)
7^5 = 16,807 (units digit of 7)
7^6 = 117,649 (units digit of 9)
7^7 = 823,543 (units digit of 3)
7^8 = 5,764,801 (units digit of 1)

Units digits written out: {7, 9, 3, 1, 7, 9, 3, 1, ...}—it's a repeating pattern with a minimum unit of repetition of four numbers {7, 9, 3, 1}

So if the units digit of 7^4 is 1, then the units digits of 7^8, 7^{12}, and 7^{16} will be 1, and then count forward to find that the units digit of 7^{18} will be a 9.

Value of Term	1	7	9
Term #	16	17	18

Note that you don't have to calculate big numbers to find the units digit pattern of any integer base. For example:

$7^1 = 7$, which ends in 7

Any number ending in 7, when multiplied by 7, will produce a number ending in 9 (because $(7)(7) = 49$, but you care only about the units digit). Any number ending in 9, when multiplied by 7, will produce a number ending in 3 (because $(9)(7) = 63$, but you care only about the units digit), etc.

Let's practice by finding the units digit of 4^{35}.

$4^1 = 4$, units digit of 4
Number ending in $(4)(4)$ will end in a 6
Number ending in $(6)(4)$ will end in a 4
Interesting: the units digit pattern of 4^n is {4, 6, 4, 6, 4, 6...}
Every odd power of 4 ends in 4, so 4^{35} will have a units digit of 4.

If you are asked to find the units digit of a quantity such as 743^{67}, don't panic! You care only about the units digit of 743, which is a 3. Why? Because:

$743^1 = 743$, which ends in a 3.
Any number ending in a $(3)(743)$ (a number ending in 3) will produce a number ending in a 9.
Any number ending in a $(9)(743)$ (a number ending in 3) will produce a number ending in a 7.
Any number ending in a $(7)(743)$ (a number ending in a 3) will produce a number ending in a 1.
Any number ending in a $(1)(743)$ (a number ending in a 3) will produce a number ending in a 3.
Pattern: {3, 9, 7, 1, 3, 9, 7, 1, ...}
So 743^{64} will end in a 1 (final units digit in the 4-number repeating pattern), so 743^{65} will end in a 3, so 743^{66} will end in a 9, and 743^{67} will end in a 7. Our answer is 7.

Another example of a patterned sequence is formed by the whole-number remainders produced by certain quotients.

Consider first of all that if an integer n is divided by 7, the whole-number remainders can consist only of the integers $\{0, 1, 2, 3, 4, 5, 6\}$. If you divide any set of consecutive integers by 7, the whole number remainders will form a pattern. Consider values of n from 7 through 14:

$\frac{7}{7}$ = remainder 0

$\frac{8}{7}$ = remainder 1

$\frac{9}{7}$ = remainder 2

$\frac{10}{7}$ = remainder 3

$\frac{11}{7}$ = remainder 4

$\frac{12}{7}$ = remainder 5

$\frac{13}{7}$ = remainder 6

$\frac{14}{7}$ = remainder 0 (pattern begins again)

Example: if n is an even positive multiple of 3, what are the possible remainders when n is divided by 12?

When $n = 6$, remainder when $\frac{6}{12} = 6$

When $n = 12$, remainder when $\frac{12}{12} = 0$

When $n = 18$, remainder when $\frac{18}{12} = 6$
Pattern: $\{6, 0, 6, 0, \ldots\}$
Answer: 0 and 6

Reminder: any time you see a question asking about units digits or remainders, it's likely that a repeating pattern is involved. If you are given very large numbers (e.g., 743^{67}) that the GRE calculator simply cannot handle, find the pattern using more manageable numbers. With units digits, all that matters is finding the pattern formed by the units digit of the base taken to the first few positive integer powers. With remainder questions, quantities like $10^{32} + x$ will behave according to patterns revealed by $10^1 + x$, $10^2 + x$, etc.

We'll end this section with a quantitative comparison question that shows the value of recognizing a repeating pattern.

Sample Question

For each positive integer n, the nth term in the sequence S is $(-1)^n$.

Quantity A   Quantity B
The sum of the first 30 terms of the sequence   The sum of the first 31 terms of the sequence

(A) Quantity A is greater.
(B) Quantity B is greater.
(C) The two quantities are equal.
(D) The relationship cannot be determined from the information given.

Solution

You can list the first few terms to see what this sequence is all about:

$(-1)^1 = -1$
$(-1)^2 = 1$
$(-1)^3 = -1$
$(-1)^4 = 1$

Based on the quantities to be compared, let's also think about the 30th and 31st terms:

$(-1)^{30} = 1$
$(-1)^{31} = -1$

You know that the sum of the first 31 terms is the sum of the first 30 terms plus the 31st term. If that 31st term is negative, as you know it to be, then the sum of the first 31 terms must be less than the sum of the first 30 terms.

Sum of first 31 terms = sum of first 30 terms – 1

Sum of first 31 terms < sum of first 30 terms

Therefore, even without computing, you know with certainty that **Quantity A is greater than Quantity B**.

Rates

Think of **rate** as a special type of ratio, the pace at which something takes place or a *price per* a certain amount of an item.

Let's look at some common ways in which rate is used:

Rate × Time = Distance
30 miles per hour × 5 hours = 150 miles

Rate × Time = Work
5 items per hour × 6 hours = 30 items

Rate × Units = Amount
$6 per bag × 4 bags = $24 total

When dealing with a rate, pay close attention to both units used in the rate. For example, in a rate × time = distance problem, if the rate is in *miles* per *hour*, then the distance used must be in *miles*, and the time used must be in *hours*. If you input a rate in *miles* per *hour* and a distance in *miles*, then the time you solve for will be in *hours*.

You will sometimes need to convert units in order to generate the correct answer to a rate question. Let's start by considering how to convert a given rate into a rate using different units.

Because rate is a ratio of two units, it's often helpful to write it as a fraction, with the word "per" indicating the fraction line between numerator and denominator. For example, 30 miles per hour can be written as $\frac{30 \text{ miles}}{1 \text{ hour}}$. This fraction is especially helpful if you need to convert a rate into different units. For example:

If a car travels 30 miles per hour, what is its rate in feet per second? Note: 1 mile = 5,280 feet.

Start with the fraction $\dfrac{30 \text{ miles}}{1 \text{ hour}}$.

You need to go from miles to feet and from hours to seconds—the order in which you handle those conversions does not matter, so let's start with miles to feet. Next to the fraction $\dfrac{30 \text{ miles}}{1 \text{ hour}}$, write the fraction $\dfrac{5,280 \text{ feet}}{1 \text{ mile}}$. Remember that when you multiply fractions, you can cross-cancel equal quantities—in this case, you can cancel the unit miles, leaving you with feet in the numerator and hours in the denominator. Then you write similar conversion fractions for hours to minutes and minutes to seconds as demonstrated below:

$$\left(\frac{30 \text{ miles}}{1 \text{ hour}} \right)\left(\frac{5,280 \text{ feet}}{1 \text{ mile}} \right)\left(\frac{1 \text{ hour}}{60 \text{ minutes}} \right)\left(\frac{1 \text{ minute}}{60 \text{ seconds}} \right)$$

Note that once you have canceled the old units and are left with just the desired units (in this case, feet in the numerator and seconds in the denominator), simply find the product of all of the numerator values, then divide by the product of all of the denominator values.

$$\frac{(30)(5,280)}{(60)(60)} = \frac{44 \text{ feet}}{1 \text{ second}}$$

You have converted the rate of 30 miles per hour into the equivalent rate of 44 feet per second.

Sometimes, however, you're better off using the rate as given and converting your answer into the desired unit. One common example is when a question gives you a rate in *hours* but asks for the answer in *minutes*:

If Bill walks at a rate of 4 miles per hour, how long, in *minutes*, will it take for Bill to walk 14 miles?

You can set up the equation $4(T) = 14$ as long as you recognize that because the rate is in miles per hour and the distance is in miles, the time (T) you solve for will be in hours. In this case, $T = 3.5$ hours. You can then use the fraction method to convert to minutes:

$$(3.5 \text{ hours})\left(\frac{60 \text{ minutes}}{1 \text{ hour}} \right) = 210 \text{ minutes}$$

Be careful when converting hours to minutes, especially if you use the calculator. For example, if you generate an answer of 2.2 hours, that is NOT equivalent to 2 hours and 20 minutes! You are used to a decimal remainder of 0.2 equaling the number 20—for example, $2.20 is 2 dollars and 20 cents. However, that's true because there are 100 cents in a dollar, so 0.2 of 100 = 20. There are 60 minutes in an hour, and 0.2 hours is equivalent to $\frac{1}{5}$ hour, which is 12 minutes $\left(\frac{60}{5} \right)$. So 2.2 hours is 2 hours and 12 minutes, or 132 minutes total. It's safest to use the fraction method you've been using:

$$(2.2 \text{ hours})\left(\frac{60 \text{ minutes}}{1 \text{ hour}} \right) = 132 \text{ minutes}$$

Rate problems also sometimes ask you to handle very large numbers that can overwhelm the limited capacity of the provided calculator. Let's review how to rewrite large numbers in order to solve such problems efficiently.

The number 40,000 can be written as $(4)(10^4)$—in other words, the leading digits times 10 to the power of the number of zeros following the leading digit.

One million can be written as 10^6, so 3 million can be written as $(3)(10^6)$. One billion can be written as 10^9, so 5.2 billion can be written as $(5.2)(10^9)$.

Example: The average distance from Earth to Mars is 140 million miles. How long, in seconds, will it take a beam of light to travel the 140 million miles from Earth to Mars if light travels at 186,000 miles per second? Please round your answer to the nearest second.

Rate × time = distance, but let's use efficient notation:
$[(186)(10^3)](T) = (140)(10^6)$—note that by using a rate of miles per second, this T will be in seconds.
$$T = \frac{(140)(10^6)}{(186)(10^3)}$$
Use exponent rules to recognize that $\frac{10^6}{10^3} = 10^3$.

Therefore, $T = \frac{(140)(10^3)}{(186)}$. The calculator can easily handle these numbers. $\frac{140,000}{186} = 753$ seconds (rounded to the nearest second).

Sample Question 1

Sam starts walking on a trail at 2:00 p.m. and maintains a speed between 3 and 4 miles per hour. If the trail is 6 miles long, at what time could Sam finish his walk?

Indicate all such times.

A 2:50 p.m.
B 3:10 p.m.
C 3:40 p.m.
D 3:50 p.m.
E 4:10 p.m.

Solution

At a rate of 3 miles per hour, it would take Sam 2 hours to walk 6 miles. At a rate of 4 miles per hour, it would take Sam 1.5 hours to walk 6 miles.

Therefore, if he starts his walk at 2:00 p.m., he will end it sometime between 3:30 and 4:00 p.m.

The answers that apply are [C] and [D].

Sample Question 2

It takes a certain machine 18 hours to create 12 widgets. The machine runs 24 hours per day.

Quantity A
The number of hours it takes the machine to create 3,200 widgets

Quantity B
The number of widgets the machine can make in 200 days, working continually

Ⓐ Quantity A is greater.
Ⓑ Quantity B is greater.
Ⓒ The two quantities are equal.
Ⓓ The relationship cannot be determined from the information given.

Solution

If the machine creates 12 widgets in 18 hours, it takes $\frac{18}{12} = 1.5$ hours per widget.

Thus, 3,200 widgets would take (3,200)(1.5) = 4,800 hours. Use the fraction method to convert hours to days.

$$(4,800 \text{ hours})\left(\frac{1 \text{ day}}{24 \text{ hours}}\right) = 200 \text{ days}.$$

Therefore, in 200 days, the machine produces 3,200 widgets. Since 4,800 is greater than 3,200, **Quantity A is greater than Quantity B**.

Solving Problems that Present Multiple Rates

You may understand and use rates all the time, and they are simple enough. However, some challenges can come when you are required to use several different rates within the same problem, especially under the time pressure of the exam. Let's illustrate this with a few examples.

Imagine that two partners are working on building a fence. Mary can build it alone in 8 hours, and Jake can build it alone in 12 hours.

If they work together, would it make sense to add up those times and say that it will take them 20 hours? Nope. Working together to complete the same job should take less time than working alone.

If they work together, you need to add up their rates, not their times: **the sum of their individual rates is the rate at which they can complete the job working together**.

If Mary takes 8 hours to build one fence, her rate is $\frac{1}{8}$ of a fence per hour. Jake's rate is $\frac{1}{12}$ of a fence per hour.

To add these rates, you need a common denominator:

$$\frac{1}{8} + \frac{1}{12} = \frac{3}{24} + \frac{2}{24} = \frac{5}{24}$$

So their combined rate working together is $\frac{5}{24}$ of a fence per hour. How do you figure out how long it will take for them to finish building the entire fence? Take the reciprocal of the combined 1-hour result, which is $\frac{24}{5}$ (or 4.8) hours.

Why does that work? Let's demonstrate using direct proportions.

$$\frac{\frac{5}{4} \text{ fence}}{1 \text{ hour}} = \frac{1 \text{ fence}}{x \text{ hours}}$$

Cross-multiply to get $\frac{5}{4}x = 1$, then solve for x by dividing both sides by $\frac{5}{24}$. $x = \frac{24}{5}$, or 4.8. Now that you've seen why it works, simply memorize that the reciprocal of the combined 1-hour fraction of a task completed will be the time it takes to accomplish the entire task.

Here's a slightly trickier example:

Imagine that a certain duck takes 2 hours to travel from one side to the other of a 4-mile-wide lake and then takes 4 hours to travel back on the same path. What was the duck's average speed?

It's tempting to mentally average the numbers and say that the duck's average was 2 miles per hour on the way there and 1 mile per hour on the way back, so the duck's average speed must have been 1.5 miles per hour overall. However, this is not correct.

If you write out the math, the duck traveled a total distance of 8 miles in a total time of 6 hours, for an average speed of $1.\overline{3}$ miles per hour. The reason the average speed is not the average of 1 and 2 is that the duck spent longer traveling at a slower speed, which pulls the average speed down below 1.5.

It's hard to be clever about anticipating every mixture "trick" that might appear; what's much more effective is to make sure that you seek to be careful and exhaustive and that you don't take unnecessary shortcuts. It's important to be methodical with these questions, rather than rush to an incorrect answer based on a faulty assumption or oversimplification.

Here are two more sample questions for you to practice that involve a mixture of traveling rates:

Sample Question 1

Train A leaves Station M at 8:10 p.m. and travels toward Station N at 40 mph. Train B leaves Station M at 8:40 p.m. and travels toward Station N at 60 mph. At what time will Train B catch up to Train A?

(A) 9:00 p.m.
(B) 9:20 p.m.
(C) 9:30 p.m.
(D) 9:40 p.m.
(E) 10:00 p.m.

Solution

By the time Train B catches up to Train A, the two trains would have traveled the same total distance as the other. Knowing this, you can set up an equation by pitting their distances against one another.

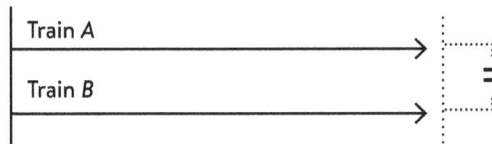

You know that Train A traveled at a rate of 40 miles per hour for an unknown period of time, so Train A's rate × time = 40t.

Train B traveled at 60 miles per hour for 30 minutes, or 0.5 hours, less than that, so Train B's rate × time = 60(t − 0.5).

Again, you know that rate × time = distance, so since you know that the distance traveled by Train A = the distance traveled by Train B, you can set up the following equation and solve for t:

$40t = 60(t - 0.5)$
$40t = 60t - 30$
$20t = 30$
$t = \dfrac{30}{20}$
$t = 1.5$

This means that it took 1.5 hours from when Train A first started traveling for Train B to catch up to Train A, which would put you at answer choice (D) 9:40 p.m. If you double-check your reasoning, Train A, driving at 40 mph, would travel 60 miles in one and a half hours, and Train B would drive 60 miles in one hour. That's when it would catch up.

Note that the math would have worked out exactly the same had you not changed out the minutes to half an hour:

$40t = 60(t - 30)$
$40t = 60t - 1800$
$20t = 1800$
$t = 90$

You just would have needed to work with greater numbers. In either case, **the correct answer is (D)**.

Sample Question 2

Wendy leaves her home and drives to work at x mph. At exactly the same time, Sam leaves the same house and drives in the opposite direction at $\frac{2}{3}x$ mph. If, after 20 minutes, Wendy and Sam are 25 miles apart, how fast is Sam driving?

Ⓐ 25 mph
Ⓑ 30 mph
Ⓒ 35 mph
Ⓓ 40 mph
Ⓔ 45 mph

<u>Solution</u>

Here Wendy and Sam are driving in opposite directions, and the 25 miles represent the total distance they've both traveled after 20 minutes.

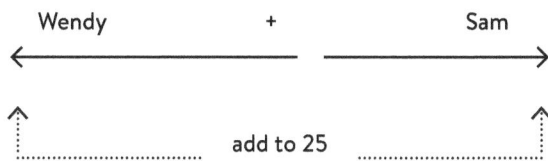

20 minutes is $\frac{1}{3}$ of an hour. Since Wendy drives at x mph, she drives a total distance of $\frac{1}{3}x$.

Since Sam drives at a rate of $\frac{2}{3}x$, Sam drives a total distance of $\left(\frac{1}{3}\right)\left(\frac{2}{3}\right)x$.

Together, they drive a combined distance of $\frac{1}{3}x + \left(\frac{1}{3}\right)\left(\frac{2}{3}\right)x$, which you know = 25, and you can use this to solve for x, and ultimately solve for Sam's speed:

$$\frac{1}{3}x + \left(\frac{1}{3}\right)\left(\frac{2}{3}\right)x = 25$$

$$\frac{1}{3}x + \frac{2}{9}x = 25$$

$$\frac{3}{9}x + \frac{2}{9}x = 25$$

$$\frac{5}{9}x = 25$$

$$x = 25\left(\frac{9}{5}\right)$$

$$x = 45$$

Once you've solved for x, you have to be careful and remember that x represents Wendy's rate. Sam's rate is $\frac{2}{3}x$, which is $\left(\frac{2}{3}\right)(45) = 30$. **(B) is the correct answer.**

Practice Questions

1. A certain souvenir stand has 3 types of items for sale: hats, pins, and stickers. Hats cost between $6 and $8, pins between $3 and $5, and stickers between $2 and $3. If the stand sold 40 items during a certain shift, 18 of which were hats, which of the following could be the total amount received from selling the 40 items?

Indicate all such amounts.

A. $100
B. $150
C. $200
D. $250
E. $300

2. In the sequence $b_1, b_2, b_3 \ldots$, the nth term is defined by $b_n = kn - 2$. If the first 5 terms of the sequence add up to 50, what is the value of k?

$k =$ _____

3. A car traveled 480 miles in 8 hours. For the first 4 hours, it traveled at a rate of 50 miles per hour.

Quantity A	Quantity B
The average speed at which the car traveled for the final 4 hours	70 mph

A. Quantity A is greater.
B. Quantity B is greater.
C. The two quantities are equal.
D. The relationship cannot be determined from the information given.

4. A car traveled 480 miles in 8 hours. For the first 240 miles, it traveled at a rate of 50 miles per hour.

Quantity A	Quantity B
The average speed at which the car traveled for the final 240 miles	70 mph

A. Quantity A is greater.
B. Quantity B is greater.
C. The two quantities are equal.
D. The relationship cannot be determined from the information given.

5. In the sequence $b_1, b_2, b_3 \ldots$, the nth term is defined by $b_n = 0.01n$. What is the sum of the first 20 terms in the sequence?

_____

6. If the sum of 16 consecutive integers is 328, what is the greatest of the integers?

A. 13
B. 17
C. 20
D. 28
E. 32

Practice Questions Continued

7. For a certain sequence, each of the 10 terms is derived by dividing the previous term by 2. The first term in the sequence is 10.

Quantity A	Quantity B
The sum of the sequence	20

(A) Quantity A is greater.
(B) Quantity B is greater.
(C) The two quantities are equal.
(D) The relationship cannot be determined from the information given.

8. A certain object travels at a constant rate. If it takes x minutes to travel y miles, how many feet does the object travel per second? (1 mile = 5,280 feet)

(A) $\dfrac{125x}{11y}$

(B) $\dfrac{11x}{125y}$

(C) $\dfrac{88y}{x}$

(D) $31,600xy$

(E) $\dfrac{11y}{125x}$

9. The sum of 6 consecutive integers is negative.

Quantity A	Quantity B
The absolute value of the least of the integers	The absolute value of the greatest of the integers

(A) Quantity A is greater.
(B) Quantity B is greater.
(C) The two quantities are equal.
(D) The relationship cannot be determined from the information given.

10. A copier prints pages at an average rate of 20 pages per minute for the first 1,000 pages of a report and then 10 pages per minute for the second 1,000 pages of the report. What was the copier's average rate for all 2,000 pages?

(A) 12 pages per minute

(B) $13\frac{1}{3}$ pages per minute

(C) 15 pages per minute

(D) $16\frac{1}{3}$ pages per minute

(E) $16\frac{2}{3}$ pages per minute

11. A certain animal travels at a constant rate of x miles per hour for y hours. The animal travels a total distance of z miles. If y is 4 more than x and z is 18 more than x, how many miles did the animal travel?

┌─────────────┐
│   │
└─────────────┘

12. Working alone, machine A can produce one badge every 5 minutes, and machine B can produce a badge every 3 minutes. How many minutes will it take them, working together, to produce 16 badges?

(A) 8 minutes
(B) 30 minutes
(C) 48 minutes
(D) 82 minutes
(E) 144 minutes

Practice Question Solutions

1. A certain souvenir stand has 3 types of items for sale: hats, pins, and stickers. Hats cost between $6 and $8, pins between $3 and $5, and stickers between $2 and $3. If the stand sold 40 items during a certain shift, 18 of which were hats, which of the following could be the total amount received from selling the 40 items?

Indicate <u>all</u> such amounts.

- [A] $100
- [B] $150
- [C] **$200**
- [D] **$250**
- [E] $300

Solution

Per the given parameters, the stand would have received the greatest amount of money if it sold 18 hats for $8 and 22 pins for $5, or (18)(8) + (22)(5) = $254.

The stand would have received the least amount of money if it sold 18 hats for $6 and 22 stickers for $2, or (18)(6) + (22)(2) = $152.

So you know that the stand received between $152 and $254.

Choices [C] and [D] are within that range and are therefore correct.

2. In the sequence $b_1, b_2, b_3 \ldots$, the nth term is defined by $b_n = kn - 2$. If the first 5 terms of the sequence add up to 50, what is the value of k?

$$k = \boxed{4}$$

Solution

The first term is equal to $(1)k - 2$, the second term is equal to $(2)k - 2$, and so on. If you know that the sum of the first 5 terms is 50, you can set up the following equation to solve for k:

$$(1k - 2) + (2k - 2) + (3k - 2) + (4k - 2) + (5k - 2) = 50$$
$$15k - 10 = 50$$
$$15k = 60$$
$$\mathbf{k = 4}$$

Solutions Continued

3. A car traveled 480 miles in 8 hours. For the first 4 hours, it traveled at a rate of 50 miles per hour.

Quantity A	Quantity B
The average speed at which the car traveled for the final 4 hours	70 mph

(A) Quantity A is greater.
(B) Quantity B is greater.
(C) **The two quantities are equal.**
(D) The relationship cannot be determined from the information given.

Solution

If the car traveled at a rate of 50 miles per hour for 4 hours, it traveled $(50)(4) = 200$ miles during that time.

That means it traveled $480 - 200 = 280$ miles in the remaining $8 - 4 = 4$ hours.

$\frac{280}{4} = 70$ miles per hour.

Quantity A and Quantity B are equal, so the correct answer is (C).

4. A car traveled 480 miles in 8 hours. For the first 240 miles, it traveled at a rate of 50 miles per hour.

Quantity A	Quantity B
The average speed at which the car traveled for the final 240 miles	70 mph

(A) **Quantity A is greater.**
(B) Quantity B is greater.
(C) The two quantities are equal.
(D) The relationship cannot be determined from the information given.

Solution

If the car traveled at 50 miles per hour for the first 240 miles, it took the car $\frac{240}{50} = 4.8$ hours to drive that distance.

This means the car traveled the remaining 240 miles in 3.2 hours.

$\frac{240}{3.2} = 75$, meaning that the car traveled at 75 miles per hour for the remaining 240 miles.

Quantity A is greater.

5. In the sequence $b_1, b_2, b_3 \ldots$, the nth term is defined by $b_n = 0.01n$. What is the sum of the first 20 terms in the sequence?

2.1

Solution

What this means is that the first term is (0.01)(1), the second term is (0.01)(2), and so on. You can write out the first few terms to get a better understanding of the given situation, and you know to end with the 20th term.

0.01, 0.02, 0.03, 0.04,… 0.18, 0.19, 0.20

As highlighted during the discussion of sequences, you can see that you have 10 equally spaced "pairs," (0.01 + 0.20), (0.02 + 0.19), (0.03 + 0.18),… that each add up to 0.21.

(10)(0.21) = 2.1, which is the answer.

6. If the sum of 16 consecutive integers is 328, what is the greatest of the integers?

(A) 13
(B) 17
(C) 20
(D) **28**
(E) 32

Solution

If the sum of 16 consecutive integers is 328, you can break this down to having 8 pairs of integers (with numbers being paired as in the instructional discussion), each of which adds up to $\frac{328}{8} = 41$.

You know that the first and last terms, which you can define as x and $x + 15$, must add up to 41, and you can set up the following equation to solve for x:

$x + (x + 15) = 41$
$2x + 15 = 41$
$2x = 26$
$x = 13$

The first of the 16 consecutive numbers is 13, and the last is 28.

The correct answer is (D).

Solutions Continued

7. For a certain sequence, each of the 10 terms is derived by dividing the previous term by 2. The first term in the sequence is 10.

Quantity A	Quantity B
The sum of the sequence	20

Ⓐ Quantity A is greater.
Ⓑ Quantity B is greater.
Ⓒ The two quantities are equal.
Ⓓ The relationship cannot be determined from the information given.

Solution

You can list the first terms of the sequence to get a better understanding of it:

10, 5, 2.5, 1.25,...

And if you were to add up the 10 terms on the list, you'd find that the sum gets closer and closer to 20 but never actually gets there. Below is a list of the first few terms and their eventual sums.

Order	Term	Sum
1	10	10
2	5	15
3	2.5	17.5
4	1.25	18.75
5	0.625	19.375
6	0.3125	19.6875

The pattern you may notice is that with each new term you add, you make up half the distance to 20, but since the terms you add keep getting lesser and lesser, as mentioned above, you'll never actually get to 20.

So Quantity B is greater.

8. A certain object travels at a constant rate. If it takes x minutes to travel y miles, how many feet does the object travel per second? (1 mile = 5,280 feet)

Ⓐ $\dfrac{125x}{11y}$

Ⓑ $\dfrac{11x}{125y}$

Ⓒ $\dfrac{88y}{x}$

Ⓓ $31,600xy$

Ⓔ $\dfrac{11y}{125x}$

Solution

Start by writing the rate as $\dfrac{y \text{ miles}}{x \text{ minutes}}$. Then convert units using the fraction method:

$$\left(\frac{y \text{ miles}}{x \text{ minutes}} \right)\left(\frac{5,280 \text{ feet}}{1 \text{ mile}} \right)\left(\frac{1 \text{ minute}}{60 \text{ seconds}} \right)$$

Then, place the product of all numerators (including the variable y) over the product of all denominators (including the variable x) and reduce the fraction to lowest terms:

$$\frac{5,280y}{60x} = \frac{88y}{x}$$

The correct answer is (C).

9. The sum of 6 consecutive integers is negative.

Quantity A
The absolute value of the least of the integers

Quantity B
The absolute value of the greatest of the integers

(A) **Quantity A is greater.**
(B) Quantity B is greater.
(C) The two quantities are equal.
(D) The relationship cannot be determined from the information given.

Solution

You can think of many examples for which Quantity A is greater than Quantity B. In fact, any set of 6 consecutive negative integers will do the trick, and in such a case, the absolute value of the least of the integers will always be greater than the absolute value of the greatest integer.

Can there be a list that meets the given parameters and in which the absolute value of the greatest of the integers is greater than the absolute value of the least? No.

If the sum of the 6 consecutive integers is negative, you know that at most you have at most 2 positive integers, 0, and 3 negative integers: 2, 1, 0, –1, –2, –3. If you had more positive integers, you wouldn't be able to have a negative overall sum as required in the question stem.

Even in such a chase, the absolute value of the least term on the list is greater than the absolute value of the greatest, and this is true for all sets of consecutive integers.

Examples of lists:

2, 1, 0, –1, –2, –3
1, 0, –1, –2, –3, –4
0, –1, –2, –3, –4, –5
–1, –2, –3, –4, –5, –6
–2, –3, –4, –5, –6, –7

The absolute value of the least is always greater than the absolute value of the greatest, so Quantity A is always greater.

10. A copier prints pages at an average rate of 20 pages per minute for the first 1,000 pages of a report and then 10 pages per minute for the second 1,000 pages of the report. What was the copier's average rate for all 2,000 pages?

(A) 12 pages per minute
(B) **$13\frac{1}{3}$ pages per minute**
(C) 15 pages per minute
(D) $16\frac{1}{3}$ pages per minute
(E) $16\frac{2}{3}$ pages per minute

Solution

If the copier prints 20 pages per minute, it takes $\frac{1,000}{20}$ = 50 minutes to print 1,000 pages.

If the copier prints 10 pages per minute, it takes $\frac{1,000}{10}$ = 100 minutes to print 1,000 pages.

So it will take the copier 150 minutes to print all 2,000 pages.

$\frac{2,000}{150}$ = $13\frac{1}{3}$ pages per minute.

(B) is the correct answer.

Solutions Continued

11. A certain animal travels at a constant rate of x miles per hour for y hours. The animal travels a total distance of z miles. If y is 4 more than x and z is 18 more than x, how many miles did the animal travel?

21

Solution

If the animal travels at x miles per hour for y hours and travels a total distance of z miles, you know that:

$$xy = z$$

If y is 4 more than x, you can substitute $x + 4$ for y. If z is 18 more than x, you can substitute $x + 18$ for z. Then, you can solve for x.

$(x)(x + 4) = x + 18$
$x^2 + 4x = x + 18$
$x^2 + 3x - 18 = 0$
$(x + 6)(x - 3) = 0$

So x = either 3 or −6

Note that in this situation, x can't be negative, so it must be 3. This means that $y = 3 + 4 = 7$, and $z = 3 + 18 = 21$.

21 is the correct answer.

12. Working alone, machine A can produce one badge every 5 minutes, and machine B can produce a badge every 3 minutes. How many minutes will it take them, working together, to produce 16 badges?

Ⓐ 8 minutes
Ⓑ 30 minutes
Ⓒ 48 minutes
Ⓓ 82 minutes
Ⓔ 144 minutes

Solution

One way to think of this is that machine A can produce 12 badges per hour, and machine B produces 20 badges per hour. Together, they can produce 32 badges per hour. If this is the case, it would take them half that time, or 30 minutes, to produce 16 badges.

(B) is the correct answer.

8

VERBAL REASONING

Single-Blank Text Completion

I will begin the study of text completion with single-blank questions (i.e., questions that require you to select the best choice to fill in one blank space in given sentences). Typically, you'll see a few single-blank questions per exam. Single-blank questions serve as a nice introduction to thinking about how to approach text completion questions in general.

Problem-Solving Strategies

You can split up your problem-solving process for text completion questions into two phases: (1) evaluating the statement and (2) choosing from the answer choices.

Evaluating the Statement

Keep in mind that the missing word or phrase is never random or accidental; the whole sentence has been created to lead you to this word or phrase. Put another way, all questions are carefully designed to enable you to anticipate the characteristics of the words or phrases needed to fill in the blank spaces.

Embedded clues about the missing word can appear anywhere in the statement—they may appear right next to the relevant blank space or (especially in longer sentences or paragraphs) in a completely different part of the text.

When you first read a statement, don't rush to the blank space—nor should you ignore it to focus exclusively on the adjacent wording. Rather, take in the statement as a whole and use every possible clue to anticipate the type of word or phrase that will fit into the blank.

Evaluating Answer Choices

Next, when you arrive at the answer choices, evaluate each one carefully and then decide to eliminate, leave, or select each one. You want to eliminate it if you are certain it's not the right answer; you want to leave it if you are unsure; and you want to select it if you feel confident it is correct. Even if you select an answer early in the process, I recommend that you carefully evaluate all of the remaining answer choices.

After that first round, review all the answer choices you didn't eliminate and choose the single best one. Even if you have an answer that you feel fairly certain about, use this second round to confirm that it is indeed better than the other options available.

Common Positive Paths

Path 1:
Able to eliminate four wrong answers and see why one answer is right.

Path 2:
Able to eliminate two wrong answers and see why one answer is right.

Path 3:
Able to eliminate two wrong answers. Down to three choices, able to see why one answer makes better sense than the other two.

Path 4:
Able to eliminate three answer choices. Down to two, able to see that one of them is clearly wrong.

Three Types of Clues

Let's take a look at how you can find the words in the sentence that provide the most useful clues about what needs to go in the blanks.

There are three key types of contextual clues to find within the sentence that tip off which word or phrase will fit best in the blank space. We can categorize these clues as **definitions**, **inferences**, and **contrasts**. Of course, during the exam, you don't have to spend time categorizing the type of clues that you are given in each sentence. However, practicing identifying and utilizing such clues before the exam is helpful, so let's get started.

Definitions

The most basic type of clue is the **definition**. The test writer will provide a definition for the missing word (or phrase) somewhere else in the text. Note that this clue can be located anywhere, and the writer will often get creative with the sentence structure to distance it from the blank space.

Here is a super-simple example to illustrate:

Imagine that the missing word is **elusive**, which means challenging to find, catch, or achieve.

You may see the definition right next to the blank:

The thief was so ____, or **difficult to find and catch**, that the police had to bring in special forces.

Or the definition may be separated from the blank:

____ thieves often require local police to bring in special forces, for such criminals are particularly **difficult to find and catch**.

Regardless of where in the sentence the hints occur, be on the lookout for words and phrases in the text that help define the missing term. Let's look at two full sample questions for which definitions play a central role in determining the correct answer.

Sample Question 1

The Great Exhibition of 1851 put innovations and ideas from all over the world on display in London's Hyde Park, celebrating the many _____ of technology and human progress that marked the Industrial Revolution.

Ⓐ manipulation
Ⓑ surrenders
Ⓒ advances
Ⓓ disclosures
Ⓔ gatherings

Solution

The key clues here are *innovations*, *ideas*, *technology*, and *progress*—these words define the subject of the exhibition and, therefore, the word in the blank. You also know the word in the blank is positive because the exhibition is *celebrating* it. Therefore, you need a word that fits the definition of <u>progress</u> and <u>innovation</u> in ideas and technology. *Innovations* can be defined as *advances* in technology, and *advances* are also virtually synonymous with *progress*, so it makes sense that **(C) is the correct answer**.

Looking at the other answer choices:

(A) No words in the text refer to *manipulations*, or controlled adjustments of technology, so you can eliminate that answer choice.

(B) Nothing in the text indicates a *surrender*, and in this context, *surrender* is too negative a word to work with *celebrating*. You can eliminate this choice as well.

(D) To disclose is to reveal, so *disclosures* could be a somewhat tempting answer because the sentence is about an exhibition. However, as depicted in the sentence, the Industrial Revolution was marked not by disclosures of progress but by progress itself—and this progress is what the exhibition is celebrating. Therefore, you can eliminate (D).

(E) Finally, though the exhibition and celebration could be defined as a gathering, *gatherings* did not mark the Industrial Revolution. You can eliminate choice (E).

Sample Question 2

British humorist P. G. Wodehouse was an enormously _____ writer, churning out 71 novels, 24 story collections, 42 plays, and 15 movie scripts in his nearly 75-year career.

(A) lugubrious
(B) prolific
(C) controversial
(D) partisan
(E) languorous

<u>Solution</u>

All of the information you are given about Wodehouse, in describing what sort of *enormously* _____ *writer* he was, deals with the vast amount of material that he produced over his long career.

In keeping with this definition, you can expect a modifier such as <u>productive</u>. Let's take a look at the answer choices.

(A) *Lugubrious* is a synonym for sad or mournful. Nothing in the sentence suggests sadness, so you can eliminate this answer choice.

(B) *Prolific* is a synonym for highly productive and is exactly the type of answer you are looking for. **(B) is correct.**

(C) No language in the sentence indicates that Wodehouse was *controversial*, so you can eliminate this answer choice. (Note: Wodehouse may indeed have been a controversial author; however, because this text does not contain any references to controversy, (C) will not be the correct answer choice. You must be careful not to bring outside information to the passage, even if you know such information to be true.)

(D) To be *partisan* is to be strongly supportive of a particular party or cause. Although Wodehouse may have been partisan, nothing in the sentence refers to partisanship or taking sides. You can confidently eliminate this answer choice as well.

(E) Finally, to be *languorous* is to lack energy, which is quite the opposite of the characteristics of Wodehouse that the sentence describes. You can eliminate answer choice (E).

Inferences

In some sentences, you'll be given clues that do not provide direct definitions but that allow you to infer the missing term. Going back to the simple example term **elusive**, meaning difficult to find or catch, let's look at the following:

The thief was so _____ that the police had to hire extra forces and purchase special equipment to apprehend her.

You aren't specifically told that the thief is difficult to find and catch, but you can infer this quality based on the information provided in the sentence—specifically that the police had to expend extra effort to capture her.

Here are a couple more examples of sentence completion questions that provide clues that allow you to infer the meaning of the missing term.

Sample Question 1

One crucial difference between real-world and online discourse is that the inherent anonymity of social media can afford us a feeling of _____ that may encourage us to give free rein to our worst impulses.

(A) congeniality
(B) perspicacity
(C) endangerment
(D) impunity
(E) self-possession

Solution

You know from the clues in the text that online discourse is *anonymous*—no one knows who we are—and that this quality may encourage us to feel *free* to do bad things we would otherwise hold ourselves back from (reins are restraints, so *to give free rein* is to choose not to use restraints). You need to infer what sort of feeling resulting from anonymity might provide such encouragement.

(A) *Congeniality* is friendliness. Nothing in the sentence refers to friendliness, and this feeling wouldn't encourage us to give in to our worst impulses, so you can eliminate this answer.

(B) *Perspicacity* is the characteristic of perceptiveness and having keen insight. No words in the sentence suggest sharp perception, and there is no inherent reason perspicacity would encourage us to give in to our worst impulses. You can eliminate this answer as well.

(C) Although the word *endangerment* has negative connotations, hence superficially fitting with the overall tone of the sentence, no words in the text refer to danger—so this choice is very unlikely to be correct. You could leave it in out of an abundance of caution, but it's not a great fit for the sentence.

(D) *Impunity*—the freedom to act without suffering the consequences of our actions (it literally means a lack of punishment)—is the exact type of word you are looking for. If online anonymity makes us feel confident that no one can identify us, feeling freedom from the risk of punishment could indeed encourage us to give free rein to our worst impulses. **You can infer that (D) is correct**.

(E) There is no reason to infer that a feeling of *self-possession*, or control of one's emotions and behavior, would encourage us to give free rein to the worst of our impulses; indeed, quite the opposite because *free rein* is a lack of control. Furthermore, self-possession is a positive quality, hence not in keeping with the tone of the sentence. You can eliminate this answer choice as well.

Sample Question 2

Sarah Hale, longtime editor of the 19th-century American women's magazine *Godey's Lady's Book*, wrote passionately about Thanksgiving, _____ national leaders to add it to the calendar of national celebrations until Lincoln finally acquiesced in 1863.

(A) discharging
(B) defraying
(C) badgering
(D) restraining
(E) promising

Solution

You can infer from *passionately* that Hale invested energy and emotion in her advocacy of Thanksgiving to national leaders. Looking at the fact that Lincoln *finally acquiesced* to Hale—or gave in to her requests after a lengthy period—we can infer that Hale petitioned for an official Thanksgiving celebration repeatedly over a long time. Therefore, you can infer that Sarah Hale perhaps pleaded for Thanksgiving to be made an official national holiday.

Let's take a look at the answer choices.

(A) To *discharge* a person is to dismiss them, which doesn't make sense in this context. No words in the sentence have anything to do with dismissal. You can eliminate this answer choice.

(B) *Defraying* means to help to pay the cost, which also doesn't make sense in this context. No language in the text refers to cost or payment. You can eliminate this answer choice as well.

(C) *Badgering* is to repeatedly ask, which is exactly the type of answer you anticipated. **Answer choice (C) is correct**.

(D) *Restraining* means holding back, the opposite of what Hale is described in this sentence as doing. You can eliminate this answer choice.

(E) Sarah Hale is not *promising* national leaders to add it to the calendar. Although this answer choice is in keeping with Hale's passionate advocacy, her *promising* could not lead Lincoln to *finally acquiesce*. You can eliminate this answer choice as well.

Contrasts

The final type of clue that you may find in a sentence completion question is a **contrast**. The missing word stands in contrast or opposition to other specific language in the text.

Be on the lookout for words that will tip off that a contrast is coming, such as the following:

unlike
despite
although
while
however
contrary
but
rather
instead
nonetheless
nevertheless
still
on the other hand

Note: On the GRE, sometimes milder words such as "unexpected," "surprising," or "incongruous" can indicate that a contrast or opposition exists in the sentence.

Going back to the simple example using the word elusive, you can see how you might set up the answer with a contrast:

Unlike her accomplice, who was fairly easy for the police to catch, Janice proved to be quite _____.

You know directly from the sentence that Janice was the opposite of *easy…to catch*, so it would make sense that she would be elusive.

Let's look at some sample questions in which contrast clues play a key role.

Sample Question 1

In stark contrast to the current _____, a disharmony exacerbated by sharp disagreements with coworkers and struggles to abide by company policies marked the beginning of Smith's time as an employee at the research laboratory.

Ⓐ competence
Ⓑ effortlessness
Ⓒ intelligence
Ⓓ intractability
Ⓔ collegiality

Solution

From the language of the text, you can infer that the word in the blank shows a stark contrast to *disharmony* in the workplace. You should be looking for a word that suggests harmony—people getting along and working well together, particularly in a professional context.

Let's look at the answer choices.

(A) *Competence* shows no contrast with *disharmony* and is very unlikely to be the correct answer. Although it does imply positive contributions to the workplace and is therefore not completely off-topic for the general meaning of the text, competence does not directly oppose the meaning of disharmony.

(B) *Effortlessness* does not contrast directly with *disharmony*, so it is unlikely to be correct. However, it is a good antonym for *struggles*, so it is worth keeping in mind if no other answer choice works better.

(C) Nothing in the text states that a lack of *intelligence* contributed to Smith's early *disharmony* or that an increase in intelligence characterizes the difference between the *disharmony* and her contrasting current situation. You can eliminate this answer choice.

(D) *Intractability* is stubbornness. Stubbornness does not contrast with *disharmony*; in fact, stubbornness would fit well with the list of things the sentence states show a contrast to the word you are looking for. You can eliminate this answer choice.

(E) *Collegiality*, which is cooperative and harmonious interaction among a group of co-workers, provides a stark contrast with *disharmony*, *disagreements*, and *struggles* in the office. This word is exactly what you are looking for; it fits the sentence far better than effortlessness, the only other choice that was still in the running. Furthermore, *collegiality* relates directly to workplace culture. **(E) is the correct answer choice**.

Sample Question 2

Although they can lead us to make grave errors, cognitive biases also help us more efficiently _____ the overwhelming flood of information we encounter each day.

(A) acknowledge
(B) process
(C) dismiss
(D) retrain
(E) disregard

<u>Solution</u>

You have a clear opposition here: *grave errors* contrast with *help* and *efficiently*.

You can expect the word in the blank to be positive, a verb that would describe how to *efficiently* <u>deal with</u> an *overwhelming flood*. A verb that means <u>manage</u>, <u>understand</u>, or <u>sort out</u> would fit into this blank.

(A) *Acknowledge* may be a somewhat tempting answer choice because it is positive and has to do with understanding. However, cognitive biases could help us efficiently *acknowledge* a flood of information, and acknowledging this flood of information would do nothing to help us deal with its overwhelming nature.

(B) Because they would impose a structure on the flood of information, cognitive biases could indeed help us efficiently *process* that information. **(B) is the correct answer**.

(C) Although it is possible (though not likely) that one would need help to *dismiss* an overwhelming flood of information, we would not seek to do so efficiently. This answer choice does not work.

(D) This answer choice is very similar to (C), and *disregard* has the same disqualifications. You can eliminate (D) as well.

(E) To *retrain* is to reteach. It would not be possible to retrain a flood of information. You can eliminate this answer choice as well.

Prediction Drill

For each of the following sentences, underline the key clues that tip off what you can expect from the missing term before then making a prediction about what the missing term might be.

1. Certain that she would soon be laid off because of her company's restructuring, Allison _____ her upcoming termination by leaving for a secure position with an industry competitor.

2. All types of houseplants can provide us with aesthetic pleasure and stress relief; however, some, including English ivy, Boston fern, peace lily, and aloe vera, also act as _____ natural filters that can significantly improve air quality in our living spaces.

3. Though modern parents generally accept rebellion as an inevitable part of adolescence, they often end up in _____ relationships with their teenage children because they abhor the ways in which this necessary process plays out.

4. In the process of _____ about the triumphs and tribulations of the past, history students become better prepared to meet the challenges of a constantly changing and increasingly complex modern world.

5. It is remarkable how much parenting norms can change from generation to generation: although the ultimate crime 50 years ago was to _____ one's children, neglecting to indulge their whims is now considered a parental sin.

6. Cats whiskers, or vibrissae, owe their incredible sensitivity to the sensory organs called proprioceptors at their tips. Although whisker sensitivity helps cats successfully _____ their environments, overstimulated proprioceptors may occasionally cause them discomfort.

7. Justin was a _____ opponent, his superficial indifference cleverly masking a calculating mind.

8. O. W. Gurley, a wealthy Black businessman, moved to Tulsa, Oklahoma, in 1905 to create economic opportunities for those _____ "the harsh oppression of Mississippi."

9. Although cars have long been _____ in our area, our great-grandmother could remember a time when a jalopy coming down the road would draw fascinated children from every nearby home.

Prediction Drill Solutions

1. <u>Certain</u> that she would <u>soon be laid off</u> because of her company's restructuring, Allison _____ her <u>upcoming termination</u> by <u>leaving for a secure position</u> with an industry competitor.

Notes: Allison knows she is about to get *laid off*, and she <u>acts ahead of time</u> to avoid this fate by *leaving for a secure position* elsewhere.

Anticipate: Allison <u>preempted</u> her upcoming termination.

2. All types of houseplants can provide us with <u>aesthetic pleasure and stress relief</u>; <u>however</u>, some, including English ivy, Boston fern, peace lily, and aloe vera, also act as _____ natural <u>filters</u> that can <u>significantly improve air quality</u> in our living spaces.

Notes: You are looking for a benefit of houseplants that is different from (*however*), but does not counteract, aesthetic pleasure and stress relief. Because they *significantly improve air quality*, you can infer that they are <u>good/powerful/strong</u> natural filters.

Anticipate: Some houseplants act as <u>effective</u> natural filters that can significantly improve air quality.

3. <u>Though</u> modern parents generally <u>accept</u> rebellion as an inevitable part of adolescence, they often end up in _____ relationships with their teenage children because they <u>abhor</u> the ways in which this necessary process plays out.

Notes: You have a couple of clues here. The part of the sentence where the blank occurs is set up to contrast (*though*) with the earlier statement that parents *accept* their children's rebellion. Further, you learn that the parents *abhor*, or hate, the way the process plays out. Therefore, you are looking for a word that conveys <u>conflict</u> and <u>unpleasantness</u>.

Anticipate: Modern parents often end up in <u>argumentative</u> relationships with their teenage children.

4. In the <u>process</u> of _____ about the <u>triumphs and tribulations of the past</u>, <u>history students</u> may become better prepared to meet the challenges of a constantly changing and increasingly complex modern world.

Notes: What *process* do *history* students take part in relation to *the past*? They <u>study</u> it and <u>learn</u> about its good times and bad times.

Anticipate: History students undertake the process of <u>studying and learning</u> about the triumphs and tribulations of the past.

5. It is remarkable how much parenting norms can <u>change</u> from generation to generation: <u>although</u> the ultimate <u>crime 50 years ago</u> was to _____ one's children, <u>neglecting to indulge</u> their whims is <u>now</u> considered a parental <u>sin</u>.

Notes: The words *change* and *although* tell you to look for a contrast in this sentence between norms *50 years ago* and norms *now*. Today, *neglecting to indulge* children is a *sin*; in contrast, 50 years ago, it would have been a *crime* to <u>indulge</u> them.

Anticipate: The ultimate crime 50 years ago was to <u>indulge or spoil</u> one's children.

6. Cat whiskers, or vibrissae, owe their <u>incredible sensitivity</u> to the <u>sensory organs</u> called proprioceptors at their tips. <u>Although</u> whisker sensitivity helps cats <u>successfully</u> _____ their <u>environments</u>, overstimulated proprioceptors may occasionally <u>cause them discomfort</u>.

Notes: Because the word in the blank is associated with *successfully* and is placed in contrast (*Although*) with *cause them discomfort*, you can infer that it is a positive/beneficial word for something cats would want or need to do in relation to their *environment*. Because the whiskers are external *sensory organs*, the verb should have something to do with what accurate perception of their surroundings would help the cats do.

Anticipate: Whisker sensitivity helps cats successfully <u>navigate</u> their environments.

7. Justin was a _____ opponent, his superficial indifference cleverly masking a calculating mind.

Notes: The underlined words in the sentence create a clear sense of the meaning of the adjective that goes in the blank. The word *opponent* shows that Justin is seeking victory in a competition. The word *superficial* (meaning only on the surface) and the phrase *cleverly masking* indicate that Justin is intentionally and skillfully creating a deceptive appearance of not working hard to win. The fact that he has a *calculating mind* shows that Justin is carefully planning his path to victory.

You are looking for a word that describes Justin as a shrewdly strategic opponent.

Anticipate: Justin was a cunning opponent.

8. O. W. Gurley, a wealthy Black businessman, moved to Tulsa, Oklahoma, in 1905 to create economic opportunities for those _____ "the harsh oppression of Mississippi."

Notes: You are told that Gurley *moved to Oklahoma* to help people who were affected by adverse conditions in *Mississippi*. If those people were in Tulsa, they too must have left Mississippi to get away from its *harsh oppression*.

Anticipate: O. W. Gurley sought to create economic opportunities for those escaping from the *harsh oppression of Mississippi*.

9. Although cars have long been _____ in our area, our great-grandmother could remember a time when a jalopy coming down the road would draw fascinated children from every nearby home.

Notes: The sentence establishes a contrast to a period when cars made people *fascinated*, so you can infer that, now, cars are fairly unexciting and ordinary.

Anticipate: Cars have long been common in our area.

Practice Questions

Select from amongst the answer choices one that best completes the given statement.

1. O. W. Gurley, a wealthy Black businessman, moved to Tulsa, Oklahoma, in 1905 to create economic opportunities for those _____ "the harsh oppression of Mississippi."

Ⓐ yearning for
Ⓑ refuting
Ⓒ fleeing
Ⓓ attesting to
Ⓔ yielding to

2. Cat whiskers, or vibrissae, owe their incredible sensitivity to sensory organs called proprioceptors at their tips. Although whisker sensitivity helps cats successfully _____ their environments, overstimulated proprioceptors may occasionally cause them discomfort.

Ⓐ naturalize
Ⓑ negotiate
Ⓒ predominate
Ⓓ forfeit
Ⓔ relish

3. All types of houseplants can provide us with aesthetic pleasure and stress relief; however, some, including English ivy, Boston fern, peace lily, and aloe vera, also act as _____ natural filters that can significantly improve air quality in our living spaces.

Ⓐ effortful
Ⓑ efficacious
Ⓒ effluent
Ⓓ effusive
Ⓔ effete

4. Justin was _____ opponent, his superficial indifference cleverly masking a calculating mind.

Ⓐ an insidious
Ⓑ a callow
Ⓒ a prosaic
Ⓓ a capricious
Ⓔ a malicious

5. Though modern parents generally accept rebellion as an inevitable part of adolescence, they often end up in _____ relationships with their teenage children because they abhor the ways in which this necessary process plays out.

Ⓐ salubrious
Ⓑ uncanny
Ⓒ rancorous
Ⓓ austere
Ⓔ unstinting

6. In the process of _____ the triumphs and tribulations of the past, history students become better prepared to meet the challenges of a constantly changing and increasingly complex modern world.

Ⓐ preparing
Ⓑ improving
Ⓒ replacing
Ⓓ transmuting
Ⓔ scrutinizing

7. Although cars have long been _____ in our area, our great-grandmother could remember a time when a jalopy coming down the road would draw fascinated children from every nearby home.

Ⓐ ubiquitous
Ⓑ cherished
Ⓒ propitious
Ⓓ unorthodox
Ⓔ compelling

8. Certain that she would soon be laid off because of her company's restructuring, Allison _____ her upcoming termination by leaving for a secure position with an industry competitor.

Ⓐ predetermined
Ⓑ predisposed
Ⓒ prevaricated
Ⓓ predominated
Ⓔ preempted

9. It is remarkable how much parenting norms can change from generation to generation: although the ultimate crime 50 years ago was to _____ one's children, neglecting to indulge their whims is now considered a parental sin.

Ⓐ rebuff
Ⓑ bemuse
Ⓒ cosset
Ⓓ undermine
Ⓔ upbraid

Practice Question Solutions

1. O. W. Gurley, a wealthy Black businessman, moved to Tulsa, Oklahoma, in 1905 to create economic opportunities for those _____ "the harsh oppression of Mississippi."

(A) yearning for
(B) refuting
(C) **fleeing**
(D) attesting to
(E) yielding to

Solution

You can infer that Gurley wanted to create opportunities for those escaping *the harsh oppression of Mississippi* to create a better life for themselves in Oklahoma. Let's evaluate the answer choices.

(A) These individuals would not be *yearning for*, or desiring, *the harsh oppression of Mississippi*, so you can eliminate this answer choice.

(B) These individuals are also not *refuting*, or proving to be false, *the harsh oppression of Mississippi*, so you can eliminate this answer choice as well.

(C) These individuals are *fleeing*, or escaping from, *the harsh oppression of Mississippi*, so **this is the correct answer**.

(D) Nothing in the sentence indicates that the people Gurley sought to help were *attesting to*, or providing evidence of, *the harsh oppression of Mississippi*. You can eliminate (D) as well.

(E) *Yielding to*, or giving in to, fits reasonably well with *the harsh oppression of Mississippi*, so it may be a tempting answer choice. However, it does not account for what these people are doing in Oklahoma, so it doesn't fulfill the function of the word in the blank. It does not fit the sentence as well as answer choice (C). You can eliminate this answer choice as well.

2. Cat whiskers, or vibrissae, owe their incredible sensitivity to sensory organs called proprioceptors at their tips. Although whisker sensitivity helps cats successfully _____ their environments, overstimulated proprioceptors may occasionally cause them discomfort.

(A) naturalize
(B) **negotiate**
(C) predominate
(D) forfeit
(E) relish

Solution

You can infer that the sensitivity of cats' whiskers helps them navigate their environment. Let's evaluate the answer choices.

(A) *Naturalize* is both awkward yet tempting—to naturalize is to cause to adapt or to adapt to a new area. This word is at least on topic for the context. However, if you plug it into the blank, the sentence tells you that the cats' whisker sensitivity helps them cause their environments to adapt. This meaning is not correct. So you can eliminate naturalize.

(B) *Negotiate* is a synonym for navigate, and **it is the correct answer**.

(C) To *predominate* means to be the primary or main element. No words in the sentence refer to relative significance or dominance of cats. You can eliminate this answer choice.

(D) Similarly, to *forfeit* means to give up, and you have no hints of this either, so you can eliminate it as well.

(E) And finally, to *relish* is to feel great enjoyment. Nothing in the sentence tells you that cats enjoy their environments (and it also doesn't go well with *successfully*), so you can eliminate this answer choice as well.

3. All types of houseplants can provide us with aesthetic pleasure and stress relief; however, some, including English ivy, Boston fern, peace lily, and aloe vera, also act as _____ natural filters that can significantly improve air quality in our living spaces.

Ⓐ effortful
Ⓑ efficacious
Ⓒ effluent
Ⓓ effusive
Ⓔ effete

Solution

The *however* indicates that, although all plants offer aesthetic pleasure and stress relief, a select few have an additional characteristic: some also act as _____ natural filters. Because they can significantly improve air quality, you can infer that they must be effective air filters.

(A) *Effortful* isn't a great match. Nothing in the sentence indicates effort. You can eliminate (A).

(B) *Efficacious* is a synonym for effective and **is, thus, the correct answer**.

(C) *Effluent* means flowing out; nothing in the sentence suggests flowing, and filters don't flow. You can eliminate this answer choice.

(D) *Effusive* means overflowing; like (C) above, this word has nothing to do with the sentence (or with filters in general). You can eliminate it.

(E) *Effete* means lacking strength or force; it is the opposite of what you are looking for. Effete filters would not significantly improve air quality. You can eliminate (E).

4. Justin was _____ opponent, his superficial indifference cleverly masking a calculating mind.

Ⓐ an insidious
Ⓑ a callow
Ⓒ a prosaic
Ⓓ a capricious
Ⓔ a malicious

Solution

You know that Justin's *superficial indifference* cleverly masks a calculating mind, so you want an answer that gives you a sense that he's deceptive, scheming, or something of that nature.

(A) *An insidious* opponent is one who is dangerous in a way that is difficult to see, crafty, and deceptive. This is a great match and **is the correct answer**.

(B) *A callow* person is one who is inexperienced or immature. This doesn't fit the description given of Justin. You can eliminate it.

(C) *A prosaic* person is one who is unimaginative or dull. This doesn't fit the description given of Justin. You can eliminate it.

(D) *A capricious* person is one who is fickle, inconstant, and always changing their mind. This also doesn't fit anything in the description given of Justin.

(E) *A malicious* person is one who wants to do harm. Though Justin does intend to deceive and is scheming to win, the text contains no indication that Justin wants to or means to do harm. You can eliminate this answer as well.

Solutions Continued

5. Though modern parents generally accept rebellion as an inevitable part of adolescence, they often end up in _____ relationships with their teenage children because they abhor the ways in which this necessary process plays out.

(A) salubrious
(B) uncanny
(C) rancorous
(D) austere
(E) unstinting

Solution

The missing word describes the type of relationships that modern parents have with their teenage children, and you have some key clues as to what to expect.

You start with a contrast, *though modern parents generally accept*, which indicates you are looking to fill in the blank with a word that indicates the opposite of acceptance. Then, you are told that the parents *abhor* the ways in which this necessary process plays out, another indication that the blank contains a negative word that implies conflict and unpleasantness.

Let's take a look at the answer choices.

(A) *Salubrious* means healthful, which is not the description the clues are pointing you to. You can eliminate it.

(B) *Uncanny* means strange or inexplicable—no words in the sentence tell you that the relationship is strange or can't be explained, so you can eliminate this answer choice as well.

(C) A *rancorous* relationship is one characterized by anger or resentment. This matches the clues—it contrasts with acceptance and matches abhorrence. **Rancorous is correct.**

(D) *Austere* means very strict and without comforts. It isn't a good match for the clues in the sentence. You can eliminate austere as well.

(E) Although *unstinting* may sound like a negative word, it actually means generous. It doesn't match up with the meaning required by the clues. (E) can be eliminated as well.

6. In the process of _____ the triumphs and tribulations of the past, history students become better prepared to meet the challenges of a constantly changing and increasingly complex modern world.

(A) preparing
(B) improving
(C) replacing
(D) transmuting
(E) scrutinizing

Solution

You are looking for something that *history students* do in relation to the *triumphs and tribulations* of the past. They study or analyze them.

Let's evaluate the answer choices.

(A) *Preparing* does not work in this context and can be eliminated.

(B) *Improving* does not work in this context and can be eliminated.

(C) *Replacing* does not work in this context and can be eliminated.

(D) To *transmute* is to change—the sentence does mention the changing world, but it does not indicate that the students are changing anything about the past, so you can eliminate transmuting.

(E) *Scrutinizing* means studying very carefully. This fits the context well, for this is what history students do. **(E) is the correct answer.**

7. Although cars have long been _____ in our area, our great-grandmother could remember a time when a jalopy coming down the road would draw fascinated children from every nearby home.

(A) **ubiquitous**
(B) cherished
(C) propitious
(D) unorthodox
(E) compelling

Solution

You expect a word synonymous with <u>unsurprising</u> or <u>ordinary</u> to contrast with the fact that cars were so unusual and interesting as to inspire fascination in the past. Let's take a look at the answer choices.

(A) *Ubiquitous* means present everywhere. **This is the correct answer.**

(B) *Cherished* doesn't provide the contrast that this sentence requires—cherishing cars would not prevent them from attracting fascination or attention. You can eliminate this answer choice.

(C) *Propitious* means favorable or promising; in context, it's tough to see what this could be contrasted against, so you can eliminate this answer choice as well.

(D) *Unorthodox* means going against the norm; this is the opposite of the answer you are looking for, so you can eliminate this answer choice, too.

(E) To be *compelling* is to be irresistible or to command respect. This is the opposite of what you are looking for; you are seeking a word that implies the car would NOT attract fascinated attention. You can eliminate answer choice (E).

8. Certain that she would soon be laid off because of her company's restructuring, Allison _____ her upcoming termination by leaving for a secure position with an industry competitor.

(A) predetermined
(B) predisposed
(C) prevaricated
(D) predominated
(E) **preempted**

Solution

By *leaving* her company for a *secure position* elsewhere, Allison would <u>preempt</u>, or act in advance to prevent, her being laid off.

Fortunately for us, *preempted* is among the answer choices, and **(E) is the correct answer.**

Let's take a quick look at the other answer choices.

(A) To *predetermine* is to decide something in advance: that does not fit the context. Allison isn't deciding her termination.

(B) To *predispose* is to make someone more likely or susceptible. It's unorthodox or incorrect phrasing to say one predisposes an action. Also, this meaning is the opposite of what you are looking for. You can safely eliminate this answer choice as well.

(C) To *prevaricate* is to lie, which doesn't make sense in this context. You can eliminate prevaricated.

(D) To *predominate* something is to be the main element in it; this meaning does not fit the context of this sentence. You can eliminate this answer choice as well.

Solutions Continued

9. It is remarkable how much parenting norms can change from generation to generation: although the ultimate crime 50 years ago was to _____ one's children, neglecting to indulge their whims is now considered a parental sin.

(A) rebuff
(B) bemuse
(C) cosset
(D) undermine
(E) upbraid

Solution

You know you have a contrast between the generations and that, now, it is considered a parental sin to neglect to *indulge* the whims of one's child. So, in contrast, you can infer that, 50 years ago, it was a crime to indulge or spoil one's children. With that in mind, let's evaluate the answer choices.

(A) To *rebuff* is to reject, which is the reverse of what you are looking for. You can eliminate this answer.

(B) To *bemuse* is to confuse or to puzzle, which doesn't fit in this context—no language in the sentence refers to confusing one's children. You can eliminate this answer choice as well.

(C) *Cosset* is a synonym for pamper or coddle. It's the exact type of word you are looking for: the opposite of *neglecting to indulge*. **(C) is correct**.

(D) *Undermining*, or trying to weaken, is not relevant to the context. It is not the opposite of neglecting to indulge and does not imply spoiling. You can eliminate this answer choice as well.

(E) To *upbraid* is to scold. To scold doesn't fit the context; it does not mean spoil or indulge. You can eliminate this answer choice as well.

9

VERBAL REASONING

Two- and Three-Blank Text Completion

In this lesson, I will discuss text completion for two or three blank spaces instead of one blank space. Most of the exam's text completion questions involve two or three blank spaces, and you can apply the same strategies you used in Chapter 8 for these questions.

Let's get started with a couple of sample questions.

Sample Question 1

Ancient myths often fulfilled the same purpose that science writing does today: to __(i)__ the most persistent mysteries of our existence. For instance, the myth of Persephone's yearly descent into the underworld was a way for ancient Greeks to ___(ii)___ the cycle of the seasons.

BLANK i

Ⓐ amplify
Ⓑ elucidate
Ⓒ perpetuate

BLANK ii

Ⓓ account for
Ⓔ debunk
Ⓕ obscure

Solution

You have enough general knowledge of ancient myths and science writing to predict the first missing term and likely know these topics help <u>explain</u>, <u>explore</u>, or <u>consider</u> *the most persistent mysteries of our existence.*

The second missing term is a continuation of this discussion—the myth was *a way for ancient Greeks to* perhaps <u>understand</u> or <u>think about</u> *the cycle of the seasons.*

Let's evaluate the answer choices for the two blank spaces.

(A) *Elucidate*, or explain, is the type of answer you predicted, and **it is correct**.

(B) To *amplify* is to make louder or more intense; that doesn't fit well with the context. Also, there is no word among the answer choices for blank ii that would work together with amplify. You can eliminate this answer choice.

(C) To *perpetuate* something is to keep it going; like answer choice (B), this one doesn't work perfectly with the meaning of the context and has no good match among the answer choices for the second blank. You can eliminate it.

For the second blank,

(D) *Account for* is the type of answer you were looking for, and **it is correct**. The myth helped the Greeks explain *the cycle of seasons*; this statement makes perfect sense and works seamlessly with the word you chose for the first blank, *elucidate*.

(E) Nothing in the sentence suggests that the ancient Greeks were trying to *debunk*, or prove false, the cycle of seasons. You can eliminate this answer choice.

(F) Similarly, no words in the text indicate that the Greeks tried to *obscure*, or hide, the cycle of seasons. You can eliminate this choice as well.

Sample Question 2

A rapidly evolving retail landscape means that brick-and-mortar stores increasingly ____(i)___ fourth-quarter sales to ___(ii)___ their bottom lines; unfortunately, this means that the holiday sales season starts earlier each year, forcing companies to risk consumer ___(iii)___ Christmas displays that come up before Halloween.

BLANK i
(A) abjure
(B) bypass
(C) depend on

BLANK ii
(D) augment
(E) offset
(F) elude

BLANK iii
(G) endorsement of
(H) backlash against
(J) requirements on

Solution

How would stores likely think about their fourth-quarter sales and bottom lines? It would make sense that stores *increasingly* want *fourth-quarter sales to* improve *their bottom lines*. You then have a statement that they are *unfortunately* going to *risk* something with *consumers*—what could that be? This blank must indicate a negative reaction of some kind. What kind of negative reaction might be caused by Christmas displays in October? Perhaps confusion, fatigue, or annoyance. Let's evaluate the answer choices.

(A) *Abjure* is to renounce or avoid, which is the opposite of what stores want to do regarding sales. You can eliminate this choice.

(B) *Bypass* means to avoid or go around—the stores are not seeking to go around fourth-quarter sales, so you can eliminate this answer choice as well.

(C) It makes sense that stores *depend on* fourth-quarter sales for their bottom lines, and **this is the correct answer for the first blank**.

For the second blank:

(D) Stores want fourth-quarter sales to *augment*, or improve, the bottom line, so **this is the correct answer**.

(E) Sales could not *offset*, or counteract, the stores' bottom lines, so you can eliminate this answer choice.

(F) Similarly, sales could not *elude*, or escape from, the bottom lines. You can eliminate (F) as well.

For the third blank:

(G) Companies are not risking customer *endorsement of* Christmas displays, so (G) is not correct.

(H) Companies are risking *backlash for* Christmas displays that are put up too early, so **(H) is correct**.

(J) Companies are not risking *requirements on* Christmas displays, so (J) is not correct.

Solving Out of Order

For the first two examples, it made sense for you to go in the order of the missing terms. However, it will often be to your advantage during text completion questions to solve the blanks in an order different from that in which they appear in the sentence; frequently, the second or third blank is much easier to fill in based on the context than the first, or the second or third term provides the key clue that informs you how to define the missing first term. For these reasons, you will often fill in missing words out of order.

Here are some examples of questions in which solving out of order proves helpful.

Sample Question 1

The study's authors ____(i)___ that their remarkable findings have not yet been ____(ii)___; they doggedly insist that further studies are needed before the drug can be administered to human volunteers.

BLANK i

Ⓐ conceal
Ⓑ caution
Ⓒ commend

BLANK ii

Ⓓ disclosed
Ⓔ replicated
Ⓕ allocated

Solution

The part of the statement that follows the semicolon—*they doggedly insist that further studies are needed before the drug can be administered to human volunteers*—tips off that the second space should be filled in with a word that indicates the results haven't yet been proven or verified. After filling in this term, you can infer that the first term should be a verb that means the scientists are communicating forcefully (to match with *doggedly insisting*) that the drug is not ready for use. Based on this information, **it would make sense that the authors would *caution*, or warn, that the findings have not been *replicated*, or repeated in a way that would prove their reliability**.

For the other answer choices for the second blank:

(D) There is nothing in the text that indicates the results have not been *disclosed*, or made known. You can eliminate this answer choice.

(F) It's unclear how findings can be *allocated*, or distributed, and the context makes no reference to distribution. You can eliminate this answer choice as well.

Going back to the other answer choices for the first blank:

(A) The context gives no hint that the authors are trying to *conceal*, or hide, this information; this answer choice would conflict with the information that they are *doggedly insisting* that more research is needed.

(B) Nor do they *commend*, or praise, the fact that their findings are not yet proven; in fact, nothing in the sentence suggests that the scientists are saying anything positive at all. You can eliminate this answer choice as well.

Sample Question 2

To say that Jones is the best attorney at the firm would be ___(i)___. Though he is unmatched as ___(ii)___ and persuasive courtroom litigator, his research skills are so __(iii)___ that he always requires a large group of research associates on his team.

BLANK i

Ⓐ unscrupulous
Ⓑ imprecise
Ⓒ uninteresting

BLANK ii

Ⓓ a deft
Ⓔ an impetuous
Ⓕ an indifferent

BLANK iii

Ⓖ paltry
Ⓗ benign
Ⓙ fungible

Solution

You can't start with the first blank because, without the information provided in the second and third blanks, you don't know what type of attorney Jones is. For the second blank, you have a positive description, something that aligns with *persuasive* and would describe a litigator in a good light. Then, when you get to the third blank, you understand from the *though* that precedes the positive description that now you will have a negative, critical description. You can anticipate something like *his research skills are so* <u>lacking</u> *that he always requires a large group of research associates on his team.* Returning to the first blank, you can now see that saying that Jones is the firm's best attorney would be <u>inaccurate</u> because he has some exceptional skills but also at least one weak point.

Let's take a look at the answer choices, moving from the second and third blanks to the first.

For the second blank:

(D) *Deft*, or skillful, fits perfectly into the context of the sentence. **This answer choice is correct.**

(E) An *impetuous* person is impulsive, one prone to acting without thought. Being *impetuous* would not make him a persuasive courtroom litigator and, therefore, does not fit into the context.

(F) An *indifferent* person is one who doesn't care and is uninterested—indifference is also not a quality that would support the description of Jones as a persuasive litigator.

For the third blank, you want a negative word that matches up with the fact that he always needs help.

(G) *Paltry*, or meager, fits what you are looking for. **(G) is correct.**

(H) *Benign* means harmless—this word is not negative and is not an appropriate description for skills.

(J) *Fungible* means interchangeable. This word does not fit the context of this sentence and can be eliminated.

Finally, going back to the first blank:

You know from the rest of the sentence that it's <u>inaccurate</u> to say he's the firm's best attorney.

(A) *Unscrupulous* means unethical. Although this is a negative word, it doesn't have quite the right meaning. The sentence doesn't tell you that it would be unethical to say Jones is the best attorney.

(B) **Imprecise is the correct answer.** Although Jones is the best (*unmatched*) in one way, he is not the best in another, so to call him the best attorney overall would be *imprecise*.

(C) The context does not tell you that calling him the best attorney would be *uninteresting*. This word does not fit the meaning of the sentence and can be eliminated.

Missing Terms Can Inform One Another

Finally, what's clever and unique about text completion questions that involve multiple missing terms is that the missing terms might be the key clues that depend on one another; without knowing at least one term, you can't fill in the remaining spot(s), and all terms together could perhaps paint either an entirely positive or a negative portrait of a situation.

Sometimes, you can tell that the two or three blanks in a sentence must have similar meanings or must have opposing meanings, but you can't necessarily tell what those meanings are. For example, you could have a sentence in which you know that two blanks must be either both positive or both negative, but nothing in the sentence indicates which one you are looking for. For these questions, you must evaluate the answer choices together and see which pair of available words works together.

Let's look at some examples.

Sample Question 1

Some educational reformers ___(i)___ a state curriculum designed first and foremost to teach ___(ii)___ skills; they ___(iii)___ that children ought to learn to pay taxes and balance a budget in their math courses, to cook a meal in chemistry, and to write corporate memos in English.

BLANK i

Ⓐ suppress
Ⓑ repudiate
Ⓒ espouse

BLANK ii

Ⓓ computational
Ⓔ utilitarian
Ⓕ analytical

BLANK iii

Ⓖ maintain
Ⓗ overlook
Ⓙ resent

Solution

Note that, before any of the blanks are filled in, you can assume the first and third blanks together indicate a positive attitude or a negative attitude toward the type of education discussed. The reformers in the sentence might support *a state curriculum designed to teach real-life skills*, or these reformers might object to such a curriculum; nothing in the sentence makes either attitude more likely.

Therefore, you need a pair of answer choices that align with each other, and **you have that with *espouse*, which means support, and *maintain*, which in this context means assert. For the second blank, you just need a word that accurately describes the skills presented in the text. They are practical, real-life skills—or *utilitarian*.**

For the first blank:

(A) To *suppress* is to forcibly limit or end, which doesn't match the rest of the text and can be eliminated.

(B) *Repudiate* means reject—this would work if the selection for the third blank aligns with it; you need to check whether there is an option that will mean something like "deny." Because there is no such option for the third blank, you can eliminate repudiate.

(C) To *espouse* means to embrace and support. For this to be the correct answer, it requires a word for the third blank that has a similar meaning. Looking at options (G), (H), and (J), you can see that *maintain* is close in meaning to espouse and is an appropriate term for blank iii.

For the third blank:

(H) *Overlook*, or fail to notice, does not fit the meaning of the sentence and can be eliminated.

(J) *Resent*, or feel personal indignation at, is too emotional for the tone of the sentence and creates an unsuitable meaning; if these reformers don't believe in this curriculum, they don't *resent* the fact that children ought to be taught practical skills but instead *disagree* that they ought to.

For the second space, there is no other evidence in the text that supports a focus on *computational* or *analytical* skills, so you can eliminate these answer choices.

(D) *Computational* means having to do with numerical calculation or computing. The sentence does not describe a curriculum that focuses on computation. This choice can be eliminated.

(E) *Utilitarian*, or focused on things that are practically useful, perfectly describes the curriculum presented in the text and, therefore, is clearly correct.

(F) *Analytical* does not match the description of the curriculum in the sentence and can be eliminated.

Sample Question 2

During World War II, Norman Rockwell's ___(i)___ painting of "Rosie the Riveter" became an enduring ___(ii)___ of the working woman—capable, strong, and patriotic.

BLANK i

Ⓐ trenchant
Ⓑ controversial
Ⓒ iconic

BLANK ii

Ⓓ reward
Ⓔ symbol
Ⓕ stereotype

Solution

Here, it makes sense that the two words would have similar meanings that have to do with the creation of a durable positive image: *Rockwell's* iconic *painting became an enduring* symbol. **Both terms are correct.**

For the first blank:

(A) To be *trenchant* is to be sharp or pointed, especially in analyzing or criticizing—we don't have clues to indicate that this is true of this painting. According to the sentence, the painting presents a positive, admiring image of the working woman—not an analytical or critical one.

(B) Similarly, no clues indicate that the painting is *controversial*. No disagreement or argument is implied. (B) can be eliminated.

For the second blank:

(D) *Reward* doesn't fit here—the painting is not a prize. This choice can be eliminated.

(F) *Stereotype* might be somewhat attractive because of its meaning; the painting is described as a standardized image of a group of people. However, the word stereotype generally has an overall negative connotation, so it doesn't fit the positive tone of the sentence as well as answer choice (E).

Practice Questions

1. As Americans grow increasingly health conscious and food scientists develop more ___(i)___ natural flavors and essences, flavored seltzer water is quickly ___(ii)___ sweetened soda as our national beverage of choice.

BLANK i

Ⓐ insipid
Ⓑ noxious
Ⓒ palatable

BLANK ii

Ⓓ supplanting
Ⓔ defaulting
Ⓕ preceding

2. Many people enjoy eating food that is ___(i)___ spicy, but true ___(ii)___ of spicy cuisine will go to great lengths to push their taste buds to their limits.

BLANK i

Ⓐ militantly
Ⓑ negligently
Ⓒ subtly

BLANK ii

Ⓓ connoisseurs
Ⓔ naysayers
Ⓕ dilettantes

3. In both major American political parties, ___(i)___ exists between hardliners who demand total ideological purity from their politicians and ___(ii)___ who simply want to support the candidate most likely to win.

BLANK i

Ⓐ congruity
Ⓑ diversion
Ⓒ enmity

BLANK ii

Ⓓ militants
Ⓔ pragmatists
Ⓕ nihilists

4. The prevailing notion that normal body temperature is an unwavering 98.6 degrees Fahrenheit is ___(i)___; one's body temperature ___(ii)___ a great deal throughout the day, trending highest in the late afternoon and evening hours and lowest during sleep.

BLANK i

Ⓐ undisputed
Ⓑ intractable
Ⓒ erroneous

BLANK ii

Ⓓ oscillates
Ⓔ ascends
Ⓕ regresses

5. Many voters were drawn to the young candidate's energy and ___(i)___ ideas, but party leadership worried that her somewhat radical stances on key issues would keep her from ___(ii)___ broad enough support to win the general election.

BLANK i

Ⓐ archaic
Ⓑ progressive
Ⓒ antediluvian

BLANK ii

Ⓓ garnering
Ⓔ construing
Ⓕ circumventing

6. Archaeologists at Stonehenge have concluded that many of the enormous stones that ___(i)___ the iconic edifice were likely ___(ii)___ about 150 miles away in a mountainous part of Wales; this suggests a meaningful ___(iii)___ between the spiritual traditions of people living in both locations.

BLANK i

Ⓐ raze
Ⓑ threaten
Ⓒ comprise

BLANK ii

Ⓓ deserted
Ⓔ quarried
Ⓕ inaugurated

BLANK iii

Ⓖ rivalry
Ⓗ concern
Ⓙ relationship

7. Superfans of Disney's EPCOT Center ___(i)___ the fact that the iconic attraction Spaceship Earth is often erroneously labeled a geodesic dome; in fact, the attraction is one of the world's only architectural examples of a geodesic sphere, supported by three enormous arms that serve as ___(ii)___.

BLANK i

Ⓐ dispute
Ⓑ execrate
Ⓒ savor

BLANK ii

Ⓓ buttresses
Ⓔ assets
Ⓕ corroborations

8. The island nation of Singapore is one of the most ___(i)___ countries in the world, yet it has managed to ___(ii)___ strict standards of cleanliness ___(iii)___ the enormous yearly influx of tourists and business travelers to its pristine streets and shores.

BLANK i

Ⓐ indigent
Ⓑ overlooked
Ⓒ visited

BLANK ii

Ⓓ circumvent
Ⓔ maintain
Ⓕ squander

BLANK iii

Ⓖ without
Ⓗ despite
Ⓙ by dint of

Practice Questions Continued

9. Despite his fervent interest in art, James refused to visit the van Gogh exhibit until it had been in town for several months, citing his ___(i)___ the many ___(ii)___ visitors who insist on crowding around the masterpieces to take selfies.

BLANK i

Ⓐ insecurity with
Ⓑ disgust with
Ⓒ attraction to

BLANK ii

Ⓓ deferential
Ⓔ erudite
Ⓕ impertinent

10. Proponents of the FCC Fairness Doctrine maintain that ___(i)___ broadcasters to give equal time to both sides of political controversies enables citizens to make informed decisions. Many such advocates ___(ii)___ the FCC for abandoning the doctrine, suggesting that the decision has given rise to political polarization. However, critics of the doctrine allege that it ___(iii)___ conspiracy theories.

BLANK i

Ⓐ disallowing
Ⓑ obliging
Ⓒ longing for

BLANK ii

Ⓓ feel indebted to
Ⓔ condemn
Ⓕ are conscious of

BLANK iii

Ⓖ legitimizes
Ⓗ runs roughshod over
Ⓙ has cast aspersions on

11. Tiny, uninhabited Henderson Island lies thousands of miles from a major population center, yet researchers estimate that it has the highest ___(i)___ of waterborne pollution of any place in the world: its location makes it a landing spot for ___(ii)___ waste from cities on the Yangtze River watershed.

BLANK i

Ⓐ ebullience
Ⓑ output
Ⓒ concentration

BLANK ii

Ⓓ mismanaged
Ⓔ undiscovered
Ⓕ recycled

12. In our era of ___(i)___ violent crime rates, it is perhaps ___(ii)___ that sheltered audiences thirsty for thrills prefer ___(iii)___ true-crime documentaries and murder podcasts over the anodyne entertainment that was popular among audiences in times past who couldn't take their safety for granted.

BLANK i

Ⓐ dwindling
Ⓑ exploding
Ⓒ immutable

BLANK ii

Ⓓ unprecedented
Ⓔ unsurprising
Ⓕ anomalous

BLANK iii

Ⓖ macabre
Ⓗ soporific
Ⓙ palliative

13. It may be tempting to think of IBM computer Deep Blue's 1997 victory over chess master Gary Kasparov as the moment when artificial intelligence began to ___(i)___human intelligence, but it is worth noting that Kasparov gave the computer a run for its money: the chess pro beat Deep Blue 4–2 in their first match in 1996 and only ___(ii)___ lost to the newly upgraded computer during their rematch.

BLANK i

Ⓐ inundate
Ⓑ outstrip
Ⓒ curtail

BLANK ii

Ⓓ narrowly
Ⓔ patently
Ⓕ appreciably

14. Robert Ballard credits his exceptional ___(i)___ underwater exploration to his ability to ___(ii)___ the ocean floor with live video he captures via remotely operated vehicles he designed in the 1980s.

BLANK i

Ⓐ success in
Ⓑ disillusionment with
Ⓒ indifference toward

BLANK ii

Ⓓ imagine
Ⓔ surveil
Ⓕ transform

15. In a world increasingly ___(i)___ by diminishing resources, a growing population, and increasing habitat ___(ii)___, the university's biology department asserts that it is ___(iii)___ that students of all ages learn about the ecology of the earth and our place in it.

BLANK i

Ⓐ challenged
Ⓑ enriched
Ⓒ diversified

BLANK ii

Ⓓ amelioration
Ⓔ value
Ⓕ degradation

BLANK iii

Ⓖ inconsequential
Ⓗ imperative
Ⓙ marginal

16. If ___(i)___ were all that it took to be a successful politician, Farber would have been reelected by a landslide. Unfortunately, his ___(ii)___ speeches were far from convincing, given his propensity to use many words to say very little.

BLANK i

Ⓐ rank demagoguery
Ⓑ tactical acuity
Ⓒ rhetorical flourishes

BLANK ii

Ⓓ anemic
Ⓔ sanguine
Ⓕ baroque

Practice Questions Continued

17. Following the attack on Pearl Harbor in 1942, education departments in many American universities announced special ___(i)___ master's programs to ___(ii)___ an ___(iii)___ shortage of teachers because of sudden mass military recruitment.

BLANK i

Ⓐ preliminary
Ⓑ extended
Ⓒ expedited

BLANK ii

Ⓓ forestall
Ⓔ facilitate
Ⓕ actualize

BLANK iii

Ⓖ extraneous
Ⓗ interrupted
Ⓙ impending

18. Confirmation bias is the often ___(i)___ act of acknowledging only those perspectives that ___(ii)___ our pre-existing views, while at the same time ignoring or dismissing opinions that ___(iii)___ our way of looking at the world.

BLANK i

Ⓐ salutary
Ⓑ subconscious
Ⓒ equivocal

BLANK ii

Ⓓ affirm
Ⓔ challenge
Ⓕ disregard

BLANK iii

Ⓖ bolster
Ⓗ indulge
Ⓙ jeopardize

Practice Question Solutions

1. As Americans grow increasingly health conscious and food scientists develop more ___(i)___ natural flavors and essences, flavored seltzer water is quickly ___(ii)___ sweetened soda as our national beverage of choice.

BLANK i

Ⓐ insipid
Ⓑ noxious
Ⓒ palatable

BLANK ii

Ⓓ supplanting
Ⓔ defaulting
Ⓕ preceding

Solution

For the first blank, you are looking for a word or phrase that would be a positive description of flavors for seltzer. For the second blank, *flavored seltzer water is quickly re-placing sweetened soda as our national beverage of choice.* Let's take a look at the answer choices.

For the first blank, *palatable*, or pleasant to taste, is the only reasonable choice, and **it is correct**.

(A) *Insipid* means lacking in flavor or interest, which does not fit.
(B) *Noxious* means harmful, which does not work here and can be eliminated.

For the second blank:

(D) *Supplanting* is a great synonym for replacing, and **it is the correct choice**.
(E) *Defaulting* means either failing to pay back a debt or falling back into an original state, and neither meaning fits here.
(F) *Preceding* means happening earlier in time; it doesn't work in the sentence.

2. Many people enjoy eating food that is ___(i)___ spicy, but true ___(ii)___ of spicy cuisine will go to great lengths to push their taste buds to their limits.

BLANK i

Ⓐ militantly
Ⓑ negligently
Ⓒ subtly

BLANK ii

Ⓓ connoisseurs
Ⓔ naysayers
Ⓕ dilettantes

Solution

It's unclear exactly what ought to go in the first space, but for the second space, you should expect a term like lovers or fans.

For the second space:

(D) *Connoisseurs*, or experts, is a terrific match for what you are looking for, and **it is correct**.
(E) *Naysayers* are those who criticize and contradict—that's not what you are looking for, so you can eliminate this choice.
(F) *Dilettantes* are those who are superficially interested in something, which would contradict the statement that these people *go to great lengths to push their limits.* You can eliminate this answer choice as well.

Going back to the first space:

(A) *Militantly,* or combatively, doesn't appropriately modify "spicy"—in fact, it's a bit scary to think of what militantly spicy food would be like. More important, though, it doesn't provide the appropriate contrast with *true connoisseurs* of the spiciest food. You can eliminate (A).

Solutions Continued

(B) *Negligently*, or neglectfully, also doesn't fit with the word spicy. Moreover, it is a negative word and does not match the tone of the clause—*many people enjoy* suggests you are looking for a neutral-to-positive descriptor.

(C) *Subtly*, or delicately, spicy is a great fit and **is correct**.

---

3. In both major American political parties, ___(i)___ exists between hardliners who demand total ideological purity from their politicians and ___(ii)___ who simply want to support the candidate most likely to win.

BLANK i

Ⓐ congruity
Ⓑ diversion
Ⓒ **enmity**

BLANK ii

Ⓓ militants
Ⓔ **pragmatists**
Ⓕ nihilists

Solution

For the first blank, you can imagine a term that might be synonymous with something like <u>division</u> or <u>conflict</u>, and **you get that with *enmity*, which is hostility**.

(A) *Congruity* is agreement or matching, which is the opposite of the meaning you are looking for. You can eliminate this answer choice.

(B) *Diversion* may be a tempting wrong answer, in that it sounds like division, but a diversion means a distraction, which does not work in this context.

For the second blank, you need something that contrasts with *ideological purity*, and you want a word that describes someone who simply wants to win—***pragmatist, or one guided by practical considerations, is a great fit here.***

(D) *Militants* fight aggressively in support of a cause they believe in—this word would describe the hardliners rather than their opposites.

(F) *Nihilists* find life meaningless and don't believe or participate in society's laws and institutions. This choice does not match the description of people who want to support the winning candidate, and it can therefore be eliminated.

---

4. The prevailing notion that normal body temperature is an unwavering 98.6 degrees Fahrenheit is ___(i)___; one's body temperature ___(ii)___ a great deal throughout the day, trending highest in the late afternoon and evening hours and lowest during sleep.

BLANK i

Ⓐ undisputed
Ⓑ intractable
Ⓒ **erroneous**

BLANK ii

Ⓓ **oscillates**
Ⓔ ascends
Ⓕ regresses

Solution

For the first blank, you don't yet have enough information to know how to describe the prevailing notion. Let's fill in the second blank first.

For the second blank, the temperature is the highest during one part of the day and lowest during another. This tells you that the temperature <u>varies</u> or <u>changes</u> throughout the day.

(D) *Oscillates* is the only choice for blank ii that fits this meaning.

This tells you that the prevailing notion is <u>inaccurate</u>, **and the best synonym for that is (C) *erroneous*.**

As for the other answer choices:

(A) To be *undisputed* is to be beyond question; because the prevailing notion is shown in the sentence to be inaccurate, this answer choice is incorrect.
(B) *Intractable* means stubborn, which doesn't fit in this context and can be eliminated.
(E) *Ascends* could be a tempting answer choice, but it tells only a part of the story—the temperature goes both up and down, so this answer choice is not as good as (D).
(F) *Regresses* has the same problem as *ascends*—it is not a complete description of what body temperature does as described in the text.

---

5. Many voters were drawn to the young candidate's energy and ___(i)___ ideas, but party leadership worried that her somewhat radical stances on key issues would keep her from ___(ii)___ broad enough support to win the general election.

BLANK i

(A) archaic
(B) progressive
(C) antediluvian

BLANK ii

(D) garnering
(E) construing
(F) circumventing

Solution

For the first space, you can expect a description that harmonizes with the candidate's *youth* and *energy* and is also consistent with her seeming, at least in some ways, to be *radical*. For the second space, you can expect a synonym for getting. Let's take a look at the answer choices.

For the first blank:

(B) *Progressive*, or advocating for reform, is a good match for the first space, and **it is correct**.
(A) *Archaic* and (C) *antediluvian* both mean old-fashioned or outdated, which are not consistent with the description of the candidate and are antonyms of what you are looking for, so they can both be eliminated.

For the second blank:

(D) *Garnering* is a synonym for getting, and **it is correct**.
(E) *Construing* means interpreting. It wouldn't make sense to say she is interpreting enough support, so you can eliminate this choice.
(F) *Circumventing* is getting around or avoiding—the opposite of the meaning the sentence requires. You can eliminate this answer choice as well.

---

6. Archaeologists at Stonehenge have concluded that many of the enormous stones that ___(i)___ the iconic edifice were likely ___(ii)___ about 150 miles away in a mountainous part of Wales; this suggests a meaningful ___(iii)___ between the spiritual traditions of people living in both locations.

BLANK i

(A) raze
(B) threaten
(C) comprise

BLANK ii

(D) deserted
(E) quarried
(F) inaugurated

BLANK iii

(G) rivalry
(H) concern
(J) relationship

Solutions Continued

Solution

You can make helpful inferences about the missing terms based on the clues in the text: *many of the enormous stones that* <u>make up</u> *the iconic edifice were likely* <u>acquired</u> *about 150 miles away…this suggests a meaningful* <u>connection</u> *between the spiritual traditions…* Let's take a look at the answer choices.

For the first blank, (C) *comprise*, or make up, makes the most sense and **is the correct answer**.
(A) To *raze* is to demolish, which does not fit the context.
(B) *Threaten* is similarly unsuitable for this sentence, so you can eliminate those two choices.

For the second blank, (E) *quarried*, or dug up from the earth, accurately expresses how stones are acquired, and **it is correct**.
(D) *Deserted* means left behind, which does not work in this sentence.
(F) To *inaugurate* is to formally commence or introduce—it doesn't make sense to say that the stones were introduced or commenced, so both of these answer choices can be eliminated.

For the third blank:

(G) *Rivalry*, or competition, doesn't work because you are looking for a word that tells you there was cooperation between the two groups. You can eliminate that answer choice.
(H) *Concern* isn't a great fit because the sentence does not give clues about a potential issue of concern.
(J) *Relationship* is the type of answer you were looking for—we have clues about a connection between the people, and **it is the correct answer**.

7. Superfans of Disney's EPCOT Center ___(i)___ the fact that the iconic attraction Spaceship Earth is often erroneously labeled a geodesic dome; in fact, the attraction is one of the world's only architectural examples of a geodesic sphere, supported by three enormous arms that serve as ___(ii)___.

BLANK i
(A) dispute
(B) execrate
(C) savor

BLANK ii
(D) buttresses
(E) assets
(F) corroborations

Solution

For the first blank, you can anticipate that superfans will <u>feel negatively</u> about the general population getting something wrong about a topic with which they are obsessed.

For the second blank, you can see from the context that the arms *serve as* <u>supports</u> to hold the structure in place.

Let's move on to the answer choices.

For blank ii:

(D) *Buttresses* are architectural supports. **(D) is the correct answer**.
(E) *Assets* are positive qualities or valuable possessions. This word does not describe the function of the supporting arms as described in the sentence.
(F) *Corroborations* are indeed supports, but they are supports for ideas (like evidence), not physical supports for buildings. This choice can be eliminated.

Going back to the first blank:

(A) *Dispute* is highly tempting because superfans would know enough about the attraction to challenge the characterization of the sphere as a dome. However, the blank describes their attitude toward *the fact* that the erroneous description exists. There is no evidence that they dispute the existence of the error. You can eliminate (A).

(B) *Execrate* means denounce or harshly criticize. It fits well with the meaning of the sentence that superfans would execrate this mistake being made. **(B) is the correct answer**.

(C) *Savor* means enjoy, which is the opposite of the meaning you are looking for. You can eliminate (C).

---

8. The island nation of Singapore is one of the most ___(i)___ countries in the world, yet it has managed to ___(ii)___ strict standards of cleanliness ___(iii)___ the enormous yearly influx of tourists and business travelers to its pristine streets and shores.

BLANK i

Ⓐ indigent
Ⓑ overlooked
Ⓒ **visited**

BLANK ii

Ⓓ circumvent
Ⓔ **maintain**
Ⓕ squander

BLANK iii

Ⓖ without
Ⓗ **despite**
Ⓙ by dint of

Solution

You can anticipate that the first blank might be filled with visited, according to the description toward the end of the sentence of an *enormous yearly influx of tourists and business travelers*. For the second and third blanks, *it has managed* to keep *strict standards of cleanliness* in spite of *the enormous yearly influx…*

Let's take a look at the answer choices.

For the first blank, (C) *visited* is the answer you anticipated, and **it is correct**.

(A) *Indigent* means poor and needy, and although this could be true of Singapore, you don't have evidence of that in this sentence.

(B) *Overlooked* means unnoticed, which is not consistent with the description of an enormous influx of tourists.

For the second blank, (E) *maintain* is a great synonym for keep, and **it is the correct answer**.

(D) *Circumvent*, or get around, does not fit with Singapore's maintaining its cleanliness, so it can be eliminated.

(F) *Squander*, or let go to waste, contradicts the information in the rest of the sentence and can be eliminated.

Finally, (H) *despite* is a great match for the third blank and **is the correct choice**.

(G) *Without* is the opposite meaning and can be eliminated.

(J) *By dint of*, or by means of, does not result in a reasonable meaning—Singapore isn't maintaining its cleanliness by means of the huge crowds of tourists, so (J) can be eliminated as well.

Solutions Continued

9. Despite his fervent interest in art, James refused to visit the van Gogh exhibit until it had been in town for several months, citing his ___(i)___ the many ___(ii)___ visitors who insist on crowding around the masterpieces to take selfies.

BLANK i

Ⓐ insecurity with
Ⓑ disgust with
Ⓒ attraction to

BLANK ii

Ⓓ deferential
Ⓔ erudite
Ⓕ impertinent

Solution

The sentence presents a contrast with James' fervent interest in art, so you can anticipate that he doesn't want to visit the exhibit because of his <u>dislike</u> for *the many <u>annoying</u> visitors who insist on crowding around the masterpieces to take selfies*.

Let's take a look at the answer choices.

For the first blank:

(A) No language in the text supports the idea that James feels *insecurity with* the other visitors, so you can eliminate that answer choice.
(B) *Disgust with* is stronger than what you anticipated, but it matches up well with the sentence, and **it is the correct choice**.
(C) He wouldn't stay away if he felt *attraction to* the other visitors, so you can eliminate that choice.

For the second blank:

(D) *Deferential*, or respectful, doesn't describe the behavior of visitors crowding around the masterpieces taking selfies—and James would not object to respectful behavior. You can eliminate this answer choice.

(E) You don't have any clues in the sentence indicating that these visitors are *erudite*, or very knowledgeable, so you can eliminate that answer choice as well.
(F) *Impertinent* people are those who don't show proper respect, and it makes sense that James would feel that the many visitors crowding around the masterpieces taking selfies weren't showing proper respect. **(F) is the correct choice**.

---

10. Proponents of the FCC Fairness Doctrine maintain that ___(i)___ broadcasters to give equal time to both sides of political controversies enables citizens to make informed decisions. Many such advocates ___(ii)___ the FCC for abandoning the doctrine, suggesting that the decision has given rise to political polarization. However, critics of the doctrine allege that it ___(iii)___ conspiracy theories.

BLANK i

Ⓐ disallowing
Ⓑ obliging
Ⓒ longing for

BLANK ii

Ⓓ feel indebted to
Ⓔ condemn
Ⓕ are conscious of

BLANK iii

Ⓖ legitimizes
Ⓗ runs roughshod over
Ⓙ has cast aspersions on

Solution

You can anticipate that the doctrine <u>required</u> *broadcasters* to cover *both sides* of controversies to allow citizens to make informed decisions and that many advocates <u>criticize</u> the FCC for abandoning this doctrine. However, critics of the doctrine could have alleged that it <u>gave rise</u> to conspiracy theories.

Let's take a look at the answer choices.

For the first blank, (B) *obliging*, which in this context means requiring, is a great match for what you anticipated, and **it is correct**.
(A) *Disallowing* is limiting or prohibiting, which is the opposite of the meaning required by the context.
(C) *Longing for* is wishing for, which is not a good fit for this situation. Both (A) and (C) can be eliminated.

For the second blank:

(E) *Condemn*, or criticize, is a great fit for what you expected, and **it is correct**.
(D) Advocates would not *feel indebted to* the FCC for abandoning the doctrine, so you can eliminate this answer.
(F) It doesn't fit the context to say that advocates *are conscious of*, or are aware of, the FCC for abandoning the doctrine. You can eliminate this answer choice as well.

For the third blank:

(G) *Legitimizes*, or made to seem more acceptable, is a great fit and **the right answer**.
(H) *To run roughshod* over is to disregard, which does not fit with what you anticipated, which was to help give rise to conspiracy theories. With this, (H) can be eliminated.
(J) *To cast aspersions on* is to insult, which does not accurately describe the critics' views as to what the doctrine did to conspiracy theories. Hence, (J) can be eliminated.

11. Tiny, uninhabited Henderson Island lies thousands of miles from a major population center, yet researchers estimate that it has the highest ___(i)___ of waterborne pollution of any place in the world: its location makes it a landing spot for ___(ii)___ waste from cities on the Yangtze River watershed.

BLANK i

Ⓐ ebullience
Ⓑ output
Ⓒ **concentration**

BLANK ii

Ⓓ **mismanaged**
Ⓔ undiscovered
Ⓕ recycled

Solution

The *yet* informs you of a contrast—Henderson Island is *tiny* and *uninhabited*, and it *lies thousands of miles from a population center, yet researchers estimate that it has the highest* <u>quantity</u> *of waterborne pollution*. It makes sense that **the correct answer is concentration**, or amount per space, because this answer makes the sentence coherent. It's a contrast that Henderson is so isolated from the causes of pollution *yet* so polluted. The second part of the statement gives you the reason why: it's a *landing spot for* <u>uncontrolled</u> *waste from the cities on the Yangtze River watershed*. And because this passage discusses pollution, **it makes sense that *mismanaged* would be the word before *waste***.

For the other answer choices for the first blank:

(A) *Ebullience* means enthusiasm or high spirits—that doesn't fit the meaning of the sentence, so you can eliminate this answer choice.
(B) *Output* does not fit with the description of Henderson Island as a landing spot for pollution from cities. You can eliminate (B).

Solutions Continued

For the second blank:

(E) If it were *undiscovered* waste, we wouldn't be discussing it.
(F) If it were *recycled*, it wouldn't be pollution, so you can eliminate both answer choices.

---

12. In our era of ___(i)___ violent crime rates, it is perhaps ___(ii)___ that sheltered audiences thirsty for thrills prefer ___(iii)___ true-crime documentaries and murder podcasts over the anodyne entertainment that was popular among audiences in times past who couldn't take their safety for granted.

BLANK i
(A) **dwindling**
(B) exploding
(C) immutable

BLANK ii
(D) unprecedented
(E) **unsurprising**
(F) anomalous

BLANK iii
(G) **macabre**
(H) soporific
(J) palliative

Solution

Of course, it very much helps to know that *anodyne* means inoffensive or dull, but even without that knowledge, you can get by with clues provided in the sentence. Knowing that today's audiences are *sheltered*, you can assume an era of <u>lower</u> *violent crime rates*, and therefore predict that it is <u>expected</u> that <u>grisly</u> *true-crime* entertainment is popular among *sheltered audiences thirsty for thrills*. Let's take a look.

For the first blank:

(A) *Dwindling* is a good match for what you expected, and **it is the correct answer**.
(B) *Exploding* is the opposite of what you anticipated, so you can eliminate it.
(C) *Immutable*, or unchangeable, doesn't have support in the text, so you can eliminate it as well.

For the second blank:

(D) *Disheartening* is not supported by the rest of the text and can be eliminated.
(E) *Unsurprising* matches what you expected and **is correct**.
(F) *Anomalous*, or unusual, is the opposite of what you are looking for—it does not describe the fact that people *thirsty for thrills* enjoy true-crime programming. (F) can be eliminated as well.

For the third blank:

(G) *Macabre* means gruesome and focused on death. It fits well with what you are looking for in this sentence. **(G) is the correct answer**.
(H) *Soporific* means sleep-inducing and is the opposite of what you are looking for—it is more akin to *anodyne* than to *thrill*-seeking.
(J) *Palliative* means relieving pain or soothing, which is also more like *anodyne* and, therefore, is the opposite of what you are looking for.

---

13. It may be tempting to think of IBM computer Deep Blue's 1997 victory over chess master Gary Kasparov as the moment when artificial intelligence began to ___(i)___ human intelligence, but it is worth noting that Kasparov gave the computer a run for its money: the chess pro beat Deep Blue 4–2 in their first match in 1996 and only ___(ii)___ lost to the newly upgraded computer during their rematch.

BLANK i

(A) inundate

(B) outstrip

(C) curtail

BLANK ii

(D) narrowly

(E) patently

(F) appreciably

Solution

You can anticipate that because the computer won, the first blank needs a word that indicates being better than *human intelligence*. Because of the words *tempting* and *but* and the fact that Kasparov *gave the computer a run for its money,* you're looking for a word that indicates barely lost for the second space. Let's take a look at the answer choices.

For the first blank:

(A) To *inundate* is to flood, which does not make sense with this sentence. You can eliminate (A).

(B) *Outstrip,* or overtake, is a great match, and **it is correct**.

(C) To *curtail* is to limit or cut short, which does not fit the context. You can eliminate (C).

For the second blank:

(D) *Narrowly* perfectly matches the answer you anticipated, and **it is correct**.

(E) *Patently* means obviously, so it does not work.

(F) *Appreciably* means significantly, which does not match the meaning you are looking for, so you can eliminate it.

14. Robert Ballard credits his exceptional ___(i)___ underwater exploration to his ability to ___(ii)___ the ocean floor with live video he captures via remotely operated vehicles he designed in the 1980s.

BLANK i

(A) success in

(B) disillusionment with

(C) indifference toward

BLANK ii

(D) imagine

(E) surveil

(F) transform

Solution

You expect a positive answer such as accomplishments in for the first blank, and *success in* **is a great match and the correct answer**.

(B) *Disillusionment* is the feeling of losing faith in something, which does not fit.

(C) *Indifference* is a lack of interest, which fails to match the other descriptions given in the sentence. Both (B) and (C) can be eliminated.

For the second blank, Ballard uses his technology to *surveil,* or closely observe, the ocean floor. **(E) is the correct answer**.

(D) He doesn't *imagine* the ocean floor because he captures it using video, so this answer choice is incorrect.

(F) You are given no evidence that he changes or *transforms* the ocean floor, so you can eliminate this answer choice as well.

Solutions Continued

15. In a world increasingly ___(i)___ by diminishing resources, a growing population, and increasing habitat ___(ii)___, the university's biology department asserts that it is ___(iii)___ that students of all ages learn about the ecology of the earth and our place in it.

BLANK i

Ⓐ **challenged**
Ⓑ enriched
Ⓒ diversified

BLANK ii

Ⓓ amelioration
Ⓔ value
Ⓕ **degradation**

BLANK iii

Ⓖ inconsequential
Ⓗ **imperative**
Ⓙ marginal

Solution

For the first blank, you can expect a word such as <u>stressed</u> or <u>pressured</u>; for the second blank, an indication of <u>harm</u> to habitats, in keeping with the list of stressors; and for the third, a word that signifies <u>importance</u>: *in a world increasingly* <u>stressed</u> *by diminishing resources... and increasing habitat* <u>harm</u>, *it is* <u>important</u> *that students of all ages learn...*

Let's take a look at the answer choices.

For the first blank, *challenged* is a good fit and **the correct answer**. It doesn't make sense to say that the world is (B) *enriched* or (C) *diversified* by diminishing resources, as both words have positive connotations. You can quickly eliminate choices (B) and (C).

For the second blank:

(D) *Amelioration* is improvement, which would not cause pressure or challenges. (D) can be eliminated.
(E) *Value* is also too positive a word for this blank; the word needs to fit into a list of things that cause difficulty. (E) can be eliminated.
(F) *Degradation* is a good match for the word you were looking for. **(F) is the correct answer choice**.

For the third blank:

(G) *Inconsequential*, or unimportant, isn't a good fit for the context, so you can eliminate it.
(H) *Imperative*, or absolutely necessary, is the **correct answer**.
(J) *Marginal*, or of minor importance, is the opposite of what the context requires.

---

16. If ___(i)___ were all that it took to be a successful politician, Farber would have been reelected by a landslide. Unfortunately, his ___(ii)___ speeches were far from convincing, given his propensity to use many words to say very little.

BLANK i

Ⓐ rank demagoguery
Ⓑ tactical acuity
Ⓒ **rhetorical flourishes**

BLANK ii

Ⓓ anemic
Ⓔ sanguine
Ⓕ **baroque**

Solution

You know Farber tends *to use many words to say very little*, so for the first space, you can anticipate an answer that means <u>talking too much</u> or <u>giving elaborate but meaningless speeches</u> and for the second, maybe something like <u>overly wordy</u>. Let's take a look.

For the first blank:

(A) *Rank demagoguery* is gaining power by arousing the emotions of a mob—we don't have evidence of this situation in the rest of the sentence, especially because Farber's speeches were *far from convincing*. You can eliminate this phrase.

(B) *Tactical acuity* is strategic intelligence. The sentence gives no support for this description. You can eliminate this choice as well.

(C) The phrase *rhetorical flourishes* indicates fanciful language, and **this is the correct answer**.

For the second blank:

(D) *Anemic* means lacking in force, which isn't the correct meaning for the sentence. You can eliminate this answer.

(E) *Sanguine* is optimistic or positive, characteristics common to political speeches in general but not ones that match the specific clues given to you in this sentence. You can also eliminate this answer.

(F) *Baroque* means overly ornate, which fits perfectly with *using many words to say very little* and with your choice for blank i, *rhetorical flourishes*. **(F) is the correct answer**.

---

17. Following the attack on Pearl Harbor in 1942, education departments in many American universities announced special ___(i)___ master's programs to ___(ii)___ an ___(iii)___ shortage of teachers because of sudden mass military recruitment.

BLANK i

(A) preliminary
(B) extended
(C) **expedited**

BLANK ii

(D) **forestall**
(E) facilitate
(F) actualize

BLANK iii

(G) extraneous
(H) interrupted
(J) **impending**

Solution

A *sudden mass military recruitment* would cause a similarly <u>sudden</u> shortage of teachers, so you can seek an appropriate synonym. For blank ii, perhaps *departments announced special master's programs to* <u>offset</u> this shortage.

Let's take a look at the answer choices.

For the first blank, (A) *preliminary*, or introductory, master's programs wouldn't be particularly helpful in this context. They wouldn't be an efficient response to the sudden and severe lack of teachers.

(B) *Extended*, or lengthened, master's programs make the problem worse, so you can eliminate both (A) and (B).

(C) *Expedited*, or sped up, isn't exactly what you anticipated, but it makes sense in this context; it would help deal with the sudden shortage of teachers in a short time. **(C) is the correct answer**.

For the second blank, (D) *forestall* means prevent and **is correct**.

(E) *Facilitate* means to help something move forward; that's the opposite of what you're looking for. Universities are not described as trying to help the shortage progress.

(F) *Actualize* means make real—they don't want to make the shortage real, so you can eliminate both (E) and (F).

Finally, for the last blank, (G) *extraneous* means irrelevant—there is no hint that the teacher shortage was irrelevant.

(H) Nothing in the text suggests that the teacher shortage was *interrupted*. Both (G) and (H) can be eliminated.

(J) It makes sense that the attack and resulting sudden military recruitment would cause an *impending* shortage of teachers—a shortage that is about to happen. **(J) is the correct answer**.

Solutions Continued

18. Confirmation bias is the often ___(i)___ act of acknowledging only those perspectives that ___(ii)___ our pre-existing views, while at the same time ignoring or dismissing opinions that ___(iii)___ our way of looking at the world.

BLANK i

Ⓐ salutary
Ⓑ subconscious
Ⓒ equivocal

BLANK ii

Ⓓ affirm
Ⓔ challenge
Ⓕ disregard

BLANK iii

Ⓖ bolster
Ⓗ indulge
Ⓙ jeopardize

Solution

You may not be sure what should go into the first space, but confirmation bias is characterized by *acknowledging only those perspectives that* <u>support</u> *our pre-existing views, while at the same time ignoring or dismissing opinions that* <u>go against</u> *our way of looking at the world.*

Let's take a look at the answer choices.

For the first blank:

It makes sense to say that confirmation bias is often a *subconscious* act, and **this is the correct answer**.
(A) *Salutary* means beneficial to health. This statement certainly doesn't indicate that confirmation bias is healthy.
(C) *Equivocal*, meaning ambiguous or not taking a stand, doesn't match the description of confirmation bias. You can eliminate both of those choices.

For the second blank:

(D) *Affirm* is a good synonym for <u>support</u>, and **it's correct**.
(E) *Challenge* and (F) *disregard* are the opposite of what you are looking for and can both be eliminated.

For the third blank, confirmation bias makes us ignore or dismiss opinions that *jeopardize*, or threaten, our view of the world; **choice (J) is correct**.
(G) *Bolster*, or support, means the opposite of something that can threaten our views.
(H) *Indulge*, or gratify, does not match the meaning you are looking for. Hence, (G) and (H) can be eliminated.

10
VERBAL REASONING

Sentence Equivalence

Sentence equivalence questions are similar to single-blank text completion questions. The difference with sentence equivalent questions is that you must identify two answer choices that give the sentence the same overall meaning.

Although the two correct answers are usually synonyms, they need not be. Two words do not need to have the same meaning to accomplish the same purpose in a sentence. You will frequently observe this case in our examples and on the official GRE. Conversely, just because you see a pair of synonyms among the answer choices does not mean that they are the correct answer choices; they can mean the same thing and both be wrong.

Recommended Strategy

Overall, use a strategy that is similar to that utilized for the text completion questions:

1. Read the entire sentence and predict the type of word that is expected to fill in the blank.

2. Evaluate the answer choices using a process of identification and elimination: select the answers that seem correct, leave the answers that you feel uncertain about, and eliminate the answers that you know are incorrect.

3. For sentence equivalence questions, make sure that the two selected answers give the sentence the same meaning and that the sentence makes sense with either of the two answer choices inserted.

Anticipating and Selecting Answers

As discussed in the text completion chapters, it is important to develop a habit of figuring out what word or group of words would fit the space best. Think about the missing words in terms of **definitions** (when the sentence directly reveals the meaning of the missing word), **inferences** (when the sentence reveals enough about the missing word that you can infer its meaning), and **contrasts** (when the sentence reveals that the missing word will be an antonym for the premise of the sentence).

Below is the first example question, which has clues that **define** the missing term. Please give it a shot before I discuss the solution.

Sample Question

Throughout his life, Mahatma Gandhi remained firmly committed to the _____ of material possessions: at his death, he owned only a pocket watch, a few pairs of sandals, a book, a pair of glasses, and some eating utensils.

A renunciation
B tabulation
C commemoration
D accrual
E acknowledgment
F eschewal

Solution

A term such as <u>rejection</u> or another term that means <u>giving up</u> can be anticipated because the second half of the sentence describes Gandhi as having few material possessions. Because the sentence reveals that he was firmly committed to his way of living, you know that his lack of possessions was a conscious choice.

Among the answer choices, **there are two synonyms for rejection or avoidance: renunciation and eschewal.**

Tabulation is counting up; *commemoration* and *acknowledgment* are associated with the recognition of something; and *accrual* means gathering or accumulating. None of these terms is a match for the context, and all can be eliminated.

Next is the second sample question. For this question, an **inference** should be made about what type of term might best fit the slot.

Sample Question

Despite having been the first pilot to break the sound barrier, Chuck Yeager never got a chance to fly in space; however, he made important contributions to space exploration in his role as a _____ to a whole generation of spaceflight pioneers.

A agitator
B mentor
C critic
D insurgent
E advisor
F rival

Solution

You can infer that Chuck Yeager was able to play some sort of <u>positive role</u> relative to this generation of spaceflight pioneers. **The two possible answer choices that match each other are *mentor* and *advisor*, which are both correct.**

Agitator, *critic*, and *rival* are the opposite of the inference and can be quickly eliminated. It does not make sense to see him as an *insurgent*, so that choice can also be eliminated.

Below is one more sample question. For this question, a **contrast** provides a hint about what to look for when filling in the space.

Sample Question

The ginkgo tree's unique fan-shaped leaves turn a stunning golden yellow in autumn; unlike the slowly falling leaves of other deciduous trees, the ginkgo's leaves all fall to the ground _____.

A variably
B concurrently
C intermittently
D randomly
E continually
F simultaneously

Solution

Here, the possible answer is a **contrast** to *the slowly falling leaves of other deciduous trees*. The pair of correct answers may not be quite what is expected, but they make perfect sense: ***concurrently* and *simultaneously* are the correct answers**. Leaves do not control the pace at which they fall, and slowly falling leaves fall from a tree at different times; that must mean the opposite of that is a tree in which the leaves <u>all fall together</u>, which is what this answer presents.

Variably, *intermittently*, and *randomly* are the opposite of the inferred meaning, and *continually* does not fit; all can, therefore, be eliminated.

Practice Questions

Select from amongst the answer choices two choices that result in sentences that mean the same thing.

1. Prone to explaining each of her decisions in great detail, the judge could never be accused of a lack of _____.

[A] apostasy
[B] transparency
[C] diffidence
[D] competence
[E] reticence
[F] candor

2. Although we are taught to associate yawning with exhaustion or boredom, intense stress can also _____ this response: many soldiers report repeatedly yawning while on alert in combat zones.

[A] dampen
[B] obstruct
[C] precipitate
[D] venerate
[E] engender
[F] depreciate

3. The investigators pored over hours of footage filmed inside the lighthouse, looking for _____ in light or sound that they could present as evidence of the paranormal.

[A] contrasts
[B] anomalies
[C] mutations
[D] adjustments
[E] aberrations
[F] juxtapositions

4. Modern Japan's embrace of all things *kawaii*, or cute, has proven to be anything but an _____ trend; its enduring popularity has made *kawaii* a billion-dollar industry that encompasses hundreds of thousands of consumer items and myriad entertainment franchises.

[A] ephemeral
[B] evanescent
[C] endemic
[D] exorbitant
[E] elliptical
[F] efficacious

5. Some patients with depression and bipolar disorder have reported significant _____ of their symptoms upon regularly wearing blue-blocking glasses for several weeks, leading some researchers to wonder whether the blue light emitted by phones, computers, and tablets has a negative effect on the mental health of all technology users.

[A] augmentation
[B] exacerbation
[C] amelioration
[D] incapacitation
[E] mitigation
[F] regeneration

6. While the weather to our west looks _____, the sun is shining brightly to our east.

[A] minatory
[B] penetrating
[C] inauspicious
[D] propitious
[E] crestfallen
[F] derogatory

Practice Questions Continued

7. Students whose teachers praise them for their exemplary effort are far more likely to take on _____ academic challenges in the future than children whose teachers merely compliment their natural intelligence.

- [A] provocative
- [B] infelicitous
- [C] limpid
- [D] formidable
- [E] arduous
- [F] mellifluous

8. While Betsy Ross may well have been _____ the construction of the first American flag, most scholars agree that the Stars and Stripes was conceived and designed by lawyer and composer Francis Hopkinson.

- [A] implicated in
- [B] instrumental in
- [C] inimical to
- [D] innocuous in
- [E] indoctrinated into
- [F] integral to

9. Though always open to compromise in his personal life, John was highly ____at work, refusing to abide by practices that differed from the conventions and regulations he held dear.

- [A] tractable
- [B] orthodox
- [C] xenophobic
- [D] intransigent
- [E] competent
- [F] amorphous

10. Our phobias often do not reflect reality: fear of flying is much more _____ than fear of driving, but the average American is far more likely to be injured or killed in a car accident than in a plane crash.

- [A] requisite
- [B] prevalent
- [C] rarefied
- [D] consummate
- [E] pervasive
- [F] plausible

11. As female authors narrow the gender gap in literature, an increasing number of bestsellers _____ a topic rarely represented in novels of earlier eras: female friendship.

- [A] overstate
- [B] foreground
- [C] denigrate
- [D] malign
- [E] romanticize
- [F] spotlight

12. When an artistic breakthrough occurs, all the glory perhaps rightly goes to the artist; however, tireless behind-the-scenes figures—spouses, patrons, and supportive friends—are often _____ to the artist's process of producing and presenting pioneering work to the world.

- [A] indispensable
- [B] subsidiary
- [C] deleterious
- [D] ancillary
- [E] imperative
- [F] inimical

13. Most mammals do not use their faces to express their emotions; to _____ a cat's emotional state, for instance, it is best to look at its tail.

A ascertain
B inhibit
C enhance
D discern
E stabilize
F safeguard

14. Despite America's urgent need for wartime workers, the cultural bias against working mothers was so difficult to _____ that Congress held off on funding child care until well into the war.

A conquer
B recant
C restore
D duplicate
E vanquish
F exchange

15. As Gold Rush mining camps grew ever more crowded, San Francisco developed a _____ economy, quickly becoming the largest and most important financial center in the American West.

A faltering
B bustling
C vibrant
D questionable
E stringent
F realistic

16. Despite a wealth of evidence of the executive director's popularity with her staff and a sheaf of impassioned letters from her supporters, the _____ board of directors refused to reconsider its recommendation that she be terminated.

A forbearing
B divergent
C fallacious
D inexorable
E clement
F obdurate

17. As unemployment spiked and the stock market plunged for the third consecutive month, the public became increasingly frustrated with Congress, which they saw as _____ in its response to the economic crisis.

A volatile
B dilatory
C discerning
D germane
E anarchic
F laggard

18. Because of its uncanny _____ to the toxic belladonna plant, foragers and cooks did not consider the tomato a food item until the mid-1800s.

A resemblance
B misconception
C incongruity
D similarity
E concurrence
F aversion

Practice Question Solutions

1. Prone to explaining each of her decisions in great detail, the judge could never be accused of a lack of ____.

- A apostasy
- **B transparency**
- C diffidence
- D competence
- E reticence
- **F candor**

Solution

What you know of the judge is that she is *prone to explaining each of her decisions in great detail*, so she could never be accused of a lack of <u>giving information</u>.

Looking at the answer choices, **the two that match and make the most sense are *transparency*, which in this context means clearness of communication, and *candor*, which has the same meaning**.

Apostasy is the renunciation of a religious belief, *diffidence* means a lack of self-confidence, *competence* is the ability to do something well, and *reticence* is the reluctance to speak, which is the opposite of the inferred meaning. None of these other terms fit the sentence and all can be eliminated.

2. Although we are taught to associate yawning with exhaustion or boredom, intense stress can also _____ this response: many soldiers report repeatedly yawning while on alert in combat zones.

- A dampen
- B obstruct
- **C precipitate**
- D venerate
- **E engender**
- F depreciate

Solution

You can anticipate a word or phrase such as <u>elicit</u> or <u>bring about</u>. Following the colon is an example of intense stress that brings about yawning. Let's take a look at the answer choices.

To *dampen* is to diminish, which is the opposite of what you are looking for, and to *obstruct* is to block, which is also not what you are looking for. You can eliminate both of these choices.

To *precipitate* is to cause, **which is one of the correct answers**.

To *venerate* is to honor, which does not make sense in this sentence.

To *engender* is also to cause; **this answer is the second correct choice**.

To *depreciate* is to diminish, which is not a fit, and you can eliminate this choice as well.

3. The investigators pored over hours of footage filmed inside the lighthouse, looking for _____ in light or sound that they could present as evidence of the paranormal.

A contrasts
B **anomalies**
C mutations
D adjustments
E **aberrations**
F juxtapositions

Solution

Evidence of the paranormal would need to include <u>highly unusual occurrences</u> in light or sound, and **the two answer choices that represent this idea are _anomalies_ and _aberrations_, which are correct**.

Contrasts, _adjustments_, and _juxtapositions_ would all be normal occurrences that would not be evidence of the paranormal and can be quickly eliminated. _Mutations_ might be, but it does not have a matching term and can be eliminated.

4. Modern Japan's embrace of all things _kawaii_, or cute, has proven to be anything but an _____ trend; its enduring popularity has made _kawaii_ a billion-dollar industry that encompasses hundreds of thousands of consumer items and myriad entertainment franchises.

A **ephemeral**
B **evanescent**
C endemic
D exorbitant
E elliptical
F efficacious

Solution

Based on the description that follows the semicolon, which indicates the immense influence and staying power of the trend, you can anticipate that the missing term will have something to do with the notion that it is _proven to be anything but_ a <u>short-term</u> or <u>limited</u> trend.

Reviewing the answer choices, **the two that match in meaning are _ephemeral_ and _evanescent_, which both mean lasting for a short period**.

Endemic means native to a certain group or area, which does not make sense in this context; _exorbitant_ means excessive, which does not make sense in this context; it's unclear what an _elliptical_ trend would be—whether it is a trend with an oval shape or a trend that is difficult to understand—regardless, the word does not match the meaning that you need; and _efficacious_ means effective, which does not make sense in this context, so all these remaining choices can be eliminated.

Solutions Continued

5. Some patients with depression and bipolar disorder have reported significant _____ of their symptoms upon regularly wearing blue-blocking glasses for several weeks, leading some researchers to wonder whether the blue light emitted by phones, computers, and tablets has a negative effect on the mental health of all technology users.

A. augmentation
B. exacerbation
C. amelioration
D. incapacitation
E. mitigation
F. regeneration

Solution

If the findings make researchers wonder about the *negative effects* of blue light, the blue-blocking glasses must have a beneficial effect on these patients, so you can anticipate an answer with a meaning such as <u>relief from</u> or <u>lessening of</u>.

Two possible answer choices are *amelioration* and *mitigation*, both of which are associated with a reduction of symptoms.

Both *augmentation* and *exacerbation* are associated with increasing symptoms and can be eliminated; *incapacitation* means a lack of ability, which does not make sense in this context and can also be eliminated; *regeneration* is regrowth, which does not fit the sentence and can be eliminated.

6. While the weather to our west looks _____, the sun is shining brightly to our east.

A. minatory
B. penetrating
C. inauspicious
D. propitious
E. crestfallen
F. derogatory

Solution

The best answer choices contrast with the notion that *the sun is shining brightly to our east*.

The pair of answers that makes sense is *minatory*, which means threatening, and *inauspicious*, which means unpromising.

It is unclear what *penetrating* weather would be like, so you can eliminate that description; *propitious* means favorable, which is not a contrast to the brightly shining sun and does not have a matching pair, so you can also eliminate this answer choice; *crestfallen* means sad—it is unclear what sad weather is like, so you can eliminate this answer choice; *derogatory* means disrespectful—it is unclear what disrespectful weather means, so you can also eliminate this answer choice.

7. Students whose teachers praise them for their exemplary effort are far more likely to take on _____ academic challenges in the future than children whose teachers merely compliment their natural intelligence.

A provocative
B infelicitous
C limpid
D formidable
E arduous
F mellifluous

Solution

You can anticipate that you will have a modifier that indicates more rigorous or more challenging *academic challenges*, which would match the students' *exemplary effort*. Let's take a look at the answer choices.

Both *formidable* and *arduous* are great synonyms for the word challenging, and these are the correct answers.

Provocative academic challenges are those that elicit strong reactions—there are no clues in the sentence to indicate that these students are likely to take on more provocative challenges, so you can eliminate this choice. *Infelicitous* means awkward or inappropriate; *limpid* academic challenges are transparent; *mellifluous* means sweet sounding. None of these descriptions fit this situation, and all can be eliminated.

8. While Betsy Ross may well have been _____ the construction of the first American flag, most scholars agree that the Stars and Stripes was conceived and designed by lawyer and composer Francis Hopkinson.

A implicated in
B instrumental in
C inimical to
D innocuous in
E indoctrinated into
F integral to

Solution

Because of the contrast presented by *while*, a phrase such as credited with can be expected. Let's examine the answer choices.

The correct matching pair that fits here is *instrumental in* and *integral to*, both of which mean centrally important. While these words are different than anticipated, they make sense in terms of fitting the sentence and contrasting with Francis Hopkinson's being the original designer.

Implicated in is somewhat tempting in that it means to be accused of something, but it has the wrong tone, and there is not a matching term for it, so it can be eliminated. *Inimical* is harmful and *innocuous* is unharmful, neither of which fit this situation; both can be eliminated. To be *indoctrinated* is to be instructed, which does not make sense in this context, and can also be eliminated.

Solutions Continued

9. Though always open to compromise in his personal life, John was highly _____ at work, refusing to abide by practices that differed from the conventions and regulations he held dear.

- A tractable
- **B orthodox**
- C xenophobic
- **D intransigent**
- E competent
- F amorphous

Solution

You have a contrast to the fact that John is *open to compromise* in some areas, and you have the modifying phrase after the comma that tells you that John *refuses to abide by practices that differ* from traditions and regulations, so you can anticipate that John is the opposite of being open to compromise in his professional life.

Reviewing the answer choices, the two that best match this description are *orthodox*, which means conforming to traditionally held beliefs, and *intransigent*, which means unwilling to change. **These are the two correct choices**.

To be *tractable* is to be easily controlled or persuaded, which is the opposite of the premise of the sentence, so you can eliminate this answer choice.

To be *xenophobic* is to be prejudiced against people of other nationalities. This answer choice can be eliminated.

There is no evidence in this sentence that John was highly *competent*, or able, in his work life. Thus, answer choice [E] can be eliminated.

Amorphous means lacking a clearly defined shape, so you can also eliminate this answer choice.

10. Our phobias often do not reflect reality: fear of flying is much more _____ than fear of driving, but the average American is far more likely to be injured or killed in a car accident than in a plane crash.

- A requisite
- **B prevalent**
- C rarefied
- D consummate
- **E pervasive**
- F plausible

Solution

You are told that *our phobias do not reflect reality* and that you are much *more likely to be injured or killed in a car accident than in a plane crash*; therefore, you can infer that the *fear of flying is much more* common *than the fear of driving*.

Of the answer choices, the two that match are *prevalent* and *pervasive*, both of which are synonyms for common.

Requisite means required, *rarefied* means relating to very few people, and *consummate* means perfectly representative. None of these terms fit the sentence and can be eliminated.

Plausible means believable, which is the opposite of what the sentence tells you about the fear of flying; it too can be eliminated.

11. As female authors narrow the gender gap in literature, an increasing number of bestsellers _____ a topic rarely represented in novels of earlier eras: female friendship.

- [A] overstate
- [B] **foreground**
- [C] denigrate
- [D] malign
- [E] romanticize
- [F] **spotlight**

Solution

The increase in female authors is creating a change in literature by narrowing the gender gap. The nature of this change is hinted at in the remainder of the sentence: the contrast between *an increasing number* and *rarely represented* solidifies the inference that these new bestsellers by women authors underline or depict *female friendship*. You can anticipate that *as female authors narrow the gender gap in literature, an increasing number of bestsellers explore a topic rarely represented in novels of earlier eras: female friendship*.

Reviewing the answer choices, *spotlight*, or focus attention on, works very well in this context; *foreground* is also correct, as it has the same meaning as spotlight: to make the focus of attention.

Nothing in the text suggests that authors *overstate*, or exaggerate, female friendship.

The sentence also gives one no reason to believe that the authors *denigrate* or *malign* it, both of which mean to say bad things about it, so you can eliminate these answers.

The sentence offers no clues that the authors *romanticize* female friendship, and there is not a matching second answer choice for this word, so you can eliminate it as well.

12. When an artistic breakthrough occurs, all the glory perhaps rightly goes to the artist; however, tireless behind-the-scenes figures—spouses, patrons, and supportive friends—are often _____ to the artist's process of producing and presenting pioneering work to the world.

- [A] **indispensable**
- [B] subsidiary
- [C] deleterious
- [D] ancillary
- [E] **imperative**
- [F] inimical

Solution

The word however indicates that the *behind-the-scenes figures are often* integral *to the artist's process*.

Reviewing the answer choices, the two that align are *indispensable* and *imperative*, both of which mean necessary.

Both *subsidiary* and *ancillary* mean secondary, which are not suitable, so both can be eliminated.

Deleterious means causing damage and *inimical* means hostile. Neither of these negative words fit for the sentence, so you can eliminate these answer choices as well.

Solutions Continued

13. Most mammals do not use their faces to express their emotions; to _____ a cat's emotional state, for instance, it is best to look at its tail.

A **ascertain**
B inhibit
C enhance
D **discern**
E stabilize
F safeguard

Solution

You can infer that the space needs to be filled with a word or phrase that indicates <u>recognize</u>. **The two answer choices that best match are *ascertain* and *discern*.**

To *inhibit* is to limit, to *enhance* is to intensify, to *stabilize* is to make steady, and to *safeguard* is to protect; none of those terms fit the given sentence, and none of them would work to create equivalent meanings. All can be eliminated.

14. Despite America's urgent need for wartime workers, the cultural bias against working mothers was so difficult to _____ that Congress held off on funding child care until well into the war.

A **conquer**
B recant
C restore
D duplicate
E **vanquish**
F exchange

Solution

You can infer that the *cultural bias against working mothers was difficult to* <u>overcome</u> or <u>lessen</u>.

Reviewing the answer choices, the two that match and make sense are *conquer* and *vanquish*, which both mean "attain victory over."

To *recant* is to take back something one has said, which is slightly tempting but not a perfect fit for the sentence and, additionally, does not have a good match.

To *restore* is to bring back, which is not related.

Duplicate and *exchange* do not make sense in this context and do not have equivalent answer choices, so you can also eliminate these answer choices.

15. As Gold Rush mining camps grew ever more crowded, San Francisco developed a _____ economy, quickly becoming the largest and most important financial center in the American West.

A faltering
B bustling
C vibrant
D questionable
E stringent
F realistic

Solution

If San Francisco is the *largest and most important financial center in the American West*, it makes sense to define it as a *bustling* or *vibrant* economy; **these are the two correct answers**.

Faltering and *questionable* are both the opposite of what has been described and can be eliminated. *Stringent* means strict, which does not have support in this sentence, and neither does *realistic*; both terms can be eliminated.

16. Despite a wealth of evidence of the executive director's popularity with her staff and a sheaf of impassioned letters from her supporters, the _____ board of directors refused to reconsider its recommendation that she be terminated.

A forbearing
B divergent
C fallacious
D inexorable
E clement
F obdurate

Solution

You can infer that the board will be described as being <u>tough</u> or <u>unyielding</u>.

The two answer choices that match are *inexorable* and *obdurate*; both mean very stubborn and refusing to relent or change one's mind or opinion.

Forbearing is patient, which does not match; *divergent* means going in different directions; *fallacious* means dishonest; and *clement* means merciful. None of these answer choices matches the necessary meaning, so all can be eliminated.

Solutions Continued

17. As unemployment spiked and the stock market plunged for the third consecutive month, the public became increasingly frustrated with Congress, which they saw as _____ in its response to the economic crisis.

A volatile
B dilatory
C discerning
D germane
E anarchic
F laggard

Solution

You can anticipate that the public saw Congress as <u>having either no effect or a negative effect</u> in its response to the economic crisis.

You want two answer choices that match each other, and the two that do are *dilatory* and *laggard*, which both mean too slow to act. Too slow to act isn't exactly what you anticipated, but it makes perfect sense in the context of the sentence, and **these two choices are correct**.

The sentence provides no clues that Congress was *volatile* in its response, nor does this word have a match among the other answer choices, so you can eliminate [A].

Nothing in the text indicates that Congress was *discerning*, or showing careful judgment, so you can also eliminate this answer choice.

Germane means relevant, which does not make sense in this context and can be eliminated. *Anarchic* means chaotic—there are no clues that Congress has been chaotic, and you do not have a match for this answer, so you can also eliminate this choice.

18. Because of its uncanny _____ to the toxic belladonna plant, foragers and cooks did not consider the tomato a food item until the mid-1800s.

A resemblance
B misconception
C incongruity
D similarity
E concurrence
F aversion

Solution

You can infer that *foragers and cooks did not consider the tomato a food item until the mid-1800s* because of its *uncanny resemblance*, or *similarity*, to the *toxic belladonna plant*. **Both of these answer choices are correct**.

Misconception is somewhat tempting in that a misconception kept the tomato from being eaten, but the word does not make an acceptable sentence, so it can be eliminated.

Incongruity means mismatch, *concurrence* is associated with happening at the same time, and *aversion* is dislike. None of the terms works in this context, and none of the terms has a match among the other answer choices; thus, all can be eliminated.

11
VERBAL REASONING

Reading Comprehension 1

Reading comprehension questions make up about half the questions in the Verbal Reasoning section. They will take up the majority of your time, and they are the most important verbal questions for you to master.

The majority of the passages will be one paragraph in length, and you'll face one or two longer passages that can be up to four or five paragraphs long. Each passage will have one to six associated questions and will relate to one of three subject areas: humanities, social sciences, and natural sciences. At the beginning of the passage, you are told how many questions will be associated with that passage.

Reading Comprehension Lessons to Come

In this lesson, I'll discuss GRE reading comprehension in general and talk about optimal **reading strategies** that put you in the best possible position to answer any and all types of questions that come your way.

Over the next three lessons, you'll practice additional passages while breaking down and discussing in detail each of the different **question types** that you might encounter.

Let's start by looking at a couple of sample passages and their associated questions. Please read through and try to answer them before I continue this discussion.

Sample Passage 1

3 Questions

Although human exposure to electromagnetic fields (EMFs) has become more prevalent since the advent of human-made EMF producers, such as home appliances, mobile phones, and power grids, exposure to electromagnetism has always been a part of life. After all, Earth and the Sun both generate their own EMFs. However, some evidence suggests that extended exposure to high-frequency EMFs can cause physical and even mental illnesses in humans. Although the science behind these claims remains controversial, EMF exposure has been associated with depression, anxiety, sleep disorders, fatigue, and difficulty with focus. In fact, some scientists believe that the ubiquity of EMFs is at least partially to blame for the increasing worldwide rates of mental illness. Although this hypothesis might seem far-fetched at first, you may recently have personally experienced the mental effects of EMFs. Many people report feelings of unease and heaviness when a severe thunderstorm is rolling in, which could be explained by the high levels of EMF emitted by lightning.

1. The passage is primarily concerned with

(A) an urgent need to reduce our exposure to high-frequency EMFs.
(B) a controversy surrounding whether Earth's electromagnetism is affecting our bodies.
(C) comparing the EMFs emitted by power grids to those emitted by lightning.
(D) presenting the hypothesis that human-made EMFs affect our mental health.
(E) dispelling myths surrounding the safety of home appliances and mobile phones.

2. It can be inferred from the passage that the author would agree with which of the following statements? Select all that apply.

[A] It is impossible to avoid all EMF exposure.
[B] High-frequency EMFs cause most mental issues, such as depression and anxiety.
[C] We should ban home appliances and electronics that emit high-frequency EMFs.

3. The author includes the last two sentences of the passage to

(A) prove that EMFs are dangerous to physical health.
(B) demonstrate that EMFs could indeed affect our mental well-being.
(C) point out that EMFs are a natural, harmless part of life on Earth.
(D) suggest that people living in storm-prone areas are at a high risk of mental illness.
(E) hypothesize that some people are more sensitive to the effects of EMFs than others.

Sample Passage 2
4 Questions

For the past 80 years, students of economics have learned about the "paradox of thrift": the idea that individuals who act responsibly and save money actually harm the economy by suppressing consumer demand and economic growth. Perhaps now we can add another paradox to economic textbooks: the "paradox of toil." First formulated by the Icelandic economist Gauti Eggertsson, the paradox of toil asserts that if too many people want to work too many hours, the resulting increased competition among workers can have dire consequences for the economy, including declining wages and demand and increased unemployment. The worst part is that the marketplace has no self-correcting mechanism for this situation. In fact, the usual market mechanism for dealing with unemployment—lower wages—would lead to a vicious cycle of lower demand and more unemployment. In a very real sense, an overzealous work ethic can become a formidable economic villain.

Of course, Eggertsson realized that the paradox of toil can occur only under a narrow range of circumstances. Most notably, interest rates must effectively be zero. When interest rates are positive, lenders are willing to expand credit, thereby propping up demand for goods and services. However, when interest rates are near the zero bound, credit cannot be offered on favorable terms for borrowers. At this point, at least according to Eggertsson, the paradox of toil comes into play. Traditionally, economists have viewed zero interest rates as nothing more than a theoretical possibility. However, in our decidedly abnormal economic times, zero interest rates are very close to reality. As we look at the current state of the economies of industrialized nations, we see stagnant wages despite very low unemployment rates, indicating that the paradox of toil may be all too real.

1. The author of the passage indicates that economists such as Eggertsson believe that

(A) workers in modern industrialized nations are too productive.
(B) the paradox of thrift remains a greater threat than the paradox of toil.
(C) the free market always leads to high unemployment rates.
(D) working too much may damage the economy.
(E) interest rates should be kept as high as possible to prevent the paradox of toil.

2. When interest rates are NOT at or near zero, which of the following can be inferred to be true? Select all that apply.

[A] It is unlikely that the paradox of toil will occur.
[B] Borrowers can usually increase credit to increase demand.
[C] Unemployment will remain at acceptable levels.

3. According to the passage, which of the following is an assumption that underlies Eggertsson's theory?

(A) Governments recognize the limits of free-market solutions.
(B) Interest rates have typically been positive in the past.
(C) Workers are incapable of understanding that their behavior is paradoxical.
(D) Lenders will not expand credit when interest rates are zero.
(E) Higher wages will lead to increased interest rates.

Sample Passage 2 Continued

For the past 80 years, students of economics have learned about the "paradox of thrift": the idea that individuals who act responsibly and save money actually harm the economy by suppressing consumer demand and economic growth. Perhaps now we can add another paradox to economic textbooks: the "paradox of toil." First formulated by the Icelandic economist Gauti Eggertsson, the paradox of toil asserts that if too many people want to work too many hours, the resulting increased competition among workers can have dire consequences for the economy, including declining wages and demand and increased unemployment. The worst part is that the marketplace has no self-correcting mechanism for this situation. In fact, the usual market mechanism for dealing with unemployment—lower wages—would lead to a vicious cycle of lower demand and more unemployment. In a very real sense, an overzealous work ethic can become a formidable economic villain.

Of course, Eggertsson realized that the paradox of toil can occur only under a narrow range of circumstances. Most notably, interest rates must effectively be zero. When interest rates are positive, lenders are willing to expand credit, thereby propping up demand for goods and services. However, when interest rates are near the zero bound, credit cannot be offered on favorable terms for borrowers. At this point, at least according to Eggertsson, the paradox of toil comes into play. Traditionally, economists have viewed zero interest rates as nothing more than a theoretical possibility. However, in our decidedly abnormal economic times, zero interest rates are very close to reality. As we look at the current state of the economies of industrialized nations, we see stagnant wages despite very low unemployment rates, indicating that the paradox of toil may be all too real.

4. Which of the following best describes the structure of the passage?

(A) A hypothesis about the economy is presented and then debunked.
(B) An economic theory is outlined, and the likelihood of a situation it predicts is discussed.
(C) Two paradoxes are compared, and one is discarded in favor of the other.
(D) A self-correcting mechanism is questioned, and a dire prediction for the economy is made.
(E) A new economic problem is outlined, and possible solutions are evaluated.

Reading Strategy

Now that you've had a little taste of what GRE reading comprehension is like, let's discuss the ideal strategy for approaching the passages and questions.

Although we all read daily, we may rarely read in a self-aware manner, nor may we *try to read well*. You also aren't used to being tested on your reading ability. Therefore, the pressure of being tested can make it difficult to achieve the calm, receptive state you need to read at your best.

Reading well versus reading poorly depends upon the communication between the author's intent and the reader's focus. You read well when you are interested in the text and aligned with the author in some way. You read poorly when you don't understand why the author wrote a passage or when your mind is elsewhere—when your focus does not connect with the content of the text.

If your goal is to read well, your best strategy should be to read with empathy. You should approach every passage with the mindset of wanting to understand not just what the passage is about but, more fundamentally, why the author decided to write it, and, more specifically, why she wrote the passage the way she did.

One challenge of GRE reading comprehension questions, especially the trickiest ones, is that they require you to see both "the forest" and "the trees"—that is, they require you to have a clear and accurate understanding of the big picture regarding the passage as a whole, as well as a nuanced mastery of specific details within the passage. In response to this challenge, test takers often overextend themselves and try to memorize everything in the passage or accomplish too many different tasks simultaneously as they read.

This is unnecessary and counterproductive. I recommend you focus on the big-picture understanding during your initial reading and check all specific details as needed when it comes time to evaluate them while answering individual questions. I'll model this in many ways in the lessons ahead, but for now, the key takeaway is to maintain a simple, clear focus during your reading of the passage: work to understand why the author wrote the passage and why each part of the passage exists relative to the overall purpose. Focusing on just this task will prevent you from getting lost and distracted during your reading, and it will put you in an optimal position to answer both general and specific questions.

> Read with empathy. Focus on why the author chose to write the passage, and worry less about capturing every detail as you read. As you read, consider how the passage is structured and the purpose of each component of the passage relative to this overall purpose.

What Not to Do

In reading, focus is key. You can do more harm than good by trying to do too many different things at once. Scattered focus makes it harder to answer questions correctly.

Here are practices you should **avoid** because they might hold you back during reading comprehension.

1. Evaluating Subjectively

Certain questions may require you to subjectively evaluate certain parts of the passage, but otherwise, it's not your job to form an opinion about the author or the passage. In fact, it's a waste of time and a harmful distraction to do so. Your job is to be objective and to seek to understand the information presented as accurately as possible without coloring it with your own experiences or opinions.

2. Jumping Ahead to Look at Questions

Before you read the passage, glance at the information supplied at the top. You'll learn how many questions will be asked about the passage. If there is just one question, it doesn't hurt to read that question before reading the text of the passage. However, if there are several questions associated with the passage, it's both counterproductive and a waste of precious time to scroll through and review these questions before reading the passage.

3. Taking Passage Notes

If you love taking notes and they improve your reading, please feel free to do so. However, I've found that notes do not aid overall comprehension (and, in fact, may hinder it) for most students. Note-taking most often slows students down, and notes are generally not helpful in answering questions.

4. Memorizing Details

I have mentioned this already, but it's important enough to mention it again.

Because some questions require you to access details from the passage, you may think you must memorize the content of the text as you read. However, you don't! Trying to master every detail can make it harder to see the big picture as clearly as you would otherwise. Give yourself a little breathing room, focus on the author's purpose, and you may be surprised to see how much easier it is to understand the passage as a whole.

Of course, you know yourself best, so feel free to disregard this advice. For most students, however, avoiding these strategies will prove critical to their success.

Let's go back to the sample passages and model the reading process. Afterward, I'll walk through how you should answer the questions. (Again, I'll have further discussion of the different question types in the lessons ahead.)

Sample Passage 1 Solutions

Here are solutions to the passages introduced earlier in this chapter.

Although human exposure to electromagnetic fields (EMFs) has become more prevalent since the advent of human-made EMF producers, such as home appliances, mobile phones, and power grids, exposure to electromagnetism has always been a part of life. After all, Earth and the Sun both generate their own EMFs. However, some evidence suggests that extended exposure to high-frequency EMFs can cause physical and even mental illnesses in humans. Although the science behind these claims remains controversial, EMF exposure has been associated with depression, anxiety, sleep disorders, fatigue, and difficulty with focus. In fact, some scientists believe that the ubiquity of EMFs is at least partially to blame for the increasing worldwide rates of mental illness. Although this hypothesis might seem far-fetched at first, you may recently have personally experienced the mental effects of EMFs. Many people report feelings of unease and heaviness when a severe thunderstorm is rolling in, which could be explained by the high levels of EMF emitted by lightning.

Background information about main topic: human exposure to EMFs.

Main point: some evidence suggests extended exposure can cause physical and even mental illness.

Support.

Comments

The passage begins by giving you background information about the topic. It then moves to the main point: there is some evidence suggesting that extended exposure to high-frequency EMFs can cause physical and even mental illness. It then moves on to several different types of support for this theory.

1. The passage is primarily concerned with

(A) an urgent need to reduce our exposure to high-frequency EMFs.

(B) a controversy surrounding whether Earth's electromagnetism is affecting our bodies.

(C) comparing the EMFs emitted by power grids to those emitted by lightning.

(D) **presenting the hypothesis that human-made EMFs affect our mental health.**

(E) dispelling myths surrounding the safety of home appliances and mobile phones.

(D) matches our solution, and it is correct.

(A) and (B) go well beyond what is stated in the text, and (C) and (E) do not represent the primary concern of the passage.

2. It can be inferred from the passage that the author would agree with which of the following statements? Select all that apply.

[A] **It is impossible to avoid all EMF exposure.**

[B] High-frequency EMFs cause most mental issues such as depression and anxiety.

[C] We should ban home appliances and electronics that emit high-frequency EMFs.

For the second question, you're asked to select all the answers that apply. For [A], you were told in the passage that EMF exposure has always been a part of life and that Earth and the Sun both generate their own EMFs, so **yes, you can infer that the author would agree with [A]**.

For [B], you don't have nearly enough evidence to support the idea that EMFs cause *most* mental illnesses; this is a great example of how a single word can make an answer choice wrong. For [C], the author takes no position in this passage regarding whether the devices should be banned. You can't infer that the author would agree with either [B] or [C].

3. The author includes the last two sentences of the passage to

(A) prove that EMFs are dangerous to physical health.

(B) **demonstrate that EMFs could indeed affect our mental well-being.**

(C) point out that EMFs are a natural, harmless part of life on Earth.

(D) suggest that people living in storm-prone areas are at a high risk of mental illness.

(E) hypothesize that some people are more sensitive to the effects of EMFs than others.

These last two sentences are used to demonstrate that EMFs could indeed affect our mental well-being, so **(B) is the correct answer**.

(A) discusses physical health, which isn't the focus here, and the word *prove* is much too strong. (C) contradicts the point being made.

(D) doesn't accurately represent the passage, which doesn't single out or emphasize people who live in storm-prone areas—and it doesn't indicate that anyone is *at a high risk of mental illness*.

(E) makes a mistake similar to the one made in answer choice (D)—the text doesn't differentiate some people from others or suggest that certain individuals are more sensitive to EMFs.

Sample Passage 2 Solutions

For the past 80 years, students of economics have learned about the "paradox of thrift": the idea that individuals who act responsibly and save money actually harm the economy by suppressing consumer demand and economic growth. Perhaps now we can add another paradox to economic textbooks: the "paradox of toil." First formulated by the Icelandic economist Gauti Eggertsson, the paradox of toil asserts that if too many people want to work too many hours, the resulting increased competition among workers can have dire consequences for the economy, including declining wages and demand and increased unemployment. The worst part is that the marketplace has no self-correcting mechanism for this situation. In fact, the usual market mechanism for dealing with unemployment—lower wages—would lead to a vicious cycle of lower demand and more unemployment. In a very real sense, an overzealous work ethic can become a formidable economic villain.

> **Background: economics students learn of paradox of thrift.**

> **Main topic: economist Eggertsson—paradox of toil—too many people working too many hours could = bad consequences for the economy.**

> **Further elaboration: no self-correction, but rather vicious cycle that gets worse.**

Of course, Eggertsson realized that the paradox of toil can occur only under a narrow range of circumstances. Most notably, interest rates must effectively be zero. When interest rates are positive, lenders are willing to expand credit, thereby propping up demand for goods and services. However, when interest rates are near the zero bound, credit cannot be offered on favorable terms for borrowers. At this point, at least according to Eggertsson, the paradox of toil comes into play. Traditionally, economists have viewed zero interest rates as nothing more than a theoretical possibility. However, in our decidedly abnormal economic times, zero interest rates are very close to reality. As we look at the current state of the economies of industrialized nations, we see stagnant wages despite very low unemployment rates, indicating that the paradox of toil may be all too real.

> **Eggertsson knew the paradox of toil is unlikely to actually happen; will only occur when interest rates are effectively at zero.**

> **Explanation of why.**

> **Traditionally, economists have viewed zero interest rates as very unlikely.**

> **But currently, this is very close to reality.**

> **The paradox of toil may currently be all too real.**

Comments

The author wrote the passage to (1) explain to us the paradox of toil, (2) discuss the unlikely characteristics (namely zero interest rates) that would make the paradox of toil possible, and finally, (3) show us that these characteristics exist in our modern age and that perhaps we may be experiencing the paradox of toil today.

1. The author of the passage indicates that economists such as Eggertsson believe that

(A) workers in modern industrialized nations are too productive.
(B) the paradox of thrift remains a greater threat than the paradox of toil.
(C) the free market always leads to high unemployment rates.
(D) **working too much may damage the economy.**
(E) interest rates should be kept as high as possible to prevent the paradox of toil.

Answer choice (D) matches the definition of the paradox of toil well, and it is the correct answer.

(A) is attractive, but *modernized industrialized nations* and *too productive* are not exact matches for what the passage tells you Eggertsson believed.

(B) The passage doesn't compare the paradoxes, so you can quickly eliminate this answer choice.

In (C), the word *always* makes this claim far too strong to be correct; the answer choice does not reflect Eggertsson's beliefs described in the passage.

(E) You haven't read any information in the passage that would enable you to infer that Eggertsson thought *interest rates should be kept as high as possible*.

2. When interest rates are NOT at or near zero, which of the following can be inferred to be true? Select all that apply.

[A] **It is unlikely that the paradox of toil will occur.**
[B] **Borrowers can usually increase credit to increase demand.**
[C] Unemployment will remain at acceptable levels.

You are told that the paradox of toil can occur only when interest rates are effectively at zero, **so you can infer [A].**

You are also told that when interest rates are positive, lenders are willing to expand credit, propping up demand for goods and services, so you can infer that borrowers can usually increase credit to increase demand, and **you can select [B] as well.**

However, the passage contains no information to indicate that when interest rates are NOT at or near zero, unemployment will remain at acceptable levels—there could be any variety of reasons why unemployment levels might run amok at any given time regardless of interest rates. Therefore, you can't select [C].

Sample Passage 2 Solutions Continued

3. According to the passage, which of the following is an assumption that underlies Eggertsson's theory?

(A) Governments recognize the limits of free-market solutions.
(B) Interest rates have typically been positive in the past.
(C) Workers are incapable of understanding that their behavior is paradoxical.
(D) **Lenders will not expand credit when interest rates are zero.**
(E) Higher wages will lead to increased interest rates.

According to the passage, an important component of Eggertsson's theory is that *when interest rates are near the zero bound, credit cannot be offered on favorable terms to borrowers.* That is a nice match for answer choice **(D), which is the correct choice**.

(A) and (C) are not discussed in the passage. Even if (B) is true and discussed, it is not something that underlies Eggertsson's theory. (E) is not discussed, nor can it be inferred from the text. Therefore, all these choices can be eliminated.

4. Which of the following best describes the structure of the passage?

(A) A hypothesis about the economy is presented and then debunked.
(B) **An economic theory is outlined, and the likelihood of a situation it predicts is discussed.**
(C) Two paradoxes are compared, and one is discarded in favor of the other.
(D) A self-correcting mechanism is questioned, and a dire prediction for the economy is made.
(E) A new economic problem is outlined, and possible solutions are evaluated.

With answer choice (A), *a hypothesis* isn't a great match, but by itself, perhaps it isn't bad enough to eliminate the answer choice; however, *debunked* is—the paradox of toil is not debunked in the passage, so you can eliminate this answer choice.

With answer choice (B), both the first and second parts align with the passage, so let's leave it for now and review the other choices.

The passage doesn't compare the two paradoxes or choose one over the other, so you can quickly eliminate answer choice (C).

With (D), no self-correcting mechanism is questioned, and *a dire prediction for the economy is made* is too dark and dramatic to describe the tone of the passage, so you can eliminate this choice as well.

Finally, you aren't given a problem and possible solutions, so you can eliminate (E).

(B) is the only viable answer. It accurately describes the structure of the passage: the first paragraph outlines a theory, and the second discusses the likelihood of the situation it predicts. **Therefore, (B) is correct.**

Practice Passage

Let's try one final three-question passage together to finish the chapter.

Nineteenth-century Prussian general and military philosopher Carl von Clausewitz famously claimed that "war is the continuation of politics by other means." In this pronouncement, Clausewitz challenged the common assumption that war is akin to a sporting competition between nations in which one side "wins" by achieving battlefield victory over a "loser" who waves a metaphorical, if not literal, white flag of surrender. For Clausewitz, the purpose of war was far more complicated. In his estimation, countries go to war to achieve economic and political goals that they have failed to achieve by other methods. However, while battlefield defeat does not imply the impossibility of achieving those goals, battlefield victory does not assure success in attaining them, either.

To choose what, at first glance, might appear a shocking example of this principle, consider Japan in 1945. From a military standpoint, few countries have ever been more thoroughly defeated: Japan faced complete destruction of its military and industrial capabilities, millions of military and civilian casualties, and the national humiliation of virtually unconditional surrender. Yet, Clausewitz might argue, Japan achieved its war aims nonetheless. Japan's primary goal in the 1930s was to create the "Greater East Asia Co-Prosperity Sphere": a strong, Japan-dominated East Asian economy. Although early 20th-century Japanese attempts to achieve this aim brought it into disastrous military conflict with the United States, after the American occupation of Japan ended, Japan began its economic domination of most of East Asia, leading to its emergence as one of the wealthiest countries on the planet.

1. Which of the following best describes the primary purpose of the passage?

(A) To criticize conventional views of warfare
(B) To illustrate the validity of a view that is at odds with conventional wisdom
(C) To argue that victory and defeat are meaningless concepts when discussing warfare
(D) To explain the motives behind Japan's involvement in World War II
(E) To analyze the assumptions underlying a prevalent theory of warfare

2. The author uses the phrase "white flag of surrender" to achieve which of the following goals?

(A) To illustrate a common viewpoint with a concrete image
(B) To illustrate the idea that formal surrender is a necessary component of military defeat
(C) To indicate that surrender is often a more complicated process than civilians typically imagine
(D) To show how wars typically ended in Clausewitz's time
(E) To illustrate the sense of deep humiliation experienced by defeated countries

3. Which of the following regarding Japan is NOT mentioned by the author?

(A) One reason for the military conflict between the United States and Japan
(B) The magnitude of Japan's military losses
(C) How Japan was able to economically dominate East Asia after World War II
(D) Japan's current economic position in the world
(E) The psychosocial consequences of Japan's defeat

Practice Passage Solutions

Nineteenth-century Prussian general and military philosopher Carl von Clausewitz famously claimed that "war is the continuation of politics by other means." In this pronouncement, Clausewitz challenged the common assumption that war is akin to a sporting competition between nations in which one side "wins" by achieving battlefield victory over a "loser" who waves a metaphorical, if not literal, white flag of surrender. For Clausewitz, the purpose of war was far more complicated. In his estimation, countries go to war to achieve economic and political goals that they have failed to achieve by other methods. However, while battlefield defeat does not imply the impossibility of achieving those goals, battlefield victory does not assure success in attaining them, either.

To choose what, at first glance, might appear a shocking example of this principle, consider Japan in 1945. From a military standpoint, few countries have ever been more thoroughly defeated: Japan faced complete destruction of its military and industrial capabilities, millions of military and civilian casualties, and the national humiliation of virtually unconditional surrender. Yet, Clausewitz might argue, Japan achieved its war aims nonetheless. Japan's primary goal in the 1930s was to create the "Greater East Asia Co-Prosperity Sphere": a strong, Japan-dominated East Asian economy. Although early 20th-century Japanese attempts to achieve this aim brought it into disastrous military conflict with the United States, after the American occupation of Japan ended, Japan began its economic domination of most of East Asia, leading to its emergence as one of the wealthiest countries on the planet.

Seems to start with main point—war is just another means of politics—Carl von Clausewitz.

Contrasts with the assumption that war is like a competition where one side wins and the other side loses.

Further explanation—for Clausewitz, war is more complicated—war is a way to achieve goals, but victory and defeat don't guarantee success or failure in the achievement of the goals.

The second paragraph serves as an example of the main point: Japan was defeated in war but achieved its desired goals after the war.

Comments

This is a more challenging text to understand, especially at the beginning. It helps to read through to the end and then reread to more fully understand the substance and purpose of the first parts of the passage. Specifically, it may have been difficult to understand what exactly was meant by Clausewitz's quotation, but when you're given further elaboration in the latter parts of the passage and the example of Japan post-WWII, it becomes much clearer.

1. Which of the following best describes the primary purpose of the passage?

(A) To criticize conventional views of warfare
(B) **To illustrate the validity of a view that is at odds with conventional wisdom**
(C) To argue that victory and defeat are meaningless concepts when discussing warfare
(D) To explain the motives behind Japan's involvement in World War II
(E) To analyze the assumptions underlying a prevalent theory of warfare

None of the answer choices for the first question may jump out as ideal, but (B) is the one you can't find fault with and by far the best available. **(B) must therefore be the correct choice.** The passage uses the first paragraph to present you with a view that is at odds with conventional wisdom (a loose synonym for *common assumption*) and the second to illustrate the validity of that view.

The passage doesn't offer criticism of conventional views of warfare, so you can eliminate (A). The author also doesn't claim that victory and defeat are meaningless concepts, so you can easily eliminate (C) as well. (D) While the passage does mention Japan's motives for entering WWII, explaining these motives cannot be described as its primary purpose. These *war aims* are mentioned for the first time at the end of the second paragraph. You can eliminate that choice.

(E) is perhaps the most tempting of the incorrect answer choices, but the passage doesn't provide an analysis of Clausewitz's underlying assumptions; rather, it gives you an explanation of the theory and an example of it playing out in the world, so you can eliminate (E) as well.

2. The author uses the phrase "white flag of surrender" to achieve which of the following goals?

(A) **To illustrate a common viewpoint with a concrete image**
(B) To illustrate the idea that formal surrender is a necessary component of military defeat
(C) To indicate that surrender is often a more complicated process than civilians typically imagine
(D) To show how wars typically ended in Clausewitz's time
(E) To illustrate the sense of deep humiliation experienced by defeated countries

For the second question, the best available answer choice is (A). You know that this is a part of the *common assumption*, or viewpoint, and the white flag does provide a *concrete image* to illustrate the point.

You have no clues to suggest that the author intends to illustrate with the white flag that surrender is a *necessary component of military defeat* or indicate that surrender is *often a more complicated process than civilians typically imagine*, so you can eliminate both of those choices.

(D) is somewhat tempting, but you only know that this was a typically held assumption, not that this is how wars *typically ended* in Clausewtiz's time, so you can eliminate this choice.

(E) overly infers the meaning of the white flag—while the passage does discuss the humiliation of defeat, it does so in a completely separate context from the white flag of surrender. You can eliminate this answer choice.

Solutions Continued

3. The author does NOT mention which of the following with regard to Japan?

(A) One reason for the military conflict between the United States and Japan
(B) The magnitude of Japan's military losses
(C) How Japan was able to economically dominate East Asia after World War II
(D) Japan's current economic position in the world
(E) The psychosocial consequences of Japan's defeat

To answer this question correctly and confidently, you must not only choose the one answer not mentioned but also find the four answer choices that are mentioned in the passage. One small advantage is that you know that the subject matter is narrowly focused on Japan, so you can focus on just the second paragraph.

(A) is discussed in the passage—we are told that Japan's primary goal and its attempts to achieve this aim put it into military conflict with the United States—so you can eliminate (A).

Multiple parts of the second paragraph discuss (B), so you can eliminate it as well.

(C) does not seem to be discussed, so let's leave it for now.

Japan's current economic position is discussed in the final sentence, so you can eliminate answer choice (D).

Finally, (E) is discussed in terms of *national humiliation*, so you can eliminate it as well.

Returning to (C), you are told that Japan was able to dominate East Asia after WWII, but the passage doesn't give you any information, directly or indirectly, about how. **Therefore, (C) was not discussed and is the correct answer**.

12

VERBAL REASONING

Reading Comprehension 2

In this chapter, the second of four GRE reading comprehension lessons, I'll start the discussion of specific question strategies by focusing on those that ask about (1) the general purpose of the passage, (2) the opinions of the author or others discussed in the passage, or (3) the reason the author included different parts of the passage. As you'll see, reading for *why* the author wrote the passage puts you in the ideal position to answer reading comprehension questions.

Before I get started, here is one more important reminder about reading GRE passages:

Don't be afraid to reread along the way.

When you understand what you read, you might think the process advances linearly—you move forward, and that's it. Time pressure may also cause anxiety about reviewing the text to verify or strengthen your understanding.

However, **all** good readers go back and forth in the text as they read, and you shouldn't be afraid to do so during the exam. GRE passages tend to be dense, and your understanding of their overall structure and the author's overall purpose is critical to your success.

Often, it can be helpful to reread the first few sentences of a passage to get a clearer sense of their meaning, to scan the first paragraph of the passage after you've read it completely, or to quickly glance back over an entire long passage after you've read it once. Taking the time to understand is always better than rushing ahead and missing the point.

Remember, your goal is to understand the author's intentions.

With that said, let's start by looking at a few sample passages. We'll then discuss different question types before modeling the reading process and answering some questions together.

Sample Passage 1

2 Questions

Candles have been lighting the way for human civilization for almost as long as civilization has existed. Evidence suggests that early candles were used in ancient Greece, Rome, China, and India, both for illumination and for religious ritual. In much of Europe, North Africa, and the Middle East, however, candles were slow to gain popularity because of the widespread availability of olive oil, an effective fuel for oil lamps. This state of affairs changed after the fall of the Roman Empire, when trade disruption stopped the flow of olive oil into Western Europe. Chandlers, or candlemakers, became an essential part of European medieval life. Although today we associate candles with pleasant scents, the tallow candles of the Middle Ages were so putrid that some towns banned candle manufacturing outright. Odorless beeswax candles were available at the time but expensive to produce, making them a luxury available only to the nobility and the church.

During the 19th century, widespread industrialization and the development of oil refineries made candles more affordable and accessible to the masses than ever before. Paraffin, an inexpensive and odorless petroleum byproduct, became the candle material of choice. For a brief moment, the candle industry boomed. However, kerosene lamps and, ultimately, incandescent light bulbs dimmed candle sales as the 20th century approached.

While far fewer candles are sold today than were sold in the 19th century, modern candle companies have transformed candlemaking from an essential craft to a fine art. Since candles are no longer used primarily for illumination, their scent has become their most important component. Many candle companies now use natural waxes and oils to produce candles that burn slowly and cleanly, allowing their fragrances to take center stage.

1. Based on the information in the passage, which of the following would the author agree with? Select all that apply.

[A] Had the Roman Empire not fallen, candles would never have become widely available in Western Europe.
[B] Finding an odorless and affordable material for candlemaking allowed the candle industry to expand.
[C] Candles have at times been considered luxury goods.

2. Which of the following best describes the purpose of this passage?

(A) To explain the importance of scent in candlemaking
(B) To trace the rise and fall of candles as illuminants
(C) To argue that candles are necessary for civilization
(D) To provide a brief history of candle manufacturing
(E) To argue that candlemaking is a fine art

Sample Passage 2

2 Questions

Comparing ancient Egypt with ancient Athens, one is tempted to assume that their political differences are embodied in the architecture that both cultures left behind. Ancient Egypt was a society ruled by kings who were considered semi-divine; these supreme rulers were honored with elaborate palaces and tombs, most notably the Great Pyramids at Giza. Reaching toward the sun, these extraordinary burial sites seem to embody the strict hierarchical organization of ancient Egyptian civilization. Conversely, ancient Athens has been hailed by democracies the world over as the birthplace of self-government. Indeed, Athens's symmetrical, rational architecture appears radically open to the modern viewer, inviting all people to participate in lively political debates.

However, these assumptions are misleading. Free women in ancient Egypt were recognized as men's equals in legal affairs, including property ownership, while women in ancient Greece were entirely banned from public life. Some ancient Egyptian men moved up the social ladder by learning to read and write and becoming government scribes, but such class mobility was rare in ancient Greece. Although architecture might provide some sense of an ancient society's preoccupations and beliefs, one should take care not to overextend these generalizations.

1. With which of the following statements would the author of this passage agree? Select all that apply.

[A] Ancient Egypt and ancient Greece were equally unjust societies.
[B] Stereotypes persist in our historical perspectives on ancient cultures.
[C] Ancient Egypt was a far superior society to ancient Athens.

2. Which of the following best represents the author's purpose in including examples of architecture in this passage?

(A) To symbolize the accomplishments of two ancient civilizations
(B) To cast aspersions on Egyptian engineering accomplishments
(C) To suggest a clear aesthetic lineage between ancient Greece and ancient Egypt
(D) To illustrate an argument about the prevalence of historical stereotypes
(E) To compare the religious building styles of ancient Egypt and ancient Greece

Question Strategies

Different types of questions present you with different types of challenges. Often, incorrect answers are wrong because they do not match the task presented to you in the question stem. Furthermore, a key trait that differentiates top scorers is the ability to get maximum benefit from the question stem. Weaker test-takers treat different types of questions as if they were all the same. However, you want to have a clear sense of what each type of question is asking and recognize that the right answer aligns with both the text presented in the passage and the task presented in the stem.

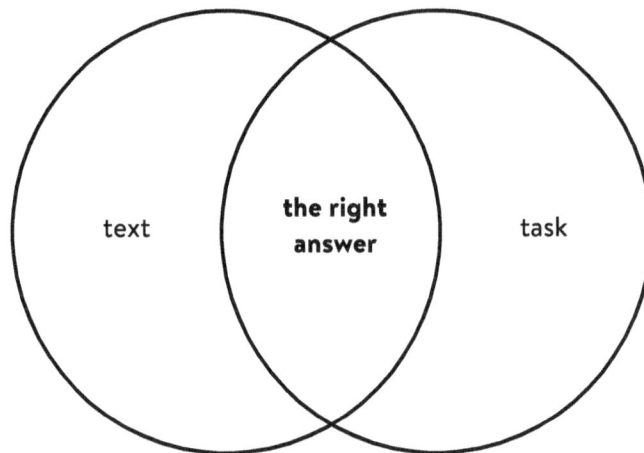

What you'll often experience when evaluating answer choices is that you can eliminate some because they don't align with the passage, and you can eliminate others because they don't align with the question. So, again, if you are strict and habitual about using both criteria, you will be in an optimal position to see why certain answer choices are more viable and others are more obviously incorrect. Now, let's talk in a bit more detail about each type of question.

General Questions

- The author of the passage is **primarily concerned** with…
- Which of the following best states the **author's main point**?
- The **primary purpose** of the passage is to…
- Which of the following best describes the **organization of the passage**?

General questions will ask about the author's primary purpose in writing the passage or the main point presented in the passage, or they will ask you about how the passage was structured. The overall strategy of reading for the author's purpose puts you in an ideal position to answer general questions.

Attractive incorrect answers will often discuss parts of the passage but fail to represent the passage as a whole, or they may misrepresent the author's reason for writing the passage in a subtle but significant way. They will also often include incorrect details about the passage that give them away.

As questions become increasingly challenging, correct answer choices will often be written in ways that are not straightforward or direct representations of the passage, the author's purpose, or the structure of the passage. The answer may represent the point of the passage in an unexpected way or describe the structure in a convoluted fashion. You want to be prepared for these challenges and feel confident that you're not doing anything wrong if you don't find the right answers written in the exact ways that you'd like them to be written.

Opinion Questions

- Which of the following best represents the **author's opinions** about the unfinished monument?
- With which of the following statements would the author **most likely agree**?
- The passage suggests that Klinke and Thomas would **likely disagree about** which of the following?

Most opinion questions ask about the opinion of the author of the passage, but some ask about the opinions of different people mentioned in the passage. Additionally, some questions will ask about the author's general opinion, while others will ask the author's opinions about specific topics mentioned in the passage. Sometimes, the question stem will tip off the specificity of the question; at other times, it may not.

In all such situations, your job is to be precise. Again, reading with the goal of understanding why the author wrote the passage will put you in a great position to answer opinion questions. Beyond this, you want to develop habits of being meticulous in assessing whose opinion is in question and confirming that the opinion is about the right subject matter, as per the question stem and the answer choice.

Role of the Passage's Parts

- Which of the following best describes the **function** of the second paragraph?
- What is the **relationship between** the research attributed to Singh and the opinion attributed to Klinger?
- The **importance of the study** mentioned in lines 24–27 is that…
- The **author mentions** Santa Fe artists primarily in order to…
- In the context in which it appears, "value" (line 6) **most nearly means**…
- **Choose the sentence** that most directly connects the critical reception of the novelist's work and its success with audiences.

Finally, these questions ask you to consider what role different parts of the passage play relative to the author's purpose. Again, as with the other question types, thinking about why the author wrote the passage as you read puts you in a perfect position to answer these questions. As questions go up the difficulty scale, the right answers can get more obscure, while wrong answers commonly remain, relatively speaking, easier to spot and eliminate.

Bonus: Critical Reasoning

- Which of the following, if true, could most help **explain the claim** made by Anderson?
- Which of the following, if true, most **weakens the claim** made by the author?
- Which of the following is most **supported by the information** in the passage?
- Which of the following is most **representative of** the type of actions discussed in the passage?

A small minority of questions will also require you to critically evaluate the information in the passage—to consider what might strengthen or weaken the claims presented in the passage or how the passage might relate to information in other parts of life. Critical reasoning questions are not particularly common, and I'll discuss them more in the fourth reading comprehension lesson.

Sample Passage 1 Solutions

Candles have been lighting the way for human civilization for almost as long as civilization has existed. Evidence suggests that early candles were used in ancient Greece, Rome, China, and India, both for illumination and for religious ritual. In much of Europe, North Africa, and the Middle East, however, candles were slow to gain popularity because of the widespread availability of olive oil, an effective fuel for oil lamps. This state of affairs changed after the fall of the Roman Empire, when trade disruption stopped the flow of olive oil into Western Europe. Chandlers, or candlemakers, became an essential part of European medieval life. Although today we associate candles with pleasant scents, the tallow candles of the Middle Ages were so putrid that some towns banned candle manufacturing outright. Odorless beeswax candles were available at the time but expensive to produce, making them a luxury available only to the nobility and the church.

> The author wrote this passage to discuss history of candle usage across various civilizations.

During the 19th century, widespread industrialization and the development of oil refineries made candles more affordable and accessible to the masses than ever before. Paraffin, an inexpensive and odorless petroleum byproduct, became the candle material of choice. For a brief moment, the candle industry boomed. However, kerosene lamps and, ultimately, incandescent light bulbs dimmed candle sales as the 20th century approached.

> Continued chronological discussion of candle usage—became more affordable and accessible.

> Boomed then faded.

While far fewer candles are sold today than were sold in the 19th century, modern candle companies have transformed candlemaking from an essential craft to a fine art. Since candles are no longer used primarily for illumination, their scent has become their most important component. Many candle companies now use natural waxes and oils to produce candles that burn slowly and cleanly, allowing their fragrances to take center stage.

> Now, scent is an important component.

Comments

The author wrote the passage to talk about the history of the candle, and the author discusses candles throughout time and across different parts of the world. The first paragraph begins with early adoption in ancient times and discusses challenges overcome. The second paragraph discusses candles at the peak of their popularity, explains how they became less essential with the advent of light bulbs, and describes how they have changed in the modern world.

Sample Passage 1 Solutions

1. Based on the information in the passage, which of the following would the author agree with? Select all that apply.

[A] Had the Roman Empire not fallen, candles would never have become widely available in Western Europe.

[B] **Finding an odorless and affordable material for candlemaking allowed the candle industry to expand.**

[C] **Candles have at times been considered luxury goods.**

[A] You can't infer whether candles would have become widely available in Western Europe, regardless of the fall of the Roman Empire, so [A] is wrong.

[B] You know that bad odors limited candle growth in previous centuries, and you are told explicitly that widespread industrialization and the development of oil refineries made candles more accessible to the masses than ever before, **so you can select [B]**.

[C] Finally, you know from the final sentence of the first paragraph that beeswax candles were considered luxury goods, **so you can select [C] as well**.

2. Which of the following best describes the purpose of this passage?

(A) To explain the importance of scent in candlemaking
(B) To trace the rise and fall of candles as illuminants
(C) To argue that candles are necessary for civilization
(D) **To provide a brief history of candle manufacturing**
(E) To argue that candlemaking is a fine art

Answer choices (A), (B), and (E) all accurately reflect individual parts of the passage but do not represent the passage as a whole.

Answer choice (C) uses the absolute term "necessary," and the author doesn't make a case for candles being necessary to civilization.

All four answer choices can be eliminated fairly easily.

Answer choice (D) provides a fairly straightforward, broad, and accurate description of the purpose of the passage, and it is correct.

Sample Passage 2 Solutions

Comparing ancient Egypt with ancient Athens, one is tempted to assume that their political differences are embodied in the architecture that both cultures left behind. Ancient Egypt was a society ruled by kings who were considered semi-divine; these supreme rulers were honored with elaborate palaces and tombs, most notably the Great Pyramids at Giza. Reaching toward the sun, these extraordinary burial sites seem to embody the strict hierarchical organization of ancient Egyptian civilization. Conversely, ancient Athens has been hailed by democracies the world over as the birthplace of self-government. Indeed, Athens's symmetrical, rational architecture appears radically open to the modern viewer, inviting all people to participate in lively political debates.

> **The author wrote this passage to discuss the correlation between architecture and politics in both ancient Egypt and Athens. Paragraph presents a simple narrative of Egyptian architecture matching Egyptian politics and Athenian architecture matching Athenian politics, but expect a transition in the second paragraph.**

However, these assumptions are misleading. Free women in ancient Egypt were recognized as men's equals in legal affairs, including property ownership, while women in ancient Greece were entirely banned from public life. Some ancient Egyptian men moved up the social ladder by learning to read and write and becoming government scribes, but such class mobility was rare in ancient Greece. Although architecture might provide some sense of an ancient society's preoccupations and beliefs, one should take care not to overextend these generalizations.

> **The second paragraph shows that simple assumptions laid out in the first paragraph are indeed off— Egypt was more democratic than it may seem on the surface, while Greece didn't offer equal rights to women.**

Comments

You can anticipate the overall purpose and structure of the passage from the first sentence: one can make assumptions about the politics of ancient Egypt and Athens based on their architecture, and the author will show examples of how to do just that. However, it would be a mistake to overgeneralize these assumptions. In the second paragraph, the author provides further reasoning for this claim as well.

Sample Passage 2 Solutions

1. With which of the following statements would the author of this passage agree? Select <u>all</u> that apply.

  [A] Ancient Egypt and ancient Greece were equally unjust societies.

  [B] Stereotypes persist in our historical perspectives on ancient cultures.

  [C] Ancient Egypt was a far superior society to ancient Athens.

With answer choice [A], to say that they were *equally* unjust societies is too strong an inference, so you can't select this choice.

You can, however, say that the author is likely to believe that stereotypes persist—the passage mentions stereotypes of Athens as the birthplace of self-government. **You can select [B]**.

Finally, the author doesn't claim that one society was better than the other, and certainly not *far superior*, so you can't select [C].

2. Which of the following best represents the author's purpose in including examples of architecture in this passage?

(A) To symbolize the accomplishments of two ancient civilizations

(B) To cast aspersions on Egyptian engineering accomplishments

(C) To suggest a clear aesthetic lineage between ancient Greece and ancient Egypt

(D) To illustrate an argument about the prevalence of historical stereotypes

(E) To compare the religious building styles of ancient Egypt and ancient Greece

The architecture is employed to discuss stereotypes of the different cultures, so **(D) does represent the author's purpose well, and it is the correct answer**.

The author does not include the architectural examples to symbolize the accomplishments of the two cultures, to cast aspersions on Egyptian engineering accomplishments, or to connect the aesthetics of Greece and Egypt, so you can eliminate (A), (B), and (C) fairly quickly. Similarly, it's not the author's purpose to discuss religious building styles, so you can quickly eliminate (E) as well.

Practice Passage 1

3 Questions

Fashions and fads have been studied in disciplines as diverse as philosophy, sociology, anthropology, and economics. Recently, fashions have received renewed attention as a source of data used to test models of cultural dynamics. In this context, fashions and fads are defined as cultural traits whose popularity undergoes striking, erratic, and often short-term fluctuations that do not have any obvious cause. Nonetheless, researchers have found some statistical regularities among fads.

Bentley et al. determined that in many cultural domains, relatively few traits are common; the vast majority are very rare. They also put forward the hypothesis that the tendency of individuals to copy one another at random is sufficient to explain this pattern. Other findings, however, challenge the idea that chance dominates cultural dynamics. Popular trends may have a consistent direction for many years, while random copying would presumably involve no correlation between years. Furthermore, rates of increase in popularity appear correlated with rates of decrease: what becomes popular rapidly is also rapidly forgotten. Berger et al. showed that the popularity of a first name is influenced by the popularity of phonetically similar names. Several models have been developed to accommodate these findings.

A recent study by Ghirlanda continued the search for quantitative data to better characterize cultural dynamics by testing whether it is possible to detect the effect of a specific class of events on fashions. Ghirlanda's team investigated whether the release of movies featuring dogs was associated with changes in the popularity of featured breeds. This choice was motivated by the high interest of the general public in both dogs and movies and by the availability of high-quality data. This study showed that, indeed, movies have had a significant impact on dog breed popularity in the U.S., sometimes influencing the sales of featured breeds for a decade or more after a film's release, although this effect was found to decline over time. Their results showed that while fashions may appear random, it is possible, at least sometimes, to identify specific underlying causes.

1. Which of the following best describes the passage?

(A) A question concerning cultural dynamics is raised and then definitively answered, with reference to experimental data.

(B) Two different positions concerning a hypothesis are described, the evidence for each is presented, and a conclusion is drawn concerning which of the two is better substantiated by data.

(C) A question concerning fashions and fads is raised, some research is cited to support one position on the question, and further research is presented that casts doubt on that position.

(D) Two different perspectives on an issue are described, and compelling research is cited to support each position.

(E) A discovery that casts doubt on a previous assumption is described, and some recent research prompted by that discovery is evaluated.

2. What is the relationship between the research attributed to Berger and the perspective attributed to Ghirlanda?

(A) The two researchers reached the same conclusion by different means.

(B) The two researchers differ in their conclusions but not their assumptions.

(C) Ghirlanda's work uses and builds upon the work of Berger.

(D) Ghirlanda's work is similar to Berger's in that it collected statistical data to better understand a phenomenon.

(E) Ghirlanda's work differs from Berger's in that Berger studied only the dynamics concerning how people's names are chosen, while Ghirlanda also studied how dogs are named.

Practice Passage 1 Continued

Fashions and fads have been studied in disciplines as diverse as philosophy, sociology, anthropology, and economics. Recently, fashions have received renewed attention as a source of data used to test models of cultural dynamics. In this context, fashions and fads are defined as cultural traits whose popularity undergoes striking, erratic, and often short-term fluctuations that do not have any obvious cause. Nonetheless, researchers have found some statistical regularities among fads.

Bentley et al. determined that in many cultural domains, relatively few traits are common; the vast majority are very rare. They also put forward the hypothesis that the tendency of individuals to copy one another at random is sufficient to explain this pattern. Other findings, however, challenge the idea that chance dominates cultural dynamics. Popular trends may have a consistent direction for many years, while random copying would presumably involve no correlation between years. Furthermore, rates of increase in popularity appear correlated with rates of decrease: what becomes popular rapidly is also rapidly forgotten. Berger et al. showed that the popularity of a first name is influenced by the popularity of phonetically similar names. Several models have been developed to accommodate these findings.

A recent study by Ghirlanda continued the search for quantitative data to better characterize cultural dynamics by testing whether it is possible to detect the effect of a specific class of events on fashions. Ghirlanda's team investigated whether the release of movies featuring dogs was associated with changes in the popularity of featured breeds. This choice was motivated by the high interest of the general public in both dogs and movies and by the availability of high-quality data. This study showed that, indeed, movies have had a significant impact on dog breed popularity in the U.S., sometimes influencing the sales of featured breeds for a decade or more after a film's release, although this effect was found to decline over time. Their results showed that while fashions may appear random, it is possible, at least sometimes, to identify specific underlying causes.

3. What is the most likely reason the passage mentions the work of Bentley et al.?

(A) To prove that cultural dynamics are governed by chance
(B) To illustrate the position that Berger and Ghirlanda attempted to substantiate
(C) To describe an earlier hypothesis that has more recently been challenged
(D) To present statistical evidence that undermines the work of Berger and Ghirlanda
(E) To qualify the conclusion that cultural dynamics are governed by chance

Practice Passage 1 Solutions

Fashions and fads have been studied in disciplines as diverse as philosophy, sociology, anthropology, and economics. Recently, fashions have received renewed attention as a source of data used to test models of cultural dynamics. In this context, fashions and fads are defined as cultural traits whose popularity undergoes striking, erratic, and often short-term fluctuations that do not have any obvious cause. Nonetheless, researchers have found some statistical regularities among fads.

Background/subject matter: Passage is about statistics regarding fashions and fads.

Bentley et al. determined that in many cultural domains, relatively few traits are common; the vast majority are very rare. They also put forward the hypothesis that the tendency of individuals to copy one another at random is sufficient to explain this pattern. Other findings, however, challenge the idea that chance dominates cultural dynamics. Popular trends may have a consistent direction for many years, while random copying would presumably involve no correlation between years. Furthermore, rates of increase in popularity appear correlated with rates of decrease: what becomes popular rapidly is also rapidly forgotten. Berger et al. showed that the popularity of a first name is influenced by the popularity of phonetically similar names. Several models have been developed to accommodate these findings.

Bentley et al. claimed mostly chance and random copying. Other findings challenged the idea that chance dominates fads and fashions. The rest of the paragraph presents evidence of regularities that go against chance.

A recent study by Ghirlanda continued the search for quantitative data to better characterize cultural dynamics by testing whether it is possible to detect the effect of a specific class of events on fashions. Ghirlanda's team investigated whether the release of movies featuring dogs was associated with changes in the popularity of featured breeds. This choice was motivated by the high interest of the general public in both dogs and movies and by the availability of high-quality data. This study showed that, indeed, movies have had a significant impact on dog breed popularity in the U.S., sometimes influencing the sales of featured breeds for a decade or more after a film's release, although this effect was found to decline over time. Their results showed that while fashions may appear random, it is possible, at least sometimes, to identify specific underlying causes.

Continuing discussion of statistical analysis of fads and trends, with specific examples of the popularity of dog breeds and the release of movies.

Comments

The passage is quite dense, and some of the specific sentences are challenging to understand fully, but if you allow yourself to step back and take more of a macro view, the picture is easier to see. The author wrote this passage to discuss the study of fads and fashions using statistical analysis. The first paragraph gives you the context for discussing this topic, the second gets into the nitty-gritty details, and the third paragraph moves on to a more specific example. Let's see what challenges they present.

Solutions Continued

1. Which of the following best describes the passage?

(A) A question concerning cultural dynamics is raised and then definitively answered, with reference to experimental data.

(B) Two different positions concerning a hypothesis are described, the evidence for each is presented, and a conclusion is drawn concerning which of the two is better substantiated by data.

(C) **A question concerning fashions and fads is raised, some research is cited to support one position on the question, and further research is presented that casts doubt on that position.**

(D) Two different perspectives on an issue are described, and compelling research is cited to support each position.

(E) A discovery that casts doubt on a previous assumption is described, and some recent research prompted by that discovery is evaluated.

You're asked which of the answer choices best describes the passage. Go through the answer choices one at a time and eliminate those you feel certain are incorrect.

In (A), while the passage arguably raises a *question concerning cultural dynamics* (whether fashion trends are driven by identifiable cultural causes), this question is not *definitively answered*. You can eliminate this answer choice.

(B) describes the second paragraph of the passage with some accuracy. Here, you do have a hypothesis (*They also put forward the hypothesis that the tendency of individuals to copy one another at random is sufficient to explain this pattern*). You could argue that two positions about this hypothesis are presented: for and against. However, no conclusion is drawn concerning which is better supported by the data. The passage is much more cautious in its description of the results of the research, telling you only that *several models have been developed to accom-*

modate these findings. Furthermore, this answer choice ignores the first and last paragraphs of the passage. You can eliminate (B).

(C) is not a great representation of the passage, but there's nothing wrong with it, so let's leave it for now.

Similarly, (D) isn't great, but it's somewhat similar to (C), so let's leave it.

Finally, with (E), there is no clear *discovery* discussed in the passage, so you can quickly eliminate this choice.

Returning to (C), you can say that the hypothesis put forth by Bentley et al.—that trends arise by chance—is the question being raised. Some research is put forth to support this claim, and further research is presented that casts doubt upon it. All of this is true of the passage, and it unfolds in that order.

Looking at (D), while there are arguably two different perspectives presented in the passage (trends are random versus trends have identifiable causes), you don't have *compelling* research cited to support each position. The research described supports one position—that trends at least sometimes have identifiable causes—and it is not strong enough to be conclusive (note the qualifying language in the passage, such as *sometimes* and *possible*).

Therefore, in terms of best describing the passage, (C) is the correct answer.

2. What is the relationship between the research attributed to Berger and the perspective attributed to Ghirlanda?

(A) The two researchers reached the same conclusion by different means.

(B) The two researchers differ in their conclusions but not their assumptions.

(C) Ghirlanda's work uses and builds upon the work of Berger.

(D) Ghirlanda's work is similar to Berger's in that it collected statistical data to better understand a phenomenon.

(E) Ghirlanda's work differs from Berger's in that Berger studied only the dynamics concerning how people's names are chosen, while Ghirlanda also studied how dogs are named.

Let's see which answer choice most accurately describes the relationship between the two perspectives.

Since the two researchers did not share the same conclusions or assumptions, you can eliminate (A) and (B). Further, you have no evidence that Ghirlanda's work builds upon Berger's work, so you can eliminate (C) as well.

With (D), you can infer that Berger researched popularity by collecting data, so (D) seems likely to be correct—let's leave it for now.

Finally, (E) misrepresents Ghirlanda in that it makes it seem that Ghirlanda continued Berger's work, which the passage does not indicate. It discusses Ghirlanda studying dog names, which the passage never mentions. (Ghirlanda studies the popularity of dog breeds, not dog names.) You can eliminate (E) as well.

Returning to (D), it's a very general statement that you can make about both Berger and Ghirlanda; therefore, it is the correct answer.

Solutions Continued

3. What is the most likely reason the passage mentions the work of Bentley et al.?

(A) To prove that cultural dynamics are governed by chance
(B) To illustrate the position that Berger and Ghirlanda attempted to substantiate
(C) **To describe an earlier hypothesis that has more recently been challenged**
(D) To present statistical evidence that undermines the work of Berger and Ghirlanda
(E) To qualify the conclusion that cultural dynamics are governed by chance

Why does the author mention Bentley et al.? Let's take a look at the answer choices and see which one fits best.

The author isn't trying to assert that cultural dynamics are indeed governed by chance, and you can eliminate (A).

Bentley et al. are on the opposite side of Berger and Ghirlanda, so (B) is false and you can quickly eliminate this choice.

(C) matches the text well, so let's leave it for now.

(D) also seems somewhat attractive, so let's leave it for now as well.

Finally, Bentley et al. aren't mentioned to *qualify* or modify the conclusion that cultural dynamics are governed by chance, but rather to illustrate it, so you can eliminate (E) as well.

Returning to (D), which seemed like the less attractive of the remaining answers, and evaluating it a bit more carefully, *statistical evidence* isn't a great match for what the reference to Bentley et al. brings to the passage. Likewise, *undermines* suggests a successful weakening of a given argument, not mere conflict with that argument. Therefore, (D) is not a great match and can be eliminated.

Looking at (C) more carefully, you see that the author uses Bentley et al.'s hypothesis as a springboard to discuss statistical methods for studying fads and trends for the rest of the passage, and it accurately describes why the author mentions the work. **(C) is the correct answer.**

Practice Passage 2

3 Questions

Given that the United States was colonized by Britain only a few hundred years ago, it may seem somewhat odd that British and American accents are so differ-
5 ent. Some of these differences are relatively simple to explain. British settlers in the New World came into contact with Native Americans and settlers from other parts of Europe early in our nation's history. These encounters would have encouraged British settlers to begin
10 speaking somewhat differently from their counterparts across the Atlantic. Furthermore, during and after the American Revolution, the United States was eager to distinguish itself from the Old World, so the rapid establishment of new speech customs was likely a point of na-
15 tional pride. However, only a few Americans are aware that when British colonists arrived in the New World, they spoke with a dialect much more similar to modern American English than to the "BBC" accent we associate with British English today. Upper-class Brits began
20 using a non-rhotic accent (one in which the "r" sound is not pronounced) shortly after the American Revolution to distinguish themselves from their commoner counterparts. Therefore, American English is, at least in part, a relic of a time when British accents sounded very different from the way they do today.

1. In the context of the passage as a whole, the word "customs" (line 13) is closest in meaning to

(A) procedures.
(B) ceremonies.
(C) manners.
(D) formalities.
(E) conventions.

2. The passage suggests which of the following about American and British accents?

(A) The evolution of American accents was entirely unconscious on the part of American English speakers.
(B) Americans would have continued speaking like their British colonizers if they had not encountered Native peoples in the New World.
(C) Americans often incorrectly assume that British accents have remained static over the past several centuries.
(D) Americans with non-rhotic accents (such as those from the Deep South) have preserved a more British way of speaking than those who speak with rhotic accents.
(E) British colonists who encountered a diverse range of accents and dialects upon arrival in the United States adapted to an American way of speaking more quickly.

3. Select the sentence that suggests that early Americans may have intentionally changed the way they speak.

Practice Passage 2 Solutions

Given that the United States was colonized by Britain only a few hundred years ago, it may seem somewhat odd that British and American accents are so different. Some of these differences are relatively simple to
5 explain. British settlers in the New World came into contact with Native Americans and settlers from other parts of Europe early in our nation's history. These encounters would have encouraged British settlers to begin speaking somewhat differently from their counterparts
10 across the Atlantic. Furthermore, during and after the American Revolution, the United States was eager to distinguish itself from the Old World, so the rapid establishment of new speech customs was likely a point of national pride. However, only a few Americans are aware
15 that when British colonists arrived in the New World, they spoke with a dialect much more similar to modern American English than to the "BBC" accent we associate with British English today. Upper-class Brits began using a non-rhotic accent (one in which the "r" sound is
20 not pronounced) shortly after the American Revolution to distinguish themselves from their commoner counterparts. Therefore, American English is, at least in part, a relic of a time when British accents sounded very different from the way they do today.

Main topic: strange that British and American accents are so different.

The reasons American settlers' accents changed.

However, the main reason for the differences has to do with Brits changing their accents.

Comments

The author wrote this passage to discuss why American and British accents are so different. The author gives some explanations for why American accents have changed but also explains why British accents have changed even more, and that's why the differences are so pronounced.

1. In the context of the passage as a whole, the word "customs" (line 13) is closest in meaning to

(A) procedures.
(B) ceremonies.
(C) manners.
(D) formalities.
(E) **conventions.**

Ceremonies and *formalities* are furthest away in meaning and can be eliminated quickly. *Procedures* and *manners* are both tempting, but neither fits well when it comes to ways of speaking. The word *conventions*, or ways in which something is usually done, is the closest in meaning to *customs*. **(E) is the correct answer**.

2. The passage suggests which of the following about American and British accents?

(A) The evolution of American accents was entirely unconscious on the part of American English speakers.
(B) Americans would have continued speaking like their British colonizers if they had not encountered Native peoples in the New World.
(C) **Americans often incorrectly assume that British accents have remained static over the past several centuries.**
(D) Americans with non-rhotic accents (such as those from the Deep South) have preserved a more British way of speaking than those who speak with rhotic accents.
(E) British colonists who encountered a diverse range of accents and dialects upon arrival in the United States adapted to an American way of speaking more quickly.

This is a **detail question**—I'll talk more in general about how to approach detail questions in the next lesson, but you can certainly try it here first. Approach the answer choices one at a time.

You know that Americans wanted to distinguish themselves and establish a new identity, so (A) is not true, and you can eliminate it. Furthermore, since many reasons were given for the change in accent, (B) is also not true, and you can eliminate it as well.

(C) is definitely alluded to in the sentence that begins, *However, few Americans realize*… so let's leave it for now.

(D) requires inferences that you lack sufficient information to make, so you can eliminate (D) as well. (E) also requires far more information than the text provides, so you can eliminate (E).

Returning to (C), you're told in the passage that few Americans realize that British accents have undergone such drastic changes. You can infer from this fact that Americans often incorrectly assume that British accents have remained static. **(C) is the correct answer**.

Solutions Continued

3. Select the sentence that suggests that early Americans may have intentionally changed the way they speak.

I discussed this a bit in the elimination of answer choice (A) for the previous question—the idea that the evolution of American accents was not unconscious but rather intentional.

There are two attractive options here:

1. *British settlers in the New World came into contact with Native Americans and settlers from other parts of Europe early in our nation's history, which would have encouraged them to begin speaking somewhat differently from their counterparts across the Atlantic.*

2. *Further, during, and after the American Revolution, the United States was eager to distinguish itself from the Old World, so the rapid establishment of new speech customs was likely a point of national pride.*

The first discusses changes in accent brought about by encounters with other cultures, while the second discusses changes in accent brought about by personal motivation. Only the second shows signs of personal intention, so the second sentence is the correct one.

Further, during and after the American Revolution, the United States was eager to distinguish itself from the Old World, so the rapid establishment of new speech customs was likely a point of national pride.

Practice Passage 3

3 Questions

What is astonishing is not that some people are skeptical of "home assistants" like the Google Home and Amazon Echo but that so many consumers blithely accept these devices in their homes without concern for the broader implications of being constantly surveilled. On the surface, home assistants are a boon for tech companies because they provide a wealth of information about precisely what people want to buy and a boon for consumers because they make daily life more convenient. But what about all the other information these devices record: our most intimate conversations, the exact times of our comings and goings, and the precise tone of our voices? It has been widely reported that these devices passively record everything around them. It is not a great leap to surmise that tech companies could be using this information for purposes that consumers may not fully understand. Even if we decide that tech companies are worthy of our trust—a dubious proposition at best— we must contend with the fact that their devices can be hacked by less trustworthy actors. Is convenience truly worth such a blatant invasion of privacy?

1. The passage is primarily concerned with which of the following?

Ⓐ Determining which home assistant provides the best privacy controls for consumers
Ⓑ Demanding reforms to tech companies' approaches to consumer research
Ⓒ Suggesting that we learn to live without technological innovation
Ⓓ Making a distinction between government and corporate surveillance
Ⓔ Arguing that we have willingly sacrificed privacy in exchange for expediency

2. Select the sentence that explains the popularity of home assistants.

3. Which of the following, if true, would most seriously undermine the argument being made in this passage?

Ⓐ In 2019, just 30% of American households made use of a home assistant.
Ⓑ Home assistants make it possible for busy families to spend more time together instead of shopping or doing chores.
Ⓒ Over the past year, only a handful of cases of home assistant hacks have been reported to U.S. law enforcement.
Ⓓ It is illegal for Big Tech to store the information that their home assistants gather.
Ⓔ In a survey, respondents rated companies like Amazon and Google as more trustworthy than government agencies such as the NSA and CIA.

Practice Passage 3 Solutions

What is astonishing is not that some people are skeptical of "home assistants" like the Google Home and Amazon Echo but that so many consumers blithely accept these devices in their homes without concern for the broader implications of being constantly surveilled. On the surface, home assistants are a boon for tech companies because they provide a wealth of information about precisely what people want to buy and a boon for consumers because they make daily life more convenient. But what about all the other information these devices record: our most intimate conversations, the exact times of our comings and goings, and the precise tone of our voices? It has been widely reported that these devices passively record everything around them. It is not a great leap to surmise that tech companies could be using this information for purposes that consumers may not fully understand. Even if we decide that tech companies are worthy of our trust—a dubious proposition at best— we must contend with the fact that their devices can be hacked by less trustworthy actors. Is convenience truly worth such a blatant invasion of privacy?

Main topic: consumers blithely accept home assistant devices without enough concern about being surveilled.

Reasons to be concerned.

Comments

The author wrote this passage to discuss concerns about home assistants and, more specifically, their ability to record things about our lives without our knowing or consent.

1. The passage is primarily concerned with which of the following?

(A) Determining which home assistant provides the best privacy controls for consumers
(B) Demanding reforms to tech companies' approaches to consumer research
(C) Suggesting that we learn to live without technological innovation
(D) Making a distinction between government and corporate surveillance
(E) **Arguing that we have willingly sacrificed privacy in exchange for expediency**

The passage is not concerned with determining which home assistant provides the best privacy controls, so you can eliminate answer choice (A).

Both (B) and (C) are too extreme relative to what the author mentions—the author does not demand reforms to tech companies nor does the author suggest we live without technological innovation, so you can eliminate both of those choices as well.

The author also didn't write the passage primarily to distinguish between government and corporate surveillance, so you can eliminate (D) as well.

This leaves you with (E), the correct answer. Although it certainly doesn't match how I would have summarized the primary concern of the passage, *expediency* is a decent match for *convenience* in the final sentence, and the passage, when taken as a whole, does match this description—the author is arguing that we have indeed potentially sacrificed privacy for this expediency.

2. Select the sentence that explains the popularity of home assistants.

The following sentence explains the popularity of home assistants:

On the surface, home assistants are a boon for tech companies because they provide a wealth of information about precisely what people want to buy and a boon for consumers because they make daily life more convenient.

The phrase *boon for tech companies* explains why these companies would make home assistants readily available, and the phrases *boon for consumers* and *make daily life more convenient* explain why they are popular devices that people want to purchase and use.

Solutions Continued

3. Which of the following, if true, would most seriously undermine the argument being made in this passage?

(A) In 2019, just 30% of American households made use of a home assistant.

(B) Home assistants make it possible for busy families to spend more time together instead of shopping or doing chores.

(C) Over the past year, only a handful of cases of home assistant hacks have been reported to U.S. law enforcement.

(D) **It is illegal for tech companies to store the information that their home assistants gather.**

(E) In a survey, respondents rated companies like Amazon and Google as more trustworthy than government agencies such as the NSA and CIA.

This is an unusual type of question that requires you to go one extra step in evaluating the author's reasoning—we call these **weaken** questions, and I'll be discussing them further in Lesson 14. Notice that the question stem tells you to take each answer choice as true, so you don't need to worry about how realistic it might be; instead, you can focus purely on how much each statement would, if true, challenge the author's claims.

To prepare, remember that the author wrote the passage out of concern that technology companies may be using *home assistant* devices to collect far more information than consumers may want them to collect. Let's evaluate the answer choices and start by eliminating the obviously incorrect ones.

With (A), the fact that *just* 30% of households made use of a home assistant doesn't hurt the argument. Whether 30% of households constitutes many households or just a few is a purely subjective assessment, and at any rate, home assistant might still represent an invasion of privacy for that 30%, so you can eliminate this answer choice.

(B) might be a positive aspect of home assistants, but the extent to which families spend quality time together doesn't address the issues the author has raised and thus does not weaken the author's argument.

(C) may appear somewhat tempting in that it relates to the author's point that devices can be hacked, but *only a handful of cases* isn't too reassuring (again, how many is that, exactly?). More importantly, that fact doesn't address the author's privacy concerns about the companies or the potential for future hacking. Let's leave (C) for now as you look for a better answer.

If (D) is true, it makes the entire argument obsolete, so (D) is very likely the correct answer. To be safe, let's check (E) before selecting (D).

Like (C), (E) is slightly tempting because it addresses one of the issues the author mentions—whether tech companies are worthy of our trust—but since you've seen (D), you know (E) isn't as strong, and you can focus on (D).

If (D) is true, then tech companies and their hackers couldn't gather any information through the home assistants, and the concerns of the author would be moot. **So (D) most undermines the argument, and (D) is the correct answer.**

13

VERBAL REASONING

Reading Comprehension 3

In this lesson, I'll focus on two reading comprehension question types that test your understanding of a passage's specifics: detail questions and inference questions. A strong sense of overall passage structure and a clear understanding of why the author wrote the passage will, as always, be of great benefit; they will not only help you weed out many incorrect answer choices but also help you be far more efficient when you return to the passage to seek out and verify information.

Here are examples of how detail and inference questions might be phrased:

Detail Questions

- The passage **addresses** which of the following issues related to Thompson's management style?
- **According to the passage**, all of the following **are true** of immigrants to Singapore between 1980 and 2000 EXCEPT
- **According to the passage**, which of the following is **true** about the first part of the twentieth century but not the second?

Inference Questions

- The passage **suggests** that Glenn's dancing displays which of the following qualities?
- It **can be inferred** from the passage that those who invested in the spring of 2018 were given information about which of the following?
- Which of the following **inferences** about George Orwell's *1984* **is best supported** by the passage?

Keep in mind that inference questions rarely, if ever, require especially shrewd thinking, or any sort of significant leap of reasoning, or understanding that strays far from the text. You shouldn't go through mental gymnastics to find the correct answer—and when you strain to do so, that could indicate that you haven't understood the question.

For all detail and inference questions, try to maximize the information you get from the question stem, return to the passage, focus on the relevant text, eliminate wrong answers, and confirm the right answer from the remaining answers. Let's practice your reading and problem-solving with the following passage and questions.

Sample Passage 1

2 Questions

The first Sears, Roebuck and Company catalog was distributed in 1894, just after the U.S. Postal Service dramatically reduced the cost of disseminating mail order publications and just before it instituted Rural Free Delivery. Suddenly, it was cost-effective for Sears to send a thick catalog of goods to households all over the country, including those located in areas where access to manufactured goods had been extremely limited, earning the company new customers all around the country. The first Sears catalog was packed with desirable items, including clothing, jewelry, home appliances, musical instruments, saddles, and guns. Not only were most of the listings painstakingly illustrated and described, but Richard Sears filled every available space on the page with glowing customer testimonials and catchy slogans designed to inspire trust and excitement in American readers. Perhaps most impressive of all was the fact that Richard Sears wrote nearly all the catalog copy himself until 1908, when he finally retired. In a young, rapidly expanding nation, the Sears catalog was an ingenious, convenient way to meet the growing demand for consumer goods. Although it was discontinued in 1993, the Sears catalog remains a truly groundbreaking development in American retail history.

1. The passage suggests that all of the following would have been found in early Sears catalogs EXCEPT

(A) slogans designed to stick to the reader's mind.
(B) photographs of each item being sold.
(C) enthusiastic customer reviews.
(D) copy written by Richard Sears himself.
(E) an extremely wide variety of goods.

2. The passage suggests that which of the following factors contributed to the success of the Sears catalog? Select all that apply.

[A] Changes in U.S. Postal Service policies
[B] The fact that many Americans lived in rural or semi-rural areas
[C] The copy and layout of the catalog itself

Sample Passage 1 Solutions

The first Sears, Roebuck and Company catalog was distributed in 1894, just after the U.S. Postal Service dramatically reduced the cost of disseminating mail order publications and just before it instituted Rural Free Delivery. Suddenly, it was cost-effective for Sears to send a thick catalog of goods to households all over the country, including those located in areas where access to manufactured goods had been extremely limited, earning the company new customers all around the country. The first Sears catalog was packed with desirable items, including clothing, jewelry, home appliances, musical instruments, saddles, and guns. Not only were most of the listings painstakingly illustrated and described, but Richard Sears filled every available space on the page with glowing customer testimonials and catchy slogans designed to inspire trust and excitement in American readers. Perhaps most impressive of all was the fact that Richard Sears wrote nearly all the catalog copy himself until 1908, when he finally retired. In a young, rapidly expanding nation, the Sears catalog was an ingenious, convenient way to meet the growing demand for consumer goods. Although it was discontinued in 1993, the Sears catalog remains a truly groundbreaking development in American retail history.

The passage was written to describe the history of the Sears catalog.

The catalog started when it became cheaper to send mail.

Packed with desirable items.

Carefully illustrated and described, filled with testimonials and slogans.

Ingenious.

Groundbreaking development in American retail history.

Sample Passage 1 Solutions Continued

1. The passage suggests that all of the following would have been found in early Sears catalogs EXCEPT

(A) slogans designed to stick to the reader's mind.
(B) **photographs of each item being sold.**
(C) enthusiastic customer reviews.
(D) copy written by Richard Sears himself.
(E) an extremely wide variety of goods.

You are told that the catalogs included *catchy* slogans— that is, *designed to stick in the reader's mind*—and the customer reviews were *glowing*, an effective synonym for *enthusiastic*, so you can quickly eliminate (A) and (C). You are also told that Sears wrote the copy and a wide variety of goods were sold, so you can eliminate (D) and (E) as well.

While the passage tells you that the catalog contained *illustrations* of *most* of its merchandise, you are not told that there were photographs of each item sold, **so the correct answer is (B).**

2. The passage suggests that which of the following factors contributed to the success of the Sears catalog? Select all that apply.

[A] **Changes in U.S. Postal Service policies**
[B] **The fact that many Americans lived in rural or semi-rural areas**
[C] **The copy and layout of the catalog itself**

You are told that changes in U.S. Postal Policies made it cost-effective for Sears to distribute catalogs, **so you can select [A]**.

You know, per the passage, that the catalog could go to places where access to manufactured goods was extremely limited, **so [B] also contributed** to the success of the catalog in that it gave Sears a customer base to serve.

Finally, the author praises the layout and copy by describing the catalog as an ingenious way of meeting consumer demand, **so you can select [C] as well**.

Practice Passage 1

3 Questions

Few linguistic theories have generated as much controversy as the so-called Sapir-Whorf hypothesis, which states that the structure of a language determines a native speaker's perception of the world. Although it was named after linguist Edward Sapir and his student Benjamin Lee Whorf, "the Sapir-Whorf hypothesis" is a bit of a misnomer. Despite their pedagogical connection, these two linguists never co-authored any works, nor did either express his views in the form of a hypothesis. To compound the confusion, the Sapir-Whorf hypothesis, also known as linguistic relativity, is itself a relative concept used to explain everything from a loose interconnection between language and thought to strict linguistic determinism.

Perhaps the most famous and well-trodden anecdote connected to this hypothesis is that of the hundreds of Inuit words for snow. Many contemporary linguists believe this connection is based on a fundamental misunderstanding of Inuit language structure. Inuktitut, the language of the Inuit, is a highly plastic language that allows for the formation of a near-infinite number of words. The profusion of words for different types of snow is thought by many to be more an example of the language's flexibility than of a particular relationship between language and perception. Linguist Geoffrey K. Pullum goes so far as to disagree with the underlying basis of the example, convincingly arguing that Inuktitut does not, in fact, possess a significantly greater number of terms for snow than most European languages. Even if Pullum were mistaken, however, any argument for linguistic relativity based purely on quantitative comparisons of concept words rests on questionable grounds. After all, since the Inuit have historically spent a great deal of time traveling across snow and ice, important differences in the qualities of both substances would be relevant for effective communication. Thicker ice, for example, would be safer to walk across than thin ice, and harder-packed snow would be more favorable for dogsledding than the softer, powdery kind. Like all experts in a field, therefore, the Inuit conceivably could have developed a more refined understanding of snow and ice than would the Standard Average European, or "SAE"—a Whorf coinage—and would have thus created terms that reflected that refinement. To argue that the Inuit are able to perceive these different types of snow and ice in a fundamentally different way than the SAE can, however, is debatable.

1. The passage suggests which of the following regarding a language's having a large number of words for a particular phenomenon?

(A) It does not represent convincing evidence that the speakers of that language are capable of perceiving more variants of the phenomenon than the average person.
(B) Speakers of that language will understand that phenomenon more fully than speakers of other less descriptive languages.
(C) It does not constitute a relevant source of evidence for any linguistic concept.
(D) Sapir used this construct as the primary source of support for his hypothesis.
(E) It is, according to the author of the passage, a rare occurrence in most languages.

2. Which of the following can be inferred from the passage regarding the Inuktitut language?

(A) It contains more words than any other language.
(B) Some supporters of linguistic relativity drew false conclusions from its sentence structure.
(C) It is limited in its ability to describe phenomena that do not occur in a cold climate.
(D) Its users are less constrained in their formation of words than users of many languages.
(E) It is spoken by all or most Inuit tribes.

3. Which of the following can be inferred from the passage regarding the principle of linguistic relativity? Select all that apply.

[A] It has generated disagreement among linguists.
[B] For a time, it was widely accepted as valid.
[C] Support for it has been based on a dubious understanding of certain linguistic structures.

Practice Passage 1 Solutions

Few linguistic theories have generated as much controversy as the so-called Sapir-Whorf hypothesis, which states that the structure of a language determines a native speaker's perception of the world. Although it was named after linguist Edward Sapir and his student Benjamin Lee Whorf, "the Sapir-Whorf hypothesis" is a bit of a misnomer. Despite their pedagogical connection, these two linguists never co-authored any works, nor did either express his views in the form of a hypothesis. To compound the confusion, the Sapir-Whorf hypothesis, also known as linguistic relativity, is itself a relative concept used to explain everything from a loose interconnection between language and thought to strict linguistic determinism.

Perhaps the most famous and well-trodden anecdote connected to this hypothesis is that of the hundreds of Inuit words for snow. Many contemporary linguists believe this connection is based on a fundamental misunderstanding of Inuit language structure. Inuktitut, the language of the Inuit, is a highly plastic language that allows for the formation of a near-infinite number of words. The profusion of words for different types of snow is thought by many to be more an example of the language's flexibility than of a particular relationship between language and perception. Linguist Geoffrey K. Pullum goes so far as to disagree with the underlying basis of the example, convincingly arguing that Inuktitut does not, in fact, possess a significantly greater number of terms for snow than most European languages. Even if Pullum were mistaken, however, any argument for linguistic relativity based purely on quantitative comparisons of concept words rests on questionable grounds. After all, since the Inuit have historically spent a great deal of time traveling across snow and ice, important differences in the qualities of both substances would be relevant for effective communication. Thicker ice, for example, would be safer to walk across than thin ice, and harder-packed snow would be more favorable for dogsledding than the softer, powdery kind. Like all experts in a field, therefore, the Inuit conceivably could have developed a more refined understanding of snow and ice than would the Standard Average European, or "SAE"—a Whorf coinage—and would have thus created terms that reflected that refinement. To argue that the Inuit are able to perceive these different types of snow and ice in a fundamentally different way than the SAE can, however, is debatable.

Main topic: controversy and confusion around Sapir-Whorf hypothesis, i.e., the structure of a language determines a native speaker's perception of the world.

Discussion of how it's a misnomer.

Specific example to illustrate: hundreds of Inuit words for snow.

Comments

The author wrote the passage to discuss the Sapir-Whorf hypothesis that a language determines a native speaker's perception of the world. They discuss the controversy surrounding this hypothesis, including inaccuracies in the name of the hypothesis. In the second paragraph, the author proceeds to focus on one often used example of the Inuit language that, in the author's opinion, fails to convincingly demonstrate that language affects perception. For example, the author doesn't seem to think there is any particularly strong evidence in the Inuit language that shows that the Inuit necessarily perceived snow and ice fundamentally differently than the SAE does.

Let's take a look at some of the detail-oriented questions that might be asked on a passage such as this one.

1. The passage suggests which of the following regarding a language's having a large number of words for a particular phenomenon?

(A) **It does not represent convincing evidence that the speakers of that language are capable of perceiving more variants of the phenomenon than the average person.**

(B) Speakers of that language will understand that phenomenon more fully than speakers of other less descriptive languages.

(C) It does not constitute a relevant source of evidence for any linguistic concept.

(D) Sapir used this construct as the primary source of support for his hypothesis.

(E) It is, according to the author of the passage, a rare occurrence in most languages.

You are told that although Inuits may have more words for ice and snow, it's debatable whether they are able to perceive snow and ice in a fundamentally different way from Standard Average Europeans. This description makes answer choice (A) a good match. You can also infer from the passage that even if a language has a large number of words for something, that does not mean that speakers of the language perceive more variants of that thing than those who speak a language with fewer words for that concept. **Therefore, (A) is the correct answer.**

With (B), there is no evidence suggesting that they will understand concepts more *fully*, so you can eliminate this answer choice.

(C) is somewhat tempting, but I don't think you can say that this characteristic of a language doesn't constitute a relevant source of evidence for *any* linguistic concept. That's too broad and extreme a statement, so you can eliminate (C) as well.

The passage does not support (D) or (E) directly or indirectly, so you can eliminate both.

2. Which of the following can be inferred from the passage regarding the Inuktitut language?

(A) It contains more words than any other language.

(B) Some supporters of linguistic relativity drew false conclusions from its sentence structure.

(C) It is limited in its ability to describe phenomena that do not occur in a cold climate.

(D) **Its users are less constrained in their formation of words than users of many languages.**

(E) It is spoken by all or most Inuit tribes.

There is nothing in the passage that allows you to infer (A), (B), or (C). (E) seems like it would be true and is therefore highly tempting, but you can't actually infer (E) from the information presented in the passage.

(D) is the correct answer. You are told that *Inuktitut, the language of the Inuit, is a highly plastic language, allowing for the formation of a near-infinite number of words*. The term *highly plastic* implies that it is more flexible than other languages, so you can infer that (D) is indeed true.

Solutions Continued

3. Which of the following can be inferred from the passage regarding the principle of linguistic relativity? Select all that apply.

[A] **It has generated disagreement among linguists.**
[B] For a time, it was widely accepted as valid.
[C] **Support for it has been based on a dubious understanding of certain linguistic structures.**

You know from the passage that linguistic relativity is another term for the Sapir-Whorf hypothesis. Let's see which of the answer choices you can infer:

[A] You know from the first sentence that the Sapir-Whorf hypothesis has generated controversy, so you can infer that linguistic relativity has generated disagreement among linguists and **select [A]**.

You have no information that tells you that the principle was widely accepted, so you cannot select [B].

Finally, you have support for (C) in the second sentence of the second paragraph, *Many contemporary linguists believe this connection to be based on a fundamental misunderstanding of Inuit language structure*, **so you can select [C] as well**.

Here's one more question for this passage, a meaning in context, which I discussed in the last chapter.

4. In the context in which it appears, "well-trodden" most nearly means which of the following?

(A) Inappropriate
(B) Hackneyed
(C) Convincing
(D) Controversial
(E) Durable

Here, the best match for *well-trodden* is *hackneyed*, which means overused and unoriginal. You know that the anecdote is famous, that *many* linguists discuss and study it, and that the author doesn't necessarily have a positive opinion of it. **Therefore, *hackneyed* fits this context well**.

Answer choice (E), *durable*, is a tempting answer choice, but its tone does not match *well-trodden* as well as choice (B) does. The emphasis in the passage is on the overuse of the snow example rather than on the snow example's being strong enough to last a long time.

Practice Passage 2

2 Questions

Given the epic scale of the Lone Star State, it should come as no surprise that many of Texas's most prominent works of art are monumental extensions of the landscape itself. One of the most famous examples of such artwork is Cadillac Ranch, a public art installation located near the Panhandle town of Amarillo. Cadillac Ranch was installed in 1974 by Chip Lord, Doug Michels, and Hudson Marquez, members of the San Francisco Ant Farm art collective. The installation, funded by eccentric Amarillo millionaire Stanley Marsh III, consists of ten Cadillacs (now heavily graffitied by decades of visitors) buried nose-first in an unassuming cow pasture just off of Interstate 40. From a distance, the cars rising out of the earth appear both out of place and inevitable: a modern-day High Plains Stonehenge. Marsh backed the Ant Farm's project because he loved to confuse and provoke the denizens of his small Texas town, but Cadillac Ranch has become a much-loved Panhandle icon.

1. According to the passage, the Cadillac Ranch

(A) was intended by the artists who created it to be provocative.
(B) has won acclaim throughout the art world.
(C) has changed in appearance since its creation.
(D) remains a controversial cultural monument.
(E) is derived from a similar cultural icon.

2. According to the passage, which of the following is the most representative example of Texas art?

(A) An immersive light installation inside a large, windowless warehouse in Houston
(B) A 12-inch-by-12-inch black and white photograph of the Chisos Mountain Range located in a gallery in Lubbock
(C) A sculpture consisting of a series of enormous concrete cubes installed in the desert outside Marfa
(D) A life-sized sculpture of Sam Houston located in a public park in Austin
(E) A miniature replica of the Alamo in a hotel lobby in San Antonio

Practice Passage 2 Solutions

Given the epic scale of the Lone Star State, it should come as no surprise that many of Texas's most prominent works of art are monumental extensions of the landscape itself. One of the most famous examples of such artwork is Cadillac Ranch, a public art installation located near the Panhandle town of Amarillo. Cadillac Ranch was installed in 1974 by Chip Lord, Doug Michels, and Hudson Marquez, members of the San Francisco Ant Farm art collective. The installation, funded by eccentric Amarillo millionaire Stanley Marsh III, consists of ten Cadillacs (now heavily graffitied by decades of visitors) buried nose-first in an unassuming cow pasture just off of Interstate 40. From a distance, the cars rising out of the earth appear both out of place and inevitable: a modern-day High Plains Stonehenge. Marsh backed the Ant Farm's project because he loved to confuse and provoke the denizens of his small Texas town, but Cadillac Ranch has become a much-loved Panhandle icon.

Background: many of Texas's most prominent works of art are extensions of the landscape.

Main topic: Cadillac Ranch, details.

Comments

The author wrote this passage to discuss Cadillac Ranch. In terms of structure, you have background information about Texas art, the main point of the passage, and further details about Cadillac Ranch.

1. According to the passage, the Cadillac Ranch

(A) was intended by the artists who created it to be provocative.
(B) has won acclaim throughout the art world.
(C) **has changed in appearance since its creation.**
(D) remains a controversial cultural monument.
(E) is derived from a similar cultural icon.

You want to find an answer that is explicitly discussed in the passage.

(A) is an extremely attractive answer because you are told that *Marsh backed the Ant Farm's project because he loved to confuse and provoke the denizens of his small Texas town*, so let's leave it for now.

(B) is also attractive because you know Cadillac Ranch is very prominent and much-loved—let's leave (B) as well.

You know for certain that answer choice (C) is true because you are told that the Cadillacs have been graffitied. Therefore, (C) must be the correct answer, and there must be something wrong with both (A) and (B).

(D) is an easier answer choice to eliminate—nothing in the passage tells you explicitly that Cadillac Ranch ever was or is now a controversial cultural monument, so you can eliminate (D).

Finally, you don't have any information that tells you that Cadillac Ranch was derived from a similar icon (just that other prominent works are also extensions of the landscape), so you can eliminate (E) as well.

Returning to (A), note that the passage claims that the project's funder, eccentric millionaire Marsh, wanted to be provocative. It says nothing about the intentions of the artists themselves, so you can eliminate this choice.

With (B), being *prominent* and *much-loved* is not the same as winning acclaim in the art world, so you can eliminate (B) as well.

(C) is the correct answer.

Solutions Continued

2. According to the passage, which of the following is the most representative example of Texas art?

(A) An immersive light installation inside a large, windowless warehouse in Houston

(B) A 12-inch-by-12-inch black and white photograph of the Chisos Mountain Range located in a gallery in Lubbock

(C) **A sculpture consisting of a series of enormous concrete cubes installed in the desert outside Marfa**

(D) A life-sized sculpture of Sam Houston located in a public park in Austin

(E) A miniature replica of the Alamo in a hotel lobby in San Antonio

Although this is a question that requires you to stay close to the passage, it's one that also requires you to use some imagination in thinking about how different scenarios might fit your criteria.

The most important description of Texas art comes right at the beginning: *monumental extensions of the landscape itself*. Therefore, you want something monumental, and you want something that is an extension of the landscape; **the only answer choice that offers this combination of features is answer choice (C), which is correct**.

14
VERBAL REASONING

Reading Comprehension 4

In this lesson, I will focus on the handful of reading comprehension questions that, in addition to testing your reading ability, test your reasoning skills. These questions require you to evaluate arguments, reconcile discrepancies, or reach conclusions based on given information. Most of these questions will be presented individually and will accompany short passages on the exam, but sometimes, as you've seen in previous examples, they can be grouped with other questions in reference to longer passages. I'll start the discussion with question types that relate to arguments and then move on to discuss other question types.

Argument-Based Questions

There are several different types of reading comprehension questions that require you to evaluate arguments presented in short passages. These include:

- Role played by the bolded questions
- Strengthen and weaken the argument questions
- Answer a key question questions
- Assumption questions
- Required assumption questions

Before I discuss each question type in detail, let's break down exactly what an argument is.

The Anatomy of an Argument

The principal components of any argument are the main point being made and the support for that main point.

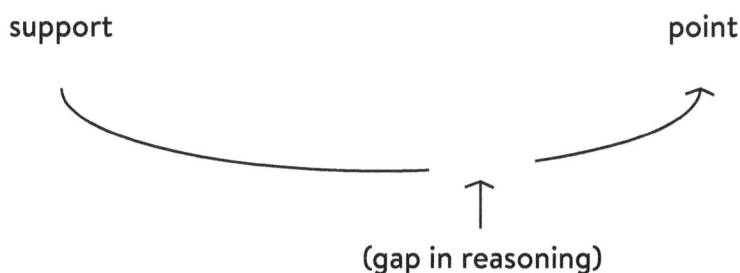

support   point

(gap in reasoning)

When you are asked to evaluate reasoning, your task is (1) to identify and focus on this argument and (2) to critically analyze the relationship between the support and the conclusion. More specifically, you want to think about the gap that exists between the support presented and the conclusion reached. Depending on the task the question stem presents, you can then strengthen the argument by filling the gap, weaken the argument by exposing the gap, and so on.

The other parts of an argument-based passage generally exist in relation to the argument and can be described in terms of the argument as support, conclusion, background information, or opinions or statements that counter the argument. For example, role played by the bolded questions, which you'll examine more closely later, test your ability to discern how these different components of a passage relate to one another.

Here are a couple of examples of short passages with basic arguments contained within them. Let's practice breaking them down.

In recent years, an increasing number of people have been switching to electronic media, such as computers and tablet devices, as their primary means of getting news. Although proponents of electronic media claim that it increases public access to information, the actual consequence of this evolution is that the public knows less about the news. Studies show that people retain more of what they read when they read on the standard gray paper that newspapers are printed on, as opposed to when they read on an electronic device.

Here, the author's main point is that because of the recent switch from print to electronic media, the public knows less about the news.

The reasoning used is that studies show that people retain more of what they read when they read on the standard gray paper that newspapers are printed on than when they read on an electronic device.

Studies show people retain more when they read on a standard gray paper rather than an electronic device	→	Evolutionary switch to electronic media means public knows less about the news

If any question asks you to think critically about the reasoning, such as how you can weaken or strengthen the argument or what assumptions are being made or required, you want to focus on this relationship between the support and the conclusion. You must think about why the support given may not completely justify the conclusion reached.

In this case, just because people retain more when reading on gray paper doesn't mean printed newspaper readers are automatically better informed. There could be countless reasons that could limit how printed newspapers affect public awareness, such as the small type, the inconvenience of trying to find articles and folding large pages, or the cost of paper newspapers. Moreover, there is a logical distinction between the number of people within a population who have access to information and how well that information is retained.

The other parts of the passage can also be considered in terms of the argument. The introductory sentence gives you relevant background information, and the clause that begins the second sentence, *While proponents of electronic media claim that it increases public access to information*, serves as a counterargument to the main claim.

Here is another example:

For the past six months, researchers have kept statistics on the surgery time for prostatectomies performed through traditional means and through a new procedure that uses robotics. The study revealed that surgeries using robotics took an average of 43 minutes, whereas traditional surgeries took an average of over 70 minutes. The study involved a variety of doctors and hospitals that were sufficient to ensure that individual surgical skills and access to specialized medical equipment were not factors in the study outcome. The researchers concluded that it is faster, in general, to perform prostatectomies robotically than it is to perform them using traditional means.

Here, the researchers' conclusion is that, in general, it is faster to perform prostatectomies robotically than it is to perform them using traditional means.

The reasoning for this is a *study revealed that surgeries using robotics took an average of 43 minutes, whereas traditional surgeries took an average of over 70 minutes.*

study revealed that surgeries using robotics took an average of 43 minutes, whereas traditional surgeries took an average of over 70 minutes	→	faster to perform prostatectomies robotically than it is to perform them using traditional means

Again, if you're asked to think critically about the reasoning, you want to focus on this relationship, and consider why the support might not guarantee the conclusion.

For example, perhaps the robotic technique is used only to perform easier prostatectomies, which are also much faster to perform. If all the traditional prostatectomies in the study were all the more challenging prostatectomies, this would skew the average times so that robotic surgeries *seem* to be faster. You certainly don't need to go into this level of detail in the moment, but again, **what's most important is that you (1) focus on the relationship between the support and the conclusion and (2) think critically about why the support given may not guarantee that conclusion reached.**

In terms of the rest of the passage, you can think of the first part as providing background: *For the past six months, researchers have kept statistics on the surgery time for prostatectomies performed through traditional means and through a new procedure that uses robotics.* The middle part, *The study involved a variety of doctors and hospitals sufficient to ensure that individual surgical skills and access to specialized medical equipment were not factors in the study outcome*, provides support for the support and counters some potential counterarguments.

I'll revisit this passage as part of a practice problem later in this lesson.

Question Types

Now, I'll briefly discuss the different types of argument-based questions that might appear on the exam. Below are sample versions of how they might be worded.

Role Played by the Bolded

- What purpose do the **two boldface sentences** serve in the passage?
- In the argument above, which of the following roles do the **two portions in boldface** play?

For these questions, two parts of the passage will be bolded, and the stem will ask you what role or purpose the bolded parts play in the passage as a whole. Almost always, these questions are presented with just one correct answer. As you might expect, tempting wrong answer choices will accurately describe the role played by one of the bolded components but not the other. Similarly, correct answer choices that are designed to appear less attractive will describe the roles played in unexpected ways.

So, as always, you want to be vigilant about your problem-solving process.

1. You need to read the text and decide for yourself what roles the bolded parts play and what you should expect to see in the correct answer choice.

2. Go through the answer choices and, in the first round, keep the ones that seem plausibly correct (or at least close to what you were looking for), and eliminate the ones you can recognize as having clearly identifiable flaws.

3. Left with answer choices that survived your elimination process, evaluate each characteristic carefully, checking details against one another and against the text as necessary, again trying to find reasons to eliminate incorrect answer choices until you feel comfortable that the one answer remaining is the best available choice.

Of course, if you are presented with a rare role played by the bolded question in which you are to select all the answers that apply, you would want to approach the question differently. In this case, you would evaluate each answer choice separately to see how well it represents the situation.

Sample Question

The makers of Celeste oatmeal cookies claim that their cookies are more healthful than those made by Ben's Oatmeal Cookie Company. **The makers of Celeste cite the use of natural ingredients and whole grains as two primary factors in their cookies' superior healthfulness.** However, their cookies have more sugar and salt than cookies created by Ben's, and most Americans consider both ingredients to be very unhealthful. **Therefore, the makers of Celeste oatmeal cookies are making false claims.**

In the argument above, which of the following roles do the two portions in boldface play?

(A) The first contains a claim made by the argument in support of a certain position; the second is that position.

(B) The first contains a claim made in support of a certain position; the second is an opposing position.

(C) The first contains the position that the argument is intended to refute, and the second is support for an opposing position.

(D) The first is the position that the argument is intended to refute; the second is an opposing position.

(E) The first contains a concession by the argument to a position that it is intended to refute; the second is support for the opposite of that position.

Solution

In the argument, the author's main point is that the makers of Celeste oatmeal cookies are making false claims, and the main reasoning for this is that *their cookies have more sugar and salt than cookies created by Ben's, and most Americans consider both ingredients to be very unhealthful.*

The first sentence of the passage—*The makers of Celeste oatmeal cookies claim that their cookies are more healthful than those made by Ben's Oatmeal Cookie Company*—is the claim that the argument is designed to go against or counter, while the second sentence—*The makers of Celeste cite the use of natural ingredients and whole grains as two primary factors in their cookies' superior healthfulness*—supports that claim.

In terms of the two bolded sentences in the question, you know that the first serves as support for the claim that the argument is meant to counter, and the second is the author's main point.

Let's evaluate the answer choices to see which one best represents the roles played.

(A) According to answer choice (A), the first bolded sentence serves to support the second bolded sentence, which isn't the case. You can eliminate this answer choice.

(B) This answer choice may not be worded in the way that you may have expected it to be, but it does seem accurate in that the first bolded sentence supports one position, and the second bolded sentence is another position, so let's leave it for now.

(C) This answer choice represents the first bolded sentence as the position the argument is meant to refute, and the second as support for the opposing position, both of which are inaccurate, so you can eliminate (C).

(D) This answer choice also represents the first bolded sentence as the position the argument is meant to refute, so you can eliminate it as well.

(E) For this answer, perhaps saying the first part is a concession might work, but it's certainly not accurate to represent the second bolded sentence as support, so you can eliminate this answer choice.

(B) is the only answer that you did not eliminate, and it accurately represents the role played by the two bolded sentences. The first bolded sentence contains support for the position that Celeste oatmeal cookies are more healthful, and the second bolded sentence represents an opposing position, which is that the makers are making false claims.

Assumption Questions

Now let's quickly discuss the next four question types: **Basic assumption, answer a key question, sufficient assumption,** and **required assumption.** These are different ways of asking you to think about the logical gap between the author's point or claim and the support the author provides. The gap represents something the author is assuming or taking for granted rather than explicitly stating in the text.

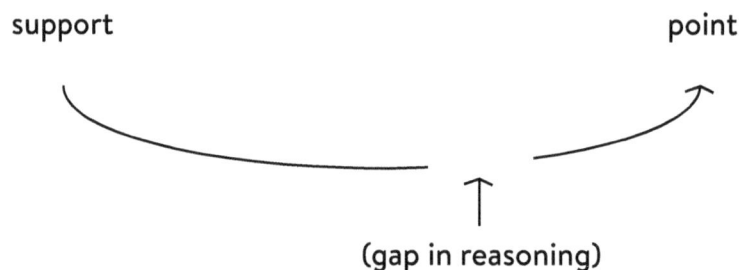

(gap in reasoning)

Basic Assumption

- The argument above **assumes** which of the following?
- The claim of the union leader **presupposes** which of the following?

You can think of a **basic assumption** as a general description of the gap in the argument's reasoning.

Answer a Key Question

- Which of the **following pieces of information would be most useful** in determining whether the conclusion is valid?
- Which of the **following would be most important to determine** before deciding whether the company should offer bonuses to new employees?

An **answer a key question** question will also serve the same function of addressing that uncertainty and filling in that gap.

Sufficient Assumption

- The conclusion drawn above **follows logically if which of the following is assumed**?
- **Which of the following, if assumed**, would allow the conclusion above to be **properly drawn**?

A **sufficient assumption** question is one that takes things one step further. Notice the language used in the question stem: the conclusion drawn above *follows logically*, would allow the conclusion above to be *properly drawn*. When you see such wording in the question stem, you know that you need an answer choice that is sufficient, or enough, to guarantee that the conclusion is logically valid.

Required Assumption

- The proponent's conclusion **depends on which of the following assumptions**?
- The argument above **relies on which of the following assumptions**?

When the question stem changes from asking for a basic or sufficient assumption to a **required assumption** by including a term or phrase such as *required* or *depends upon,* it changes your task a bit. Instead of thinking about what might fill the gap that exists between the support and conclusion, you should figure out what needs to be true in order to fill the gap between the support and conclusion; that is, instead of thinking about what is important, these questions ask you to think about what is required.

As an analogy, it can be helpful to think about your college admissions process: there were certain criteria that were important to admissions, such as your GPA, and certain criteria required, such as that you graduated from high school. **Keep in mind that when you see terminology that asks for a required assumption, you should switch your focus from seeking an assumption that is *important* for filling your gap to one that is *necessary*.**

Sample Question

For the past six months, researchers have kept statistics on the surgery time for prostatectomies performed through traditional means and through a new procedure that uses robotics. The study revealed that surgeries using robotics took an average of 43 minutes, whereas traditional surgeries took an average of over 70 minutes. The study involved a variety of doctors and hospitals that were sufficient to ensure that individual surgical skills and access to specialized medical equipment were not factors in the study outcome. The researchers concluded that it is faster, in general, to perform prostatectomies robotically than it is to perform them using traditional means.

Which of the following pieces of information would be most useful in determining whether the researchers' conclusion is valid?

(A) Are there significant differences in recovery time between those who have prostatectomies performed robotically and those who have prostatectomies performed through traditional means, and, if so, which method offers advantages?

(B) Depending on the criteria used to determine a successful outcome, are there significant differences between success rates between prostatectomies performed robotically and those performed through traditional methods, and if so, which method offers advantages?

(C) Are there any significant differences between the types of prostatectomies performed robotically and those performed through traditional methods that would affect the average time it takes to perform the surgeries using these methods?

(D) Do patients prefer one surgery method over the other, and if so, should patient preferences play a part in future decision-making regarding which surgeries are offered?

(E) Was the range and the standard deviation for how long surgeries performed robotically greater than the range and the standard deviation for how long surgeries performed through traditional methods took?

Solution

Our task here is to consider why the support of the argument presented might not guarantee the conclusion. As I mentioned before, the unspoken assumption—which is tied to what the author is failing to consider—is that there were potentially different types of prostatectomies performed robotically and through traditional means. It thus follows that the average speeds wouldn't give you an indication of one mode being *faster* than the other.

To illustrate this reasoning with a simple analogy, imagine you ride your bike to errands close by, and you drive to ones farther away. On average, it takes you 20 minutes to ride your bike to errands and 30 minutes to drive to errands. It would be a mistake to conclude from this information that you can perform errands faster on a bike than you can in a car.

In the same way, if you imagine that robotic technology has developed only to the point of performing basic prostatectomies and that all advanced ones need to be performed through traditional means, it would make sense that a recorded shorter average duration wouldn't necessarily indicate a faster pace.

Should you expect to be able to think of all this in the moment? It's fantastic when you can, but even when you can't, what's most important is to focus on the support/conclusion relationship and to think about it critically: why doesn't the support justify the conclusion? Remember, the right answer to this batch of question types will address this gap in one way or another, so you want to put your focus on the support/conclusion relationship.

For this particular question, your task is to figure out which piece of information would be most useful in determining whether the researcher's conclusion is valid. Another way to think about this is to identify which piece of information helps you evaluate whether the support justifies the conclusion. The answer to the question in the right answer choice will address the gap in the argument.

Let's evaluate each of the answer choices.

(A) Notice that (A) is about recovery time, which is not what the author's conclusion is about, so you can eliminate this answer choice.

(B) Similarly, (B) is about success rates, which, while certainly important to patients, are not relevant to the author's particular argument, which is about the time it takes to complete the surgery, so you can eliminate (B).

(C) This answer choice addresses the gap discussed earlier and is likely correct. Let's leave it for now.

(D) If patient preferences were somehow tied into average times, this could be an attractive answer choice, but as is, it doesn't directly relate to the amount of time the surgery takes, so you can eliminate (D) as well.

(E) is somewhat tempting in that it relates to the pace of surgery; however, neither the range of times nor the standard deviation affects the connection the author makes between average surgery times and pace, so you can eliminate (E) as well.

Returning to (C), if you were to find out that there were significant differences in the type of prostatectomies that affected average times, that would certainly weaken the author's reasoning. And if you were to find out that there were not significant differences, that would strengthen the author's reasoning. Therefore, the answer to (C) would be useful in determining whether the author's conclusion is valid, so **(C) is the correct answer**.

Sample Question

A primatologist observing a chimpanzee community from a distance noticed chimpanzees carrying objects to neighboring chimpanzee communities and inferred that the chimpanzees were bringing food to their neighbors. Subsequent observation from a closer vantage point, however, revealed that these chimpanzees were emptying their own community's dumping site. Thus, the primatologist was wrong.

The conclusion follows logically if which one of the following is assumed?

(A) Chimpanzee societies do not interact in all the same ways that human societies interact.
(B) There is only weak evidence for the view that chimpanzees have the capacity to make use of objects as gifts.
(C) The chimpanzees to whom the articles were brought never carried the objects into their own communities.
(D) Chimpanzee dumping sites do not contain objects consisting of edible food.
(E) The primatologist cited retracted his conclusion when it was determined that the objects the chimpanzees carried came from their dumping site.

<u>Solution</u>

For this question, you're asked to find an answer that, if assumed, enables the conclusion to follow logically. What that means is that the right answer must completely fill whatever reasoning gaps exist in the original argument to guarantee that the conclusion can logically be drawn from the argument's reasoning.

In the original argument, a primatologist inferred that chimpanzees were bringing food to their neighbors, and the author's conclusion is that the primatologist was wrong. **Therefore, the conclusion you want to support is that the chimpanzees were NOT bringing food to their neighbors**.

What reasoning does the author use? The fact that the chimpanzees were emptying their own dumping sites. Here's the argument isolated from the passage:

Chimpanzees were emptying their own dumping sites → **They were not bringing food to their neighbors**

Again, the question stem sets up a very specific task, which is that you need a choice that leads you logically all the way from the support to the conclusion.

If you look at the answer choices with those factors in mind, (A), (B), and (E) are easy to eliminate quickly because they do not directly address the issue of bringing food to neighbors.

(C) is somewhat tempting, but a careful reading shows that it's about the chimpanzees who receive the food, as opposed to the ones who bring it, and that's one of the reasons you can eliminate (C).

Notice that if (D) is true and you plug it in between the support and the conclusion, it enables the conclusion to follow logically. If the chimpanzees were emptying their dumping grounds and these dumping grounds don't have any food, then it follows logically that they weren't bringing food.

(D) is correct.

Sample Question

On a certain day, five scheduled surgeries at Metropolitan Hospital were canceled. Most often, when a surgical procedure is canceled at this hospital, the cause is a malfunction of the anesthesiology equipment that was to be used for that procedure. However, since it is unlikely that this hospital would have mechanical problems with more than one or two anesthesiology devices on a single day, some of the five cancellations were probably due to something else.

The argument depends on which of the following assumptions?

Ⓐ Metropolitan Hospital has fewer problems with its anesthesiology equipment than do other hospitals of a similar size.
Ⓑ Each of the canceled procedures would have been longer than the average surgery at Metropolitan Hospital.
Ⓒ More than one or two anesthesiology devices were scheduled to be used for the five canceled surgeries.
Ⓓ Metropolitan Hospital had never before canceled more than one or two scheduled surgeries on a single day.
Ⓔ All of the anesthesiology equipment scheduled for the canceled surgeries is located in the same operating room.

Solution

The question stem asks you to find an assumption upon which the argument depends. This means that you are looking for an answer that needs to be true in order for the argument to be reasonable.

In the argument, you're told that the hospital had five cancellations in a single day, and that since it's unlikely that the hospital would have mechanical problems with more than one or two devices, the cancellations were probably due to something else.

5 cancellations + unlikely mechanical problems with more than 1 or 2 devices	→	cancellations were probably due to something else

What is the author assuming in making this argument, and which of the answer choices needs to be true for the argument to be valid?

It seems the author is assuming that the surgeries must have been using different devices and couldn't have been using just one or two.

Let's evaluate the answer choices.

If you think through the lens of what needs to be true for the argument to work, you can quickly eliminate (A), (B), (D), and (E), none of which needs to be true for the argument to be valid.

However, (C) does need to be true for the argument to be valid, and one way for you to test this premise is to imagine if (C) weren't true: if just one or two devices were scheduled to be used, the support/conclusion relationship would be destroyed. **(C) is the correct answer**.

Strengthen the Argument

- Which of the following, if true, **most strongly supports** the claim made about the recreation center?
- Each of the following, if true, would **strengthen** the conclusion above EXCEPT

Weaken the Argument

- Which of the following, if true, **casts the most doubt** on the validity of the argument above?
- Which of the following, if true, would **most seriously weaken** the conclusion drawn above?

For **strengthen** or **weaken** questions, you are expected to understand the relationship between the support and the conclusion and identify the reasoning gap that exists between the two. From there, your task is to determine how the answer choices affect that relationship.

If you have a clear understanding of the argument, you'll find most of the time that you can eliminate some answer choices because they do not directly affect the argument. Then, you can eliminate the remaining incorrect answer choices because they don't affect the argument in the way the question asks.

Keep in mind that you won't need to gauge different degrees of weakening or strengthening. Even if the question stem asks which answer choice will *most* weaken or *most* strengthen the argument, you will never have to compare how much the answers strengthen or weaken the argument relative to one another. Instead, your focus should always be on finding one answer choice that strengthens or weakens.

You also want to remember that you don't need to question the validity of the answer choices or consider how realistic or practical they might be. You are asked to assume that the answers are true, so you should work from there.

Sample Question

Although video game sales have consistently increased over the past three years, a reversal of this trend is predicted for the very near future. Historically, over three quarters of video games sold have been purchased by people from 13 to 16 years of age, and the number of people in this age group is expected to decline steadily over the next 10 years.

Which of the following, if true, most strongly supports the prediction made about video game sales in the near future?

(A) More and more customers are choosing to purchase their games online, which is leading to the closure of many of the traditional physical stores where customers used to purchase games.
(B) Studies show that people who play video games today are more likely to purchase and play a greater variety of video games than people who played video games a generation ago.
(C) It is highly unlikely that the same games that are bestselling today will continue to be bestselling over the next 10 years.
(D) It is highly unlikely that the demographics related to the ages of video game buyers will change over the next 10 years.
(E) Customers who purchase games often sell them after playing them, so video game manufacturers should expect sales to decrease over time once a game is released.

Solution

We're asked to select the answer choice that, if true, most strongly supports the prediction made about video game sales in the near future.

This prediction is that the trend of consistently increasing video game sales is likely to reverse in the near future.

What's the reasoning given? The population of people in the age group that purchases the majority of video games will decrease over the next 10 years.

Before moving on to the answers, let's pause and focus on the support/conclusion relationship. Be sure to think carefully and critically about why the support given might not guarantee the conclusion reached.

In this case, perhaps it could be that people of different age groups might become more interested in playing video games and offset this particular shrinking segment of the population. Or, perhaps an increase in the number of games purchased per individual would be great enough to offset any population changes. The shrinking of that one particular segment of potential buyers isn't enough, without knowing more, to reach such a broad conclusion about actual buyers as a whole.

Of course, there could certainly be other factors involved, but having carefully considered gaps in the author's reasoning and with your focus firmly on the author's specific conclusion, you're in an optimal position to evaluate answer choices.

Let's see which one, if you assume it to be true, would help address the reasoning issues you saw in the argument and strengthen the prediction that was made.

(A) Without further information, whether customers purchase games online or in stores and whether stores close or stay open will have no direct bearing on whether sales will continue to trend upward or not, so (A) does not strengthen the conclusion. You can eliminate it.

(B) compares the present to the past, as opposed to comparing the future to the present, and it's tough to see how this answer choice could be used to support a claim of decreasing game sales. You can eliminate (B) as well.

(C) pertains to specific games, whereas the passage is about the industry as a whole. Therefore, without further information, details about specific games will not have any direct bearing on a general claim about the industry as a whole, so you can eliminate (C).

If true, (D) strengthens the relationship between the support given and the conclusion reached. In making his initial argument, the author assumed that the age demographics of the people who bought the most video games wouldn't be changing. Therefore, he said that since the population of those who purchase most video games will be shrinking, the number of video games purchased will likely shrink as well.

What (D) tells you is that the demographics as they pertain to age likely will not change. Again, if that's true, as you are to assume, it certainly strengthens the author's reasoning. (D) definitely seems correct, so let's leave it for now.

(E) explains why sales of one game could be expected to decrease over time, but without more information, it doesn't explain why sales in the entire industry would be expected to decrease over time, so you can eliminate this answer choice as well.

You are thus able to eliminate the four wrong answer choices and see why **(D) is indeed the correct answer**.

Responds By

- Birdy **responds** to Wilden's statement **by** …

This is a rare question type, and I've included it here because it is related to argument-based questions. In these questions, one person makes an argument, and another person responds. The question then asks what sort of argumentative strategy the respondent uses.

For these questions, you want to follow the strategy of breaking down the initial argument in terms of the author's conclusion, the support for the conclusion, and the gap that exists between the two. You then consider how the response relates to your understanding of the argument and find the answer choice that best matches.

Resolve a Discrepancy or Paradox

- Which of the following, if true, best **resolves the paradox** in the above passage?
- Which of the following pieces of evidence, if true, would provide the best explanation for the **apparent discrepancy**?

These questions present you with two ideas or statements that could be seen, at least initially, as going against each other. Your job is to identify one answer choice that could explain how these two ideas or statements could both be true at the same time.

One helpful tool for thinking about these questions is to ask yourself the question, "How come?" as in, "How come my family tells me they love my cooking but never wants seconds?" Each stimulus will have a paradox or discrepancy that can be phrased in such terms, and the more specific your understanding of the paradox, the easier it will be to see which answer choice can help explain the apparent paradox and which answer choices have no relevance to it.

Sample Question

Janet claims to have sent Terry a fax, and yet Janet does not own or have access to a fax machine.

Which of the following, if true, most helps to resolve the apparent discrepancy described above?

(A) Fax machines were once far more important to businesses than they are now.
(B) Janet has the capacity to send a fax through her computer without the aid of a fax machine.
(C) Janet used to own a fax machine, but she gave it to her sister.
(D) A day earlier, Janet said she had left a phone message.
(E) Most faxes are sent through fax machines.

Solution

How could Janet have sent a fax without access to a fax machine? **The only answer that attempts to answer that question is the correct answer: answer choice (B).** (A), (C), and (E) shed no light on this particular situation, and (D) has nothing to do with faxing. If (B) is true, it explains how Janet could have sent a fax even though she doesn't own or have access to a fax machine.

Inference and Conclusion Questions

- Which of the **following conclusions can be properly drawn** from the statements above?
- If the above statements are true, **which of the following inferences** would they support?
- Which of the **following most logically completes** the argument?

Inference and **conclusion** questions ask you which of the five answer choices must be true or can most reasonably be concluded to be correct based on the information provided. These overlap with and function very much like the detail questions in the previous chapter in both the language used in the question stem and the fact that you need right answers that don't stray from the given text. What's a bit different about individual inference and conclusion questions about short passages is that they often ask you to find answers that either summarize the passage or reach some sort of conclusion to a chain of reasoning. In other words, they ask you to find an answer that *most logically completes the argument* or something similar.

As always, you want to go through a meticulous process of eliminating incorrect answers and verifying all elements of the correct answer choice.

Sample Question

Art historians assert that one of the most challenging problems they regularly face is the attribution of artworks to particular creators, especially in the case of artworks created before the 17th century. Conflicting attributions from various commonly accepted historical sources complicate their task. When multiple different attributions exist from separate historical sources, art historians should try to determine which of these historical sources was deemed most reliable at the time the attribution was made and eliminate from consideration any and all other historical sources. Often, however, even after such attempts, there may still be two or more different attributions considered equally reliable at the time they were originally made. In such situations, experts try, occasionally without success, to use other means to establish an accurate attribution without reference to conflicting sources.

Which of the following inferences is most strongly supported by the information above?

(A) There is no way to establish a plausible attribution for most artworks created before the 17th century.

(B) There is no conclusive attribution for at least some artworks created before the 17th century for which art historians have tried to find the creator.

(C) Establishing an accurate attribution for any artwork created before the 17th century entails determining which of several attributions is the most reliable.

(D) Trying to determine who created a work of art without reference to pre-existing sources is an ineffective method of establishing an accurate attribution.

(E) The most effective way to determine the correct attribution of an artwork created before the 17th century is to eliminate as many historical sources of attribution as possible.

Solution

Here, your task is to identify an answer that is most supported by the information provided in the passage.

The passage has to do with the challenge of attributing certain historical works of art to their rightful creators, and it describes the process that historians undergo in trying to make an accurate assessment.

Let's see which of the answers is most supported by what you've been told.

(A) is far too strong in its language—the passage doesn't inform you that there is *no way* to plausibly establish attribution for *most* artworks, and you can eliminate this choice.

(B) definitely has support in the final sentence, *occasionally without success*—let's leave it for now.

(C), like (A), is too absolute in its language; the passage doesn't state this, and it could certainly be true that some works of art are unquestionably attributed to a single artist. You can eliminate (C) as well.

(D) is too general a statement. The passage describes how to determine attribution in a specific situation, not attribution in general, and it doesn't support this claim, so you can eliminate (D) as well.

Finally, the passage states that one ought to try to eliminate sources other than the most reliable, not eliminate all sources altogether, so you can eliminate (E) as well.

(B) was the only attractive answer, and it's a classic right answer to a most-supported question. It's not directly relevant to the author's main point, but it is justifiable based on the given text. You are told that art historians sometimes try without success, meaning that there must be no conclusive attribution for at least some artworks.

(B) is the correct answer.

Practice Questions

1. The collection of taxes is one of the fundamental responsibilities of a democratic government. Without tax revenue, the necessary protections and services that allow a body politic to flourish cannot be funded. Yet, in most countries, taxes are not taken directly from individuals; rather, citizens voluntarily contribute taxes, albeit under the threat of penalty. A complex system of taxation featuring a dizzying array of tax rates and exemptions gives individuals an incentive to avoid paying their full tax burdens. When individuals do not pay what they owe, the system breaks down, leading to a vicious cycle that engenders greater and greater levels of tax evasion. A simple tax system is therefore necessary for the citizens of a democracy to thrive.

Which of the following is an assumption upon which this argument relies?

Ⓐ Some citizens will avoid paying taxes if they have an incentive to do so.
Ⓑ There is an optimal tax rate that can ensure nearly full compliance with tax laws.
Ⓒ The simpler the tax system, the stronger a country's economy.
Ⓓ Citizens' sole motivation to pay taxes is the threat of penalty.
Ⓔ Tax compliance is the clearest measure of a country's prosperity.

2. An unnamed philosopher writing in the fifth century BCE tells the story of Rana, an island where an ancient people famous for producing textiles made from extremely fine wool flourished before being destroyed by a series of devastating earthquakes. It has traditionally been assumed that **Rana was nothing more than a product of the philosopher's imagination**. However, archaeologists now believe that seismic activity razed a small but prosperous civilization on an island southeast of Italy around the time when Rana was supposedly destroyed. Because this island also had an unusually large population of sheep prized for their wool, some scholars now contend that the island was the same Rana described by the philosopher. Yet, the fact remains that historians writing before the fifth century BCE never mention a Rana or a lost civilization similar to it. Since they certainly would have written of such a civilization if it had existed, **the traditional estimation of the Rana story is correct**.

In this argument, the two highlighted excerpts play which of the following roles?

Ⓐ The first is a position that the author repudiates, while the second is a conclusion that the author draws to justify that repudiation.
Ⓑ The first is a point of view that the author evaluates; the second provides evidence to strengthen the author's assessment of that position.
Ⓒ The first is a point of view that the author considers, while the second states the author's ultimate conclusion concerning that position.
Ⓓ The first presents evidence that supports the author's perspective, while the second outlines that perspective.
Ⓔ The first represents the author's position, while the second presents the author's conclusion concerning a separate position.

3. Alaskan homeowners often weatherize their homes by sealing gaps that can cause drafts and adding insulation. Until recently, many Alaskans used a popular form of insulation that releases isocyanate, a chemical that can cause breathing problems, skin allergies, and even cancer. Such insulation is now banned. Nevertheless, it is still possible to introduce dangerous levels of isocyanate into a home by insulating it, since restricting airflow in and out of the home increases the concentration of any chemical in the air of the house, and _____.

Which of the following most logically completes the argument?

(A) many common household items also release measurable quantities of isocyanate.

(B) any insulation installed before the ban has long since ceased releasing isocyanate.

(C) almost all of the fresh air that enters a weatherized house enters through HVAC vents.

(D) most other kinds of insulation present similar health risks if used inappropriately.

(E) the insulation that releases isocyanate was easy to install in an existing house.

4. Ancient records show that the government of Nenea imposed its first sales tax on bottles of wine. Despite the fact that the population remained steady, revenues from the Nenean wine tax fell precipitously over the first three years that the policy was in effect. Thus, a significant proportion of the Nenean population must have failed to pay taxes on the wine they purchased.

Which of the following statements, if true, would most seriously weaken the argument given?

(A) The amount of wine consumed by Nenean households increased after the government levied the tax.

(B) During the first two years after the tax went into effect, Nenean law required wine merchants to sell wine in bottles of the same size as before the tax was instituted.

(C) The penalty for failing to pay tax on a bottle of wine was not much greater than the price of the bottle of wine itself.

(D) The proportion of Nenean households that produced their own wine increased significantly after the government instated the tax.

(E) Even including tax, the total cost of a bottle of wine for a Nenean household declined steadily in the several years before and after the tax came into effect.

Practice Questions Continued

5. Professor Howard: Undergraduate students should not be permitted to fulfill the university's mathematics requirements by taking calculus. More than half of the undergraduate students at the university took calculus in high school. Therefore, calculus is not college-level mathematics, and for this reason alone, no student should be allowed to satisfy the requirements by taking it.

Professor Wing: According to your argument, undergraduate students shouldn't be allowed to fulfill the university's literature requirements by studying Shakespeare, since more than half of our undergraduate students have studied Shakespeare in high school. Yet, many students currently satisfy the literature requirement by taking the English department's popular Shakespeare survey course, and it would be ridiculous to prohibit them from doing so.

Professor Wing responds by:

(A) criticizing Howard's reasoning in order to question the value of the university's academic requirements.
(B) challenging Howard's conclusion by presenting a situation analogous to the one described by Howard and demonstrating its absurdity.
(C) reinterpreting the evidence presented by Howard in order to support an alternate conclusion.
(D) using statistical data to raise doubts about the validity of the university's approach to academic requirements.
(E) calling into question a justification for changing a policy by demonstrating that the change would be ineffective in solving the problem it seeks to address.

6. Throughout much of the professional world, formal performance evaluations are an important way of maintaining quality. To be effective, these performance reviews are conducted through realistic simulations of professional situations. During the evaluations, as they would in real-world professional practice, subjects are permitted to use the references they rely on in their work: physicians consult medical texts, lawyers refer to law books and case records, and engineers look up information in manuals. Therefore, students working to obtain degrees in these fields should have access to their textbooks whenever they take exams.

The argument above assumes which of the following?

(A) What is permitted in one type of evaluation should be permitted in another type of evaluation.
(B) Any evaluation that relies on realistic simulations of real-world conditions will be effective in maintaining quality.
(C) If students are not permitted to use textbooks when taking exams, the results of these exams are not valid assessments of their abilities.
(D) No examination during which students are not permitted to consult textbooks is similar to a professional evaluation in the field the students are studying.
(E) If exams in a given field are similar to professional evaluations in that same field, they will be effective in serving their intended purpose.

Practice Questions Solutions

1. The collection of taxes is one of the fundamental responsibilities of a democratic government. Without tax revenue, the necessary protections and services that allow a body politic to flourish cannot be funded. Yet, in most countries, taxes are not taken directly from individuals; rather, citizens voluntarily contribute taxes, albeit under the threat of penalty. A complex system of taxation featuring a dizzying array of tax rates and exemptions gives individuals an incentive to avoid paying their full tax burdens. When individuals do not pay what they owe, the system breaks down, leading to a vicious cycle that engenders greater and greater levels of tax evasion. A simple tax system is therefore necessary for the citizens of a democracy to thrive.

Which of the following is an assumption upon which this argument relies?

(A) **Some citizens will avoid paying taxes if they have an incentive to do so.**
(B) There is an optimal tax rate that can ensure nearly full compliance with tax laws.
(C) The simpler the tax system, the stronger a country's economy.
(D) Citizens' sole motivation to pay taxes is the threat of penalty.
(E) Tax compliance is the clearest measure of a country's prosperity.

This passage discusses general methods of tax collection and makes the claim that a simple tax system is necessary for citizens of a democracy to thrive. The question stem asks for an assumption upon which the argument relies, so you need an answer choice that must be true for the argument to be valid.

Let's take a look at the answer choices.

(A) seems like it needs to be true for the author's statements to make sense—let's leave it for now.

The author makes no claim or reference to (B), and (B) does not need to be true for the argument to work, so you can eliminate it.

(C) is somewhat tempting, but it overgeneralizes, and you don't know this to be true about all countries in general, so you can eliminate (C).

For (D), you don't know if citizens have other motivations, such as national pride or morality, that govern the paying of taxes, so you can eliminate answer choice (D).

Finally, you have no indication that (E) must be true for the argument to be valid—there could be many other better measures of a country's prosperity, and the argument would work just fine—so you can eliminate (E) as well.

(A) was the only attractive answer, so let's return to it. You're told that there is a dizzying array of tax rates and exemptions that gives individuals an incentive to avoid paying their fair tax burden, and you're told that there is a threat of penalty. This is enough to infer that some citizens will avoid paying taxes if they have an incentive to do so, and it shows that the argument wouldn't be valid unless you assume this to be the case. **Therefore, (A) is the correct answer**.

Solutions Continued

2. An unnamed philosopher writing in the fifth century BCE tells the story of Rana, an island where an ancient people famous for producing textiles made from extremely fine wool flourished before being destroyed by a series of devastating earthquakes. It has traditionally been assumed that **Rana was nothing more than a product of the philosopher's imagination**. However, archaeologists now believe that seismic activity razed a small but prosperous civilization on an island southeast of Italy around the time when Rana was supposedly destroyed. Because this island also had an unusually large population of sheep prized for their wool, some scholars now contend that the island was the same Rana described by the philosopher. Yet, the fact remains that historians writing before the fifth century BCE never mention a Rana or a lost civilization similar to it. Since they certainly would have written of such a civilization if it had existed, **the traditional estimation of the Rana story is correct**.

In this argument, the two highlighted excerpts play which of the following roles?

(A) The first is a position that the author repudiates, while the second is a conclusion that the author draws to justify that repudiation.

(B) The first is a point of view that the author evaluates; the second provides evidence to strengthen the author's assessment of that position.

(C) **The first is a point of view that the author considers, while the second states the author's ultimate conclusion concerning that position.**

(D) The first presents evidence that supports the author's perspective, while the second outlines that perspective.

(E) The first represents the author's position, while the second presents the author's conclusion concerning a separate position.

The passage is about the island of Rana and whether it was merely a product of a philosopher's imagination or an actual place.

The question asks you about the role played in the argument by two boldfaced statements. The first boldfaced statement sets up the claim that the passage is written to discuss whether Rana was nothing more than a product of the philosopher's imagination. Then the passage provides you with much evidence that contradicts this idea and hints at the possibility that Rana was a real place. The passage then ends with support for the opposite view and the author's conclusion: Rana was indeed nothing more than a product of the philosopher's imagination.

Let's evaluate the answer choices.

For (A), the author does not repudiate the first boldface portion, so you can eliminate it.

For (B), the second boldface portion is not evidence used to strengthen the author's assessment but is, instead, the author's position, so you can eliminate (B) as well.

(C) matches your understanding of the text and is therefore the correct answer.

(D) states that the first boldface portion is offered as support for the author's perspective, which is incorrect, so you can eliminate (D).

Finally, (E) incorrectly states that the first boldface portion is the author's position, and the second boldface portion is the author's conclusion on a separate position, which is not true, so you can eliminate (E) as well.

3. Alaskan homeowners often weatherize their homes by sealing gaps that can cause drafts and adding insulation. Until recently, many Alaskans used a popular form of insulation that releases isocyanate, a chemical that can cause breathing problems, skin allergies, and even cancer. Such insulation is now banned. Nevertheless, it is still possible to introduce dangerous levels of isocyanate into a home by insulating it, since restricting airflow in and out of the home increases the concentration of any chemical in the air of the house, and _____.

Which of the following most logically completes the argument?

(A) **many common household items also release measurable quantities of isocyanate.**
(B) any insulation installed before the ban has long since ceased releasing isocyanate.
(C) almost all of the fresh air that enters a weatherized house enters through HVAC vents.
(D) most other kinds of insulation present similar health risks if used inappropriately.
(E) the insulation that releases isocyanate was easy to install in an existing house.

The passage is about Alaskan home insulation releasing isocyanate, a chemical that causes health problems and was eventually banned. You need an answer choice that helps logically explain how it is still possible to introduce dangerous levels of isocyanate into a home by insulating it.

(A) could certainly help explain how, so let's leave it for now.

(B) doesn't explain how isocyanate would continue to get released, so you can eliminate it.

(C) doesn't help explain how dangerous levels of isocyanate can get into a home, so you can eliminate it.

(D) doesn't help explain how dangerous levels of isocyanate can get into a home, so you can eliminate it.

Finally, (E) doesn't help explain how dangerous levels of isocyanate can continue to get into the home, so you can eliminate it as well.

Returning to (A), since airflow is now restricted, it makes sense that insulating, combined with household items releasing quantities of isocyanate, can lead to dangerous levels of isocyanate building up in the air of the house. **(A) is the correct answer**.

Solutions Continued

4. Ancient records show that the government of Nenea imposed its first sales tax on bottles of wine. Despite the fact that the population remained steady, revenues from the Nenean wine tax fell precipitously over the first three years that the policy was in effect. Thus, a significant proportion of the Nenean population must have failed to pay taxes on the wine they purchased.

Which of the following statements, if true, would most seriously weaken the argument given?

(A) The amount of wine consumed by Nenean households increased after the government levied the tax.

(B) During the first two years after the tax went into effect, Nenean law required wine merchants to sell wine in bottles of the same size as before the tax was instituted.

(C) The penalty for failing to pay tax on a bottle of wine was not much greater than the price of the bottle of wine itself.

(D) The proportion of Nenean households that produced their own wine increased significantly after the government instated the tax.

(E) Even including tax, the total cost of a bottle of wine for a Nenean household declined steadily in the several years before and after the tax came into effect.

Ancient records show that Nenea's revenues from the wine tax fell precipitously over the first three years that the policy was in effect. The author claims that a significant portion of the population must have failed to pay taxes on the wine they purchased.

You want to weaken this claim, and you can do so by showing that there could have been some other reason for the significant decrease in wine tax revenue, such as a large decrease in wine sales. Let's take a look at the answer choices.

If (A) is true, it wouldn't help explain a decrease in taxes collected, so you can eliminate (A).

(B) also doesn't help explain why tax revenue would decrease, so you can eliminate (B) as well.

It's unclear what impact (C) has on the conclusion—if anything, it makes not paying taxes perhaps slightly more attractive, so you can eliminate it.

(D) is the type of answer you were looking for and is likely correct.

(E) is also attractive, so let's look at (D) and (E) more carefully.

If (D) is true and the proportion of households making their own wine *increased significantly*, that could explain the decrease in tax revenue without the need for people failing to pay taxes; people who make their own wine don't need to buy it and, therefore, wouldn't pay the wine tax. This would definitely weaken the author's argument.

(E) could help explain tax revenue going down *steadily*, but not *precipitously*, so it isn't as great an answer for weakening the author's argument. **(D) is the correct answer.**

5. Professor Howard: Undergraduate students should not be permitted to fulfill the university's mathematics requirements by taking calculus. More than half of the undergraduate students at the university took calculus in high school. Therefore, calculus is not college-level mathematics, and for this reason alone, no student should be allowed to satisfy the requirements by taking it.

Professor Wing: According to your argument, undergraduate students shouldn't be allowed to fulfill the university's literature requirements by studying Shakespeare, since more than half of our undergraduate students have studied Shakespeare in high school. Yet, many students currently satisfy the literature requirement by taking the English department's popular Shakespeare survey course, and it would be ridiculous to prohibit them from doing so.

Professor Wing responds by:

(A) criticizing Howard's reasoning in order to question the value of the university's academic requirements.

(B) challenging Howard's conclusion by presenting a situation analogous to the one described by Howard and demonstrating its absurdity.

(C) reinterpreting the evidence presented by Howard in order to support an alternate conclusion.

(D) using statistical data to raise doubts about the validity of the university's approach to academic requirements.

(E) calling into question a justification for changing a policy by demonstrating that the change would be ineffective in solving the problem it seeks to address.

Professor Howard argues that undergraduate students should not be permitted to fulfill the university's mathematics' requirements by taking calculus.

Instead of directly addressing Professor Howard's reasoning, Professor Wing responds by presenting a similar situation that is meant to show the weakness of Howard's reasoning.

Answer choice (B) represents this well and is correct.

Though it might be argued that Wing criticizes Howard's reasoning, he certainly does not question the value of the university's requirements, so you can eliminate (A).

Wing does not reinterpret the evidence presented by Howard, and he doesn't present an alternative conclusion, so you can eliminate (C).

Wing doesn't use statistical data to raise doubts about the validity of the university's approach, so you can eliminate (D) as well.

For (E), Wing does not claim that the change Howard suggests would not solve the problem; he simply says that Howard's suggestion is similar to an analogous situation that would be ridiculous, without specifically acknowledging that a problem exists at all. You can eliminate (E) as well.

Again, (B) represents your understanding of the response and is the correct answer.

Solutions Continued

6. Throughout much of the professional world, formal performance evaluations are an important way of maintaining quality. To be effective, these performance reviews are conducted through realistic simulations of professional situations. During the evaluations, as they would in real-world professional practice, subjects are permitted to use the references they rely on in their work: physicians consult medical texts, lawyers refer to law books and case records, and engineers look up information in manuals. Therefore, students working to obtain degrees in these fields should have access to their textbooks whenever they take exams.

The argument above assumes which of the following?

(A) **What is permitted in one type of evaluation should be permitted in another type of evaluation.**
(B) Any evaluation that relies on realistic simulations of real-world conditions will be effective in maintaining quality.
(C) If students are not permitted to use textbooks when taking exams, the results of these exams are not valid assessments of their abilities.
(D) No examination during which students are not permitted to consult textbooks is similar to a professional evaluation in the field the students are studying.
(E) If exams in a given field are similar to professional evaluations in that same field, they will be effective in serving their intended purpose.

You're asked about what is being assumed in the argument. The author's point is that students working to obtain degrees in specific fields should have access to their textbooks whenever they take exams. The reasoning given is that their real-world counterparts have access to whatever reference materials they need in their professional evaluations. The author assumes that what applies in these real-world situations should also apply during student exams. Let's review the answer choices.

(A) is a great match for what you anticipated, so let's leave it for now.

(B) goes further than the argument does; the argument does not assume that *any* such evaluation will be effective in maintaining quality, so you can eliminate this choice.

(C) also goes further than the argument does; although the argument is in favor of allowing students access to textbooks, it doesn't claim that not getting access to textbooks would result in invalid assessments, so you can eliminate this choice as well.

(D) is too absolute in its statements—we don't know if there are any examinations that are similar to professional evaluations, with or without textbooks, so you can eliminate (D) as well.

Finally, the text tells you nothing about the *intended purpose* of exams or whether these purposes are fulfilled. You can therefore eliminate (E).

(A) matches what you anticipated and is the only attractive answer; it's correct. The author assumes that because certain things are permitted for the performance evaluations of professionals, those same things should be allowed for students working to obtain degrees in those fields.

15

QUANTITATIVE REASONING

Statistics and Sets

Welcome back to quant! In this group of lessons, I'll focus on statistics, sets, combinatorics, tables and graphs, and geometry. I'll start in this lesson by discussing the basics of statistics and sets.

Statistics

For any given set of data, there are 6 computations, or determinations, that you are expected to be comfortable with and able to solve for: mean, median, mode, range, interquartile range, and probability. I'll define each of these briefly, then discuss some further considerations before I jump into practice questions.

The **mean** (or arithmetic mean) of a set of terms is the average of those terms. You can derive this average by adding up all terms and dividing the sum by the total number of terms.

The **median** of a set of terms is the number in the middle of the list created by ordering the terms from least to greatest. If the list has an even number of terms and therefore has no one "middle" term, the median is the average of the two terms in the middle.

The **mode** is the term that appears most frequently in the list. A given set may have no mode, one mode, or more than one mode.

The **range** is the positive difference between the greatest and least terms in the list.

The **interquartile range** is the positive difference between the 25th and 75th percentiles of the data in the set. I'll discuss quartiles and percentiles further below.

Finally, **probability** is the likelihood of choosing one or more specific terms out of the total group.

Let's take a closer look at each of these computations.

You're familiar with the usefulness of averages, or **means**. You also calculate them fairly routinely by adding up the terms in a set, then dividing by the number of terms. For example, the average of {10, 25, 55} is $\frac{90}{3}$, or 30. Note that the average of a set does NOT have to be a member of the set: 30 is the mean of the set, but 30 is not a member of the set.

Let's think about that calculation $\frac{90}{3}$ = 30. What if you were asked what number you had to add to the set in order to make the average of the new set 50? You can use a variable: $\frac{10 + 25 + 55 + x}{4}$ = 50. If you multiply both sides by 4 and add the known terms, you get 90 + x = 200, so x = 110. But note that the key piece of information is that in order to generate a target average of 50 with 4 terms, the terms must add up to (4)(50), or 200.

That method is useful in situations where you are told that a set of 6 numbers has an average of 12. You don't want to set up an equation with 6 variables! Instead, you want to recognize that $\frac{sum}{6}$ = 12, so the sum of the 6 terms must be 72.

Something conceptual to recognize about averages is that if you add to a set a new element that is equal to the current average of the set, the average of the new set will remain the same. For example, if a set of 5 numbers averages 20 (sum = 100), then adding the number 20 to the set will result in the new set of 6 numbers keeping the same average of 20 (sum = 120).

Finally, it's useful to recognize situations in which averages aren't as useful as other statistical measures. Averages can be highly skewed by outliers, numbers that are much less or much greater than other numbers in the set. For example, if you have 3 people with the ages of {8, 9, 13}, the average age of those people is 10. However, if a 70-year-old person enters the room, the average age jumps to 25, a number that doesn't do a very good job of representing the actual ages of the people in the room.

That's precisely why the **median** of a set can, at times, be more useful in describing a given set than its mean. The median of a set is less impacted by outliers. In the example of the ages of people in the room, the median of the original set {8, 9, 13} is 9, the middle value. In the set {8, 9, 13, 70}, the new median is the average of 9 and 13, or 11. The median of 11 does a better job of describing the ages of the people in the room than the mean of 25!

Note that the median of a set does NOT have to be a member of the set, as seen in the set {8, 9, 13, 70}, which has a median of 11.

Unlike the situation with averages, it is theoretically possible to determine the median of a set of values from knowing the value of just one member of the set! Consider a set of 35 terms arranged from least to greatest. Each "half" of the set is 17.5 numbers, which means you'll have two sets of 17 numbers on either side of the middle number—the 18th number from either end of the set—which is the median. If you happen to know that the value of the 18th term is, for example, 34, then the median of the set is 34!

Value of Term		34	
Term #	1–17	18	19–35

There's one other aspect of medians to be aware of. Let's say that you are presented with the following set of 5 terms ordered from least to greatest:

Value of Term	1		5		11
Term #	1	2	3	4	5

The median of the set is 5. But let's consider the range of possible values for the second and fourth terms in the set. The second term can be any of the following: {1, 2, 3, 4, 5}. Don't make the mistake of thinking that a number to the left of the median must be less than the median! It simply has to be less than or equal to the median. Similarly, the fourth term in the set must be greater than or equal to the median, so it can have any value from 5 through 11, inclusive. If a question asked for the least possible average of the 5-member set above, you would select the least possible values for the second and fourth terms to generate this set: {1, 1, 5, 5, 11}, which has a mean of $\frac{23}{5}$, or 4.6. If a question asked for the greatest possible average of the 5-member set above, you would select the greatest possible values for the second and fourth terms to generate this set: {1, 5, 5, 11, 11}, which has a mean of $\frac{33}{5}$, or 6.6.

The **mode** of a set is relatively easy to determine, though be aware that a set can have more than one mode. Unlike the case with the mean or median of a set, the mode of a set must be a member of the set. For example:

The set {1, 4, 4, 5, 7} has a mode of 4.
The set {–3, 5, 5, 9, 12, 12, 18} has modes of 5 and 12.

The **range** of a set is simply the greatest value minus the least value. The range of a set changes only if a new member added to the set is less than the current least term or greater than the current greatest term. For example:

The set {–4, 0, 9, 24} has a range of [24 – (–4)], or 28. That range changes only if you add to the set a term with a value of less than –4 or greater than 24.

There is a slightly more complicated measure of range called **interquartile range**, which is the positive difference between the 25th and 75th percentiles of the data in the set. Let's delve more deeply into the concepts of quartiles and percentiles.

As the name suggests, *quartiles* are quarters. Each quartile consists of one-fourth of the data points, starting with the lowest when the points are arranged in numerical order. Quartiles can also be described in percentile terms; if you think of a complete set of terms as 100% of the terms, then each quartile is composed of 25% of the terms in the set. The median of a set is the 50th percentile of the set.

For example, in a set of 20 terms arranged from least to greatest, terms 1–5 are the first quartile, terms 6–10 are the second quartile, terms 11–15 are the third quartile, and terms 16–20 are the fourth quartile. In this example, the "second highest value of the first quartile" would be the value of the fourth term. The "lowest value in the third quartile" would be the value of the 11th term.

For the purposes of the GRE, to generate the 25th percentile of a set of data, you find the median of the subset of numbers to the left of the set's median (50th percentile). To generate the 75th percentile of a set of data, you find the median of the subset of numbers to the right of the set's median (50th percentile). Let's look at two examples:

Example 1: What is the interquartile range of the set {3, 5, 5, 6, 9, 10, 14, 29}?

Step 1: find the median. This set is arranged from least to greatest, so the median of a set of 8 numbers is the average of the fourth and fifth numbers. In this case, the average of 6 and 9 is 7.5, so the median (50th percentile value) is 7.5.

List the numbers to the left of the median. Note that because the median is 7.5, you'd include 6 in the numbers to the left of the median: {3, 5, 5, 6}. The median of this set of 4 numbers is the average of the second and third numbers, so 5. That's the 25th percentile value.

List the numbers to the right of the median: {9, 10, 14, 29}. The median of this set is the average of 10 and 14, so 12. That's the 75th percentile value.

The interquartile range of this set is 12 − 5, or 7.

Example 2: What is the interquartile range of the set {−3, 0, 5, 6, 9, 15, 22}?

Step 1: the median in this case is the fourth number, so 6.
Step 2: the median of the numbers to the left of the median {−3, 0, 5} is 0, so 0 is the 25th percentile value.
Step 3: the median of the numbers to the right of the median {9, 15, 22} is 15, so 15 is the 75th percentile value.

The interquartile range of this set is 15 − 0, or 15.

The **probability** covered in this chapter is simple probability—we will look at advanced probability topics in the next chapter. Here are a few fundamental probability concepts to keep in mind.

Probability is expressed as a number from 0 through 1. A probability of 0 indicates an event that cannot happen, and a probability of 1 indicates an event that is certain to happen. Probabilities between 0 and 1 can be expressed as fractions (e.g., $\frac{1}{4}$), or as decimals (e.g., 0.25). Note that probabilities are not expressed using percentages—e.g., the probability of an event certain to happen is 1, not 100%.

The sum of all probabilities in a given situation must add up to 1. Example:

A bag contains only red, blue, and green marbles. If the probability of choosing a red marble is $\frac{1}{3}$ and the probability of choosing a blue marble is $\frac{1}{7}$, what is the probability of choosing a green marble?

$\frac{1}{3} + \frac{1}{7} + x = 1$

Use a common denominator: $\frac{7}{21} + \frac{3}{21} + x = \frac{21}{21}$

$x = \frac{11}{21}$, the probability of choosing a green marble

Note that this indicates that the minimum number of marbles in the bag is 21, and the number of marbles must be a multiple of 21. Otherwise, you'd have a non-integer number of green marbles, which is not possible.

The simplest way to calculate and express probability is to create a fraction in which the numerator is the number of elements or events that meet the conditions you're looking for ("working" elements or arrangements) and the denominator is the total number of elements or events possible. A shorthand way to express this fraction is $\frac{\text{working}}{\text{total}}$.

Let's practice with some sample questions.

High Temperatures

Below is a table of high temperatures in a certain area over the course of 2 full weeks:

Day	Sun	Mon	Tues	Wed	Thur	Fri	Sat	Sun	Mon	Tues	Wed	Thur	Fri	Sat
High Temp	78	80	82	84	83	82	76	72	70	68	71	72	78	82

Solve for the following for all 14 days:

Mean:
Median:
Mode:
Range:

Sample Questions

If 1 day during the 2 weeks is selected at random, what is the probability that the high for that day will be 80° or greater?

Ⓐ $\frac{1}{14}$

Ⓑ $\frac{1}{7}$

Ⓒ $\frac{2}{7}$

Ⓓ $\frac{5}{14}$

Ⓔ $\frac{3}{7}$

Quantity A
The average temperature of the 5 days with the lowest highs

Quantity B
The median temperature of the 5 days with the lowest highs

Ⓐ Quantity A is greater.
Ⓑ Quantity B is greater.
Ⓒ The two quantities are equal.
Ⓓ The relationship cannot be determined from the information given.

Dancing Competition

A dancer received the following scores from a set of 8 judges:

Judge:	1	2	3	4	5	6	7	8
Score:	9.0	9.4	8.8	9.4	8.9	9.5	9.4	9.2

Solve for the following:

Mean:
Median:
Mode:
Range:

Sample Questions

Quantity A

The range of the 5 lowest scores

Quantity B

The range of the 5 highest scores

(A) Quantity A is greater.
(B) Quantity B is greater.
(C) The two quantities are equal.
(D) The relationship cannot be determined from the information given.

If the competition has a 9th judge whose score is worth twice as much as that of each of the other 8 judges, what is the minimum score the dancer can receive from the 9th judge to maintain an average score of 9.0 or greater?

High Temperatures Solutions

In Order:	68	70	71	72	72	76	78	78	80	82	82	82	83	84

Mean: 77

The average of all the terms is $\frac{68 + 70 + 71 + 72 + 72 + 76 + 78 + 78 + 80 + 82 + 82 + 82 + 83 + 84}{14} = 77$.

Median: 78

To find the median of 14 terms, take the average of the 7th and 8th greatest terms. In this case, both the 7th and 8th terms are 78, so 78 is the median.

Mode: 82

The mode is 82. 82 appears 3 times on the list, which is more times than any other term.

Range: 16

The highest high temperature was 84, and the lowest high temperature was 68. The difference between them is 84 – 68 = 16, which represents the range.

Sample Question Solutions

If 1 day during the 2 weeks is selected at random, what is the probability that the high for that day will be 80° or greater?

(A) $\frac{1}{14}$

(B) $\frac{1}{7}$

(C) $\frac{2}{7}$

(D) $\frac{5}{14}$

(E) $\frac{3}{7}$

You can see that 6 of the 14 days had temperatures of 80° or greater. Here, $\frac{6}{14}$ can be reduced to $\frac{3}{7}$, and **(E) is the correct answer**.

Quantity A

The average temperature of the 5 days with the lowest highs

Quantity B

The median temperature of the 5 days with the lowest highs

(A) Quantity A is greater.
(B) **Quantity B is greater.**
(C) The two quantities are equal.
(D) The relationship cannot be determined from the information given.

The 5 lowest high temperatures are 68, 70, 71, 72, and 72. The median of these 5 temperatures is 71. You can infer that the average temperature must be lower than that because 68 and 70 are farther away from the median than are 72 and 72, but you can also calculate the average as follows: $\frac{68 + 70 + 71 + 72 + 72}{5} = 70.6$.

You can see that the median temperature is greater than the average temperature, so **Quantity B is greater**.

Dancing Competition Solutions

In Order:	8.8	8.9	9.0	9.2	9.4	9.4	9.4	9.5

Mean: 9.2

You can derive the average of the scores by adding them all up and dividing the sum by 8:

$$\frac{8.8 + 8.9 + 9.0 + 9.2 + 9.4 + 9.4 + 9.4 + 9.5}{8} = 9.2.$$

Median: 9.3

Here, because there are 8 scores on the list, the median is the average of the 4th and 5th scores, which are 9.2 and 9.4, respectively. The halfway point between those 2 scores is 9.3.

Mode: 9.4

The score 9.4 appears 3 times, which is more than any other score.

Range: 0.7

The lowest score is 8.8, and the highest is 9.5, so the range of scores is $9.5 - 8.8 = 0.7$.

Sample Question Solutions

Quantity A	Quantity B
The range of the 5 lowest scores	The range of the 5 highest scores

(A) **Quantity A is greater.**
(B) Quantity B is greater.
(C) The two quantities are equal.
(D) The relationship cannot be determined from the information given.

For the 5 lowest scores, the range is $9.4 - 8.8 = 0.6$.
For the 5 highest scores, the range is $9.5 - 9.2 = 0.3$.
Therefore, **Quantity A is greater.**

If the competition has a 9th judge whose score is worth twice as much as that of each of the other 8 judges, what is the minimum score the dancer can receive from the 9th judge to maintain an average score of 9.0 or greater?

8.2

You can imagine the ninth judge's score as counting twice, which, added to the initial scores, would give you 10 scores in total.

For the 10 scores to average at least a 9.0, you need them to add up to at least 90.

The 8 scores you already have add up to $8.8 + 8.9 + 9.0 + 9.2 + 9.4 + 9.4 + 9.4 + 9.5 = 73.6$.

To get to 90, you need the final 2 scores to be at least $90 - 73.6 = 16.4$.

For those 2 scores to be 16.4, each must be at least $\frac{16.4}{2} = 8.2$

So, if the ninth judge gives at least an 8.2, their score will count double, which will add 16.4 to the total of all scores, and $16.4 + 73.6 = 90$, which, divided by 10, gives you an average score of at least 9.0.

Again, **the correct answer is 8.2**.

Additional Considerations

Very commonly, you are asked to relate these stats to one another. You may also be asked to infer something about one stat or about the group as a whole from another stat. In doing so, there are two particular issues that require a second layer of thought:

Mean vs. Median

The GRE writers love creating questions that require you to consider the relationship between the mean and the median of a set of terms. To illustrate how to think about these questions, let's look at two different sample sets of terms, each presented in order:

List 1: 4, 6, 12, 13, 14

List 2: 11, 12, 12, 15, 19

Notice that, for both, the median is 12.

When you look at list 1, you can see that the numbers below the median are significantly farther away from it than are the numbers above the median. Thus, the average will be less than the median, and you can verify this with some computation:

$$\frac{4 + 6 + 12 + 13 + 14}{5} = 9.8$$

If you look at list 2, you can see that the numbers above the median are significantly farther away from it than are the numbers below the median. Thus, the average will be greater than the median, and you can again verify this with some computation:

$$\frac{11 + 12 + 12 + 15 + 19}{5} = 13.8$$

When asked to compare mean vs. median, you want to consider how numbers less than and greater than the median relate to it. If you notice a heavy bias one way or the other, it can tip off the relationship between the mean and the median.

Combining Averages

Sometimes problems will present you with the averages of two or more sets. It's very important to keep in mind that *you cannot simply average different averages*—the reason is that if the sets contain different numbers of items, then they need to be properly weighted.

Let's consider a situation that makes this concept clear: In a class that gives 10 equally weighted tests, a student scores an average of 70 on the first 8 tests, then scores an average of 90 on the final 2 tests. What is the student's overall test average?

You cannot simply average the two averages of 70 and 90 to generate a test score average of 80—that gives too much weight to the final 2 tests.

Instead, in situations with multiple averages, you always want to calculate the sum of all the test scores, then divide by the number of tests.

But how do you generate the sum of the scores if you don't know each individual score? Well, consider that the average formula is $\frac{\text{sum}}{\text{number of items}}$ = average. In the case of the first 8 tests, you know that $\frac{\text{sum}}{8}$ = 70, so if you multiply both sides by 8, you get a sum of 560 points. Similarly, the equation for the final 2 tests is $\frac{\text{sum}}{2}$ = 90. So the overall sum of the student's scores is 560 + 160, or 740. Now, you can calculate the average across all 10 tests by doing $\frac{740}{10}$ = average, for an overall test average of 74. Note that the overall average of 74 is lower than the incorrect average of averages outcome of 80 because there were more tests in the lower-scoring category than in the higher, so the overall average was pulled down toward the average of the lower set.

Now, let's look at what, at first glance, appears to be a very different question, but it actually hinges on the same concept that *different averages cannot simply be averaged*.

Imagine that you drove for 1 hour at 20 miles per hour and then drove for 5 more hours at 100 miles per hour. If you wanted to compute the average speed for the entire trip, you can't just average 20 and 100 because you spent a lot more time driving at 100 miles per hour than you did at 20 miles per hour. You would have to come up with the average speed by first calculating the total distance traveled and then dividing it by the total number of hours.

Total distance traveled: 1(20) + 5(100) = 520 miles

Total number of hours: 1 + 5 = 6 hours

Therefore, the average speed would be $\frac{520}{6}$, which is close to 87 miles per hour.

GRE writers can be very clever in tempting you to improperly average averages, even against your better judgment. Here's a final illustration:

A man drives to work at 40 miles per hour. He returns by the same route at 60 miles per hour. What was his average speed for the trip?

Based on the limited information given, it might be very tempting to simply average 40 and 60 and say that his average speed was 50 miles per hour.

However, this would be incorrect.

And that's because even though it's true that he traveled the *same distance* both ways, it's not true that he spent the same amount of *time* traveling both ways. In fact, he must have spent more time traveling at 40 miles per hour than at 60 miles per hour because he was driving more slowly.

To illustrate with concrete terms, let's imagine that his work is 120 miles away (the math will work out the same regardless of the distance you choose).

In this case, he would travel a total of 240 miles going to work and coming back.

At 40 miles per hour, it would take him 3 hours to get to work. And at 60 miles per hour, it would take him 2 hours to get back home. So, he would spend 5 total hours traveling.

$$\frac{\text{total distance}}{\text{total time}} = \frac{240}{5} = 48 \text{ miles per hour}$$

So, his average speed for the trip would actually be 48 miles per hour.

Questions like these may leave you nervous that you have to look out for traps. You don't. Instead, what's most important is to remember that you should not average different averages. When confronted with the types of situations exemplified above, make sure to fully work out the math: always find the sum of all the terms to be averaged and divide by the total number of terms.

Practice Questions

1. A storage facility receives 2 types of packages: package type A, each weighing exactly x pounds, and package type B, each weighing exactly $x + 12$ pounds.

If the facility receives 10 of package type A and 20 of package type B, which of the following represents the average weight of all packages received that day?

(A) $\dfrac{x + 6}{25}$

(B) $x + 8$

(C) $2x + 4$

(D) $\dfrac{30x + 24}{30}$

(E) $\dfrac{x}{2} + 8$

2. A list of terms includes the numbers x, x^2, and 0.75, and $0 < x < 1$. If the range of the terms is 0.5, what is the value of x?

$x = \boxed{}$

3. List A: $x - 4, x, x + 4, x + 8, x + 10$

List B (not shown) consists of 6 terms, all of which were derived by adding 4 to each term in list A.

Quantity A	Quantity B
The median of list B	The mean of list B

(A) Quantity A is greater.
(B) Quantity B is greater.
(C) The two quantities are equal.
(D) The relationship cannot be determined from the information given.

4. l, m, n, o, and p are all multiples of 3, and $0 < l < m < n < o < p$. The average of the 5 terms is 9.6.

Quantity A	Quantity B
p	18

(A) Quantity A is greater.
(B) Quantity B is greater.
(C) The two quantities are equal.
(D) The relationship cannot be determined from the information given.

5. A list has 4 numbers. The average of the 4 numbers is equal to the median and the range. If the greatest of the 4 numbers is 12 more than the average of the 4 numbers, what is the least of the 4 numbers?

```
┌──────────────┐
│              │
└──────────────┘
```

6. A certain experiment has 3 mutually exclusive potential outcomes. Their respective probabilities are x, y, and z. If $x = 2y$ and $y = 3z$, what is the value of y?

Ⓐ $\frac{1}{10}$

Ⓑ $\frac{1}{8}$

Ⓒ $\frac{1}{5}$

Ⓓ $\frac{1}{4}$

Ⓔ $\frac{3}{10}$

7. List A: 22, 16, 12, 4, 18, 30

Which of the following sets of numbers has the same median as list A above?

Indicate all such sets.

Ⓐ 41, –3, 0, –1, –5, 32
Ⓑ 91, 36, 5, 9, 10, 24
Ⓒ 16, 16, 16, 16, 18, 14
Ⓓ 14, 20, 16, 17, 17, 15
Ⓔ 26, 17, 16, 17, 19, 13

8. Mrs. Watson teaches 2 history classes. Her first class has a total of 23 students, whose average grade is 86. Her second class has a total of 26 students, whose average grade is 90.

Quantity A	Quantity B
The average grade for all 49 students	88

Ⓐ Quantity A is greater.
Ⓑ Quantity B is greater.
Ⓒ The two quantities are equal.
Ⓓ The relationship cannot be determined from the information given.

Practice Questions Continued

9. A certain online clothing store gives customers the option of rating items on a scale of 1 to 5 stars, with 1 star being the lowest rating and 5 being the highest rating. A certain item at the store received the following ratings from reviewers:

Number of Stars	Number of Reviewers
1	1
2	0
3	4
4	2
5	5

If the item were to get only 5-star reviews going forward, how many consecutive 5-star reviews would be required in order for the item to achieve an average star rating greater than 4?

(A) 1
(B) 2
(C) 3
(D) 4
(E) 5

10. A list of terms has a range of 16 and includes the numbers 18, 23, and 29. Which of the following terms could also be on the list?

Indicate all such terms.

A 8
B 14
C 26
D 32
E 36

Practice Question Solutions

1. A storage facility receives 2 types of packages: package type A, each weighing exactly x pounds, and package type B, each weighing exactly $x + 12$ pounds.

If the facility receives 10 of package type A and 20 of package type B, which of the following represents the average weight of all packages received that day?

(A) $\frac{x + 6}{25}$

(B) $x + 8$

(C) $2x + 4$

(D) $\frac{30x + 24}{30}$

(E) $\frac{x}{2} + 8$

Solution

To calculate the average weight of all the packages, you have to first come up with the total weight of all packages, and then divide that by the total number of packages.

The total weight of all packages should be equal to $10(x)$ $+ 20(x + 12)$, which $= 10x + 20x + 240 = 30x + 240$

And you will be dividing that by 30, since there are 30 packages in total.

$$\frac{30x + 240}{30} = x + 8$$

(B) is the correct answer.

2. A list of terms includes the numbers x, x^2, and 0.75, and $0 < x < 1$. If the range of the terms is 0.5, what is the value of x?

$x = \boxed{.5}$

Solution

As I've discussed in previous lessons, when numbers are between 0 and 1, they become lesser and lesser when squared and taken to greater and greater exponents. So, you know that x^2 must be less than x.

According to the given parameters, there are initially two ways to get to a range of 0.5: x could be the greatest term and x^2 the least, or 0.75 could be the greatest term and x^2 the least.

By trying out some numbers such as 0.8 or 0.9 (which, when squared, lead to 0.64 and 0.81, respectively), you can quickly infer that you can't get a range of 0.5 when x is the greatest term and x^2 the least. The only way for you to have a range of 0.5 is for 0.75 to be the greatest term and x^2 to be the least.

That means that, since the greatest term is 0.75 and the range is 0.5, you can use the following to solve for x^2, the least term:

$$x^2 = 0.75 - 0.5 = 0.25$$

And if $x^2 = 0.25$, $x = \sqrt{0.25} = \mathbf{0.5}$

Solutions Continued

3. List A: $x - 4, x, x + 4, x + 8, x + 10$

List B (not shown) consists of 6 terms, all of which were derived by adding 4 to each term in list A.

Quantity A | Quantity B
The median of list B | The mean of list B

(A) **Quantity A is greater.**
(B) Quantity B is greater.
(C) The two quantities are equal.
(D) The relationship cannot be determined from the information given.

Solution

You can add 4 to each of the elements in list A and imagine list B as follows:

List B: $x, x + 4, x + 8, x + 12, x + 14$

For these 5 terms, the median is $x + 8$.

The average is $\dfrac{x + x + 4 + x + 8 + x + 12 + x + 14}{5} = \dfrac{5x + 38}{5} = x + \dfrac{38}{5}$.

You know that $\dfrac{38}{5}$ is less than 8, so the average must be less than the median.

Quantity A is greater.

Note that adding 4 to each element on the list did not change the relationship between the median and the mean. If you were able to see this upfront, you could have chosen to start your work by evaluating the initial terms given in list A.

4. $l, m, n, o,$ and p are all multiples of 3, and $0 < l < m < n < o < p$. The average of the 5 terms is 9.6.

Quantity A | Quantity B
p | 18

(A) Quantity A is greater.
(B) Quantity B is greater.
(C) **The two quantities are equal.**
(D) The relationship cannot be determined from the information given.

Solution

For the average of the 5 terms to equal 9.6, the 5 terms must add up to $(9.6)(5) = 48$.

Let's think of multiples of 3, in order: 3, 6, 9, 12, 15, 18, 21…

The numbers rise quickly, and you can see that you're fairly limited in terms of picking 5 terms that add to 48.

Trying out the first 5 terms, you can see that they add to $3 + 6 + 9 + 12 + 15 = 45$. The only way to get to a total of 48 is to keep the first 4 terms as is and to switch the last one to 18, so that the total list is: $3 + 6 + 9 + 12 + 18 = 48$. 5 terms that add to 48 give you an average of 9.6.

So, the greatest of the 5 terms must be 18, and the two quantities are therefore equal. **The correct answer is (C)**.

5. A list has 4 numbers. The average of the 4 numbers is equal to the median and the range. If the greatest of the 4 numbers is 12 more than the average of the 4 numbers, what is the least of the 4 numbers?

12

Solution

If the greatest of the 4 numbers is 12 more than the average and the average is equal to the median, then you know that the greatest of the numbers is 12 more than the median.

If the average is equal to the median, you can also infer that the 2 middle terms, when the numbers are placed in order, must be "equidistant" from the average, for if they weren't (e.g., if one term was 3 away from the average and the other 4 away), the average and the median wouldn't equal one another.

If the 2 middle terms must be equidistant from the average, then so must the 2 outer terms—the least and the greatest (if the other 2 terms weren't equidistant from the average, you'd then arrive at a different average).

Since the greatest term is 12 greater than the average, the least must also be 12 less than the average. So, the range must be 24, and, per the initial conditions, you know that the mean and median must also be 24.

If the least term is 12 less than 24, it must equal 24 – 12 = 12.

6. A certain experiment has 3 mutually exclusive potential outcomes. Their respective probabilities are x, y, and z. If $x = 2y$ and $y = 3z$, what is the value of y?

Ⓐ $\frac{1}{10}$

Ⓑ $\frac{1}{8}$

Ⓒ $\frac{1}{5}$

Ⓓ $\frac{1}{4}$

Ⓔ $\frac{3}{10}$

Solution

You know that all possible outcome probabilities must add up to 100%, or fractionally speaking, $\frac{1}{1}$.

So, $x + y + z = 100\%$, or $x + y + z = 1$ (whichever you prefer).

If $x = 2y$ and $y = 3z$, you know that x must equal $6z (x = 2(3z))$.

So, $x + y + z = 6z + 3z + z = 100\%$; $10z = 100\%$; $z = 10\%$.

If $z = 10\%, y = 30\%$ and $x = 60\%$.

Since you are asked to solve for y, and 30% is equivalent to $\frac{3}{10}$, **(E) is the correct answer.**

Solutions Continued

7. List A: 22, 16, 12, 4, 18, 30

Which of the following sets of numbers has the same median as list A above?

Indicate all such sets.

A 41, –3, 0, –1, –5, 32
B 91, 36, 5, 9, 10, 24
C 16, 16, 16, 16, 18, 14
D 14, 20, 16, 17, 17, 15
E 26, 17, 16, 17, 19, 13

Solution

When you put the elements in list A in order, 22, 16, 12, 4, 18, 30 becomes 4, 12, 16, 18, 22, 30, then you can see that the median = $\frac{16 + 18}{2}$ = 17.

Let's put each of the answer choices in order to see what their respective medians are:

[A] 41, –3, 0, –1, –5, 32 becomes –5, –3, –1, 0, 32, 41, which has a median of $\frac{-1 + 0}{2}$ = –0.5.
[B] 91, 36, 5, 9, 10, 24 becomes 5, 9, 10, 24, 36, 91, which has a median of $\frac{10 + 24}{2}$ = 17.
[C] 16, 16, 16, 16, 18, 14 becomes 14, 16, 16, 16, 16, 18, which has a median of 16.
[D] 14, 20, 16, 17, 17, 15 becomes 14, 15, 16, 17, 17, 20, which has a median of $\frac{16 + 17}{2}$ = 16.5.
[E] 26, 17, 16, 17, 19, 13 becomes 13, 16, 17, 17, 19, 26, which has a median of 17.

Therefore, answer choices [B] and [E] have medians that equal the median of list A and are the correct answers.

8. Mrs. Watson teaches 2 history classes. Her first class has a total of 23 students, whose average grade is 86. Her second class has a total of 26 students, whose average grade is 90.

Quantity A	Quantity B
The average grade for all 49 students	88

Ⓐ **Quantity A is greater.**
Ⓑ Quantity B is greater.
Ⓒ The two quantities are equal.
Ⓓ The relationship cannot be determined from the information given.

Solution

Since 88 is halfway between 86 and 90, and you have more students at 90 than at 86, you can infer that the average will be greater than 88 and that Quantity A will therefore be greater.

If you are not sure, or would like to verify, you could calculate the average as follows:

$$\frac{(23)(86) + (26)(90)}{49} \approx 88.12$$

Again, Quantity A is greater.

9. A certain online clothing store gives customers the option of rating items on a scale of 1 to 5 stars, with 1 star being the lowest rating and 5 being the highest rating. A certain item at the store received the following ratings from reviewers:

Number of Stars	Number of Reviewers
1	1
2	0
3	4
4	2
5	5

If the item were to get only 5-star reviews going forward, how many consecutive 5-star reviews would be required in order for the item to achieve an average star rating greater than 4?

(A) 1
(B) 2
(C) 3
(D) 4
(E) 5

Solution

Let's start by computing the current total number of stars, the number of ratings, and the average.

There are (1)(1) + (0)(2) + (4)(3) + (2)(4) + (5)(5) = 46 = 46 total stars.

There are 1 + 0 + 4 + 2 + 5 = 12 total ratings.

The current average is $\frac{46}{12}$, which is about 3.8.

If the store receives another 5-star rating, the average would go up to $\frac{51}{13}$, which is about 3.9.

If the store receives 2 more 5-star ratings, the average would go up to $\frac{56}{14}$, which is exactly 4.0.

Since you need an average higher than 4.0, you know you need more than 2 additional 5-star ratings, **so (C) is the correct answer.**

With three 5-star ratings, the average would go up to $\frac{61}{15}$, which is a little more than 4.

You can also set up an inequality to get the answer. Piggy-backing off some of the work you've done so far, knowing that you have 14 reviews that add up to 56 stars, that all the new reviews would be 5 stars, and you need an average greater than 4, you can set up the following inequality:

$$\frac{46 + 5x}{12 + x} > 4$$

This tells you to look for a number of 5-star reviews, which, when added to what you already have, will give you an average greater than 4.

You can solve the equation for x:

$$\frac{46 + 5x}{12 + x} > 4$$
$$46 + 5x > 4(12 + x)$$
$$46 + 5x > 48 + 4x$$
$$x > 2$$

This also gives you the correct answer of 3, which is (C).

Solutions Continued

10. A list of terms has a range of 16 and includes the numbers 18, 23, and 29. Which of the following terms could also be on the list?

Indicate <u>all</u> such terms.

A 8
B 14
C 26
D 32
E 36

Solution

It can often be helpful to take a moment to think about extremes—the least or greatest values based upon the information given to us, and that's true here.

If the list has a range of 16 and you imagine that 18 is the least number on the list, the greatest possible would be $18 + 16 = 34$.

If you imagine that 29 is the greatest number on the list, the least possible number would be $29 - 16 = 13$.

Taken together, you know that other numbers on the list must be greater than or equal to 13 and less than or equal to 34.

Answer choices [B], [C], and [D] fit into that range and are therefore correct.

Sets

Now, let's talk briefly about sets, or, more specifically, the issue of overlapping sets.

A set is simply a group of terms. If a question mentions two or more sets, it is possible that the sets are **mutually exclusive**, in which case no term can be included in more than one set. I'll say more about this situation when I discuss advanced probability in the next chapter.

Sometimes, a term may be a member of more than one set. Here are some indications that you are dealing with overlapping sets:

The sum of the set totals is greater than the total number of terms or elements in the problem. For example:

In a group of 50 students, 30 take math and 40 take physics. Well, 30 + 40 = 70, and there are only 50 students, so some students must be taking both (and are therefore included in both set totals).

The question uses the words *both* and/or *neither*, as in "How many students take *both* classes?" or "How many students take *neither* class?"

When sets potentially overlap, it is helpful to represent the situation with a **Venn diagram**, in which overlapping circles indicate the possibility that terms might be members of only one set, both sets, or neither set. Note that in an earlier chapter you used Venn diagrams to help you find the **greatest common factor** and **least common multiple** for two numbers; in this chapter, you'll use them to solve problems asking you to identify how many elements are in each possible position when sets overlap.

Here's a basic Venn diagram showing the potential overlap of two sets labeled *A* and *B*.

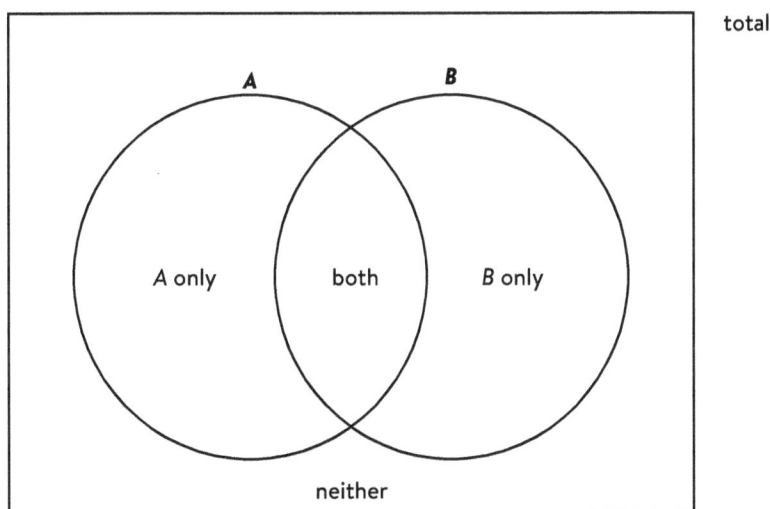

The diagram helps remind you that the total number or terms or elements in set *A*—which should be written *above* or *below* the circle—does not indicate whether those elements are in set *A* only or in both set *A* and set *B*. It also reminds you that it is possible for some elements to be in neither set.

The basic Venn diagram formula, using the notation from the diagram above, is
A + B – both + neither = total

Let's look more closely at this formula, which efficiently solves many problems involving overlapping sets. Remember that the value of *A* (the total number of elements in circle *A*) can be expressed as "*A* only + both," and the value of *B* (the total number of elements in circle *B*) can be expressed as "*B* only + both." So *A* + *B* can be expressed as "*A* only + both + *B* only + both," which *double counts the elements in both sets*, and that's why the basic Venn formula subtracts the "both" quantity *once*, to eliminate that double counting. Once you add in the neithers, which are not included anywhere in the *A* or *B* circles, then you have the total number of elements.

Note that if you are asked, "How many elements are in sets *A* or *B*?," that "or" is *inclusive*, meaning that the elements in both sets should be included in your answer. Every element except the neithers is in set *A* or *B*. The phrase "*A* or *B*" is the same as the phrase "*A* or *B* or both" (which the test writers can also use).

The calculation *A* + *B* – both will give you the number of elements in *A* or *B* or both. In formal notation, $A \cup B$ (the union of sets *A* and *B*) is equivalent to "*A* or *B* or both."

If the test writers want to *exclude* the elements in both sets, in other words, to find the sum "*A* only + *B* only," they will ask a question phrased in one of the following ways (not a complete list):

"How many elements are in sets *A* or *B*, but not both?"
"How many elements are in exactly one set?"

Using Venn diagram notation, the formula for finding *A* or *B*, but not both, would be:

$A + B – 2(\text{both}) = A \text{ only} + B \text{ only}$

Remember that "$A + B$" double counts the boths, so if you want to remove them entirely, you have to subtract them *twice* from the sum $A + B$.

The formal notation $A \cup B$ (the intersection of sets A and B) is the same as the "both" category on the basic diagram.

Let's look at the context for a typical problem involving overlapping sets.

There are 200 people in a room. 140 of them have brown hair, 90 have curly hair, and 50 have neither brown nor curly hair.

$140 + 90 = 230$, and there are only 200 people in total, so the brown hair and curly hair sets must overlap. The word "neither" is also an indicator of a problem in which a Venn diagram can be useful.

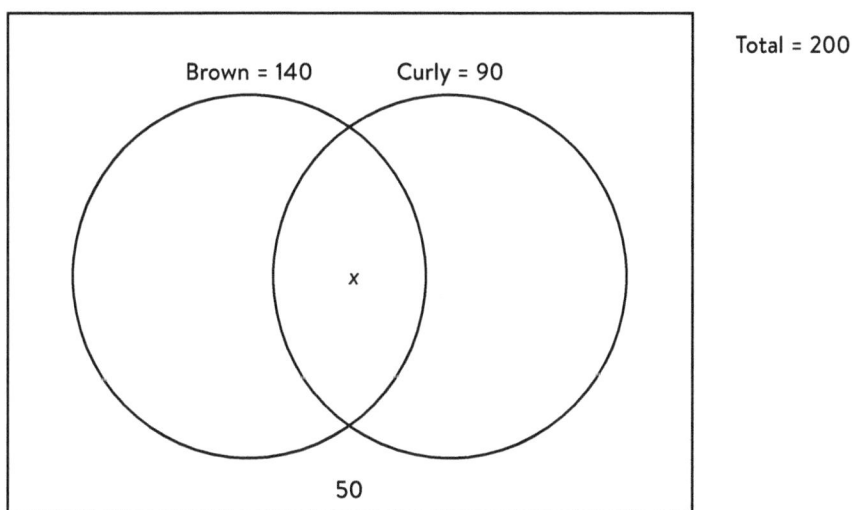

Total = 200

Let's use the formula $A + B -$ both $+$ neither $=$ total

$140 + 90 - x + 50 = 200$

$280 - x = 200$, so $x = 80$. 80 people have both brown and curly hair.

Depending on the question asked, it might be helpful to fill in all of the positions in your Venn diagram:

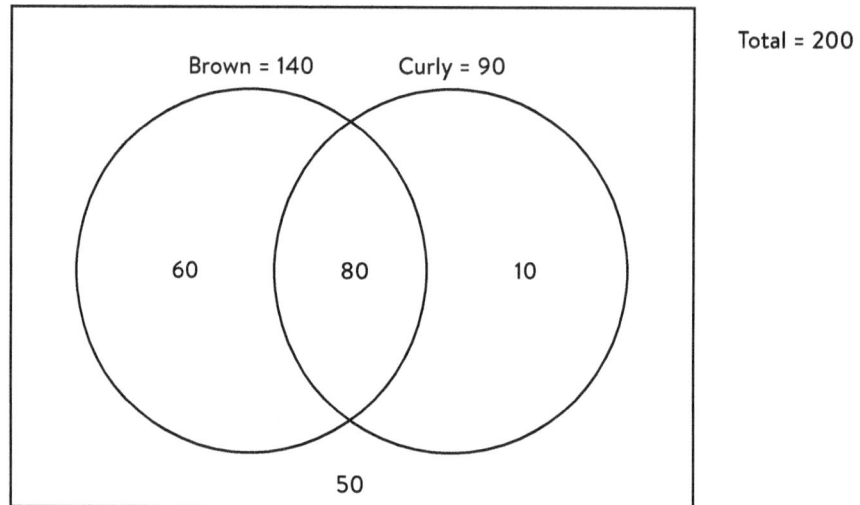

Note that once all of the non-overlapping positions are filled in, you can check your work by making sure that *A* only + both + *B* only + neither = total. In this case, 60 + 80 + 10 + 50 = 200, so that's good.

You can now answer any question asked, including "How many people have brown hair or curly hair, but not both?" That would be *A* only + *B* only, or 60 + 10 = 70, the same answer you'd get if you did *A* + *B* – 2(both), 140 + 90 – 2(80) = 70.

Overlapping set questions are often presented entirely in percentage terms. For example: Of the students in a school, 75% have brown hair, 40% have curly hair, and 5% have neither brown nor curly hair. What percent of the students have both brown and curly hair? The best way to handle these questions is to set the total number of students at 100, which turns 75% into the number 75, etc. So *A* is 75, *B* is 40, and neither is 5. 75 + 40 – both + 5 = 100, so both = 20, which you then convert back to 20%.

Sometimes the amount of overlap between two sets is not a fixed quantity but rather something that the test writers will ask you to maximize or minimize. A good indicator of this type of problem is phrasing such as "What is the greatest (or least) number of people who could be in both sets (or neither set)?"

In addressing such problems, let's start with some theoretical basics. You'll note below that the categories of both and neither are linked in a way that might initially seem strange: when you increase the boths, you increase the neithers (and vice versa), and when you decrease the boths, you decrease the neithers (and vice versa).

Maximizing the Boths and Neithers

The greatest number of elements that can be in both sets is the lesser of the two circle totals A and B. For example, if in a group of 100 students, 30 take math and 60 take physics, then the maximum number of students who could be in both classes is 30, the lesser of the two circle totals. In that case, you have 0 math only, 30 both, 30 physics only, and 40 neithers. Note that maximizing the boths also maximized the neithers.

Minimizing the Boths and Neithers

The number of elements in both sets can be 0 (mutually exclusive sets), but only if the sum of the two set totals (the circle totals we've been calling A and B) is less than or equal to the overall total. For example, if in a group of 100 students, 30 take math and 60 take physics, it's possible that there is 0 overlap between the groups: 30 take math only, 60 take physics only, and 10 take neither.

If the sum of the two set totals is greater than the overall total, then it is not possible for the boths to be 0. In this case, the way to minimize the boths is to set the neithers to 0, then use the formula to solve for the boths. For example, if in a group of 100 students, 50 take math and 70 take physics, then the boths can't be 0. So, set the neithers to 0 and use the formula: 50 + 70 – both + 0 = 100.

120 – both = 100

Both = 20. This is the minimum possible value for the boths.

Let's look at a sample problem:

In a certain school, the Math Club has 40 members, and the Physics Club has 47 members. At least 3 members of the Math Club are not in the Physics Club. Which of the following could be the number of members in the Physics Club who are not in the Math Club?

Let's start by setting the value of the Math Club-only students at the minimum of 3. The other 37 members of the Math Club can be assigned to both clubs (because the number 37 is less than the Physics Club set total of 47), leaving 10 students in Physics Club only.

Now, let's maximize the Math Club-only students at 40, leaving 0 students in both clubs. All 47 Physics club students are therefore in Physics Club only.

The range of possible values for Physics Club-only students (the ones in Physics club but not in Math Club) is from 10 through 47. The format of this question would probably be multiple choice (all that apply), and you would choose all answers in that range.

It's possible, though unlikely, that a GRE question will involve 3 potentially overlapping sets. In that case, use the following Venn diagram:

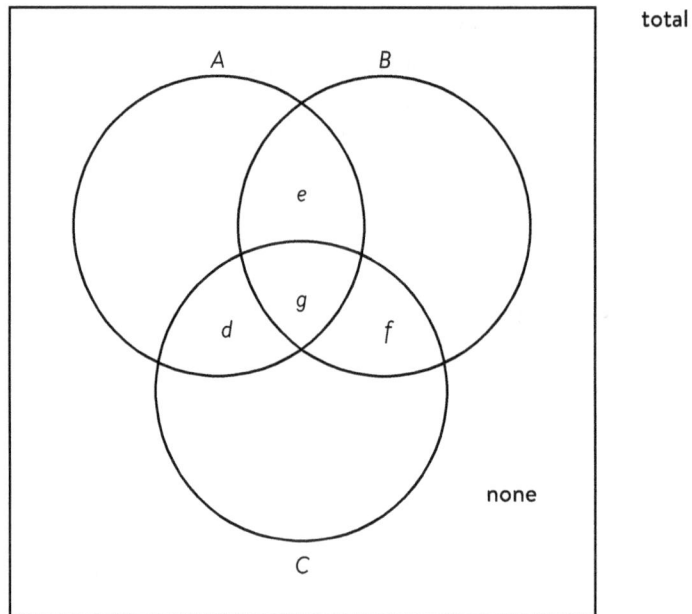

The formula for this diagram is $A + B + C - (d + e + f) - 2(g) + \text{none} = \text{total}$

This formula operates on principles similar to the 2-circle formula. $A + B + C$ double counts the elements in positions d, e, and f (2-circle overlaps) and triple counts the elements in position g (3-circle overlaps). Therefore, you need to subtract the double counted elements once and the triple-counted elements twice to make sure that everything is counted only once.

Note that if you are told that 40 elements are in both sets A and B, those 40 elements could (unless otherwise noted) be in positions e (the overlap of just A and B) or g (the overlap of all 3 sets). So, if you know that there are 5 elements in position g, subtract those 5 from 40 to generate a total of 35 items in position e.

Practice Questions

1. 18 people attended a cookout. Each person ate a burger, a hot dog, or both. If 12 people ate a burger and 12 people ate a hot dog, how many people ate both burgers and hot dogs?

(A) 4
(B) 6
(C) 8
(D) 10
(E) It cannot be determined.

2. Set A: All multiples of 4 less than or equal to 1,000
Set B: All multiples of 5 less than or equal to 1,000

Quantity A	Quantity B
The number of terms that are in set A that are not in set B	The number of terms that are in set B that are not in set A

(A) Quantity A is greater.
(B) Quantity B is greater.
(C) The two quantities are equal.
(D) The relationship cannot be determined from the information given.

3. There are 623 people in the Fairfax County database who have received a driving ticket, a parking ticket, or both in the past year. If at least 400 of those people received a parking ticket and an equal or greater number of them received a driving ticket, which of the following could be the number of drivers who received both a driving ticket and a parking ticket in the past year?

Indicate all such values.

A 136
B 187
C 223
D 426
E 623

Practice Question Solutions

1. 18 people attended a cookout. Each person ate a burger, a hot dog, or both. If 12 people ate a burger and 12 people ate a hot dog, how many people ate both burgers and hot dogs?

- (A) 4
- **(B) 6**
- (C) 8
- (D) 10
- (E) It cannot be determined.

Solution

If you add up the number of burgers and hot dogs eaten, you get 12 + 12 = 24, which is 6 more than the 18 people who attended. This must mean that these 6 people must have eaten both a burger and a hot dog, and **(B) is the correct answer**.

---

2. Set A: All multiples of 4 less than or equal to 1,000
Set B: All multiples of 5 less than or equal to 1,000

Quantity A	Quantity B
The number of terms that are in set A that are not in set B	The number of terms that are in set B that are not in set A

- (A) **Quantity A is greater.**
- (B) Quantity B is greater.
- (C) The two quantities are equal.
- (D) The relationship cannot be determined from the information given.

Solution

If you divide 1,000 by 4, you get 250. This tells you that there are 250 multiples of 4 that are less than or equal to 1,000.

If you divide 1,000 by 5, you get 200. This tells you that there are 200 multiples of 5 that are less than or equal to 1,000.

The terms that are elements in both lists are those that are multiples of both 4 and 5: multiples of 20.

If you divide 1,000 by 20, you get 50. This tells you that there are 50 multiples of 20 that are less than or equal to 1,000.

The number of terms that are in set A that are not in set B is therefore 250 – 50 = 200.

Similarly, the number of terms that are in set B that are not in set A is therefore 200 – 50 = 150.

The correct answer is (A).

---

3. There are 623 people in the Fairfax County database who have received a driving ticket, a parking ticket, or both in the past year. If at least 400 of those people received a parking ticket and an equal or greater number of them received a driving ticket, which of the following could be the number of drivers who received both a driving ticket and a parking ticket in the past year?

Indicate <u>all</u> such values.

- [A] 136
- **[B] 187**
- **[C] 223**
- **[D] 426**
- **[E] 623**

Solution

If at least 400 people also received a driving ticket, you know that the overlap between the two categories must be at least 400 + 400 – 623 = 177.

In terms of the maximum overlap, there is nothing in the question stem that makes it impossible for all 623 people in the database to have received both a driving and parking ticket.

Therefore, answer choices [B], [C], [D], and [E] could all be viable numbers for the overlap.

16 Distribution and Combinatorics

QUANTITATIVE REASONING

In this lesson, I'll continue to explain how to manage and interpret data. I'll start by discussing ways to measure how it's distributed, or spread out. I'll then discuss different ways of combining elements in a data set and bring this together with a discussion of probability (which I already talked about a bit in the last lesson).

Please note that some of these topics can be quite challenging; true and thorough mastery would require a great deal of in-depth study. You must weigh your investment of energy against what the GRE require: these particular topics don't tend to be tested too often, and when they are, the questions are usually limited in their scope. As always, I will do my best to provide you with the right type of information and the right level of emphasis.

Distribution

If you have a set of data that you arrange in order from least to greatest, there are a variety of ways in which the data can be distributed along this range. The data can be clustered around the mean, evenly distributed, or randomly inconsistent.

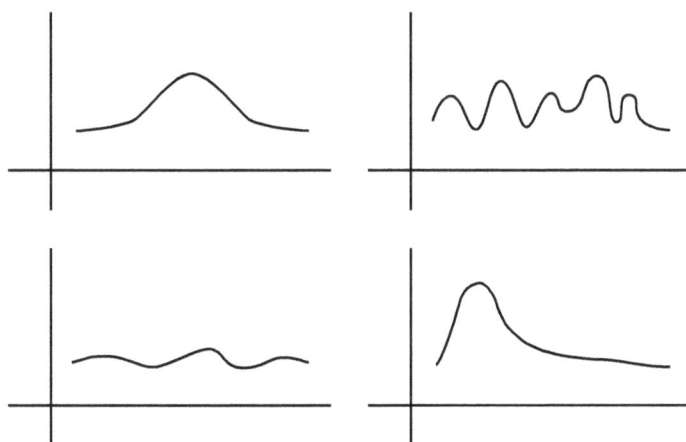

Let's imagine that the four charts above provide information about rainfall in different parts of the country. The x-axis shows inches of rain in a day, and the y-axis shows the number of days when a city got that amount of rainfall. This type of chart is known as a **frequency distribution**.

I'll discuss tables and charts in greater detail in the next two lessons, but for now, you can familiarize yourself with these examples illustrating how varied frequency distributions can be.

Sample (Non-Normal) Distribution Question

200 adults were polled about how many monthly subscriptions they carried, and the relative frequency of different responses is listed below.

# of monthly subscriptions	Relative frequency
0	12%
1	8%
2	14%
3	26%
4	18%
5	15%
6	7%

Which of the following represents the number of polled adults who have 1 or 0 monthly subscriptions?

(A) 20
(B) 24
(C) 32
(D) 40
(E) 48

Solution

Per the given table, you can see that 20% of all those polled, 12% + 8%, have 0 or 1 subscription.

20% of 200 individuals = (0.2)(200) = 40, so **(D) is the correct answer.**

Standard Deviation

Standard deviation is a statistical method of describing the amount of distance, or deviation, between each data point and the mean for that set of data.

Here's how to compute the standard deviation:

1. Calculate the mean of the values.
2. Find the difference between each of the values and this mean.
3. Square each of these differences.
4. Take the average of the squares.
5. Square root this average of the squares.

Although I've included the calculation process here for your reference, **it is important to note that the computations required to derive the standard deviation for a set of data are too particular and time-consuming for the context of the GRE, and you will not be required to compute standard deviation on the exam.**

Rather, you will be expected to understand standard deviation on a conceptual level and be able to utilize information that you are given about standard deviation to make basic calculations.

On a conceptual level, it's important to remember that standard deviation does not depend on how great or less the mean is, but rather, how close or far away all the terms are from this mean. If, for example, all of the terms in a certain set either increased or decreased by a specific amount, the mean would change, but the standard deviation would not.

For example, if for the set of numbers $\{x, y, z\}$, the standard deviation is s, then for the set of numbers $\{x + 5, y + 5, z + 5\}$, the standard deviation would remain s. The set of values was merely moved 5 units to the right on the number line, and thus, the mean increased by 5, but the distance of the terms from the mean did not change.

However, if you modify a set of terms in a way that changes their distance from the set's mean, then the standard deviation does change. For example, if for the set of numbers $\{x, y, z\}$ the standard deviation is s, then for the set of numbers $\{4x, 4y, 4z\}$, the standard deviation would become $4s$. Similarly, the set of numbers $\{0.5x, 0.5y, 0.5z\}$ would have a standard deviation of $0.5s$.

Combining the concepts above, if for the set of numbers $\{x, y, z\}$, the standard deviation is s, then for the set of numbers $\{4x + 5, 4y + 5, 4z + 5\}$, the standard deviation would become $4s$. Multiplication of each term in the set has the same multiplicative effect on the standard deviation, but moving each term left or right on the number line via addition or subtraction does not affect the standard deviation.

Generally, you want to think of standard deviation as "closeness" to the mean. To be within 1 standard deviation of the mean is to be within one level of closeness. A term that is 2 standard deviations away from the mean would be farther away from it.

To illustrate with specific numbers, imagine you have a set whose mean is 15 and standard deviation is 2. Being within 1 standard deviation of the mean would mean that a number is at most 2 away from 15, or between 13 and 17. Being between 1 and 2 standard deviations from the mean would mean that the number is between 2 and 4 units away from the mean: between 11 and 13 or between 17 and 19. Finally, if you were to evaluate how the number 18 relates to the mean, you could say that since it's 3 away from 15, and since the standard deviation is 2, it's $\frac{3}{2} = 1.5$ standard deviations away from the mean.

Sample Scenario

Let's look at one more example to discuss these concepts further. Imagine that 4 students in a class obtained the following 5 scores, ordered, on their exams:

Student Scores

Alex   72, 81, 86, 92, 94
Barb   83, 86, 88, 90, 93
Carol   87, 88, 88, 88, 89
Dave   94, 95, 95, 95, 96

Your calculator will tell you that Barb and Carol have the same average. However, you can see that Barb's scores vary far more from that average than Carol's do; therefore, Barb's scores have a greater standard deviation than Carol's scores.

You can also note that Carol and Dave have different averages but the same distribution of scores relative to those averages. Therefore, Carol's and Dave's scores have equal standard deviations.

Sample Questions

1. List A: $x - 4, x - 2, x, x + 4, x + 6$
List B: $y - 4, y - 2, y, y + 4, y + 9$

Quantity A

The standard deviation of the numbers in list A

Quantity B

The standard deviation of the numbers in list B

Ⓐ Quantity A is greater.
Ⓑ Quantity B is greater.
Ⓒ The two quantities are equal.
Ⓓ The relationship cannot be determined from the information given.

Solution

Note that to consider standard deviation, you don't need to know the relationship between x and y; it doesn't matter. Instead, you need to think about how the elements on each list relate to one another.

Comparing list A and list B, you can see that the deviation within the lists is almost identical; the only difference is the final element on each list: $x + 6$ and $y + 9$. Since this final element shows greater deviation in list B than in list A, and all other elements in both lists show the same amount of deviation, list B must have a greater standard deviation than list A. **(B) is the correct answer**.

2. A certain list of numbers has a mean of 26.4 and a standard deviation of 2.2. Which of the following terms is not within 2 standard deviations of the mean?

Indicate all such terms.

A 21.5
B 23.4
C 24.3
D 28.9
E 30.9

Solution

If the mean is 26.4 and the standard deviation is 2.2, then, to be within 2 standard deviations of the mean, a number must be at least 26.4 – 2.2 – 2.2 = 22 and no more than 26.4 + 2.2 + 2.2 = 30.8.

The two terms on the list not within these 2 standard deviations are answer choices [A] and [E].

3. 300 students took a certain exam; the mean score was 60, and the standard deviation was 8. How many standard deviations away from the mean is a score of 80?

(A) 1.2
(B) 1.5
(C) 1.8
(D) 2.2
(E) 2.5

Solution

A score of 80 is 80 – 60 = 20 away from the mean. If the standard deviation is 8, then a score of 80 is $\frac{20}{8}$ = 2.5 standard deviations away from the mean. **The correct answer is (E).**

Normal Distribution

When it comes to the distribution of data, the GRE writers expect you to be familiar with the concept of a *normal distribution*. In statistics, a normal distribution describes a particular and common way in which data is distributed relative to the mean: it takes the familiar shape of a bell curve. In a normal distribution, percentages of the data align predictably with distances from the mean expressed in standard deviations.

Here is the standard normal distribution curve and its associated data percentiles. The GRE writers expect you to be familiar with the percentages of data associated with each standard deviation from the mean, so make sure to memorize this diagram.

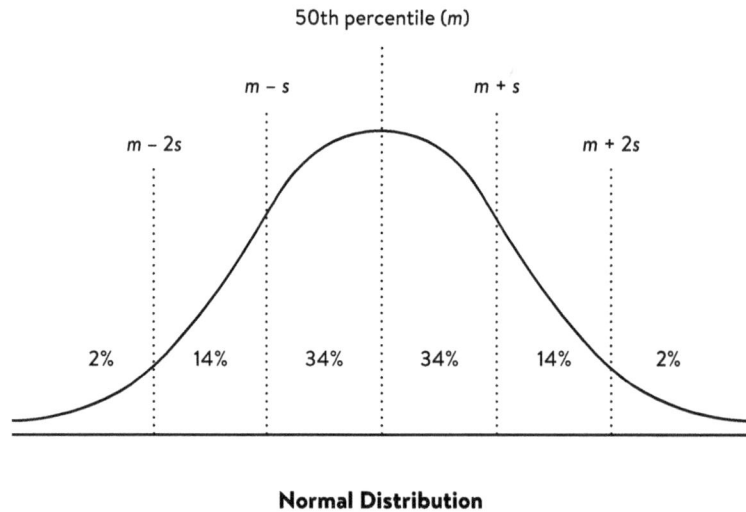

Normal Distribution

You are expected to know that normally distributed data have four major characteristics:

1. The mean, median, and mode are all nearly equal and can all be approximated by m.
2. The data are grouped fairly symmetrically about the mean (m).
3. About $\frac{2}{3}$ of the data are within 1 standard deviation of the mean (between $m - s$ and $m + s$).
4. Almost all of the data, over 95%, are within 2 standard deviations of the mean (between $m - 2s$ and $m + 2s$).

Sample Questions

1. A random variable X is normally distributed with a mean of 160 and a standard deviation of 15.

Quantity A
The probability of the event that X is between 145 and 175

Quantity B
The probability of the event that X is less than 160

Ⓐ Quantity A is greater.
Ⓑ Quantity B is greater.
Ⓒ The two quantities are equal.
Ⓓ The relationship cannot be determined from the information given.

Solution

Quantity A represents terms that are within one standard deviation of 160. With normal distribution, you can expect roughly $\frac{2}{3}$ of all terms to fall within this range.

Quantity B represents terms that are less than the mean. With normal distribution, you can expect roughly $\frac{1}{2}$ of all terms to fall within this range.

Therefore, **Quantity A is greater than Quantity B**.

2. 6,000 trees were planted in a certain region. After 2 years, the heights of these trees are approximately normally distributed, with an average height of 42 inches and a standard deviation of 6 inches.

Which of the following is the best approximation for how many of the trees are smaller than 30 inches?

Ⓐ 10
Ⓑ 100
Ⓒ 500
Ⓓ 1,000
Ⓔ 1,500

Solution

Note that the test writers do not expect you to calculate this exactly; they are testing your conceptual understanding (hence the variation in the answer choices).

You know that a tree smaller than 30 inches is a tree that's more than 2 standard deviations away from the mean; if the heights are normally distributed, this roughly represents about 0.0228% of all the trees planted, which is about 136 of the 6,000 total trees that were planted. **The answer closest to this is (B), which is correct**.

Combinatorics

Imagine that you have a certain number of terms, or elements, to put into an order, or to put into groups. Combinatorics is the study of how to compute the different numbers of options that are available to us.

The Multiplication Principle

The fundamental idea behind all combinatorics is that if you have x options for how to make selection one and y options for how to make selection two, you have $(x)(y)$ unique ways to make a combination of both selections.

Examples to illustrate:

- If you have 3 options for an appetizer and 4 for the main course, you have (3)(4) = 12 options for different ways to combine an appetizer and a main course.

- If you have 5 shirts and 2 ties, you have (5)(2) = 10 options for different ways to pick a shirt and combine it with a tie.

- If a movie theater is playing 6 different films, each 4 times per day, there are (6)(4) = 24 different options to go and see a movie at that theater.

Per the multiplication principle, you'll often start combinatorics questions by writing out _ × _ or _ × _ × _ as your base equation, with a slot for each of the selections you have to make. You will then fill in each slot with the number of options available for that selection.

$$\underline{\quad} \times \underline{\quad} \times \underline{\quad} \times \underline{\quad}$$

Draw a slot for each decision
to be made

Note that in each of these examples, the probability of making any one exact combination of selections is equal to 1 divided by the number of options. So, for the first example, there is a $\frac{1}{12}$ chance that a particular appetizer and main course combination will be selected; for the second example, there is a $\frac{1}{10}$ chance that a particular shirt and tie combination will be selected; and for the final example, there is a $\frac{1}{24}$ chance that a particular film at a particular time will be chosen.

Sample Question

A certain license plate consists of the letters T and M and the numbers 7, 3, and 6. Each letter and number is used once, and no other letters or numbers are used. If the license plate starts with a letter, what is the probability that it is T7M36?

(A) $\frac{1}{24}$

(B) $\frac{1}{48}$

(C) $\frac{1}{96}$

(D) $\frac{1}{192}$

(E) $\frac{1}{248}$

Solution

You can solve for the probability of getting that one particular result by first calculating all the different possibilities that are available per the parameters given to us.

You can start by thinking about the number of decisions you have to make and the number of options that you have for each decision.

Here, there are 5 decisions to be made for each of the 5 positions in the license plate, so you can start with this:

$$\_ \times \_ \times \_ \times \_ \times \_$$

Now you can think about the number of options you have for each position, and here's a tip: **whenever there are limits imposed on what can fill a particular position, you want to start your calculations at that position.**

In this case, you're told that the first position must be filled by a letter. You have only two possibilities, T and M, for this first selection:

$$2 \times \_ \times \_ \times \_ \times \_$$

Once the first position is filled, you have 4 elements left to fill the second position, which can be either a letter or a number, 3 elements left for the third position, 2 elements left for the fourth, and 1 final element left for the fifth:

$$2 \times 4 \times 3 \times 2 \times 1 = 48$$

That means there are 48 different options for how to arrange the 2 letters and 3 numbers per the parameters given, and the odds of getting the one specific license plate are therefore $\frac{1}{48}$. **The correct answer is (B).**

Complications

Combinatorics problems become a bit more complicated when you have to consider whether items can or can't repeat and when you have to determine whether elements are being selected for individual or group distinctions.

Selecting for a Group vs. Individual Appointments

The most important decision you'll face when dealing with a tough combinatorics question is whether you are selecting for a group with no particular order or for a specific arrangement of assignments.

To illustrate, imagine that a company was going to hire 2 new employees from among 4 candidates: one for a full-time position and one for a part-time position. If you label the candidates A, B, C, and D, you can see that you have the following **12** options for the different ways in which you can fill the positions:

Full-time	A	A	A	B	B	B	C	C	C	D	D	D
Part-time	B	C	D	A	C	D	A	B	D	A	B	C

Now, let's imagine that instead of hiring for 2 separate positions, the company was just hiring 2 of the 4 candidates. Instead of having 12 options for different ways in which you could hire a pair of candidates, you'd have just **6**:

2 positions	A&B	A&C	A&D	B&C	B&D	C&D

This is because in the first situation, hiring A full-time and B part-time is a different outcome from hiring B full-time and A part-time; in the second situation, hiring A and B as a pair is the same as hiring B and A as a pair, so there are fewer different options.

In formal terms, an arrangement with specific items in specific positions (such as letters or numbers in a password or people in a ranked hierarchy) is known as a **permutation**, while a selection of a set of items in no particular order (such as selecting a group of people for a team or committee where everyone has the same rank) is known as a **combination**.

Before I go any further, let's discuss a piece of mathematical notation that frequently arises in calculating both permutations and combinations: the factorial.

The multiplication principle at the heart of combinatorics frequently leads to a situation in which a positive integer is multiplied by every positive integer less than itself down to 1, for example, (4)(3)(2)(1). This situation is so common that we describe it as a factorial and use an exclamation point as its symbol. 4! (pronounced "four factorial") is equivalent to (4)(3)(2)(1), and therefore has a numerical value of 24. 6! = (6)(5)(4)(3)(2)(1), or 720. (I'll talk a bit more about factorials later in the chapter.)

To find the number of possible combinations, you want to first compute the number of possible permutations, and then divide that number by the factorial of the number of positions to be filled. This factorial in the denominator represents the number of possible ordered arrangements (or permutations) that you can make out of each group (or combination).

So, for example, if you are selecting for a group of 2, you want to divide by 2!, or $(2)(1)$ because you'll end up with $\frac{1}{(2)(1)}$ = half as many combinations as the number of permutations you would have had selecting for individual positions.

Let's illustrate by returning to the example of selecting employees. If you wanted to select for 2 positions, you know that you have 2 decisions to make, so you can start off by drawing 2 slots:

$\_ \times \_$

Since you have 4 candidates, you have 4 options for the first position. Once that first selection has been made, you have 3 options for the second position.

$\underline{4} \times \underline{3} = 12$

Therefore, according to the multiplication principle, you have 12 total options for your decision.

If you were selecting for a group of 2 employees instead of 2 separate positions, you'd want to divide your answer by 2! or (2)(1):

$$\frac{(4)(3)}{2!} =$$

$$\frac{(4)(3)}{(2)(1)} = 6$$

If you are selecting for a group of 3, you want to divide by 3!, or (3)(2)(1), because you'll end up with $\frac{1}{(3)(2)(1)} = \frac{1}{6}$ as many different *combinations* as the number of *permutations* you would have had selecting for individual positions.

If you are selecting for a group of 4, you want to divide by 4!, or (4)(3)(2)(1), because you'll end up with $\frac{1}{(4)(3)(2)(1)} = \frac{1}{24}$ as many *combinations* as the number of *permutations* you would have had, and so on.

Permutation

Number of possibilities when specific positions are considered

↓

Product of the number of options you have for each position

Combination

Number of possibilities when selecting for groups

↓

Product of the number of options you have for each position divided by a factorial of the number of items in the combination

Sample Scenario

To illustrate, let's imagine that you have a game for which you have 6 tiles numbered 1, 2, 3, 4, 5, and 6. These tiles are placed into a bag. 3 tiles are selected at random, one at a time, to create a 3-digit number.

Let's think about some different questions that you might be asked and how to answer them.

1. If each tile is put back into the bag after it is selected (so that it can potentially be selected again), how many different 3-digit numbers can you get?

2. If the tiles are not put back into the bag after each selection, how many different 3-digit numbers can you get?

3. If the tile is put back into the bag after each selection, what is the probability of getting one specific 3-digit number?

4. If the tiles are put back into the bag after each selection, what is the probability of getting one specific set of 3 digits, regardless of order?

5. If the tiles are not put back into the bag after each selection, what is the probability of getting one specific 3-digit number?

6. If the tiles are not put back into the bag after each selection, what is the probability of getting one specific set of 3 digits, regardless of order?

<u>Solutions</u>

1. If each tile is put back into the bag after it is selected (so that it can potentially be selected again), how many different 3-digit numbers can you get?

If tiles are put back after each selection, you have 6 different options for each of the 3 selections of tiles. Therefore, you have (6)(6)(6) = **216 possible options** for the number.

2. If the tiles are not put back into the bag after each selection, how many different 3-digit numbers can you get?

If tiles are not replaced, then you have 6 different options for the first selection, 5 different options for the second selection, and 4 different options for the third. Therefore, you have (6)(5)(4) = **120 possible options** for the number.

3. If the tile is put back into the bag after each selection, what is the probability of getting one specific 3-digit number?

Since tiles are replaced, you know that there are $(6)(6)(6) = 216$ possible numbers. Therefore, the probability of getting one specific result would be $\frac{1}{216}$.

4. If the tiles are put back into the bag after each selection, what is the probability of getting one specific set of 3 digits, regardless of order?

To compute the total number of combinations, regardless of order, you have to divide the total number of possible ordered permutations, which you know to be 216, by a factorial of the number of positions, in this case 3, so 3!

$$\frac{216}{3!} = \frac{216}{(3)(2)(1)} = \frac{216}{6} = 36$$

So, if order doesn't matter, there are 36 unique combinations of 3 digits, and the probability of getting any one specific set is, therefore, $\frac{1}{36}$.

5. If the tiles are not put back into the bag after each selection, what is the probability of getting one specific 3-digit number?

If the tiles are not put back into the bag after each selection, you know from your previous work that there are 120 possible permutations. Therefore, the probability of obtaining one specific result would be $\frac{1}{120}$.

6. If the tiles are not put back into the bag after each selection, what is the probability of getting one specific set of 3 digits, regardless of order?

Again, if order doesn't matter, then to calculate the total number of possible combinations, you have to divide the total number of ordered permutations by the factorial of the number of decisions, in this case 3!, or $(3)(2)(1) = 6$.

$$\frac{120}{6} = 20.$$

So, there are 20 combinations when digits cannot be repeated and order does not matter.

The probability of getting any one of those combinations is $\frac{1}{20}$.

Combinatorics Thought-Process Flowchart

1. First, consider the number of selections to be made and the total number of options for each selection.
2. Next, consider whether one selection impacts the number of options left for another selection. If so, adjust the numbers accordingly.
3. Finally, consider whether you are selecting for a group or a specific arrangement. If selecting for a specific arrangement, leave as is.
4. If selecting for a group, divide by the factorial of the number in the group (for example, if you are choosing for a group of 4, you would divide by 4!).

Alternative Combinatorics Notation

The GRE expects you to be comfortable with combinatorics notation that uses n to denote the pool of objects available and k to denote the number of objects being arranged in a specific order (permutations) or selected in no particular order (combinations).

Specifically, the notation $_nP_k$ denotes that you have a total of n options from which to select k items for a specific arrangement. Note that $_nP_k$ is associated with the formula $\frac{n!}{(n-k)!}$, but this formula generates the same result as the multiplication principle procedure. For example, $_5P_3$ can be calculated as $\frac{5!}{(5-3)!}$, which simplifies to $\frac{5!}{2!}$, which is the same result you get using the method $(5)(4)(3) = 60$ permutations.

The notation $_nC_k$ and $\binom{n}{k}$ denote that you have a total of n options from which to select k items in no particular order for a group. The formula associated with $_nC_k$ is $\frac{n!}{(k!)(n-k)!}$, which again gives the same results as the method outlined above. For example, $_5C_3$ can be calculated as $\frac{5!}{(3!)(5-3)!}$, which gives the same result as the method $\frac{(5)(4)(3)}{3!}$.

The following expressions and calculations all represent choosing a team of 4 people from a group of 9, and all give the same numerical result:

$$_9C_4, \binom{9}{4}, \frac{9!}{(4!)(9-4)!}, \frac{(9)(8)(7)(6)}{(4)(3)(2)(1)}$$

Here are a couple of sample questions to get some practice with these notations.

Sample Questions

1. Jed will take 3 of his 5 watches with him on his trip. Which of the following represents the number of different combinations of watches that he can choose?

    (A) $_3C_5$

    (B) $_3C_8$

    (C) $_5C_3$

    (D) $_8C_5$

    (E) $_8C_3$

Solution

When you represent combinations in the notation given in the answer choices, you want to put the total number of options before "C" and the total number selected after "C", so **the correct answer is answer choice (C).**

2. Jed will also take with him 2 of his 6 jackets and 4 of his 7 sweaters. Which of the following represents the number of different combinations of sweaters and jackets that he can take with him?

Ⓐ $\left(\begin{array}{c}2\\6\end{array}\right)\left(\begin{array}{c}4\\7\end{array}\right)$

Ⓑ $\left(\begin{array}{c}4\\6\end{array}\right)\left(\begin{array}{c}3\\7\end{array}\right)$

Ⓒ $\left(\begin{array}{c}6\\2\end{array}\right)\left(\begin{array}{c}7\\4\end{array}\right)$

Ⓓ $\dfrac{\left(\begin{array}{c}2\\6\end{array}\right)}{\left(\begin{array}{c}4\\7\end{array}\right)}$

Ⓔ $\dfrac{\left(\begin{array}{c}6\\2\end{array}\right)}{\left(\begin{array}{c}7\\4\end{array}\right)}$

Solution

When you represent combinations in the notation given in the answer choices, you want to put the total number of options on top and the total number selected on the bottom; thus, the correct representation of selecting 2 of 6 jackets is $\left(\begin{array}{c}6\\2\end{array}\right)$ and 4 of 7 jackets is $\left(\begin{array}{c}7\\4\end{array}\right)$. If you want a combination of these options, you should multiply them, so the total number of selections would be $\left(\begin{array}{c}6\\2\end{array}\right)\left(\begin{array}{c}7\\4\end{array}\right)$, **which is answer choice (C)**.

Combinatorics with Multiple Cases

You will occasionally come across combinatorics questions that require making and combining separate calculations. Let's look at two examples so that you can identify and address these types of problems.

Permutations with Multiple Cases

Example: A security passcode contains 6 distinct letters: A, B, C, D, E, F. The letter E MUST be the 4th letter, and the letter B CANNOT be next to the letter E. How many passcodes are possible?

Because you are making specific arrangements, you know that you need to calculate permutations. Let's start by creating a diagram based on the multiplication principle:

_ × _ × _ × _ × _ × _

You know that the 4th blank from the left must contain the letter E, so there's only one option there. The issue is that the letter B is more constrained than the remaining letters A, C, D, F, so you cannot say that you have 5 choices for the remaining 5 spots.

Instead, let's create one working arrangement of the E and B:

B _ _ E _ _

Because the remaining 4 letters are similarly unconstrained, this arrangement of the B and E would result in the following number of overall arrangements:

B _ _ E _ _ = (1)(4)(3)(1)(2)(1), or 24 permutations.

Now let's do another working arrangement for B and E:

_ B _ E _ _ = (4)(1)(3)(1)(2)(1), or 24 permutations.

So, each working arrangement of the B and E letters results in 24 permutations. How many arrangements of B and E are there? Well, E must be 4th, and B cannot be 3rd or 5th, so B must be 1st, 2nd, 3rd, or 6th. There are 4 places for B, so (4)(24) = **96 overall permutations**.

Combinations with Multiple Cases

In a class with 8 juniors and 5 seniors, the teacher wants to create groups of 4 students, with each group having at least 2 seniors. How many such groups can be created?

Let me begin by saying that any time you see the phrase "at least" in a combinatorics problem, (1) you are dealing with a difficult problem and (2) it is important that you pause to consider carefully the impact of that phrase on your approach.

In this case, you know that because you are creating groups in which the members all have the same rank, you are calculating combinations. However, the phrase "with each group having *at least* 2 seniors" complicates matters as it makes several structures possible for the groups of 4. Let's start with a quick table of possible group structures:

Structure	Juniors	Seniors	Total
A	2	2	4
B	1	3	4
C	0	4	4

Let's consider structure A, 2 juniors and 2 seniors. Let's start with 2 juniors from a group of 8. Remember that people by definition are not put back into the pool once selected, so each selection does impact the number of options left.

$\frac{(8)(7)}{2!}$, or 28 possible combinations of 2 juniors

$\frac{(5)(4)}{2!}$, or 10 possible combinations of 2 seniors

Now, remember that any of the 28 combinations of 2 juniors can be placed with any of the 10 combinations of 2 seniors, so the number of overall groups of 4 in structure A is (28)(10) = 280. The "and" in the phrase "2 juniors and 2 seniors" implies multiplication.

Let's calculate the combinations possible in structure B:

$\frac{8}{1!}$ = 8 groups of one junior

$\frac{(5)(4)(3)}{3!}$ = 10 groups of 3 seniors

(8)(10) = 80 overall groups of 4 in structure B

Let's calculate the combinations possible in structure C:

Be careful with 0 juniors—0! has a value of 1. It has to do with the "empty set" being a possible subset of any set; in other words, mathematically there is 1 way to choose 0 juniors out of 8. Any time you are selecting 0 items from a pool, there is 1 way to do that.

So there's 1 group of 0 juniors.

$\frac{(5)(4)(3)(2)}{4!}$ = 5 groups of 4 seniors

(1)(5) = 5 overall groups of 0 juniors and 4 seniors

Now what? Well, the teacher is going to choose structure A or structure B or structure C, and the word "or" implies addition. She can choose one of the 280 groups from structure A, one of 80 from structure B, or one of 5 from structure C. 280 + 80 + 5 = **365 overall possible groups of 4**, given the constraints.

Additional Applications for Factorials

Factorials can also appear in problem types other than calculations of combinations and permutations. Let's consider some additional concepts related to factorials. First, a few additional examples of factorials and what they represent—the ellipses (three dots) are used to represent the pattern continuing through the number 1, which is the final term in any factorial.

$100! = (100)(99)(98)\ldots(1)$

$n! = (n)(n-1)(n-2)\ldots(1)$

There's also one special definition you should know for the purposes of the GRE:

$0! = 1$

It is sometimes helpful to rewrite factorials in prime factored form, as you'll see in a moment. Here's how you can do that, in this case for 8!:

Write out the integer components of 8!

$8! = (8)(7)(6)(5)(4)(3)(2)(1)$

Prime factor each integer element—let's go left to right breaking down each non-prime integer element into prime factors. (Ignore the final 1, as 1 is not prime.)

$[(2)(2)(2)]\,(7)\,[(2)(3)]\,(5)\,[(2)(2)]\,(3)\,(2)$

Combine like prime factors: $8! = (2^7)(3^2)(5)(7)$

Sample Questions

What is the value of $\dfrac{7!}{4!}$?

$$\dfrac{(7)(6)(5)(4)(3)(2)(1)}{(4)(3)(2)(1)}$$

Cancel the matching (4)(3)(2)(1) quantities from the fraction's numerator and denominator, leaving you with (7)(6)(5), or 210.

What expression is equivalent to $\dfrac{n!}{(n-2)!}$?

$$\dfrac{(n)(n-1)(n-2)(n-3)\ldots(1)}{(n-2)(n-3)\ldots(1)}$$

Cancel the matching terms from the fraction's numerator and denominator, leaving you with $(n)(n-1)$, or $n^2 - n$.

If $f(x) = x!$, what is the value of $\dfrac{f(f(3))}{f(3)}$?

If $f(x) = x!$, then $f(3) = 3! = (3)(2)(1) = 6$.

You can substitute this into the original question so that $\dfrac{f(f(3))}{f(3)}$ becomes $\dfrac{f(6)}{6}$.

$f(6) = 6! = (6)(5)(4)(3)(2)(1)$

$$\dfrac{f(6)}{f(3)} = \dfrac{6!}{3!} = \dfrac{6!}{6} = \dfrac{(6)(5)(4)(3)(2)(1)}{6} = (5)(4)(3)(2)(1) = 120$$

What is the greatest possible value of n for which 8! is divisible by 2^n?

Remember that divisibility of a greater number by a lesser number is demonstrated by setting up a fraction in which the greater numerator number (in this case, 8!) can absorb the entire lesser denominator number (in this case, 2^n). This is most easily demonstrated, as discussed earlier, via prime factorization.

Using the prime factorization of 8! demonstrated above, the fraction is:

$$\dfrac{(2^7)(3^2)(5)(7)}{2^n}$$

The 2^n quantity in the denominator can only be absorbed or canceled by the 2^7 quantity in the numerator—none of the other prime factors in the numerator are relevant. So, n can be as great as 7, but no greater. The answer is 7.

There's one more factorial concept that can be a bit of a brain melter. Let's dive in.

If you take a simple factorial such as 3! and write it as (3)(2)(1), it makes sense that its numerical value of 6 is divisible by 3 and 2; after all, the number 6! was formed by multiplying 3, 2, and 1. The number 6 on the number line happens to be a place where the sets of multiples of 2 and multiples of 3 coincide in a single number.

If I ask you to consider the quantity (3! − 1), it's evident that its value is 5, which is NOT divisible by 2 or 3. There's a reason for that: all multiples of 2 are 2 units apart on the number line, and all multiples of 3 are 3 units apart, so if you start on a number that IS divisible by 2 and 3 and then move one unit to the left, you *cannot* land on a number divisible by 2 or 3.

Now, consider the number 26!; its numerical value is so great that it overwhelms the limited parameters of the GRE calculator. Let's write it using ellipses:

26! = (26)(25)(24)(23)…(1)

By analogy with 3!, you can conclude that 26! is divisible by every single integer from 1 through 26. 26! occupies a place on the number line where all of those sets of multiples converge in a single very great number. Let's generalize that as a rule:

The number n! is divisible by every integer from 1 through n.

In the case of 26!, you can extend its known divisibility beyond the integers from 1 through 26. You know that 26! is divisible by 27 because 27 = (9)(3), and 26! contains (9)(3). Same thing with 28 = (14)(2). It's only when you reach the prime number 29 that you have an integer that does not go evenly into 26! Let's generalize that too:

The number n! is divisible by every integer from 1 through n and by all subsequent integers until the first prime number greater than n is reached.

But now let's consider the number (26! − 1). By analogy to 3!, you know that number is NOT divisible by any integer from 2 through n. The least integer that *might* go into 26! − 1 evenly is 29, the first prime number greater than 26.

The number (n! − 1) is NOT divisible by any integer from 2 through n; the first integer that might go evenly into it is the first prime number greater than n.

How might that show up on the GRE?

Sample Question

Which of the following ranges contains n, the least integer that is a factor of (50! − 1)?

Ⓐ 1 < n < 8

Ⓑ 9 < n < 17

Ⓒ 18 < n < 31

Ⓓ 32 < n < 52

Ⓔ 52 < n

Solution

The answer is (E) because no integer from 1 through 52 can be a factor of (50! − 1). Remember that 51 = (17)(3), and 52 = (26)(2), so 51 and 52 are factors of 50! and are therefore not factors of (50! − 1). You don't know what that least factor n is, but you know it must be 53 or greater.

Advanced Probability

I've already talked about some basic probability scenarios. I'll build on that by discussing some more complex probability situations, specifically those that involve more than one selection to be made.

In the examples that follow, you'll note that I sometimes explain two solution methods. When a problem involves making more than one selection, you can continue to use the method of placing the number of outcomes (or "paths") that work over the total number of outcomes (or "paths"). Alternatively, you can calculate the probability of each sequential event and then multiply those probabilities—remember that if you need event A and event B to happen, the word *and* denotes *multiplication* of the probabilities of event A and event B happening.

Another thing that's important to note—as I will ahead—is that the way that to calculate the total number of outcomes (or "paths") in the following sample problems often draws upon either the multiplication principle of combinatorics or the overlapping set techniques I explained using Venn diagrams.

To illustrate, once again pretend you have a bag filled with tiles numbered 1, 2, 3, 4, 5, and 6.

Example 1: Independent Events

If you return the tile to the bag after each selection, what is the probability that you will first select a 3 and then a 4?

These are independent events because the result of the first selection does not influence the probability of the second selection. Because the tile is returned to the bag after the first selection, you are choosing from 6 options each time. Using the multiplication principle, you know that the total number of outcomes is (6)(6), or 36 different outcomes. Your probability of getting the exact outcome of a 3 and then a 4 is $\frac{1}{36}$.

Alternatively, you can recognize that the probability of getting a 3 on the first selection is $\frac{1}{6}$, and the probability of getting a 4 on the second selection is also $\frac{1}{6}$. Because you need a 3 and then a 4, you multiply those probabilities: $\left(\frac{1}{6}\right)\left(\frac{1}{6}\right) = \frac{1}{36}$. You have a $\frac{1}{36}$ probability of the outcome you are seeking.

Example 2: Dependent Events

If you don't return the tile to the bag after each selection, what is the probability that you will first select a 3 and then a 4?

Here you have dependent events—because you don't return the tile to the bag after the first selection, the probability of the second selection is changed due to the lesser number of total tiles in the bag. Once again, you know how to handle this situation using the multiplication principle; the total number of outcomes is (6)(5), or 30. The probability of following the exact path of selecting a 3 and then a 4 is $\frac{1}{30}$.

Alternatively, the probability for the first selection is $\frac{1}{6}$, but the probability for the second selection is $\frac{1}{5}$. The probability of the desired outcome using this "fraction method" is therefore $\left(\frac{1}{6}\right)\left(\frac{1}{5}\right) = \frac{1}{30}$.

Example 3: Overlapping Probabilities

If you return selected tiles to the bag after each selection, and if you select twice, what is the probability that you will select a 3 at least once?

You might recall my warning in the combinatorics discussion that the phrase "at least" signals a high level of difficulty, and its implications must be carefully considered. That warning applies to probability questions as well, and it alerts you to the fact that several different "paths" lead to the desired outcome. You can meet the conditions of the question by getting a 3 on the first selection (but not the second), a 3 on the second selection (but not the first), or a 3 on both the first and second selections.

We know that the probability of selecting a 3 on the first selection is $\frac{1}{6}$, and the probability of selecting a 3 on the second selection is also $\frac{1}{6}$. However, you can't simply combine those two probabilities to get the answer. The word "both" should call to mind overlapping sets, and indeed, this is a situation in which you have to account for overlapping probabilities.

The good news is that you can easily calculate the probability of selecting a 3 in both selections: $\left(\frac{1}{6}\right)\left(\frac{1}{6}\right) = \frac{1}{36}$. At this point, it might help to actually make a Venn diagram to illustrate this situation:

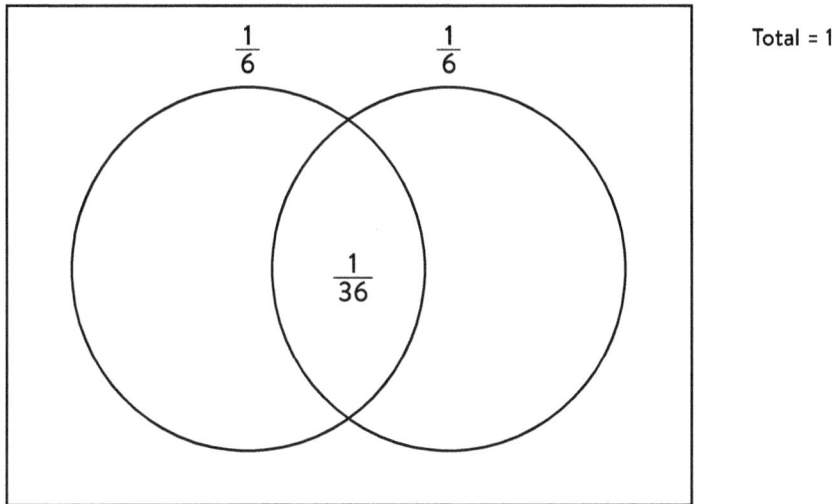

From here, you can use your Venn diagram knowledge to recognize that calculating $A + B$, or in this case $\frac{1}{6} + \frac{1}{6}$, will double count the probability of both A and B, but you can adjust that by subtracting it once from the $A + B$ total.

Therefore, you know to do $\frac{1}{6} + \frac{1}{6} - \frac{1}{36}$ in order to get the answer. Let's work that out by forming common denominators: $\frac{6}{36} + \frac{6}{36} - \frac{1}{36} = \frac{11}{36}$. The answer is $\frac{11}{36}$.

If you prefer, you can use the calculated probability of getting a 3 on both selections to calculate the probabilities of getting a 3 only on the first selection and a 3 only on the second selection. Here's that diagram:

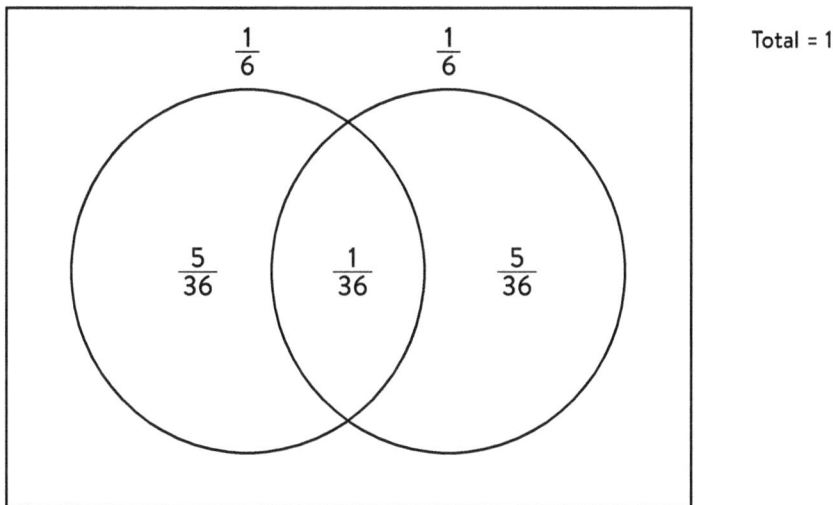

From this diagram, you can calculate the combined probability of the separate positions A only + B only + both: $\frac{5}{36} + \frac{5}{36} + \frac{1}{36} = \frac{11}{36}$.

Note that if the question asked about the probability of getting a 3 either on the first selection or on the second selection but not on both selections, then you can either do $A + B - 2(\text{both})$, or $\frac{1}{6} + \frac{1}{6} - 2\left(\frac{1}{36}\right) = \frac{10}{36}$, or you can do A only $+ B$ only, or $\frac{5}{36} + \frac{5}{36} = \frac{10}{36}$.

Example 4: Overlapping Probabilities with an Unknown Amount of Overlap

For this problem type, which is about as difficult as the GRE gets, I need to retire the bag of tiles for a more theoretical situation.

In a probability experiment, the probability that event A will occur is $\frac{1}{3}$, and the probability that event B will occur is $\frac{1}{5}$. Which of the following values could be the probability that $A \cup B$ (that is, the event A or B or both) will occur?

Indicate <u>all</u> such values.

A $\frac{3}{7}$

B $\frac{7}{15}$

C $\frac{2}{3}$

<u>Solution</u>

Both the wording of the question ("Which of the following values could be the probability") and the possibility of multiple answers indicate that you can't simply calculate the definite probability of both A and B occurring the way you did in Example 3. Instead, you need to break out the maximizing and minimizing skills you learned in the discussion of Venn diagrams!

Let's begin with the fact that the maximum probability for "both A and B" is the lesser of the two circle totals. In this case, $\frac{1}{5}$. Let's make a Venn diagram, insert $\frac{1}{5}$ for the probability of both, and calculate the A-only and B-only probabilities.

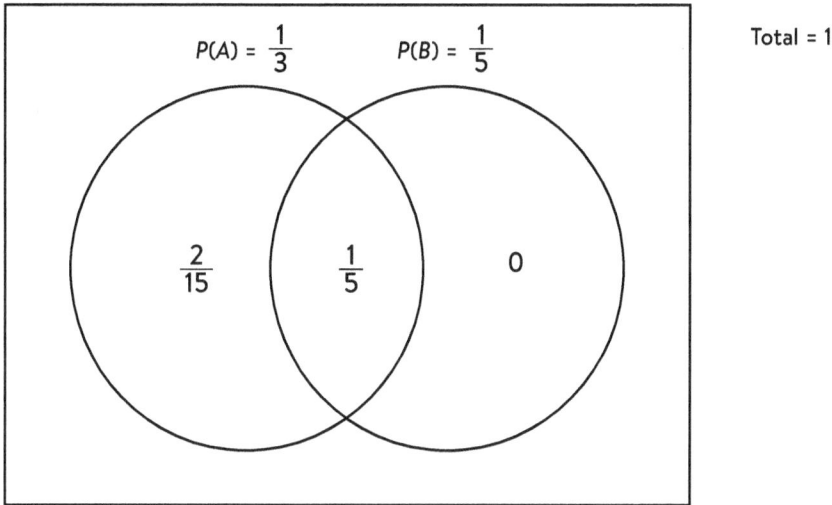

Total = 1

$P(A) = \frac{1}{3}$ $P(B) = \frac{1}{5}$

$\frac{2}{15}$ $\frac{1}{5}$ 0

Note that the A-only calculation came from doing $\frac{1}{3} - \frac{1}{5}$, which becomes $\frac{5}{15} - \frac{3}{15} = \frac{2}{15}$.

When you maximize the overlap (the probability of A and B both happening), you can answer the question by doing A only + B only + both, or $\frac{2}{15} + 0 + \frac{1}{5}$. Using a common denominator, that's $\frac{2}{15} + \frac{3}{15}$, or $\frac{5}{15}$, which reduces to $\frac{1}{3}$.

Now, let's minimize the overlap. In this case, given that $\frac{1}{3} + \frac{1}{5} = \frac{8}{15}$, which is less than 1, there doesn't need to be any overlap at all. Here's that diagram:

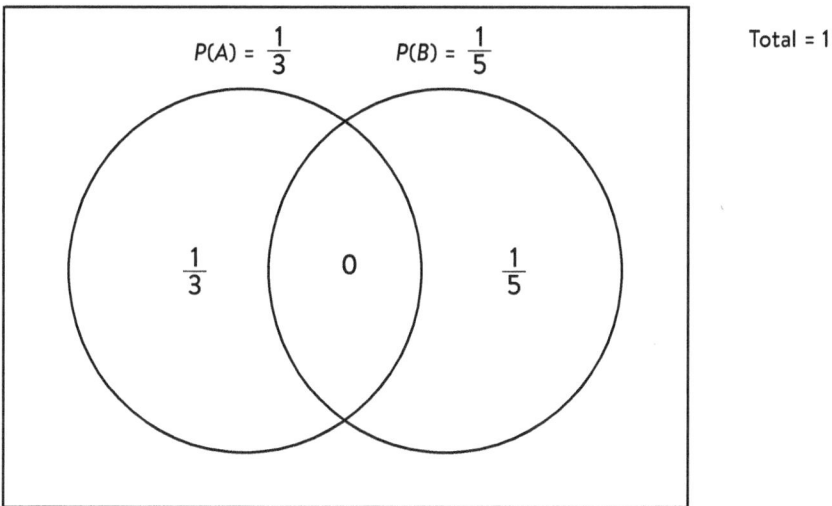

Total = 1

$P(A) = \frac{1}{3}$ $P(B) = \frac{1}{5}$

$\frac{1}{3}$ 0 $\frac{1}{5}$

With the overlap minimized, the calculation of A only + B only + both gives you $\frac{1}{3} + \frac{1}{5} + 0$. Using a common denominator, you get $\frac{5}{15} + \frac{3}{15} = \frac{8}{15}$.

That means that given the information presented in the question, the probability of A or B or both ranges from a minimum of $\frac{1}{3}$ to a maximum of $\frac{8}{15}$. Now, let's consider the answer choices—and recognize that it might be easier in this case to work with decimal values. $\frac{1}{3}$ is roughly 0.33, and $\frac{8}{15}$ is roughly 0.53.

[A] $\frac{3}{7}$ is roughly 0.428, so that is in the range of possible values

[B] $\frac{7}{15}$ is roughly 0.47, so that is in the range of possible values

[C] $\frac{2}{3}$ is roughly 0.67, so that is NOT in the range of possible values

The answer choices [A] and [B] are correct.

Note that you can derive the range of possible values for the probability of neither A nor B from the work you did. In the case where the probability of A or B or both was $\frac{1}{3}$, the probability of neither is $\frac{2}{3}$. In the case where the probability of A or B or both was $\frac{8}{15}$, the probability of neither is $\frac{7}{15}$. So, the probability of neither A nor B could range from a minimum of $\frac{7}{15}$ (or roughly 0.47) to a maximum of $\frac{2}{3}$ (or roughly 0.67).

Complementary Probability

If the probability that event F will occur is x, then the probability that event F will not occur is $1 - x$.

For example, if the probability that it will rain in a certain town on a certain day is 30%, or 0.3, then the probability that it will not rain in that certain town on that certain day is $1 - 0.3$, or 0.7.

The GRE can combine complementary probability with a multiple event scenario to create some fun problems. For example, if the probability of rain in a certain town on a certain day is 0.3, what is the probability that over consecutive days Monday through Thursday it will rain only on Thursday in that town?

Solution: $(0.7)(0.7)(0.7)(0.3)$, or 0.1029

Sample Question

If the probability that event A will occur is m, and the probability that event B will occur is n, and if events A and B are independent of one another, which of the following represents the probability that either event A or B will occur, but not both?

(A) $m + n$
(B) $2mn - n$
(C) $2m + 2n - mn$
(D) $m + n - 2mn$
(E) $m + n + 2mn$

Solution

First, let's consider the probability of A occurring without B occurring.

The probability that event A will occur is m. Since the probability that event B will occur is n, the probability that event B will not occur is $1 - n$.

Thus, the probability that event A will occur and event B will not is $(m)(1 - n)$. Now, let's consider the probability of B occurring without A occurring.

The probability that event B will occur is n, and the probability that event A will occur is $(1 - m)$.

Therefore, the probability that event B will occur but event A will not is $n(1 - m)$.

The odds that either of these events will happen are the sum of both options:

$m(1 - n) + n(1 - m) =$
$m - mn + n - nm =$
$m - 2mn + n =$
$m + n - 2mn$

(D) is the correct answer.

I'll conclude this discussion of complementary probability by noting that it gives you a powerful tool for answering certain probability questions that use the phrase "at least." Let's return to example 3: If you return selected tiles to the bag after each selection, and if you select twice, what is the probability that you will select a 3 at least once?

In a typical 2-event situation like this one, you can follow any of the following 4 paths:

Path 1: select a 3, then don't select a 3 (A, then not B)
Path 2: don't select a 3, then select a 3 (not A, then B)
Path 3: select a 3, then select a 3 (A, then B, or "both" in Venn terms)
Path 4: don't select a 3, then don't select a 3 (not A, then not B, or "neither" in Venn terms).

In the original explanation, you directly calculated the probability of A or B or both—in other words, you calculated the combined probability of paths 1, 2, and 3.

But complementary probability offers another approach. Let's call the probability of path 4 (getting a 3 on neither selection) the probability of "neither." Well, the probability of getting a 3 on at least one selection is 1 − neither. In other words, once you figure out the probability of path 4, then 1 − (path 4) is the sum of paths 1 through 3.

Let's try it. You'll first calculate the probability of not selecting a 3 on either selection—this is relatively straightforward: $\left(\frac{5}{6}\right)\left(\frac{5}{6}\right)$, or $\frac{25}{36}$. The probability of selecting at least one 3 is therefore $1 - \frac{25}{36}$, or $\frac{11}{36}$—precisely the answer you got above.

There's one more probability question type I want to address. I could have included this question type with earlier discussions of fractions or percents, but because it's mostly presented in probability terms, I'll address it here.

If a bag of 50 marbles contains 20 blue marbles, how many blue marbles must be added so that the probability of randomly selecting a blue marble from the bag is 0.6?

Let's start by noting that the current probability of selecting a blue marble is $\frac{20}{50}$. It's important in this question type to keep the original numbers rather than reducing that fraction. You're going to add an unknown number of blue marbles to the bag; you'll use the variable x to represent that unknown number. But keep in mind that if you add blue marbles to the bag, you're also adding that same number of marbles to the total number of marbles in the bag, and of course, that has to be taken into account in any probability question. So, let's represent the probability situation with the unknown number of blue marbles added to the bag:

$$\frac{20 + x}{50 + x}$$

That fraction represents the new probability of randomly selecting a blue marble from the bag, but you know that the new probability has to equal 0.6. Let's represent 0.6 as a fraction for ease of calculator. You can start by writing 0.6 as $\frac{6}{10}$, but you can reduce that to $\frac{3}{5}$. Note that the fraction indicating the final probability can be a reduced fraction, as the fraction on the left side of the equation simply needs to equal that value.

$$\frac{20 + x}{50 + x} = \frac{3}{5}$$

Now cross-multiply:

$(20 + x)(5) = (50 + x)(3)$
$100 + 5x = 150 + 3x$
$2x = 50$
$x = 25$, and that's the answer.

You can check your math by calculating that you'd now have 45 blue marbles out of a total of 75 marbles. $\frac{45}{75}$ reduces to $\frac{3}{5}$, which is equivalent to 0.6.

Note that the question could have been presented in percent terms: If a bag of 50 marbles contains 20 blue marbles, how many blue marbles must be added so that exactly 60% of the marbles in the bag are blue? The solution path would be the same because you would write the target fraction on the right side of the equation as $\frac{60}{100}$, which reduces to $\frac{3}{5}$.

Practice Questions

1. Let A, B, and C be independent events for which $P(A \text{ or } B) = 0.44$, $P(B \text{ or } C) = 0.54$, and $P(C) = 2P(A)$.

What is $P(B)$?

(A) 0.1
(B) 0.2
(C) 0.22
(D) 0.34
(E) 0.74

2. A child is allowed to select exactly 1 toy from bin A, 1 toy from bin B, and 1 toy from bin C. If bin A has 3 toys, bin B has 5 toys, and bin C has 7 toys, and if all the toys are different and unique, in how many different ways can the child make his selection?

[ ]

3. $S = \{0, 1, 2, 3, 4, 5\}$

If m represents the number of 3-member subsets of S and n represents the number of 4-member subsets of S, then what is the value of $m - n$?

(A) 5
(B) 8
(C) 10
(D) 20
(E) 40

4. An experiment has 4 potential mutually exclusive outcomes: A, B, C, and D. The probability that A will occur is 0.21, the probability that B will occur is 0.17, and the probability that C will occur is 0.31.

Quantity A
The probability that A or B will occur

Quantity B
The probability that D will occur

(A) Quantity A is greater.
(B) Quantity B is greater.
(C) The two quantities are equal.
(D) The relationship cannot be determined from the information given.

5. A bag contains 4 red balls, 6 green balls, and nothing else. If 3 balls are pulled out of the bag one at a time, randomly and without being replaced, what is the probability that 3 consecutive red balls will be selected?

[ ]
———
[ ]

6. A bag contains 4 red balls and 6 green balls. If 2 balls are pulled out at random, what is the probability that 1 is red and 1 is green?

[ ]
———
[ ]

Practice Questions Continued

7. A coach selects 5 players to start a basketball game from the 8 total players on the team. How many different options does the coach have for the starting group of 5?

(A) 56
(B) 81
(C) 336
(D) 362
(E) 1,344

8. For a certain probability experiment, the probability that event A will occur is $\frac{1}{2}$, the probability that event B will occur is $\frac{1}{4}$, and the probability that event C will occur is $\frac{1}{8}$.

Quantity A	Quantity B
The probability that event A or B or both occur.	The probability that event A or C or both occur.

(A) Quantity A is greater.
(B) Quantity B is greater.
(C) The two quantities are equal.
(D) The relationship cannot be determined from the information given.

9. A child splatters paint on a canvas. She covers at least $\frac{1}{4}$ of the canvas in yellow paint, at least $\frac{1}{2}$ of the canvas in red paint, and at least $\frac{2}{3}$ of the canvas in green paint.

If 1 spot on the canvas is selected at random, which of the following could be the probability that spot would be blank and devoid of any of the child's paint splatter?

Indicate all such values.

A $\frac{1}{8}$

B $\frac{1}{4}$

C $\frac{2}{5}$

D $\frac{1}{2}$

10. For a certain carnival game, a player gets 2 attempts to throw a ball through a hoop. If the probability of getting the ball through the hoop is 80% on any 1 attempt, what is the likelihood that a player will get the ball through the hoop at least once in 2 attempts?

(A) 0.36
(B) 0.64
(C) 0.8
(D) 0.92
(E) 0.96

11. If an integer from 0 to 999 is selected at random, what is the probability that it will have at least one 8 as one of its digits?

(A) 24.2%
(B) 27.2%
(C) 28%
(D) 28.1%
(E) 30%

Practice Question Solutions

1. Let A, B, and C be independent events for which $P(A \text{ or } B) = 0.44$, $P(B \text{ or } C) = 0.54$, and $P(C) = 2P(A)$.

What is $P(B)$?

Ⓐ 0.1
Ⓑ 0.2
Ⓒ 0.22
Ⓓ 0.34
Ⓔ 0.74

Solution

Notice that replacing "A" in $P(A \text{ or } B)$ with "C" in $P(B \text{ or } C)$ increased the odds from 0.44 to 0.54. This tells you that the difference of $P(C) - P(A) = 0.1$. If $P(C) = 2P(A)$, you can infer that $P(C) = 0.2$, and $P(A) = 0.1$ (because $P(C)$ has to be twice $P(A)$ and also 0.1 greater).

Here's the long way to compute this:

$2P(A) + P(B) = 0.54$
$-(P(A) + P(B) = 0.44)$
$P(A) = 0.1$

If $P(A) = 0.1$, $P(C) = 0.2$, and $P(B) = 0.44 - 0.1 = 0.34$. **(D) is correct.**

2. A child is allowed to select exactly 1 toy from bin A, 1 toy from bin B, and 1 toy from bin C. If bin A has 3 toys, bin B has 5 toys, and bin C has 7 toys, and if all the toys are different and unique, in how many different ways can the child make his selection?

$$\boxed{105}$$

Solution

If bin A has 3 toys, bin B has 5 toys, and bin C has 7 toys, there are $(3)(5)(7) =$ **105 different ways for the child to make his selection**.

Solutions Continued

3. $S = \{0, 1, 2, 3, 4, 5\}$

If m represents the number of 3-member subsets of S and n represents the number of 4-member subsets of S, then what is the value of $m - n$?

(A) 5
(B) 8
(C) 10
(D) 20
(E) 40

Solution

For the 3-member subset, you know you have 6 options for the first selection, 5 options for the second, and 4 for the third, and since you are selecting 3 items and order doesn't matter, you have to divide all this by 3!:

$$\frac{(6)(5)(4)}{(3)(2)(1)} = 20, \text{ so } m = 20$$

For 4 member subsets, you have 6 options for the first selection, 5 for the second, 4 for the third, and 3 for the last, and since you are selecting for 4 items and order doesn't matter, divide it all by 4!:

$$\frac{(6)(5)(4)(3)}{(4)(3)(2)(1)} = 15, \text{ so } n = 15$$

Thus, $m - n = 20 - 15 = 5$, and the correct answer is (A).

4. An experiment has 4 potential mutually exclusive outcomes: A, B, C, and D. The probability that A will occur is 0.21, the probability that B will occur is 0.17, and the probability that C will occur is 0.31.

Quantity A	Quantity B
The probability that A or B will occur	The probability that D will occur

(A) **Quantity A is greater.**
(B) Quantity B is greater.
(C) The two quantities are equal.
(D) The relationship cannot be determined from the information given.

Solution

Since all are mutually exclusive outcomes, to calculate the probability that A or B will occur, you simply need to add up their individual probabilities, in this case $0.21 + 0.17 = 0.38$.

You can calculate the probability that D will occur by subtracting all other probabilities from 1:

$$1 - 0.21 - 0.17 - 0.31 = 0.31.$$

Therefore, Quantity A is greater.

5. A bag contains 4 red balls, 6 green balls, and nothing else. If 3 balls are pulled out of the bag one at a time, randomly and without being replaced, what is the probability that 3 consecutive red balls will be selected?

$$\boxed{1}$$
$$\overline{}$$
$$\boxed{30}$$

Solution

The probability that the first ball selected is red is $\frac{4}{10}$.

Since the balls are not replaced, once the red ball is selected, the probability that another red ball is selected is $\frac{3}{9}$.

The probability that a third red ball is then selected is $\frac{2}{8}$.

Therefore, the probability of selecting 3 consecutive red balls is:

$$\left(\frac{4}{10}\right)\left(\frac{3}{9}\right)\left(\frac{2}{8}\right) = \left(\frac{2}{5}\right)\left(\frac{1}{3}\right)\left(\frac{1}{4}\right) = \frac{2}{60} = \mathbf{\frac{1}{30}}.$$

6. A bag contains 4 red balls and 6 green balls. If 2 balls are pulled out at random, what is the probability that 1 is red and 1 is green?

$$\boxed{8}$$
$$\overline{}$$
$$\boxed{15}$$

Solution

There are a few different ways you can approach this problem. Here are two:

Option 1: You can calculate the odds of first selecting a red ball and then a green ball and the odds of first selecting a green ball followed by a red ball. You then add the 2 odds together.

Red then green: $\left(\frac{4}{10}\right)\left(\frac{6}{9}\right) = \left(\frac{2}{5}\right)\left(\frac{2}{3}\right) = \frac{4}{15}$

Green then red: $\left(\frac{6}{10}\right)\left(\frac{4}{9}\right) = \frac{4}{15}$

$$\frac{4}{15} + \frac{4}{15} = \frac{8}{15}$$

Option 2: You can calculate the odds of selecting 2 reds and the odds of selecting 2 greens, and subtract both from 1, leaving the odds of getting one red and one green.

Odds of getting 2 reds: $\left(\frac{4}{10}\right)\left(\frac{3}{9}\right) = \left(\frac{2}{5}\right)\left(\frac{1}{3}\right) = \frac{2}{15}$

Odds of getting 2 greens: $\left(\frac{6}{10}\right)\left(\frac{5}{9}\right) = \left(\frac{3}{5}\right)\left(\frac{5}{9}\right) = \frac{1}{3}$

$$\frac{2}{15} + \frac{1}{3} = \frac{2}{15} + \frac{5}{15} = \frac{7}{15}; 1 - \frac{7}{15} = \mathbf{\frac{8}{15}}$$

Solutions Continued

7. A coach selects 5 players to start a basketball game from the 8 total players on the team. How many different options does the coach have for the starting group of 5?

Ⓐ **56**
Ⓑ 81
Ⓒ 336
Ⓓ 362
Ⓔ 1,344

Solution

There are $(8)(7)(6)(5)(4) = 6{,}720$ permutations of the 8 players.

Since you are selecting for a simple group of 5, a combination in no particular order, you want to divide that number by 5!, which is $(5)(4)(3)(2)(1) = 120$.

$\frac{6,720}{120} = 56$, and **(A) is the correct answer.**

8. For a certain probability experiment, the probability that event A will occur is $\frac{1}{2}$, the probability that event B will occur is $\frac{1}{4}$, and the probability that event C will occur is $\frac{1}{8}$.

Quantity A	Quantity B
The probability that event A or B or both occur.	The probability that event A or C or both occur.

Ⓐ Quantity A is greater.
Ⓑ Quantity B is greater.
Ⓒ The two quantities are equal.
Ⓓ **The relationship cannot be determined from the information given.**

Solution

You don't know the relation between the different events, so it could be, for example, that event B happens every time event A occurs, or only occurs every time event A doesn't, and so on.

If event B always occurs with event A, the probability that events A or B or both occur is $\frac{1}{2}$. If event B never occurs with event A, the probability that events A or B or both occur is $\frac{1}{2} + \frac{1}{4} = \frac{3}{4}$.

If event C always occurs with event A, the probability that events A and C or both occur is $\frac{1}{2}$. If event C never occurs with event A, the probability that events A and C or both occur is $\frac{1}{2} + \frac{1}{8} = \frac{5}{8}$.

Without further information, you can't tell which quantity is greater, and the correct answer is (D).

9. A child splatters paint on a canvas. She covers at least $\frac{1}{4}$ of the canvas in yellow paint, at least $\frac{1}{2}$ of the canvas in red paint, and at least $\frac{2}{3}$ of the canvas in green paint. If 1 spot on the canvas is selected at random, which of the following could be the probability that spot would be blank and devoid of any of the child's paint splatter?

Indicate all such values.

[A] $\frac{1}{8}$

[B] $\frac{1}{4}$

[C] $\frac{2}{5}$

[D] $\frac{1}{2}$

Solution

Here, without more information, you don't know how the probabilities or proportions of the different colors relate to one another. You can imagine extreme scenarios in which the paint splatters overlap as little as possible and are thus able to cover the entire canvas, leaving no blank spots at all, OR, by contrast, the splatters overlap as *much* as possible, in which case all of the red and yellow paint overlap with the green paint and leave $\frac{1}{3}$ of the canvas completely blank. All of the other possibilities fall between these two extremes; **the probability of landing on blank space is between 0 and $\frac{1}{3}$, so answer choices [A] and [B] are the only possibilities that could work**.

10. For a certain carnival game, a player gets 2 attempts to throw a ball through a hoop. If the probability of getting the ball through the hoop is 80% on any 1 attempt, what is the likelihood that a player will get the ball through the hoop at least once in 2 attempts?

(A) 0.36
(B) 0.64
(C) 0.8
(D) 0.92
(E) 0.96

Solution

Option 1: To calculate the probability that the player will make at least 1 throw, you want to add up the odds that they will make the first or the second throw, and then subtract from that the likelihood of making both. Note that you aren't saying they aren't allowed to make both; it's just that you've already accounted for it when adding up the other likelihoods.

Likelihood of making first + likelihood of making second – likelihood of making both =

$0.8 + 0.8 - 0.64 =$ **0.96**.

Option 2: Here's a conceptual way to think about the same situation:

Imagine that the player tries the carnival game 100 times.

During those 100 times, you can expect that they will make the first throw 80 times, satisfying the condition of making 1 or more throws.

And for the 20 times they don't make the first throw, they should make the second throw $(0.8)(20) = 16$ times, or $\frac{16}{20}$.

So, out of 100 times, you can expect the player to make at least 1 throw 80 + 16 = 96 times.

Solutions Continued

11. If an integer from 0 to 999 is selected at random, what is the probability that it will have at least one 8 as one of its digits?

(A) 24.2%
(B) 27.2%
(C) 28%
(D) **28.1%**
(E) 30%

Solution

To calculate this, you have to think about all of the integers with at least one 8, and then consider the overlap of integers with more than one 8.

To begin, you know that there are 100 integers that have an 8 in the hundreds place—all of those integers from 800 to 899.

You also know that there are 100 integers that have 8 in the tens place and 100 integers that have 8 in the ones place (one way to think about this is that $\frac{1}{10}$ of all the integers, which are 1,000 total, will have one of the 10 digits in a certain position).

So far, you have 100 + 100 + 100 = 300. However, you now must subtract the overlap.

First, for integers with 8 in the hundreds digit place, you must subtract the numbers that have 8 in the tens digit place: 880 through 889. There are 10 such integers total, and they also include the term 888, which has 8 in all digits.

Next, you have to think about the integers that have 8 in the tens digit and also the units digit. There are 10 such numbers (188, 288, 388, etc.), but you've already accounted for one of them (888), so this actually adds 9 more integers to the list of those with more than one 8.

So, you started out with 100 (the number of terms with 8 as the hundreds digit) + 100 (the number of terms with 8 as the tens digit) + 100 (the number of terms with 8 as the units digit) = 300, and from this you must subtract 10 and 9 more, which represented the "overlap" of integers with more than one 8 as a digit. You end up with 300 − 10 − 9 = 281 integers from 0 through 999 that have at least one 8.

Since there are 1,000 integers total from 0 to 999 inclusive, that means the probability of selecting an integer with an 8 in it is $\frac{281}{1,000}$, or 28.1%, **which is answer choice (D)**.

17
QUANTITATIVE REASONING

Tables and Graphs, Part 1

Tables and graphs are very common on the GRE, and your ability to correctly utilize them is fundamental to your success in the quantitative sections. The GRE's tables and graphs are not especially difficult to understand or interpret. The challenge is that they contain a lot of information, and you need to ensure you are consistently careful and correct in both your understanding of the task and your reading of these tables and graphs.

The numerical information presented in the tables and graphs will either be qualitative in nature (describing the characteristics of something, such as, for example, the weights or heights of various animals in a zoo), or they will give you information about frequency (e.g., the number of each type of animal in the zoo) or relative frequency (e.g., the same data about the number of animals at the zoo, but presented in terms of the percentage they represent of the total zoo population).

This information will most commonly be presented in the form of tables, bar graphs, segmented bar graphs, line graphs, or circle graphs. You will practice examples of each in this chapter. Information can also be presented in other, less common graphical ways; I'll cover those in the next chapter.

Questions will ask you to interpret the data or utilize it in some way: to perform simple computations, identify ratios or proportions, or solve for different types of statistics. You will practice examples of all these types of questions here as well.

To begin, let's look at a few sample situations and review the ways in which the same information can be presented in different tables and graphs.

Price of Item X and Price of Item Y Over Time

Imagine that you are given the following information about the price of two items, Item X and Item Y, and how they've changed over time. Here are three different ways in which the same information can be presented:

Year	Price of Item X	Price of Item Y
1990	$1.25	$1.00
2000	$1.50	$1.75
2010	$1.75	$2.00
2020	$2.00	$2.50

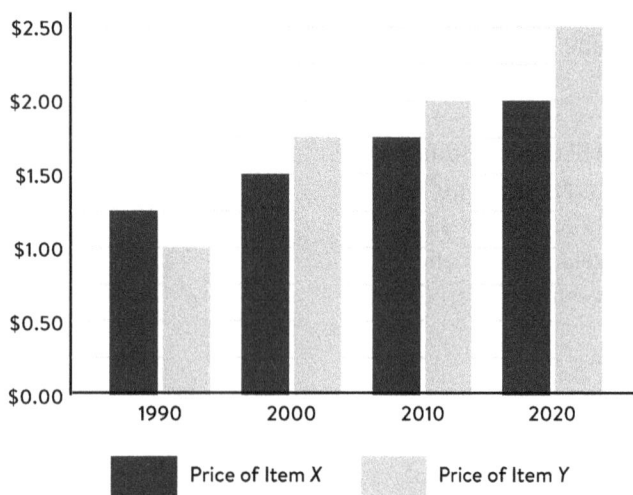

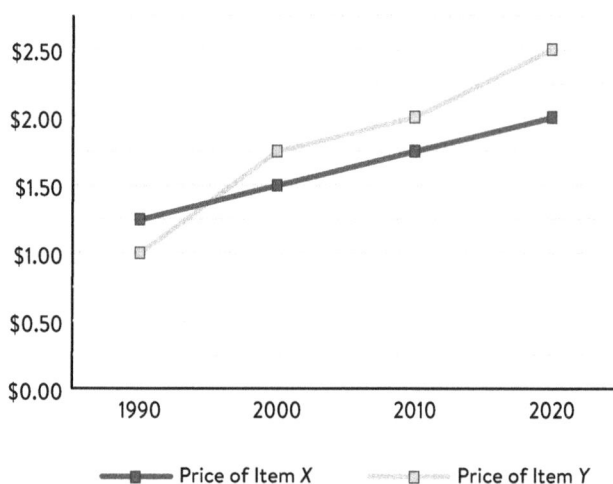

Here is the same information, presented in both bar and line graphs in which the x-axis represents the year, and the y-axis represents the price of each item. Please note that on the real exam, you won't be presented with multiple views of the same information as you are here, and the questions will vary depending on how the information is presented.

Now let's look at some examples of the types of questions that you might be asked regarding this information.

1. How much more would it have cost to purchase 20 of item Y in 2020 than 20 of item Y in 1990?

- (A) $10
- (B) $20
- (C) $30
- (D) $40
- (E) $50

Solution

In 2020, it would have cost $2.50 per item times 20 items = $50 to purchase 20 of item Y. In 1990, it would have cost $1.00 per item times 20 items = $20 to purchase 20 of item Y. The difference between those prices is $50 – $20 = $30, so **(C) is the correct answer.**

2. The price of item X increased by what percent between 1990 and 2010?

(A) 20%
(B) 25%
(C) 37.5%
(D) 40%
(E) 60%

Solution

In 1990, the price of item X was $1.25. In 2010, the price of item X was $1.75. The price increased 0.50, which represents $\frac{0.50}{1.25} = 0.4$, or a 40% increase. **(D) is the correct answer.**

---

3. How much greater is the increase in price for item Y between 1990 and 2010 than the increase in price for item X between 1990 and 2020?

(A) $0.25
(B) $0.50
(C) $0.65
(D) $0.75
(E) $1.00

Solution

Item Y increased from $1.00 in 1990 to $2.00 in 2010, a difference of $1.00. Item X increased from $1.25 in 1990 to $2.00 in 2020, a difference of $0.75. Therefore, the increase in price for item Y between 1990 and 2010 was $0.25 greater than the increase in price for item X between 1990 and 2020. **(A) is the correct answer.**

4. The ratio of the price of item X in 1990 to the price of item X in 2020 is greater than which of the following ratios?

Indicate <u>all</u> such ratios.

[A] Price of item X in 1990 to the price of item Y in 2010
[B] Price of item Y in 1990 to the price of item Y in 2010
[C] Price of item Y in 1990 to the price of item X in 2010
[D] Price of item X in 2000 to the price of item Y in 2010
[E] Price of item Y in 2000 to the price of item Y in 2020

Solution

The price of item X in 1990 is $1.25, and the price of item X in 2020 is $2.00, so the ratio of the two is $\frac{1.25}{2} = \frac{5}{8}$.

For [A], the ratio is $\frac{1.25}{2} = \frac{5}{8}$. This is not greater than the initial ratio.

For [B], the ratio is $\frac{1}{2}$. This is not greater than the initial ratio.

For [C], the ratio is $\frac{1}{1.75} = \frac{4}{7}$. This is not greater than the initial ratio.

For [D], the ratio is $\frac{1.5}{2} = \frac{3}{4}$. This is greater than the initial ratio.

Finally, for [E], the ratio is $\frac{1.75}{2.5} = \frac{7}{10}$. This is greater than the initial ratio.

Thus, answer choices [D] and [E] are correct.

Weekend Shop Sales

A certain shop is open for two weekend days, Saturday and Sunday, and it sells exactly five types of items: appetizers, sandwiches, soups, desserts, and drinks. The following table and graphs show the number of each type of item sold on each day.

Item	Saturday	Sunday
appetizers	43	41
sandwiches	82	86
soups	42	48
desserts	62	33
drinks	75	82

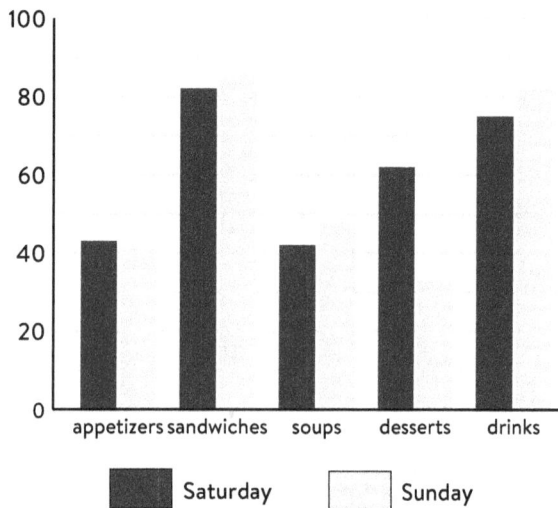

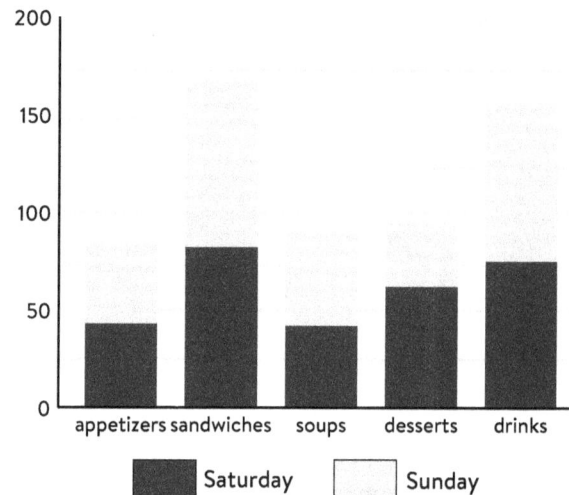

A segmented bar graph helps you see how components add up to a total.

1. Which of the following accurately represents the ratio of the total number of appetizers sold over the weekend to the total number of sandwiches sold over the weekend?

(A) 1:4
(B) 10:22
(C) 1:2
(D) 11:21
(E) 41:74

Solution

There were a total number of $43 + 41 = 84$ appetizers sold over the weekend and a total of $82 + 86 = 168$ sandwiches sold over the weekend. The ratio of appetizers sold to sandwiches sold is, therefore, $\frac{84}{168} = \frac{1}{2}$. **The correct answer is (C).**

---

2. For which of the following types of items was the total number of sales the least over the entire weekend?

(A) Appetizers
(B) Sandwiches
(C) Soups
(D) Desserts
(E) Drinks

Solution

You can fairly quickly see that sandwiches and drinks are out of the running. Comparing appetizers to soups, you can see that the store sold fewer appetizers (1 more appetizer on Saturday but 7 fewer on Sunday). Comparing appetizers to desserts, there were a lot more desserts sold on Saturday, and some more appetizers sold on Sunday, but overall there were fewer appetizers sold than desserts (appetizers = $43 + 41 = 84$; desserts = $62 + 33 = 95$). Therefore, **(A) is the correct answer.**

3. If the store earned a net profit of $2.25 per sandwich sold, how much more profit did it earn from the sale of sandwiches on Sunday than it earned from the sale of sandwiches on Saturday?

$ [   ]

Solution

The store sold 4 more sandwiches on Sunday than it did on Saturday ($86 - 82 = 4$). Therefore, **it earned (4)($2.25) = $9.00 more in profit off sandwiches sold on Sunday than on Saturday**.

---

4. Appetizers represent approximately what percentage of all items sold on Sunday?

(A) 10%
(B) 15%
(C) 20%
(D) 25%
(E) 30%

Solution

There were 41 appetizers sold on Sunday, and a total of $41 + 86 + 48 + 33 + 82 = 290$ items were sold. $\frac{41}{290} = 0.141$, which is closest to 15%. **(B) is the correct answer.**

Acme Co.

Total revenue in 2010: $500,000; Total revenue in 2020: $725,000

PERCENTAGE OF INCOME PER INCOME STREAM

	2010	2020
Online	24	42
Wholesale	44	33
Retail	10	15
Institutional	12	7
Other	10	3

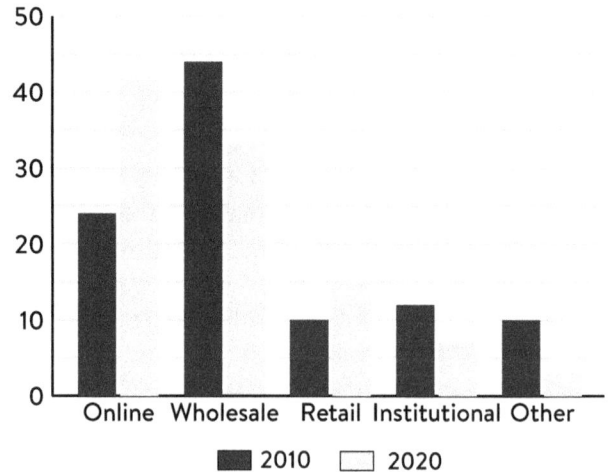

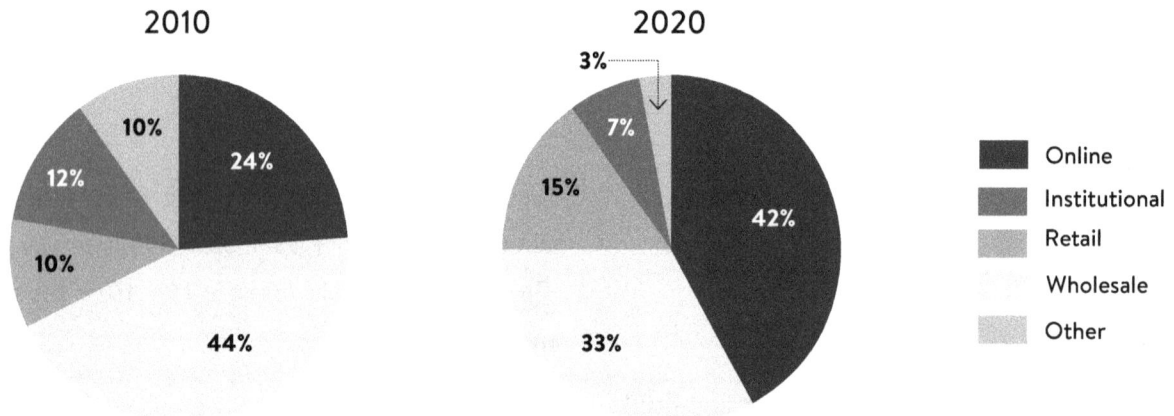

2010

2020

1. How much more total revenue did Acme Co. earn through retail sales in 2020 than in 2010?

(A) $24,500
(B) $36,250
(C) $47,550
(D) $58,750
(E) $225,000

Solution

Acme Co. earned (0.15)($725,000) = $108,750 through retail sales in 2020 and (0.10)($500,000) = $50,000 through retail sales in 2010. Therefore, Acme Co. earned $108,750 – $50,000 = $58,750 more in retail sales revenue in 2020 than it did in 2010. **The correct answer is (D).**

2. Which income streams had a greater total revenue in 2010 than in 2020?

Indicate all such income streams.

A Online
B Wholesale
C Retail
D Institutional
E Other

Solution

For online and retail sales, the total revenue of the company and their portion of that total revenue both went up between 2010 and 2020, so you know that their revenue was greater in 2020 than it was in 2010.

For wholesale, in 2010 revenue was (0.44)($500,000) = $220,000. In 2020, wholesale revenue was (0.33)($725,000) = $239,250. Therefore, total revenue from wholesale was greater in 2020.

For institutional, in 2010 revenue was (0.12)($500,000) = $60,000. In 2020, institutional revenue was (0.07)($725,000) = $50,750. Therefore, total revenue from institutional was greater in 2010.

For other, in 2010, the revenue was (0.10)($500,000) = $50,000. In 2020, other revenue was (0.03)($725,000) = $21,750. Therefore, total revenue from other was greater in 2010.

Therefore, the two departments that had greater total revenue in 2010 were [D] institutional and [E] other.

---

3. Which income stream has the greatest ratio of total revenue earned in 2020 to total revenue earned in 2010?

Ⓐ Online
Ⓑ Wholesale
Ⓒ Retail
Ⓓ Institutional
Ⓔ Other

Solution

You are looking for the stream whose revenue grew the most, proportionally speaking, between 2020 and 2010; this stream will have the highest ratio of revenue earned in 2020 to that earned in 2010. The only two likely streams are online and retail sales, since both grew as a percentage of overall sales while the other streams did not.

For online sales, the ratio of revenue earned in 2020 to 2010 is:

$$\frac{(0.42)(725,000)}{(0.24)(500,000)}, \text{ or } \frac{304,500}{120,000} \approx \frac{2.5}{1}$$

For retail sales, the ratio of revenue earned in 2020 to 2010 is:

$$\frac{(0.15)(725,000)}{(0.10)(500,000)}, \text{ or } \frac{108,750}{50,000} \approx \frac{2.2}{1}.$$

So, the ratio of total revenue earned from online sales is greatest, and (A) is the correct answer.

---

4. Which of the following represents the total range of revenue earned from each of the different income streams in 2010?

Ⓐ $50,000
Ⓑ $70,000
Ⓒ $122,000
Ⓓ $170,000
Ⓔ $220,000

Solution

In 2010, Acme Co. earned the most total revenue through wholesale sales, which accounted for 44% of $500,000 = $220,000 in total revenue. It earned the least through retail and other sales, which each accounted for 10% of $500,000 = $50,000 in total revenue.

The range of revenue for the different income streams was therefore $220,000 – $50,000 = $170,000, and **(D) is the correct answer.**

Suggested Strategies

Compared to their counterparts, quantitative questions that involve the use of tables and charts tend to be fairly straightforward. Even at the highest adaptive levels, they typically don't require clever inferences, understanding of advanced math rules, or efficient answer choice strategies.

Instead, success on these questions typically requires the following:

1. Comfort and familiarity. The last thing you want to do is run into an unfamiliar type of graph during your official timed exam. A key to success is to have previous experience working with all the different types of tables and graphs that you might encounter on test day.

2. Exactness. For these questions, you're typically provided with a lot more information than you are for other types of questions, so it's easier than usual to either misread or lose sight of the task, misinterpret the given information, or mismatch the two. **Therefore, you want to practice not rushing and being attentive to detail to avoid careless errors**.

3. Mastery of underlying math rules. Nearly every question you'll see related to tables and graphs will test either your ability to read the information correctly or your ability to utilize the given information to solve for ratios, proportions, or various statistics.

On the pages to come are three sample sets of table and graph questions. The first set includes four questions that focus on **reading correctly**, the second set includes four examples of **ratio and proportion** questions, and the final set includes four examples of **statistics** questions. By the time you're done, you should have a good sense of what to expect from table and graph questions and how to be successful with them.

Study Regimen

A certain student has decided to follow a strict study regimen that includes 3 daily study sessions: 1 in the morning, 1 in the afternoon, and 1 in the evening. At each study session, the student will devote a certain percentage of time to learning, a certain percentage of time to practice, and a certain percentage to review. The student will go through 3 stages of studying, during which she plans to change the time spent studying at each study session, as well as the allocation of that time to each priority, in the following manner:

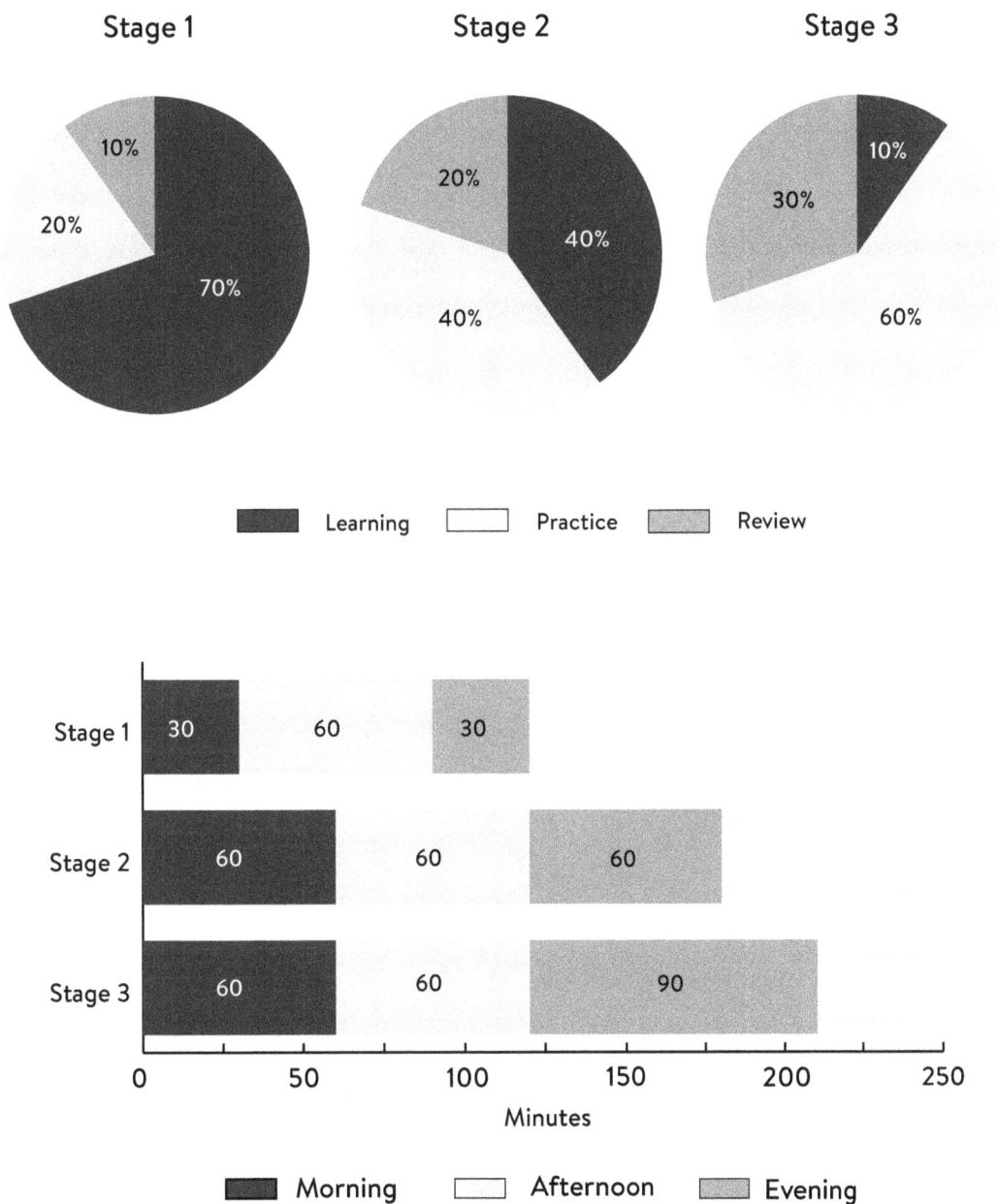

Practice Questions

1. The study regimen recommends what percentage increase in daily study time between stage 1 and stage 3?

(A) 25%
(B) 50%
(C) 75%
(D) 100%
(E) 175%

2. Assuming that the regimen's recommendations for the percentage of time spent on learning, practice, and review apply to each study session of each day, how much time is recommended for practice in the afternoon session during stage 3?

(A) 12 minutes
(B) 20 minutes
(C) 24 minutes
(D) 30 minutes
(E) 36 minutes

3. How many more minutes per day will the student spend reviewing during stage 2 than they will during stage 1?

```

```

4. Assuming that the study regimen's recommendations for percentage of time allocated to learning, practice, and review apply to each study session of each day, for which of the following study sessions are the greatest number of minutes allocated to learning?

(A) A morning in stage 1
(B) An evening in stage 1
(C) An afternoon in stage 2
(D) A morning in stage 3
(E) An evening in stage 3

Practice Question Solutions

1. The study regimen recommends what percentage increase in daily study time between stage 1 and stage 3?

(A) 25%
(B) 50%
(C) 75%
(D) 100%
(E) 175%

Solution

In stage 1, the total daily recommended study time was 30 + 60 + 30 = 120. In stage 3, the total jumps to 60 + 60 + 90 = 210.

The difference is 210 − 120 = 90.

$\frac{90}{120} = \frac{3}{4} = 75\%$ increase.

(C) is the correct answer.

---

2. Assuming that the regimen's recommendations for the percentage of time spent on learning, practice, and review apply to each study session of each day, how much time is recommended for practice in the afternoon session during stage 3?

(A) 12 minutes
(B) 20 minutes
(C) 24 minutes
(D) 30 minutes
(E) 36 minutes

Solution

From the circle graph, you know that it is recommended that the student spend 60% of their study time during stage 3 on practice. If an afternoon session is 60 minutes long, the student would spend. (6)60 = 36 minutes of that on practice, so **(E) is the correct answer.**

3. How many more minutes per day will the student spend reviewing during stage 2 than they will during stage 1?

```
24
```

Solution

During stage 1, the student studies a total of 120 minutes per day, 10% of which they spend reviewing, which equates to 12 minutes per day.

During stage 2, the student studies a total of 180 minutes per day, 20% of which they spend reviewing, which equates to 36 minutes per day.

Thus, **the student will spend 24 minutes more per day reviewing during stage 2 than they did during stage 1.**

4. Assuming that the study regimen's recommendations for percentage of time allocated to learning, practice, and review apply to each study session of each day, for which of the following study sessions are the greatest number of minutes allocated to learning?

(A) A morning in stage 1
(B) An evening in stage 1
(C) An afternoon in stage 2
(D) A morning in stage 3
(E) An evening in stage 3

Solution

In stage 1, the regimen recommends spending 70% of one's studying time on learning. In stage 1, the morning and evening sessions are both 30 minutes, so for both (A) and (B), the portion devoted to learning = (0.7)(30) = 21 minutes.

For afternoon in stage 2, learning = (0.4)(60) = 24 minutes.
For morning in stage 3, learning = (0.1)(60) = 6 minutes.
For evening in stage 3, learning = (0.1)(90) = 9 minutes.

(C) is the greatest and the correct answer.

Districts

A certain city comprises 4 districts: A, B, C, and D. The following table lists the population of each of the 4 districts in the city both in 2015 and in 2020.

District	2015	2020
A	3,201	3,992
B	5,422	5,664
C	5,640	5,286
D	6,043	6,120

Practice Questions

1. Approximately what percentage of the city's population lived in District D in 2020?

Ⓐ 25%
Ⓑ 29%
Ⓒ 32%
Ⓓ 34%
Ⓔ 36%

2. Which of the following is closest to the ratio of the population of District A in 2015 to the population of District A in 2020?

Ⓐ 2:3
Ⓑ 3:4
Ⓒ 32:39
Ⓓ 4:5
Ⓔ 16:19

3. The increase in population in District B represents approximately what percent of the total increase in population for the entire city between 2015 and 2020?

Ⓐ 18%
Ⓑ 32%
Ⓒ 42%
Ⓓ 64%
Ⓔ 71%

4. If the ratio of the population in District A to the population in District C had stayed roughly consistent between 2015 and 2020, and if District A had a population of 3,992 in 2020, what population is expected in District C in 2020?

Ⓐ 4,890
Ⓑ 6,440
Ⓒ 7,030
Ⓓ 7,260
Ⓔ 8,340

Practice Question Solutions

1. Approximately what percentage of the city's population lived in District D in 2020?

(A) 25%
(B) 29%
(C) 32%
(D) 34%
(E) 36%

Solution

There were a total of $3{,}992 + 5{,}664 + 5{,}286 + 6{,}120 = 21{,}062$ residents in the city in 2020, and 6,120 of them live in District D. $\frac{6{,}120}{21{,}062} \approx 29\%$, and **(B) is the correct answer**.

2. Which of the following is closest to the ratio of the population of District A in 2015 to the population of District A in 2020?

(A) 2:3
(B) 3:4
(C) 31:39
(D) 4:5
(E) 16:19

Solution

The ratio of the population of District A in 2015 to 2020 is 3,201:3,992, which is roughly equivalent to 32:40. You can simplify this by dividing both parts of the ratio by 8, which gives you 4:5. Alternatively, you could have used a calculator to see that $\frac{3{,}201}{3{,}992} \approx 80.2\%$, which, again, is closest to the ratio 4:5. **The correct answer is (D).**

3. The increase in population in District B represents approximately what percent of the total increase in population for the entire city between 2015 and 2020?

(A) 18%
(B) 32%
(C) 42%
(D) 64%
(E) 71%

Solution

District B increased by $5664 - 5422 = 242$.

Meanwhile, in 2015, the total population for the city was $3{,}201 + 5{,}422 + 5{,}640 + 6{,}043 = 20{,}306$.

In 2020, it was $3{,}992 + 5{,}664 + 5{,}286 + 6{,}120 = 21{,}062$.

$21{,}062 - 20{,}306 = 756$.

$\frac{242}{756} \approx 32\%$

(B) is the correct answer.

4. If the ratio of the population in District A to the population in District C had stayed roughly consistent between 2015 and 2020, and if District A had a population of 3,992 in 2020, what population is expected in District C in 2020?

(A) 4,890
(B) 6,440
(C) 7,030
(D) 7,260
(E) 8,340

Solutions Continued

Solution

The ratio of the population of District A to the population of District C in 2015 is $\dfrac{3,201}{5,640}$.

If District A has a population of 3,992 in 2020 and the two districts continue to have the same ratio, you can use the following proportional equation to solve for the population of District C in 2020:

$$\frac{3,201}{5,640} = \frac{3,992}{x}$$

$$3,201x = (3,992)(5,640)$$

$$x = \frac{(3,992)(5,640)}{3,201}$$

x = 7,033.7, which is closest to 7,030 in answer choice (C).

Grades

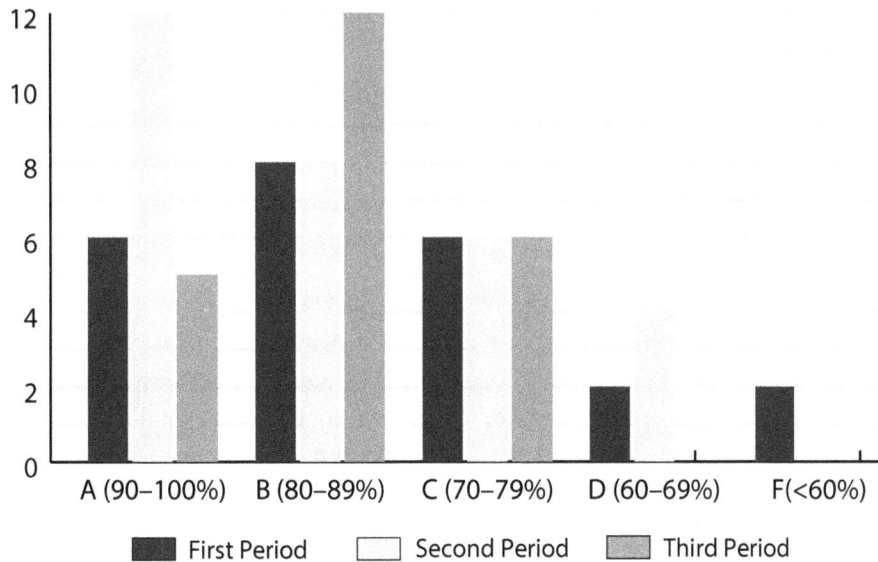

Practice Questions

1. Which of the following represents the average (arithmetic mean) number of students per period who received either an A or a B?

Ⓐ 8
Ⓑ 13
Ⓒ 17
Ⓓ 19
Ⓔ 22

2. Which of the following could be the median percent grade for the first period?

Indicate all such scores.

Ⓐ 76%
Ⓑ 78%
Ⓒ 81%
Ⓓ 89%
Ⓔ 92%

3. For which periods is the range of grades greater than 35%?

Ⓐ First
Ⓑ Second
Ⓒ Third
Ⓓ First and second only
Ⓔ It cannot be determined.

4. Which of the following must be true?

Indicate all such statements.

Ⓐ The range of grades was greater in the first period than in the second period.
Ⓑ The range of grades was greater in the second period than in the third period.
Ⓒ The range of grades was greater in the first period than in the third period.

Sample Question Solutions

1. Which of the following represents the average (arithmetic mean) number of students per period who received either an A or a B?

Ⓐ 8
Ⓑ 13
Ⓒ 17
Ⓓ 19
Ⓔ 22

Solution

In the first period, 6 + 8 = 14 students received either an A or a B. In the second period, 12 + 8 = 20 students received an A or a B. Finally, in the third period, 5 + 12 = 17 students received either an A or a B. Thus, a total of 14 + 20 + 17 = 51 students received either an A or a B, for an average of $\frac{51}{3}$ = 17 such students per period. **(C) is the correct answer.**

2. Which of the following could be the median percent grade for the first period?

Indicate all such scores.

Ⓐ 76%
Ⓑ 78%
Ⓒ 81%
Ⓓ 89%
Ⓔ 92%

Solution

There are 6 + 8 + 6 + 2 + 2 = 24 total grades given out in the first period, and you know the median percent grade must be the average of the 12th and 13th highest grades. Per what you know about the grades for this period, you can infer that the 12th and 13th highest grades must have been B's, which you are told are between 80 and 89%. **Thus, both [C] and [D] could represent the median percent grade for the period.**

3. For which periods is the range of grades greater than 35%?

Ⓐ First
Ⓑ Second
Ⓒ Third
Ⓓ First and second only
Ⓔ It cannot be determined.

Solution

If a class has students with A's and F's, the range can be as great as 100 or as small as 90 – 59 = 31. Therefore, you cannot determine if any ranges are greater than 35%, and **(E) is the correct answer**.

4. Which of the following must be true?

Indicate all such statements.

Ⓐ The range of grades was greater in the first period than in the second period.
Ⓑ The range of grades was greater in the second period than in the third period.
Ⓒ The range of grades was greater in the first period than in the third period.

Solution

The range of grades for the first period could be as great as 100 – 0 = 100 or as small as 90 – 59 = 31%.

The range of grades for the second period could be as great as 100 – 60 = 40 or as small as 90 – 69 = 21%.

The range of grades for the third period could be as great as 100 – 70 = 30 or as small as 90 – 79 = 11%.

Thus, the only statement that must be true is [C], so **[C] is the correct answer.**

18
QUANTITATIVE REASONING

Tables and Graphs, Part 2

Welcome to the second of two lessons on tables and graphs. In this lesson, I'll focus on the more obscure types of graphs that appear on the GRE: scatterplots, boxplots, and histograms. I'll also use this opportunity to further discuss concepts of dispersion and distribution.

The types of graphs discussed here appear on the GRE far less frequently than the ones I discussed in the previous lesson. They may also be less familiar to you than some of the more common data presentation methods. While you shouldn't allocate too much of your study time to these types of graphs, you should invest enough attention so you understand these graphs and feel comfortable with them in case they do appear on your exam.

To begin, let's imagine the following set of sample data, which represents the height, in inches, and age, in years, of a group of high school students.

Age	13	14	14	14	15	15	16	16	16	16	16	17	17	17	18	18
Hgt	65	68	60	63	66	62	67	68	70	72	68	63	66	75	67	71

Let's think about how this information might be presented using different types of graphing methods, starting with scatterplots.

Scatterplot Graphs

If you graph the ages and heights of the students using age for the x-axis and height for the y-axis, you get a scattering of positions, as exhibited below.

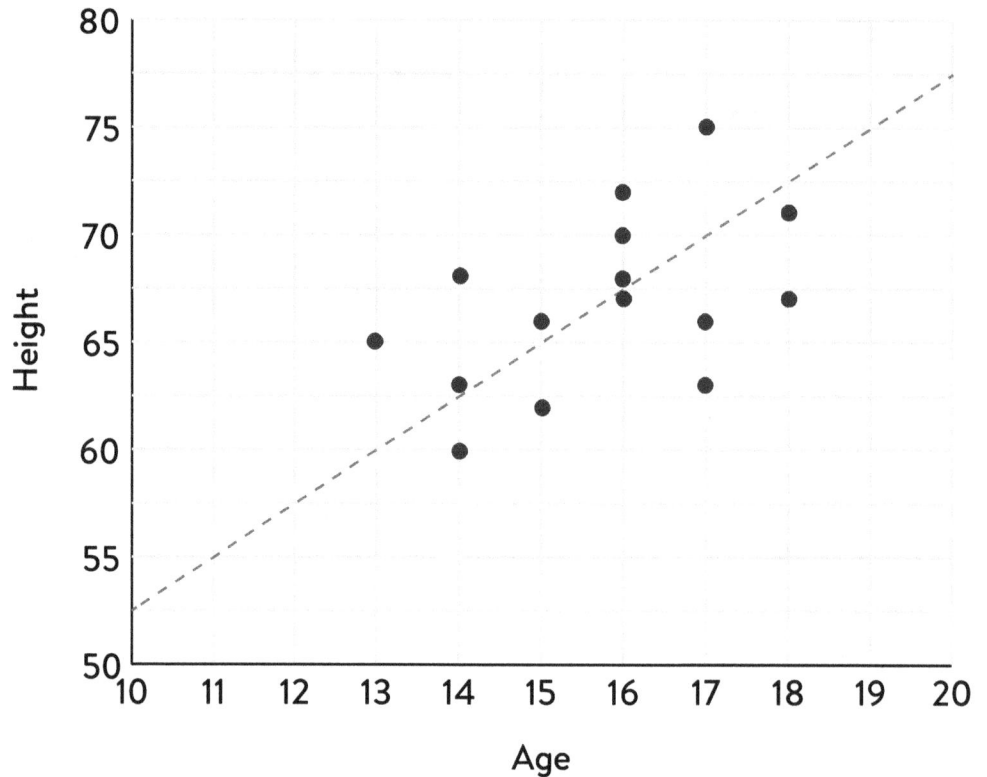

Age	13	14	14	14	15	15	16	16	16	16	16	17	17	17	18	18
Hgt	65	68	60	63	66	62	67	68	70	72	68	63	66	75	67	71

The line that's drawn on the graph is known as a **trendline**. A trendline is the line that best fits and best generalizes the aggregate data.

Note that coming up with an equation for a trendline based on given data is beyond the scope of the GRE and is NOT required of you.

However, you will sometimes be expected to determine the equation for a trendline that's already drawn or about which some information is provided (e.g., its slope or x-intercept). This will simply require an understanding of how lines are defined on a coordinate plane, which I will cover in the next lesson.

You'll also be expected to understand how given points relate to the trendline (e.g., which points are above or below it).

Sample Question

Which age group has the greatest number of students who are over the expected height according to the trendline?

(A) 14
(B) 15
(C) 16
(D) 17
(E) 18

Solution

There are four 16-year-old students whose heights are above what you would expect of a 16-year-old student per the trendline. No other age group has so many members who are above the expected height, so **(C) is the correct answer**.

Boxplots

Boxplots, or box-and-whisker plots, are useful for representing the dispersion, or spread, of data. To illustrate, use the data about the students again, but this time, focus just on their heights and not their ages.

Age	13	14	14	14	15	15	16	16	16	16	16	17	17	17	18	18
Hgt	65	68	60	63	66	62	67	68	70	72	68	63	66	75	67	71

If you order the heights numerically from shortest to tallest, you end up with this list:

60, 62, 63, 63, 65, 66, 66, 67, 67, 68, 68, 68, 70, 71, 72, 75

To create a boxplot from this data, you need five pieces of information: the minimum, the maximum, the median, the 25th percentile, and the 75th percentile figures, all of which will help split up the data and make it easier to interpret.

For your list, you can see that the minimum is 60, and the maximum is 75.

Because there are 16 total heights, the median will be the average of the 8th and 9th tallest students. Our 8th and 9th tallest students are both 67 inches tall, so the median is 67.

Quartiles are quarters. Each quartile consists of one-fourth of the data points, starting with the lowest when the points are arranged in numerical order. Because you have a total of 16 data points in this set, each quartile will contain 4 data points. The first quartile marker is the boundary between the first quartile (the bottom quarter of the data points) and the second quartile (the next lowest quarter of the data points—the one right below the median). Therefore, the first quartile marker for this set will be the average of the fourth and fifth numbers in the ordered list, which are 63 and 65:

$$\frac{63 + 65}{2} = 64$$

The second quartile marker is the median of the set.

The third quartile marker is the boundary between the third quartile (the quarter immediately above the median) and the fourth quartile (the top quarter of the data points). The third quartile marker for this set will be the average of the 12th and 13th numbers in the ordered list, which are 68 and 70:

$$\frac{68 + 70}{2} = 69$$

Now that you have everything you need:

Minimum: 60
First quartile marker: 64
Median: 67
Third quartile marker: 69
Maximum: 75

You can go ahead and create a boxplot.

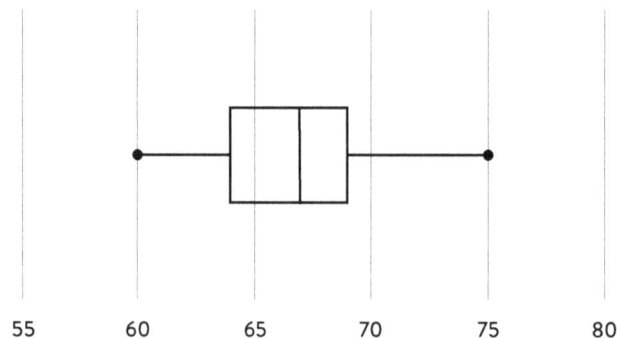

Again, these graphs can be useful for insight into how spread out or concentrated the data might be.

Note that the leftmost black dot at 60 represents the minimum, and the rightmost black dot at 75 represents the maximum—the lines connecting from the central box to the minimum and maximum values are the "whiskers" in the term "box and whiskers plot." The central box is bounded on the left and right by vertical lines representing the 25th and 75th percentile values, and the vertical line inside the box represents the 50th percentile, or median, value.

Sample Question

If $Q1$ denotes the end of the first quartile, M denotes the median, and $Q3$ denotes the end of the third quartile, which range of students represents the greatest difference in height?

Ⓐ Between the shortest student and $Q1$
Ⓑ Between $Q1$ and M
Ⓒ Between M and $Q3$
Ⓓ Between $Q1$ and $Q3$
Ⓔ Between $Q3$ and the tallest student

Solution

There is a difference of 4 inches between the shortest student and $Q1$, 3 inches between $Q1$ and M, 2 inches between M and $Q3$, 5 inches between $Q1$ and $Q3$, and 6 inches between $Q3$ and the tallest student. So, the greatest difference in height is between $Q3$ and the tallest student, and **(E) is the correct answer**.

Histograms

A histogram is very much like a standard bar graph, but it has a few specific defining characteristics. First, histograms often highlight intervals, or ranges of values, rather than single values. Second, unlike a bar graph, a histogram has no space between bars; if there is an empty space on a histogram, it's indicative of an empty interval (one into which none of the data points fall). To illustrate, let's once again use the information about student heights, and again let's ignore the data about their ages:

Age	13	14	14	14	15	15	16	16	16	16	16	17	17	17	18	18
Hgt	65	68	60	63	66	62	67	68	70	72	68	63	66	75	67	71

And, as you did before, let's go ahead and arrange the heights in order from least to greatest:

60, 62, 63, 63, 65, 66, 66, 67, 67, 68, 68, 68, 70, 71, 72, 75

Now, let's imagine that you split up the range of these heights (60–75) into four equal increments, or intervals:

60–63 inches tall
64–67 inches tall
68–71 inches tall
72–75 inches tall

And count the number of students who fall into each interval:

60–63 inches tall: 4
64–67 inches tall: 5
68–71 inches tall: 5
72–75 inches tall: 2

And represent this information in a histogram:

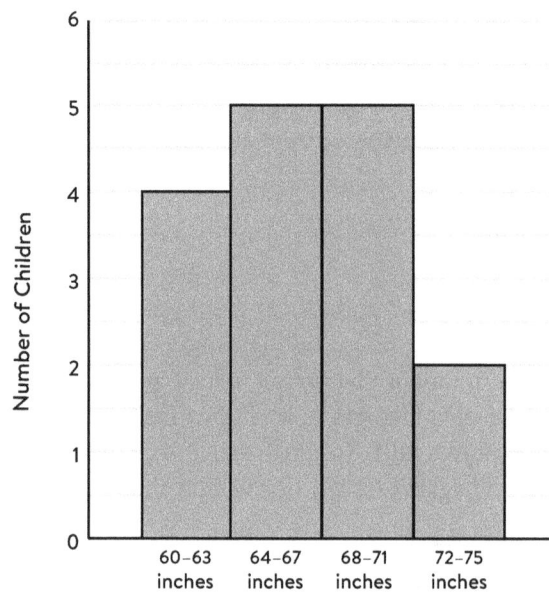

Sample Question

If a student is selected at random, what is the probability that the student will be 67 inches tall or shorter?

```
┌─────────┐
│         │
└─────────┘
─────────────
┌─────────┐
│         │
└─────────┘
```

Solution

As you can see in the histogram, there are 5 + 4 = 9 students who are 67 inches or shorter, so the probability of selecting a student 67 inches or shorter is $\frac{9}{16}$.

Practice Questions

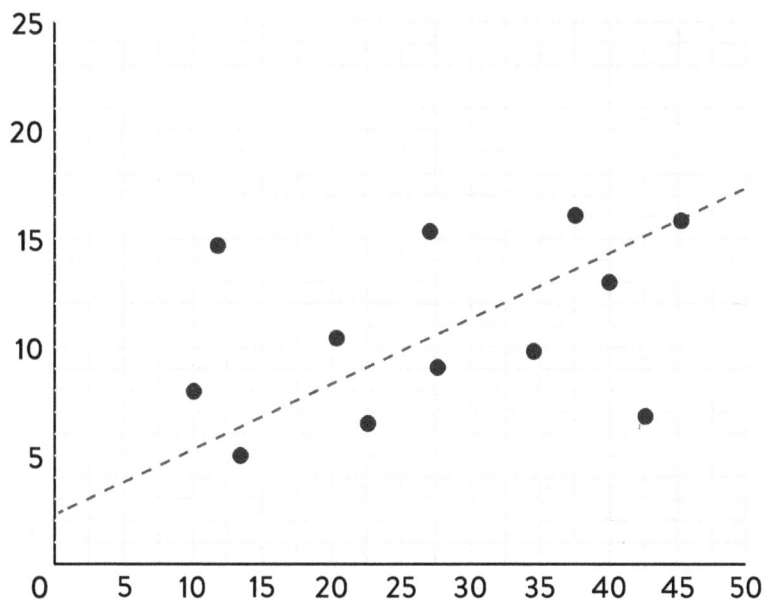

$$y = \frac{3}{10}x + 2.2$$

1. Per the trendline, what value of x would give a y-value of 3.2?

Ⓐ $\frac{8}{3}$

Ⓑ 3

Ⓒ $\frac{10}{3}$

Ⓓ $\frac{11}{3}$

Ⓔ $\frac{11}{4}$

2. Which of the following points is farthest away from the trendline?

Ⓐ (0.5, 2.45)
Ⓑ (1, 2.4)
Ⓒ (1.5, 2.45)
Ⓓ (2, 2.85)
Ⓔ (2.5, 3.2)

Practice Questions Continued

Curb Weights of Different Types of Automobiles (in pounds)

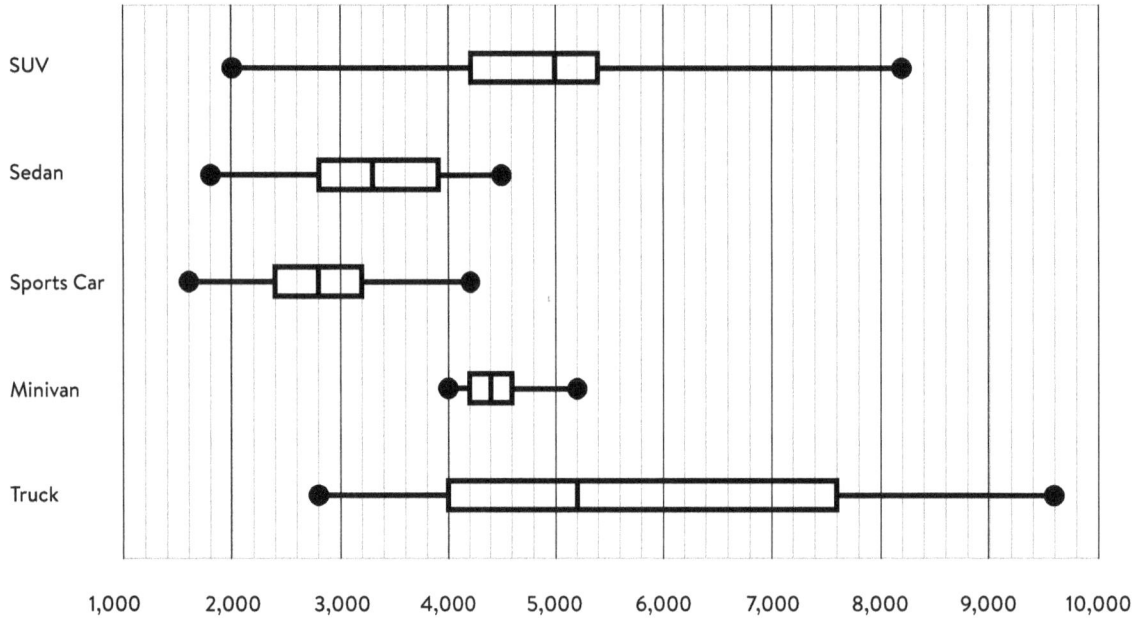

3. For which type of car is the range between the 25th percentile weight and the 75th percentile weight the least?

Ⓐ SUV
Ⓑ Sedan
Ⓒ Sports car
Ⓓ Minivan
Ⓔ Truck

4. The weight of a truck in the 25th percentile is approximately what percentage of the weight of a minivan in the 75th percentile?

Ⓐ 68%
Ⓑ 87%
Ⓒ 92%
Ⓓ 106%
Ⓔ 115%

Practice Question Solutions

1. Per the trendline, what value of x would give a y-value of 3.2?

Ⓐ $\frac{8}{3}$

Ⓑ 3

Ⓒ $\frac{10}{3}$

Ⓓ $\frac{11}{3}$

Ⓔ $\frac{11}{4}$

Solution

If $y = 3.2$, then you can use the following equation to solve for x:

$$3.2 = \frac{3}{10x} + 2.2$$

$$1 = \frac{3}{10x}$$

$$x = \frac{10}{3}$$

(C) is the correct answer.

2. Which of the following points is farthest away from the trendline?

Ⓐ (0.5, 2.45)
Ⓑ (1, 2.4)
Ⓒ (1.5, 2.45)
Ⓓ (2, 2.85)
Ⓔ **(2.5, 3.2)**

Solution

Per the given equation, when $x = 0.5$, you should expect that $y = \left(\frac{3}{10}\right)(0.5) + 2.2 = 2.35$. (A) is 0.1 away from this expected value.

When $x = 1$, you should expect that $y = \left(\frac{3}{10}\right)(1) + 2.2 = 2.5$. (B) is also 0.1 away from its expected value.

When $x = 1.5$, you should expect that $y = \left(\frac{3}{10}\right)(1.5) + 2.2 = 2.65$. (C) is 0.2 away from this expected value.

When $x = 2$, you should expect that $y = \left(\frac{3}{10}\right)(2) + 2.2 = 2.8$. (D) is 0.05 away from this expected value.

Finally, when $x = 2.5$, you should expect that $y = \left(\frac{3}{10}\right)(2.5) + 2.2 = 2.95$. (E) is 0.25 away from this expected value.

Since (E) is farthest away from its expected value, it is the correct answer.

Solutions Continued

3. For which type of car is the range between the 25th percentile weight and the 75th percentile weight the least?

Ⓐ SUV
Ⓑ Sedan
Ⓒ Sports car
Ⓓ **Minivan**
Ⓔ Truck

Solution

You can calculate the interquartile range of each type of car as follows:

SUV: 5,400 – 4,200 = 1,200
Sedan: 3,900 – 2,800 = 1,100
Sports car: 3,200 – 2,400 = 800
Minivan: 4,600 – 4,200 = 400
Truck: 7,600 – 4,000 = 3,600

Minivans have the least difference between the 25th percentile and the 75th percentile weight, and **(D) is the correct answer**.

4. The weight of a truck in the 25th percentile is approximately what percentage of the weight of a minivan in the 75th percentile?

Ⓐ 68%
Ⓑ **87%**
Ⓒ 92%
Ⓓ 106%
Ⓔ 115%

Solution

The 25th percentile weight truck is 4,000 pounds, and the 75th percentile minivan is 4,600 pounds. This is closest to 87%, and **(B) is the correct answer**.

19

QUANTITATIVE REASONING

Coordinate Planes

I'll start the three geometry lessons by discussing the **coordinate plane** beginning with basic terminology.

- The **rectangular coordinate system** is also known as the **xy-coordinate system** or the **xy-plane**.
- The **origin** represents the intersection of the x- and y-axes and the center of the coordinate plane. It has the coordinates $(0, 0)$.
- The **x-axis** is a horizontal number line that determines the side-to-side positioning of a point.
- The **y-axis** is a vertical number line that determines the up-and-down positioning of a point.
- A point on the coordinate plane is represented by an **ordered pair** of numbers (x, y). The first number, x, represents the x-coordinate of that point, and the second number, y, represents the y-coordinate of that point.
- The **x-coordinate** of a point represents the horizontal positioning of that point.
- The **y-coordinate** of a point represents the vertical positioning of that point.
- The coordinate plane can be split into four **quadrants**, as shown in the following diagram.

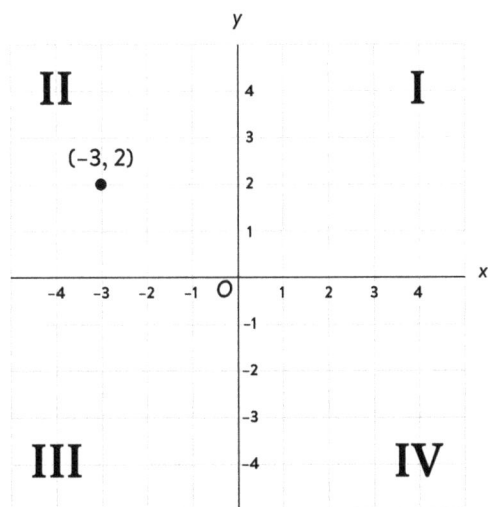

The point $(-3, 2)$ is positioned where it is because the -3 tells you that it is 3 positions to the left of the origin, and the 2 tells you that it is 2 positions up from the origin.

Reflections

On the exam, you may be asked to consider where points might end up if they are reflected over the x-axis, the y-axis, or the origin. You can think of reflection over the origin as a sequence of two reflections, either:

Across the x-axis, then across the y-axis
Across the y-axis, then across the x-axis

Please consider the diagram below; before you read the text beneath the diagram, note where you think the quadrant II point $(-3, 2)$ will end up if reflected over the x-axis, the y-axis, and the origin.

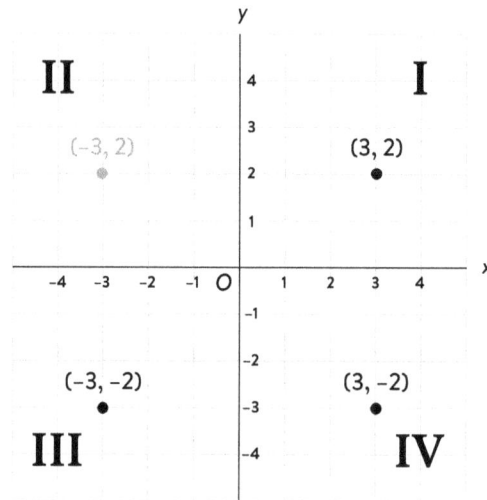

$(-3, 2)$ reflected over the x-axis becomes $(-3, -2)$ in quadrant III.
$(-3, 2)$ reflected over the y-axis becomes $(3, 2)$ in quadrant I.
$(-3, 2)$ reflected over the origin becomes $(3, -2)$ in quadrant IV.

It might help to generalize what happens when points are reflected on the xy-plane:

Reflection across the x-axis preserves the original x-coordinate but negates the original y-coordinate; therefore, (x, y) becomes $(x, -y)$.

Reflection across the y-axis negates the original x-coordinate but preserves the original y-coordinate; therefore, (x, y) becomes $(-x, y)$.

Reflection across the origin negates both the original x-coordinate and the original y-coordinate; therefore, (x, y) becomes $(-x, -y)$.

Distance

Sample Question

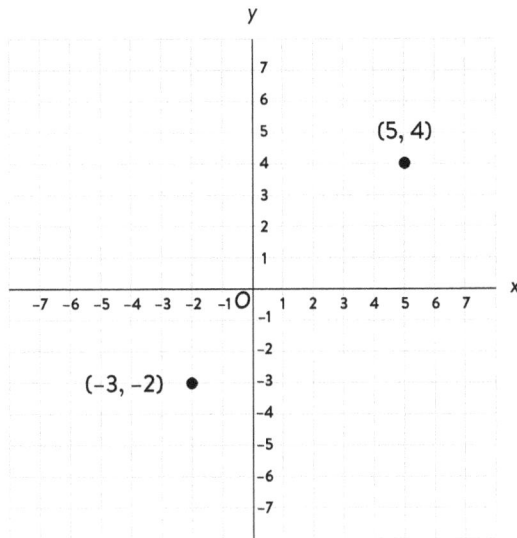

Which of the following represents the distance between the two labeled points on the coordinate plane diagram above?

(A) 8

(B) 10

(C) $8\sqrt{2}$

(D) $8\sqrt{3}$

(E) 12

Solution

If you are asked to find the distance between two points on the coordinate plane, you can do so with the Pythagorean theorem (which I'll cover more in the next lesson).

If you are asked to find the distance between (5, 4) and (−3, −2), you can start by creating an imaginary right triangle, as in the following diagram:

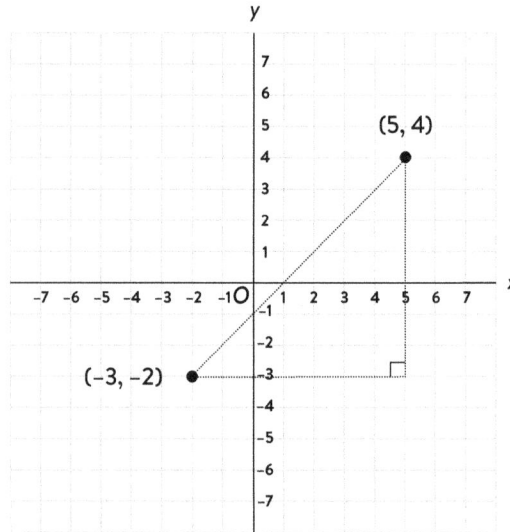

The length of the horizontal leg of the right triangle is equal to the distance between the x-coordinates of the given points: $5 - (-3) = 8$. The length of the vertical leg of the right triangle is equal to the distance between the y-coordinates of the given points: $4 - (-2) = 6$. Once you know the lengths of the right triangle's two legs, you can use the Pythagorean theorem to find the length of the hypotenuse, which is also the straight-line distance between the two given points:

$$8^2 + 6^2 = c^2$$
$$64 + 36 = c^2$$
$$100 = c^2$$
$$10 = c$$

Thus, the distance between the points $(5, 4)$ and $(-3, -2)$ is 10.

If you are already comfortable with this, you can jump straight to using the distance formula, which is an adaptation of the Pythagorean theorem.

$$c = \sqrt{(y_2 - y_1)^2 + (x_2 - x_1)^2}$$
$$= \sqrt{[5 - (-3)]^2 + [4 - (-2)]^2}$$
$$= \sqrt{(5 + 3)^2 + (4 + 2)^2}$$
$$= \sqrt{8^2 + 6^2}$$
$$= \sqrt{64 + 36}$$
$$= \sqrt{100}$$
$$= 10$$

Note that memorizing some common right triangles called Pythagorean triples, which I will discuss further in the next chapter, can save you from having to perform the calculation above. In this case, 6-8-10 is simply a doubling of the 3-4-5 Pythagorean triple. In other words, a right triangle with legs of 6 and 8 will always have a hypotenuse of 10.

Graphing on the XY-Plane

You may well encounter several different kinds of graphs presented on the *xy*-plane. As I proceed, I'll discuss terminology specific to each type, but first, let's define some general terms pertaining to creating and interpreting graphs on the *xy*-plane.

A graph on the *xy*-plane is a way of visualizing the relationship between the variables in the equation represented by the graph.

A **y-intercept** is a point where the graph intersects with the *y*-axis. A *y*-intercept will, therefore, always have an *x*-coordinate of 0.

An **x-intercept** is a point where the graph intersects with the *x*-axis. An *x*-intercept will, therefore, always have a *y*-coordinate of 0.

If a point is on a particular graph (that is, if the graph touches or passes through that point), then the (x, y) coordinates of that point constitute a **solution** to the equation that produced the graph.

Therefore, if a point is referred to as a solution to an equation, that point will be on the graph that represents that equation.

Line Graphs and Linear Equations

Graphs of **lines** on the *xy*-plane are produced by **linear equations** that contain no terms with an exponent greater than 1.

Horizontal lines are produced by equations like $y = 3$. Note that in the absence of an *x* variable, *y* equals 3 for any value of *x*, producing a horizontal line across the entire *xy*-plane where *y* equals 3. Horizontal lines have a slope of 0.

Vertical lines are produced by equations like $x = 3$. Note that in the absence of a *y* variable, *x* equals 3 for any value of *y*, producing a vertical line across the entire *xy*-plane where *x* equals 3. Vertical lines have a slope that is undefined.

A line that is neither perfectly horizontal nor perfectly vertical has a defined **slope** that is not equal to 0. The slope of a line can be found by identifying two points on the line—call them (x_1, y_1) and (x_2, y_2)—and calculating $\frac{y_2 - y_1}{x_2 - x_1}$. It does not matter which point you label (x_1, y_1) and which you label (x_2, y_2), but you must keep the same order in the numerator and the denominator of the slope calculation.

Note that sometimes the slope calculation is referred to as $\frac{\text{rise}}{\text{run}}$, meaning that you are determining how much you have to rise (or fall) and how much you have to run (left or right) in order to move from one point on a line to another point on the same line. Rise indicates a positive numerator, while fall indicates a negative numerator; run to the right indicates a positive denominator, run to the left indicates a negative denominator.

Be careful about starting at one point on a linear graph and counting how many tick marks up/down and left/right you have to move to reach another point on the same graph. This method will work if the spacing between tick marks is the same on both axes; in other words, moving up or down one tick mark on the y-axis represents the same number of units as moving left or right one tick mark on the x-axis. If the two axes are scaled differently, then you must use the formula given on the previous page to calculate slope.

Let's return to the $\frac{\text{rise}}{\text{run}}$ calculation to discuss the slopes of horizontal and vertical lines. A horizontal line has no rise but infinite run, so it has a slope of $\frac{0}{\infty}$, which simplifies to 0. A vertical line has an infinite rise but no run, so it has a slope of $\frac{\infty}{0}$, and any fraction with a denominator of 0 has a value that is undefined!

Imagine that you are running a lemonade stand and selling cups of lemonade for 50 cents each. And imagine that you start the day with $5.00 in your cash box.

If you think of the number of lemonades that you sell as x and the total amount of money in your cash box as y, you can set up the following equation relating the two to each other: $y = 0.5x + 5$, and graph it:

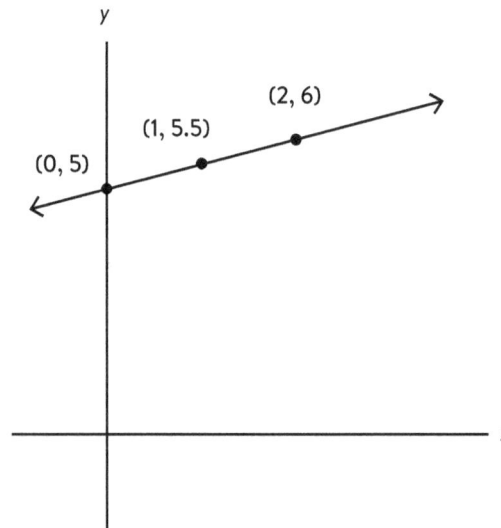

The total amount of money that you'll have in the cash box will be equal to the $5.00 you started with, plus $0.50 for each lemonade sold. After you sell one lemonade, you'll have $5.50, and after you sell two lemonades, you'll have $6.00, and so on.

This example represents the essence of drawing lines in the coordinate plane. You have an input (*x*) and an output (*y*); you have a starting point (*b*), in this case $5.00; and you have a rate (*m*) by which the output changes as the input changes—in this case, you gain an extra $0.50 for each lemonade sold.

y = mx + b

Using coordinate plane terminology, you can think of the starting point, **b**, as the **y-intercept**, and you can think of the rate of change, **m**, as the **slope** of the line. Let's look at an example in which you are given a graph on the *xy*-plane and asked to interpret it.

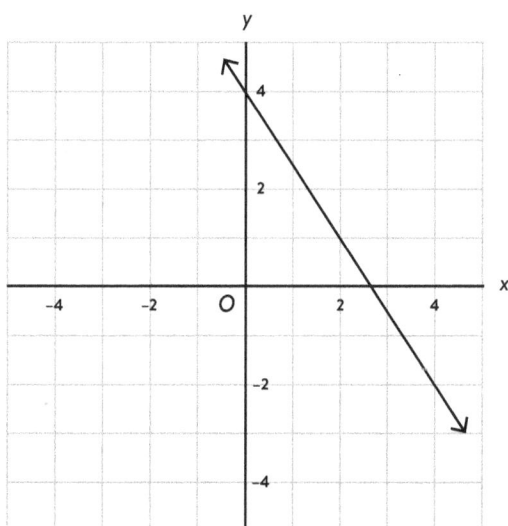

You can see that the line hits the *y*-axis at 4. That *y*-intercept represents the point (0, 4). You can also identify (2, 1) as another point on the same line. Let's calculate the slope of the line in two different ways:

Because the tick marks on each axis are equally proportioned—each tick mark represents 1 unit—you can derive the slope from the path you take from (0, 4) to (2, 1). You have to go down 3 units and to the right 2 units, for a $\frac{\text{rise}}{\text{run}}$ of $\frac{-3}{2}$. Note that if you started at (2, 1), you'd need to go up 3 units and go left 2 units, for a $\frac{\text{rise}}{\text{run}}$ of $\frac{3}{-2}$, which simplifies to the same result of $-\frac{3}{2}$.

You can label (0, 4) as (x_1, y_1) and (2, 1) as (x_2, y_2). The formula gives you $\frac{1-4}{2-0}$, or $\frac{-3}{2}$. Note that if you labeled (2, 1) as (x_1, y_1) and (0, 4) as (x_2, y_2), the formula would give you $\frac{4-1}{0-2}$, or $\frac{3}{-2}$, which simplifies to $-\frac{3}{2}$.

Therefore, you can represent the above graph with the following equation:

$$y = -\frac{3}{2}x + 4$$

Imagine you're given a sample question based on the preceding graph.

Sample Question

What is the value of y when x is 4?

- (A) 2
- (B) 0
- (C) −1
- (D) −2
- (E) −3

Solution

Using the graph and your calculation that in moving from (0, 4) to (2, 1), you moved down 3 units for each 2 units moved to the right, you can move down 3 units and right 2 units from (2, 1) to (4, −2). Therefore, when x is 4, y is −2. (D) is the correct answer.

Alternatively, you can generate the equation for this line as you did above, then input 4 for x and solve for y:

$$y = \left(-\frac{3}{2}\right)x + 4$$
$$y = \left(-\frac{3}{2}\right)(4) + 4$$
$$y = -6 + 4$$
$$y = -2$$

(D) is the correct answer.

Parallel Lines

Parallel lines have the same slope as one another and will never intersect.

Sample Question

Line A has equation $3y - 2x = 3$. Line B is parallel to line A and has a y-intercept of -2. What is the equation of line B?

(A) $y = -2x + 1$

(B) $y = \frac{2}{3}x + 2$

(C) $y = \frac{2}{3}x - 2$

(D) $y = -\frac{2}{3}x + 2$

(E) $y = -\frac{3}{2}x - 2$

<u>Solution</u>

You can convert the equation for line A to the $y = mx + b$ form to find its slope:

$3y - 2x = 3$
$3y = 2x + 3$
$y = \frac{2}{3}x + 1$

So, the slope of line A is $\frac{2}{3}$. Line B, which is parallel to line A, must have the same slope.

If line B's y-intercept is -2, you can set up the following equation for line B:

$y = \frac{2}{3}x - 2$, so **(C) is the correct answer.**

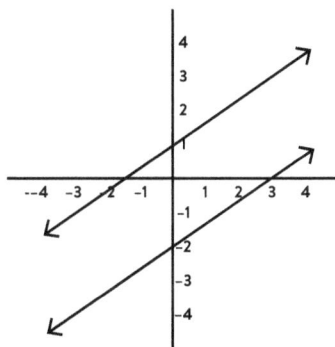

a graph of the parallel lines
for reference

Perpendicular Lines

Perpendicular lines intersect one another at right, or 90°, angles. Perpendicular lines have negative reciprocal slopes: for example, if one line has a slope of $\frac{3}{7}$, a line perpendicular to it will have a slope of $-\frac{7}{3}$. The original fraction $\frac{3}{7}$ was both written in the reciprocal $\frac{7}{3}$ and negated in that its sign went from positive to negative.

Another example: if a line has a slope of –2, a line perpendicular to it will have a slope of $\frac{1}{2}$. Note that because –2 can be written as $-\frac{2}{1}$, its reciprocal is $-\frac{1}{2}$, which you can then negate to form $\frac{1}{2}$.

Sample Question

Line A has equation $3y - 2x = 3$. Line B is perpendicular to line A and has a y-intercept of 3. What is the equation of line B?

(A) $y = \frac{3}{2}x + 3$

(B) $y = \frac{2}{3}x - 3$

(C) $y = 3x + 1$

(D) $y = -\frac{2}{3}x + 3$

(E) $y = -\frac{3}{2}x + 3$

<u>Solution</u>

From the work you did on the previous question, you know that the equation for line A can be rewritten as $y = \frac{2}{3}x + 1$, and line A has a slope of $\frac{2}{3}$.

If line B is perpendicular to line A, you know it must have the negative reciprocal slope, or $-\frac{3}{2}$.

With a slope of $-\frac{3}{2}$ and a y-intercept of 3, the equation of line B is $y = -\frac{3}{2}x + 3$, so **(E) is the correct answer**.

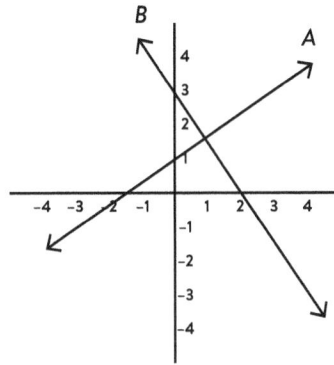

a graph of the perpendicular
lines for reference

Interpreting the Line *y* = *x*

A very important linear equation graph that you might be asked to work with is the graph of the line *y* = *x*, as shown below. The line *y* = *x* is sometimes referred to as "the 45-degree line" because it cuts the right angles of quadrants I and III into equal 45-degree angles.

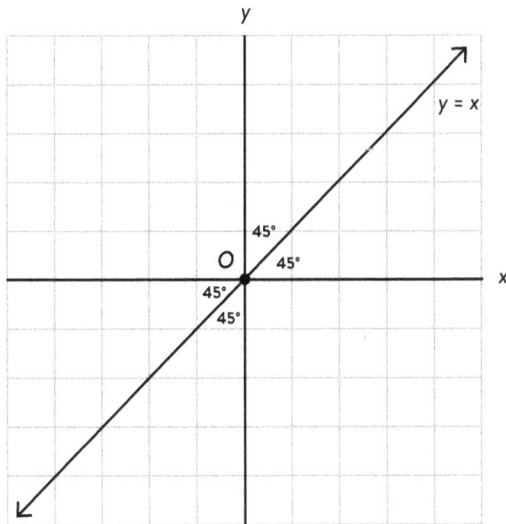

The line *y* = *x* passes through the origin and has a slope of 1. More important, every point on the line has ordered pair coordinates in which the *x* and *y* coordinates are equal—in other words, (3, 3) is on the line, as is (−4, −4). If a point is on the line *y* = *x*, its *x* and *y* coordinates are equal. But there's additional information you can derive from this graph, as I'll demonstrate using the following diagram:

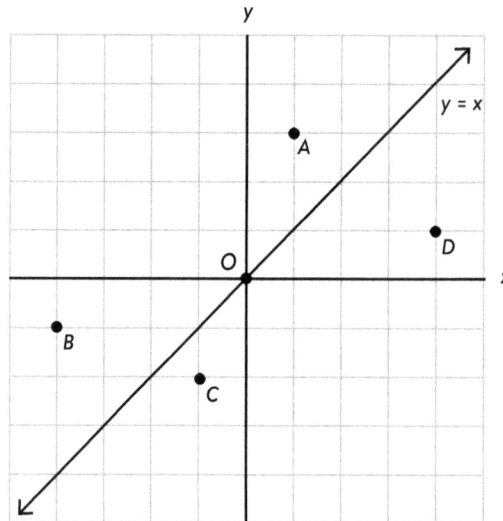

Any point above the line $y = x$ has a y-coordinate that is greater than its x-coordinate; any point below the line $y = x$ has an y-coordinate that is less than its x-coordinate. After all, if its x- and y-coordinates were exactly equal, it would be on the line $y = x$!

In this diagram, points A and B are above the line $y = x$, and points C and D are below the line $y = x$. Without knowing the exact coordinates of those points, you can conclude that points A and B have y-coordinates that are greater than their x-coordinates, while points C and D have y-coordinates that are less than their x-coordinates.

It might seem strange that you can draw the above conclusions for points such as C and D, so let's examine these two points. Let's say that point C has an x-coordinate of -1. If its y-coordinate were also -1, point C would be on the line $y = x$. But you have to go farther down below the line, so the y-coordinate must be something like -2. Remember that because -1 is farther to the right than -2 on a two-dimensional number line, -1 is greater than -2, so point C's y-coordinate is less than its x-coordinate, just as expected from a point below the line $y = x$. Point D might have coordinates like $(-4, -1)$. Because -1 is greater than -4, point D has a y-coordinate greater than its x-coordinate, just as expected from a point above the line $y = x$. Now, let's consider a slight tweak to the diagram and a question that might accompany it.

Sample Question

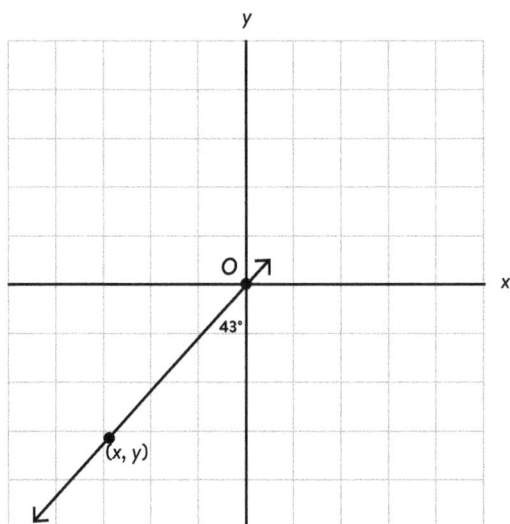

Quantity A

x

Quantity B

y

Ⓐ Quantity A is greater.
Ⓑ Quantity B is greater.
Ⓒ The two quantities are equal.
Ⓓ The relationship cannot be determined from the information given.

Solution

Note that the line segment containing the point with coordinates (x, y) forms a 43-degree angle with the negative y-axis. Recall that the line $y = x$ would form a 45-degree angle with the negative y-axis, as shown via the dotted line below:

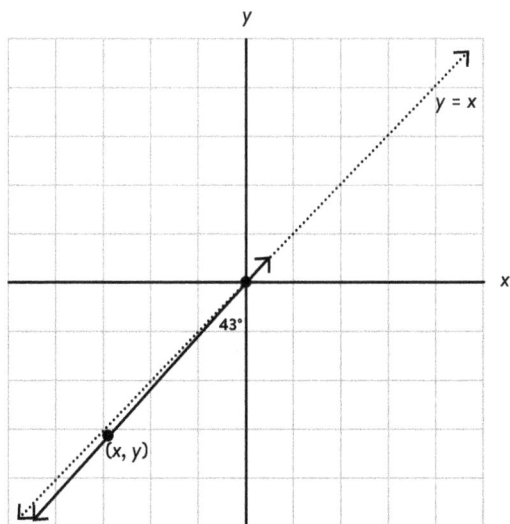

Note that the line segment in this diagram is below the dotted line $y = x$ at every point to the left of the origin. Therefore, the point with coordinates (x, y) is below the line $y = x$, and its y-coordinate is less than its x-coordinate. Therefore, **(A) is the correct answer**. Without knowing the exact values of x and y, you can conclude that x is greater than y because of the point's relationship to the line $y = x$.

Inequalities

Let's imagine that instead of being given the previous graph and equation, you were asked to consider a related inequality, such as:

$$y < -\frac{3}{2}x + 4$$

In such situations, start by graphing the line $y = -\frac{3}{2}x + 4$. In other words, you graph the line as if the equation had an equal sign rather than an inequality sign.

In graphing this line, however, you need to indicate whether the initial inequality contains a less than (<) or greater than (>) sign, in which case you graph a dashed line, or whether the initial inequality contains a less than or equal to ($\leq$) or greater than or equal to ($\geq$) sign, in which case you graph a solid line.

If the original inequality states that y is greater than a certain result, that means that y lies above the solid or dashed line. If the inequality shows that y is less than a certain result, y lies below the solid or dashed line.

greater than = above the line
less than = below the line

One quick reminder: if you have to manipulate an inequality to isolate the y variable, remember that if you multiply or divide both sides of an inequality by a negative number, you must flip the direction of the inequality sign!

Sample Question

Which of the following points satisfies the inequality $y < -\frac{3}{2}x + 4$?

Indicate all such points.

A (0, 0)
B (0, 3)
C (0, 4)
D (0, 5)
E (2, 3)

Solution

Our given inequality contains a *less than* sign, so let's graph a dashed line at $y = -\frac{3}{2}x + 4$, and then use shading to indicate the region *below* that line, as shown in the following diagram:

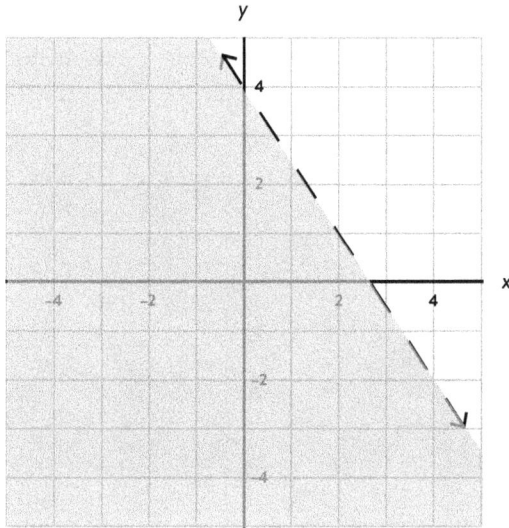

You can see that points [A] (0, 0) and [B] (0, 3) are clearly located within the shaded region.

(0, 4) would be eligible if the inequality sign were less than or equal to, but because it isn't, (0, 4) doesn't satisfy the inequality.

If you aren't sure of any of the points—for example, point (2, 3)—we can substitute its coordinates into the inequality to see whether the result is a true statement:

Is $2 < \left(-\frac{3}{2}\right)(3) + 4$?
Is $2 < -4.5 + 4$?
Is $2 < -0.5$?

No. Therefore, (2, 3) does not satisfy the inequality.

The correct answers are [A] and [B].

Systems of Inequalities

Certain questions require you to consider a system of inequalities, which is a combination of two or more inequalities. In such cases, you want to identify answers that satisfy **both** or **all** of the inequalities given to us.

Sample Question

Which of the following graphs accurately represents solutions that satisfy the following system of inequalities?

$$y \leq \frac{2}{3}x + 1$$

$$y \leq -\frac{3}{2}x + 3$$

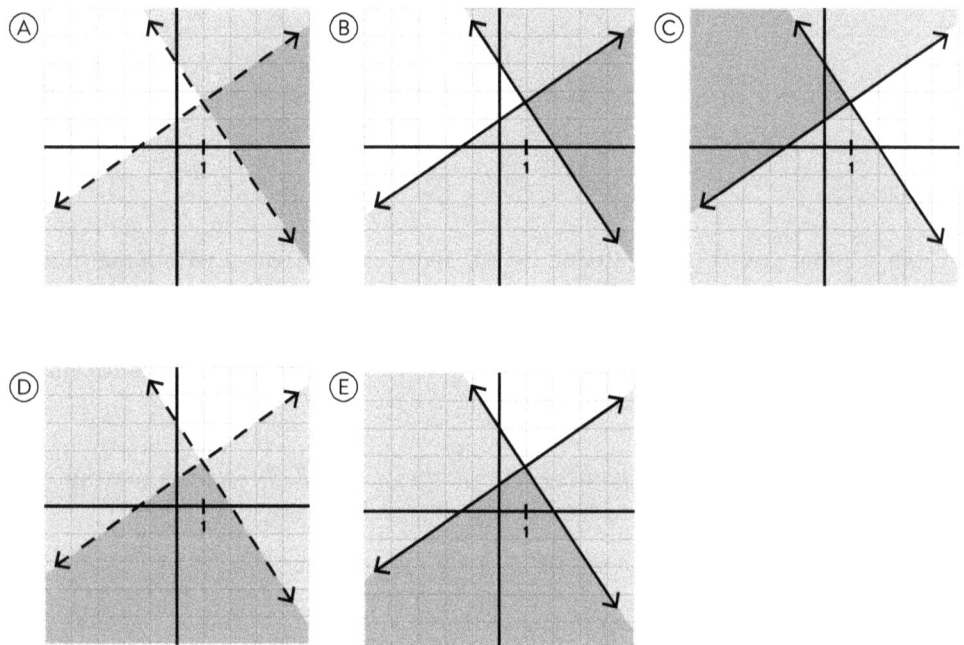

Solution

You know from the first equation that you are looking for answers on or below the line $y = \frac{2}{3}x + 1$, and you know from the second that you are looking for answers on or below the line $y = -\frac{3}{2}x + 3$. The only graph that satisfies both of these conditions is answer choice (E).

Wrong answers (A) and (B) both indicate that the area is above the line $y = -\frac{3}{2}x + 3$, (C) incorrectly indicates that the area is above the line $y = \frac{2}{3}x + 1$, and (A) and (D) both incorrectly fail to indicate the "or equal to" criteria with their dashed lines. Therefore, **the correct answer is (E)**.

Parabola Graphs and Quadratic Equations

Interpreting quadratic equations and creating the parabola graphs that result from them are in-depth topics on which I could spend a lot of time; however, these questions are fairly rare on the GRE and cover a limited set of concepts.

Let's highlight the essentials:

Quadratic equations contain one term in which the unknown or variable is taken to the second power (i.e., squared), and no term is raised to a higher power.

Quadratic equations form parabolas when graphed. A parabola is U-shaped, and the point where a parabola "turns" is called its vertex. In a typical vertically oriented parabola, if the parabola opens upward, then the y-coordinate of the vertex is the parabola's minimum (least y-value); if the parabola opens downward, then the y-coordinate of its vertex is the parabola's maximum (greatest y-value).

The **standard form** of a quadratic equation is

$y = ax^2 + bx + c$

A parabola graphed from a standard form quadratic equation will have the following characteristics:

Its y-intercept will be $(0, c)$, because in the standard equation when $x = 0$, $y = c$. The x-coordinate of its vertex will be $-\frac{b}{2a}$.

If a is positive, the parabola opens upward; if a is negative, the parabola opens downward.

Standard form quadratic equations are usually easily factorable, and from the factored form, you can derive further information about the appearance of the resulting parabola. For example:

$y = x^2 + 2x - 15$

Because you're interested in the x-intercepts of the parabola, let's set $y = 0$ and factor.

$0 = (x + 5)(x - 3)$

In order for the product of the factors to equal 0, one or both factors must equal 0. If $x + 5 = 0$, then $x = -5$, so -5 is one of the parabola's x-intercepts (also called roots, solutions, or zeros). If $x - 3 = 0$, then $x = 3$ is the parabola's other x-intercept.

You know that you're dealing with a parabola with x-intercepts of -5 and 3, and you know that it opens upward and has a y-intercept of -15.

Note that you might be asked to interpret a quadratic equation given as follows:

$$(x + a)(x + b) = x^2 + cx + d$$

If you FOILed the left side, you'd get:

$$x^2 + ax + bx + ab = x^2 + cx + d$$

You know that the middle terms on the left ($ax + bx$) combine to form the cx term on the right, so $ax + bx = cx$, which you can simplify to $a + b = c$.

You also know that ab on the right equals d on the left, so $ab = d$.

You also need to be familiar with the **vertex form** of a quadratic equation that will graph as a parabola:

$$y = a(x - h)^2 + k$$

What can you learn about a parabola graph from the vertex form?

a: As in the standard form, the value of a tells you about the shape of the parabola. If a is positive, the parabola will open upward, and if it's negative, the parabola will open downward. As $|a|$ becomes greater, the parabola gets narrower; as $|a|$ becomes less, the parabola gets wider.

h: The value of h is also the x-coordinate of the vertex. It's important to remember that the equation gives $(x - h)^2$, so, for example, if the equation says $(x + 4)^2$, then the x-coordinate of the vertex will be -4.

k: The value of k is also the y-coordinate of the vertex.

From the vertex form, you can conclude that the vertex of the resulting parabola is (h, k). Note that k will be either the highest or lowest y-value on the graph—and therefore either the maximum or minimum of the parabola—while the h will be the x-coordinate at which the parabola reaches its minimum or maximum value. For example:

In the parabola $y = 2(x - 5)^2 + 7$, the parabola opens upward (a is positive) from a vertex of $(5, 7)$. The parabola's minimum is 7, and the x-coordinate at which the parabola reaches its minimum is 5.

In the parabola $y = -(x + 3)^2 - 9$, the parabola opens downward (a is negative) from a vertex of (−3, −9). The parabola's maximum is −9, and the x-coordinate at which the parabola reaches its maximum is −3.

Sample Question

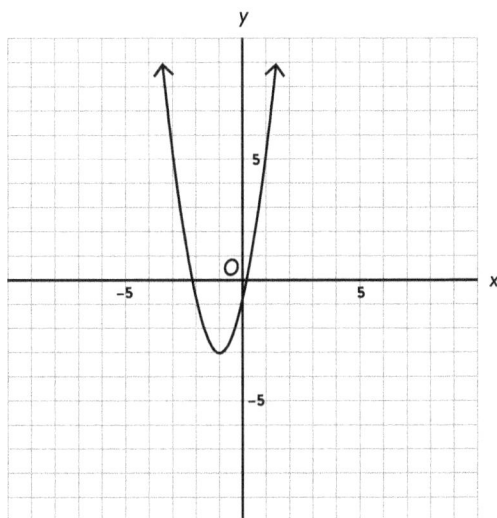

Which of the following equations accurately represents the given parabola?

(A) $y = -2(x - 1)^2 - 3$
(B) $y = 2(x - 1)^2 - 3$
(C) $y = 2(x + 1)^2 - 3$
(D) $y = 2(x - 1)^2 + 3$
(E) $y = 2(x + 1)^2 + 3$

<u>Solution</u>

You can see that the vertex of the parabola is at (−1, −3), which means you should have $(x + 1)^2 - 3$ in the answer, and since the parabola opens up, you know that the coefficient must be positive. This leads you to (C), the correct answer.

Alternatively, if you weren't sure of the vertex formula or you wanted to verify your work, you could try plugging the coordinates of points you know are on the parabola into the answer choice equations. Recall that the coordinates of a point that is on a given graph must correctly solve the equation for that graph! For example, if you try plugging in (0, −1), you get the following results for each of the answer choices:

(A) $y = -2(0 - 1)^2 - 3 = -2 - 3 = -5$ doesn't work
(B) $y = 2(0 - 1)^2 - 3 = 2 - 3 = -1$ works
(C) $y = 2(0 + 1)^2 - 3 = 2 - 3 = -1$ works
(D) $y = 2(0 - 1)^2 + 3 = 2 + 3 = 5$ doesn't work
(E) $y = 2(0 + 1)^2 + 3 = 2 + 3 = 5$ doesn't work

From there, you could try one more of the points, such as (–2, –1) or (–1, –3), to see whether (B) or (C) is correct. Let's try plugging in the vertex (–1, –3):

(B) $y = 2(-1 - 1)^2 - 3 = 2(4) - 3 = 5$ doesn't work
(C) $y = 2(-1 + 1)^2 - 3 = 2(0) - 3 = -3$ works

So, you can confirm that **(C) matches the diagram and is the correct answer**.

More on Functions

Why are some equations and their resulting graphs presented to you as functions using terms such as $f(x)$ in place of the variable y? Why are you sometimes presented with the equation $y = 2x + 3$ and other times with the linear function $f(x) = 2x + 3$?

Well, there is a mathematical definition of a function that differentiates it from some other types of equations and graphs. In a function, there can be only one y-value for any particular x-value. In a function, you cannot have two points such as (2, 3) and (2, 7), because that results in having two y-values associated with a single x-value. You may recall from a long-distant math class the concept of the "vertical line test": if you can draw a vertical line on the xy-plane that intersects with a graph in more than one place, that graph is NOT the graph of a function.

However, there's a second, simpler explanation for the use of function notation on the GRE—it allows the test writers to refer to an equation without defining it. For example, they can say something like "if $f(x)$ passes through the point (3, 5)," you know that they're referring to some kind of graph, but you don't know whether it's a line, a parabola, or some other kind of graph. I'll say more about that below.

There are some terms specific to functions with which you must be familiar.

The **domain** of a function refers to the set of permissible inputs, or x-values. In general, the domain of a function is "all real numbers" with some familiar exceptions:

(1) Any number that would result in the denominator of a fractional function having the value of 0

Example: If $f(x) = \frac{x}{x-1}$, then the domain will be all real numbers except $x = 1$. The graph of $f(x)$ will not have a y-value associated with the x-value of 1.

(2) Any number that would result in a negative number under an even radical (e.g., square root, 4th root, 6th root, etc.)

Example: If $f(x) = \sqrt{x - 3}$, then the domain will be all x greater than or equal to 3. The graph of $f(x)$ will not show any y-values for any x-value less than 3. In other words, the graph will appear to "start" at $x = 3$ and proceed to the right on the xy-plane.

The **range** of a function refers to the set of potential outputs, or y-values. In general, the best way to determine the range of a function is to graph it—as such, questions about range are rare on the GRE. That said:

What is the range of $f(x) = (x - 4)^2 + 3$?

This is the vertex form of a quadratic equation that will produce a parabola. This parabola is going to open upward (a is positive) from a vertex of (4, 3). Therefore, the range of the function is $y \geq 3$.

Function Graph Translation and Reflection

Remember how the test writers can use $f(x)$ to refer to a function about which little else is known? That leads to questions that ask you to understand simply that an original function $f(x)$ is being **translated** (moved) a certain distance left, right, up, or down, or **reflected** across an axis or across the origin.

When an original function $f(x)$ is translated or reflected, all points on $f(x)$, such as its y-intercept or x-intercepts, would be translated or reflected in the same manner.

Given the original function $f(x)$:

$f(x + a)$ moves $f(x)$ a units to the left
$f(x - a)$ moves $f(x)$ a units to the right
$f(x) + a$ moves $f(x)$ a units up
$f(x) - a$ moves $f(x)$ a units down

Given the original function $f(x)$:

$f(-x)$ reflects $f(x)$ across the y-axis
It helps to remember that in function notation, what's inside the parentheses is the x-value, so turning (x) into $(-x)$ negates all the x-values, which takes a point with an x-value of 3 and moves it to an x-value of -3, thereby reflecting it across the y-axis.

$-f(x)$ reflects $f(x)$ across the x-axis
It helps to remember that in function notation, $f(x)$ represents the y-values, so turning $f(x)$ into $-f(x)$ negates all the y-values, which takes a point with a y-value of 3 and moves it to a y-value of -3, thereby reflecting it across the x-axis.

$-f(-x)$ reflects $f(x)$ across the origin
Here you are negating both the x- and y-values, thereby reflecting $f(x)$ across both axes, which, as discussed earlier, results in a reflection across the origin.

Let's consider a few simple sample questions dealing with function graph translation and reflection.

If $f(x)$ has a y-intercept of 12, what will be the y-intercept of $f(x) - 3$?

You're asked to move $f(x)$ down 3 units, so the original y-intercept of 12 will now occur at $y = 9$, 3 units lower.

If $f(x)$ is a parabola with roots at -2 and 3, what are the roots of $f(x - 4)$?

Recall that a "root" is an x-intercept of a parabola. You're asked to move $f(x)$ 4 units to the right, so the root at $x = -2$ will move 4 units right to 2, and the root at $x = 3$ will move to 7. The new roots are 2 and 7.

Now, let's consider a more difficult question that—fortunately for us—presents an opportunity to solve it creatively:

Sample Question

Which of the following functions f defined for all numbers x has the property that $f(x) = f(-x)$ for all numbers x?

(A) $f(x) = 3x + 2$
(B) $f(x) = -2x - 4$
(C) $f(x) = 3(x - 4)^2 + 1$
(D) $f(x) = 2x^2 + 1$
(E) $f(x) = (x)(x^3 - 1)$

<u>Solution</u>

It's true the question asks you to identify a function in which the graph of $f(x)$ would be the same as the graph of $f(-x)$, the original graph reflected across the y-axis. You're looking for a function $f(x)$ that is symmetrical about the y-axis—in other words, reflecting $f(x)$ across the y-axis wouldn't change the graph at all. However, it would be tough to solve the problem that way, as it's difficult to look at function equations (especially those in answers such as (E)) and recognize whether they have certain forms of symmetry.

What can you do instead? You can plug in numbers! Let's make a quick table and see what happens in each function when you plug in the number $x = 3$:

f(x)	f(3)	f(–3)	Test	Passes Test?
$3x + 2$	$3(3) - 2 = 7$	$3(-3) + 2 = -7$	$7 = -7$	NO
$-2x - 4$	$-2(3) - 4 = -10$	$-2(-3) - 4 = 2$	$-10 = 2$	NO
$3(x - 4)^2 + 1$	$3(3 - 4)^2 + 1 = 4$	$3(-3 - 4)^2 + 1 = 148$	$4 = 148$	NO
$2x^2 + 1$	$2(3^2) + 1 = 19$	$2(-3^2) + 1 = 19$	$19 = 19$	YES
$(x)(x^3 - 1)$	$(3)(3^3 - 1) = 78$	$(-3)(-3^3 - 1) = 84$	$78 = 84$	NO

Cool! **The answer is (D)** because only that answer choice function gives $f(3) = f(-3)$. Only (D) has the property that $f(x) = f(-x)$ for all values of x.

Sample Question

Which of the following graphs accurately represents $f(x) = |x - 2| + 1$?

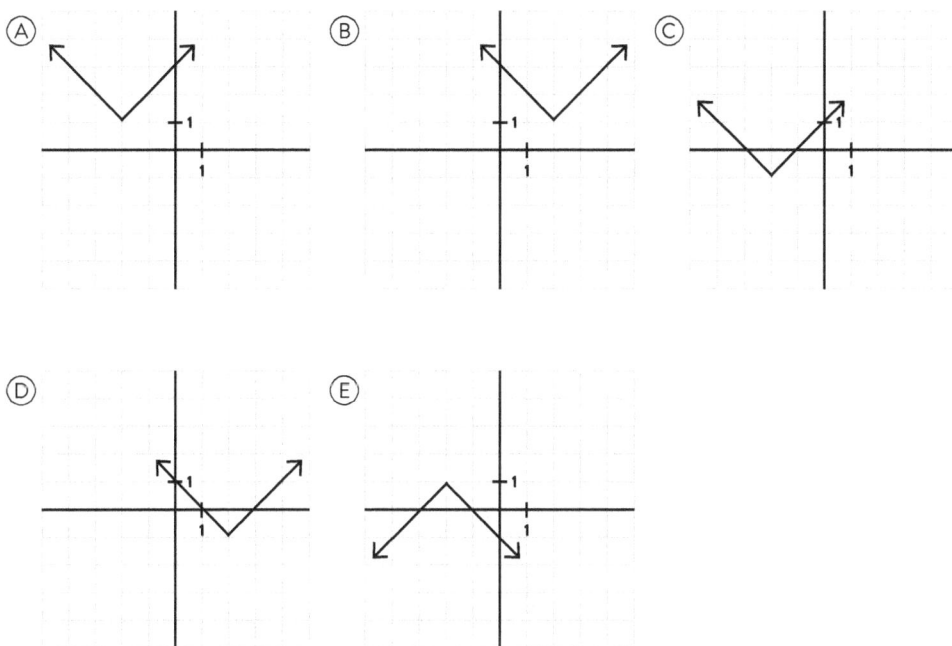

Solution

One way to answer graphing questions is by testing numbers, as you did for the previous question. For example, you can plug 0 in for x in the given equation and see that $f(0) = |0 - 2| + 1 = 3$ and know that $(0, 3)$ must be a point on the graph. If you plug in 2 for x, you can see that $f(x) = |2 - 2| + 1 = 1$, and you know that $(2, 1)$ must be a point on the graph.

Armed with this information, you can see that **answer choice (B) is the only choice that contains those two points, and it is the correct answer**.

Coordinate Plane Drill

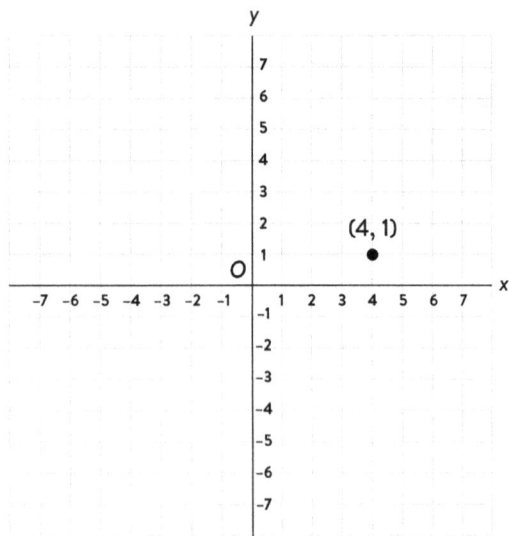

1. Reflect the point (4, 1) over:

A. x-axis
B. y-axis
C. origin
D. line $y = x$
E. line $y = -1$

2. Match the following equations to their graphs:

A. $y = -\frac{1}{2}x + 2$

B. $y = \frac{1}{2}x + 2$

C. $y = \frac{1}{2}x - 2$

D. $y = 2x + 2$

1.
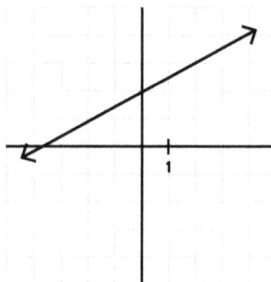

2.
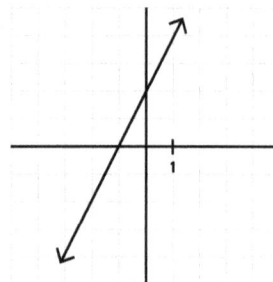

3.
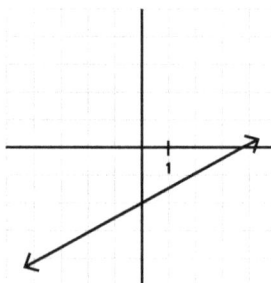

4.
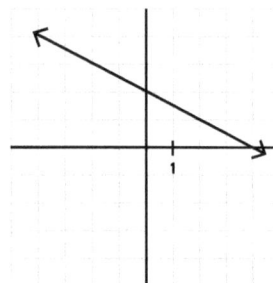

3. Match the following systems with their respective graphs:

A. $y \geq -2x - 4$

   $y \leq \frac{1}{2}x + 1$

B. $y \geq -2x - 4$

   $y \geq \frac{1}{2}x + 1$

C. $y \leq -2x - 4$

   $y \leq \frac{1}{2}x + 1$

D. $y \leq -2x - 4$

   $y \geq \frac{1}{2}x + 1$

1.

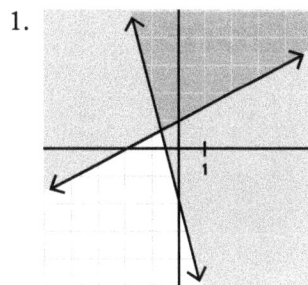

2.

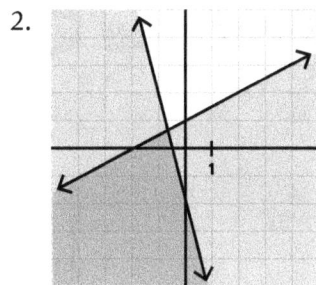

3.

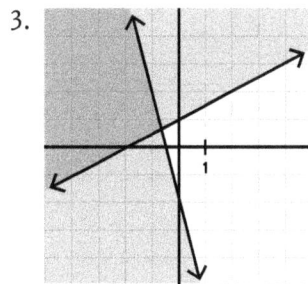

4.

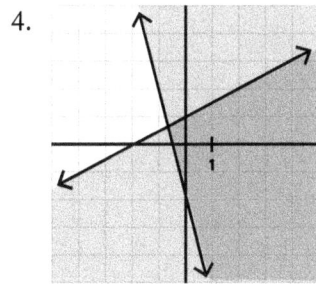

SOLUTIONS

1.	2.	3.
A. (4, –1)	A. 4	A. 4
B. (–4, 1)	B. 1	B. 1
C. (–4, –1)	C. 3	C. 2
D. (1, 4)	D. 2	D. 3
E. (4, –3)		

Practice Questions

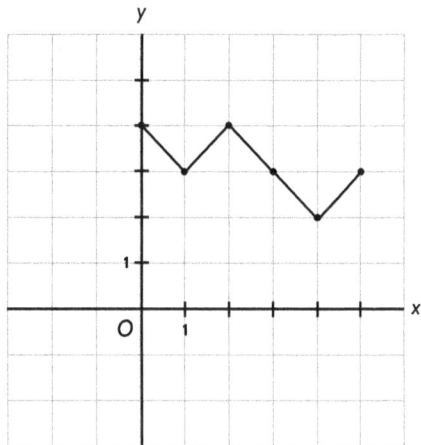

1. The above graph represents function $f(x)$. What is $f(f(4))$?

(A) 1
(B) 2
(C) 3
(D) 4
(E) 5

2. Which of the following graphs accurately represents solutions to the equation $y = -x^2 + 4$?

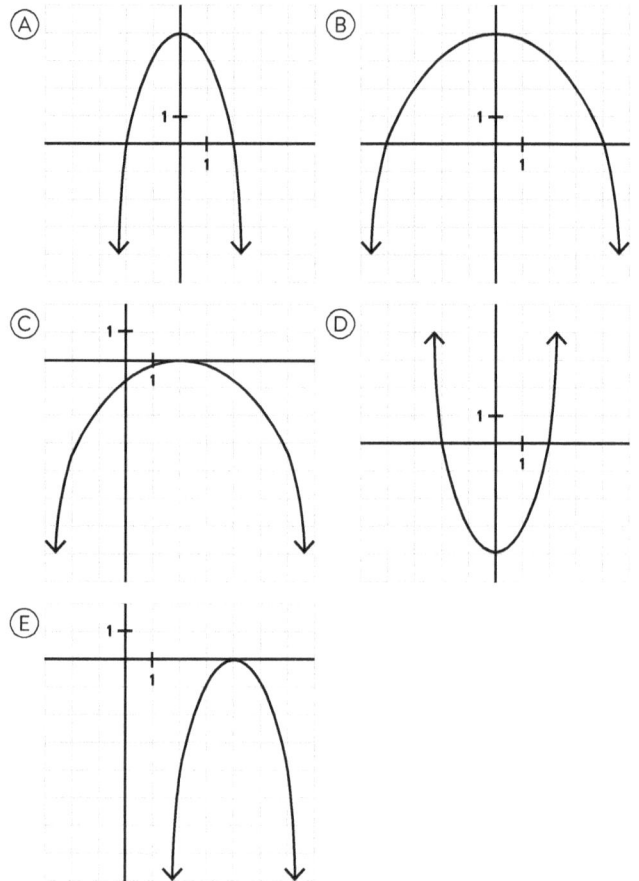

3. If a square with vertices (3, 5), (–1, 5), (3, 9), and (–1, 9) is reflected over the *x*-axis, which of the following would be the vertices of the reflected image?

Indicate <u>all</u> such points.

A (–3, 5)
B (3, –5)
C (–1, –9)
D (1, 9)
E (1, –9)

4. Line *a* is parallel to line *b*. Line *b* passes through points (5, 2) and (9, 4). Point (3, 2) is on line *a*. What is the *y*-intercept of line *a*?

5. Line *l* has equation $y = -2x + 4$, and line *m* is perpendicular to line *l*, with the same *x*-intercept as line *l*. Which of the following graphs represents line *m*?

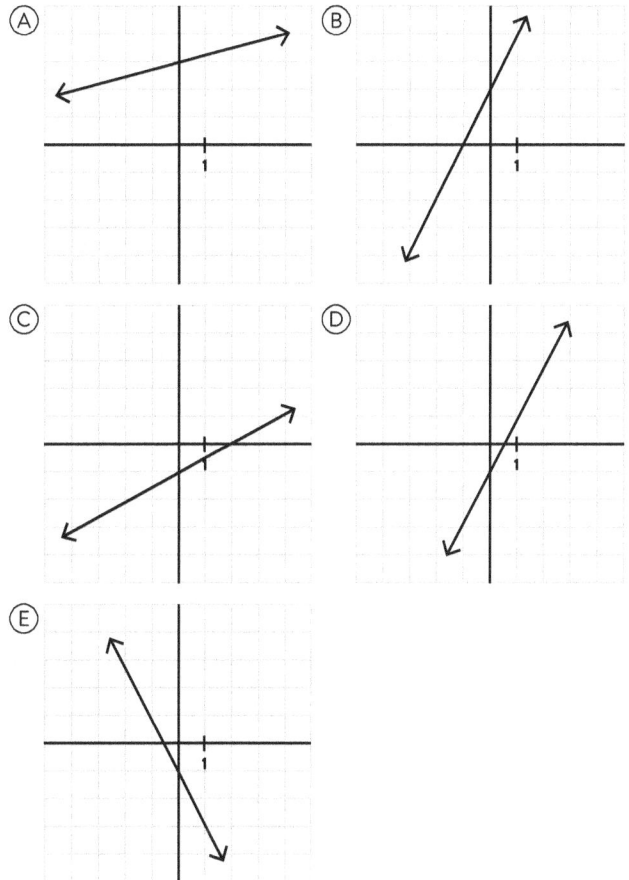

(A)

(B)

(C)

(D)

(E)

Practice Question Solutions

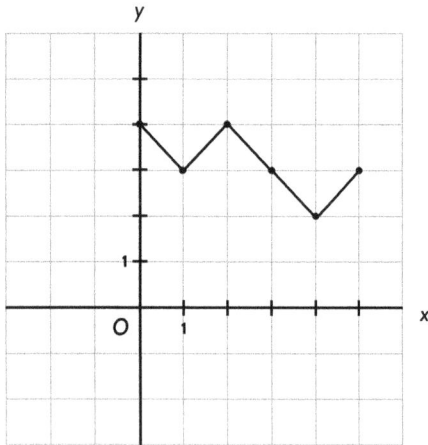

1. The above graph represents function $f(x)$. What is $f(f(4))$?

(A) 1
(B) 2
(C) 3
(D) 4
(E) 5

Solution

$f(4)$, or the result when the input is 4, is 2.

$f(2)$, or the result when the input is 2, is 4.

Therefore, $f(f(4)) = 4$, and **(D) is the correct answer**.

2. Which of the following graphs accurately represents solutions to the equation $y = -x^2 + 4$?

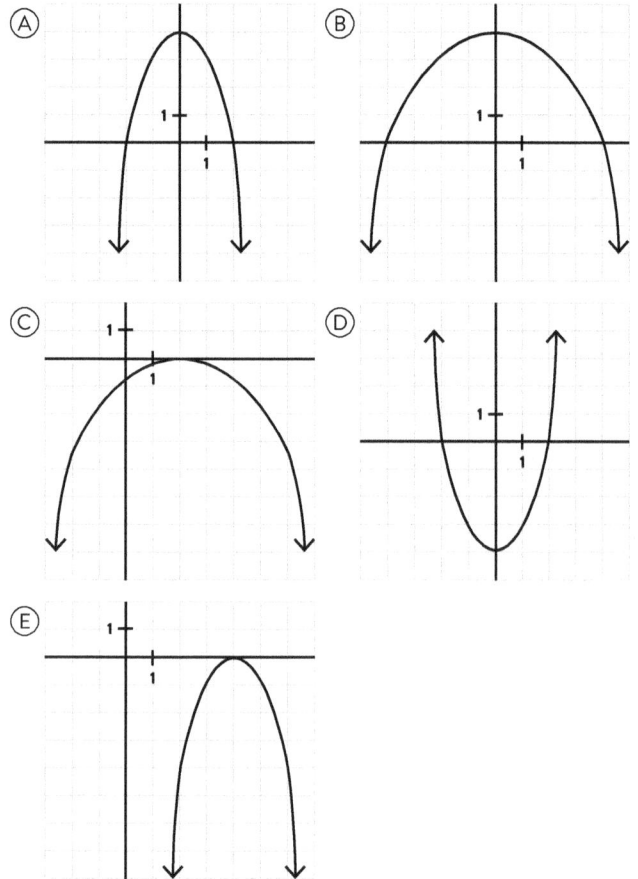

Solution

You know that the y-intercept is 4, with a vertex of $(0, 4)$. This leaves you with (A) and (B).

One way to check which is correct is to consider the x-intercepts. You can see that when $x = 2$ or -2, per the given equation, $y = -(2)^2 + 4 = 0$. So, the two x-intercepts are $(2, 0)$ and $(-2, 0)$. Looking at the graphs, you can see that **(A) matches that information, and it is the correct answer**.

3. If a square with vertices (3, 5), (–1, 5), (3, 9), and (–1, 9) is reflected over the x-axis, which of the following would be the vertices of the reflected image?

Indicate all such points.

A (–3, 5)
B (3, –5)
C (–1, –9)
D (1, 9)
E (1, –9)

Solution

You can visualize, either mentally or on paper, the initial square and the reflected square as follows:

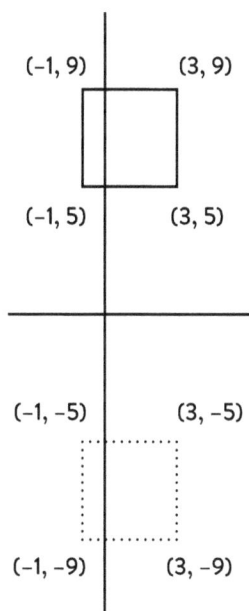

If you reflect over the x-axis, you can expect for the x-coordinate to remain the same and for the y-coordinate to switch to its opposite orientation (from positive to negative or vice versa).

You can see that the reflected vertices are (3, –5), (–1, –5), (3, –9), and (–1, –9), so answer choices [B] and [C] are correct.

4. Line a is parallel to line b. Line b passes through points (5, 2) and (9, 4). Point (3, 2) is on line a. What is the y-intercept of line a?

0.5

Solution

If line b goes through points (5, 2) and (9, 4), you know that it has a slope of $\frac{4-2}{9-5} = \frac{2}{4} = \frac{1}{2}$.

So, you know that line a must also have a slope of $\frac{1}{2}$.

If line a goes through point (3, 2), you can insert that point into the $y = mx + b$ equation to solve for the y-intercept:

$$2 = \left(\frac{1}{2}\right)(3) + b$$
$$2 = 1.5 + b$$
$$\mathbf{0.5 = b}$$

Solutions Continued

5. Line l has equation $y = -2x + 4$, and line m is perpendicular to line l, with the same x-intercept as line l. Which of the following graphs represents line m?

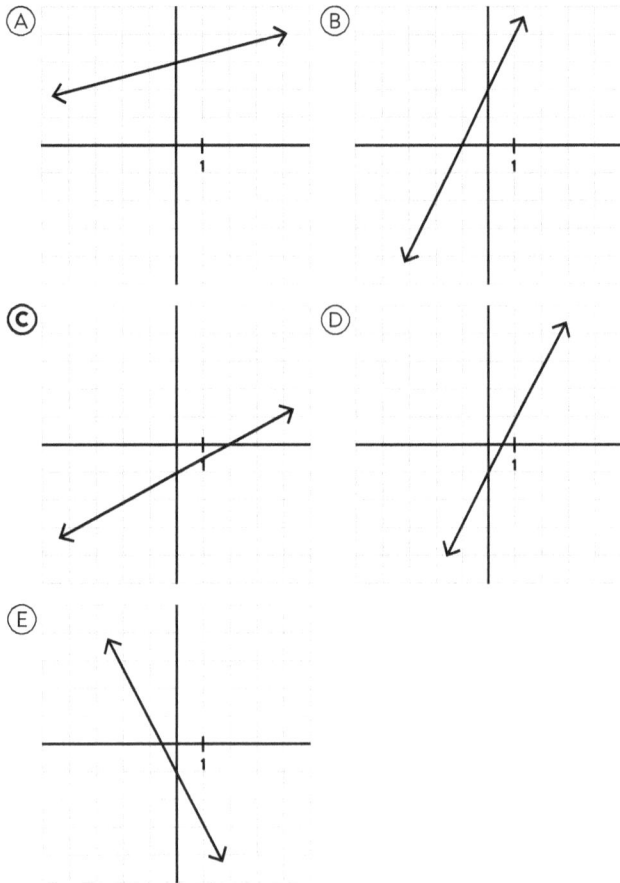

Solution

If line l has equation $y = -2x + 4$, you know it has a slope of -2. If line m is perpendicular to line l, you know it must have a slope of $\frac{1}{2}$.

To find the x-intercept for line l, you can input 0 for y and solve for x as follows:

$y = -2x + 4$
$0 = -2x + 4$
$2x = 4$
$x = 2$

Since you are told that both lines share an x-intercept, you now know that line m has an x-intercept of 2 as well.

Knowing both of these characteristics, **select answer choice (C) as the correct representation of line m**.

20 Lines, Angles, and Triangles

QUANTITATIVE REASONING

In this lesson, I'll dive deeper into geometry by discussing the basics of lines, angles, and triangles. Again, you are probably already familiar with the concepts I'm about to discuss, but it may have been a while since you've seen or thought about them. Let's make sure to get you reacclimated before test day.

Let's start by noting that on the GRE, geometric figures are not necessarily drawn to scale—we cannot assume that quantities such as lengths and angle measures are as they appear in a figure. This is particularly important to remember when approaching quantitative comparison questions.

Points on a Line

If a GRE question simply states that, for example, points A, B, C, and D are collinear or on the same straight line, do not assume that they appear in that order from left to right. Assume that you know the relative positions of the points if you are told that "points A, B, C, and D lie on a line in the order given" or if you are presented with a diagram labeling the points.

If all points lie on the same line, as in the diagram below, you can infer distances between points through addition or subtraction.

Sample Question

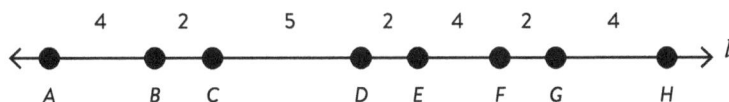

Points A, B, C, D, E, F, G, and H all lie on line l. Which of the following line segments is the longest?

Ⓐ AD
Ⓑ BE
Ⓒ CF
Ⓓ DG
Ⓔ EH

<u>Solution</u>

To get the distance between points A and D, you can add up all of the shorter segments that add up to AD, specifically, $AB + BC + CD$, which is $4 + 2 + 5 = 11$.

You can use the same process for each of the other line segments in question, and when you do, you get the following lengths:

$BE = 9$
$CF = 10$
$DG = 7$
$EH = 9$

Of the 5 lengths in question, AD is the longest, and **(A) is the correct answer.**

Lines and Angles

Supplementary Angles

When a straight line is intersected by a transversal, as in the figure below, it creates two supplementary angles that must add up to 180°.

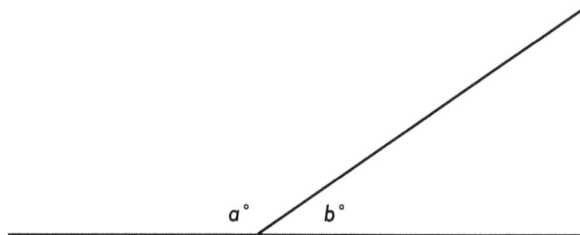

In the figure above, $\angle a$ and $\angle b$ are supplementary angles. If $\angle a = 3\angle b$, what is the degree measure of $\angle a$?

(A) 45°
(B) 60°
(C) 90°
(D) 120°
(E) 135°

Solution

If $\angle a$ and $\angle b$ are supplementary, you know that they add up to 180°. Thus, you can solve:

$\angle a + \angle b = 180°$; all supplementary angles add to 180°.
$3\angle b + \angle b = 180°$; you can substitute $3b$ for a.
$4\angle b = 180°$; now you can add up the $\angle b$'s and solve.
$\angle b = 45°$; now you can use this information to solve for $\angle a$.
$\angle a + 45° = 180°$; all supplementary angles add to 180°.
$\angle a = 135°$.

(E) is the correct answer.

Intersecting Lines

If two straight lines intersect each other, they will create four angles, as in the figure below.

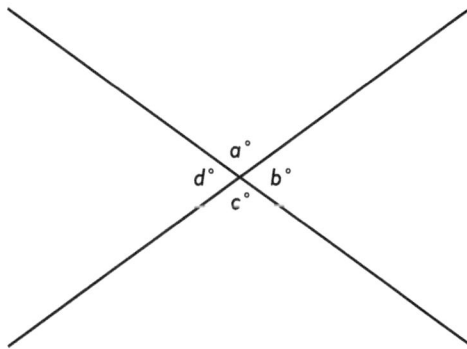

In such situations, it must be true that:

1. Vertical angles (those on opposite sides of the point of intersection) are congruent, or equal to each other.
2. Adjacent angles (those right next to each other) are supplementary, or add up to 180°.
3. All angles together add up to 360°.

Sample Question

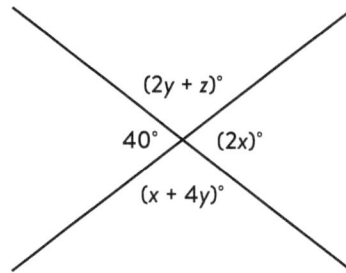

What is the value of z?

$z =$ ☐

Solution

There are several ways to go about solving this problem; you can take advantage of the fact that opposite angles are equal, that adjacent angles add up to 180°, and/or that all angles add up to 360°.

Let's start by first recognizing that opposite angles must be equal to each other, and, therefore:

$2x = 40$
$x = 20$

Next, knowing the value of x, you can use your understanding of adjacent angles to set up the following equation and solve for y:

$40 + (x + 4y) = 180$
$40 + (20 + 4y) = 180$
$60 + 4y = 180$
$4y = 120$
$y = 30$

Finally, now that you know the value of y, use your understanding of the adjacent angles once more to find the value of z:

$40 + (2y + z) = 180$
$40 + [(2)(30) + z] = 180$
$40 + 60 + z = 180$
$100 + z = 180$
$z = 80$

80 is the correct answer.

Parallel Lines Cut by a Transversal

If a set of parallel lines is cut by a transversal, as in the image below, it creates two sets of four congruent angles.

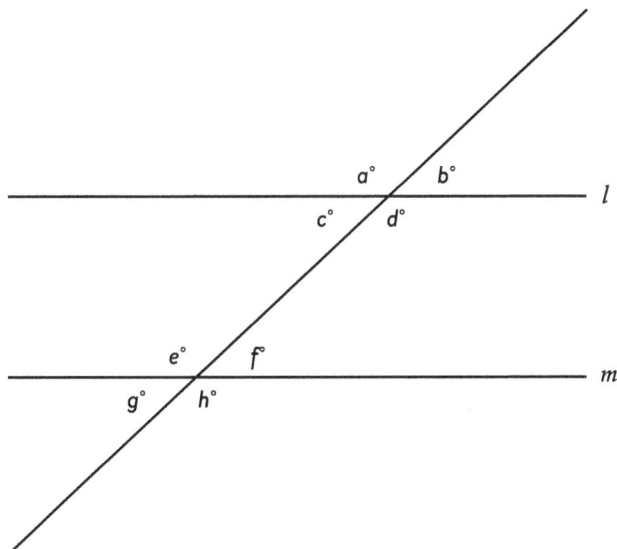

Let's discuss some terminology related to this diagram of parallel lines cut by a transversal.

$\angle c$ and $\angle f$ are congruent and are called **alternate interior angles**—that is, they are interior to the parallel lines but on alternate sides of the transversal. $\angle d$ and $\angle e$ are also congruent for the same reason.

Because $\angle b$ and $\angle c$ are congruent vertical angles, $\angle b$, $\angle c$, $\angle f$, and $\angle g$ are all congruent. Similarly, $\angle a$, $\angle d$, $\angle e$, and $\angle h$ are all congruent.

Note that you can derive the two sets of angle equivalences using just the concepts of congruent vertical angles and congruent alternate interior angles. That said, here are some other terms you might come across:

The following pairs of congruent angles are called **corresponding angles** due to positions that correspond to each other relative to the parallel lines and the transversal: $\angle a$ and $\angle e$, $\angle b$ and $\angle f$, $\angle c$ and $\angle g$, $\angle d$ and $\angle h$.

The following pairs of congruent angles are called **alternate exterior angles** because they are exterior to the parallel lines but on alternate sides of the transversal: $\angle a$ and $\angle h$, $\angle b$ and $\angle g$.

The following pairs of angles are supplementary (sum to 180°) and are called **same-side interior angles** because they are interior to the parallel lines but on the same side of the transversal: $\angle c$ and $\angle e$, $\angle d$ and $\angle f$. I'll outline an interesting application of the same-side interior angle relationship in the next chapter.

Sample Question

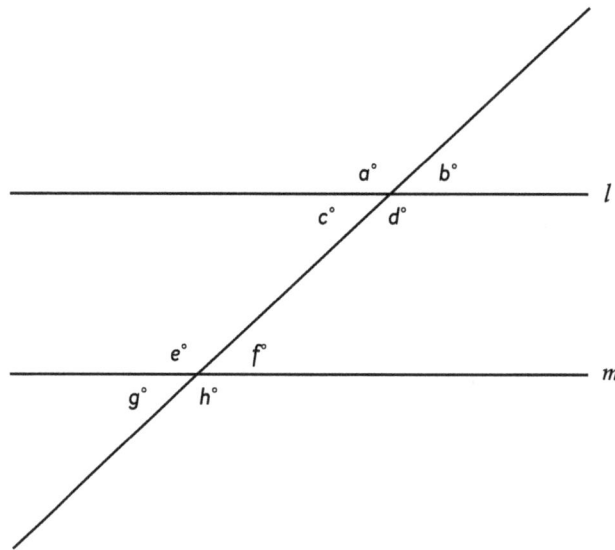

If *l* and *m* are parallel lines and $\angle a = 140°$, which other angles must also equal 140°?

Indicate all such angles.

[A] $\angle c$
[B] $\angle d$
[C] $\angle e$
[D] $\angle f$
[E] $\angle g$

Solution

As discussed above, $\angle a$, $\angle d$, $\angle e$, and $\angle h$ must be congruent, and $\angle b$, $\angle c$, $\angle f$, and $\angle g$ must be congruent. Therefore, from the set of options you've been given, **the answers [B] and [C] are correct**.

Triangles

Now, let's move on to triangles. The triangle is arguably the most important shape in geometry, and the properties of triangles allow you to solve for lengths and angles that you wouldn't be able to solve for otherwise. **Even when a question presents itself as being about another shape, such as a quadrilateral, a hexagon, or a cube, very often the key to success is understanding and applying the rules of triangles.** Triangle rules are essential to your mastery of geometry, and I'll cover everything you need to know about them for the GRE.

First, let's cover some basic triangle terms and relationships:

- The sum of a triangle's three interior angles is 180°.
- The perimeter of a triangle is the sum of all side lengths.
- The area of a triangle is $\left(\frac{1}{2}\right)$(base)(height). Any side of a triangle can be used as its base, but note that the height (or altitude) must be perpendicular to that base.
- Sides opposite equal angles are equal, and angles opposite equal sides are equal.
- The longest side of the triangle will be opposite the greatest angle, and the shortest side will be opposite the least angle.
- In a **right** triangle, one angle is exactly 90°. In an **acute** triangle, all angles are less than 90°. In an **obtuse** triangle, one angle is greater than 90°.

Now let's look at some triangle rules and relationships that require a bit more explanation.

Exterior Angles

In the diagram below, $\angle a$, $\angle b$, and $\angle c$ are interior angles, and $\angle d$, $\angle e$, and $\angle f$ are exterior angles. An **exterior angle** is defined as an angle supplementary to an interior angle.

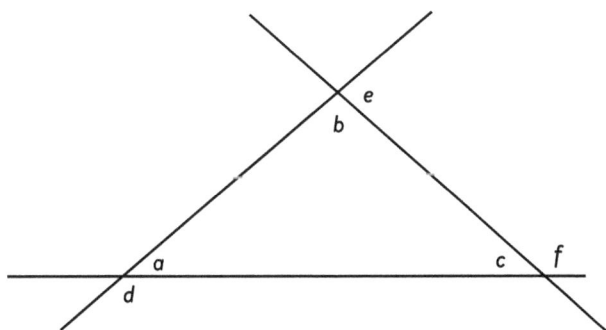

The sum of a triangle's three exterior angles is 360°. You can demonstrate that by imagining that the three interior angles each measure 60°. Each supplementary exterior angle would then equal 120°, and the three exterior angles would add up to 360°.

In addition, any exterior angle is equal to the sum of the two **remote interior angles** (i.e., the two non-adjacent interior angles). In the diagram above, $\angle d = \angle b + \angle c$, $\angle e = \angle a + \angle c$, and $f\angle = \angle a + \angle b$. Why? Well, remember that adjacent angles along a line add up to 180° and the three interior angles of a triangle add up to 180°—any interior angle (e.g., $\angle a$) adds up to 180° with its adjacent exterior angle (e.g., $\angle d$) and also adds up to 180° with the other two interior angles (e.g., $\angle b + \angle c$). Therefore, $\angle d = \angle b + \angle c$.

Triangle Inequality Theorem

Given two sides of any triangle, the third side must be less than the sum of the other two sides but greater than the difference. For example, if you know that a triangle has sides of length 4, 7, and x, then the third side (x) must obey the following rule:

$7 - 4 < x < 7 + 4$

$3 < x < 11$

The third side of this triangle must be between 3 and 11 units in length. Note that it cannot be equal to either 3 or 11, but must fall between them. If x is an integer, it must be a member of the set $\{4, 5, 6, 7, 8, 9, 10\}$.

Here are some sample questions that involve these triangle concepts:

Sample Question 1

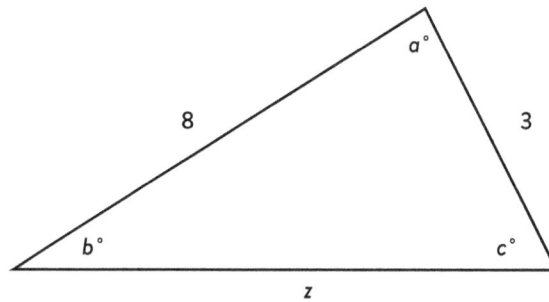

If $\angle b < \angle a < \angle c$, which of the following could be the value of z?

Indicate all such values.

A 2
B 5
C 6
D 7
E 10

Solution

You know that in a triangle, the longest side is opposite the greatest angle, and the shortest side is opposite the least angle. $\angle a$ is greater than $\angle b$ but less than $\angle c$, so you know that the side opposite $\angle a$, which is z, must be greater than the side opposite $\angle b$, which is 3, and less than the side opposite $\angle c$, which is 8.

You also know that any two sides of a triangle must add up to be greater than the third side, so z could not equal 5, as in answer choice [B].

Therefore, the two answers that would work here are answer choices [C] and [D].

Sample Question 2

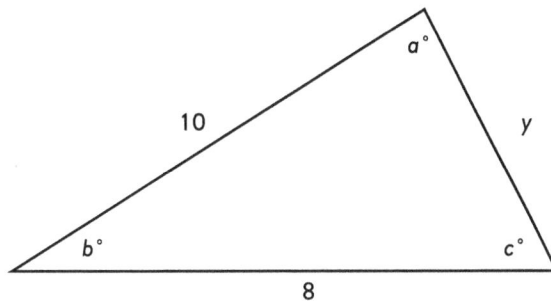

If $\angle b < \angle a < \angle c$, which of the following could be the value of y?

Indicate <u>all</u> such values.

- A 1
- B 2
- C 3
- D 4
- E 5

<u>Solution</u>

Here, you are asked to infer information about the length of side y, which is opposite $\angle b$. You know that $\angle b$ is the least of the group, so y must be shorter in length than the other two sides, which are 8 and 10, respectively. So, $y < 8$.

You also know that y must be great enough that the sum of the lengths of any two sides is greater than the length of the third side. Since $y + 8 > 10$, you know that y must be greater than 2.

Putting this together, you can see that 3, 4, and 5 are viable options for the length of side y.

Isosceles Triangles

Isosceles triangles have at least two sides of equal length. In an isosceles triangle, the two angles opposite the two congruent sides will also be equal.

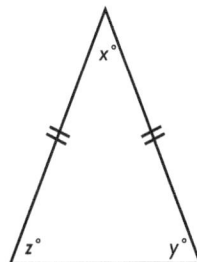

Sample Question

For the triangle above, if the measure of $\angle y = 6a - 20$ and the measure of $\angle z = 4a + 10$, what is the measure of $\angle x$?

x = [ ]

Solution

From the information you've been given, you know that this is an isosceles triangle and that $\angle y$ and $\angle z$ are equal to each other. You can also answer the question by setting the measures of $\angle y$ and $\angle z$ equal to each other and then solving for a:

$6a - 20 = 4a + 10$
$2a = 30$
$a = 15$

If a is 15, then the measure of $\angle y = 6(15) - 20 = 90 - 20 = 70°$, which is also the measure of $\angle z$. **Therefore, the measure of $\angle x$ = 180 – 70 – 70 = 40°.**

Equilateral Triangles

Equilateral triangles have three congruent sides and three congruent angles, each 60°. Often, when you are asked to solve for unknown lengths in an equilateral triangle, you will do so by splitting it in half and creating two 30°-60°-90° triangles, which I'll discuss shortly.

Sample Question (Challenge)

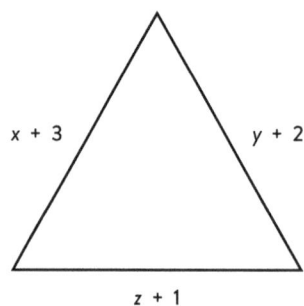

If the given triangle is equilateral, which of the following is the greatest?

(A) $x + y$
(B) $x + z$
(C) $y + z$
(D) $2x$
(E) $2y$

Solution

There are several different ways to think about this question. One method is to think of all variables in terms of one variable. Let's express all of the variables above in terms of x.

So, you know that one side is $x + 3$.

You know that another side, $y + 2$, is equal to $x + 3$, so you can say that:

$y + 2 = x + 3$
$y = x + 1$

Finally, you know that the final side, $z + 1$, is also equal to $x + 3$, so you can say that:

$z + 1 = x + 3$
$z = x + 2$

Armed with this information, you can compare the answers to one another.

$x + y = x + (x + 1) = 2x + 1$
$x + z = x + (x + 2) = 2x + 2$
$y + z = (x + 1) + (x + 2) = 2x + 3$
$2x = 2x$
$2y = 2(x + 1) = 2x + 2$

Regardless of the value of x, **answer choice (C) will always be greatest, and it is the correct answer.**

Congruent Triangles

Two triangles are congruent if they have the exact same side lengths and angles. Note that congruent shapes do not need to share the same orientation; that is, one shape could be a mirror reflection of another, and as long as all angles and lengths are the same, the two shapes will still be considered congruent.

Sample Question

A triangle is drawn on a coordinate plane with vertices at points (–4, 1), (–5, –2), and (–1, –2). If a second triangle is to be drawn congruent with the first, with points (3, 4) and (7, 4) as two of its vertices, which of the following could be its third vertex?

Indicate all such points.

A (2, 7)
B (4, 7)
C (6, 7)
D (4, 1)
E (6, 1)

<u>Solution</u>

(4, 7)   (6, 7)

(−4, 1)   (3, 4)   (7, 4)

(4, 1)   (6, 1)

(−5, −2)   (−1, −2)

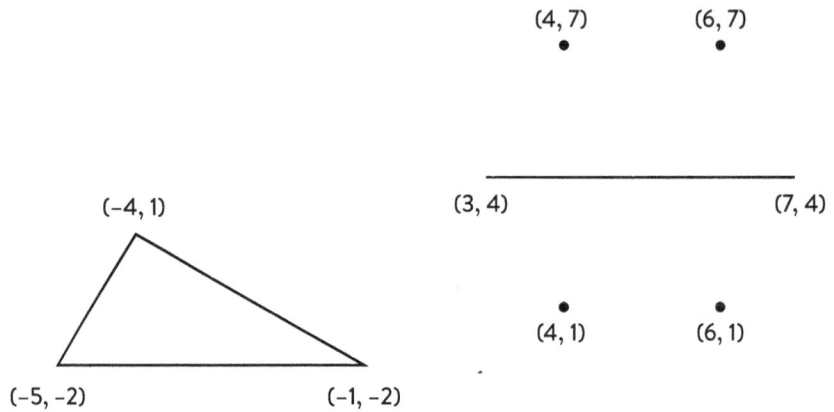

If the second triangle is congruent to the first, then you know that the missing point from the second triangle must have an x-coordinate that is between those of the two given vertices and is 1 away from one of them and 3 away from the other (that is, the x-coordinate must be either 4 or 6), and it also must have a y-coordinate that is 3 greater than or 3 less than that of the two given vertices (that is, either $4 + 3 = 7$ or $4 - 3 = 1$). **The points mentioned in answer choices [B], [C], [D], and [E] all match those conditions and are correct.**

Similar Triangles

Similar polygons are those that share the same shape but not necessarily the same size. Two triangles are similar if they have the same three angle measures. Similar triangles have sides that are proportional to one another. For example, if you know that two triangles are similar and that one side of the larger triangle is twice the length of its corresponding side on the smaller triangle, each side of the larger triangle will be twice the length of its respective corresponding side on the smaller triangle.

As a side note, it is helpful to remember that as lengths change proportionally, areas change exponentially. For example, if there are two similar triangles, one of which has sides that are twice as long as the sides of the other, the larger triangle will have an area that is $2^2 = 4$ times as large. If the sides are 3 times as long, the area will be $3^2 = 9$ times as great.

Sample Question

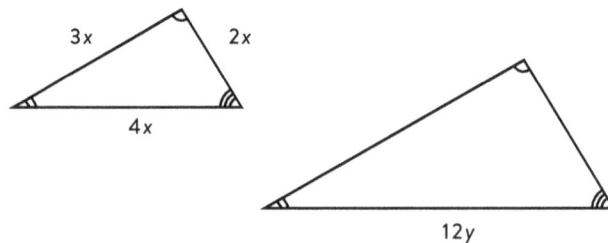

3x   2x

4x

12y

If the two triangles on the preceding page are similar, which of the following is equal to the perimeter of the second triangle?

Ⓐ 26y
Ⓑ 27y
Ⓒ 28y
Ⓓ 29y
Ⓔ 30y

Solution

Since you know the two triangles are similar, if $4x$ corresponds to $12y$, you can infer that $2x$ must correspond to $6y$, and $3x$ corresponds to $9y$.

Therefore, the perimeter of the second triangle must be $12y + 6y + 9y = 27y$, so **(B) is the correct answer**.

Right Triangles

Right triangles, or triangles that include a 90° angle, are extremely useful in all of geometry for calculating unknown lengths and angles.

What's most important to know about a right triangle is that the lengths of the sides must relate to one another as expressed in the Pythagorean theorem:

$$a^2 + b^2 = c^2$$

a and b are the two sides, or legs, that form the right angle. c, which is known as the hypotenuse, is always the longest side of any right triangle because it is opposite the 90° angle (which is also the greatest angle).

There are four types of right triangles that appear most commonly on the GRE, and I will highlight and practice them specifically.

3-4-5 and 5-12-13 Right Triangles

It's not easy to find integers that fit cleanly into the formula $a^2 + b^2 = c^2$. The simplest trios of lengths that fit the Pythagorean theorem are variants of 3-4-5 and 5-12-13:

$$3^2 + 4^2 = 5^2$$
$$5^2 + 12^2 = 13^2$$

These sets of numbers and their multiples, known as Pythagorean triples, appear frequently in GRE questions, and recognizing them will save you a lot of time.

$$3^2 + 4^2 = 5^2$$
$$6^2 + 8^2 = 10^2$$
$$30^2 + 40^2 = 50^2$$

Sample Question

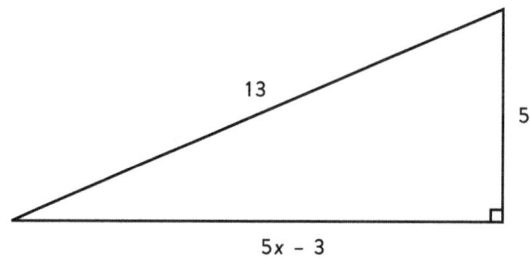

What is the value of x?

$x = $ [   ]

<u>Solution</u>

If you don't recognize this to be a 5-12-13 triangle, you can use the Pythagorean theorem and solve for x:

$(5x - 3)^2 + 5^2 = 13^2$
$(5x - 3)^2 + 25 = 169$
$(5x - 3)^2 = 144$
$5x - 3 = 12$
$5x = 15$
$x = 3$

If you recognized early on that this was a 5-12-13 triangle, you could have started from $5x - 3 = 12$ instead.

30°-60°-90° and 45°-45°-90° Right Triangles

Whereas Pythagorean triples are defined by the ratio of their sides, the next two special types of right triangles are defined by their interior angles.

What's valuable about these two types of right triangles is that they have sides with fixed proportions relative to one another, proportions that we are expected to know, and you can use these proportions to solve for unknown lengths.

In a 30°-60°-90° triangle, the sides will always match the ratio x, $x\sqrt{3}$, $2x$, with the shortest side, x, opposite the least angle, which is 30°; $x\sqrt{3}$ opposite 60°; and the longest side, $2x$, opposite the greatest angle, 90°.

In a 45°-45°-90° triangle, the sides will always align with the ratio x, x, $x\sqrt{2}$, with the two shortest sides, x, opposite the two 45° angles and the longest side, $x\sqrt{2}$, opposite the right angle.

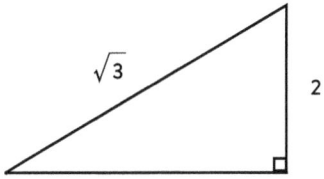

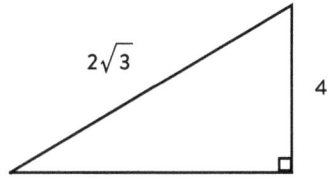

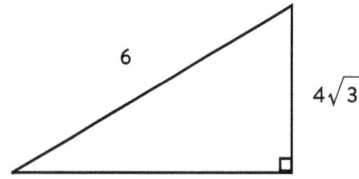

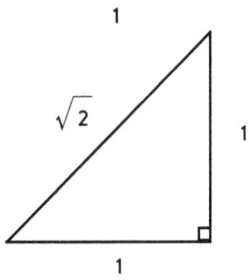

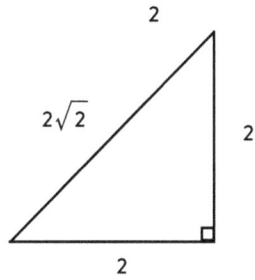

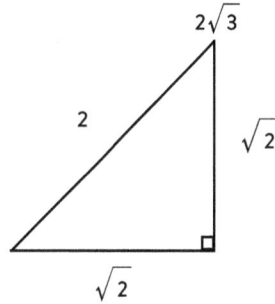

Sample Question 1

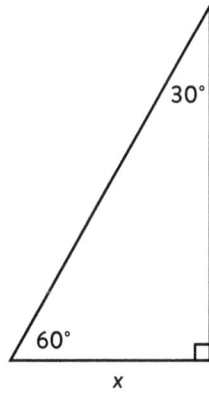

If the area of the given triangle is $18\sqrt{3}$, what is the value of x?

(A) 6

(B) $6\sqrt{3}$

(C) 9

(D) $9\sqrt{3}$

(E) 18

<u>Solution</u>

You know that the two legs of a 30-60-90 triangle are, proportionally speaking, x and $x\sqrt{3}$. You can therefore use the triangle area formula to solve for x:

$$\frac{x(x\sqrt{3})}{2} = 18\sqrt{3}$$
$$x(x\sqrt{3}) = 36\sqrt{3}$$
$$(x^2)\sqrt{3} = 36\sqrt{3}$$
$$x^2 = 36$$
$$x = 6$$

(A) is the correct answer.

Sample Question 2

What's the area of an equilateral triangle with side length 6?

First, let's create a drawing, making sure to label not only the side lengths of the equilateral triangle but also the angle measures.

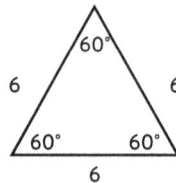

In order to calculate the area of this triangle, you need a height (or altitude) that is perpendicular to the base. Note that when you draw that altitude from the top vertex angle down to the base, you form two 30°-60°-90° triangles.

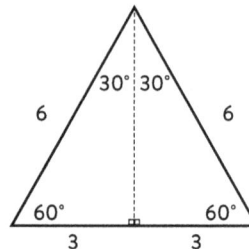

Now, you can use side ratios to find the triangle's height. Sometimes, it helps to line up the angle measures, side ratios, and known side values as follows:

30°	60°	90°
x	$x\sqrt{3}$	$2x$
3	$3\sqrt{3}$	6

Using this chart, you can determine that the height, which is across from the 60° angle and is thus the $x\sqrt{3}$ side, measures $3\sqrt{3}$.

Therefore, **the area of the triangle is $\left(\frac{1}{2}\right)(6)(3\sqrt{3})$, or $9\sqrt{3}$**. Note that despite splitting the equilateral triangle into two 30°-60°-90° triangles to calculate the height, you need to use the length of the original equilateral triangle's entire base (6) when calculating its area.

Sample Question 3

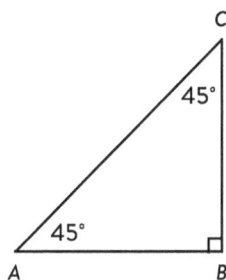

If the length of $AC = 8\sqrt{2}$, what is the perimeter of triangle ABC?

Ⓐ $16\sqrt{2}$

Ⓑ $16 + 8\sqrt{2}$

Ⓒ 24

Ⓓ $24\sqrt{2}$

Ⓔ $24 + 8\sqrt{2}$

Solution

You know that the sides of an isosceles right triangle, proportionally speaking, must be x, x, and $x\sqrt{2}$, with the longest side, $x\sqrt{2}$, serving as the hypotenuse. Since you are told that the hypotenuse is $8\sqrt{2}$, you know that each of the sides must equal 8.

$8 + 8 + 8\sqrt{2} = 16 + 8\sqrt{2}$

(B) is the correct answer.

Practice Questions

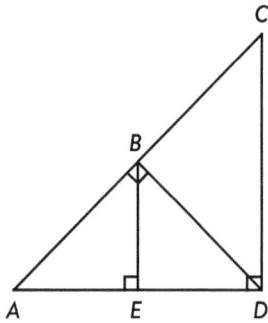

1. If $EB = ED = 2$, $AB = BD$, and $AD = CD$, what is the value of AC?

Ⓐ 4
Ⓑ $4\sqrt{2}$
Ⓒ 8
Ⓓ $8\sqrt{2}$
Ⓔ 16

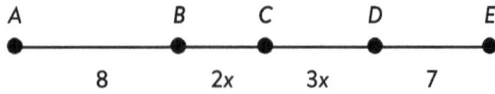

2. If $AD = CE + 5$, what is the length of BD?

Ⓐ 2
Ⓑ 4
Ⓒ 6
Ⓓ 8
Ⓔ 10

3. $\angle O > \angle NPO; \angle MNP > \angle NMP$

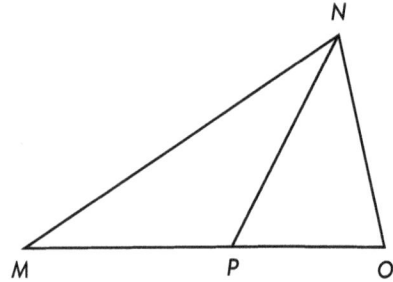

Quantity A	Quantity B
MP	PO

Ⓐ Quantity A is greater.
Ⓑ Quantity B is greater.
Ⓒ The two quantities are equal.
Ⓓ The relationship cannot be determined from the information given.

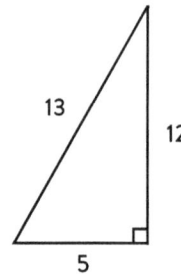

4. If the two triangles above are similar, what is the value of $4x + 2$?

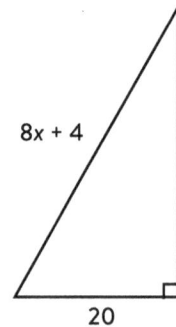

5. An equilateral triangle on a coordinate plane has two vertices at points (5, 4) and (5, –2), respectively. Which of the following could be the third vertex?

Ⓐ $(2\sqrt{3}, 1)$
Ⓑ $(3\sqrt{3}, 1)$
Ⓒ $(5 - 3\sqrt{3}, 1)$
Ⓓ $(8, 1)$
Ⓔ $(5, 4 - 3\sqrt{3})$

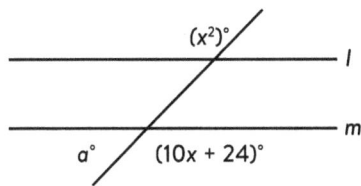

6. If lines l amd m are parallel, which of the following could be the value of a?

Indicate all such values.

Ⓐ 36
Ⓑ 72
Ⓒ 144
Ⓓ 176

7. Sean draws 3 lines on his computer screen and uses them to create an isosceles right triangle. If 1 of those lines has length $4\sqrt{2}$, which of the following could be the area of the triangle?

Ⓐ $4\sqrt{2}$
Ⓑ $8\sqrt{2}$
Ⓒ 12
Ⓓ 16
Ⓔ 32

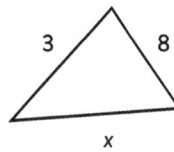

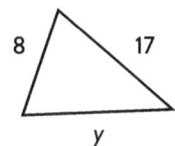

8. x and y are both integers.

Quantity A	Quantity B
x	y

Ⓐ Quantity A is greater.
Ⓑ Quantity B is greater.
Ⓒ The two quantities are equal.
Ⓓ The relationship cannot be determined from the information given.

Practice Question Solutions

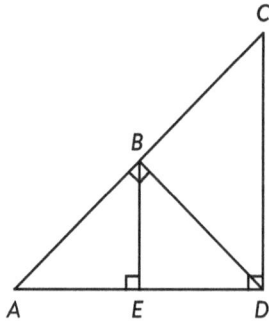

1. If $EB = ED = 2$, $AB = BD$, and $AD = CD$, what is the value of AC?

(A) 4
(B) **$4\sqrt{2}$**
(C) 8
(D) $8\sqrt{2}$
(E) 16

Solution

If $EB = ED$, $AB = BD$, and $AD = CD$, you can infer that you are dealing with a series of 45°-45°-90° right triangles, which all have sides with proportions x: x: $x\sqrt{2}$.

Therefore, if EB and $ED = 2$, you know that $BD = 2\sqrt{2}$.

If $BD = 2\sqrt{2}$, $AD = (2\sqrt{2})(\sqrt{2}) = (2)(2) = 4$.

If $AD = 4$, then $AC = 4\sqrt{2}$, and **(B) is the correct answer.**

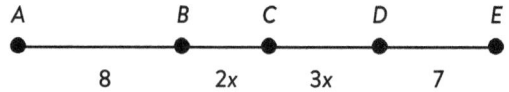

2. If $AD = CE + 5$, what is the length of BD?

(A) 2
(B) 4
(C) 6
(D) 8
(E) **10**

Solution

You know that AD is made up of $AB + BC + CD$, which equals, per the given information, $8 + 2x + 3x$, or $8 + 5x$.

You know that CE is made up of $CD + DE$, which equals, per the given information, $3x + 7$.

If $AD = CE + 5$, then you know that:

$8 + 5x = 3x + 7 + 5$

You can solve for x:

$8 + 5x = 3x + 7 + 5$
$2x = 4$
$x = 2$

If $x = 2$, you know that $BC = 2(2) = 4$, and $CD = 3(2) = 6$, so $BD = 10$. **(E) is the correct answer.**

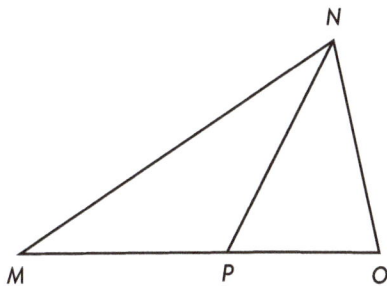

3. $\angle O > \angle NPO$; $\angle MNP > \angle NMP$

Quantity A	Quantity B
MP	PO

Ⓐ **Quantity A is greater.**
Ⓑ Quantity B is greater.
Ⓒ The two quantities are equal.
Ⓓ The relationship cannot be determined from the information given.

Solution

Per the given information, you know that in triangle NPO, because $\angle O$ is greater than $\angle PNO$, side NP must be longer than side PO.

Similarly, in triangle MNP, if $\angle MNP$ is greater than $\angle NMP$, side MP must be greater than side NP.

If $MP > NP$, and $NP > PO$, you can infer that $MP > PO$, and **(A) is the correct answer.**

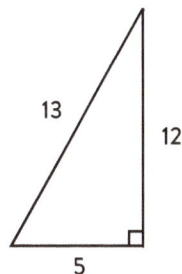

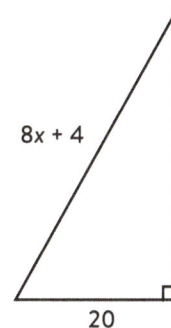

4. If the two triangles above are similar, what is the value of $4x + 2$?

26

Solution

Since you know these are similar triangles, you can infer from the relationship between 20 and 5 that each side of the larger triangle must be 4 times the size of each side of the smaller triangle.

Therefore, you know that:

$8x + 4 = 4(13)$

$8x + 4 = 52$

At this point, you could solve for x and then figure out $4x + 2$. Alternatively, you can simply divide both sides of the equation by 2, which gives you:

$4x + 2 = 26$

26 is the correct answer.

Solutions Continued

5. An equilateral triangle on a coordinate plane has two vertices at points (5, 4) and (5, –2), respectively. Which of the following could be the third vertex?

Ⓐ $(2\sqrt{3}, 1)$
Ⓑ $(3\sqrt{3}, 1)$
Ⓒ $(5 - 3\sqrt{3}, 1)$
Ⓓ $(8, 1)$
Ⓔ $(5, 4 - 3\sqrt{3})$

Solution

You can draw the two points:

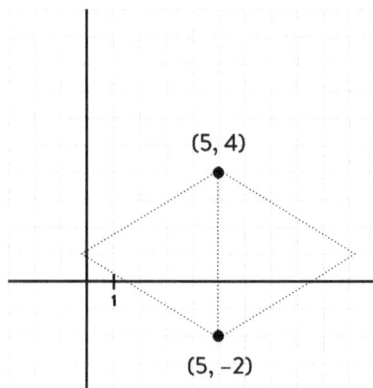

You can imagine the third point of the equilateral triangle falling to the left or right of the two given points, as you've drawn out in the image.

Now, you need to find the coordinates of that third point.

You know that the y-coordinate of the third point must be halfway between the two original points, or $\frac{4 + (-2)}{2} = 1$.

To figure out the x-coordinates of the potential third points, you can split up the equilateral triangles into 30-60-90 triangles:

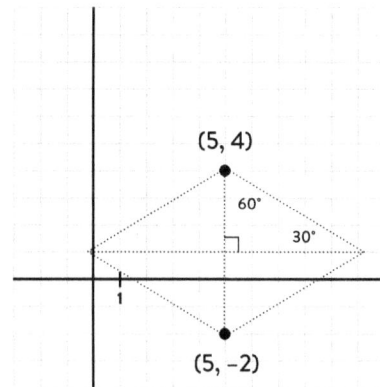

You know that the shortest leg of one of the 30-60-90 triangles must be half the total length of the side, or $\frac{6}{2} = 3$, so the second leg of the 30-60-90 triangle must be $3\sqrt{3}$.

Since you are starting at an x-coordinate of 5 and going $3\sqrt{3}$ either way, you can end up at either $(5 - 3\sqrt{3}, 1)$ or $(5 + 3\sqrt{3}, 1)$ for the third point, as shown in the image below.

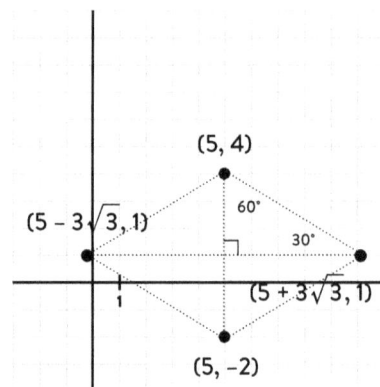

(C) is the correct answer.

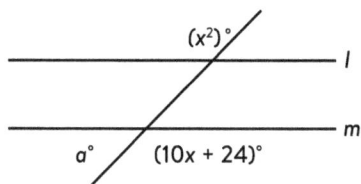

6. If lines l amd m are parallel, which of the following could be the value of a?

Indicate all such values.

[A] **36**
[B] 72
[C] 144
[D] **176**

Solution

You know that since lines l and m are parallel, x^2 must be equal to $10x + 24$. You can use this information to set up an equation and solve for x:

$x^2 = 10x + 24$

$x^2 - 10x - 24 = 0$

$(x - 12)(x + 2) = 0$

$x = 12$ or -2

If $x = 12$, $10x + 24$ would $= 144$, and a would $= 180 - 144 = 36$.

If $x = -2$, $10x + 24$ would $= (10)(-2) + 24 = 4$, and a would $= 180 - 4 = 176$.

So, the correct answers are [A] and [D].

7. Sean draws 3 lines on his computer screen and uses them to create an isosceles right triangle. If 1 of those lines has length $4\sqrt{2}$, which of the following could be the area of the triangle?

(A) $4\sqrt{2}$
(B) $8\sqrt{2}$
(C) 12
(D) **16**
(E) 32

Solution

Per the given information, there are two possibilities for this isosceles right triangle: either $4\sqrt{2}$ is its hypotenuse, or $4\sqrt{2}$ is the length of one of its sides.

In a right isosceles triangle, the side lengths match the ratio $x: x:x\sqrt{2}$.

If $4\sqrt{2}$ is the hypotenuse, then the sides would be 4 each, and the area of the triangle would then be equal to $\frac{(4)(4)}{2} = 8$. Unfortunately, you don't have 8 among the answer choices.

If $4\sqrt{2}$ is one of the sides, then the area of the triangle would be equal to $\frac{(4\sqrt{2})(4\sqrt{2})}{2} = \frac{32}{2} = 16$.

(D) is the correct answer.

Solutions Continued

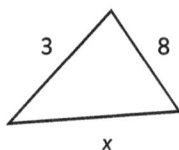

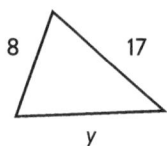

8. x and y are both integers.

Quantity A	Quantity B
x	y

Ⓐ Quantity A is greater.
Ⓑ Quantity B is greater.
Ⓒ The two quantities are equal.
Ⓓ **The relationship cannot be determined from the information given.**

Solution

Since any two sides of a triangle must always add up to a sum greater than the length of the third side, you know that x must be greater than 5 but less than 11.

Similarly, y must be greater than 9 but less than 25.

Based on this information, you can't tell whether x or y is greater, so (D) is correct.

21

QUANTITATIVE REASONING

Other Geometric Shapes

In this chapter, the final lesson on geometry, I'll discuss general polygon rules and the properties of different types of quadrilaterals, circles, and three-dimensional shapes.

The Importance of Triangles

Whether a question is about parallelograms, hexagons, or even cylinders, very often the key to success will be your ability to utilize the rules of triangles to infer information that is not directly stated.

For many geometry-based questions, your workflow should consist of the following:

1. Reading some information about a scenario.
2. Being asked about an unknown component, such as a length or an angle.
3. Using your understanding of the situation and of triangle rules to solve for that unknown.

You'll see many examples of questions that require such a workflow in this lesson.

Polygons

Polygon is a broad term for any shape with multiple sides. Although you won't be tested on rules of specific polygons other than triangles and quadrilaterals, you are expected to know the following general rules about all polygons:

- As with all shapes, the perimeter represents the distance around the outline of the shape, and the area represents the space inside the shape.
- A **regular** polygon is one in which all sides have the same length and all angles have the same measure.
- **The interior angles of a polygon add up to (180)(n − 2)**, where n = the number of sides for that polygon. Thus, a 4-sided figure has interior angles that add up to $(180)(4 − 2) = (180)(2) = 360°$, a 7-sided figure has interior angles that add up to $(180)(7 − 2) = (180)(5) = 900°$, and so on.
- As with all shapes, an **exterior angle** is defined as an angle supplementary to an interior angle and created by extending one of the sides of the polygon. The sum of the exterior angles for any polygon (including triangles) is 360°.

This last rule makes possible some interesting quantitative comparison questions. Consider the following diagrams.

Sample Question 1

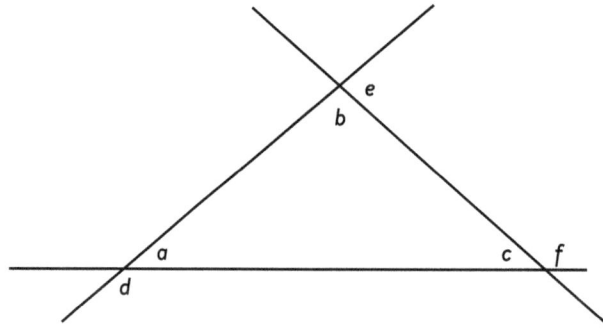

Quantity A

$a + b + c$

Quantity B

$d + e + f$

Solution

Despite lacking any concrete numbers, you know that the sum of the interior angles of a triangle is 180°, and the sum of the exteriors is 360°. Therefore, **Quantity B is greater**.

Sample Question 2

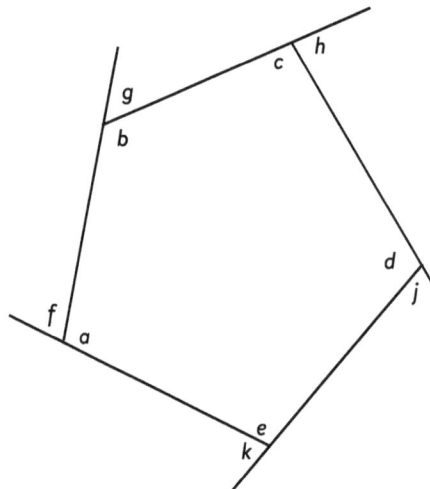

Quantity A

$a + b + c + d + e$

Quantity B

$f + g + h + j + k$

Solution

In this case, the sum of the exterior angles is still 360°. However, as shown above, the sum of the interior angles of a 5-sided polygon is 180°(5 – 2), or 540°. Therefore, **Quantity A, the sum of the interior angles, is greater than Quantity B, the sum of the exterior angles**.

A Brief Note on Regular Hexagons

A 6-sided polygon is called a hexagon, and using the $180(n - 2)$ formula, the interior angles of a hexagon add up to 720°. If a hexagon is regular, then each interior angle is equal to 120° (720° divided into 6 equal interior angles). If you draw a line from each vertex to the center of the hexagon, you bisect each of these 120° angles, forming a shape composed of 6 equilateral triangles.

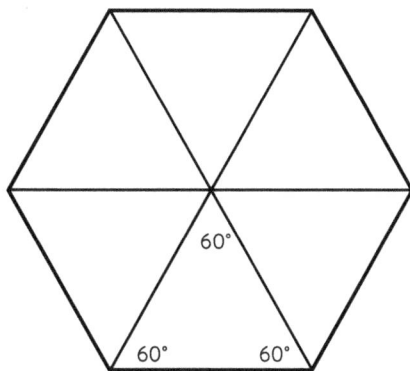

You can, therefore, find the area of a regular hexagon by finding the area of one of the equilateral triangles (as demonstrated in the previous chapter) and then multiplying that result by 6.

Now, consider the top half of the regular hexagon. Note that if the hexagon has side length s, then the perimeter of the shape below is $5s$.

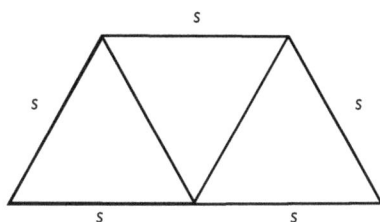

Sample Question 1

If 2 vertices of an octagon are selected at random, what are the odds that they will be adjacent to each other?

(A) $\frac{1}{8}$

(B) $\frac{1}{7}$

(C) $\frac{1}{4}$

(D) $\frac{2}{7}$

(E) $\frac{2}{5}$

Solution

There are 8 vertices in an octagon. If you pick any of the vertices, there are 7 other vertices from which to choose the second. Of these, 2 will be adjacent to the original vertex. Therefore, the probability of picking 2 vertices at random and having them adjacent to each other is $\frac{2}{7}$.

The correct answer is choice (D).

Sample Question 2

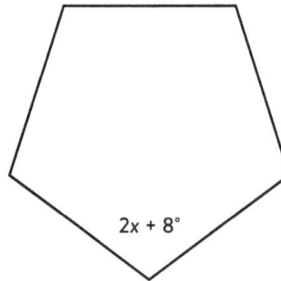

2x + 8°

If one internal angle of a regular pentagon is equal to $2x + 8$, what is the value of x?

$x =$ ☐

Solution

You know that all internal angles of a pentagon must add up to a sum of $(5 - 2)(180) = 540$.

Since this is a regular pentagon, all 5 angles are congruent, so each angle must measure $\frac{540}{5} = 108$.

If $2x + 8 = 108$, then $x =$ **50**.

Quadrilaterals

Quadrilaterals are shapes with four sides. For all quadrilaterals, the sum of the measure of the interior angles is $360°$. Certain quadrilaterals have additional qualities that help you define them further, as I'll discuss shortly.

Sample Question

A quadrilateral has angles with values equal to x, $x + 20$, $2x$, and $2(x + 20)$. What is the value of x?

Ⓐ 45
Ⓑ 50
Ⓒ 55
Ⓓ 60
Ⓔ 65

Solution

You know that the sum of the measures of the four angles of a quadrilateral must equal $360°$, so you can set up the following equation to solve for x:

$x + x + 20 + 2x + 2(x + 20) = 360$
$4x + 20 + 2x + 40 = 360$
$6x + 60 = 360$
$6x = 300$
$x = 50$

The correct answer is (B).

Parallelograms

A parallelogram is a quadrilateral that has two pairs of parallel sides. Note that rectangles and squares are parallelograms, so don't assume from the word itself that a parallelogram must look like the one in the diagram below.

For all parallelograms, the diagonally opposite angles are equal to each other, and adjacent angles are supplementary (they add up to 180°). How do you know that adjacent angles are supplementary? Do you recall the parallel line term **same-side interior angles**? Any side of a parallelogram is a transversal running between two parallel lines, and adjacent angles are, therefore, same-side interior angles adding up to 180°. A parallelogram, therefore, has four pairs of adjacent same-side interior supplementary angles.

The area of a parallelogram is the length of the base multiplied by the height. (Note that the height, like the height of a triangle, is a perpendicular altitude that runs from the base to the opposite side. Unless the parallelogram is a rectangle, the height is not equal to one of the parallelogram's sides.)

Sample Question

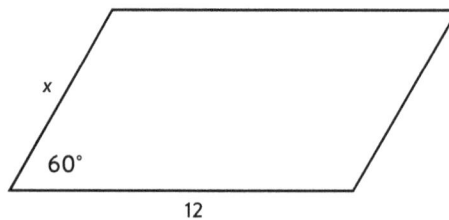

If the area of the given parallelogram is 72, what is the value of x?

(A) 3
(B) 4
(C) $4\sqrt{3}$
(D) $6\sqrt{3}$
(E) 12

Solution

If the area of the given parallelogram is 72, you know that it must have a height of 6. You can draw in that height and create a 30°-60°-90° triangle as below.

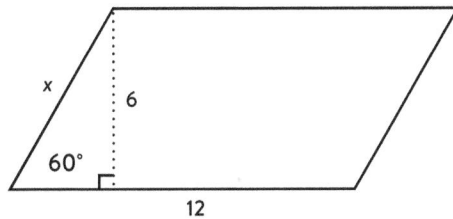

For the 30°-60°-90° triangle, the other base must be $\dfrac{6}{\sqrt{3}} = \dfrac{6\sqrt{3}}{3} = 2\sqrt{3}$, and, therefore, the hypotenuse, which is twice the length of the shortest side, must be $4\sqrt{3}$.

The correct answer is (C).

Trapezoids

Trapezoids are quadrilaterals that have at least one set of parallel sides. For any trapezoid, the area is equal to the average length of the bases (the two parallel sides) multiplied by the height, or

$$\left(\frac{b_1 + b_2}{2}\right)h.$$

Additionally, each pair of angles created by cutting the parallel sides with transversals adds up to 180°.

Sample Question

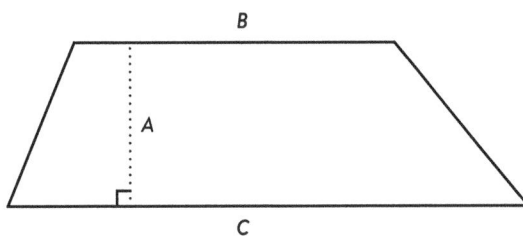

If $B = 2A$ and $C = 2B$, what is the area of the given trapezoid when $A = 5$?

Ⓐ 25
Ⓑ 40
Ⓒ 50
Ⓓ 75
Ⓔ 150

<u>Solution</u>

If $A = 5$, you know that $B = 2(5) = 10$, and $C = 2(10) = 20$. Armed with this information, you can calculate that the area of the trapezoid must be $\left(\frac{10 + 20}{2}\right)(5) = 75$.

Therefore, the correct answer is (D).

If a question mentions an **isosceles trapezoid**, then you know that the two non-parallel sides are equal in length and form equal angles with the parallel bases of the trapezoid. The following diagram shows an isosceles trapezoid and the information you can derive from that term:

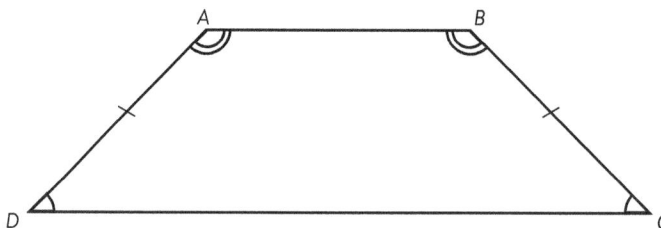

Side AD is equal in length to side BC, $\angle A$ and $\angle B$ are equal in measure, and $\angle C$ and $\angle D$ are equal in measure.

If you drew heights from vertices A and B to the base CD, you would create congruent triangles AED and BFC, as shown below:

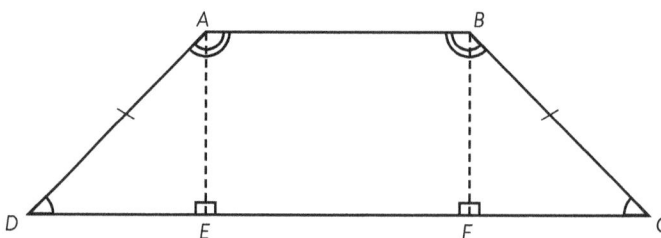

One final word of advice: unless a trapezoid is presented as an isosceles trapezoid, don't try to find its area by breaking it down into triangles and rectangles. Instead, use the trapezoid area formula, using triangle rules to determine the trapezoid's height.

Rectangles

Rectangles are parallelograms with four 90° angles. If you label the adjacent sides of a rectangle as the length and width, you know that the area of a rectangle equals the length multiplied by the width, and the perimeter is equal to the sum of 2 times the length and 2 times the width.

Note that squares are considered rectangles, so if a question asks you about, say, a rectangle with an area of 100, then a square with side length 10 would meet that definition.

Sample Question

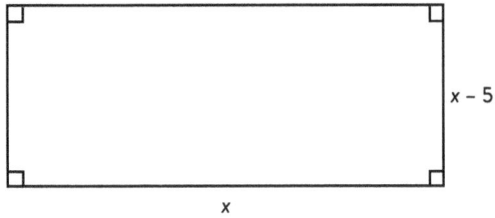

If the area of the given rectangle is 36, what is the value of x?

(A) 4
(B) 5
(C) 6
(D) 7
(E) 9

Solution

If you know that the area of the rectangle is 36, you can use the following equation to solve for x:

$(l)(w) = 36$

$x(x - 5) = 36$

$x^2 - 5x = 36$

$x^2 - 5x - 36 = 0$

$(x - 9)(x + 4) = 0$

$x = 9$ or -4

In this case, since a length can't be negative, x must therefore be equal to 9, and **(E) is the correct answer**.

Alternatively, you could have solved this by identifying two numbers 5 apart that can be multiplied to give 36, which in this case would be 9 and 4, and knowing that they would have to correspond to x and $x - 5$, respectively.

Squares

A square is a rectangle that, in addition to having four congruent 90° angles, has four congruent sides.

If you call the side length of a square s, the perimeter of the square would be $4s$ and the area s^2.

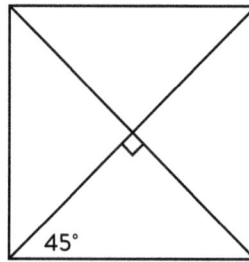

45°

Additionally, if you draw a diagonal in the square, it will create two 45-45-90 triangles, and if you draw two diagonals in a square, they will intersect at a right angle.

Sample Question

A square field measures 6 miles along the diagonal from one corner to the opposite corner. What is the perimeter of the field?

(A) $9\sqrt{2}$
(B) $12\sqrt{2}$
(C) 18
(D) 24
(E) $24\sqrt{2}$

<u>Solution</u>

The diagonal of a square splits the square into two 45-45-90 triangles, which have sides that are, proportionally speaking, x, x, and $x\sqrt{2}$.

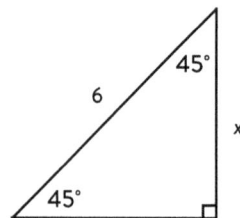

If you know that the hypotenuse is 6, you can use the following equation to solve for one of the sides, which you can call x:

$$x\sqrt{2} = 6$$

$$x = \frac{6}{\sqrt{2}}$$

$$x = \frac{6\sqrt{2}}{2}$$

$$x = 3\sqrt{2}$$

If each side of the square has length $3\sqrt{2}$, then the perimeter must be $(4)(3\sqrt{2}) = 12\sqrt{2}$.

The correct answer is (B).

Circles

Let's turn our attention to circles.

- A circle is defined as all points that are a given distance from a **center**.
- The **radius** of a circle, r, is the distance from the center of the circle to any point on its circumference (perimeter).
- The **diameter** of a circle, d, is the distance across the widest part of the circle and is equal to $2r$. The diameter must pass through the center of the circle.
- The **circumference** of a circle is the distance around the circle, and it's always equal to πd or $2\pi r$.
- Pi (π) is the constant ratio of the circumference of any circle and its diameter, approximately 3.14 or $\frac{22}{7}$.
- The **area** of a circle can be calculated using the formula πr^2.
- A **chord** is a line segment joining any two points on the circumference of a circle. A diameter is the longest chord in any circle. The distance of a chord from the center of a circle is the length of the shortest perpendicular line segment joining the center of the circle and the chord. As the distance of the chord from the center of a circle increases, its length decreases.
- The formula $(x - h)^2 + (y - k)^2 = r^2$ defines the graph of a circle on the xy-plane. From this formula you can derive the coordinates of the center of the circle (h, k), and its radius r. For example, the formula $(x + 4)^2 + (y - 2)^2 = 9$ indicates a circle with a center at $(-4, 2)$ and a radius of 3.

Sector Areas and Arc Lengths

There are several circle diagrams with which you should be familiar. I'll begin with a diagram that marks off portions of a circle; a pie-shaped portion of the whole area is called a sector, and a portion of the curved circumference line is called an arc.

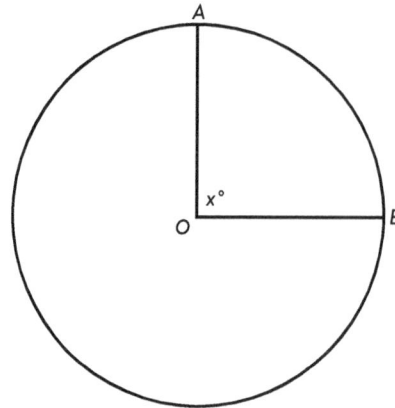

In this diagram, the center of the circle is labeled O, and A and B are points on the circumference of the circle. $\angle AOB$, with an indicated measure of $x°$, is called a **central angle** because it has a vertex at the center of the circle and rays extending to points on the circumference. That central angle creates both arc AB, a portion of the curved circumference line, and a sector AOB, a portion of the area of the circle.

Because circles contain 360 degrees, the proportion of the central angle to the $360°$ of the circle is equal to the proportion of the intercepted arc to the circumference and also equal to the proportion of the area of a sector to the area of the circle. In other words, from the diagram above, you can set up the following proportions:

$$\frac{x°}{360°} = \frac{\text{arc } AB}{2\pi r}, \text{ and } \frac{x°}{360°} = \frac{\text{area of sector } AOB}{\pi r^2}$$

The arc of a circle can be described in degree terms (e.g., an $80°$ arc) or in unit terms based on the unit length of the circle's radius. A central angle's degree measure is equal to the degree measure of its intercepted arc, so if arc AB were an $80°$ arc, then $\angle AOB$ would have a measure of $80°$.

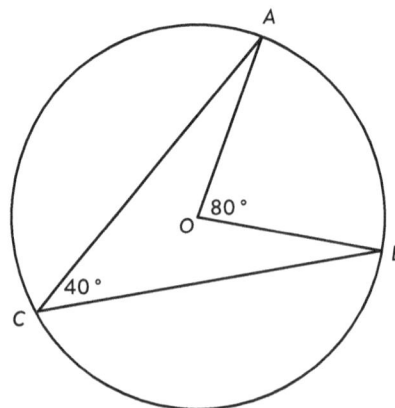

In the diagram above, $\angle ACB$ is called an inscribed angle because its vertex is on the circumference of the circle. Note that $\angle ACB$ still intercepts arc AB, just like $\angle AOB$ does. **An inscribed angle has a measure that is exactly half that of the central angle that intercepts the same arc.** Therefore, given that $\angle AOB$ has a measure of $80°$, $\angle ACB$ has a measure of $40°$.

Inscribed angles can be tricky to memorize—just remember that all three points that constitute an inscribed angle will be on the circumference of the circle. Note the following diagram:

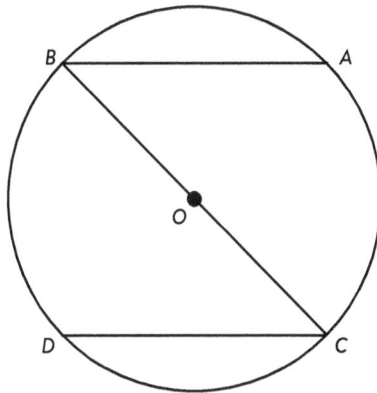

Angles *ABC* and *BCD* are inscribed angles. The degree measure of ∠*ABC* would be half of the degree measure of arc *AC*, and the degree measure of ∠*BCD* would be half of the degree measure of arc *BD*. If line segments *AB* and *CD* are parallel, then you can use parallel line angle rules to derive even more information.

Here's a final diagram related to inscribed angles that you should memorize:

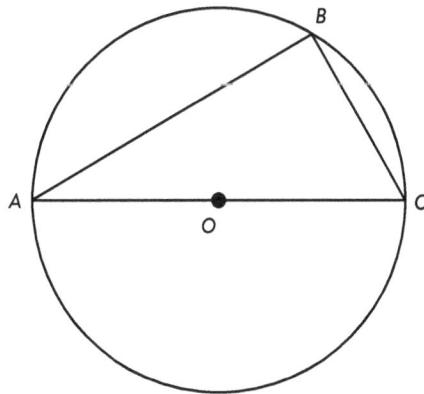

This diagram shows a triangle (*ABC*) inscribed in a semicircle. *O* is the center of the circle, points *A* and *C* are endpoints of the diameter, and point *B* is on the circumference of the circle. You are expected to recognize that a triangle inscribed in a semicircle, as in the diagram above, is always a right triangle: ∠*ABC* is a right angle. How do you know? Well, ∠*ABC* is an inscribed angle that intercepts the bottom half of the circle, which is a 180° arc. ∠*ABC* is, therefore, half the measure of 180°, or 90°. Once you label ∠*ABC* as a right angle, you can apply your right triangle knowledge in order to answer whatever question you are asked.

Lines Tangent to a Circle

A line is tangent to a circle if it touches the circle at exactly one point (the point of tangency). Any time you are presented with a line tangent to a circle, draw a radius from the center of the circle to the point of tangency—those two line segments always meet at a right angle (90°).

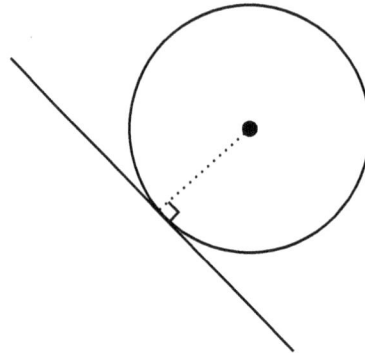

Let's look at a diagram you might see on the GRE, accompanied by the information that line segments AB and BC are tangent to the circle at points A and C, respectively.

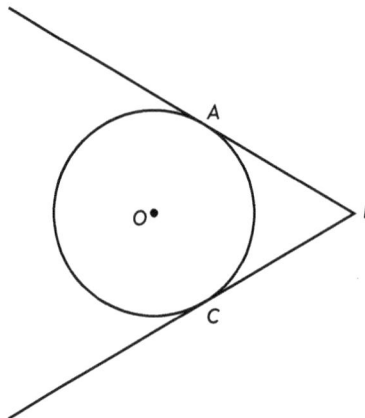

Let's first draw lines from the center to the points of tangency and establish 90° angles:

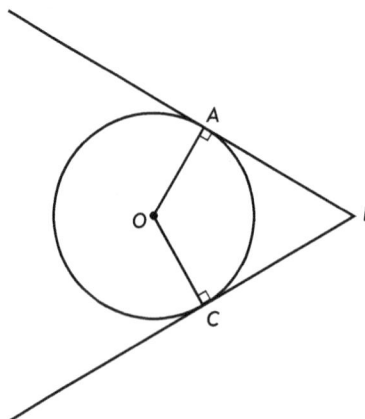

Note that the shape *AOCB* is a quadrilateral (4-sided polygon) that has interior angles that add up to 360°. Because angles *A* and *C* are each 90°, you know that the sum of ∠*AOC* (a central angle) and ∠*ABC* must be 180°. If you draw a straight line from *B* to *O*, you form two right triangles, and you know that the sides *AO* and *CO* are radiuses of the circle. From there, you will have enough given information (e.g., the length of the radius, the degree measure of arc *AC*, etc.) to answer the question.

Circle Drill

Because the various measurements for a circle are all related to one another, you are often given certain details about a circle or sector and asked to determine other details. Let's practice doing so here. Below is a table that includes clues about different circles. Please fill in the missing information.

Radius	Circumference	Area	Central Angle	Arc Length	Sec Area
4			180		
		36π			3π
	18π				9π
			45	3π	
		225π	72		
			120	20π	

Triangles in Circles

Let's consider the fairly common case of triangles drawn with one vertex at the center of a circle and the other two vertices on the circumference. Here are three possible diagrams, each of which provides different information.

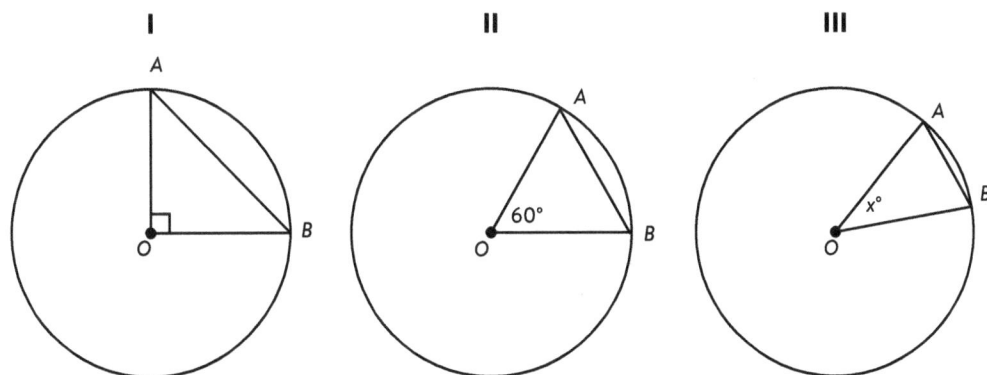

Always remember when dealing with circles that any line segment drawn from the center to the circumference is a radius! In all three diagrams above, line segments *AO* and *BO* are radiuses that are equal in length, so the triangles in all three diagrams above are at least isosceles (two equal sides).

In diagram I, you are given the information that ∠*AOB* is a right angle. Because you know that sides *AO* and *BO* are equal in length, you have a right isosceles triangle, otherwise known as a 45°-45°-90° triangle.

In diagram II, you are given the information that $\angle AOB$ has a measure of 60°. Because sides AO and BO are equal in length, the angles opposite those two sides must be equal, which means they must both have a measure of 60°, so triangle AOB is an equilateral triangle!

In diagram III, all you know is that triangle AOB is isosceles, and that angles OAB and OBA are equal in measure.

Circle Drill Solutions

Radius	Circumference	Area	Central Angle	Arc Length	Sec Area
4	**8π**	**16π**	180	**4π**	**8π**
6	**12π**	36π	**30**	π	3π
9	18π	**81π**	40	**2π**	9π
12	**24π**	**144π**	45	3π	**18π**
15	**30π**	225π	72	**6π**	**45π**
30	**60π**	**900π**	120	20π	**300π**

Inscribed and Circumscribed Shapes

An **inscribed** shape is drawn inside another shape in such a way that its boundaries are determined by the boundaries of the outer shape. A shape that **circumscribes** another is drawn around, or outside, another shape in a way that determines the boundaries of the inside shape. Saying that a square is inscribed in a circle is the same as saying that a circle circumscribes a square.

Earlier, I discussed the case of a triangle inscribed in a semicircle. In that case, the boundaries of the inscribed triangle were determined by the boundaries of the circumscribed semicircle.

Here are three other situations that you should recognize and know how to interpret or address.

First, let's consider a triangle inscribed in a rectangle:

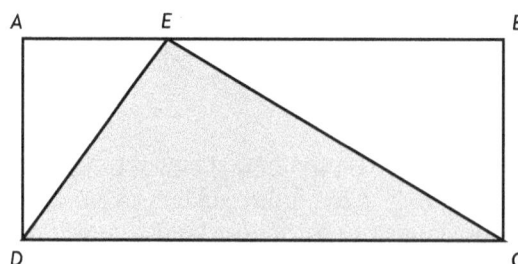

In this diagram, triangle *DEC* is inscribed in rectangle *ABCD*. I've shaded the region representing the area of triangle *DEC*. When you see this diagram, you can conclude immediately that the area of the inscribed triangle is exactly one half the area of the circumscribed rectangle! Why? Well, let's label segment *DC* the length (*l*) of the rectangle and segment *AD* the width (*w*) of the rectangle. The rectangle's area is, therefore, (length)(width), or *lw*. And the area of the triangle? It's $\left(\frac{1}{2}\right)$(base)(height), or $\left(\frac{1}{2}\right)$(*AB*)(*AD*), or $\left(\frac{1}{2}\right)$(*l*)(*w*). The height (or altitude) of the triangle is a line drawn from vertex *E* perpendicularly to the base *CD*, and the length of that line will always be equal to the width of the circumscribed rectangle.

Now let's consider a circle inscribed in a square:

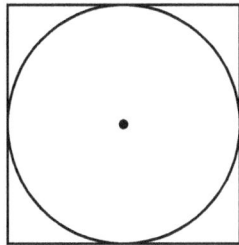

Because the circle's boundaries are limited only by the square's, the diameter of the circle will equal the side of the square.

Finally, let's consider a square inscribed in a circle:

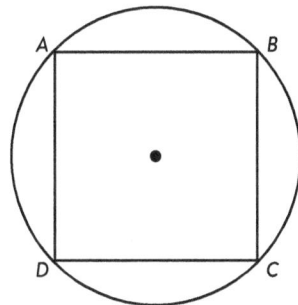

This one's a bit tougher, but the key is to draw the diagonal line *BD* or *AC*—that line is both the diagonal of the inscribed square (and the hypotenuse of a 45°-45°-90° triangle formed with the sides of the square as its legs) and the diameter of the circle.

Sample Question

A circle circumscribes a rectangle with sides of lengths 12 and 16. If all vertices of the rectangle are on the circle, what is the area of the circle?

(A) 10π
(B) 20π
(C) 100π
(D) 200π
(E) 400π

Solution

If a circle is circumscribed around a rectangle, with the vertices of the rectangle on the circle itself, then the diagonal of the rectangle must equal the diameter of the circle. One way to infer this is by recognizing that any two adjacent legs of the rectangle create a 90°-inscribed angle, which confirms that the diagonal opposite must split the circle into two equal components.

If the rectangle has sides of 12 and 16, you know that its diagonal must be 20. You can figure this out either by using the Pythagorean theorem or by recognizing that you have a version of a 3-4-5 triangle in which each number is multiplied by 4, so it must be 12-16-20.

Since the diameter is 20, the radius must be 10, and the area of the circle must be $(10^2)\pi$, or 100π.

The correct answer is (C).

Sometimes, the test writers give you diagrams in which one shape is inside another, though not in a way that constitutes an inscribed or circumscribed shape.

Sample Question

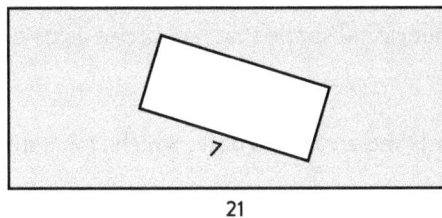

If the 2 rectangles in the given image are similar and the area of the larger rectangle is 126 cm², what is the area of the shaded region, in cm²?

Ⓐ 112
Ⓑ 105
Ⓒ 98
Ⓓ 21
Ⓔ 14

Solution

If the larger rectangle has an area of 126 and one side is 21, the other side must be $\frac{126}{21} = 6$.

If the two triangles are similar, then you can use the proportion $\frac{6}{21} = \frac{x}{7}$, which shows that the smaller rectangle must have a short side of length 2.

The smaller rectangle therefore has an area of 14, and the shaded region equals:

126 – 14 = 112.

(A) is the correct answer.

3D Shapes

Finally, you may be asked to work with two types of three-dimensional shapes: cylinders and prisms.

A cylinder is a three-dimensional shape that has circles as its two bases. A soda can is a common example of a cylinder.

The volume of a cylinder is the area of its base, which is πr^2, multiplied by its height, h.

Volume of a cylinder: $(\pi r^2)h$

For the surface area of a cylinder, first calculate the area of each of the bases, πr^2, and add them together, which gives you $2\pi r^2$. Then, calculate the area of the outside curved surface, which equals the perimeter of the base ($2\pi r$) multiplied by the height of the cylinder, h. (One helpful visual for the surface area of the side of a cylinder is to think of the paper that would be required to go around a can: it would be a rectangle whose length would equal the circumference of the can and whose height would equal the height of the can.)

Surface area of a cylinder: $2\pi r^2 + (2\pi r)h$

A prism is the general term for any three-dimensional shape with two opposite bases that are congruent.

To find the volume of a prism, you simply need to find the area of its base and multiply that by the prism's height (the height is the length of the perpendicular altitude running from one base to the opposite base).

Volume of a rectangular prism: $(l \times w)h$

To find the surface area of a prism, you want to find the area of each face and add them all together.

Surface area of a rectangular prism: $2(l \times w) + 2(l \times h) + 2(w \times h)$

Sample Question

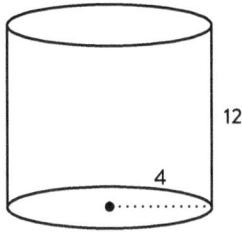

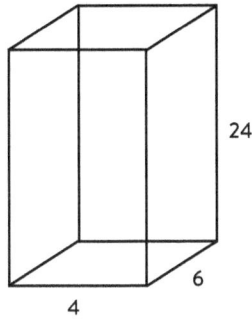

Quantity A
Volume of a cylinder with a base with a radius
of 4 and a height of 12

Quantity B
Volume of a rectangular prism with dimensions
4 by 6 by 24

Ⓐ Quantity A is greater.
Ⓑ Quantity B is greater.
Ⓒ The two quantities are equal.
Ⓓ The relationship cannot be determined from the information given.

Solution

The cylinder has a base with area 16π and a height of 12. Therefore, its volume is:

$(16π)(12) = 192π$, or roughly $(192)(3.14) \approx 602.88$

The rectangular prism has a base of area 24 and a height of 24. Therefore, its volume
is 576.

Therefore, the volume of the cylinder is greater, and **(A) is correct**.

Practice Questions

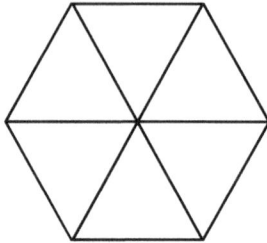

1. If a regular hexagon with a perimeter of 54 is split into 6 congruent triangles, as pictured, what is the perimeter of each resultant triangle?

(A) 18
(B) $18\sqrt{3}$
(C) 27
(D) $27\sqrt{3}$
(E) 36

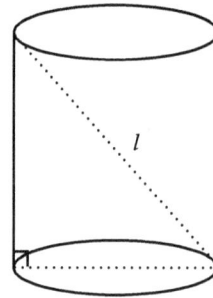

3. If the cylinder above has a volume of $108\sqrt{2}\pi$ and a base with area 18π, what is the length of line l?

(A) 8
(B) 12
(C) $8\sqrt{2}$
(D) $12\sqrt{2}$
(E) $16\sqrt{2}$

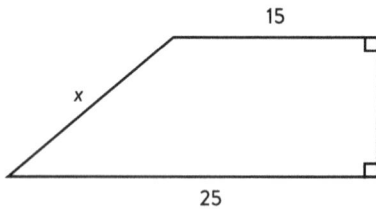

2. If the area of the above trapezoid is 480, what is the value of x?

(A) 10
(B) $18\sqrt{2}$
(C) 24
(D) 26
(E) 32

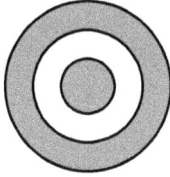

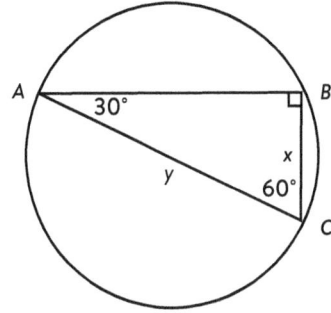

4. The above image includes 3 concentric circles, the innermost with a radius of 1 cm, the next with a radius of 2 cm, and the largest with a radius of 3 cm. What is the area of the shaded regions?

(A) 4π
(B) 5π
(C) 6π
(D) 7π
(E) 8π

5. If (4, 4) and (4, –2) are 2 vertices of a square, which of the following could be additional vertices of the same square?

Indicate all such points.

A (–2, 4)
B (–2, –2)
C (7, 1)
D (4, 1)
E (10, 4)
F (10, –4)

6. Triangle ABC is inscribed in a circle with an area of less than 36π, and x is greater than 2.

Quantity A	Quantity B
Least possible value of y	Greatest possible value of x

(A) Quantity A is greater.
(B) Quantity B is greater.
(C) The two quantities are equal.
(D) The relationship cannot be determined from the information given.

Practice Question Solutions

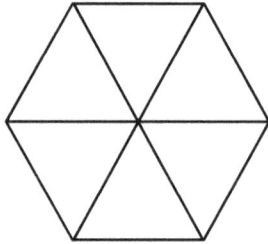

1. If a regular hexagon with a perimeter of 54 is split into 6 congruent triangles, as pictured, what is the perimeter of each resultant triangle?

A) 18
B) $18\sqrt{3}$
C) 27
D) $27\sqrt{3}$
E) 36

Solution

If the hexagon is regular and its perimeter is 54, you know that each of its sides must equal $\frac{54}{6} = 9$.

If this hexagon is split into 6 congruent triangles, you end up with 6 equilateral triangles.

The perimeter of each equilateral triangle equals $9 + 9 + 9 = 27$, so **(C) is the correct answer**.

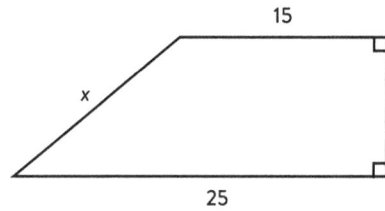

2. If the area of the above trapezoid is 480, what is the value of x?

A) 10
B) $18\sqrt{2}$
C) 24
D) 26
E) 32

Solution

If the area of the trapezoid is 480, you can use the trapezoid area formula to find its height:

$$\frac{15 + 25}{2}h = 480$$

$$20h = 480$$

$$h = 24$$

Now, you can draw in the height, and taking advantage of the difference between the lengths of the bases, you can create a right triangle and use it to find the value of x.

You can either use the Pythagorean theorem or recognize that this is a multiple of the 5-12-13 triangle; in this case, the triangle is 10-24-26, so $x = 26$.

(D) is the correct answer.

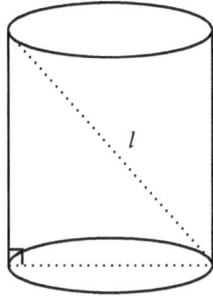

3. If the cylinder above has a volume of $108\sqrt{2}\pi$ and a base with area 18π, what is the length of line l?

Ⓐ 8
Ⓑ **12**
Ⓒ $8\sqrt{2}$
Ⓓ $12\sqrt{2}$
Ⓔ $16\sqrt{2}$

Solution

If the base of the cylinder has an area 18π, it means that the height of the cylinder must be $\dfrac{108\sqrt{2}\,\pi}{18\pi}$, or $6\sqrt{2}$.

If the base of the cylinder has an area of 18π, it also means that it must have a radius of $\sqrt{18}$, which simplifies to $3\sqrt{2}$.

If the base has a radius of $3\sqrt{2}$, it must have a diameter twice that, or $6\sqrt{2}$.

Now you know 2 sides of the right triangle, and they are both $6\sqrt{2}$. You can either use the Pythagorean theorem here to solve for the third side, or you can recognize this as a 45-45-90 triangle, and know that the hypotenuse is just one of the sides multiplied by $\sqrt{2}$, or $(6\sqrt{2})(\sqrt{2}) = (6)(2) = 12$.

The correct answer is (B).

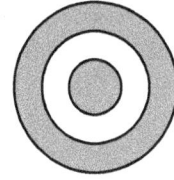

4. The above image includes 3 concentric circles, the innermost with a radius of 1 cm, the next with a radius of 2 cm, and the largest with a radius of 3 cm. What is the area of the shaded regions?

Ⓐ 4π
Ⓑ 5π
Ⓒ **6π**
Ⓓ 7π
Ⓔ 8π

Solution

To solve for the area of the shaded regions, you can first find the area of the largest circle, then subtract from it the area of the second largest, and then add back the area of the smaller circle.

The largest circle has a radius of 3; therefore, it has an area of 9π.

The second largest circle has a radius of 2; therefore, it has an area of 4π.

The smallest circle has a radius of 1; therefore, it has an area of 1π.

The area of the shaded regions $= 9\pi - 4\pi + 1\pi = 6\pi$.

(C) is the correct answer.

Solutions Continued

5. If (4, 4) and (4, −2) are 2 vertices of a square, which of the following could be additional vertices of the same square?

Indicate all such points.

A (−2, 4)
B (−2, −2)
C (7, 1)
D (4, 1)
E (10, 4)
F (10, −4)

Solution

If you consider (4, 4) and (4,−2) to be adjacent vertices of a square, you can imagine the other 2 vertices being either to the left or to the right of the given points.

Since the initial points are 6 places apart (4 − (−2) = 6), you know that the new points must be 6 places from the given points.

If you go to the left, that takes you to (−2, 4) and (−2, −2).

If you go to the right, that takes you to (10, 4) and (10, −2).

If you consider (4, 4) and (4, −2) to be opposite vertices of a square, you can imagine the other vertices as existing between the 2 points and to the left and right, respectively.

One way to identify the exact coordinates of those 2 other vertices is to consider the midpoint of (4, 4) and (4, −2), which is (4, 1). You know that the given vertices are 3 away from this midpoint, and you can infer that the new vertices must also be 3 spaces away, getting you to (1, 1) and (7, 1).

Based on this information, answer choices [A], [B], [C], and [E] could all be vertices of the square.

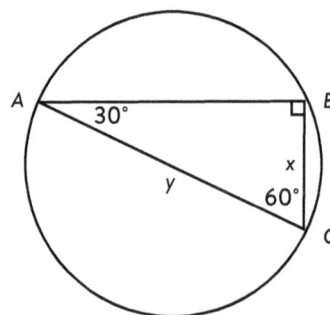

6. Triangle ABC is inscribed in a circle with an area of less than 36π, and x is greater than 2.

Quantity A
Least possible value of y

Quantity B
Greatest possible value of x

A Quantity A is greater.
B **Quantity B is greater.**
C The two quantities are equal.
D The relationship cannot be determined from the information given.

Solution

Since ABC is a 30°-60°-90° triangle, y must equal $2x$. Since x is greater than 2, y must be, at the least, greater than 4.

Per the given parameters regarding the area of the circle, the largest that the radius could be is less than 6, and the largest the diameter could be is less than 12. In this case, the greatest that x could be is less than 6.

The greatest possible value of x is greater than the least possible value of y, so (B) is correct.

22 Analytical Writing Measure

Now, let's discuss the Analytical Writing measure. The Analytical Writing measure will appear first on your exam and consists of one 30-minute "Analyze an Issue" essay. The essay is not part of your 130–170 scaled score. Instead, it is scored on a separate scale from zero to six in half-point increments.

Although the essay is primarily intended to test your writing skills, your critical reasoning skills will also be evaluated. You should write the essay to the best of your abilities, showcasing both sets of skills. Please note that the essay does not require specific knowledge in any particular field, so it is important to avoid writing as if you know more than you do.

Analyze an Issue Task

For your essay, you will be asked to evaluate a simple statement or claim similar to one of the following examples:

- As artificial intelligence grows, it will fulfill many of the duties that were previously required of human employees. Therefore, we can expect that the growth of artificial intelligence will inevitably lead to a shrinking workforce.

- Question-and-answer discussion is always a better method of instruction than pure lectures.

You will then be asked to write an essay in which you explain why you agree or disagree with the given claim or statement and provide evidence to support your position.

The instructions for each essay will differ slightly, so it is important to read them carefully. Please note that ETS publishes *all* potential issue topics that you might see on your exam! They are available at: ets.org/pdfs/gre/issue-pool.pdf

Grading Criteria for Essays

According to ETS, "Analyze an Issue" essays are graded according to the following criteria:

- Ability to articulate a clearly defined, well-considered, insightful position on the issue in accordance with the assigned task
- Ability to develop a position with compelling and persuasive reasons and/or examples
- Ability to organize the essay in a focused and cohesive manner that serves its main purpose
- Ability to clearly communicate using a variety of words and sentence structures
- Command over the conventions and rules of standard written English

Essay Strategies

For the essay, it is important to have a lot to say.

Yes, you want to write a coherent and well-written essay. You don't want to come across as inauthentic, use awkward language, or sound too casual. However, you should also avoid being overly careful about your diction or writing too little.

Although multiple spelling and grammatical errors will negatively impact your score, the graders will overlook occasional errors. The focus of your energy should be on the content of your essay, such as an abundance of strong and relevant ideas and supporting points. Avoid filling your essay with fluff or unnecessary words; rather, focus on using as much strong text as possible in the time allotted.

The primary emphasis of the grading will be on your critical thinking and analytical writing skills, i.e., your ability to correctly understand a situation and explain your understanding, your ability to critically evaluate the situation and explain your evaluation in words, and your ability to imagine or consider how evidence or external factors could influence the given situation or argument.

Based on this information, here are some key strategies for writing your essay:

1. Pay careful attention to the full scenario presented before the instructions. The scenario often provides essential context to understand the instructions.

2. Pay careful attention to the specific instructions that accompany your issue. The instructions will vary slightly from prompt to prompt, and you will be evaluated partly on how well you stick to the precise, assigned task.

3. Take a few minutes before you write to brainstorm ideas on your scratch paper. Do not rush this step. Remember, the stronger the content, the higher the score. Once you feel that you have enough content to write the essay, determine how you want to organize the information. You can then outline this in writing or keep note of it in your head, whichever approach is more comfortable for you.

4. Note that there is no "right" answer, so you do not have to worry about finding one. Instead, consider the prompt, see what types of examples and ideas come to mind and what side your opinions naturally fall on, and go from there. By the way, if you are nervous about coming up with relevant support for your arguments on the spot, you can go in with some examples in mind that you know can apply to a variety of prompts.

5. Keep in mind that this is an exercise in critical thinking and persuasive writing. Do your best to write as compelling an essay as you can and to provide as much supporting evidence as possible.

6. The evidence that you provide can be derived from history or your past experiences. You can also include general truths and hypotheticals, although the latter risks being weak unless sufficiently detailed and reasoned.

7. It is also very helpful to be mindful of the other side of the argument (situations where your opinion might not hold true or evidence that could be used to support another position) and to discuss your consideration of counterarguments and opposing viewpoints. Of course, many prompts will specifically instruct you to do this.

8. Organize your essay into distinct paragraphs. Each paragraph should have a specific purpose. You do not have to worry about including a certain number of sentences in each paragraph. Unless you feel a compelling need to stray, a simple structure of an introductory paragraph, supporting paragraphs, and a concluding paragraph should be sufficient.

9. When you have finished writing your essay, spend two minutes reviewing it for grammatical and spelling errors.

A Note about the Software

You will type your essay using word processing software similar to Microsoft Word or Google Docs. You will have functions that allow you to insert, delete, cut, paste, and undo text. However, a spell checker or grammar checker will not be available. I recommend that you familiarize yourself with the interface before test day.

On the following pages are a sample "Analyze an Issue" essay prompt, some blank space in case you'd like to practice preparing a response and/or responding to the prompt yourself, and examples of responses at different score levels.

Claim: The opinions that the citizens of a particular country hold of their leadership are the best way to measure the effectiveness of that leadership.

Write a response in which you discuss the extent to which you agree or disagree with the claim. In developing and supporting your position, be sure to address the most compelling reasons and/or examples that could be used to challenge your position.

Sample Score: 5.5–6

The claim that we can measure the effectiveness of leadership based on the opinions of citizens is certainly a strong one; whether the opinions of citizens are the best way to measure the effectiveness of leadership is far more questionable.

The task of leading any country is incredibly complicated. Therefore, the judgment of effective leadership is inherently subjective and dependent on both the criteria used, and how each criterion is weighted. One person might view foreign relations as an insignificant factor, while another might see it not only as important but critical for determining leadership, and there is arguably no objective way to determine a correct answer.

One thing that is true is that throughout history, there have been many leaders who have been popular with their own citizens in their own time that we would not hold up as representative of effective leadership today. For example, it is reported that many North Koreans revered their founding father, dictator Kim Il Sung, until his death, and many genuinely felt that he was a wonderful leader. However, most others outside the country view his leadership record in a severely different fashion.

Another complicating factor is that of passing time and evolving perspectives. For example, American citizens, as a whole, felt mixed emotions about Abraham Lincoln during his presidency, but generally feel a sense of reverence toward him today. If how a country feels about its leaders is indeed the best measure of that leadership, we wouldn't expect the measurement to be so fluid.

Too often, those in power forget who they are meant to serve, and, if a leader is effective, of course the citizens should feel happy with the leadership. However, this does not mean that how the citizens feel about their leadership is the best representation of the leadership. Instead, I believe that there may be other indicators, such as those that measure the well-being of the citizens, the opportunities that they have, and their freedoms, that I find to be more objective and effective.

Sample Score: 4

While I do believe that how citizens feel about their leadership is an important way to measure the effectiveness of that leadership, I think that there are other ways of measuring leadership that are better. Sometimes leaders can be effective but unpopular, and sometimes popular leaders are ineffective.

For example, in the United States, it is often said that voters feel positively about the president when the economy is doing well and negatively about the president when the economy is doing poorly, even though the actions of the president may not have any direct impact on the economy. Politicians add to this by falsely taking credit or assigning blame, growing the disconnect between how we feel about them and what they've actually done.

Additionally, leaders often use propaganda to try to manipulate how the citizens feel. This is especially true in countries where the government controls the media or where access to information is very limited, such as North Korea. Surely, no one would claim that how the citizens of North Korea feel about their leadership would excuse what their leadership has done to their country, and North Korea stands as an example of how a government can use propaganda to manipulate how citizens feel.

In conclusion, I live in a democracy where the feelings of a population play such a critical role in determining who gets to govern and would hate to live somewhere where the feelings of the citizens are not taken into as much consideration. However, I don't feel that the feelings of citizens are the best way to judge the effectiveness of leadership.

Sample Score: 2

The opinions that citizens of a country have of their leader are not useful for measuring the effectiveness of that leadership. If they were, we could simply use a popularity contest for a listing of the greatest leaders of all time. The truth of the matter is that sometimes, in order to be a good leader, you have to make tough decisions, and tough decisions can make one unpopular. Therefore, sometimes, in order to be a good leader, sometimes you have to be unpopular. Other times, leaders will make bad decisions in order to remain popular, and we won't even know it until it's too late.

It's easier to make a popular decision than it is a unpopular but right decision. I'd rather have leaders who are willing to make the right decisions, and not the ones who want to be most popular.

23. Text Completion and Sentence Equivalence Practice

1. The superintendent's district-wide school uniform mandate did not come out of nowhere; the change in policy was _____ by her recent appearance on the local news, where she lamented students' standards of dress and conduct.

(A) belied
(B) buttressed
(C) propelled
(D) obscured
(E) prefigured

2. No strangers to the _____ of midwestern weather, the rural family gathered their valuables and ran to the storm shelter as soon as the sky turned the unmistakable yellow-green that presages a tornado.

(A) lucidity
(B) japes
(C) congruence
(D) vagaries
(E) respites

3. The runaway success of the true-crime podcast surprised everyone but its creator, a former journalist who knew that the public's thirst for stories of murder and mayhem can never be _____.

(A) stabilized
(B) slaked
(C) piqued
(D) conceived
(E) divulged

4. Although many early Black historians _____ the official credentials of their discipline, they boldly declared themselves historians nonetheless, carefully chronicling the stories of their communities for the benefit of future generations.

(A) possessed
(B) bestowed
(C) impacted
(D) lacked
(E) required

5. The professor's most recent work is informed by the university library's collection on the history of women in America, which places particular _____ the interplay between gender, race, and citizenship status.

(A) reverence for
(B) disdain for
(C) emphasis on
(D) desecration toward
(E) ignorance of

6. The Flehmen response allows an animal to _____ sensory information using its vomeronasal organ, a specialized pheromone-sensing mechanism located between its palate and the roof of its mouth.

(A) rescind
(B) sanction
(C) abscond
(D) assimilate
(E) generate

7. Agriculture in the 1930s exploited existing patterns of racial competition and hierarchy for profit; newly formed multiracial alliances were ___(i)___ the divide-and-conquer mentality ___(ii)___ by industry leaders.

BLANK i

Ⓐ anticipated by
Ⓑ anathema to
Ⓒ aligned with

BLANK ii

Ⓓ cultivated
Ⓔ dismissed
Ⓕ prevented

8. Although the number of patients with Celiac disease, an immune reaction to gluten that ___(i)___ the lining of the small intestine, has remained relatively ___(ii)___ in recent years, patients who report non-Celiac gluten sensitivity, a little-understood and far more subjective diagnosis, have more than quadrupled.

BLANK i

Ⓐ ameliorates
Ⓑ vitiates
Ⓒ bedecks

BLANK ii

Ⓓ static
Ⓔ harrowing
Ⓕ variable

9. Many voters were drawn to the young candidate's energy and ___(i)___ ideas, but party leadership worried that her radical stances on key issues like healthcare and immigration would keep her from ___(ii)___ broad enough support to win the general election.

BLANK i

Ⓐ extremist
Ⓑ progressive
Ⓒ fanatical

BLANK ii

Ⓓ garnering
Ⓔ construing
Ⓕ circumventing

10. Perhaps the most celebrated Vietnamese dish in the West is pho, a beef noodle soup served in a rich broth ___(i)___ spices, made ___(ii)___ with chili sauce, limes, and fresh herbs.

BLANK i

Ⓐ redolent with
Ⓑ derelict of
Ⓒ reeking of

BLANK ii

Ⓓ urbane
Ⓔ benign
Ⓕ piquant

11. The media's focus on male participants in the 1968 walkout, particularly those who were arrested in a dramatic fashion, ___(i)___ the critical participation of countless girls and women and ___(ii)___ their organizational contributions to the walkout's success.

BLANK i

Ⓐ minimized
Ⓑ overstated
Ⓒ dispersed

BLANK ii

Ⓓ misrepresented
Ⓔ aggrandized
Ⓕ condoned

12. World War II directly ___(i)___ over one-third of the output of American industry during the first half of the 1940s, but expanded productivity also ___(ii)___ that ordinary Americans saw a remarkable increase in the supply of consumer goods after the war.

BLANK i

Ⓐ conserved
Ⓑ consumed
Ⓒ dismantled

BLANK ii

Ⓓ ensured
Ⓔ threatened
Ⓕ discounted

13. On the first day of a new expedition, Meriwether Lewis and William Clark ___(i)___ traveled just a few hours from home base before establishing camp so that they could discover whether they had forgotten any essential provisions and easily return to their ___(ii)___ to fetch them.

BLANK i

Ⓐ always
Ⓑ never
Ⓒ rarely

BLANK ii

Ⓓ starting point
Ⓔ culmination
Ⓕ subsequent station

14. Although I didn't always agree with him, the speaker's approach to his discipline challenged my own habits of thinking; I found his ideas both ___(i)___ and __(ii)___ in ways I couldn't always explain but also couldn't shake.

BLANK i

Ⓐ vexing
Ⓑ soothing
Ⓒ indulging

BLANK ii

Ⓓ indecent
Ⓔ mellow
Ⓕ compelling

15. ___(i)___ predictions that public libraries would quickly grow ___(ii)___ with the rise of the internet have failed to materialize; in fact, libraries have successfully ___(iii)___ to meet the changing needs of the public, offering computer literacy courses, job search resources, and community programming for citizens of all ages.

BLANK i

Ⓐ Lugubrious
Ⓑ Propitious
Ⓒ Equivocal

BLANK ii

Ⓓ imperative
Ⓔ ponderous
Ⓕ superannuated

BLANK iii

Ⓖ floundered
Ⓗ evolved
Ⓙ ossified

16. Returning to his hometown for the first time since he was a child, Jack was surprised at how little ___(i)___ he felt. The reception he received from his relatives was, by and large, ___(ii)___; it was almost as if the intervening years had erased the ___(iii)___ that had initially riven them.

BLANK i

Ⓐ nostalgia
Ⓑ lassitude
Ⓒ hostility

BLANK ii

Ⓓ benign
Ⓔ truculent
Ⓕ unbiased

BLANK iii

Ⓖ mutual antipathy
Ⓗ haughty affectation
Ⓙ profound reverence

17. Tech firms tend to follow a predictable life cycle. There is an initial period of ___(i)___, during which a loose company culture and rapid growth allows the firm to recruit top talent, followed by a period of ___(ii)___, when the firm reaches a sustainable size and its employees wait for the firm to go public or be sold. Finally, there is the long-awaited ___(iii)___ or, if that fails to materialize, a swift and perilous downfall.

BLANK i

Ⓐ dynamism
Ⓑ precarious
Ⓒ unease

BLANK ii

Ⓓ retrenchment
Ⓔ equilibrium
Ⓕ catharsis

BLANK iii

Ⓖ phenomenon
Ⓗ boon
Ⓙ explosion

18. Creative Writing Professor Jeremy Benson is the latest ___(i)___ the university's controversial Pass-Fail pilot program, which allows instructors to ___(ii)___ using letter grades to evaluate their students. "Writing is about exploration and experimentation," Professor Benson said. "The most promising and ambitious work I see from my students is often the ___(iii)___. Should a student be penalized with a poor grade for taking a creative risk?"

BLANK i

Ⓐ detractor of
Ⓑ guest of
Ⓒ convert to

BLANK ii

Ⓓ opt out of
Ⓔ flout
Ⓕ advocate for

BLANK iii

Ⓖ least visionary
Ⓗ most professional
Ⓙ least polished

19. Although a ___(i)___ intellect is a great ___(ii)___ when it comes to academic success, a willingness to work hard and institute effective study habits is even more ___(iii)___ to success in school.

BLANK i

Ⓐ diminutive
Ⓑ keen
Ⓒ trustworthy

BLANK ii

Ⓓ liability
Ⓔ obstacle
Ⓕ asset

BLANK iii

Ⓖ negligible
Ⓗ crucial
Ⓙ inept

20. The speaker argued that a company's stated commitment to diversity in hiring is ___(i)___; employees from all backgrounds also need to feel ___(ii)___ and have the opportunity to make meaningful ___(iii)___ to company culture throughout their careers.

BLANK i

Ⓐ objective
Ⓑ insufficient
Ⓒ obsolete

BLANK ii

Ⓓ surrounded
Ⓔ respected
Ⓕ targeted

BLANK iii

Ⓖ exceptions
Ⓗ scruples
Ⓙ contributions

21. At a time when Americans seem to worship at the altar of ___(i)___ more than ever, organization consultant Marie Kondo's mission to declutter our lives may seem like an ___(ii)___ national fascination; perhaps we are beginning to realize that our accumulated stuff is not bringing us ___(iii)___ or clarity.

BLANK i

Ⓐ minimalism
Ⓑ nationalism
Ⓒ consumerism

BLANK ii

Ⓓ unlikely
Ⓔ indisputable
Ⓕ unsparing

BLANK iii

Ⓖ tribulation
Ⓗ contentment
Ⓙ resources

22. Scientists have discovered two viruses that appear to ___(i)___ single-celled micro algae that play an important role in the health of coral; these viruses may be ___(ii)___ the dangerous ___(iii)___ of coral ecosystems around the world.

BLANK i

Ⓐ repel
Ⓑ infect
Ⓒ enervate

BLANK ii

Ⓓ hampering
Ⓔ revamping
Ⓕ catalyzing

BLANK iii

Ⓖ decline
Ⓗ proliferation
Ⓙ distortion

23. No matter how well I think I know something, further study will typically ___(i)___ new possibilities. The key to wisdom is remaining open to new ideas that can ___(ii)___ if only we are willing to ___(iii)___ them.

BLANK i

Ⓐ preclude
Ⓑ spread
Ⓒ reveal

BLANK ii

Ⓓ emerge
Ⓔ fade
Ⓕ stabilize

BLANK iii

Ⓖ reflect
Ⓗ confront
Ⓙ consider

24. In the late eighteenth century, American women of all classes were considered responsible for ___(i)___ life; thus, our earliest First Ladies understood that our young democracy required a national ___(ii)___ who could present herself as both ___(iii)___ and queen.

BLANK i

Ⓐ national
Ⓑ domestic
Ⓒ public

BLANK ii

Ⓓ celebrity
Ⓔ duchess
Ⓕ hostess

BLANK iii

Ⓖ royalty
Ⓗ commoner
Ⓙ devotee

25. Like many politically ___(i)___ artists in the 1950s, entertainer Lena Horne found herself ___(ii)___ and ___(iii)___ performing on television or in the movies because of her civil rights activism.

BLANK i

Ⓐ correct
Ⓑ diplomatic
Ⓒ engaged

BLANK ii

Ⓓ lauded
Ⓔ blacklisted
Ⓕ overexposed

BLANK iii

Ⓖ limited to
Ⓗ barred from
Ⓙ contemplating

26. Many of America's most important government sites have been ___(i)___ of attack, from the British razing of Washington during the War of 1812 to the September 11, 2001, assault on the Pentagon. Political violence has unfortunately rendered these places more ___(ii)___ and less ___(iii)___ to the public than their architects likely intended.

BLANK i

Ⓐ memorials
Ⓑ temples
Ⓒ targets

BLANK ii

Ⓓ protected
Ⓔ penetrable
Ⓕ welcoming

BLANK iii

Ⓖ diverting
Ⓗ uninspiring
Ⓙ accessible

27. Confirmation bias is the often ___(i)___ act of referencing only those perspectives that ___(ii)___ our preexisting views while at the same time ignoring or dismissing opinions that ___(iii)___ our way of looking at the world.

BLANK i

Ⓐ salutary
Ⓑ subconscious
Ⓒ time-honored

BLANK ii

Ⓓ affirm
Ⓔ challenge
Ⓕ disregard

BLANK iii

Ⓖ bolster
Ⓗ indulge
Ⓙ jeopardize

28. Most people know that the Great Red Spot, the planet Jupiter's most ___(i)___ characteristic, is ___(ii)___ anticyclonic storm that has been ___(iii)___ for at least several hundred years; however, many do not realize that the storm has been steadily shrinking for a century.

BLANK i

Ⓐ vexed
Ⓑ provisional
Ⓒ conspicuous

BLANK ii

Ⓓ an unpresuming
Ⓔ a titanic
Ⓕ an indented

BLANK iii

Ⓖ dwindling
Ⓗ raging
Ⓙ regressing

29. The university's part-time instructors ___(i)___ the department's policy of tying promotions to favorable teacher evaluations, ___(ii)___ that students with substandard grades tend to unfairly take their ___(iii)___ out on the instructors and TAs responsible for grading their poorly written essays.

BLANK i

Ⓐ remonstrated against
Ⓑ acceded to
Ⓒ fathomed

BLANK ii

Ⓓ recommending
Ⓔ contravening
Ⓕ contending

BLANK iii

Ⓖ trepidation
Ⓗ seclusion
Ⓙ acrimony

30. Shunning the _____ high school reading list that had failed to engage her students the previous year, the teacher took a new approach, assigning her students just one book to explore for the entire semester: Leo Tolstoy's *War and Peace*.

A unorthodox
B mystifying
C hackneyed
D controversial
E timeworn
F suggestive

31. If these more conservative projections are correct, the economy, far from hurtling toward recession, is on track for a modest _____.

A improvement
B downturn
C detour
D swoon
E furrow
F eruption

32. Campers are sent home immediately for serious infractions like drug use, sexual misconduct, or violent behavior. On the other hand, counselors tend to take a lax attitude toward _____ wrongdoings like staying up past curfew or playing harmless pranks on other campers.

A indefensible
B venial
C sagacious
D irrepressible
E vehement
F negligible

33. A new study found that 54% of those wrongly convicted of a crime are themselves victims of official _____, either by police, prosecutors, or both.

A diligence
B wrongdoing
C intervention
D fascination
E misconduct
F impartiality

34. Impressionism originated with a group of Paris-based artists whose independent art exhibitions brought them _____ during the 1870s and 1880s.

A distinction
B infamy
C obscurity
D renown
E secrecy
F custody

35. The prevalence of commercial whaling in New England resulted in widespread overfishing by the early 1700s: the right whale population was near extinction in 1935, when international _____ measures for right whales finally came into effect.

A preservation
B acceptance
C integration
D demand
E conservation
F allocation

36. By 1849, word of the California gold rush had spread; many farmers _____ their fields in favor of seeking their fortunes.

A transplanted
B relinquished
C enriched
D rotated
E shrouded
F abandoned

37. Scientists have known since ancient times that liver tissue has a remarkable ability to _____ itself after incurring damage, but how it does so remains a mystery.

A regenerate
B renew
C renovate
D contract
E diverge
F recapitulate

38. At the turn of the twentieth century, concern over childhood malnutrition inspired some philanthropic groups to provide _____ lunches to public school students free of charge.

A leftover
B hygienic
C balanced
D healthful
E elaborate
F bland

39. Perhaps U.S. Secretary of State Madeleine Albright's greatest diplomatic achievement was her _____ push for NATO military intervention during the 1999 humanitarian crisis in Kosovo.

A abortive
B effective
C unexpected
D intractable
E successful
F ceremonious

40. Throughout the late 1950s, television-obsessed viewers were _____ by a series of scandals related to high-stakes quiz shows that had been cleverly rigged by their producers.

A fascinated
B shaken
C infuriated
D consoled
E riveted
F besieged

41. In 1940, President Roosevelt acknowledged that he would have trouble convincing Americans to go to war: many complacent citizens had simply closed their eyes to the dangers of the European conflict, while others _____ American defense preparations for political reasons.

A supported
B resisted
C ignored
D falsified
E opposed
F converted

42. To _____ the widespread dissemination of knowledge and advancement of wisdom, a university must allow for the free expression of ideas.

A apprehend
B sustain
C balance
D foster
E impede
F ascertain

43. _____ popular belief, Michelangelo did not paint the Sistine Chapel ceiling lying down: rather, he painted in a standing position, supported by a unique system of platforms that he attached to the walls with brackets.

A In line with
B Counter to
C Pertaining to
D Unencumbered by
E Consistent with
F Contrary to

44. During the contentious summer debate, Senator Jones appeared _____ and irritated as he addressed his opponent's cutting remarks about his voting record.

A rattled
B amused
C vacuous ·
D bumptious
E unnerved
F satisfied

45. America's food deserts are typically found in low-income areas, a situation that dooms locals to struggle against _____ of both money and healthy food choices.

A a surfeit
B a quota
C a paucity
D an array
E a dearth
F an allowance

46. The mayor was willing to consider several innovative proposals for repurposing the site of the _____ amusement park, but he refused to consider reopening the park to the public, citing the prohibitive cost of bringing old attractions up to code.

A defunct
B lucrative
C obsolete
D nostalgic
E prevailing
F prodigious

47. Persistent budget issues _____ the performing arts magnet school's ambitious plans for a four-week musical theater summer camp.

A stimulated
B heartened
C scotched
D sublimated
E scuppered
F enervated

48. Reverend Gibson was hoping to collect $20 for his mission from that evening's prayer meeting, so he was stunned by the congregation's _____ when he discovered five $100 bills in the offering plate.

A indigence
B insouciance
C parsimony
D abstemiousness
E munificence
F liberality

Solutions

1. The superintendent's district-wide school uniform mandate did not come out of nowhere; the change in policy was _____ by her recent appearance on the local news, where she lamented students' standards of dress and conduct.

(A) belied
(B) buttressed
(C) propelled
(D) obscured
(E) prefigured

The key clue here is that the superintendent's mandate *did not come out of nowhere*; it was *prefigured*, or indicated beforehand, by her *recent appearance on the local news, where she lamented students' standards of dress and conduct*, so **(E) is the correct answer**.

To *belie* is to give a false impression, which she wasn't doing here.

To *buttress* is to support, and to *propel* is to move forward. Both answers are somewhat attractive, but neither matches the meaning of *did not come out of nowhere* as well as prefigured does, so you can eliminate both.

To *obscure* is to conceal, and that isn't what the superintendent is doing here, so you can eliminate (D) as well.

2. No strangers to the _____ of midwestern weather, the rural family gathered their valuables and ran to the storm shelter as soon as the sky turned the unmistakable yellow-green that presages a tornado.

(A) lucidity
(B) japes
(C) congruence
(D) vagaries
(E) respites

The key clue here is that the family *ran to the storm shelter as soon as the sky turned the unmistakable yellow-green that presages a tornado*. You know you're looking for a modifier that, ideally, indicates a sudden change in weather that requires quick action.

Looking at the answer choices, *lucidity* means clearness, which isn't a match for what you need and can be eliminated.

Japes are practical jokes, and without some clear indication of irony, this doesn't work here either, so you can eliminate japes, too.

Congruence has to do with alliance or the coming together of things, which doesn't fit the situation and you can eliminate that answer choice as well.

Vagaries are unexpected changes, a modifier that's very apt for this situation, whereas *respites* are peaceful breaks, almost the opposite of a tornado; thus, **vagaries is correct**.

3. The runaway success of the true-crime podcast surprised everyone but its creator, a former journalist who knew that the public's thirst for stories of murder and mayhem can never be _____.

(A) stabilized
(B) slaked
(C) piqued
(D) conceived
(E) divulged

If the true-crime podcast is a runaway success, you can infer that you are looking for something like *the public's thirst for stories of murder and mayhem can never be* satisfied. Let's see which of the answer choices provides the best match.

Stabilized isn't what you expected, but it's somewhat tempting—maybe it can't ever get to a stable level because it can't ever get satisfied. Not ideal, but let's leave it for now.

To *slake* is to quench or satisfy, so slaked is a much better match than stabilized, and ***slaked* is the correct answer**.

Piqued means stimulated—it would go against the intended meaning to say that the public's thirst can never be stimulated.

Conceived means imagined or created—it doesn't make sense to say that the public's thirst can't be thought of or created.

Finally, *divulged* means revealed, and it doesn't match the intended meaning to say that the public's thirst can't be revealed.

4. Although many early Black historians _____ the official credentials of their discipline, they boldly declared themselves historians nonetheless, carefully chronicling the stories of their communities for the benefit of future generations.

Ⓐ possessed
Ⓑ bestowed
Ⓒ impacted
Ⓓ lacked
Ⓔ required

The key clue here is that *they boldly declared themselves historians nonetheless*. What *nonetheless* tells you is that they suffered some sort of deficiency in this respect, such as not having the official credentials. **Choice (D), *lacked*, describes this situation precisely and is the correct answer**.

Looking at the other answer choices, if they *possessed* the official credentials, they wouldn't need to boldly declare themselves historians *nonetheless*, and there is no evidence in the passage to suggest that they *bestowed*, or presented, *impacted*, or *required* the official credentials of their discipline, so you can eliminate all of these choices as well.

5. The professor's most recent work is informed by the university library's collection on the history of women in America, which places particular _____ the interplay between gender, race, and citizenship status.

Ⓐ reverence for
Ⓑ disdain for
Ⓒ emphasis on
Ⓓ desecration toward
Ⓔ ignorance of

Because the professor's *work is informed by the university library's collection*, you can infer that it must be significant, and you can also imagine that this collection places particular *emphasis on* the interplay between gender, race, and citizenship status, so **(C) is the correct answer**.

(A) is also somewhat attractive, but libraries are not necessarily places to show *reverence* or deep respect for their subjects but rather to gather information on and study them.

Disdain is the sense that something is not worthy of one's respect, which doesn't match the intended meaning. *Desecration* is the act of damaging or showing a lack of respect, which also doesn't match, and it doesn't make sense to say that the professor's work is informed by something that places particular *ignorance of* something, so you can eliminate all those answer choices as well.

6. The Flehmen response allows an animal to _____ sensory information using its vomeronasal organ, a specialized pheromone-sensing mechanism located between its palate and the roof of its mouth.

Ⓐ rescind
Ⓑ sanction
Ⓒ abscond
Ⓓ assimilate
Ⓔ generate

You know that the *Flehmen response allows an animal to* do something with sensory information—<u>process</u> it, <u>combine</u> it, <u>experience</u> it—or something similar. Let's see what you are given in the answer choices.

It doesn't make sense that an animal would *rescind*, or cancel, sensory information, so you can eliminate that choice, and it also doesn't make sense that an animal would *sanction*, or approve of, sensory information, so you can eliminate that choice as well. (Note that a secondary definition of *sanction*, i.e., to punish, also doesn't work here.)

Assimilate, which means bring together, matches what you anticipated. *Generate* is somewhat attractive, but you're told it's a *specialized pheromone-sensing mechanism*, and it's unclear why animals would need to create such sensory information within themselves. **Assimilate is therefore a much better match for the information presented and is the correct answer.**

7. Agriculture in the 1930s exploited existing patterns of racial competition and hierarchy for profit; newly formed multiracial alliances were ___(i)___ the divide-and-conquer mentality ___(ii)___ by industry leaders.

BLANK i

Ⓐ anticipated by
Ⓑ anathema to
Ⓒ aligned with

BLANK ii

Ⓓ cultivated
Ⓔ dismissed
Ⓕ prevented

You are told that *agriculture in the 1930s exploited existing patterns of racial competition and hierarchy for profit*. Therefore, you can anticipate that multiracial *alliances were* in contrast with *the divide-and-conquer mentality* supported *by industry leaders*.

Looking at the answer choices, for the first blank, **anathema to, which means intensely disliked by or denounced by, is a great match for what you expected, and it is correct.** You have no sense that these alliances were *anticipated by* the mentality of the leaders, so you can eliminate that choice, and to say that these alliances were *aligned with* the mentality of the leaders would be the opposite of the intended meaning; you can eliminate that choice as well.

For the second blank, **cultivated is also a great match for what you expected, and it is correct.** You know that the industry leaders wanted this mentality, so *dismissed* and *prevented* are incorrect and can be eliminated.

8. Although the number of patients with Celiac disease, an immune reaction to gluten that ___(i)___ the lining of the small intestine, has remained relatively ___(ii)___ in recent years, patients who report non-Celiac gluten sensitivity, a little-understood and far more subjective diagnosis, have more than quadrupled.

BLANK i

Ⓐ ameliorates
Ⓑ vitiates
Ⓒ bedecks

BLANK ii

Ⓓ static
Ⓔ harrowing
Ⓕ variable

The number of patients with Celiac disease is being compared in a contrasting way to those who report *non-Celiac gluten sensitivity*, and you can anticipate that, for the second blank, this number of patients has *remained relatively* static *in recent years*, which **is the correct answer for the second blank.** You have no evidence that the number of patients is *harrowing*, or scary, and *variable* is the opposite of what to expect per the given clues.

The first space is far more difficult to fill, mainly because of the challenging nature of the answer choices. To *ameliorate* is to improve, to *vitiate* is to impair, and to *bedeck* is to decorate. **Vitiates clearly fits the meaning best and is correct.**

9. Many voters were drawn to the young candidate's energy and ___(i)___ ideas, but party leadership worried that her radical stances on key issues like healthcare and immigration would keep her from ___(ii)___ broad enough support to win the general election.

BLANK i

Ⓐ extremist
Ⓑ progressive
Ⓒ fanatical

BLANK ii

Ⓓ garnering
Ⓔ construing
Ⓕ circumventing

For the first blank, because of *but* at the beginning of the second clause, you know that the word should contrast with the candidate's *radical stances*. *Extremist* and *fanatical* are quite close to *radical* in meaning, so you can eliminate choices (A) and (C). *Progressive*, or promoting progress or reform, is a good match, and **(B) is the correct answer**.

For the second blank, the clues give you a sense that you need a word such as <u>getting</u>, and *garnering* is a great synonym. **It is the correct answer.** *Construing* means interpreting, which doesn't fit in this situation, and *circumventing* has to do with getting around something, which also doesn't fit here.

10. Perhaps the most celebrated Vietnamese dish in the West is pho, a beef noodle soup served in a rich broth ___(i)___ spices, made ___(ii)___ with chili sauce, limes, and fresh herbs.

BLANK i

Ⓐ redolent with
Ⓑ derelict of
Ⓒ reeking of

BLANK ii

Ⓓ urbane
Ⓔ benign
Ⓕ piquant

For the first blank you know that the broth is *rich* and includes *spices*, so **it makes sense to describe it as** ***redolent***, or fragrant with spices. *Derelict* means run down, which doesn't work here, and *reeking* also pertains to smell, but the word has a negative connotation that doesn't fit the context.

For the second blank, to be *urbane* is to be polite or polished, and to be *benign* is to be mild or harmless, whereas to be *piquant* is to be spicy or engaging. Clearly, if you are using chili sauce, limes, and herbs, ***piquant*** **is the best choice here**.

11. The media's focus on male participants in the 1968 walkout, particularly those who were arrested in a dramatic fashion, ___(i)___ the critical participation of countless girls and women and ___(ii)___ their organizational contributions to the walkout's success.

BLANK i

Ⓐ minimized
Ⓑ overstated
Ⓒ dispersed

BLANK ii

Ⓓ misrepresented
Ⓔ aggrandized
Ⓕ condoned

You can infer that if the *media's focus* was on *male participants*, it must have <u>underrepresented</u> *the critical participation of girls and women*, and for the first blank, ***minimized*** **matches the anticipated meaning**. *Overstated* is the opposite of what you expect, and *dispersed*, or spread out, doesn't fit in this context.

For the second blank, again, because of an emphasis on the contributions of male participants, **it makes sense that the contributions of women were *misrepresented*, which is correct**. You don't have clues that indicate that the contributions of women were *aggrandized*, or made greater, or *condoned*, or allowed.

12. World War II directly ___(i)___ over one-third of the output of American industry during the first half of the 1940s, but expanded productivity also ___(ii)___ that ordinary Americans saw a remarkable increase in the supply of consumer goods after the war.

BLANK i

Ⓐ conserved
Ⓑ consumed
Ⓒ dismantled

BLANK ii

Ⓓ ensured
Ⓔ threatened
Ⓕ discounted

For the first blank, **it makes sense that *World War II directly* consumed *over one-third of the output of American industry* because the materials would be necessary for war**. It doesn't make sense to say the war *conserved* industry, and there is no evidence in the sentence that suggests World War II *dismantled*, or took apart, the output of American industry.

For the second blank, if there is *expanded productivity*, it makes sense that it would *ensure that ordinary Americans saw an increase in the supply of consumer goods*, so **ensured is the correct answer**. It wouldn't make sense for expanded productivity to *threaten* or *discount* such an outcome, and you can eliminate both options.

13. On the first day of a new expedition, Meriwether Lewis and William Clark ___(i)___ traveled just a few hours from home base before establishing camp so that they could discover whether they had forgotten any essential provisions and easily return to their ___(ii)___ to fetch them.

BLANK i

Ⓐ always
Ⓑ never
Ⓒ rarely

BLANK ii

Ⓓ starting point
Ⓔ culmination
Ⓕ subsequent station

Starting with the second blank, *on the first day of a new expedition*, if they discover they had *forgotten any essential provisions*, **they would return to their *starting point***, not their *culmination*, which is the end, or the *subsequent station*.

You have fewer clues and less certainty for the first blank, but it makes sense they would make a habit of *always* following this routine. Furthermore, if you try to insert *never* or *rarely*, it creates some ambiguity and awkwardness around the modifier *so they could discover whether they had forgotten any essential provisions*. **So always is correct for the first blank**.

14. Although I didn't always agree with him, the speaker's approach to his discipline challenged my own habits of thinking; I found his ideas both ___(i)___ and ___(ii)___ in ways I couldn't always explain but also couldn't shake.

BLANK i

Ⓐ vexing
Ⓑ soothing
Ⓒ indulging

BLANK ii

Ⓓ indecent
Ⓔ mellow
Ⓕ compelling

You know that the speaker's approach to his discipline challenged the author's own habits of thinking, and she found the speakers ideas ____ and ____ *in ways I couldn't always explain but also couldn't shake*. You want to find answers for the blanks that match those descriptions.

For the first blank, ***vexing*, or causing frustration, is a good match**—we often feel frustrated when we can't explain or shake something easily, especially something that goes against our nature. *Soothing* isn't a good match for the descriptors that you've been given, nor is *indulging*, so you can eliminate both.

For the second blank, the author finds the speaker's ideas *compelling* in that she can't shake them, and, **juxtaposed with *vexing*, *compelling* makes a great match**. You don't have a sense that the author finds the ideas *indecent*, or inappropriate, or *mellow*, so you can eliminate both choices.

15. ___(i)___ predictions that public libraries would quickly grow ___(ii)___ with the rise of the internet have failed to materialize; in fact, libraries have successfully ___(iii)___ to meet the changing needs of the public, offering computer literacy courses, job search resources, and community programming for citizens of all ages.

BLANK i

Ⓐ **Lugubrious**
Ⓑ Propitious
Ⓒ Equivocal

BLANK ii

Ⓓ imperative
Ⓔ ponderous
Ⓕ **superannuated**

BLANK iii

Ⓖ floundered
Ⓗ **evolved**
Ⓙ ossified

The third blank is the easiest to fill in first; **it makes sense that libraries *successfully* evolved *to meet the changing needs of the public*,** rather than *floundered*, which means struggled, or *ossified*, which means became rigid.

For the first blank, ***lugubrious*, or gloomy, is the best fit**. *Propitious*, or favorable, doesn't make sense, nor does *equivocal*, which means ambiguous.

For the second, **it makes sense that libraries were predicted to grow *superannuated***, or obsolete, rather than *imperative*, which means very important, or *ponderous*, which means labored and weighty.

16. Returning to his hometown for the first time since he was a child, Jack was surprised at how little ___(i)___ he felt. The reception he received from his relatives was, by and large, ___(ii)___; it was almost as if the intervening years had erased the ___(iii)___ that had initially riven them.

BLANK i

Ⓐ nostalgia
Ⓑ lassitude
Ⓒ **hostility**

BLANK ii

Ⓓ **benign**
Ⓔ truculent
Ⓕ unbiased

BLANK iii

Ⓖ **mutual antipathy**
Ⓗ haughty affectation
Ⓙ profound reverence

If the first blank were a question by itself, it might be tempting to select several of the answers but difficult to choose one with certainty. Similarly, if the second blank were a question by itself, it might be very hard to find any answer attractive for any reason. However, the third blank is far more clearly defined, and if you start there, it informs you of what to do for the other two blanks.

For the third blank, you're told *it was almost as if the intervening years had erased the ____ that had initially riven them*. To be *riven* is to be violently torn apart, so you know that this family separated in an unhappy way—for the third blank, ***mutual antipathy*, or dislike, makes the most sense**, as opposed to *haughty affectation* or *profound reverence*.

Knowing this, returning to the first blank, **it makes the most sense to infer Jack was surprised at how little *hostility* he felt**, as opposed to *nostalgia* or *lassitude*, which is similar to weariness.

For the second blank, **it makes sense that his reception was *benign***, or gentle and kindly, as opposed to *truculent*, or eager to fight, or *unbiased*, which means free of prejudice.

17. Tech firms tend to follow a predictable life cycle. There is an initial period of ___(i)___, during which a loose company culture and rapid growth allows the firm to recruit top talent, followed by a period of ___(ii)___, when the firm reaches a sustainable size and its employees wait for the firm to go public or be sold. Finally, there is the long-awaited ___(iii)___ or, if that fails to materialize, a swift and perilous downfall.

BLANK i

(A) **dynamism**
(B) precarious
(C) unease

BLANK ii

(D) retrenchment
(E) **equilibrium**
(F) catharsis

BLANK iii

(G) phenomenon
(H) **boon**
(J) explosion

The key clue you're told upfront is that tech firms tend to follow *a predictable life cycle*—you can use this and the new information to come to fill in the blanks as best you can.

For the first blank, *precariousness* and *unease* might aptly describe many initial periods for new tech terms, but they don't go well with descriptions such as *loose company culture*, *rapid growth*, and, most important, *allows the firm to recruit top talent*. **Dynamism, which is characterized by vigorous activity and rapid progress, is a great match for an initial period that allows the firm to recruit top talent**.

For the second blank, **once a firm reaches a sustainable size, *equilibrium* makes a lot of sense**. *Retrenchment*, or the reduction of spending, is perhaps tempting, but you aren't given any specific indication in the sentence that there is a decrease at this stage in the cycle, so you can eliminate it. You also don't have any indication that companies predictably go through a period of *catharsis*, which means the release of repressed emotions, so you can eliminate that answer choice as well.

For the third blank, although *explosion* is somewhat tempting, it's a very general word, and it's unclear how it applies to this situation. **Boon, which means something of great benefit, is a much better fit in this context**. *Phenomenon*, like *explosion*, is a bit too general to be correct here.

18. Creative Writing Professor Jeremy Benson is the latest ___(i)___ the university's controversial Pass-Fail pilot program, which allows instructors to ___(ii)___ using letter grades to evaluate their students. "Writing is about exploration and experimentation," Professor Benson said. "The most promising and ambitious work I see from my students is often the ___(iii)___. Should a student be penalized with a poor grade for taking a creative risk?"

BLANK i

(A) detractor of
(B) guest of
(C) **convert to**

BLANK ii

(D) **opt out of**
(E) flout
(F) advocate for

BLANK iii

(G) least visionary
(H) most professional
(J) **least polished**

A key clue comes at the end with Professor Benson's rhetorical question, which implies that, for the first blank, the professor is the latest *convert to* the university's program, as opposed to being a *detractor of* it. It doesn't make sense to say the professor is a *guest of* the program. **(C) is correct**.

For the second blank, **it makes sense that the Pass-Fail program would allow *instructors to* opt out of *using letter grades to evaluate students***. The clues you are given do not suggest that instructors *advocate for* or *flout* using letter grades, so you can eliminate both choices.

For the third blank, *least polished* may not seem to have much support, but it does contrast with *promising and ambitious*, as the grammatical construction of the sentence requires. Moreover, **it's a much better fit than the other answer choices**; *least visionary* doesn't match as a contrast to "*promising and ambitious*," and neither does *most professional*, which wouldn't be likely to cause grading dilemmas.

19. Although a ___(i)___ intellect is a great ___(ii)___ when it comes to academic success, a willingness to work hard and institute effective study habits is even more ___(iii)___ to success in school.

BLANK i

Ⓐ diminutive
Ⓑ keen
Ⓒ trustworthy

BLANK ii

Ⓓ liability
Ⓔ obstacle
Ⓕ asset

BLANK iii

Ⓖ negligible
Ⓗ crucial
Ⓙ inept

Because you're leading up to *academic success*, you can infer that **you want a *keen*, or sharp, intellect and that this is a great *asset*.**

For the first blank, *diminutive* is the opposite of what you would need, and *trustworthy* is attractive but not quite as strong a match as *keen*.

For the second blank, it wouldn't make sense that the keen intellect is either a *liability* or an *obstacle* to intellectual success, so both options can be eliminated.

For the third blank, you are told that these other characteristics are *even more ____ to success in school*, and **the word that makes the most sense here is *crucial*.** *Negligible* is the opposite of what you need, and *inept*, or showing no skill, doesn't fit this situation.

20. The speaker argued that a company's stated commitment to diversity in hiring is ___(i)___; employees from all backgrounds also need to feel ___(ii)___ and have the opportunity to make meaningful ___(iii)___ to company culture throughout their careers.

BLANK i

Ⓐ objective
Ⓑ insufficient
Ⓒ obsolete

BLANK ii

Ⓓ surrounded
Ⓔ respected
Ⓕ targeted

BLANK iii

Ⓖ exceptions
Ⓗ scruples
Ⓙ contributions

The key clue is the word *also* in the statement *employees from all backgrounds also need to feel.*

For the first blank, **the company's stated commitment to diversity in hiring is insufficient, or not enough.** You don't have support in the sentence that indicates that the company's stated commitment is *objective* or *obsolete*, so you can eliminate both choices.

For the second and third blanks, **it makes sense that employees from all backgrounds also need to feel respected *and have the opportunity to make meaningful contributions to company culture throughout their careers*.**

It makes little sense to state that these employees would need to feel *surrounded* or *targeted*, or to say that they need to feel the opportunity to make *exceptions* or *scruples*, which are concerns, so you can eliminate all of those choices.

21. At a time when Americans seem to worship at the altar of ___(i)___ more than ever, organization consultant Marie Kondo's mission to declutter our lives may seem like an ___(ii)___ national fascination; perhaps we are beginning to realize that our accumulated stuff is not bringing us ___(iii)___ or clarity.

BLANK i

Ⓐ minimalism
Ⓑ nationalism
Ⓒ consumerism

BLANK ii

Ⓓ unlikely
Ⓔ indisputable
Ⓕ unsparing

BLANK iii

Ⓖ tribulation
Ⓗ contentment
Ⓙ resources

If you insert *consumerism* in the first blank and *unlikely* in the second, it **creates a nice contrast between Americans working at the altar of consumerism and Marie Kondo's mission to declutter.**

You don't have any indications for *nationalism* in the first blank, and *minimalism* goes against clues in the sentence, such as *our accumulated stuff*.

For the second, you don't have clues that tell you that Marie Kondo's mission is an *indisputable* or *unsparing national fascination*, so you can eliminate both.

Finally, for the third blank, **it goes along with the rest of the passage and makes sense to say that perhaps we are beginning to realize that our accumulated stuff is not bringing us contentment or clarity.**

Neither *tribulation*, which is suffering, nor *resources* make much sense in this context and can both be eliminated.

22. Scientists have discovered two viruses that appear to ___(i)___ single-celled micro algae that play an important role in the health of coral; these viruses may be ___(ii)___ the dangerous ___(iii)___ of coral ecosystems around the world.

BLANK i

Ⓐ repel
Ⓑ infect
Ⓒ enervate

BLANK ii

Ⓓ hampering
Ⓔ revamping
Ⓕ catalyzing

BLANK iii

Ⓖ decline
Ⓗ proliferation
Ⓙ distortion

For the first blank, **it makes sense that viruses *infect* the single-celled micro algae.** You don't have an indication that the viruses *repel*, or drive the micro algae away. *Enervate*, or drain of energy, is somewhat attractive, but *infect* is certainly a better a choice.

For the second and third blanks, if these *micro algae play an important role in the health of coral* and the viruses are infecting the micro algae, **it makes sense that *these viruses may be* catalyzing *the dangerous* decline of coral ecosystems around the world*.**

For the second blank, *hampering* could have worked if *proliferation* were put into the third blank, but *proliferation* doesn't fit into the third blank for other reasons, primarily the modifier *dangerous*. So *hampering* doesn't work for the second blank. *Revamping* also doesn't have any support and can be eliminated.

For the third blank, again, because of the modifier *dangerous*, *proliferation* doesn't work, and it's unclear what the *distortion* of coral ecosystems would entail, so you can eliminate that choice as well.

23. No matter how well I think I know something, further study will typically ___(i)___ new possibilities. The key to wisdom is remaining open to new ideas that can ___(ii)___ if only we are willing to ___(iii)___ them.

BLANK i

Ⓐ preclude
Ⓑ spread
Ⓒ reveal

BLANK ii

Ⓓ emerge
Ⓔ fade
Ⓕ stabilize

BLANK iii

Ⓖ reflect
Ⓗ confront
Ⓙ consider

The sentence starts with *no matter*, so you know you'll have a contrast—**no matter how well I think I know something, further study will typically reveal new possibilities makes a lot of sense and is correct**.

Spread is also somewhat attractive but not as clean a fit as reveal, and *preclude*, which means to prevent, doesn't match the situation.

For the second blank, **it makes sense for new ideas to emerge, or come about**, rather than *fade* or *stabilize*.

For the third blank, although *confront* is a somewhat attractive choice, you don't have the support for such a dramatic term, and **consider is a better match**. *Reflect on* might have been attractive, but *reflect*, by itself, doesn't fit and can be eliminated.

24. In the late eighteenth century, American women of all classes were considered responsible for ___(i)___ life; thus, our earliest First Ladies understood that our young democracy required a national ___(ii)___ who could present herself as both ___(iii)___ and queen.

BLANK i

(A) national
(B) **domestic**
(C) public

BLANK ii

(D) celebrity
(E) duchess
(F) **hostess**

BLANK iii

(G) royalty
(H) **commoner**
(J) devotee

Here, the first and second blanks influence and inform each other; **American women were *responsible for domestic life*, so *our earliest First Ladies understood that our young democracy required a national* hostess**; in this role, **it makes sense that the First Lady would present herself as both a commoner and queen**.

For the first blank, there is nothing in the text to suggest that American women would be responsible for *national* life or *public* life, and for the second blank, you don't have clues that indicate First Ladies understood that a young democracy required a national *celebrity* or *duchess*.

Finally, for the third blank, *royalty* wouldn't contrast with queen, and you don't have support for the idea that the First Lady would be a *devotee* (given that it's unclear to what she would be devoted), so you can eliminate both of those answers.

25. Like many politically ___(i)___ artists in the 1950s, entertainer Lena Horne found herself ___(ii)___ and ___(iii)___ performing on television or in the movies because of her civil rights activism.

BLANK i

(A) correct
(B) diplomatic
(C) **engaged**

BLANK ii

(D) lauded
(E) **blacklisted**
(F) overexposed

BLANK iii

(G) limited to
(H) **barred from**
(J) contemplating

You know from the end of the sentence that Lena Horne was active in civil rights, so for the first blank, **politically engaged makes the most sense**. Political *correctness* is a colloquial term; taken in a literal sense, there is nothing that suggests that her politics were right, and you can eliminate this choice; there is also nothing in the sentence that suggests that her politics were *diplomatic*, or intended to improve relations without upsetting anyone, so you can eliminate that answer choice as well.

The second and third blanks are combined, so **it makes sense that _Lena Horne found herself_ blacklisted _and barred from_ performing**.

Moving on to the third blank, because television and movies are such desirable mediums, _limited to_ makes little sense, and it's tough to see how _contemplating_ could work here. Both can be eliminated.

For the second blank, it wouldn't make sense that she was _lauded_, or praised, while being barred, and it also wouldn't make sense that she was _overexposed_, or exposed too much, so you can eliminate both of those choices as well.

26. Many of America's most important government sites have been ___(i)___ of attack, from the British razing of Washington during the War of 1812 to the September 11, 2001, assault on the Pentagon. Political violence has unfortunately rendered these places more ___(ii)___ and less ___(iii)___ to the public than their architects likely intended.

BLANK i

Ⓐ memorials
Ⓑ temples
Ⓒ targets

BLANK ii

Ⓓ protected
Ⓔ penetrable
Ⓕ welcoming

BLANK iii

Ⓖ diverting
Ⓗ uninspiring
Ⓙ accessible

For the first blank, **the only answer choice that makes sense is _targets_**, and the examples that follow illustrate that the sites have been targets. Though you might memorialize certain events, the text is referring to the attacks themselves, not _memorials_ to them. Similarly, it makes no sense to create _temples_ of attack, so you can eliminate both choices.

The correct answer to the second blank is less clear until you fill in the third; **the answers align if you say that the places are more _protected_ and less _accessible_, which are the two correct answers**. If they are less accessible, it wouldn't make sense to say they are more _penetrable_ or _welcoming_.

For the third blank, the architects likely did not intend for their works to be _diverting_ or _uninspiring_, so once you recognize this, you can eliminate both.

27. Confirmation bias is the often ___(i)___ act of referencing only those perspectives that ___(ii)___ our pre-existing views while at the same time ignoring or dismissing opinions that ___(iii)___ our way of looking at the world.

BLANK i

Ⓐ salutary
Ⓑ subconscious
Ⓒ time-honored

BLANK ii

Ⓓ affirm
Ⓔ challenge
Ⓕ disregard

BLANK iii

Ⓖ bolster
Ⓗ indulge
Ⓙ jeopardize

For the first blank, **subconscious, or outside of conscious recognition, works best**. You don't have clues in the sentence that tell you that confirmation bias is _salutary_, or beneficial, or _time-honored_, so you can eliminate both choices.

For the second blank, **referencing only those perspectives that affirm our pre-existing views aligns best with confirmation bias**, whereas _challenge our pre-existing views_ and _disregard our pre-existing views_ are practically the opposite of what you are looking for.

For the final blank, **it makes the most sense to say *dismissing opinions that jeopardize our way of looking at the world***; confirmation bias wouldn't lead you to *dismiss* opinions that bolster or *indulge* our way of looking at the world.

28. Most people know that the Great Red Spot, the planet Jupiter's most ___(i)___ characteristic, is ___(ii)___ anticyclonic storm that has been ___(iii)___ for at least several hundred years; however, many do not realize that the storm has been steadily shrinking for a century.

BLANK i

Ⓐ vexed
Ⓑ provisional
Ⓒ conspicuous

BLANK ii

Ⓓ an unpresuming
Ⓔ a titanic
Ⓕ an indented

BLANK iii

Ⓖ dwindling
Ⓗ raging
Ⓙ regressing

For the first blank, **it makes the most sense to say that the Great Red Spot is Jupiter's most *conspicuous*, or noticeable, characteristic**, as opposed to *vexed*, meaning problematic (who says it's a problem?) or *provisional*, meaning temporary or tentative.

For the second blank, **because it's Jupiter's most notable characteristic, *titanic* works best here.** *Unpresuming* and *indented* don't fit what you know of the storm.

Finally, for the third blank, ***raging* makes the most sense**; *dwindling* doesn't contrast with *however* in the final part of the original sentence, and *regressing*, which means returning to a previous state, also doesn't work.

29. The university's part-time instructors ___(i)___ the department's policy of tying promotions to favorable teacher evaluations, ___(ii)___ that students with substandard grades tend to unfairly take their ___(iii)___ out on the instructors and TAs responsible for grading their poorly written essays.

BLANK i

Ⓐ remonstrated against
Ⓑ acceded to
Ⓒ fathomed

BLANK ii

Ⓓ recommending
Ⓔ contravening
Ⓕ contending

BLANK iii

Ⓖ trepidation
Ⓗ seclusion
Ⓙ acrimony

Once you've read the entire sentence, **it's clear that the part-time instructors would not be in favor of this plan, so *remonstrated against*, or protested against, makes the most sense and is correct.**

In terms of the other answers, *acceded to*, or agreed to, could have worked, but it doesn't match up with the rest of the sentence, especially the part where they are making arguments against the students. *Fathomed*, or understood, doesn't work here because the sentence is saying more than that the instructors simply grasped the policy's meaning.

For the second blank, **the teachers are *contending*, or stating, that such students are doing this**, rather than *recommending* this or *contravening*, which means denying the veracity of something.

And for the final blank, **these students with substandard grades are unfairly taking their *acrimony*, or bad feeling, out on the instructors**, rather than their *trepidation*, which means nervousness, or their *seclusion*.

30. Shunning the _____ high school reading list that had failed to engage her students the previous year, the teacher took a new approach, assigning her students just one book to explore for the entire semester: Leo Tolstoy's *War and Peace*.

- [A] unorthodox
- [B] mystifying
- [C] **hackneyed**
- [D] controversial
- [E] **timeworn**
- [F] suggestive

You're looking for a modifier for the high school reading list, and you know the list was used in the previous year and failed to engage students. **Two words that match are *hackneyed* and *timeworn*.** *Unorthodox*, or nonconforming, doesn't have support from the rest of the sentence, nor do *mystifying*, *controversial*, or *suggestive*.

31. If these more conservative projections are correct, the economy, far from hurtling toward recession, is on track for a modest _____.

- [A] improvement
- [B] **downturn**
- [C] detour
- [D] **swoon**
- [E] furrow
- [F] eruption

The key clue here is that you are contrasting a *recession* with a more *modest* _____. **The two terms that fit best are *downturn* and *swoon*, the latter of which, in this context, means fade.**

Improvement might have worked, but there is no equivalent for it; *detour* doesn't work because it indicates too significant a change and doesn't fit with the modifier *modest*; *furrow* means groove or wrinkle—it's unclear how it could apply here and doesn't fit; and finally, modest *eruption* doesn't match well, so this last answer choice can be eliminated as well.

32. Campers are sent home immediately for serious infractions like drug use, sexual misconduct, or violent behavior. On the other hand, counselors tend to take a lax attitude toward _____ wrongdoings like staying up past curfew or playing harmless pranks on other campers.

- [A] indefensible
- [B] **venial**
- [C] sagacious
- [D] irrepressible
- [E] vehement
- [F] **negligible**

The phrase *on the other hand* indicates that you have a contrast, and the contrast is between the *serious infractions* mentioned in the first sentence and something like *minor wrongdoings like staying up past curfew or playing harmless pranks on other campers*. **You can therefore anticipate that what will fill the blank is a synonym for minor, and the two terms that fit are *venial* and *negligible*.**

Per the other information in the statement, these wrongdoings don't seem *indefensible*, they are not *sagacious*, or wise, they are not *irrepressible*, or unrestrained, and they are also not *vehement*.

33. A new study found that 54% of those wrongly convicted of a crime are themselves victims of official _____, either by police, prosecutors, or both.

- [A] diligence
- [B] **wrongdoing**
- [C] intervention
- [D] fascination
- [E] **misconduct**
- [F] impartiality

The structure of the sentence gives away what to expect—*those wrongly convicted of a crime are themselves victims of official _____*. **You need to fill the space with a pair of terms that function similarly to crime, and you get that with *wrongdoing* and *misconduct*.**

It wouldn't make sense to say that these individuals are *victims* of *diligence*, *intervention*, *fascination*, or *impartiality*, so you can eliminate these answer choices.

34. Impressionism originated with a group of Paris-based artists whose independent art exhibitions brought them _____ during the 1870s and 1880s.

[A] **distinction**
[B] infamy
[C] obscurity
[D] **renown**
[E] secrecy
[F] custody

Here, context doesn't clearly define exactly what you need from the right answers; instead, **you also need to use the fact that *distinction* and *renown* match each other to inform you that they are both correct.**

Infamy is being known for bad qualities, and you don't have clues for that or a matching word; *obscurity* is the quality of being unknown, and you don't have clues or a match for that; the same goes for *secrecy* and *custody*.

35. The prevalence of commercial whaling in New England resulted in widespread overfishing by the early 1700s: the right whale population was near extinction in 1935, when international _____ measures for right whales finally came into effect.

[A] **preservation**
[B] acceptance
[C] integration
[D] demand
[E] **conservation**
[F] allocation

The key clues are that there was previously *overfishing* and *near extinction* until ____ measures finally came into effect. Therefore, **these measures would combat overfishing and near extinction, and the two that match are *preservation* and *conservation*.**

It's unclear what international *acceptance* or *integration* measures would mean for right whales. International *demand* and *allocation* measures could perhaps be attractive if considered in certain ways, but they fit awkwardly with the rest of the sentence (*demand* in particular) and don't work nearly as well as the correct choices in terms of aligning with the clues in the text.

36. By 1849, word of the California gold rush had spread; many farmers _____ their fields in favor of seeking their fortunes.

[A] transplanted
[B] **relinquished**
[C] enriched
[D] rotated
[E] shrouded
[F] **abandoned**

Once word of the gold rush spread, **it makes sense that many farmers relinquished or abandoned (i.e., left) their fields in favor of seeking their fortunes.**

The farmers could have *transplanted*, *enriched*, *rotated*, or *shrouded* their fields, but none of these align with the clues given in the sentence, and none have a match in terms of the function played in the sentence.

37. Scientists have known since ancient times that liver tissue has a remarkable ability to _____ itself after incurring damage, but how it does so remains a mystery.

[A] **regenerate**
[B] **renew**
[C] renovate
[D] contract
[E] diverge
[F] recapitulate

Here, the key clue is that it's something that *liver tissue* would have a *remarkable ability* to do after incurring damage, and **the two answers that match best are *regenerate* and *renew*.**

Renovate is somewhat attractive but indicates change, and you don't have a sense that the liver changes after damage; you also don't have any indication that the liver *contracts*, *diverges*, or *recapitulates*, which means repeats, so you can eliminate those choices as well.

38. At the turn of the twentieth century, concern over childhood malnutrition inspired some philanthropic groups to provide _____ lunches to public school students free of charge.

A leftover
B hygienic
C **balanced**
D **healthful**
E elaborate
F bland

Though *balanced* and *healthful* aren't synonyms, they serve the same purpose here and create equivalent sentences; thus, **they are correct**.

It makes little sense that these philanthropic groups would provide *leftover*, *hygienic*, or *bland* lunches to combat malnutrition, and while *elaborate* might appear tempting, it has no obvious match, so all of these choices can be eliminated.

39. Perhaps U.S. Secretary of State Madeleine Albright's greatest diplomatic achievement was her _____ push for NATO military intervention during the 1999 humanitarian crisis in Kosovo.

A abortive
B **effective**
C unexpected
D intractable
E **successful**
F ceremonious

You know you are looking for positive terms because it's her *greatest diplomatic achievement*, and **two that work and match each other well are *effective* and *successful***.

Abortive, *unexpected*, *intractable* (which means hard to manage), and *ceremonious* have little support in the passage and no match among the answer choices.

40. Throughout the late 1950s, television-obsessed viewers were _____ by a series of scandals related to high-stakes quiz shows that had been cleverly rigged by their producers.

A **fascinated**
B shaken
C infuriated
D consoled
E **riveted**
F besieged

Several of the answer choices could work here independently, but in terms of finding a pair that produce sentences alike in meaning, **the two choices that match up are *fascinated* and *riveted***.

Shaken and *infuriated* don't have matches, and *consoled* and *besieged* don't make sense in this context.

41. In 1940, President Roosevelt acknowledged that he would have trouble convincing Americans to go to war: many complacent citizens had simply closed their eyes to the dangers of the European conflict, while others _____ American defense preparations for political reasons.

A supported
B **resisted**
C ignored
D falsified
E **opposed**
F converted

The key clue is that *President Roosevelt acknowledged that he would have trouble convincing Americans to go to war*; based on this information, **it makes sense to say others resisted or opposed American defense preparations**.

Supported doesn't work based on context, *ignored* doesn't have a match, and it's tough to see what could be meant by *falsified* or *converted*.

42. To _____ the widespread dissemination of knowledge and advancement of wisdom, a university must allow for the free expression of ideas.

A apprehend
B sustain
C balance
D foster
E impede
F ascertain

You can assume that a university would want to spread knowledge and wisdom. **Although *sustain* and *foster* are not synonyms, they provide the sentence with roughly the same meaning and are the correct pair.**

In this context, *apprehend* is likely meant to mean understand, which is a decent synonym for *ascertain*; as a pair, they are somewhat attractive but certainly not as strong a fit as the pair of correct choices. It's unclear why knowledge and wisdom would need to be *balanced* or *impeded*, so you can eliminate those choices as well.

43. _____ popular belief, Michelangelo did not paint the Sistine Chapel ceiling lying down: rather, he painted in a standing position, supported by a unique system of platforms that he attached to the walls with brackets.

A In line with
B Counter to
C Pertaining to
D Unencumbered by
E Consistent with
F Contrary to

Here, the terms used to indicate contrast are themselves in question. You know the terms should indicate contrast because of the clues *not* and *rather*.

Based on this, **the correct answers are *counter to* and *contrary to*.**

Per the given clues about contrast, it wouldn't make sense to say is the second part of the sentence is *in line with* or *consistent with* popular belief, and *pertaining to* and *unencumbered by* have no support in the sentence and no match among the answer choices.

44. During the contentious summer debate, Senator Jones appeared _____ and irritated as he addressed his opponent's cutting remarks about his voting record.

A rattled
B amused
C vacuous
D bumptious
E unnerved
F satisfied

You know that the debate was *contentious* and the opponent's remarks were *cutting*; **you're looking for a modifier that combines well with irritated, so *rattled* and *unnerved* fit well here.**

There are no indications in the text that the senator would be *amused*, or *vacuous*, meaning mindless, or *bumptious*, meaning brash, or *satisfied*.

45. America's food deserts are typically found in low-income areas, a situation that dooms locals to struggle against _____ of both money and healthy food choices.

A a surfeit
B a quota
C a paucity
D an array
E a dearth
F an allowance

You are told that *America's food deserts are typically found in low-income areas*, which *dooms locals to struggle against _____ of both money and healthy food choices*. There is a parallel between the first part of the sentence and the last, so you can expect that what fills the blank will indicate a lack of *money and healthy food choices*: **both *a paucity* and *a dearth* do that and are correct.**

The other near-pairs don't fit the context of the sentence. *A surfeit* would mean an overabundance, and *an array* would mean several, which you don't have here. Meanwhile, *a quota* would be an amount set by a rule, and *an allowance* would be a preestablished number, neither of which is indicated by the text.

46. The mayor was willing to consider several innovative proposals for repurposing the site of the _____ amusement park, but he refused to consider reopening the park to the public, citing the prohibitive cost of bringing old attractions up to code.

- [A] **defunct**
- [B] lucrative
- [C] **obsolete**
- [D] nostalgic
- [E] prevailing
- [F] prodigious

You know that the park would need to be reopened, so it makes sense that it is *defunct* or *obsolete*.

If it were *lucrative*, that would mean the cost would not be *prohibitive*, and there isn't a match for the term. One might feel *nostalgic* about the park, but it doesn't make sense to describe the park as *nostalgic*. *Prevailing*, or current, might make a bit of sense but doesn't have a match, and *prodigious*, or large, could also perhaps make sense but doesn't have support or a match.

47. Persistent budget issues _____ the performing arts magnet school's ambitious plans for a four-week musical theater summer camp.

- [A] stimulated
- [B] heartened
- [C] **scotched**
- [D] sublimated
- [E] **scuppered**
- [F] enervated

Persistent budget issues can't be a good thing, and in this case, it makes sense that the school stopped their plans. **Scotched, meaning put an end to, and scuppered, meaning sank, therefore both fit well**.

It wouldn't make sense to say that the budget issues *stimulated* or *heartened* the plans. There are no indications that the plans were *sublimated*, or modified, and there isn't a match for the term. *Enervated*, or weakened, could work here, but it doesn't have a match.

48. Reverend Gibson was hoping to collect $20 for his mission from that evening's prayer meeting, so he was stunned by the congregation's _____ when he discovered five $100 bills in the offering plate.

- [A] indigence
- [B] insouciance
- [C] parsimony
- [D] abstemiousness
- [E] **munificence**
- [F] **liberality**

The reverend was expecting $20 and received $500, so you can anticipate that *he was stunned by the congregation's* generosity. Let's take a look at the answer choices.

Indigence means poverty, and *insouciance* means lack of concern, neither of which works here. *Parsimony*, meaning stinginess or reluctance to spend money, and *abstemiousness*, meaning frugality or self-restraint, might be considered a pair, but they are the opposite of your anticipated meaning.

Munificence is the quality of being generous, as is, in this context, liberality, and they are both correct.

24. Reading Comprehension Practice

Passage 1
3 Questions

Synesthesia is a little understood phenomenon in which stimulation of one sense leads to the involuntary stimulation of another. Synesthetes have been known to see sounds, taste words, and hear smells. One of the most common forms of synesthesia is grapheme-color synesthesia. People with this form of synesthesia see letters and numbers as "tinted" or "shaded" colors. The mental association between character and color appears to be stable and inherent: a synesthete will consistently associate the same grapheme with the same color. Although grapheme-color synesthetes do not universally perceive the same colors in association with the same graphemes, studies with large sample sizes have shown that there are some commonalities among synesthetes' perceptions: a significant number of synesthetes, for example, see the letter "A" as red. Although the neurological causes of synesthesia are unclear, it has been suggested that the condition develops early in life when children are introduced to abstract concepts for the first time. Some researchers believe that grapheme-color synesthesia is a common form of the condition because letters and numbers are the first abstract concepts most children are exposed to in school.

1. According to the passage, which of the following is true of people with grapheme-color synesthesia?

Ⓐ Each letter in the alphabet is tinted a different color.
Ⓑ Most perceive the same colors in conjunction with the same letters.
Ⓒ There is some consistency in their perceptions of specific graphemes.
Ⓓ They gradually lose their grapheme-color synesthesia as they approach adulthood.
Ⓔ Many experience other forms of synesthesia as well.

2. Which of the following statements, if true, would undermine the suggestion being made in the passage about the neurological underpinnings of grapheme-color synesthesia?

Ⓐ Grapheme-color synesthesia affects only 5% of the world's population.
Ⓑ People who learn to read earlier than expected are not more likely to develop grapheme-color synesthesia.
Ⓒ A significant percentage of grapheme-color synesthetes develop their condition after the age of 20.
Ⓓ Grapheme-color synesthesia does not typically present in illiterate patients.
Ⓔ People who have well-developed reading and writing skills are slightly more likely to exhibit grapheme-color synesthesia than people who do not.

3. Choose the sentence that provides empirical evidence for a claim about how grapheme-color synesthesia presents itself in a population.

Passage 2
2 Questions

Among the strangest and most intriguing of all living creatures is the tardigrade, also known as the moss piglet or water bear. This tiny, segmented, eight-legged micro-animal might appear unassuming, but the tardigrade is a paragon of resilience. Tardigrades have survived all five of Earth's mass extinctions, through which they have evolved a wide variety of survival characteristics. Individual tardigrade species are capable of thriving in every habitat on Earth: inside volcanoes, on the tops of mountains, under layers of solid permafrost, and at the bottom of the sea. Tardigrades can even survive in outer space for up to 10 days. They can withstand extreme temperatures and pressures, starvation, dehydration, air deprivation, and even radiation and toxin exposure. The main reason why tardigrades are such excellent survivors is that they are capable of suspending their metabolisms, for years if necessary, when they enter an inhospitable environment. As we look toward a future of climate change, increasing pollution, and species loss, there is much we can learn from the indefatigable tardigrade.

4. According to the passage, which of the following situations could a tardigrade survive? Select all that apply.

A Being inserted into a radioactive environment deep within Earth
B Being exposed to temperatures near absolute zero
C Being isolated from sources of food and hydration for several weeks

5. What is the purpose of the final sentence of the passage?

A To suggest that only tardigrades will survive Earth's next mass extinction event
B To warn that tardigrades are in danger of extinction because of climate change and pollution
C To suggest that humans must learn how to suspend our metabolisms as tardigrades do
D To remind the reader that Earth is facing unprecedented environmental threats
E To propose that tardigrades be studied to determine whether their survival mechanisms could help other species cope with a changing environment

Passage 3
3 Questions

The most iconic structure at Disney World's EPCOT Center is Spaceship Earth, a geodesic sphere inspired by the work of architect and futurist Buckminster Fuller. Spaceship Earth may appear perfectly spherical from a distance, but up close it reveals itself to be a complex polyhedron: each of its faces is divided into three isosceles triangles that come together to form a point. In all, the structure is made up of 11,324 facets. The sphere is comprised of two enormous interior domes. The bottom dome is held in place by six legs anchored deep in the soft Florida soil. The upper dome sits on a steel ring extending around Spaceship Earth's circumference. These domes are covered by cladding, to which the silver facets are attached. One of Spaceship Earth's most formidable foes is rain, which is a common occurrence in South Florida. If its designers hadn't devised a clever drainage

system, Spaceship Earth would shed water in torrents from its curved sides and spring a multitude of hard-to-fix leaks. To prevent this, engineers spaced the facets of Spaceship Earth one inch apart, creating gaps that catch rainwater and channel it into the nearby World Showcase Lagoon.

6. Which of the following best describes the structure of the passage?

A An architectural landmark is identified, and its many engineering defects are enumerated.
B The exterior of a favorite Disney World attraction is contrasted with its interior.
C An attraction is described from a distance and then examined in closer detail.
D A curious structure is described aesthetically and then mathematically.
E The structural integrity of a landmark is called into question, and solutions are offered.

7. Choose the sentence that makes it clear that the exterior faces of Spaceship Earth are not attached directly to the structural domes.

8. The author of the passage suggests that which of the following aspects of Spaceship Earth's environment affected its design? Select all that apply.

A The soft, wet soil of South Florida
B The millions of people who would visit the park each year
C The availability of a human-made lake nearby

Passage 4
3 Questions

Most students know Pythagoras as the mathematician responsible for his eponymous theorem concerning the side lengths of right triangles. However, Pythagoras's contemporaries knew him best for the communal, ascetic religion he founded in the 6th century BCE. One of Pythagoras's most interesting teachings was known as *musica universalis*, or "the music of the spheres." According to this belief, the sun, the moon, and the other planets all move around Earth according to strict ratios that cause them to emit "hums" based on the speeds and lengths of their orbital revolutions. Pythagoras compared the music of the spheres to the different tones that plucked strings create depending upon their lengths. The inaudible music of the spheres was believed to affect all manner of terrestrial things, an idea that may seem far-fetched today but was widely embraced well into the Renaissance.

9. For one to accept the idea of *musical universalis* as it is described in the passage, which of the following belief systems would one also have to accept as true? Select <u>all</u> that apply.

- [A] A geocentric model of the cosmos
- [B] The idea that the universe functions according to a mathematical pattern
- [C] Monotheistic religion

10. Choose the sentence that describes *musica universalis* by comparing it to a more terrestrial phenomenon.

11. The author approaches the concept of *musica universalis* with which of the following?

(A) Engaged curiosity
(B) Frustrated skepticism
(C) Dutiful acceptance
(D) Bittersweet nostalgia
(E) Intense scorn

Passage 5
1 Question

Toxoplasmosis is a disease caused by the parasite *toxoplasma gondii*. This parasite can reproduce only in the Felidae family, but it can infect any warm-blooded animal. Some researchers estimate that up to half of the world's population is infected with toxoplasmosis, but the vast majority of infections are asymptomatic. Young children and those who suffer from compromised immune systems are at greatest risk for severe symptoms, which can include seizures, fever, and loss of muscle coordination.

Pregnant women are encouraged to take steps to avoid infection because infection during pregnancy can cross the placenta and infect the fetus, possibly resulting in birth defects, miscarriage, or stillbirth. *T. gondii* is typically transmitted through improperly prepared food or drink or through contact with the feces of an infected

cat. In recent years, the media have emphasized a potential connection between toxoplasmosis and mental illness by labeling the disease "crazy cat-lady syndrome." Although there is little proof that cat ownership significantly increases the risk of a *T. gondii* infection, there is some evidence that suggests a link between toxoplasmosis and schizophrenia.

12. Which of the following findings, if true, would best strengthen the link between toxoplasmosis and schizophrenia?

(A) A study of patients diagnosed with schizophrenia found that half of such patients tested positive for toxoplasmosis.
(B) The children of mothers treated for symptomatic toxoplasmosis are found to be three times more likely to be diagnosed with schizophrenia than those whose mothers had not been exposed to toxoplasmosis prior to becoming pregnant.
(C) Research concludes that children who experience seizures before the age of 12 are more likely to be diagnosed with schizophrenia later in life than children who do not.
(D) A study of people who live in households with three or more pets find that they are not more likely to be treated for schizophrenia than those without pets.
(E) One of the symptoms of toxoplasmosis is a high fever that can be accompanied by hallucinations or delusions.

Passage 6
3 Questions

On September 1, 1859, English amateur astronomer Richard Carrington saw something through his optical telescope that had never before been observed by human eyes: a solar flare. Solar flares occur when accelerated, charged particles interact with the sun's plasma, tangling and reorganizing magnetic field lines near a sunspot. Such events are often accompanied by a coronal mass ejection (CME), a bubble of radiation and particles that bursts into space at a very high speed. When these particles enter an outer layer of Earth's atmosphere called the ionosphere, they cause the phenomenon *aurora borealis*, or northern lights. In certain situations, solar flares can pose a threat: intense CMEs that are oriented toward Earth can trigger geomagnetic storms that may interfere with radio transmissions, radar signals, and satellites and even disable parts of the terrestrial power grid in extreme cases. Though few people understand the danger of solar flares, the chances of such an event occurring in our lifetimes is not remote. In 2014, scientist Pete Riley estimated that there is a 12% chance that a massive, potentially damaging solar storm may impact Earth in the next 10 years.

13. It can be inferred that no one witnessed a solar flare before 1859 for which of the following reasons?

(A) Few astronomers before the 19th century acknowledged that the sun was at the center of the solar system.
(B) The widespread belief that the sun was completely unchanging discouraged scientists from studying it in detail.
(C) Telescope technology had not yet improved to the point that solar flares were distinguishable to the astronomer.
(D) Solar flares were extremely uncommon throughout the 17th and 18th centuries.
(E) The power grid and communications technology were undeveloped before the 1850s, making it impossible to note the effects of CMEs on Earth.

14. Which of the following, if true, would most seriously weaken the claim made in the passage about the likelihood of a destructive solar flare?

(A) A massive CME oriented toward outer space fails to cause problems with communications or power on Earth.
(B) Engineers are hard at work improving the worldwide terrestrial power grid to better withstand the effects of a CME.
(C) Solar activity waxes and wanes in relatively predictable nine-year cycles.
(D) CMEs have never caused worldwide power and communication disruptions on Earth before.
(E) A new study proves that CMEs powerful enough to disrupt communications and power on Earth occur roughly once every one million years.

15. To interfere with human life on Earth, CMEs must be which of the following? Select all that apply.

[A] Oriented toward Earth
[B] Visible as the aurora borealis
[C] Powerful enough to enter our atmosphere

Passage 7
3 Questions

While nearly everyone who has taken a world history course or visited a museum knows that ancient Egyptians were sometimes mummified, the history of animal mummification in ancient Egypt is less well known. Egyptians began mummifying animals around 1500 BCE. Cats were especially common subjects for mummification because of their exalted status in ancient Egyptian culture, but archaeologists have also found mummified dogs, baboons, cows, lions, birds, even hippopotamuses. While the motivations behind animal mummification remain a mystery, Egyptologists have suggested several hypotheses. Egyptians were animists who believed that their gods could dwell in anything, including animals. Mummified animals may, therefore, have been worshiped by devout Egyptians. Alternately, mummified animals could have been presented to particular gods or goddesses as votive offerings. Other Egyptologists believe that animals were mummified to provide their owners with companionship or a source of nutrition in the afterlife, where Egyptians believed all souls reside after death.

16. With which of the following statements is the author most likely to agree?

(A) Ancient Egyptians had a profound, often religious relationship with animals.
(B) Mummification was performed as a way of keeping the body intact so that it could be physically reanimated.
(C) After 1500 BCE, all cats in ancient Egypt were mummified.
(D) Mummification has been part of ancient Egyptian culture since its beginnings.
(E) Animal mummification is not well understood because Egyptians did not depict it in their art or literature.

17. Select the sentence that makes it clear that Egyptologists are not certain why ancient Egyptians mummified animals.

18. Which of the following situations aligns with a hypothesis mentioned in the passage that Egyptologists have proposed for why ancient Egyptians mummified animals? Select all that apply.

⬜ A A prince is buried with mummified cows and goats to provide him with sustenance as he travels to the afterlife.

⬜ B A little girl is mummified alongside a monkey she kept as a beloved pet.

⬜ C A lion that killed several people is mummified to be sent to the underworld for punishment.

Passage 8
4 Questions

Scientists have long believed that the Black Death, a pandemic that killed an estimated 100 million people in 14th-century Eurasia, was caused by the bubonic plague, a disease spread by the bacterium *Yersinia pestis*. This terrifying infection spread rapidly through the population and killed many of its victims in mere days. First-hand accounts of the Black Death describe symptoms similar to those of the bubonic plague: the emergence of buboes (sores) on the skin, rashes, fever, and vomiting. However, some scientists believe that the Black Death was caused by an agent other than *Y. pestis*. Bubonic plague is spread from rats to fleas; fleas then bite human hosts and infect them with the bacteria. No accounts of the time mention a massive drop in the rat population, an event that would typically precede a bubonic plague infection. In fact, many scientists suspect that parts of Northern Europe would have been too cold for the fleas that spread the plague to survive. What's more, both the speed of infection and the death rates during the Black Death were much higher than those of more recent outbreaks of bubonic plague. Thus, the true origins of the Black Death remain something of a mystery.

19. Which of the following, if true, would most effectively weaken the argument that the Black Death was not caused by *Y. pestis*?

Ⓐ Bubonic plague continues to periodically reappear in contemporary society.

Ⓑ Scientists have found several historical variants of *Y. pestis*, some of which are no longer contagious today.

Ⓒ Manuscripts from medieval Germany describe symptoms of the Black Death that do not match those of modern bubonic plague.

Ⓓ Climatologists discover evidence to suggest that average temperatures in 14th-century Europe were significantly lower than they are there today.

Ⓔ Human remains from a 14th-century mass grave contain signs of bubonic plague infection in recovered DNA.

20. Which of the following best describes the author's attitude toward the hypothesis that the Black Death was caused by an infection other than bubonic plague?

Ⓐ Passionate support
Ⓑ Existential concern
Ⓒ Bitter exasperation
Ⓓ Engaged curiosity
Ⓔ Stubborn closed-mindedness

21. The passage mentions all of the following elements of the Black Plague that distinguish it from typical bubonic plague EXCEPT for what?

Ⓐ The lack of a recorded mass decline in the rodent population

Ⓑ Its proliferation of infection in regions with cold climates

Ⓒ Its extremely high rate of infection

Ⓓ Its quick and near-certain deadliness

Ⓔ The appearance of buboes and rashes on patients' skin

22. Which of the following, if true, would make it difficult for epidemiologists to establish the true cause of the Black Death? Select all that apply.

A Different outbreaks of the same disease can cause patients to experience a different combination of symptoms.
B Accounts of the Black Death from the 14th century likely do not contain entirely reliable scientific information about infection.
C Bodies of Black Death victims are often too poorly preserved to yield useful information about cause of death.

Passage 9
3 Questions

After days of punishing heat, a miracle occurs: clouds amass overhead, and a healing rain falls over the parched earth. Just imagining this scene can call to mind a distinctive scent that most recognize but few can name: the earthy, irresistible petrichor. Petrichor, a combination of two Greek words, *petros* (stone) and *ichor* (the blood of the gods), was coined by two Australian scientists in 1964. According to more recent research, this scent is composed of up to three elements. One is an oil released by plants during dry weather and absorbed by soil and rocks. Another is geosmin, a metabolic by-product of certain bacteria that are found in wet soil. Human beings are incredibly sensitive to geosmin, able to detect it in amounts as small as five parts per trillion. Finally, ozone can contribute to the scent of petrichor, especially if the rainstorm that triggers it includes lightning. In 2015, MIT scientists determined the mechanism by which petrichor is released. When a raindrop hits a porous surface, small air bubbles form that float to the surface and release aerosols that carry the scents that make up petrichor.

23. The passage identifies which of the following as factors contributing to humans' ability to smell petrichor? Select all that apply.

A Periods of dry weather
B Sensitivity to geosmin
C Aerosols that occur during rainfall

24. What is the function of the first sentence of the passage? Select all that apply.

A To draw the reader in with an image that appeals to the senses
B To cause the reader to imagine the scent of petrichor without necessarily having prior knowledge of it
C To suggest that petrichor is something we imagine, not a real sensory experience

25. Which of the following best describes the structure of the passage?

Ⓐ A chemical process is defined, and its potential hazards are identified.
Ⓑ A fantastical scene is presented and then debunked using scientific terms.
Ⓒ A word is defined, and the theories behind its meaning are presented.
Ⓓ Early explanations of a phenomenon are presented and described using modern research.
Ⓔ A familiar phenomenon is described, and the science behind it is explained.

Passage 10
3 Questions

The continuation of moon research and the development of new exploration technologies require moondust, or a suitable simulant, for tests and experiments. Moondust, however, is unique. It is sharp and jagged, it is superfine, it sticks to absolutely everything, and it has the troubling tendency to jam machinery and abrade everything it touches. For these reasons, it poses a threat to lunar missions, not to mention futuristic plans to establish a colony on the moon. Indeed, Apollo 16 Commander John Young once stated that "dust is the number one concern in returning to the moon." Moondust has peculiar qualities that Earth dust lacks because the conditions on the moon are so different from those on Earth: moondust is electrostatically charged because it's constantly being hit by solar wind and cosmic rays, and it is jagged because micrometeoroids are continuously bombarding the lunar soil, causing it to melt, splash, and then refreeze. Scientists are developing simulated moondust using samples from Hawaiian volcanoes, Arizona desert, and Montana prairie, and they hope to refine their simulants even further, developing prototypes that mimic the different dusts found in disparate regions of the moon.

26. Which of the following represent reasons that moondust would make it hard to colonize the moon? Select all that apply.

A It would make it difficult for transport systems to function properly.

B It would cause respiratory problems in organisms who breathe it in.

C It could quickly weather structures left exposed to the elements.

27. Which of the following is the primary purpose of the passage?

Ⓐ To explain why the moon is not a suitable place for human colonization

Ⓑ To indicate why scientists must create simulated moondust for space research

Ⓒ To list the conditions that make moondust such a frustrating material to deal with

Ⓓ To argue that we need to return to the moon immediately to collect more moondust

Ⓔ To explore the different types of moondust that exist in different regions of the moon

28. Which of the following can be inferred from the passage? Select all that apply.

A Montana prairie dust is remarkably similar to moondust.

B Solar wind and cosmic rays are made up of charged particles.

C Commander John Young believed that moon exploration should end.

Passage 11
2 Questions

Recent breakthroughs in medical technology have made it possible for doctors to keep terminally ill and gravely injured people alive longer than ever before. However, these advancements have deepened a long-standing moral quandary: How do we know that such people would even want to be kept alive and, if so, for how long? At what point does keeping an unconscious person alive go against the directive to do no harm? An advance healthcare directive, or living will, is a legal document that allows one to specify what sorts of medical decisions should be made for one in the event of incapacitation or illness. It allows one to detail how they should be treated—or not treated—if they are on life support with no possibility of recovery or if they have entered a coma with little chance of waking. These increasingly common documents are part of a larger movement toward more compassionate and intentional end-of-life care that attempts to empower patients, even when they are unable to speak for themselves.

29. With which of the following statements would the author most likely agree? Select all that apply.

A The feelings and desires of a gravely ill or injured person should always supersede the advice of a doctor.

B The completion of an advance healthcare directive should be mandatory.

C It is incorrect to assume that all critically ill or injured patients want to be kept alive as long as possible.

30. Which of the following, if true, could represent a reason that advance healthcare directives are becoming increasingly common in the United States? Select all that apply.

A Americans have become increasingly health conscious about their diets.

B Studies have revealed that people can feel pain, hear, and think while comatose.

C A majority of Americans now die in a hospital setting.

Passage 12
4 Questions

For a generation accustomed to SUVs and minivans, the aesthetics of American cars of the 1960s might seem very strange indeed. The Big Three automakers' advertising mantra in that decade was "longer, lower, wider." The cars of the day were sleek and sweeping, designed to "look fast standing still," as auto journalists would say. In contrast, modern vehicles announce: "I can crush boulders with ease." The epitome of 1960s car aesthetics was the appropriately dubbed "fastback" body style, characterized by a roofline that descended in a continuous slope to the rear bumper. It was clunky compared to more recent sedans and coupes, but the fastback looked aerodynamic. The Oldsmobile Toronado was the fast-back par excellence: a massive 1960s American vehicle whose dramatic rear roofline was matched by a front hood that seemed to stretch into the next zip code.

The purpose of such styling was to present the illusion of flight, even if the cars of that era still struggled with such basic tasks as turning and braking. In their design, the cars looked as much like jet planes and rocket ships as any conveyance with wheels possibly could, an aesthetic that fit the 1960s obsession with all things aeronautical. The space program was in its heyday during the 1960s, and jet travel had only recently become a possibility for the average American. Oldsmobile even used a NASA spokesperson in its early advertisements for the Toronado. And this aeronautical theme was not restricted to cars: the far-out 1960s "Googie" architectural style could be seen in hamburger stands, drive-in theaters, and motels designed to look as though they could actually fly. Americans of the time desperately wanted to take wing, even if they had never before left Earth.

31. The phrase "crush boulders with ease" in the first paragraph suggests which of the following?

(A) All modern SUVs can handle rugged terrain without difficulty.
(B) Automotive styling continues to suggest that a car may be capable of tremendous feats.
(C) Cars of the 1960s were not made with passenger safety in mind.
(D) Automotive advertising is unusually deceptive.
(E) There is an increasing emphasis on mechanical perfection in the car industry.

32. The author suggests which of the following about American cars of the 1960s? Select all that apply.

[A] They often had major deficiencies in performance.
[B] They tended to have more extreme styling features than contemporary cars do.
[C] Their design was influenced by cultural touchpoints of the time.

33. The phrase "Hamburger stands, drive-in theaters, and motels designed to look as though they could actually fly" in the second paragraph emphasizes which of the following? Select all that apply.

[A] The creativity of 1960s architects
[B] The somewhat absurd nature of the Googie style
[C] The desire among many Americans to establish a colony on another planet

34. Which of the following answers best describes the primary purpose of the passage?

(A) To suggest that we have lost interest in space exploration over the past several decades
(B) To dismiss a particular automotive design as old-fashioned and frivolous
(C) To compare the automotive and architectural implications of a particular design philosophy
(D) To examine the effect of a cultural phenomenon on design
(E) To criticize the 1960s tendency to privilege aesthetics over practicality

Passage 13
3 Questions

From the late 19th to the early 20th centuries, scientists debated the merits of two doctrines that sought to describe the nature of the connections in the nervous system. Anatomists, who studied the morphology of neurons and brains, held that the nervous system was a reticulum: a continuous network of cells. At the time, microscopy allowed anatomists to distinguish individual neuronal cell bodies and branches but was not advanced enough to allow them to discern how exactly these bodies were connected with one another. The adherents of the so-called reticular doctrine argued that it was impossible to explain how electrical signals (a major mode of transmission of neural signals) could be carried throughout the nervous system without direct connections between cells. On the other hand, physiologists, who studied the functions of neurons, theorized that neurons were discrete, separate cells, existing independently but connected functionally with one another at points of near-contact called synapses. They knew that neurons released diffusible chemical signals, which we now call neurotransmitters, and that the signals from one set of cells could influence another set of cells not directly connected to the first. The proponents of the so-called neuron doctrine reasoned that, for the nervous system to be self-regulating, cells needed to be separated so that the strength of their connections could change.

This debate was partially resolved in the 1950s with the advent of electron microscopy, which revealed the presence of narrow spaces between most neuron pairs, now called synaptic clefts. These clefts were clear manifestations of the points of noncontact junctures proposed by the adherents of the neuron doctrine. At the synaptic cleft, one neuron communicates with its partner through the release of chemical neurotransmitters from tiny sacs called vesicles. For a time, it seemed this debate had been put to rest. However, further studies revealed that some neurons are connected to one another directly, membrane to membrane, by protein pores called gap junctions. Experiments on neurons connected by gap junctions revealed that these junctions connect neurons electrically, allowing mutual electrical excitation (or inhibition) between them without the need for an intermediate chemical signal.

35. Which of the following experimental results would most directly support the reticular doctrine?

(A) An experiment using a light microscope finds no evidence of a separation between individual neurons.
(B) A neuron located on one side of the brain is found to excite a neuron located on the other side.
(C) Ions causing electrical excitation are discovered to flow directly between the branches of two neurons.
(D) A previously undiscovered set of neurotransmitters is found to dampen electrical activity in the brain.
(E) Electrical signals that represent a key mode of neural signaling are discovered to flow throughout the nervous system.

36. As discussed in the passage, which of the following pieces of evidence presented the greatest challenge to the reticular doctrine?

(A) The nature of the connections between neurons could not be elucidated at the microscopic level.
(B) Chemical signals from one neuron were found to affect the behavior of other neurons.
(C) Scientists discovered a space between neurons that were in communication with one another.
(D) Scientists knew that electrical signals generally require continuity of the conducting medium for transmission.
(E) Separate neuronal cell bodies were visible by light microscopy.

37. Select the sentence that best supports the neuron doctrine.

Passage 14
2 Questions

Animal behaviors result from a complex interaction between genetic and environmental factors, commonly known as nature and nurture, respectively. Although clearly distinct genetic factors are predetermined and generally fixed, environmental ones are ever-changing; it is impossible to determine for any given action where one ends and the other begins.

The genetic component of an organism's behavior results from the effects that genes have on an organism's development. Genetic programs result in very specific wiring of the neural circuits that drive behavior. Genes also dictate which neurotransmitters and hormones (signaling molecules) an organism's endocrine and nervous systems produce and use and what effects those signaling molecules will have on their receptors, and by extension, their target cells and organs.

An organism's environment, on the other hand, consists of the material in the natural world immediately outside the organism's body. Although the term nurture suggests the primary importance of early childhood experiences, an organism's environment can also include chemicals—both natural and human produced—that may affect an organism's behavior. For example, certain insect repellents make use of chemical signals that induce insects to move away from a treated area. Of course, the environment can also include the influence of other organisms. A male mountain goat is likely to behave differently in the presence of a female mountain goat than it will in the presence of a rival.

But only by looking at both parts simultaneously can one hope to understand the true nature of animal behavior. A change in environment, such as the arrival of a predator, will trigger the secretion of various signaling molecules by one organism (a direct result of the activity of its genes and related proteins) that create chemical signals in the environment that may in turn influence the behavior of other organisms.

38. According to the information in the passage, which of the following would NOT be considered an example of nurture?

Ⓐ A song sung by a mother intended to soothe her child

Ⓑ The production of neurotransmitters that target specific receptors

Ⓒ The presence of a sexually receptive female fish in a tank

Ⓓ Toxic chemicals in a river that affect frog development

Ⓔ A display of violence by an older male gorilla toward a younger one

39. Which of the following statements most closely represents the main argument of the passage?

Ⓐ The genetic and environmental components that factor into animal behavior are clearly separable.

Ⓑ Genetics plays the most important role in establishing neuronal connections in an animal's nervous system.

Ⓒ Genetic and environmental factors exert interdependent influences on animal behavior.

Ⓓ Many different types of external stimuli can influence an organism's behavioral responses.

Ⓔ Chemical signals from both neural/hormonal signaling pathways and the environment play key roles in dictating an animal's responses to external stimuli.

Passage 15
3 Questions

Ever since Charlotte, Emily, and Anne Brontë emerged as a literary troika, their sisterhood has often caused their work to be shortchanged by consideration in the aggregate and blinded critics to their very different styles, temperaments, and legacies.

Charlotte, the eldest of the three sisters, is best known for *Jane Eyre*, her first published novel and a surprise best-seller. Because of its style (a heady blend of Victorian naturalism and gothic romance) and its revolutionary focus on female self-determination, *Jane Eyre* made Charlotte Brontë a household name. Though Charlotte's novels were accessible to a Victorian public accustomed to Dickens and Thackeray, her steadfast attention to her characters' interiority gives her work a decidedly modern feel.

Emily, perhaps the most idiosyncratic of the Brontë sisters, published only one novel in her short life, though its modern reputation may eclipse even that of *Jane Eyre*. *Wuthering Heights* is passionate and stormy—a multigenerational Shakespearean tragedy on the moors. Its eerie intensity and formal innovations continue to surprise and enthrall readers today.

Anne published two novels in her life: *Agnes Grey* and *The Tenant of Wildfell Hall*. The youngest Brontë, and the only sister to have been educated entirely at home by the girls' strict Methodist aunt, Anne wrote novels more mannered than Charlotte's or Emily's: quieter, subtler, and more explicitly moral. These qualities meant that her work was often upstaged by that of her sisters. Had she not been in direct competition with them, her writing would perhaps be better appreciated today.

The Brontë sisters grew up in the same isolated Yorkshire parsonage and had many of the same life experiences and influences, yet their works are remarkably distinctive. A discerning reader would never mistake the writing of one sister for that of another. Spending time with each sister's work is like looking at the same fascinating vista through three very different lenses.

40. With which of the following would the author most likely agree?

(A) The environment in which the Brontë sisters were raised did not impact the style or settings of their work.
(B) Some critical analyses of the Brontë's work have focused on the similarities among the sisters' work.
(C) Emily Brontë was more influenced by the works of Shakespeare than were her sisters.
(D) Female autonomy was a popular emerging theme in Victorian literature.
(E) Though less well critically received, Anne Brontë was a more prolific author than either of her sisters.

41. Which of the following can be inferred from the passage? Select all that apply.

[A] *Jane Eyre*'s most prominent literary influences were the novels of William Thackeray and Charles Dickens.
[B] Emily Brontë's *Wuthering Heights* contains formal innovations that are appreciated by modern readers.
[C] An intense focus on the interior lives of characters is more common in contemporary literature than it was in the fiction of earlier eras.

42. Choose the sentence that connects one of the Brontë sisters' life experiences and her writing style.

Passage 16
3 Questions

That life can be a struggle is more than a cliché. We encounter dissonance in disagreements at work, discord among team members, conflict between mates, and competition among companies. Fortunately, psychology has given us tools for insight into the most frustrating friction of all: the everyday dissonance that occurs within ourselves.

When we simultaneously hold multiple ideas or feelings that conflict, the internal clash can produce emotional or cognitive dissonance. This inner discord can be painful,

thus demanding recognition and resolution. If there is a villain in this clash, it is our ability to creatively justify mutually exclusive ideas. Whether it is conscious or unconscious, this mechanism can allow us to deceive ourselves in an attempt to satisfy incompatible desires. For instance, we might know that smoking is harmful for our health, but we might still justify a social smoking habit by telling ourselves that giving in to the urge every once in a while is acceptable. However, we can overcome this bad mental habit. Properly harnessed, cognitive or emotional dissonance can act as an opportunity to mobilize our best selves, recognize and resolve dilemmas, and better understand our motivations.

43. The passage suggests that when attempting to evaluate human nature, one must recognize which of the following? Select all that apply.

[A] Psychological dissonance can cause people to behave in a self-defeating manner.
[B] People are typically unhappy.
[C] People can tolerate varying levels of psychological dissonance, depending on their mental health.

44. Select the sentence that mentions a positive aspect of cognitive or psychological dissonance.

45. Which of the following is an example of "creatively justify[ing] mutually exclusive ideas?" Select all that apply.

[A] A student needs to complete an assignment by Sunday night but spends all weekend at the beach because it is summer.
[B] A child contemplates stealing candy from the corner store but decides to refrain because it would be morally wrong.
[C] A homeowner needs to save money for a new roof but makes plans to vacation in Europe because he found a great deal on plane tickets.

Passage 17
4 Questions

One of the first American religions began in the upstate New York bedroom of two teenage girls. In 1848, young Maggie and Kate Fox told their parents that they were in contact with a spirit named Mr. Splitfoot. What's more, they provided proof: when they asked Mr. Splitfoot questions, he would respond intelligently by "rapping" on the walls or furniture, wowing the Fox family and, later, sellout crowds all over the Northeast. Thus, the Fox sisters became a phenomenon, and Spiritualism, a religion based loosely on the tenets of Christianity but incorporating a belief in spirit communication, was born. Even when the Fox sisters came out as frauds in 1888 (they produced those rapping sounds by surreptitiously popping their joints against hard surfaces), Spiritualism remained popular for decades. Especially during the Civil War, Spiritualism provided a balm for grieving families who wanted to continue communicating with their lost loved ones from beyond the grave. However, there was another reason for Spiritualism's popularity: its progressive emphasis on women's voices. A religion founded by mischievous teenage girls and practiced by thousands of mostly female spirit mediums was almost predestined to become an outlet for women who were eager to be heard.

46. The passage suggests that the Fox sisters achieved widespread success as mediums for which of the following reasons?

(A) They provided disillusioned Christians with an alternative religious faith.
(B) They were outspoken feminists at a moment when women's suffrage was in vogue.
(C) They convinced audiences that they were in contact with an intelligent spirit.
(D) They were capable of making Mr. Splitfoot appear before audiences on command.
(E) The fact that they were young girls made people trust them more.

47. Select the sentence that connects the popularity of Spiritualism with a historical event.

48. The author suggests that the Fox sisters introduced the world to Mr. Splitfoot to

(A) further their goal of starting a new religion.
(B) help grieving families make contact with deceased loved ones.
(C) play a cruel joke on the people who believed them.
(D) garner attention and praise.
(E) give women more power in American society.

49. The author would likely assert that Spiritualism was a proto-feminist movement for which of the following reasons? Select all that apply.

[A] Early feminists were more likely to be Spiritualists than Christians.
[B] Spiritualism began with the revelations of ordinary teenage girls.
[C] Spiritualism put female spirit mediums in the public eye.

Passage 18
3 Questions

It is unfortunate that James Joyce's *Ulysses*, considered by many to be the most important modernist novel, is remembered today more for its difficulty than for its brilliance and bravery. Though the book is indeed daunting for readers unused to textual density and experimentation, its virtues are manifold. On the surface level, Joyce's novel tells the story of an ordinary man's movements through the city of Dublin on one ordinary day: June 16, 1904, now known as Bloomsday. However, this seemingly mundane story conceals near infinite hidden depth. Each chapter of *Ulysses* is based on an event in Homer's *The Odyssey* and is written in an entirely different mode from the chapters preceding and following it. The novel is densely allusive, and the different styles Joyce uses hearken back to various watershed moments in English literary history. However, it is possible to enjoy and learn from the novel without understanding every obscure reference or being able to follow every sentence. The language of *Ulysses* is the book's true protagonist. It is jubilant, playful, and innovative, more poetry than prose. More than any novel before it, *Ulysses* captures what it feels like to think and exist in the world.

50. The author of the passage regards Joyce's *Ulysses* with which of the following?

(A) Bemusement
(B) Flippancy
(C) Trepidation
(D) Pretension
(E) Veneration

51. With which of the following literary traditions does *Ulysses* engage? Select all that apply.

A Homeric epic
B The English canon
C Stream of consciousness

52. The author implies that which of the following contribute to *Ulysses'* reputation for difficulty? Select all that apply.

A The fact that the book covers the events of just one day
B The book's innovative and unique structure
C The book's dense intertextuality

Passage 19
4 Questions

The terrifying *Nosferatu: A Symphony of Horror* was released by German filmmaker F. W. Murnau in 1922. The film, an unauthorized adaptation of Bram Stoker's *Dracula*, told the suspiciously *Dracula*-esque story of a suspiciously *Dracula*-esque vampire called Count Orlok. Although copyright controversy plagued the film upon its release, E. Elias Merhige's 2000 film *Shadow of the Vampire* imagines a darker secret history for the film. In *Shadow*, Murnau keeps the true origins of his film's lead actor, Max Schreck, a secret from his cast. Schreck only appears on set at night, in character, and in full makeup. As the shoot progresses, other actors realize that Schreck is a real vampire that Murnau discovered in the Czechoslovakian castle where *Nosferatu* was filmed. Although *Shadow of the Vampire* is fictional, it is strangely convincing. The real Schreck was no vampire, but he was an eccentric and mysterious character; his portrayal of a bloodthirsty ghoul remains deeply unsettling, even in our age of guts, gore, and CGI jump scares. Perhaps, it is the spectral quality of old film or the doomed Weimar strangeness of its art direction, but something about *Nosferatu* makes it feel far darker than any film should.

53. The author of the passage repeats the phrase "suspiciously *Dracula*-esque" twice to

(A) suggest that the film was more terrifying than Bram Stoker's novel.
(B) convince readers that F. W. Murnau was incapable of inventing his own stories.
(C) imply that it is unnecessary to see *Nosferatu* if one is familiar with the story of *Dracula*.
(D) emphasize the copyright controversy that plagued *Nosferatu* upon its release.
(E) inject a whimsical tone into an otherwise serious passage.

54. Select the sentence from the passage that compares *Nosferatu* to modern horror films.

55. According to the passage, Merhige's *Shadow of the Vampire* was a

(A) documentary film that outs Max Schreck as a real-life vampire.
(B) film based on real events surrounding the production of *Nosferatu*.
(C) fictional film that capitalizes on the eerie strangeness of *Nosferatu*.
(D) documentary film in which some details are changed for copyright reasons.
(E) fictional film that liberally borrowed from Bram Stoker's *Dracula*.

56. The author would agree that all of the following aspects of *Nosferatu* make it scary EXCEPT the

(A) strange performance of Max Schreck as Count Orlok.
(B) unsettling, abstract quality of its set design.
(C) imperfections of old film stock.
(D) fraught historical context of the film's production.
(E) film's reliance on jump scares to shock the audience.

Passage 20
3 Questions

Lyme disease is a common bacterial infection transmitted by black-legged ticks that causes flu-like symptoms; it is often accompanied by a distinctive "bull's-eye" rash. Most cases of Lyme disease can be cured with a standard course of antibiotics. However, there is another Lyme-related diagnosis that is less robustly supported by mainstream medicine: chronic Lyme. Chronic Lyme patients report vague but debilitating symptoms, such as extreme fatigue, muscle pain, and mental fog. However, chronic Lyme patients do not present any sign of the Lyme infection they blame for their symptoms when tested. Some doctors believe that these patients suffer from an autoimmune disease that may have been triggered by Lyme disease. Others accuse chronic Lyme patients of blatantly manufacturing their symptoms. Many members of the medical community express frustration with chronic Lyme because "Lyme-literate" doctors have begun prescribing long-term intravenous antibiotic therapy to these patients, a therapy that is not just unproven but also dangerous. Doctors worry that chronic Lyme patients are hastening the worldwide rise of antibiotic resistance in an ill-fated attempt to find relief from their mysterious symptoms.

57. According to the passage, Lyme disease and chronic Lyme differ in which of the following ways? Select all that apply.

[A] The duration and severity of symptoms
[B] The efficacy of antibiotics for treatment
[C] The medical community's consensus on it

58. The author regards chronic Lyme patients with

(A) a complete lack of compassion.
(B) outrage that their illness is not being treated more aggressively.
(C) skepticism that their illness has a physical cause.
(D) exasperation at their poor choice of doctors.
(E) concern with the implications of their treatments.

59. According to the passage, which of the following aspects of chronic Lyme makes doctors skeptical of it? Select all that apply.

[A] The lack of a bull's-eye rash on chronic Lyme patients
[B] Its similarity to an autoimmune disorder
[C] The fact that chronic Lyme patients test negative for Lyme infection

Passage 21
4 Questions

We have been investigating the paranormal for centuries, but the forms of our fascination with spirit manifestations have changed over time. Perhaps unsurprisingly, 21st-century ghost hunters use a variety of gadgets and gizmos to attempt to capture proof of paranormal activity. Many of these devices are nothing more than simple video or audio recorders. However, one of the latest technological innovations popular with ghost hunters—the spirit box—is far stranger. The spirit box is essentially a radio scanner that rapidly jumps between frequencies. When ghost hunters believe they are in the presence of a spirit, they ask it questions and then listen to the noise generated by the spirit box, hoping to hear a ghostly answer in the static. Believers allege that spirits can use the sound issuing from the box to speak to us from beyond the grave. Skeptics suggest that ghost hunters are simply hearing what they want to hear. Although it is quite unlikely that the spirit box actually connects seekers with the spirit world, it does demonstrate one of the human mind's most uncanny abilities: the ability to perceive sophisticated patterns in a welter of meaningless noise.

60. The author of the passage regards paranormal investigation with which of the following?

(A) Indignant dismissal
(B) Astonished credulity
(C) Amused skepticism
(D) Intellectual admiration
(E) Exasperated befuddlement

61. Which of the following questions is NOT addressed by the passage? Select all that apply.

[A] What are some of the other gadgets that paranormal investigators use to capture proof of the paranormal?
[B] How do paranormal investigators explain the mechanism a ghost uses to "speak" through the spirit box?
[C] How long have people been investigating the paranormal?

62. Choose the sentence from the passage that demonstrates how ghost hunters use the spirit box during an investigation.

63. Which of the following is most similar to the situation described in the final sentence of the passage?

(A) An archaeologist investigates a site that she is sure will yield a great discovery but is disappointed to find nothing there.
(B) A man reports that he has been abducted by aliens but rescinds his statement after being diagnosed with and treated for paranoid schizophrenia.
(C) A child thinks she sees a monster under her bed but is reassured when her father checks and finds nothing there.
(D) A frightened child in a dark forest repeatedly mistakes the shapes and sounds of the leaves and branches for those of an attacker.
(E) A skeptic debunks a supposed Bigfoot print by pointing out that the foot does not have any ridges or wrinkles in it.

Passage 22
1 Question

Scientists were surprised to find that mice injected with laboratory cultures of *Borrelia burgdorferi*, the bacterium that causes Lyme disease, had different immune system responses than humans infected with the same bacterium as a result of a tick bite. However, when mice were infected with *B. burgdorferi* via tick bite, their immune response was identical to that of humans infected in the same way. Therefore, it is likely that the bacterium in the ticks takes a different form from the laboratory-produced bacterium.

64. Which of the following is an assumption that underlies the argument?

(A) The human immune response to injection with lab cultures of *B. burgdorferi* would be identical to the mouse's immune system response to injection.
(B) No laboratory-cultured bacteria could cause the mouse's immune system to react as it does when infected with *B. burgdorferi* by tick bite.
(C) In other mammals, the immune system responses to *B. burgdorferi* infections both by injection and by tick bite are identical to those in mice.
(D) In the wild, ticks at least occasionally infect mice with Lyme disease.
(E) The way in which the *B. burgdorferi* infection enters the body does not explain the difference in the mouse's immune system response.

Passage 23
1 Question

Most existing decorated artifacts from the early Middle Ages were items designed for church use. However, even those existing decorated artifacts from the early Middle Ages that have no obvious ecclesiastical function are predominantly adorned with Biblical iconography. This evidence suggests that, during this time, artisans were strongly discouraged from decorating objects with secular motifs.

65. Which of the following statements, if true, most weakens the argument above?

(A) Some of the most skillfully decorated objects of the early Middle Ages were artifacts with no apparent church use.
(B) Unlike domestic objects found in castles and private homes, objects stored in churches of the Middle Ages were generally treated with respect by invaders.
(C) Almost all of the existing artifacts of the early Middle Ages that were not decorated by artisans had no obvious ecclesiastical function.
(D) Because monasteries in the early Middle Ages were often centers of education, even manuscripts that covered secular subject matter were typically produced by monks.
(E) Artifacts of the early Middle Ages decorated with religious symbols were as prevalent in private homes as they were in religious sanctuaries.

Passage 24
3 Questions

In 1565, an enormous deposit of solid graphite was found near the English town of Seathwaite in Cumbria, England. The graphite found there was unusually pure and strong—so strong that it could be removed in thin, grippable sticks. Thus, the forerunner of the modern pencil was born. Artists immediately took note of the find; graphite pencils represented an enormous improvement over silverpoint, the antiquated drawing technique that had been the standard for draftsmen since the Middle Ages. Before an Italian couple designed the wood encasement that we recognize in modern pencils, graphite sticks were often wrapped in materials like string or sheepskin for stability and ease of use. There was, however, a more serious catch: graphite immediately became commercially valuable because it was the perfect material with which to cast cannonball molds. The Crown eventually took over the Seathwaite deposit and guarded it closely, even flooding it to prevent theft when not in use. Until 1662, when Italian inventors found a way to reconstitute solid sticks from graphite powder—a far more abundant resource—graphite pencils had to be smuggled and were jealously guarded by their owners. By the end of the 17th century, however, the graphite pencil was an important part of any artist's toolkit.

66. Which of the following represent reasons that pencils did not become common as soon as the Seathwaite graphite deposit was found? Select all that apply.

- [A] Cannonballs are made of graphite, so the English government took over the mines.
- [B] It took years for inventors to discover how to turn graphite powder into sticks.
- [C] Pencils were relatively inconvenient for artists to use before wood was added to their exteriors.

67. The passage suggests which of the following about the Seathwaite graphite deposit?

- (A) It remains the only source of solid graphite in the world.
- (B) It is no longer in use because the British Crown flooded it after mining it.
- (C) It is now considered inferior to graphite deposits found in Italy.
- (D) The unique properties of its graphite inspired artists to imagine a tool similar to the modern pencil.
- (E) Its graphite powder was far more useful to artists than the sticks that were originally quarried from it.

68. Select the sentence that describes a forerunner of the graphite pencil.

Passage 25
2 Questions

Safe-cracking is the process of opening a safe without a combination or key. The safe-cracking method seen most often in movies is lock manipulation, which involves determining how to open a safe without damaging it. Lock manipulation requires little special equipment and can be done in silence, which can help a safe-cracker evade capture. However, it can be time-consuming and requires a great deal of skill and practice to master. To manipulate a combination lock, safe-crackers carefully turn it while listening or feeling for tiny imperfections within the mechanism, imperfections that can help determine the combination number by number. Safe owners make this process easier when they fail to change their safe's combination from the easily guessable factory preset, or "try-out combination."

Safe manufacturers and safe-crackers are always attempting to stay one step ahead of each other. For instance, some safe-crackers may take an X-ray of a lock to determine its code, but one lock manufacturer has added a lead shield around their locks to inhibit this strategy. Of course, brute force methods are also available to safe-crackers if they can drill, torch, or detonate explosives near a safe without attracting the attention of the police. However, only the most daring criminal would have the nerve to undertake such a risky maneuver.

69. Which of the following is a reason a safe-cracker might rely on lock manipulation rather than brute force methods? Select all that apply.

[A] A safe must sometimes be cracked when people are within earshot.

[B] A safe-cracker cannot always bring equipment to a job without inviting suspicion.

[C] A safe-cracker does not always know what to expect when confronting a new safe.

70. Select the sentence that provides an example of an action safe-makers could take to evade a particular safe-cracking technique.

Passage 26
3 Questions

The most popular of the recently promulgated mini-fasting regimens involves limiting food intake to an eight-hour period each day. Dieters skip breakfast and eat their first meal at mid-day. They can continue eating nutritious meals and snacks during the daytime hours, but after a relatively early dinner, they must fast throughout the night. Nutritionists who champion mini-fasting say that such a regimen improves sleep, helps the body regulate glucose, and can even stave off chronic diseases such as cancer and heart disease. Dieters like the plan because it doesn't leave them feeling deprived of the food they enjoy. Skeptics, on the other hand, point out that much of the research on the benefits of intermittent fasting has been performed only on animal populations or on human subjects who were monitored for only a short time. Others suggest that, although there may be some benefits to the regimen, weight loss is not among those best supported by science.

71. Choose the sentence that best captures a reason for why mini-fasting might be easier to stick with than other diet plans.

72. Mini-fasting challenges which of the following pieces of conventional wisdom about nutrition? Select all that apply.

[A] One's diet has a tremendous effect on one's susceptibility to chronic disease.

[B] Eating a healthy breakfast immediately upon waking is essential for good health.

[C] Losing weight is purely a matter of ingesting fewer calories.

73. Which of the following people would be the *least* likely to find mini-fasting helpful?

(A) A woman in her 50s who has been warned by her doctor that she is prediabetic

(B) A young man whose job requires him to work irregular hours with few breaks

(C) A man who resists dieting because he does not want to give up his favorite foods

(D) A woman whose struggles with insomnia affect her work performance and mood

(E) A young woman at a healthy weight who wants to live a long and healthy life

---

Passage 27
3 Questions

Agatha Christie is known the world over as the most successful mystery writer of all time. However, many of her fans do not realize that she was once involved in a highly publicized mystery of her own. Christie had been married to her husband, Archie, for more than 10 years when, in 1926, he asked her for a divorce after falling in love with another woman. On December 3 of that year, after quarreling with Archie—who then left home to spend the weekend with his mistress—Christie disappeared from her home, leaving behind a short note mentioning that she was headed for Yorkshire. Ominously, her car, which contained a suitcase full of clothes and an expired driver's license, was later found abandoned at a rock quarry 15 miles away. Christie's disappearance caused a national outcry. Manhunts involving thousands of police officers and troupes of concerned citizens ensued. Christie was not found until December 14, when she turned up in a Yorkshire hotel registered under an assumed name. Doctors called to the scene announced that Christie had been suffering from amnesia and had no idea how she came to be staying at the hotel. Skeptics suggested that she must have been attempting to frame her husband for murder or was engaged in an elaborate and poorly conceived publicity stunt. The world will likely never know precisely what happened to Christie: her posthumous 1977 autobiography mentions nothing of the affair.

74. Which of the following is the best example of irony in the passage?

(A) Christie was a famous mystery novelist, but she felt it necessary to stage a publicity stunt to increase her readership.
(B) Christie left a note saying she was going to Yorkshire and ended up in a Yorkshire hotel.
(C) Christie is famous for her 1926 disappearance but fails to mention it in her autobiography.
(D) Christie's husband left home to see his mistress, but Christie herself stayed away from home far longer than he did.
(E) Christie was a world famous writer of mystery novels, but the mystery of her disappearance was never solved.

75. Choose the sentence that provides the best evidence that Christie's disappearance spurred many ordinary Britons to action.

76. It can be inferred that Christie's diagnosis of amnesia may have been which of the following? Select all that apply.

[A] A cover story meant to account for her disappearance
[B] A false diagnosis based on symptoms that Christie, who would have known about amnesia from her work, reported to doctors
[C] The true reason that Christie went missing for as long as she did

Passage 28
2 Questions

There is no better illustration of the notion that Victorian England was the historical epicenter of sentimentalism than the elaborate national mourning surrounding the death of Queen Victoria's Prince Consort Albert in 1861. Prince Albert was underappreciated in the British Empire during his lifetime because of his German ancestry and lack of personal magnetism. However, he was the power behind Queen Victoria's throne, lending his judgment and expertise to foreign and domestic affairs alike. Queen Victoria loved him to the point of obsession. When Prince Albert passed away at the age of 42, the Queen sank into a deep depression. Elaborate mourning rituals with strict rules concerning etiquette, home décor, and dress were already an integral part of Victorian culture, but Queen Victoria pushed those practices to an extreme when she determined to remain in deep mourning for the rest of her life, isolate herself from all but her most trusted advisors, and cancel all public appearances for several years. For a time, the British Empire followed suit: the British public realized how they had taken the dynamic and wise Prince Albert for granted and sank into mourning alongside the Queen. Sales of jet jewelry, black crepe dresses, and black-edged stationery skyrocketed in the years following Prince Albert's demise.

77. The passage implies that which of the following are aspects of Victorian sentimentalism? Select all that apply.

[A] The elaborate ritualization of emotions
[B] A willingness to mourn publicly for someone one does not personally know
[C] A lack of regard for people who do not hail from one's country of origin

78. Which of the following likely contributed to the public outpouring of grief for Prince Albert?

(A) His illustrious German ancestry
(B) Queen Victoria's strict adherence to etiquette and form
(C) Britain's widespread influence on the world stage
(D) A sense that the Prince was underappreciated during his life
(E) The softening effect the Prince had on the Queen's stern public image

Passage 29
3 Questions

Tornadoes have been known to occur on every continent, but these terrifying phenomena are most numerous and violent in the Great Plains of the United States because of a perfect confluence of climatic and geographic factors. This confluence has earned the swath of North America that extends from Central Texas to Saskatchewan and from the Rockies to the Appalachians the moniker "Tornado Alley." Tornadoes are most common during the spring, but they can occur at any time of year. To form tornadoes, air masses that differ widely from one another in humidity and temperature must meet explosively. South of Tornado Alley, the Gulf of Mexico provides abundant warm, humid air ripe for low-level moisture to the Great Plains. To the north, as frigid air moves south from the Arctic, the Rockies filter out moisture and bend the cold airstream downward, shooting a strong band of dry, chilly air toward the center of the continent. In this way, the unique topography of the United States fuels unusually strong and long-lived storm systems in Tornado Alley that are sometimes perfect for cyclonic development.

79. For a tornadic storm to develop, which of the following is a circumstantial requirement? Select all that apply.

A The storm must occur during the spring months.
B The storm must be located over the center of the country.
C A cold, dry air mass and a warm, wet air mass must meet.

80. It can be inferred that tornadoes are the most common and most deadly in Tornado Alley for all of the following reasons EXCEPT

A the Rocky Mountains filter moisture out of cold air from the Arctic.
B North America is located roughly halfway between the North Pole and the Equator, so is subject to both cold and hot air masses.
C the Great Plains is flat and sparsely populated, so people can see severe thunderstorms from far away.
D there is a source of abundant tropical moisture available to the Great Plains from the south.
E thunderstorms in general are extremely common in the Great Plains.

81. Select the sentence that identifies the geographic location of Tornado Alley.

Passage 30
2 Questions

Daylight Saving Time has been legally sanctioned in the United States since 1918. However, vast swaths of the world, including all of Africa and Asia, do not observe it. The practice makes little sense near the equator, where sunrise and sunset times vary little throughout the year, or near the poles, where working hours will often be wildly out of sync with sunlight hours, no matter what manipulations one makes to the clock. In the travel and transport industries, Daylight Saving Time can cause major complications in scheduling and logistics. The agricultural sector also opposes the practice because it increases the amount of time farm workers must spend working each day in the summer. However, Daylight Saving Time does have benefits. Proponents suggest that it allows people to spend more time enjoying the outdoors after work in the summer. The retail and entertainment industries love it because it gives people more leisure time to spend money at the movies or mall. Daylight Saving Time can also decrease energy costs by reducing the need for artificial light in the evenings.

82. Which of the following people would be most likely to have a favorable opinion of Daylight Saving Time?

A An employee of an airline who handles logistics
B An African executive who must teleconference with clients all over the United States and Europe
C A nurse in Brazil who works highly unpredictable hours
D The CEO of an American theme park that features many water rides
E An Inuit ice fisherman who lives near the Arctic Circle

83. What is the purpose of the passage?

A To argue that Daylight Saving Time is more trouble than it's worth
B To discuss the controversies that surround Daylight Saving Time
C To outline the history of seasonal clock manipulation
D To suggest that a seemingly simple cultural practice is actually very complex
E To explain why countries with temperate climates are more likely to observe Daylight Saving Time

Solutions

Passage 1
3 Questions

Synesthesia is a little understood phenomenon in which stimulation of one sense leads to the involuntary stimulation of another. Synesthetes have been known to see sounds, taste words, and hear smells. One of the most common forms of synesthesia is grapheme-color synesthesia. People with this form of synesthesia see letters and numbers as "tinted" or "shaded" colors. The mental association between character and color appears to be stable and inherent: a synesthete will consistently associate the same grapheme with the same color. Although grapheme-color synesthetes do not universally perceive the same colors in association with the same graphemes, studies with large sample sizes have shown that there are some commonalities among synesthetes' perceptions: a significant number of synesthetes, for example, see the letter "A" as red. Although the neurological causes of synesthesia are unclear, it has been suggested that the condition develops early in life when children are introduced to abstract concepts for the first time. Some researchers believe that grapheme-color synesthesia is a common form of the condition because letters and numbers are the first abstract concepts most children are exposed to in school.

Why did the author write this passage?

The author wrote this passage to describe synesthesia and to explain grapheme-color synesthesia; she details what individuals with grapheme-color synesthesia experience, identifies some commonalities among those who experience it, and suggests some potential correlations in its development in children.

1. According to the passage, which of the following is true of people with grapheme-color synesthesia?

(A) Each letter in the alphabet is tinted a different color.
(B) Most perceive the same colors in conjunction with the same letters.
(C) **There is some consistency in their perceptions of specific graphemes.**

(D) They gradually lose their grapheme-color synesthesia as they approach adulthood.
(E) Many experience other forms of synesthesia as well.

You are asked to find an answer that is true, according to the passage, for those with grapheme-color synesthesia. Let's take a look at the answer choices.

(A) is tempting, but it doesn't actually state in the passage that people with grapheme-color synesthesia see each letter of the alphabet tinted a different color. It's probably wrong, but let's not eliminate it for now.

(B) is too strong an inference, going well beyond what is stated, so it can be quickly eliminated—we don't know that most perceive the same colors with the same letters.

(C) requires far less from you for proof than (B): *some consistency* requires any degree of commonality, whereas (B) requires that the majority of grapheme-color synesthetes share a common experience.

Moreover, the text does provide you with the proof you need for (C) in the line, *a significant number of synesthetes, for example, see the letter "A" as red*, which shows that, indeed, there is some consistency in their perceptions of the colors of specific graphemes. (C) is likely the correct answer, but let's move on.

You have no indication that (D) is true, so you can eliminate it, and nothing in the text hints at (E) either, so you can eliminate it as well.

Going back to (A) and turning to the text to confirm one more time, you can see that there is no mention of each specific letter having a specific tint, so (A) is incorrect, and **(C) is the correct answer**.

2. Which of the following statements, if true, would undermine the suggestion being made in the passage about the neurological underpinnings of grapheme-color synesthesia?

(A) Grapheme-color synesthesia affects only 5% of the world's population.

(B) People who learn to read earlier than expected are not more likely to develop grapheme-color synesthesia.

(C) **A significant percentage of grapheme-color synesthetes develop their condition after the age of 20.**

(D) Grapheme-color synesthesia does not typically present in illiterate patients.

(E) People who have well-developed reading and writing skills are slightly more likely to exhibit grapheme-color synesthesia than people who do not.

You're asked to find an answer that would weaken the *suggestion being made… about the potential neurological underpinnings of grapheme-color synesthesia.* The part of the passage most relevant to this question is the final section:

Although the neurological causes of synesthesia are unclear, it has been suggested that the condition develops early in life when children are introduced to abstract concepts for the first time. Some researchers believe that grapheme-color synesthesia is a common form of the condition because letters and numbers are the first abstract concepts most children are exposed to in school.

Let's evaluate which of the answer choices would do the most to weaken this proposition.

With (A), the fact that grapheme-color synesthesia affects only 5% of the population has no impact on the claim made about how the synesthesia might come about, so you can quickly eliminate (A).

For (B), it's unclear why, in relation to the author's claim, those who read earlier than normal ought to be more likely to develop grapheme-color synesthesia, and it's tough to see how this could weaken the author's suggestion, so you can eliminate this answer choice as well.

If (C) is true, then the claim that the synesthesia develops as children first learn letters and colors as abstract concepts certainly would be significantly weakened, so (C) is very likely the correct answer. Let's leave it for now and keep looking.

Illiterate is not exactly the same as not knowing letters, and more importantly, it's tough to see how (D) could

weaken the author's suggestion, so you can quickly eliminate (D) as well.

Finally, again, it's difficult to see how (E) can be used to weaken the author's claim, so you can quickly eliminate (E) as well.

(C) is the only attractive answer, and it certainly makes sense why it could undermine the author's suggestion. **(C) is correct**.

3. Choose the sentence that provides empirical evidence for a claim about how grapheme-color synesthesia presents itself in a population.

Although grapheme-color synesthetes do not universally perceive the same colors in association with the same graphemes, studies with large sample sizes have shown that there are some commonalities among synesthetes' perceptions: a significant number of synesthetes, for example, see the letter "A" as red.

You are asked to find the sentence that provides *empirical*, or specific, evidence about how grapheme-color synesthesia presents itself *in a population*.

The sentence highlighted above specifically mentions the observed characteristics of the population at large and is thus the correct answer.

Passage 2
2 Questions

Among the strangest and most intriguing of all living creatures is the tardigrade, also known as the moss piglet or water bear. This tiny, segmented, eight-legged micro-animal might appear unassuming, but the tardigrade is a paragon of resilience. Tardigrades have survived all five of Earth's mass extinctions, through which they have evolved a wide variety of survival characteristics. Individual tardigrade species are capable of thriving in every habitat on Earth: inside volcanoes, on the tops of mountains, under layers of solid permafrost, and at the bottom of the sea. Tardigrades can even survive in outer space for up to 10 days. They can withstand extreme temperatures and pressures, starvation, dehydration, air deprivation, and even radiation and toxin exposure. The main reason why tardigrades are such excellent survivors is that they are capable of suspending their metabolisms, for years if necessary, when they enter an inhospitable environment. As we look toward a future of climate change, increasing pollution, and species loss, there is much we can learn from the indefatigable tardigrade.

Why did the author write this passage?

The author wrote this passage to share an intriguing characteristic about tardigrades: their remarkable resilience. He gives examples that illustrate just how resilient the tardigrade is before discussing the main reason for their ability to survive. Finally, he concludes that there is much we can learn from tardigrades.

4. According to the passage, which of the following situations could a tardigrade survive? Select <u>all</u> that apply.

A. **Being inserted into a radioactive environment deep within Earth**

B. **Being exposed to temperatures near absolute zero**

C. **Being isolated from sources of food and hydration for several weeks**

You are asked to identify situations a tardigrade could survive, and you are told to select all answers that apply. Let's evaluate each answer to see which ones have textual support.

For [A], you are told in the passage that tardigrades can survive radiation and that they can survive every habitat on Earth; therefore, **[A] presents a situation tardigrades can survive, and you can select it**.

For [B], because you are told that tardigrades can survive in extreme temperatures, outer space, and under solid permafrost, you have enough support to say that they can survive being exposed to temperatures near absolute zero, so **you can select [B] as well**.

Finally, for [C], because tardigrades can suspend their metabolism for years, if necessary, they can certainly survive being isolated from sources of food and hydration for several weeks, so **you can select [C] as well**.

5. What is the purpose of the final sentence of the passage?

A. To suggest that only tardigrades will survive Earth's next mass extinction event

B. To warn that tardigrades are in danger of extinction because of climate change and pollution

C. To suggest that humans must learn how to suspend our metabolisms as tardigrades do

D. To remind the reader that Earth is facing unprecedented environmental threats

E. **To propose that tardigrades be studied to determine whether their survival mechanisms could help other species cope with a changing environment**

After spending the passage discussing the amazing characteristics of the tardigrade, in the final sentence, the author proposes that there is much we can learn from it. Let's see which of the answer choices best captures the intention of this final sentence.

For (A), there is no indication the author believes that only tardigrades will survive the next mass extinction, so you can quickly eliminate this choice.

For (B), the author doesn't think tardigrades are in danger of extinction and isn't trying to warn us, so you can eliminate this choice as well.

(C) is too specific, and the author isn't stating that humans need to be able to suspend our metabolisms, so you can eliminate this choice.

(D) somewhat matches the first part of the final sentence, but it doesn't align with the passage as a whole or with the second part of the final sentence. Hence, you can eliminate it.

(E) does a great job of representing the purpose of the sentence as a whole: it discusses the broader context of our changing environment and the author's point that tardigrades ought to be studied. **(E) is the correct answer**.

Passage 3
3 Questions

The most iconic structure at Disney World's EPCOT Center is Spaceship Earth, a geodesic sphere inspired by the work of architect and futurist Buckminster Fuller. Spaceship Earth may appear perfectly spherical from a distance, but up close it reveals itself to be a complex polyhedron: each of its faces is divided into three isosceles triangles that come together to form a point. In all, the structure is made up of 11,324 facets. The sphere is comprised of two enormous interior domes. The bottom dome is held in place by six legs anchored deep in the soft Florida soil. The upper dome sits on a steel ring extending around Spaceship Earth's circumference. These domes are covered by cladding, to which the silver facets are attached. One of Spaceship Earth's most formidable foes is rain, which is a common occurrence in South Florida. If its designers hadn't devised a clever drainage system, Spaceship Earth would shed water in torrents from its curved sides and spring a multitude of hard-to-fix leaks. To prevent this, engineers spaced the facets of Spaceship Earth one inch apart, creating gaps that catch rainwater and channel it into the nearby World Showcase Lagoon.

Why did the author write this passage?

The author wrote this passage to describe the intricacies of the design of Spaceship Earth at EPCOT Center.

6. Which of the following best describes the structure of the passage?

(A) An architectural landmark is identified, and its many engineering defects are enumerated.
(B) The exterior of a favorite Disney World attraction is contrasted with its interior.
(C) **An attraction is described from a distance and then examined in closer detail.**
(D) A curious structure is described aesthetically and then mathematically.
(E) The structural integrity of a landmark is called into question, and solutions are offered.

Several of these answer choices are attractive and similar to one another. You need to carefully weed them out one at a time until only the best answer remains.

Answer choice (B) is attractive because parts of the exterior and interior are discussed, but the passage is not structured to contrast the exterior and interior of the attraction.

(D) and (E) are fairly obviously incorrect—the passage is not set up to describe the structure aesthetically then

mathematically, and there aren't questions presented and solutions offered.

Down to (A) and (C). The passage is more about describing Spaceship Earth in detail and less about enumerating engineering defects. Furthermore, it's much easier to claim that Spaceship Earth is an attraction as opposed to an architectural landmark, so (C) is the stronger answer. **(C) is correct.**

7. Choose the sentence that makes it clear that the exterior faces of Spaceship Earth are not attached directly to the structural domes.

These domes are covered by cladding, to which the silver facets are attached.

You know that the exterior faces are made up of 11,324 facets. The above sentence tells you that the domes are covered by cladding; therefore, the exterior faces do not attach directly to the domes.

8. The author of the passage suggests that which of the following aspects of Spaceship Earth's environment affected its design? Select all that apply.

[A] **The soft, wet soil of South Florida**
[B] The millions of people who would visit the park each year
[C] **The availability of a human-made lake nearby**

You are told that the *bottom dome is held in place by six legs anchored deep in the soft Florida soil*, so **you know that [A] affected its design.**

[B] is tempting because it makes sense that an attraction would be designed with its visitors in mind, but there is nothing in the passage itself that suggests that the anticipated number of visitors impacted the design of Spaceship Earth. You can therefore eliminate [B].

Finally, while you might quickly consider dismissing [C], you are told that *engineers spaced the facets of Spaceship Earth one inch apart, creating gaps that catch rainwater and channel it into nearby World Showcase Lagoon.* The Lagoon can be considered a human-made lake, and because it impacted the design of Spaceship Earth, **you should select [C] as well.**

Passage 4
3 Questions

Most students know Pythagoras as the mathematician responsible for his eponymous theorem concerning the side lengths of right triangles. However, Pythagoras's contemporaries knew him best for the communal, ascetic religion he founded in the 6th century BCE. One of Pythagoras's most interesting teachings was known as *musica universalis*, or "the music of the spheres." According to this belief, the sun, the moon, and the other planets all move around Earth according to strict ratios that cause them to emit "hums" based on the speeds and lengths of their orbital revolutions. Pythagoras compared the music of the spheres to the different tones that plucked strings create depending upon their lengths. The inaudible music of the spheres was believed to affect all manner of terrestrial things, an idea that may seem far-fetched today but was widely embraced well into the Renaissance.

Why did the author write this passage?

The author wrote the passage to discuss the religion founded by Pythagoras, highlighting the fact that it was what Pythagoras was best known for in his time and detailing one of its most interesting teachings: the music of the spheres.

9. For one to accept the idea of *musical universalis* as it is described in the passage, which of the following belief systems would one also have to accept as true? Select all that apply.

☒ **A geocentric model of the cosmos**
☒ **The idea that the universe functions according to a mathematical pattern**
☐ Monotheistic religion

You get key details about the idea from the following sentence: *According to this belief, the sun, the moon, and the other planets all move around Earth according to strict ratios that cause them to emit "hums" based on the speeds and lengths of their orbital revolutions.*

From this sentence, **you can see that in order to believe in this concept, one must believe in both answer choices [A] and [B]**: [A] because you are told that *the sun, moon and other planets move around Earth* and [B]

because you are told they do so according to *strict ratios*.

There is no mention of a requirement for monotheistic religion (a religion that proscribes a belief in a single god), so you can eliminate [C].

10. Choose the sentence that describes *musica universalis* by comparing it to a more terrestrial phenomenon.

Pythagoras compared the music of the spheres to the different tones plucked strings create depending upon their lengths.

Plucking strings of different lengths in order to create different tones is something that we would do on Earth, so this sentence is one where *musica universalis*, or the music of the spheres, is described by comparing it to a more terrestrial phenomenon.

The sentence that follows is somewhat tempting in large part because it includes the term *terrestrial*, but it doesn't function by *comparing musica universalis* to an earthly phenomenon and is, therefore, not correct.

11. The author approaches the concept of *musica universalis* with which of the following?

Ⓐ **Engaged curiosity**
Ⓑ Frustrated skepticism
Ⓒ Dutiful acceptance
Ⓓ Bittersweet nostalgia
Ⓔ Intense scorn

The author is both engaged with the topic and curious about it; (A) represents his mindset well.

There is little hint that the author is frustrated or that he is approaching the topic with *skepticism*, so you can eliminate (B).

With (C), the author does not appear to believe in the concept of *musica universalis*, and there is no apparent duty for him to show *acceptance*, so you can eliminate this answer choice as well.

There is no hint the author feels *nostalgic* for the music of the spheres, so you can eliminate (D). Similarly, the author doesn't feel scorn, and certainly not *intense scorn*, for the topic, so you can eliminate (E) as well.

(A) is the only attractive choice remaining, and **(A) is correct**.

Passage 5
1 Question

Toxoplasmosis is a disease caused by the parasite *toxoplasma gondii*. This parasite can reproduce only in the Felidae family, but it can infect any warm-blooded animal. Some researchers estimate that up to half of the world's population is infected with toxoplasmosis, but the vast majority of infections are asymptomatic. Young children and those who suffer from compromised immune systems are at greatest risk for severe symptoms, which can include seizures, fever, and loss of muscle coordination.

Pregnant women are encouraged to take steps to avoid infection because infection during pregnancy can cross the placenta and infect the fetus, possibly resulting in birth defects, miscarriage, or stillbirth. *T. gondii* is typically transmitted through improperly prepared food or drink or through contact with the feces of an infected cat. In recent years, the media have emphasized a potential connection between toxoplasmosis and mental illness by labeling the disease "crazy cat-lady syndrome." Although there is little proof that cat ownership significantly increases the risk of a *T. gondii* infection, there is some evidence that suggests a link between toxoplasmosis and schizophrenia.

12. Which of the following findings, if true, would best strengthen the link between toxoplasmosis and schizophrenia?

Ⓐ A study of patients diagnosed with schizophrenia found that half of such patients tested positive for toxoplasmosis.

Ⓑ **The children of mothers treated for symptomatic toxoplasmosis are found to be three times more likely to be diagnosed with schizophrenia than those whose mothers had not been exposed to toxoplasmosis prior to becoming pregnant.**

Ⓒ Research concludes that children who experience seizures before the age of 12 are more likely to be diagnosed with schizophrenia later in life than children who do not.

Ⓓ A study of people who live in households with three or more pets find that they are not more likely to be treated for schizophrenia than those without pets.

Ⓔ One of the symptoms of toxoplasmosis is a high fever that can be accompanied by hallucinations or delusions.

You are asked to select an answer that would most strengthen the connection between toxoplasmosis and schizophrenia. Let's take a look at the answer choices.

(A) might sound attractive at first, but because you are told in the passage that half of the general population tests positive for toxoplasmosis, this doesn't provide any support that testing positive for toxoplasmosis makes one more likely to be diagnosed with schizophrenia. You can eliminate this choice.

(B) If this answer choice is true, it shows a strong correlation between toxoplasmosis and schizophrenia. (B) is likely the correct answer. Let's leave it for now.

Neither (C), (D), nor (E) help link schizophrenia with toxoplasmosis, so you can eliminate them.

Returning to **(B), if this is true, it strengthens the connection between toxoplasmosis and schizophrenia and, therefore, is the correct answer.**

Passage 6
3 Questions

On September 1, 1859, English amateur astronomer Richard Carrington saw something through his optical telescope that had never before been observed by human eyes: a solar flare. Solar flares occur when accelerated, charged particles interact with the sun's plasma, tangling and reorganizing magnetic field lines near a sunspot. Such events are often accompanied by a coronal mass ejection (CME), a bubble of radiation and particles that bursts into space at a very high speed. When these particles enter an outer layer of Earth's atmosphere called the ionosphere, they cause the phenomenon *aurora borealis*, or northern lights. In certain situations, solar flares can pose a threat: intense CMEs that are oriented toward Earth can trigger geomagnetic storms that may interfere with radio transmissions, radar signals, and satellites and even disable parts of the terrestrial power grid in extreme cases. Though few people understand the danger of solar flares, the chances of such an event occurring in our lifetimes is not remote. In 2014, scientist Pete Riley estimated that there is a 12% chance that a massive, potentially damaging solar storm may impact Earth in the next 10 years.

Why did the author write this passage?

The author wrote this passage to discuss solar flares. She starts off with a general introduction to the topic and then talks specifically about the types of solar flares that cause geomagnetic storms which can in turn pose a threat to us on Earth and the likelihood of such storms.

13. It can be inferred that no one witnessed a solar flare before 1859 for which of the following reasons?

Ⓐ Few astronomers before the 19th century acknowledged that the sun was at the center of the solar system.

Ⓑ The widespread belief that the sun was completely unchanging discouraged scientists from studying it in detail.

Ⓒ **Telescope technology had not yet improved to the point that solar flares were distinguishable to the astronomer.**

Ⓓ Solar flares were extremely uncommon throughout the 17th and 18th centuries.

Ⓔ The power grid and communications technology were undeveloped before the 1850s, making it impossible to note the effects of CMEs on Earth.

At the beginning of the passage, you're told that Richard Carrington was the first person to observe a solar flare in 1859. You know from the rest of the text that solar flares are events that do occur periodically, so let's see which of the answer choices best addresses why he was the first human to see one with his own eyes.

Whether or not astronomers acknowledge that the sun is the center of the solar system has no bearing on whether one can or cannot see a solar flare, so you can quickly eliminate (A).

There is no information presented in the text that indicates that there was widespread belief that the sun was

completely unchanging or that scientists were discouraged from studying it in detail, nor is there any indication given that such a belief or such discouragement would have prevented people from seeing solar flares, so you can eliminate (B) as well.

(C) makes great sense. Though there is no direct mention in the text of telescope technology, you do know that a telescope was required, and you can infer from your understanding of scientific history that improvements in telescopes would allow us to see things that we couldn't before. Let's leave it for now.

(D) might explain why it was rare to see solar flares during those specific periods but not why no one had ever seen one in any time period, so you can eliminate this answer choice.

Though (E) might seem tempting, the effect of CMEs on Earth is not what is being discussed, and you don't need to measure their impact to observe solar flares, so you can eliminate (E) as well.

(C) was the only viable answer choice, and **(C) is correct**.

14. Which of the following, if true, would most seriously weaken the claim made in the passage about the likelihood of a destructive solar flare?

Ⓐ A massive CME oriented toward outer space fails to cause problems with communications or power on Earth.

Ⓑ Engineers are hard at work improving the worldwide terrestrial power grid to better withstand the effects of a CME.

Ⓒ Solar activity waxes and wanes in relatively predictable nine-year cycles.

Ⓓ CMEs have never caused worldwide power and communication disruptions on Earth before.

Ⓔ **A new study proves that CMEs powerful enough to disrupt communications and power on Earth occur roughly once every one million years.**

You want to start by identifying the claim in question, and you can do so by locating the sentence in which the author makes an argument about the likelihood of damage from solar flares. You find it in this sentence here:

Though few people understand the danger of solar flares, the chances of such an event occurring in our lifetimes is not remote.

From the text presented earlier in the passage, you've learned that solar flares pose danger to us when they are accompanied by intense CMEs, which are oriented toward Earth.

Let's see which of the answer choices would do the most to weaken the author's claim.

You are told in the text that only CMEs oriented toward Earth pose a threat. So, knowing that (A) is true doesn't weaken the author's claim, and you can eliminate this choice.

Whether (B) is true or not doesn't impact the chances of a certain natural event happening, so you can eliminate (B) as well.

It's difficult to see how (C) could weaken the author's claim or make it seem that the odds of a *destructive* solar flare are any less remote, so you can eliminate (C).

(D) may be somewhat tempting, but it's less so when you consider how recently worldwide power and communications systems have been put into place. The fact that dangerous solar flares have not yet disrupted these systems doesn't necessarily make the chances that they won't in our lifetime any more remote.

You are told in the passage that solar flares are dangerous when they lead to intense CMEs that are oriented toward Earth—(E) tells you this only happens once every 1,000,000 years. (E) directly contradicts the claim that the chances that a dangerous solar flare could occur in our lifetime are not remote—once every 1,000,000 years makes the chances of a dangerous solar flare occurring in our lifetime very remote, and **(E) is the correct answer**.

15. To interfere with human life on Earth, CMEs must be which of the following? Select <u>all</u> that apply.

[A] **Oriented toward Earth**
[B] Visible as the aurora borealis
[C] **Powerful enough to enter our atmosphere**

You're asked for the characteristics required for CMEs to interfere with human life. The sentence with the key information to answer this question is this one: *In certain situations, solar flares can pose a threat: intense CMEs that are oriented toward Earth can trigger geomagnetic storms that may interfere with radio transmissions…*

Evaluating the answer choices, you know that [A] must be true—a CME must be oriented toward Earth to pose a threat to us. **You can select [A]**.

[B] does not have to be true—aurora borealis is mentioned before the author narrows her focus to CMEs that impact our lives, and you don't have any text that confirms that you must be able to see a CME as aurora borealis for it to be significant enough to interfere with human life on Earth. So, you cannot select [B].

Finally, to interact with radio transmissions, radar signals, and other terrestrial technology, the flares would have to be powerful enough to enter our atmosphere, so **you can select [C] as well**.

Passage 7
3 Questions

While nearly everyone who has taken a world history course or visited a museum knows that ancient Egyptians were sometimes mummified, the history of animal mummification in ancient Egypt is less well known. Egyptians began mummifying animals around 1500 BCE. Cats were especially common subjects for mummification because of their exalted status in ancient Egyptian culture, but archaeologists have also found mummified dogs, baboons, cows, lions, birds, even hippopotamuses. While the motivations behind animal mummification remain a mystery, Egyptologists have suggested several hypotheses. Egyptians were animists who believed that their gods could dwell in anything, including animals. Mummified animals may, therefore, have been worshiped by devout Egyptians. Alternately, mummified animals could have been presented to particular gods or goddesses as votive offerings. Other Egyptologists believe that animals were mummified to provide their owners with companionship or a source of nutrition in the afterlife, where Egyptians believed all souls reside after death.

Why did the author write this passage?

The author wrote this passage to discuss Egyptian mummification of animals and the various hypotheses for what motivated it.

16. With which of the following statements is the author most likely to agree?

Ⓐ **Ancient Egyptians had a profound, often religious relationship with animals.**
Ⓑ Mummification was performed as a way of keeping the body intact so that it could be physically reanimated.
Ⓒ After 1500 BCE, all cats in ancient Egypt were mummified.
Ⓓ Mummification has been part of ancient Egyptian culture since its beginnings.
Ⓔ Animal mummification is not well understood because Egyptians did not depict it in their art or literature.

You are asked to find an answer choice with which the author is most likely to agree.

For (A), you know from the passage that Egyptians viewed cats with exalted status and that Egyptians were animists who believed that gods could dwell in animals—both statements supporting the idea that *ancient Egyptians had a profound, often religious relationship with animals*. (A) is a strong answer choice.

The first part of answer choice (B) is very attractive, but there is no support in the passage for the end of answer choice (B), *so it could be physically reanimated*, so you can eliminate this answer choice.

For (C), you have no support for the extreme claim that *all cats in ancient Egypt were mummified*, and you can quickly eliminate this choice. Note the use of the absolute word *all*.

There is also no evidence in the text that shows that mummification was a part of ancient Egyptian culture since its beginnings, so you can eliminate answer choice (D).

Finally, there is nothing stated in the passage about Egyptians not depicting animal mummification in their art or literature, so you can eliminate (E) as well.

(A) is the only answer with supporting evidence in the passage. **(A) is correct**.

17. Select the sentence that makes it clear that Egyptologists are not certain why ancient Egyptians mummified animals.

While the motivations behind animal mummification remain a mystery, Egyptologists have suggested several hypotheses.

With the phrase *remain a mystery*, the above sentence clearly establishes that there is some uncertainty about why ancient Egyptians mummified their animals.

18. Which of the following situations aligns with a hypothesis mentioned in the passage that Egyptologists have proposed for why ancient Egyptians mummified animals? Select all that apply.

Ⓐ **A prince is buried with mummified cows and goats to provide him with sustenance as he travels to the afterlife.**
Ⓑ **A little girl is mummified alongside a monkey she kept as a beloved pet.**
Ⓒ A lion that killed several people is mummified to be sent to the underworld for punishment.

You want to see if the answer choices presented match any of the hypothesized reasons for mummification presented in the passage.

For [A], one possibility mentioned in the passage is that animals were mummified to provide their owners with nutrition in the afterlife. **[A] matches this well, so you can select it**.

[B] matches the idea that animals were mummified for companionship, so **you can select [B] as well**.

[C] does not match any of the reasons given for mummification in the passage, so there is no reason to select it.

Passage 8
4 Questions

Scientists have long believed that the Black Death, a pandemic that killed an estimated 100 million people in 14th-century Eurasia, was caused by the bubonic plague, a disease spread by the bacterium *Yersinia pestis*. This terrifying infection spread rapidly through the population and killed many of its victims in mere days. First-hand accounts of the Black Death describe symptoms similar to those of the bubonic plague: the emergence of buboes (sores) on the skin, rashes, fever, and vomiting. However, some scientists believe that the Black Death was caused by an agent other than *Y. pestis*. Bubonic plague is spread from rats to fleas; fleas then bite human hosts and infect them with the bacteria. No accounts of the time mention a massive drop in the rat population, an event that would typically precede a bubonic plague infection. In fact, many scientists suspect that parts of Northern Europe would have been too cold for the fleas that spread the plague to survive. What's more, both the speed of infection and the death rates during the Black Death were much higher than those of more recent outbreaks of bubonic plague. Thus, the true origins of the Black Death remain something of a mystery.

Why did the author write this passage?

The author wrote the passage to discuss the possibility that the Black Death, commonly believed to be caused by bubonic plague, was caused by something else. The author then goes on to give various reasons that support the idea that bubonic plague was not in fact the cause of the Black Death.

19. Which of the following, if true, would most effectively weaken the argument that the Black Death was not caused by *Y. pestis*?

(A) Bubonic plague continues to periodically reappear in contemporary society.
(B) Scientists have found several historical variants of *Y. pestis*, some of which are no longer contagious today.
(C) Manuscripts from medieval Germany describe symptoms of the Black Death that do not match those of modern bubonic plague.
(D) Climatologists discover evidence to suggest that average temperatures in 14th-century Europe were significantly lower than they are there today.

(E) Human remains from a 14th-century mass grave contain signs of bubonic plague infection in recovered DNA.

You must assume that the answer choices are true and see which one would do the most to weaken the author's argument. Let's evaluate the answer choices one at a time, being careful to keep in mind that bubonic plague and *Y. pestis* are synonymous but bubonic plague and Black Death are not.

Whether or not bubonic plague continues to reappear does not directly strengthen or weaken the claim that the Black Death was caused by *Y. pestis*, so you can eliminate (A).

Whether certain historical variants of *Y. pestis* are no longer contagious does not directly impact the claim that Black Death was caused by *Y. pestis*, so you can eliminate (B) as well.

If anything, this answer choice would strengthen the claim that Black Death was not caused by bubonic plague, or *Y. pestis*, so you can eliminate (C).

The passage states that colder temperatures in fact make it less likely for plague to spread, so you can eliminate (D).

If (E) is true, it strengthens the connection between the Black Death and bubonic plague, or *Y. pestis*, and weakens the claim that the Black Death was not caused by bubonic plague. **(E) is the correct answer**.

20. Which of the following best describes the author's attitude toward the hypothesis that the Black Death was caused by an infection other than bubonic plague?

(A) Passionate support
(B) Existential concern
(C) Bitter exasperation
(D) **Engaged curiosity**
(E) Stubborn closed-mindedness

You are asked to describe the author's attitude toward the hypothesis that the Black Death was caused by something other than bubonic plague. Let's evaluate the answer choices.

(A) is phrased too strongly. The author is interested in the topic, but you don't have text that shows the author feels *passionate* for the topic, so you can eliminate (A).

(B) doesn't match the author's attitude, which doesn't seem particularly concerned and certainly doesn't show existential concern, or concern with meaning and existence in relation to the topic of Black Death and bubonic plague. You can eliminate (B).

(C) also doesn't match the author's attitude, which is neither bitter nor exasperated, so you can quickly eliminate this choice.

(D) represents the author's attitude toward the opinion nicely. The author is both engaged and curious, so let's leave it for now.

Finally, the author displays neither stubbornness nor closed-mindedness, so you can quickly eliminate answer choice (E).

(D) is the only attractive choice, and **(D) is the correct answer**.

21. The passage mentions all of the following elements of the Black Plague that distinguish it from typical bubonic plague EXCEPT for what?

(A) The lack of a recorded mass decline in the rodent population
(B) Its proliferation of infection in regions with cold climates
(C) Its extremely high rate of infection
(D) Its quick and near-certain deadliness
(E) **The appearance of buboes and rashes on patients' skin**

You are asked about the characteristics that distinguish Black Plague from typical bubonic plague. The key contrasting details come in the middle of the passage, starting with, *No accounts of the time...* Let's evaluate the answer choices.

You're told in the passage that Black Plague didn't include a recorded mass decline in the rodent population and that this distinguished it from typical bubonic plague, so you can eliminate (A).

You're also told that Northern Europe would have been *too cold for the fleas that spread the plague to survive*, so you can eliminate (B) as well.

You can also eliminate (C) and (D) based on how the Black Death is contrasted with more recent outbreaks of bubonic plague.

However, with answer choice (E), you are told in the passage that the appearance of buboes and rashes on the patients' skin are conditions common to both Black Plague and typical bubonic plague, so (E) does not describe symptoms that distinguish Black Plague from typical bubonic plague. **(E) is the correct answer**.

22. Which of the following, if true, would make it difficult for epidemiologists to establish the true cause of the Black Death? Select all that apply.

[A] **Different outbreaks of the same disease can cause patients to experience a different combination of symptoms.**
[B] **Accounts of the Black Death from the 14th century likely do not contain entirely reliable scientific information about infection.**
[C] **Bodies of Black Death victims are often too poorly preserved to yield useful information about cause of death.**

You are asked to select answer choices that would make it more difficult for epidemiologists to establish the true cause of the Black Death and are asked to select all answer choices that apply.

If [A] is true, it would be more difficult for epidemiologists to determine whether the same disease was responsible for different outbreaks and, therefore, to establish the true cause of the Black Death, so **you can select [A]**.

If [B] is true, it certainly makes it more difficult for epidemiologists to study the root source information and get a definitive sense of the truth, so **you can select [B] as well**.

Finally, if [C] is true, it could be more difficult to gather useful scientific data regarding the true cause of the Black Death, so **you can select [C] as well**.

Passage 9

3 Questions

After days of punishing heat, a miracle occurs: clouds amass overhead, and a healing rain falls over the parched earth. Just imagining this scene can call to mind a distinctive scent that most recognize but few can name: the earthy, irresistible petrichor. Petrichor, a combination of two Greek words, *petros* (stone) and *ichor* (the blood of the gods), was coined by two Australian scientists in 1964. According to more recent research, this scent is composed of up to three elements. One is an oil released by plants during dry weather and absorbed by soil and rocks. Another is geosmin, a metabolic by-product of certain bacteria that are found in wet soil. Human beings are incredibly sensitive to geosmin, able to detect it in amounts as small as five parts per trillion. Finally, ozone can contribute to the scent of petrichor, especially if the rainstorm that triggers it includes lightning. In 2015, MIT scientists determined the mechanism by which petrichor is released. When a raindrop hits a porous surface, small air bubbles form that float to the surface and release aerosols that carry the scents that make up petrichor.

Why did the author write this passage?

The author wrote the passage to discuss petrichor, a unique scent that comes with rain. The author specifies the elements that comprise the scent, how the scent gets released, and how sensitive humans are to the scent.

23. The passage identifies which of the following as factors contributing to humans' ability to smell petrichor? Select all that apply.

A | **Periods of dry weather**
B | **Sensitivity to geosmin**
C | **Aerosols that occur during rainfall**

You are looking for reasons the passage offers for why humans are able to perceive the scent of petrichor. Let's evaluate the answer choices.

[A] The passage notes that *an oil released by plants during dry weather* is one of the components that make up the scent of petrichor, so periods of dry weather do contribute to the ability to smell it. **You can select [A].**

Likewise, the passage notes our extreme sensitivity to geosmin, which also contributes to the scent of petrichor, so **you can select [B] as well**.

Finally, you are told that the aerosols that occur when *a raindrop hits a porous surface* are the *mechanism by which petrichor is released*, so **[C] makes a lot of sense; you can select it.**

24. What is the function of the first sentence of the passage? Select all that apply.

A | **To draw the reader in with an image that appeals to the senses**
B | **To cause the reader to imagine the scent of petrichor without necessarily having prior knowledge of it**
C | To suggest that petrichor is something we imagine, not a real sensory experience

You are asked to select answers that represent the function of the first sentence. Let's evaluate the answer choices one at a time.

The first sentence does draw you in with an image that appeals to your sense of the punishing heat and the healing rain, so **you can select [A].**

[B] also describes the function of the first sentence, and it matches the language the author uses at the beginning of the second sentence to elaborate on the first sentence. **You can select [B] as well.**

Finally, [C] is incorrect. Petrichor is a real sensory experience, so you can eliminate [C].

25. Which of the following best describes the structure of the passage?

Ⓐ A chemical process is defined, and its potential hazards are identified.
Ⓑ A fantastical scene is presented and then debunked using scientific terms.
Ⓒ A word is defined, and the theories behind its meaning are presented.
Ⓓ Early explanations of a phenomenon are presented and described using modern research.

(E) **A familiar phenomenon is described, and the science behind it is explained.**

You're asked to identify the answer choice that best describes the structure of the passage. Let's evaluate the answer choices one at a time.

(A) starts off well in that what might be described as a *chemical process* is defined, but there are no *potential hazards* identified, so you can eliminate it.

(B) talks of *debunking* a fantastical scene, which isn't the purpose of the passage, so you can eliminate (B) as well.

(C) might be tempting, but the passage is not concerned with *theories* about the *meaning* of petrichor; rather, it gives you detailed scientific information about how petrichor actually occurs, so you can eliminate (C) as well.

For (D), *Early explanations of a phenomenon* isn't a great match for the passage, which explains the origins of the word *petrichor* to describe the phenomenon but not the early explanations of the phenomenon, and certainly not using *modern research*. You can eliminate (D).

(E) is the only answer you haven't eliminated, and (E) matches the structure of the passage quite well. The passage starts off by describing a phenomenon, the scent petrichor, which is described as being familiar. The passage then goes on to explain the science behind the phenomenon—what the scent is composed of, the mechanism by which it is released, and how sensitive human beings are to it. **(E) is correct.**

Passage 10
3 Questions

The continuation of moon research and the development of new exploration technologies require moondust, or a suitable simulant, for tests and experiments. Moondust, however, is unique. It is sharp and jagged, it is superfine, it sticks to absolutely everything, and it has the troubling tendency to jam machinery and abrade everything it touches. For these reasons, it poses a threat to lunar missions, not to mention futuristic plans to es-

tablish a colony on the moon. Indeed, Apollo 16 Commander John Young once stated that "dust is the number one concern in returning to the moon." Moondust has peculiar qualities that Earth dust lacks because the conditions on the moon are so different from those on Earth: moondust is electrostatically charged because it's constantly being hit by solar wind and cosmic rays, and it is jagged because micrometeoroids are continuously bombarding the lunar soil, causing it to melt, splash, and then refreeze. Scientists are developing simulated moondust using samples from Hawaiian volcanoes, Arizona desert, and Montana prairie, and they hope to refine their simulants even further, developing prototypes that mimic the different dusts found in disparate regions of the moon.

Why did the author write this passage?

The author wrote the passage to discuss the importance and uniqueness of moondust. He discusses its unusual characteristics and the challenges it presents to both lunar missions and future plans to colonize the moon. He then goes on to describe why moondust has the unique characteristics it has and the fact that scientists are attempting to simulate dust found in disparate regions of the moon using samples from different areas around the world.

26. Which of the following represent reasons that moondust would make it hard to colonize the moon? Select all that apply.

[A] **It would make it difficult for transport systems to function properly.**
[B] It would cause respiratory problems in organisms who breathe it in.
[C] **It could quickly weather structures left exposed to the elements.**

You are told in that passage that moondust *has the troubling tendency to jam machinery and abrade everything it touches.* Based on this, **you can select answer choices [A] and [C]**: moondust would make it difficult for transport systems to function properly because it has the tendency to jam up machinery, and it could quickly weather structures because it has the tendency to abrade everything it touches.

You haven't been given specific indications that it would cause respiratory problems, so you can't select [B].

27. Which of the following is the primary purpose of the passage?

(A) To explain why the moon is not a suitable place for human colonization
(B) **To indicate why scientists must create simulated moondust for space research**
(C) To list the conditions that make moondust such a frustrating material to deal with
(D) To argue that we need to return to the moon immediately to collect more moondust
(E) To explore the different types of moondust that exist in different regions of the moon

You're asked to find an answer that represents the primary purpose of the passage. Let's evaluate the answer choices one at a time.

The passage was not primarily written to discuss why the moon is not a suitable place for human colonization; **you can eliminate answer choice (A)**.

(B) seems to match the passage fairly well. Leave it for now.

(C) is also fairly attractive but doesn't seem to represent the passage as a whole. Leave it for now.

The author wasn't making a case for (D) directly or indirectly, and this wasn't the primary purpose of the passage, so you can eliminate (D) quickly.

Finally, the passage wasn't written to explore the different types of moondust that exist in different regions of the moon, so you can eliminate (E) as well.

Returning to (B) and (C) and comparing them against the full text again, it makes more sense that (B) better represents the passage as a whole, whereas (C) represents certain characteristics of the passage but not the first or last sentence, so **(B) is the correct answer**.

28. Which of the following can be inferred from the passage? Select all that apply.

A Montana prairie dust is remarkably similar to moondust.
B **Solar wind and cosmic rays are made up of charged particles.**
C Commander John Young believed that moon exploration should end.

Let's evaluate each answer choice carefully.

Although you know that Montana prairie dust is part of the mixture being used to simulate moondust, you cannot infer from this that Montana prairie dust is *remarkably similar* to moondust, so you can't select [A].

In the passage, you are told that *moondust is electrostatically charged because it's constantly being hit by solar wind and cosmic rays*. You can infer from this that solar wind and cosmic rays are made up of charged particles and **select [B]**.

There is nothing in the passage that indicates that John Young believed that moon exploration should end, so you can't infer [C].

Passage 11
2 Questions

Recent breakthroughs in medical technology have made it possible for doctors to keep terminally ill and gravely injured people alive longer than ever before. However, these advancements have deepened a long-standing moral quandary: How do we know that such people would even want to be kept alive and, if so, for how long? At what point does keeping an unconscious person alive go against the directive to do no harm? An advance healthcare directive, or living will, is a legal document that allows one to specify what sorts of medical decisions should be made for one in the event of incapacitation or illness. It allows one to detail how they should be treated—or not treated—if they are on life support with no possibility of recovery or if they have entered a coma with little chance of waking. These increasingly common documents are part of a larger movement toward more compassionate and intentional end-of-life care that attempts to empower patients, even when they are unable to speak for themselves.

Why did the author write this passage?

The author wrote the passage to discuss the issue of accommodating personal preferences in medical care, a tool—an advanced healthcare directive—that allows one to set personal preferences, and the increasing commonality and importance of this tool in our modern world.

29. With which of the following statements would the author most likely agree? Select all that apply.

A. The feelings and desires of a gravely ill or injured person should always supersede the advice of a doctor.

B. The completion of an advance healthcare directive should be mandatory.

C. It is incorrect to assume that all critically ill or injured patients want to be kept alive as long as possible.

[A] overinfers from the information in the passage; *always* is too strong a statement, and you can't say that the author feels that the feelings and desires of the patient should always supersede the advice of a doctor.

Similarly, [B] also overinfers; nothing in the passage implies that the advance healthcare directive should be *mandatory*, so you can eliminate [B] as well.

Finally, because the passage presents the question of whether some patients would prefer not to be kept alive and because the advance healthcare directive offers instructions on a particular issue, you can infer that the author would agree that it's incorrect to infer that all patients want to be kept alive as long as possible, so **you can select [C].**

30. Which of the following, if true, could represent a reason that advance healthcare directives are becoming increasingly common in the United States? Select all that apply.

A. Americans have become increasingly health conscious about their diets.

B. Studies have revealed that people can feel pain, hear, and think while comatose.

C. A majority of Americans now die in a hospital setting.

It's unclear what impact answer choice [A] would have on the situation being discussed, so you can quickly eliminate it.

If [B] is true, it makes a lot of sense that people would be more interested in making decisions about how they want to be treated while comatose and create legal documents to that effect, so **you can select [B].**

Similarly, if [C] is true, it makes sense that people would be increasingly interested in creating legal documents that specify how they would like to be treated in these particular situations, so **you can select [C] as well.**

Passage 12
4 Questions

For a generation accustomed to SUVs and minivans, the aesthetics of American cars of the 1960s might seem very strange indeed. The Big Three automakers' advertising mantra in that decade was "longer, lower, wider." The cars of the day were sleek and sweeping, designed to "look fast standing still," as auto journalists would say. In contrast, modern vehicles announce: "I can crush boulders with ease." The epitome of 1960s car aesthetics was the appropriately dubbed "fastback" body style, characterized by a roofline that descended in a continuous slope to the rear bumper. It was clunky compared to more recent sedans and coupes, but the fastback looked aerodynamic. The Oldsmobile Toronado was the fastback par excellence: a massive 1960s American vehicle whose dramatic rear roofline was matched by a front hood that seemed to stretch into the next zip code.

The purpose of such styling was to present the illusion of flight, even if the cars of that era still struggled with such basic tasks as turning and braking. In their design, the cars looked as much like jet planes and rocket ships as any conveyance with wheels possibly could, an aesthetic that fit the 1960s obsession with all things aeronautical. The space program was in its heyday during the 1960s, and jet travel had only recently become a possibility for the average American. Oldsmobile even used a NASA spokesperson in its early advertisements for the Toronado. And this aeronautical theme was not restricted to cars: the far-out 1960s "Googie" architectural style could be seen in hamburger stands, drive-in theaters, and motels designed to look as though they could actually fly. Americans of the time desperately wanted to take wing, even if they had never before left Earth.

Why did the author write this passage?

The author wrote this passage to discuss the aesthetics of 1960s automobiles. She compares them to the cars of today, discusses how they were inspired by the aeronautical industry, and then broadens the discussion to talk about how the design of other things was also inspired by travel to space.

31. The phrase "crush boulders with ease" in the first paragraph suggests which of the following?

(A) All modern SUVs can handle rugged terrain without difficulty.
(B) **Automotive styling continues to suggest that a car may be capable of tremendous feats.**
(C) Cars of the 1960s were not made with passenger safety in mind.
(D) Automotive advertising is unusually deceptive.
(E) There is an increasing emphasis on mechanical perfection in the car industry.

(A) is somewhat tempting, but the passage is about design and perception rather than actual performance, and *all* is too strong a word—neither the passage nor the design of modern vehicles suggests that all modern SUVs can handle rugged terrain without difficulty, so you can eliminate (A).

(B) is a safe and attractive answer. Let's leave it for now.

(C) would be attractive only if you grossly overinferred from the given information; the statement is about the ruggedness of current cars, as opposed to the safety of older cars, so you can eliminate (C).

Similarly, (D) and (E) would be applicable only if you overinferred from the given information, which states nothing directly about deceptive advertising or the desire for mechanical perfection, so you can eliminate both choices.

Returning to (B), the only attractive choice, *crushing boulders with ease* would be an example of a tremendous feat, and it would be something that the styling of the car would suggest, just as the look of the 1960s cars suggested they could be fast standing still. (B) is a good match for the passage, and **(B) is correct**.

32. The author suggests which of the following about American cars of the 1960s? Select <u>all</u> that apply.

[A] **They often had major deficiencies in performance.**
[B] **They tended to have more extreme styling features than contemporary cars do.**
[C] **Their design was influenced by cultural touchpoints of the time.**

Let's evaluate each of the answer choices independently.

You are told that 1960s cars were clunky compared to those of today and that some struggled with basic tasks such as turning and braking, so **it certainly suggests answer choice [A]**.

The entire passage is about the unique styling of 1960s cars, and it begins with the author telling you that, *for a generation accustomed to SUVs and minivans, the aesthetics of American cars in the 1960s might seem very strange indeed*, which is more than enough to suggest that they had more extreme styling features than contemporary cars do, so **you can select [B] as well**.

Finally, you know that car styling was influenced by space travel, so **you can select [C] as well**.

33. The phrase "Hamburger stands, drive-in theaters, and motels designed to look as though they could actually fly" in the second paragraph emphasizes which of the following? Select <u>all</u> that apply.

[A] **The creativity of 1960s architects**
[B] **The somewhat absurd nature of the Googie style**
[C] The desire among many Americans to establish a colony on another planet

You are told that the aeronautical theme was *not restricted to cars: the far-out 1960s "Googie" architectural style could be seen in hamburger stands…* From the phrases *not* restricted and *far-out*, you can conclude that these examples are meant to emphasize both the creativity of the architects and the somewhat absurd nature of the Googie style. **You can select [A] and [B]**.

You have no support for the claim that many Americans desired to establish a colony on another planet, so you can't select [C].

34. Which of the following answers best describes the primary purpose of the passage?

(A) To suggest that we have lost interest in space exploration over the past several decades
(B) To dismiss a particular automotive design as old-fashioned and frivolous
(C) To compare the automotive and architectural implications of a particular design philosophy
(D) **To examine the effect of a cultural phenomenon on design**
(E) To criticize the 1960s tendency to privilege aesthetics over practicality

Let's see which of the answer choices best represents the primary purpose of the passage.

The author did not write this to discuss the fact that we have lost interest in space exploration over the past several decades, so you can quickly eliminate (A).

The first part of (B) starts off okay, but the author certainly doesn't see 1960s automobile style as old-fashioned and frivolous, so you can eliminate (B) as well.

(C) is somewhat attractive, but the author is not comparing the implications of a design philosophy in cars and architecture, so you can eliminate this choice as well.

Though (D) may not be what you anticipated, it represents the passage correctly. The passage examines the effect of a cultural phenomenon—namely the introduction of space travel—on design. Let's leave it for now.

The author doesn't criticize anything, so you can quickly eliminate (E).

(D) was the only attractive answer, and though it may not be how you might summarize the purpose of the passage, it is accurate. **(D) is correct**.

Passage 13
3 Questions

From the late 19th to the early 20th centuries, scientists debated the merits of two doctrines that sought to describe the nature of the connections in the nervous system. Anatomists, who studied the morphology of neurons and brains, held that the nervous system was a reticulum: a continuous network of cells. At the time, microscopy allowed anatomists to distinguish individual neuronal cell bodies and branches but was not advanced enough to allow them to discern how exactly these bodies were connected with one another. The adherents of the so-called reticular doctrine argued that it was impossible to explain how electrical signals (a major mode of transmission of neural signals) could be carried throughout the nervous system without direct connections between cells. On the other hand, physiologists, who studied the functions of neurons, theorized that neurons were discrete, separate cells, existing independently but connected functionally with one another at points of near-contact called synapses. They knew that neurons released diffusible chemical signals, which we now call neurotransmitters, and that the signals from one set of cells could influence another set of cells not directly connected to the first. The proponents of the so-called neuron doctrine reasoned that, for the nervous system to be self-regulating, cells needed to be separated so that the strength of their connections could change.

This debate was partially resolved in the 1950s with the advent of electron microscopy, which revealed the presence of narrow spaces between most neuron pairs, now called synaptic clefts. These clefts were clear manifestations of the points of noncontact junctures proposed by the adherents of the neuron doctrine. At the synaptic cleft, one neuron communicates with its partner through the release of chemical neurotransmitters from tiny sacs called vesicles. For a time, it seemed this debate had been put to rest. However, further studies revealed that some neurons are connected to one another directly, membrane to membrane, by protein pores called gap junctions. Experiments on neurons connected by gap junctions revealed that these junctions connect neurons electrically, allowing mutual electrical excitation (or inhibition) between them without the need for an intermediate chemical signal.

Why did the author write this passage?

The author wrote this passage to discuss two possible explanations for how neurons communicate electrical signals: the reticular doctrine and neuron doctrine. The author spends the first paragraph explaining both and the second paragraph offering evidence that first supports the neuron doctrine before giving evidence that suggests that the reticular doctrine could also have some truth to it.

35. Which of the following experimental results would most directly support the reticular doctrine?

Ⓐ An experiment using a light microscope finds no evidence of a separation between individual neurons.
Ⓑ A neuron located on one side of the brain is found to excite a neuron located on the other side.
Ⓒ **Ions causing electrical excitation are discovered to flow directly between the branches of two neurons.**
Ⓓ A previously undiscovered set of neurotransmitters is found to dampen electrical activity in the brain.
Ⓔ Electrical signals that represent a key mode of neural signaling are discovered to flow throughout the nervous system.

The reticular doctrine holds that cells, or neurons, communicate directly with one another without space or interference in between. Let's see which of the results would most support the doctrine.

(A) is somewhat attractive, but it doesn't show communication in any way, so you can eliminate it.

(B) doesn't show communication between cells in direct contact with one another, so you can eliminate it.

(C) shows direct communication between two cells. Let's leave it for now.

Neither (D) nor (E) have any direct relationship to communication between connected cells and can be eliminated.

(C) is not written how you expect, but it's telling you that electric signals grow from one neuron to another without space between the cells and without an external helper involved, so **(C) is the correct answer**.

36. As discussed in the passage, which of the following pieces of evidence presented the greatest challenge to the reticular doctrine?

Ⓐ The nature of the connections between neurons could not be elucidated at the microscopic level.
Ⓑ Chemical signals from one neuron were found to affect the behavior of other neurons.
Ⓒ **Scientists discovered a space between neurons that were in communication with one another.**
Ⓓ Scientists knew that electrical signals generally require continuity of the conducting medium for transmission.
Ⓔ Separate neuronal cell bodies were visible by light microscopy.

The reticular doctrine holds that neurons communicate directly with one another and with no space between one another.

Answer choice **(C) clearly countered the doctrine and presented the greatest challenge to it and is therefore the correct choice**.

The nature of the connections not being elucidated at the microscopic level isn't necessarily a challenge to the doctrine—just to finding out whether it's true or not—so you can eliminate (A).

The doctrine acknowledges that chemical signals from one neuron affect the behavior of other neurons, so (B) doesn't weaken this doctrine.

For (D), without knowing more about the relationship between the conducting medium and doctrine, it's tough to say how this impacts the argument; you can eliminate this choice.

The fact that separate cells were visible doesn't weaken the idea that cells communicate directly with other cells that they are touching, so you can eliminate (E).

37. Select the sentence that best supports the neuron doctrine.

This debate was partially resolved in the 1950s with the advent of electron microscopy, which revealed the presence of narrow spaces between most neuron pairs, now called synaptic clefts.

The previous sentence, the last one of the first paragraph, gives you a very specific understanding of the neuron doctrine: *The proponents of the so-called neuron doctrine reasoned that, for the nervous system to be self-regulating, cells needed to be separated so that the strength of their connections could change.*

Thus, this first sentence of the second paragraph, which gives you evidence of the space between cells, is the best support for the neuron doctrine.

Passage 14
2 Questions

Animal behaviors result from a complex interaction between genetic and environmental factors, commonly known as nature and nurture, respectively. Although clearly distinct genetic factors are predetermined and generally fixed, environmental ones are ever-changing; it is impossible to determine for any given action where one ends and the other begins.

The genetic component of an organism's behavior results from the effects that genes have on an organism's development. Genetic programs result in very specific wiring of the neural circuits that drive behavior. Genes also dictate which neurotransmitters and hormones (signaling molecules) an organism's endocrine and nervous systems produce and use and what effects those signaling molecules will have on their receptors, and by extension, their target cells and organs.

An organism's environment, on the other hand, consists of the material in the natural world immediately outside the organism's body. Although the term nurture suggests the primary importance of early childhood experiences, an organism's environment can also include chemicals—both natural and human produced—that may affect an organism's behavior. For example, certain insect repellents make use of chemical signals that induce insects to move away from a treated area. Of course, the environment can also include the influence of other organisms. A male mountain goat is likely to behave differently in the presence of a female mountain goat than it will in the presence of a rival.

But only by looking at both parts simultaneously can one hope to understand the true nature of animal behavior. A change in environment, such as the arrival of a predator, will trigger the secretion of various signaling molecules by one organism (a direct result of the activity of its genes and related proteins) that create chemical signals in the environment that may in turn influence the behavior of other organisms.

Why did the author write this passage?

The author wrote this passage to discuss the relationship between nature and nurture and how they are clearly intertwined yet distinct. She describes the impact of both separately and then gives examples of the importance of seeing how they influence each other.

38. According to the information in the passage, which of the following would NOT be considered an example of nurture?

(A) A song sung by a mother intended to soothe her child
(B) The production of neurotransmitters that target specific receptors
(C) The presence of a sexually receptive female fish in a tank
(D) Toxic chemicals in a river that affect frog development
(E) A display of violence by an older male gorilla toward a younger one

According to the passage, nurture has to do with factors external to oneself, and answer choices (A), (C), (D), and (E) all represent examples of nurture. (B) is the only answer choice that does not, so **(B) is the correct answer**.

39. Which of the following statements most closely represents the main argument of the passage?

(A) The genetic and environmental components that factor into animal behavior are clearly separable.
(B) Genetics plays the most important role in establishing neuronal connections in an animal's nervous system.
(C) Genetic and environmental factors exert interdependent influences on animal behavior.
(D) Many different types of external stimuli can influence an organism's behavioral responses.

(E) Chemical signals from both neural/hormonal signaling pathways and the environment play key roles in dictating an animal's responses to external stimuli.

You're asked to find the answer choice that best represents the main argument of the passage. You know that the author's main argument was that nature and nurture are intertwined. Looking at the answer choices, (A) states the opposite, (B) emphasizes the genetics and does not represent the main point, and (D) emphasizes the environment and does not represent the main point. (E) is far too specific and doesn't represent everything discussed in the passage.

Answer choice (C) matches what you anticipated and is the correct choice.

Passage 15
3 Questions

Ever since Charlotte, Emily, and Anne Brontë emerged as a literary troika, their sisterhood has often caused their work to be shortchanged by consideration in the aggregate and blinded critics to their very different styles, temperaments, and legacies.

Charlotte, the eldest of the three sisters, is best known for *Jane Eyre*, her first published novel and a surprise best-seller. Because of its style (a heady blend of Victorian naturalism and gothic romance) and its revolutionary focus on female self-determination, *Jane Eyre* made Charlotte Brontë a household name. Though Charlotte's novels were accessible to a Victorian public accustomed to Dickens and Thackeray, her steadfast attention to her characters' interiority gives her work a decidedly modern feel.

Emily, perhaps the most idiosyncratic of the Brontë sisters, published only one novel in her short life, though its modern reputation may eclipse even that of *Jane Eyre*. *Wuthering Heights* is passionate and stormy—a multi-generational Shakespearean tragedy on the moors. Its eerie intensity and formal innovations continue to surprise and enthrall readers today.

Anne published two novels in her life: *Agnes Grey* and *The Tenant of Wildfell Hall*. The youngest Brontë, and the only sister to have been educated entirely at home by the girls' strict Methodist aunt, Anne wrote novels more mannered than Charlotte's or Emily's: quieter, subtler, and more explicitly moral. These qualities meant that her work was often upstaged by that of her sisters. Had she not been in direct competition with them, her writing would perhaps be better appreciated today.

The Brontë sisters grew up in the same isolated Yorkshire parsonage and had many of the same life experiences and influences, yet their works are remarkably distinctive. A discerning reader would never mistake the writing of one sister for that of another. Spending time with each sister's work is like looking at the same fascinating vista through three very different lenses.

Why did the author write this passage?

The author wrote the passage to highlight the unique and distinguishing characteristics of the three Brontë sisters and their literary works. He starts by saying that they are often aggregated, focuses on them individually, and then concludes by saying that each sister offers a distinctive perspective on the same environment.

40. With which of the following would the author most likely agree?

(A) The environment in which the Brontë sisters were raised did not impact the style or settings of their work.
(B) **Some critical analyses of the Brontë's work have focused on the similarities among the sisters' work.**
(C) Emily Brontë was more influenced by the works of Shakespeare than were her sisters.
(D) Female autonomy was a popular emerging theme in Victorian literature.
(E) Though less well critically received, Anne Brontë was a more prolific author than either of her sisters.

You're asked to find an answer with which the author is most likely to agree. Let's evaluate the answer choices one at a time.

The passage is full of examples of how the environment influenced the Brontë sisters' work, so the author would likely not agree with (A), and you can eliminate it.

(B) seems a good match for the start of the passage, so let's leave it for now.

(C) overinfers from the fact that *Wuthering Heights* is a Shakespearean tragedy—we don't know whether Emily was more influenced by the works of Shakespeare than her sisters, and you can eliminate (C) as well.

For (D), you're told in the passage that Charlotte's focus on female self-determination was *revolutionary*, so you don't have enough evidence to infer that female autonomy was a *popular* emerging theme in Victorian literature.

You don't have evidence that Anne was more prolific, and though you know her work was upstaged, you don't necessarily know it was less critically received, so you can't infer (E).

Returning to answer choice (B), at the start of the passage, you are told that their sisterhood often caused their work to be *shortchanged by consideration in the aggregate and blinded critics to their very different styles, temperaments, and legacies.* This is enough support to say that the author most likely agrees that some critical analysis has focused on the similarities among the sisters' work, so **(B) is the correct answer**.

41. Which of the following can be inferred from the passage? Select all that apply.

[A] *Jane Eyre*'s most prominent literary influences were the novels of William Thackeray and Charles Dickens.

[B] **Emily Brontë's *Wuthering Heights* contains formal innovations that are appreciated by modern readers.**

[C] **An intense focus on the interior lives of characters is more common in contemporary literature than it was in the fiction of earlier eras.**

You're asked to identify the answer choices that can be inferred from the passage. Let's evaluate the answer choices one at a time.

For [A], the passage does not tell you that *Jane Eyre* was influenced by the novels of William Thackeray and Charles Dickens but rather that the reading public was used to novels by such writers, so [A] is not correct.

You are told in the passage that Wuthering Heights *contains formal innovations that continue to surprise and enthrall readers today*, so **you can infer [B]**.

Finally, you are told that Charlotte's *steadfast attention to their characters' interiority gives her work a decidedly modern feel*, **which allows you to infer [C]**.

42. Choose the sentence that connects one of the Brontë sisters' life experiences and her writing style.

The youngest Brontë and the only sister who had been educated entirely at home by the girls' strict Methodist aunt, Anne wrote novels that were more mannered than Charlotte's or Emily's: quieter, subtler, and more explicitly moral.

You are asked to find a sentence that connects one of the sisters' life experiences with her writing style. The sentence above does just that, matching Anne's strict and moral upbringing with her writing.

Passage 16
3 Questions

That life can be a struggle is more than a cliché. We encounter dissonance in disagreements at work, discord among team members, conflict between mates, and competition among companies. Fortunately, psychology has given us tools for insight into the most frustrating friction of all: the everyday dissonance that occurs within ourselves.

When we simultaneously hold multiple ideas or feelings that conflict, the internal clash can produce emotional or cognitive dissonance. This inner discord can be painful, thus demanding recognition and resolution. If there is a villain in this clash, it is our ability to creatively justify mutually exclusive ideas. Whether it is conscious or unconscious, this mechanism can allow us to deceive ourselves in an attempt to satisfy incompatible desires. For instance, we might know that smoking is harmful for our health, but we might still justify a social smoking habit by telling ourselves that giving in to the urge every once in a while is acceptable. However, we can overcome this bad mental habit. Properly harnessed, cognitive or emotional dissonance can act as an opportunity to mobilize our best selves, recognize and resolve dilemmas, and better understand our motivations.

Why did the author write this passage?

The author wrote this passage to discuss internal cognitive dissonance. She begins with a general paragraph about the dissonance in our lives overall and then, in the second paragraph, zeroes in on the primary topic: the dissonance within ourselves. She talks about our ability to creatively deceive ourselves to satisfy incompatible desires and ends by saying that, properly harnessed, dissonance can act as an opportunity to mobilize our best selves.

43. The passage suggests that when attempting to evaluate human nature, one must recognize which of the following? Select <u>all</u> that apply.

A **Psychological dissonance can cause people to behave in a self-defeating manner.**
B People are typically unhappy.
C People can tolerate varying levels of psychological dissonance, depending on their mental health.

You are asked to evaluate each answer choice independently regarding what the passage suggests about human nature.

You are told that *this mechanism can allow us to deceive ourselves in an attempt to satisfy incompatible desires*, and then, you are given an example of justifying smoking while knowing it is bad for our health. This suggests that psychological dissonance can cause people to behave in a self-defeating manner, so **you can select [A]**.

Nothing in the passage indicates that people are typically unhappy, so there is no reason to select [B].

The passage is not about how much psychological dissonance people can tolerate, and the author makes no distinctions about variations on mental health, so there is no reason to select [C].

44. Select the sentence that mentions a positive aspect of cognitive or psychological dissonance.

Properly harnessed, cognitive or emotional dissonance can act as an opportunity to mobilize our best selves, recognize and resolve dilemmas, and better understand our motivations.

The above sentence, which is the final of the passage, tells you a positive aspect of cognitive dissonance.

Fortunately, psychology has given us tools for insight into the most frustrating friction of all: the everyday dissonance that occurs within us, from the end of the first paragraph was probably the most attractive second choice, but it doesn't directly tell you a positive aspect of cognitive dissonance.

45. Which of the following is an example of "creatively justify[ing] mutually exclusive ideas?" Select <u>all</u> that apply.

A **A student needs to complete an assignment by Sunday night but spends all weekend at the beach because it is summer.**
B A child contemplates stealing candy from the corner store but decides to refrain because it would be morally wrong.
C **A homeowner needs to save money for a new roof but makes plans to vacation in Europe because he found a great deal on plane tickets.**

You know from the passage that creatively justifying mutually exclusive ideas is what the author called the *villain* in the clash, the one that allowed the person in the example to make the excuse and smoke a cigarette.

You are looking for examples where people justify making bad decisions, and **[A] and [C] match what you are looking for and are correct**, while [B] does not and is not correct.

Passage 17
4 Questions

One of the first American religions began in the upstate New York bedroom of two teenage girls. In 1848, young Maggie and Kate Fox told their parents that they were in contact with a spirit named Mr. Splitfoot. What's more, they provided proof: when they asked Mr. Splitfoot questions, he would respond intelligently by "rapping" on the walls or furniture, wowing the Fox family and, later, sellout crowds all over the Northeast. Thus, the Fox sisters became a phenomenon, and Spiritualism, a religion based loosely on the tenets of Christianity but incorporating a belief in spirit communication, was born. Even when the Fox sisters came out as frauds in 1888 (they produced those rapping sounds by surreptitiously popping their joints against hard surfaces), Spiritualism remained popular for decades. Especially during the Civil War, Spiritualism provided a balm for grieving families who wanted to continue communicating with their lost loved ones from beyond the grave. However, there was another reason for Spiritualism's popularity: its progressive emphasis on women's voices. A religion founded by mischievous teenage girls and practiced by thousands of mostly female spirit mediums was almost predestined to become an outlet for women who were eager to be heard.

Why did the author write this passage?

The author wrote the passage to discuss how Spiritualism came about and why it remained popular.

46. The passage suggests that the Fox sisters achieved widespread success as mediums for which of the following reasons?

(A) They provided disillusioned Christians with an alternative religious faith.
(B) They were outspoken feminists at a moment when women's suffrage was in vogue.
(C) **They convinced audiences that they were in contact with an intelligent spirit.**
(D) They were capable of making Mr. Splitfoot appear before audiences on command.
(E) The fact that they were young girls made people trust them more.

The question asks why the Fox sisters achieved widespread success. Let's evaluate the answer choices.

You don't have evidence suggesting that Spiritualism appealed to disillusioned Christians or that they saw it as an alternative religious faith, so you can eliminate (A).

(B) misappropriates a different part of the passage, and you don't have evidence that the Fox sisters were themselves outspoken feminists so you can eliminate (B).

You do have support for the fact they faked being able to talk with a spirit who would *intelligently* communicate back with them, so **(C) is the correct answer**.

The passage doesn't state that or suggest that they made Mr. Splitfoot appear, so you can eliminate (D).

Finally, the passage also doesn't state or suggest that people trusted them more because they were young girls, so you can eliminate (E) as well.

47. Select the sentence that connects the popularity of Spiritualism with a historical event.

Especially during the Civil War, Spiritualism provided a balm for grieving families who wanted to continue communicating with their lost loved ones from beyond the grave.

You know from the passage that one reason Spiritualism was popular was because it provided a balm for families grieving for loved ones lost from the Civil War.

48. The author suggests that the Fox sisters introduced the world to Mr. Splitfoot to

(A) further their goal of starting a new religion.
(B) help grieving families make contact with deceased loved ones.
(C) play a cruel joke on the people who believed them.
(D) **garner attention and praise.**
(E) give women more power in American society.

You have no evidence in the passage that suggests that the Fox sisters wanted to start a new religion, help grieving families, or give women more power in society.

Play a cruel joke is perhaps the most attractive of the wrong answers, in part because you are told that the girls are mischievous, but mischievous is not nearly enough support for *cruel joke*, and (C) doesn't fit the passage nearly as well as (D) does.

The Fox sisters did this to wow their parents, and they lied about Mr. Splitfoot to sellout crowds—this suggests that they introduced Mr. Splitfoot to garner attention and praise; **(D) is the correct answer**.

49. The author would likely assert that Spiritualism was a proto-feminist movement for which of the following reasons? Select <u>all</u> that apply.

[A] Early feminists were more likely to be Spiritualists than Christians.
[B] **Spiritualism began with the revelations of ordinary teenage girls.**
[C] **Spiritualism put female spirit mediums in the public eye.**

You are told at the end of the passage that one of the reasons for Spiritualism's popularity was its progressive emphasis on women's voices. It then gives reasons why this might be the case: it was founded by mischievous teenage girls and practiced by thousands of mostly female spirit mediums.

Knowing this, **you can select both [B] and [C]**. You don't have any support for [A] and can't select it.

Passage 18
3 Questions

It is unfortunate that James Joyce's *Ulysses*, considered by many to be the most important modernist novel, is remembered today more for its difficulty than for its brilliance and bravery. Though the book is indeed daunting for readers unused to textual density and experimentation, its virtues are manifold. On the surface level, Joyce's novel tells the story of an ordinary man's movements through the city of Dublin on one ordinary day: June 16, 1904, now known as Bloomsday. However, this seemingly mundane story conceals near infinite hidden depth. Each chapter of *Ulysses* is based on an event in Homer's *The Odyssey* and is written in an entirely dif-ferent mode from the chapters preceding and following it. The novel is densely allusive, and the different styles Joyce uses hearken back to various watershed moments in English literary history. However, it is possible to enjoy and learn from the novel without understanding every obscure reference or being able to follow every sentence. The language of *Ulysses* is the book's true protagonist. It is jubilant, playful, and innovative, more poetry than prose. More than any novel before it, *Ulysses* captures what it feels like to think and exist in the world.

Why did the author write this passage?

The author wrote this passage to discuss how *Ulysses* is a book of many virtues despite its reputation for being difficult to read. He then goes on to discuss some of its remarkable qualities.

50. The author of the passage regards Joyce's *Ulysses* with which of the following?

(A) Bemusement
(B) Flippancy
(C) Trepidation
(D) Pretension
(E) **Veneration**

The author regards Joyce's *Ulysses* with a tremendous amount of awe and respect, and **(E) represents that the best**.

Bemusement, or puzzlement, isn't a good match, nor is flippancy (a lack of respect), trepidation (nervousness), or pretension.

51. With which of the following literary traditions does *Ulysses* engage? Select <u>all</u> that apply.

[A] **Homeric epic**
[B] **The English canon**
[C] **Stream of consciousness**

You are told that each chapter of *Ulysses* is based on an event in Homer's *The Odyssey* and that different styles Joyce uses hearken back to various watershed moments in English literary history, which **covers answer choices [A] and [B]**. Finally, you're told in the final sentence that *Ulysses* captures what it feels like to think and exist in the world, which **covers answer choice [C]**.

52. The author implies that which of the following contribute to *Ulysses'* reputation for difficulty? Select <u>all</u> that apply.

[A] The fact that the book covers the events of just one day
[B] **The book's innovative and unique structure**
[C] **The book's dense intertextuality**

The fact that the book covers the events of just one day doesn't, in and of itself, make the book inherently difficult to read.

You are told that *Ulysses* is *daunting for readers unused to textual density and experimentation.* Throughout the passage, you are reminded of the novel's innovative and unique structure and its dense intertextuality, so **you can select both [B] and [C]**.

Passage 19
4 Questions

The terrifying *Nosferatu: A Symphony of Horror* was released by German filmmaker F. W. Murnau in 1922. The film, an unauthorized adaptation of Bram Stoker's *Dracula*, told the suspiciously *Dracula*-esque story of a suspiciously *Dracula*-esque vampire called Count Orlok. Although copyright controversy plagued the film upon its release, E. Elias Merhige's 2000 film *Shadow of the Vampire* imagines a darker secret history for the film. In *Shadow*, Murnau keeps the true origins of his film's lead actor, Max Schreck, a secret from his cast. Schreck only appears on set at night, in character, and in full makeup. As the shoot progresses, other actors realize that Schreck is a real vampire that Murnau discovered in the Czechoslovakian castle where *Nosferatu* was filmed. Although *Shadow of the Vampire* is fictional, it is strangely convincing. The real Schreck was no vampire, but he was an eccentric and mysterious character; his portrayal of a bloodthirsty ghoul remains deeply unsettling, even in our age of guts, gore, and CGI jump scares. Perhaps, it is the spectral quality of old film or the doomed Weimar strangeness of its art direction, but something about *Nosferatu* makes it feel far darker than any film should.

Why did the author write this passage?

The author wrote this passage to discuss the horror film *Nosferatu* and the 2000 film *Shadow of the Vampire*, which imagines a secret history for the original film: that the star was actually a vampire. The author discusses the storyline of *Shadow of the Vampire* and the fact that it is deeply unsettling.

53. The author of the passage repeats the phrase "suspiciously *Dracula*-esque" twice to

(A) suggest that the film was more terrifying than Bram Stoker's novel.
(B) convince readers that F. W. Murnau was incapable of inventing his own stories.
(C) imply that it is unnecessary to see *Nosferatu* if one is familiar with the story of *Dracula*.
(D) **emphasize the copyright controversy that plagued *Nosferatu* upon its release.**
(E) inject a whimsical tone into an otherwise serious passage.

The author mentions before using the phrase that the film was an unauthorized adaptation of Bram Stoker's *Dracula*, and you're also told that copyright controversy plagued the film upon its release. Thus, you can infer that this is the purpose for the repetition of the phrase, and **(D) is the correct answer**.

The repetition of the phrase does nothing to help suggest that the film is more terrifying than the novel. The author does not intend to imply that F. W. Murnau is incapable of inventing his own stories or that it is unnecessary to see *Nosferatu* if one is familiar with the story of *Dracula*. And finally, there is no evidence that the author intends to inject a whimsical tone into the passage or that using this phrase twice is meant to serve this purpose, so all other answer choices can be eliminated.

54. Select the sentence from the passage that compares *Nosferatu* to modern horror films.

The real Schreck was no vampire, but he was an eccentric and mysterious character; his portrayal of a bloodthirsty ghoul remains deeply unsettling even in our age of guts, gore, and CGI jump scares.

Schreck's portrayal was in the original *Nosferatu*, and *our age of guts, gore, and CGI jump scares* describes modern horror films.

55. According to the passage, Merhige's *Shadow of the Vampire* was a

(A) documentary film that outs Max Schreck as a real-life vampire.
(B) film based on real events surrounding the production of *Nosferatu*.
(C) **fictional film that capitalizes on the eerie strangeness of *Nosferatu*.**
(D) documentary film in which some details are changed for copyright reasons.
(E) fictional film that liberally borrowed from Bram Stoker's *Dracula*.

You are told in the passage that *Shadow of the Vampire* is a fictional film. This allows you to eliminate (A) and (D), which describe it as a documentary.

Looking at the details more carefully, nowhere in the passage does it state that the film is based on the real events surrounding the production of *Nosferatu* or that the film borrows from *Dracula*, so you can eliminate (B) and (E). You know that it plays on the strangeness of *Nosferatu*, so **(C) is the correct answer**.

56. The author would agree that all of the following aspects of *Nosferatu* make it scary EXCEPT the

(A) strange performance of Max Schreck as Count Orlok.
(B) unsettling, abstract quality of its set design.
(C) imperfections of old film stock.
(D) fraught historical context of the film's production.
(E) **film's reliance on jump scares to shock the audience.**

Most of what you need to answer this question comes in the final sentence of the passage: *Perhaps it is the spectral quality of old film or the doomed Weimar strangeness of its art direction, but something about* Nosferatu *makes it feel far darker than any film should*. And the right answer, one thing that isn't mentioned in association with *Nosferatu*, is related to what was mentioned right before: the *CGI jump scares* representative of our age.

You're told a sentence before that one that Max Schreck's performance is unsettling, and in that final sentence, you have support for (B), (C), and (D) contributing to the dark nature of the film.

So again, **(E) is the correct answer**.

Passage 20
3 Questions

Lyme disease is a common bacterial infection transmitted by black-legged ticks that causes flu-like symptoms; it is often accompanied by a distinctive "bull's-eye" rash. Most cases of Lyme disease can be cured with a standard course of antibiotics. However, there is another Lyme-related diagnosis that is less robustly supported by mainstream medicine: chronic Lyme. Chronic Lyme patients report vague but debilitating symptoms, such as extreme fatigue, muscle pain, and mental fog. However, chronic Lyme patients do not present any sign of the Lyme infection they blame for their symptoms when tested. Some doctors believe that these patients suffer from an autoimmune disease that may have been triggered by Lyme disease. Others accuse chronic Lyme patients of blatantly manufacturing their symptoms. Many members of the medical community express frustration with chronic Lyme because "Lyme-literate" doctors have begun prescribing long-term intravenous antibiotic therapy to these patients, a therapy that is not just unproven but also dangerous. Doctors worry that chronic Lyme patients are hastening the worldwide rise of antibiotic resistance in an ill-fated attempt to find relief from their mysterious symptoms.

Why did the author write this passage?

The author wrote this passage to discuss the challenges presented by chronic Lyme patients: the symptoms they suffer, how difficult it can be to diagnose and treat them, and the consequences for the population at large.

57. According to the passage, Lyme disease and chronic Lyme differ in which of the following ways? Select all that apply.

A | The duration and severity of symptoms
B | The efficacy of antibiotics for treatment
C | The medical community's consensus on it

This first question asks you to find details that, according to the passage, differentiate chronic Lyme from typical Lyme disease.

Per the passage, you know that chronic Lyme lasts longer and presents more severe symptoms, so **you can select [A]**; you know that, for Lyme disease, antibiotics are effective, but for chronic Lyme sufferers, antibiotics *are not just unproven but also dangerous*, so **you can select [B] as well**. Finally, for [C], it is implicit there are generally accepted methods for treating Lyme disease, but it is mentioned that there is disagreement about how to treat chronic Lyme, so **you can select [C] as well**.

58. The author regards chronic Lyme patients with

(A) a complete lack of compassion.
(B) outrage that their illness is not being treated more aggressively.
(C) skepticism that their illness has a physical cause.
(D) exasperation at their poor choice of doctors.
(E) **concern with the implications of their treatments.**

This question asks how the author regards chronic Lyme patients. Let's evaluate each answer choice.

The author shows compassion, so (A) is not a good match.

The author does not show outrage, and sometimes the illness is treated too aggressively, so (B) is not a good match.

The author believes that their illness has a physical cause and isn't skeptical of this, so (C) isn't a good match.

There is no hint that the author believes they have chosen poor doctors, so (D) isn't a good match.

Finally, the author does show concern about the implications, or consequences, of patients' treatments, both for the patients and population in general, so **(E) is the correct choice.**

59. According to the passage, which of the following aspects of chronic Lyme makes doctors skeptical of it? Select all that apply.

A | The lack of a bull's-eye rash on chronic Lyme patients
B | Its similarity to an autoimmune disorder
C | **The fact that chronic Lyme patients test negative for Lyme infection**

You are asked to find aspects of chronic Lyme that make doctors skeptical of it. Let's evaluate the answer choices one at a time.

For [A], although you are told that Lyme disease is often accompanied by a distinctive "bull's-eye" rash, this rash is not discussed regarding chronic Lyme patients. You can't infer that doctors are skeptical because of a lack of this rash, so you can eliminate [A].

[B] is somewhat tempting because it is stated in the text that doctors believe patients may be suffering from an autoimmune disease that may have been triggered by Lyme; however, this belief is very different from doctors being skeptical of chronic Lyme, so there is no reason to select [B].

Finally, you are told that *chronic Lyme patients do not present any sign of the Lyme infection they blame for their symptoms when tested*, which is a reason that makes doctors skeptical, so **you can select [C]**.

Passage 21
4 Questions

We have been investigating the paranormal for centuries, but the forms of our fascination with spirit manifestations have changed over time. Perhaps unsurprisingly, 21st-century ghost hunters use a variety of gadgets and gizmos to attempt to capture proof of paranormal activity. Many of these devices are nothing more than simple video or audio recorders. However, one of the latest technological innovations popular with ghost hunters—the spirit box—is far stranger. The spirit box is essentially a radio scanner that rapidly jumps between frequencies. When ghost hunters believe they are in the presence of a spirit, they ask it questions and then listen to the noise generated by the spirit box, hoping to hear a ghostly answer in the static. Believers allege that spirits can use the sound issuing from the box to speak to us from beyond the grave. Skeptics suggest that ghost hunters are simply hearing what they want to hear. Although it is quite unlikely that the spirit box actually connects seekers with the spirit world, it does demonstrate one of the human mind's most uncanny abilities: the ability to perceive sophisticated patterns in a welter of meaningless noise.

Why did the author write this passage?

The author wrote the passage to discuss the spirit box, a tool used by modern ghost hunters in an attempt to communicate with the spirit world. The author discusses how the spirit box is designed, what believers allege, and what skeptics suggest before giving his own perspective: although it is unlikely that the spirit box actually works, it demonstrates the human capacity to perceive patterns in meaningless noise.

60. The author of the passage regards paranormal investigation with which of the following?

Ⓐ Indignant dismissal
Ⓑ Astonished credulity
Ⓒ **Amused skepticism**
Ⓓ Intellectual admiration
Ⓔ Exasperated befuddlement

This question asks you to consider how the author regards paranormal investigation.

Indignant is showing anger or annoyance—we don't have that here, so indignant dismissal doesn't work, and you can eliminate (A).

The author isn't astonished, and the author doesn't show credulity (i.e., an eagerness to believe), so you can eliminate (B) as well.

Amused skepticism is a nice representation of the author's opinion, so let's leave (C) for now.

There is no evidence of the author having intellectual admiration for paranormal investigation, so you can eliminate (D).

And finally, the author is not exasperated (i.e., frustrated), and he is not befuddled (i.e., confused), so exasperated befuddlement doesn't work; you can eliminate (E).

(C) is the only attractive answer. The author does find the subject amusing, using terms such as *far stranger* and *uncanny*, and he shows skepticism, using terms like *quite unlikely*, so **(C) is the correct choice**.

61. Which of the following questions is NOT addressed by the passage? Select all that apply.

☐A What are some of the other gadgets that paranormal investigators use to capture proof of the paranormal?
☒B **How do paranormal investigators explain the mechanism a ghost uses to "speak" through the spirit box?**
☐C How long have people been investigating the paranormal?

At the beginning of the passage, the author discusses other types of gadgets used and the fact that we've been investigating the paranormal for centuries, so you can eliminate answer choices [A] and [C].

How ghosts speak through the spirit box is never discussed, so **you can select [B]**.

62. Choose the sentence from the passage that demonstrates how ghost hunters use the spirit box during an investigation.

When ghost hunters believe they are in the presence of a spirit, they ask it questions and then listen to the noise generated by the spirit box, hoping to hear a ghostly answer in the static.

Other sentences describe how the spirit box works or what others think of it, but the above sentence is the only one that illustrates how ghost hunters use the spirit box during an investigation.

63. Which of the following is most similar to the situation described in the final sentence of the passage?

Ⓐ An archaeologist investigates a site that she is sure will yield a great discovery but is disappointed to find nothing there.
Ⓑ A man reports that he has been abducted by aliens but rescinds his statement after being diagnosed with and treated for paranoid schizophrenia.

(C) A child thinks she sees a monster under her bed but is reassured when her father checks and finds nothing there.

(D) **A frightened child in a dark forest repeatedly mistakes the shapes and sounds of the leaves and branches for those of an attacker.**

(E) A skeptic debunks a supposed Bigfoot print by pointing out that the foot does not have any ridges or wrinkles in it.

In the final sentence, the author speaks of the human mind's ability to perceive sophisticated patterns in a welter of meaningless noise. **The answer choice that represents a situation most similar to this is (D)**, in which a frightened child mistakes the sounds of the sounds of branches and leaves for those of an attacker. None of the other answer choices involve interpreting sounds as being something other than what they are.

Passage 22
1 Question

Scientists were surprised to find that mice injected with laboratory cultures of *Borrelia burgdorferi*, the bacterium that causes Lyme disease, had different immune system responses than humans infected with the same bacterium as a result of a tick bite. However, when mice were infected with *B. burgdorferi* via tick bite, their immune response was identical to that of humans infected in the same way. Therefore, it is likely that the bacterium in the ticks takes a different form from the laboratory-produced bacterium.

64. Which of the following is an assumption that underlies the argument?

(A) The human immune response to injection with lab cultures of *B. burgdorferi* would be identical to the mouse's immune system response to injection.

(B) No laboratory-cultured bacteria could cause the mouse's immune system to react as it does when infected with *B. burgdorferi* by tick bite.

(C) In other mammals, the immune system responses to *B. burgdorferi* infections both by injection and by tick bite are identical to those in mice.

(D) In the wild, ticks at least occasionally infect mice with Lyme disease.

(E) **The way in which the *B. burgdorferi* infection enters the body does not explain the difference in the mouse's immune system response.**

You are asked to find an assumption that underlies the argument. The author's conclusion is that the bacterium in the ticks that bit the mice likely take a different form than the laboratory-produced bacterium that infected other mice. His reasoning is that mice infected with the laboratory-produced bacterium had different immune responses than human beings did, whereas those bitten by ticks had the same immune response as human beings do.

The author is assuming that, because the mice reacted differently, *it must have been because the bacterium took a different form*. However, the different reaction could very well have been due to other factors, including the different ways in which the bacteria entered the bodies of mice (i.e., injection versus tick bite).

(E) addresses this assumption and is the correct answer.

For the author to reach his conclusion, no assumption would need to be made about human immune response, so you can eliminate (A). There is also no reason (B), (C), or (D) would have been assumed.

Passage 23
1 Question

Most existing decorated artifacts from the early Middle Ages were items designed for church use. However, even those existing decorated artifacts from the early Middle Ages that have no obvious ecclesiastical function are predominantly adorned with Biblical iconography. This evidence suggests that, during this time, artisans were strongly discouraged from decorating objects with secular motifs.

65. Which of the following statements, if true, most weakens the argument above?

(A) Some of the most skillfully decorated objects of the early Middle Ages were artifacts with no apparent church use.

Ⓑ **Unlike domestic objects found in castles and private homes, objects stored in churches of the Middle Ages were generally treated with respect by invaders.**

Ⓒ Almost all of the existing artifacts of the early Middle Ages that were not decorated by artisans had no obvious ecclesiastical function.

Ⓓ Because monasteries in the early Middle Ages were often centers of education, even manuscripts that covered secular subject matter were typically produced by monks.

Ⓔ Artifacts of the early Middle Ages decorated with religious symbols were as prevalent in private homes as they were in religious sanctuaries.

Your task is to find an answer choice that, if true, weakens the given argument. The author concludes that the evidence suggests artisans of the early Middle Ages were strongly discouraged from decorating objects with secular, or nonreligious, motifs. What's her reasoning? Most existing decorated artifacts from the early Middle Ages, even if they are not designed for church use, are adorned with Biblical images.

Before jumping into the answer choices, you should think about the gap in the author's reasoning. How could it be true that most existing artifacts have Biblical images without the conclusion being the case? Well, maybe only certain types of artifacts have survived for some reason, or maybe artisans weren't discouraged but chose to create these types of works of their own free will.

With a clear sense of the argument and an understanding of the reasoning gap, you can think about which of the answers, if true, would most weaken it.

(A) would give an explanation for decorative items existing that have no church use, but it doesn't have anything to do with the gap in the argument reasoning, so you can eliminate it.

(B) directly addresses a gap in the argument's reasoning, and if (B) is true, it explains why more items with religious motifs may have survived to our modern day. Let's leave (B) for now.

(C) doesn't impact whether these items had religious motifs on them or not and can quickly be eliminated.

(D) is somewhat attractive, but you don't know how many of the decorative objects are manuscripts, and you don't know if monks would produce secular material adorned with Biblical iconography, so you can eliminate (D).

Finally, it's tough to see how (E) could be used to weaken the argument, and you can eliminate this answer choice quickly as well.

(B) is the only attractive answer. Let's return to it and think about how it impacts the argument. If (B) is true, it gives a potential explanation for why so many artifacts, even those remaining artifacts that lack an obvious religious function, have religious motifs on them—they were objects stored in churches; if this is the case, it's reasonable to believe they might have more religious images on them then would decorative artifacts from the population at large. **(B) is the correct answer**.

Passage 24
3 Questions

In 1565, an enormous deposit of solid graphite was found near the English town of Seathwaite in Cumbria, England. The graphite found there was unusually pure and strong—so strong that it could be removed in thin, grippable sticks. Thus, the forerunner of the modern pencil was born. Artists immediately took note of the find; graphite pencils represented an enormous improvement over silverpoint, the antiquated drawing technique that had been the standard for draftsmen since the Middle Ages. Before an Italian couple designed the wood encasement that we recognize in modern pencils, graphite sticks were often wrapped in materials like string or sheepskin for stability and ease of use. There was, however, a more serious catch: graphite immediately became commercially valuable because it was the perfect material with which to cast cannonball molds. The Crown eventually took over the Seathwaite deposit and guarded it closely, even flooding it to prevent theft when not in use. Until 1662, when Italian inventors found a way to reconstitute solid sticks from graphite powder—a far more abundant resource—graphite pencils had to be smuggled and were jealously guarded by their owners. By the end of the 17th century, however, the graphite pencil was an important part of any artist's toolkit.

Why did the author write this passage?

The author wrote this passage to discuss the discovery of the graphite deposit at Seathwaite and its importance to the history of the pencil. She mentions how it was prized by artists, how the graphite was then taken over by the Crown, and how graphite pencils eventually became ubiquitous.

66. Which of the following represent reasons that pencils did not become common as soon as the Seathwaite graphite deposit was found? Select <u>all</u> that apply.

A Cannonballs are made of graphite, so the English government took over the mines.
B It took years for inventors to discover how to turn graphite powder into sticks.
C Pencils were relatively inconvenient for artists to use before wood was added to their exteriors.

You are asked why pencils didn't become common as soon as the deposit was found. Two possible reasons not mentioned are restricted access to graphite and quantity.

Of the reasons given, [A] is very tempting, but you are specifically told in the passage that the government eventually took over the mines, whereas the question asks about what happened as soon as the deposits were found, so [A] is not a good match.

[B] is about graphite powder, which is not related to the Seathwaite graphite deposit found, so you can eliminate [B] as well.

The inconvenience of using graphite pencils is a reason given for why they were not popular, and the author specifically mentions that adding wood to the exterior was a convenience that helped with their stability and ease of use, so **you can select [C]**.

67. The passage suggests which of the following about the Seathwaite graphite deposit?

Ⓐ It remains the only source of solid graphite in the world.
Ⓑ It is no longer in use because the British Crown flooded it after mining it.
Ⓒ It is now considered inferior to graphite deposits found in Italy.

Ⓓ **The unique properties of its graphite inspired artists to imagine a tool similar to the modern pencil.**
Ⓔ Its graphite powder was far more useful to artists than the sticks that were originally quarried from it.

You're asked to find an answer that represents something suggested about the Seathwaite graphite deposit.

You have no indication that it's the only source of solid graphite in the world, so you can eliminate (A).

You also have no reason to believe it is no longer in use because the British Crown flooded it, for they would seemingly have little reason to make it permanently unusable, so you can eliminate (B) as well.

You also have no supporting evidence for (C) given in the passage and can eliminate it.

(D) is interesting—let's leave it for now.

(E) incorrectly combines various elements of the text—there was no graphite power taken from Seathwaite, so you can quickly eliminate it.

Returning to (D), you are told that *the forerunner of the modern pencil was born*, and the passage discusses how artists were attracted to graphite and how it eventually inspired pencils created from more abundant materials, so **(D) is a solid match and the correct answer**.

68. Select the sentence that describes a forerunner of the graphite pencil.

Artists immediately took note of the find; graphite pencils represented an enormous improvement over silverpoint, the antiquated drawing technique that had been the standard for draftsmen since the Middle Ages.

The above sentence discusses silverpoint, a forerunner of the graphite pencil.

Passage 25
2 Questions

Safe-cracking is the process of opening a safe without a combination or key. The safe-cracking method seen most often in movies is lock manipulation, which involves determining how to open a safe without damaging it. Lock manipulation requires little special equipment and can be done in silence, which can help a safe-cracker evade capture. However, it can be time-consuming and requires a great deal of skill and practice to master. To manipulate a combination lock, safe-crackers carefully turn it while listening or feeling for tiny imperfections within the mechanism, imperfections that can help determine the combination number by number. Safe owners make this process easier when they fail to change their safe's combination from the easily guessable factory preset, or "try-out combination."

Safe manufacturers and safe-crackers are always attempting to stay one step ahead of each other. For instance, some safe-crackers may take an X-ray of a lock to determine its code, but one lock manufacturer has added a lead shield around their locks to inhibit this strategy. Of course, brute force methods are also available to safe-crackers if they can drill, torch, or detonate explosives near a safe without attracting the attention of the police. However, only the most daring criminal would have the nerve to undertake such a risky maneuver.

Why did the author write this passage?

The author wrote this passage to discuss safe-cracking. She spends the first paragraph discussing a specific method of safe-cracking—lock manipulation—and then spends the second paragraph discussing how safe manufactures and safe-crackers try to stay one step ahead of each other.

69. Which of the following is a reason a safe-cracker might rely on lock manipulation rather than brute force methods? Select all that apply.

[A] **A safe must sometimes be cracked when people are within earshot.**
[B] **A safe-cracker cannot always bring equipment to a job without inviting suspicion.**
[C] A safe-cracker does not always know what to expect when confronting a new safe.

You are told that a safe-cracker might rely on lock manipulation because it can be done in silence and requires little equipment. For these reasons, **you can select answer choices [A] and [B]**.

Lock manipulation does not provide an advantage when it comes to confronting the unexpected, so you can't select [C].

70. Select the sentence that provides an example of an action safe-makers could take to evade a particular safe-cracking technique.

For instance, some safe-crackers may take an X-ray of a lock to determine its code, but one lock manufacturer has added a lead shield around their locks to inhibit this strategy.

The second paragraph is where you get the steps safe-makers and safe-crackers take to stay a step ahead of one another, and it's where you get the above sentence, which gives an example of an action safe-makers take to evade a particular safe-cracking technique.

Passage 26
3 Questions

The most popular of the recently promulgated mini-fasting regimens involves limiting food intake to an eight-hour period each day. Dieters skip breakfast and eat their first meal at mid-day. They can continue eating nutritious meals and snacks during the daytime hours, but after a relatively early dinner, they must fast throughout the night. Nutritionists who champion mini-fasting say that such a regimen improves sleep, helps the body regulate glucose, and can even stave off chronic diseases such as cancer and heart disease. Dieters like the plan because it doesn't leave them feeling deprived of the food they enjoy. Skeptics, on the other hand, point out that much of the research on the benefits of intermittent fasting has been performed only on animal populations or on human subjects who were monitored for only a short time. Others suggest that, although there may be some benefits to the regimen, weight loss is not among those best supported by science.

Why did the author write this passage?

The author wrote this passage to discuss mini-fasting, which he later describes as intermittent fasting. He describes what it entails, why nutritionists and dieters champion it, and the reasons some skeptics give for doubting its effectiveness.

71. Choose the sentence that best captures a reason for why mini-fasting might be easier to stick with than other diet plans.

Dieters like the plan because it doesn't leave them feeling deprived of food they enjoy.

The sentence prior to this one gives you a reason why nutritionists might like the plan but not why it might be easier to stick with; this sentence is the only one that gives you a specific reason why mini-fasting might be easier to stick with than other diet plans.

72. Mini-fasting challenges which of the following pieces of conventional wisdom about nutrition? Select <u>all</u> that apply.

A One's diet has a tremendous effect on one's susceptibility to chronic disease.
B **Eating a healthy breakfast immediately upon waking is essential for good health.**
C **Losing weight is purely a matter of ingesting fewer calories.**

There is nothing about mini-fasting that contrasts with statement [A], and in fact, you're told that mini-fasting encourages nutritious meals. You are told that dieters skip breakfast, which runs contrary to [B], and the focus of mini-fasting has to do with restricting calories to a specific time period, which runs contrary to [C], so **you can select both [B] and [C]**.

73. Which of the following people would be the *least* likely to find mini-fasting helpful?

Ⓐ A woman in her 50s who has been warned by her doctor that she is prediabetic
Ⓑ **A young man whose job requires him to work irregular hours with few breaks**

Ⓒ A man who resists dieting because he does not want to give up his favorite foods
Ⓓ A woman whose struggles with insomnia affect her work performance and mood
Ⓔ A young woman at a healthy weight who wants to live a long and healthy life

You know that nutritionists claim that mini-fasting can help regulate glucose, so you can eliminate (A).

It's tough to see how mini-fasting could help the person mentioned in (B), so let's leave it for now.

You're told specifically that dieters like the plan because it doesn't leave them deprived of the foods they enjoy, so it will likely help the man mentioned in (C), so you can eliminate that choice.

The nutritionist mentioned that it can improve sleep, so it can help the woman mentioned in (D), so you can eliminate this choice as well.

Finally, you know that it isn't supported for weight loss and can stave off chronic diseases. Therefore, it seems a good fit for the young woman mentioned in (E), so you can eliminate this choice.

The person mentioned in (B) was the only one whose characteristics were not a good match for the specifics mentioned in the passage, so the diet is least likely to help this individual. **(B) is the correct choice.**

Passage 27
3 Questions

Agatha Christie is known the world over as the most successful mystery writer of all time. However, many of her fans do not realize that she was once involved in a highly publicized mystery of her own. Christie had been married to her husband, Archie, for more than 10 years when, in 1926, he asked her for a divorce after falling in love with another woman. On December 3 of that year, after quarreling with Archie—who then left home to spend the weekend with his mistress—Christie disappeared from her home, leaving behind a short note mentioning that she was headed for Yorkshire. Ominously, her car, which contained a suitcase full of clothes and an expired driver's license, was later found abandoned at a rock quarry 15 miles away. Christie's disappearance caused a national outcry. Manhunts involving thousands of police officers and troupes of concerned citizens ensued. Christie was not found until December 14, when she turned up in a Yorkshire hotel registered under an assumed name. Doctors called to the scene announced that Christie had been suffering from amnesia and had no idea how she came to be staying at the hotel. Skeptics suggested that she must have been attempting to frame her husband for murder or was engaged in an elaborate and poorly conceived publicity stunt. The world will likely never know precisely what happened to Christie: her posthumous 1977 autobiography mentions nothing of the affair.

Why did the author write this passage?

The author wrote this passage to tell the real-life mystery story of the disappearance and reappearance of mystery writer Agatha Christie.

74. Which of the following is the best example of irony in the passage?

(A) Christie was a famous mystery novelist, but she felt it necessary to stage a publicity stunt to increase her readership.
(B) Christie left a note saying she was going to Yorkshire and ended up in a Yorkshire hotel.
(C) Christie is famous for her 1926 disappearance but fails to mention it in her autobiography.
(D) Christie's husband left home to see his mistress, but Christie herself stayed away from home far longer than he did.
(E) **Christie was a world famous writer of mystery novels, but the mystery of her disappearance was never solved.**

Irony occurs when the state of events represents the opposite of what is expected. Answer choices (A), (B), (C), and (D) do not represent examples of irony, but **answer choice (E) does and is the correct choice**.

75. Choose the sentence that provides the best evidence that Christie's disappearance spurred many ordinary Britons to action.

Manhunts involving thousands of police officers and troupes of concerned citizens ensued.

Other sentences in the passage discuss actions or opinions by individuals, but the above sentence is the only one that represents how Christie's disappearance spurred many Britons to action.

76. It can be inferred that Christie's diagnosis of amnesia may have been which of the following? Select all that apply.

A **A cover story meant to account for her disappearance**
B A false diagnosis based on symptoms that Christie, who would have known about amnesia from her work, reported to doctors
C **The true reason that Christie went missing for as long as she did**

You are told that we may never know what precisely happened to Christie. You are given clues that perhaps she did not have amnesia, and if this is the case, you can infer that it was a cover story meant to account for her disappearance. Therefore, **you can select [A]**.

You don't have enough information to infer [B]. All you are told is that doctors diagnosed Christie with amnesia—how they came to this conclusion is beyond the scope of this passage, and you can't conclude this.

Finally, if in fact she did suffer from amnesia, it could have been the reason Christie went missing for as long as she did, so **you can select [C] as well**.

Passage 28
2 Questions

There is no better illustration of the notion that Victorian England was the historical epicenter of sentimentalism than the elaborate national mourning surrounding the death of Queen Victoria's Prince Consort Albert in 1861. Prince Albert was underappreciated in the British Empire during his lifetime because of his German ancestry and lack of personal magnetism. However, he was the power behind Queen Victoria's throne, lending his judgment and expertise to foreign and domestic affairs alike. Queen Victoria loved him to the point of obsession. When Prince Albert passed away at the age of 42, the Queen sank into a deep depression. Elaborate mourning rituals with strict rules concerning etiquette, home décor, and dress were already an integral part of Victorian culture, but Queen Victoria pushed those practices to an extreme when she determined to remain in deep mourning for the rest of her life, isolate herself from all but her most trusted advisors, and cancel all public appearances for several years. For a time, the British Empire followed suit: the British public realized how they had taken the dynamic and wise Prince Albert for granted and sank into mourning alongside the Queen. Sales of jet jewelry, black crepe dresses, and black-edged stationery skyrocketed in the years following Prince Albert's demise.

Why did the author write this passage?

The author wrote this passage to describe how Victorian England went into national mourning after the death of Prince Albert in 1861. It discusses who he was, how much the Queen loved him, and the Victorian rituals that characterized the mourning of his death.

77. The passage implies that which of the following are aspects of Victorian sentimentalism? Select all that apply.

A **The elaborate ritualization of emotions**
B **A willingness to mourn publicly for someone one does not personally know**
C A lack of regard for people who do not hail from one's country of origin

The description of Victorian sentimentalism includes many examples of the elaborate ritualization of emotions, from the behavior of the Queen herself to the sale of particularly colored items, so **you can select [A]**. Moreover, with all those in the British public mourning Prince Albert, a person they did not know personally, **you can select [B] as well**.

You don't have evidence for [C], and in fact, the British public held Prince Albert in high regard, even though he didn't hail from England, so you can't select [C].

78. Which of the following likely contributed to the public outpouring of grief for Prince Albert?

(A) His illustrious German ancestry
(B) Queen Victoria's strict adherence to etiquette and form
(C) Britain's widespread influence on the world stage
(D) **A sense that the Prince was underappreciated during his life**
(E) The softening effect the Prince had on the Queen's stern public image

You are told in the passage that *the British public realized how they had taken the dynamic and wise Prince Albert for granted and sank into mourning alongside the Queen.* This fact supports the idea that the public's underappreciation of the Prince during his lifetime likely contributed to the outpouring of grief for him after he died, so **(D) is the correct answer**.

You are told that he was underappreciated because of his German ancestry, so (A) doesn't work; it's unclear how the public's outpouring could be the result of Queen Victoria's strict adherence to etiquette and form, so you can eliminate (B) as well. For (C), because you're only discussing the British public, Britain's influence on the world stage isn't relevant. The Prince's softening of the Queen's image is not mentioned, so (E) is also not relevant.

Passage 29
3 Questions

Tornadoes have been known to occur on every continent, but these terrifying phenomena are most numerous and violent in the Great Plains of the United States because of a perfect confluence of climatic and geographic factors. This confluence has earned the swath of North America that extends from Central Texas to Saskatchewan and from the Rockies to the Appalachians the moniker "Tornado Alley." Tornadoes are most common during the spring, but they can occur at any time of year. To form tornadoes, air masses that differ widely from one another in humidity and temperature must meet explosively. South of Tornado Alley, the Gulf of Mexico provides abundant warm, humid air ripe for low-level moisture to the Great Plains. To the north, as frigid air moves south from the Arctic, the Rockies filter out moisture and bend the cold airstream downward, shooting a strong band of dry, chilly air toward the center of the continent. In this way, the unique topography of the United States fuels unusually strong and long-lived storm systems in Tornado Alley that are sometimes perfect for cyclonic development.

Why did the author write this passage?

The author wrote this passage to describe the various unique topographical characteristics that cause Tornado Alley to have its unusual weather.

79. For a tornadic storm to develop, which of the following is a circumstantial requirement? Select <u>all</u> that apply.

- [A] The storm must occur during the spring months.
- [B] The storm must be located over the center of the country.
- [C] **A cold, dry air mass and a warm, wet air mass must meet.**

You're told that tornadoes typically occur in the spring but that they can occur at any time, so [A] does not have to be true; you are not told that tornadic storms must occur over the center of the country, so you can't select [B].

You are told in the passage that, for a tornado to occur, *air masses that differ widely from one another in humidity and temperature must meet explosively*. What is then described is cold dry air and warm wet air meeting. Thus, **[C] must be true**.

80. It can be inferred that tornadoes are the most common and most deadly in Tornado Alley for all of the following reasons EXCEPT

- (A) the Rocky Mountains filter moisture out of cold air from the Arctic.
- (B) North America is located roughly halfway between the North Pole and the Equator, so is subject to both cold and hot air masses.
- (C) **the Great Plains is flat and sparsely populated, so people can see severe thunderstorms from far away.**
- (D) there is a source of abundant tropical moisture available to the Great Plains from the south.
- (E) thunderstorms in general are extremely common in the Great Plains.

This question asks for reasons why tornadoes are the most common and deadly in Tornado Alley, and you need to select the one answer that *doesn't* contribute to this.

You know from the passage that the Rocky Mountains filter out moisture from the cold Arctic air, and this is part of the reason for the creation of tornadoes, so you can eliminate (A).

You also know that the location of North America puts Tornado Alley in position for a meeting of the different air masses, so you can eliminate (B).

You aren't told anything related to (C), so let's leave it for now.

The moisture mentioned in (D) is also mentioned in the passage as a reason for the increased likelihood of tornadic storms, so you can eliminate (D).

Finally, because the entire passage is about how the topography of the area leads to common thunderstorms, you can eliminate (E) as well.

The fact that the plains are flat and sparsely populated and that people can see severe thunderstorms are all concerns not related to what is mentioned in the passage, so **(C) is the correct answer**.

81. Select the sentence that identifies the geographic location of Tornado Alley.

This confluence has earned the swath of North America that extends from Central Texas to Saskatchewan and from the Rockies to the Appalachians the moniker "Tornado Alley."

The first sentence gives general information about tornadoes occurring in the Great Plains of the United States, and the final sentence allows you to locate Tornado Alley in the United States, but the above sentence most accurately gives specific details about the geographic location of Tornado Alley.

Passage 30
2 Questions

Daylight Saving Time has been legally sanctioned in the United States since 1918. However, vast swaths of the world, including all of Africa and Asia, do not observe it. The practice makes little sense near the equator, where sunrise and sunset times vary little throughout the year, or near the poles, where working hours will often be wildly out of sync with sunlight hours, no matter what manipulations one makes to the clock. In the travel and transport industries, Daylight Saving Time can cause major complications in scheduling and logistics. The agricultural sector also opposes the practice because it increases the amount of time farm workers must spend working each day in the summer. However, Daylight Saving Time does have benefits. Proponents suggest that it allows people to spend more time enjoying the outdoors after work in the summer. The retail and entertainment industries love it because it gives people more leisure time to spend money at the movies or mall. Daylight Saving Time can also decrease energy costs by reducing the need for artificial light in the evenings.

Why did the author write this passage?

The author wrote the passage to discuss the pros and cons of Daylight Saving Time, looking at for whom the practice makes sense, and, through examples, for whom it doesn't.

82. Which of the following people would be most likely to have a favorable opinion of Daylight Saving Time?

Ⓐ An employee of an airline who handles logistics
Ⓑ An African executive who must teleconference with clients all over the United States and Europe
Ⓒ A nurse in Brazil who works highly unpredictable hours
Ⓓ **The CEO of an American theme park that features many water rides**
Ⓔ An Inuit ice fisherman who lives near the Arctic Circle

You're asked to select the person most likely to have a favorable opinion of Daylight Saving Time.

For (A), you know that airlines find Daylight Saving Time challenging, and for (B), you know that Africa doesn't follow it, so the executive would find this situation challenging. For (C), Brazil is, relatively speaking, near the equator, and with work hours inconsistent with daylight hours, Daylight Saving Time changes probably aren't a welcome adjustment for the nurse. For (E), near the Arctic Circle, you are told Daylight Saving Time makes little sense.

For the CEO of the American theme park, Daylight Saving Time is great because it gives people more time to spend outdoors in the summer and more leisure time to spend money at the park. **(D) is the correct choice**.

83. What is the purpose of the passage?

Ⓐ To argue that Daylight Saving Time is more trouble than it's worth
Ⓑ **To discuss the controversies that surround Daylight Saving Time**
Ⓒ To outline the history of seasonal clock manipulation
Ⓓ To suggest that a seemingly simple cultural practice is actually very complex
Ⓔ To explain why countries with temperate climates are more likely to observe Daylight Saving Time

You're asked to identify the purpose of the passage. The passage tells you of those who benefit little from Daylight Saving Time and those who benefit far more from it, and the author doesn't give a personal opinion on the matter. **The answer choice that best represents this is (B)**.

The author does not claim that Daylight Saving Time is more trouble than it is worth, so you can eliminate (A). (C) is somewhat attractive, but you don't get a history of manipulation, so you can eliminate it. (D) is also slightly attractive, but Daylight Saving Time is not represented as simple or complex, so it is also incorrect. Finally, (E) is also somewhat tempting because the benefits of Daylight Saving Time in temperate versus non-temperate areas of Earth are discussed, but (E) doesn't represent the overall purpose of why the author wrote the passage, so it, too, can be eliminated.

We're All Done!

Congratulations on completing *The GRE Trainer*. This journey has been demanding, but I'm confident it will prove invaluable. Our mission is to provide you with the most effective, efficient, and powerful study methods available, and we want nothing more than to see you perform at your absolute best on exam day. Good luck!

Thank-Yous

The GRE Trainer represents the culmination of several years of research, development, and refinement. This work benefited from the contributions of many exceptional individuals, including Visala Alagappan, Sarah Bernbach, Patrick Connolly, Annie Hall, Charles Loxton, Jessica McCormack, Kayla Moody, Matthew Pattillo, Sarah Pilliard, and John Roberts. I am deeply grateful for their insight and support.

- Mike Kim

www.ingramcontent.com/pod-product-compliance
Lightning Source LLC
Chambersburg PA
CBHW080546270326
41929CB00019B/3215